The Historical Guide to
NORTH AMERICAN
RAILROADS
THIRD EDITION

KALMBACH BOOKS

Kalmbach Books
21027 Crossroads Circle
Waukesha, Wisconsin 53186
www.Kalmbach.com/Books

Published in 2014
24 23 22 21 20   5 6 7 8 9

Manufactured in China

ISBN: 978-0-89024-970-3
EISBN: 978-1-62700-157-1

Editors: Jeff Wilson, Randy Rehberg
Art Director: Tom Ford
Designer: Patti Keipe
Illustrators: Rick Johnson, Jay Smith

Cataloging-In-Publication Data
The historical guide to North American railroads / editor, Jeff Wilson.
  -- 3rd ed.

    p. : col. ill. ; cm. -- (Trains books)

  Includes index.
  Issued also as an ebook.
  ISBN: 978-0-89024-970-3

  1. Railroads--United States--History--Encyclopedias. 2. Railroads--Canada--History--
Encyclopedias. 3. Railroads--Mexico--History--Encyclopedias. I. Wilson, Jeff, 1964-
II. Title: North American railroads

TF22 .H57 2014
385/.097

On the cover

In a 1940s scene that captures the essence of the golden era of railroading, a Union
Pacific Mikado lays down a plume of smoke as it rolls its freight train eastward
along the railroad's double-track main line in Nebraska. *Photo by Linn Westcott*

  On the facing page, the first diesel streamliner, the Burlington's *Zephyr* (later
renamed *Pioneer Zephyr*), is on the last leg of its final revenue run from Galesburg,
Ill., to Chicago on March 20, 1960—26 years and more than 3 million miles after
entering service in 1934. *Photo by Bill Caflisch*

  The back cover shows a westbound BNSF export coal train, led by a GE ES44AC,
headed for Roberts Bank, British Columbia, crossing the Clark Fork River west of
Noxon, Mont. *Photo by Tom Danneman*

Contents

Foreword

Passenger diesels of the Chesapeake & Ohio, Pennsylvania, and New York Central stand on the service tracks at Cincinnati Union Terminal in September 1952. *Wallace W. Abbey*

As far back as I can remember, one of life's simple joys has been to watch a passing freight train through a car windshield. Every encounter has been a history lesson, borne on the sides of boxcars by a procession of compelling company names. When I was young, I was captivated by the familiar: Great Northern, Pennsylvania, Wabash, Baltimore & Ohio. Or mesmerized by the exotic: Pere Marquette, Bangor & Aroostook, or Quanah, Acme & Pacific. Together they implied something romantic and far-flung, a national railroad empire, all of it linked to the very track I could see merely 25 feet away.

That's part of the enduring appeal of this classic reference book, that it makes sense of a sprawling and sometimes remote part of American and Canadian history. First published in 1985 and now in its third edition, the *Historical Guide to North American Railroads* is an indispensable tool for understanding where the industry came from, and where it's going. The book unlocks the secrets of 171 essential railroads.

A new edition of the book is timely, for today's six giant systems remain the sum totals of all the flags that flew before them. High technology and international economics changed the game, making the Union Pacific or CSX or Canadian National of 2014 quite different than the old Class I carriers of the 1940s or '50s. But these companies haven't completely shed the past. Today's Norfolk Southern still carries with it some of the traditions of the Southern, Nickel Plate, Norfolk & Western and all the other roots of its family tree. BNSF, one of America's largest privately held corporations, exhibits a pride very much rooted in that most glamorous of its predecessors, the Atchison, Topeka & Santa Fe.

This book has been a labor of love for two generations of railroad editors at Kalmbach Publishing Co. To begin with, it never would have been possible without the company library that was first organized by founder Al Kalmbach and expanded by former *Trains* magazine Editor David P. Morgan, for whom the library is named. And the book is a monument to the man who plowed through thousands of books and documents to create the first edition, George H. Drury, longtime company librarian. Today's editors at Kalmbach Books can be credited with taking the *Historical Guide* to a new, contemporary level.

Meanwhile, this marvelous book continues to serve readers with its remarkable ability to connect the dots in North America's deep and fascinating railroad business. For all those flavorful names on all those passing boxcars, the mysteries have been solved.

Kevin P. Keefe
Vice President-Editorial
Kalmbach Publishing Co.

Introduction

Norfolk Southern honored its heritage by painting several new diesels in paint schemes of its predecessor railroads. Here SD70ACe 1069, in Virginian yellow and black, leads hot westbound double-stack train 22A in rural Tennessee in August 2013. *Samuel Phillips*

The *Historical Guide to North American Railroads, Third Edition* is not meant to be a complete history for each railroad, nor is it a railfan's guide of locomotive rosters and paint scheme information. Instead, each entry provides a capsule summary of the history of the railroad: when it was chartered, where it ran, how it grew, when it acquired (or was acquired by) other railroads, and whether it still exists or how it became part of another system. All of these entries together tell the story of how the North American rail system of today evolved.

Before heading straight to the individual entries, you might want to start with a short history of railroading in the U. S., Canada, and Mexico, which begins on the next page.

Previous editions of the *Historical Guide* covered railroads that no longer existed at the time of publishing. This edition also includes listings for railroads currently in operation—previously these would have appeared in the now out-of-print *Train-Watcher's Guide to North American Railroads*. Railroad entries are based on those in previous editions of the *Historical Guide* or *Train-Watcher's Guide*, with updates as needed to reflect changes that have occurred over the past 15 years.

It would have been impossible to include all the railroads that have ever existed. Current Class 1 and significant Class 2 freight railroads are included. For railroads that no longer exist, we limited the listings to railroads that existed from 1930 (the start of the Great Depression) onward, which were at the time Class 1 railroads, railroads at least 50 miles long, or lines with other historical significance. There are 171 main entries, with dozens of additional railroads included as sub-entries within the main railroad listings.

Each entry includes a historical description along with a map and one or more photos. Information and data largely came from various issues of *Poor's Railroads* and *Moody's Transportation Manual,* as well as *The Pocket List of Railroad Officials, The Official Guide,* and *The Official Railway Equipment Register.* Heralds or logos are included for railroads that had them.

The maps are intended as overviews rather than detailed guides. Their purpose is to show how each railroad fit into the North American railroad network. It would be impossible to show all connecting railroads and all cities and towns mentioned in the text. Some railroads are shown in more than one map: the

detailed maps of today's surviving Class 1 railroads show many predecessor lines. Most other maps are taken from previous editions, but if detailed maps were available from the pages of *Trains* or *Classic Trains* magazines, we used them.

Although there are fewer railroad companies today than in 1930 (or 1950 or 1990), they—and their histories and legacies—are just as fascinating and colorful. Start turning the pages to find out where they went and what they were—and perhaps how much remains of them.

Acknowledgements

This book would have been impossible to put together without the assistance of many individuals who helped by updating text, providing photos, proofreading, and drawing maps. Thanks go to Tom Danneman, Peter Hansen, Tom Hoffmann, J. David Ingles, Rob McGonigal, Bill Metzger, Matt Van Hattem, and Jim Wrinn. Thanks also go to the many photographers whose work resides in Kalmbach's David P. Morgan Library, and whose photos grace the pages of this book throughout.

A Brief History of North American Railroading

Shortly after the ceremony celebrating the driving of the Golden Spike on May 10, 1869, the two locomotives were moved closer and christened with champagne. *Andrew Russell*

North America's railroads did not develop in isolation. They connected with each other, shared many characteristics, and were shaped by the events of their time. A review of North America's railroad history furnishes a framework for the individual railroad histories and affords an understanding of why and when things happened.

The first U. S. railroads

In 1825, as goods and people moved west, the completion of the Erie Canal helped establish the city of New York as the chief port and largest city in the northeast United States. As a result, other Atlantic port cities recognized the need for improved transportation to the interior, but Baltimore could see that a canal to the west would be impractical. Therefore, on Feb. 28, 1827, the Baltimore & Ohio Railroad was chartered to

be built to the Ohio River and funnel commerce to the city. The B&O was the first railroad in the United States, and ground was broken for the railroad on July 4, 1828, by Charles Carroll, the last surviving signer of the Declaration of Independence. ("Railroad" means an incorporated common carrier offering freight and passenger service on regular schedules rather than a simple mine or quarry tramway.)

Also in 1828, the commonwealth of Pennsylvania chartered the Main Line of Public Works (an ancestor of the Pennsylvania Railroad), a line of railroads and canals running from Philadelphia to the Ohio River. Within a decade, other railroads pushed inland from Boston and Charleston, S. C., and west from Albany along the Erie Canal. Railroad development along the coast was almost as rapid. By 1838, it was possible to travel from

New York to Washington by a combination of boats and trains.

In 1852, the B&O attained its goal and reached the Ohio River at Wheeling, Va., and the Pennsylvania Railroad met the Ohio River at Pittsburgh. By early 1854, rails stretched from the East Coast to the Mississippi River at Rock Island, Ill., and three years later, a rail route opened from Charleston to Memphis, Tenn.

Transcontinental railroad and expansion

When California became a state in 1850, a railroad was necessary to connect it to the rest of the nation. Five potential routes were surveyed between 1853 and 1855:

- A northern route that was later followed by Northern Pacific and Great Northern
- A central route from Omaha to San Francisco following the Platte River

C&LE 125, one of the 10 Cincinnati-built Red Devils with a solarium lounge at the rear, is at Springfield, Ohio, during a Cincinnati–Columbus *Golden Eagle* run in May 1936. By this time, interurban traffic was in decline. *David P. Morgan Library collection*

across Nebraska and passing through Salt Lake City

- A route from Kansas City to San Francisco across southern Colorado and Utah, then north over Tehachapi Pass into the San Joaquin Valley
- A route from Fort Smith, Ark., to Los Angeles, which was followed by the Rock Island and the Santa Fe
- A route across central Texas through El Paso to Los Angeles that both the Texas & Pacific and the Southern Pacific followed

As these various possibilities were being explored, the Civil War settled the question of the route. When the South seceded, the advocates of the southern routes went with it. The railroads of the South were built primarily to tie inland areas to the coast rather than form a railroad network. Southern railroads seemed loath to arrange through service or even use joint stations in a city—matters that had to be hastily corrected during the war.

On July 1, 1862, President Abraham Lincoln signed an act authorizing the construction of a railroad from the Missouri River to the Pacific Ocean. Its track gauge was set at 4'-8½", which was later to become standard for North America.

Central Pacific broke ground in Sacramento in January 1863, and Union Pacific did the same near Omaha at the end of that year. Construction went slowly because of the lack of capital and because of the Civil War, which was occupying the resources of the nation. In July 1865, the Union Pacific laid its first rails, while the Central Pacific had progressed east out of the foothills and into the Sierra Nevada. After 1,775 miles of track were laid, the last spike, a gold one, was driven on May 10, 1869, at Promontory, Utah, and the first transcontinental railroad was complete. (The term "transcontinental" in U. S. railroad usage refers only to the west half or third of the continent—Omaha to Sacramento, for example, or even Salt Lake City to Oakland, as in the case of the Western Pacific.)

Many of the railroads that opened the West received grants of alternate sections of federally owned land along their route. The grants stipulated that the railroads had to provide reduced-rate transportation for government property, mail, and employees, a provision not repealed until 1946. By then, the government had received more than ten times the value of the land it had granted.

The 1870s and 1880s saw a tremendous increase in railroad mileage. Every town needed a railroad, and two railroads were even better. If capital were not available locally, it was in Europe, especially from prosperous industrial England, which had more capital than it could invest at home. The railroads of the western U. S. and Canada also got more than capital from Europe—they also recruited colonists to inhabit the land they were opening.

Several rail routes to the Pacific Ocean were completed in the early 1880s. In 1881, the Santa Fe met the Southern Pacific at Deming, N. M. Then in 1883, three more routes were completed: Santa Fe's own route across northern New Mexico and Arizona, SP's line between New Orleans and Los Angeles, and the Northern Pacific from Duluth, Minn., to Portland, Ore. A year later, the Union Pacific route to Oregon opened, and Canadian Pacific's route across Canada was completed in 1885.

As freight and passengers moved across the U. S. and Canada, efficient rail transportation needed a uniform time-keeping system instead of having to deal with thousands of local times. In November 1883, the railroads divided the continent into four zones with uniform times an hour apart. Gradually, others adopted the standard time of the railroads, and standard time was established in 1918 by the Standard Time Act.

Narrow gauge boom

Standard gauge was not standard in the beginning. Early railroads were built to almost any track gauge. The most common gauge in the North was 4'-8½", and railroads in the South were usually built to a 5-foot gauge (they were changed to standard gauge in 1886). Narrower gauges, such as 3 feet and 2 feet, were chosen for reasons of economy; wider gauges, such as the 6-foot gauge of the Erie Railroad, were adopted for more obscure reasons. Sometimes the reason for choosing a different gauge was so cars could not be interchanged with neighboring railroads. It took time for railroads to realize that interchanging cars was easier than transloading freight.

The narrow gauge boom, part of the overall railroad boom, ran from roughly 1870 to 1890. The reason usually given for preferring narrow gauge to standard gauge was economy as smaller locomotives and cars cost less. Another view is that narrow gauge railroads were fresh and new at a time when standard gauge railroads had fallen out of favor with the public (the 6-foot gauge Erie was worst of all).

The advantage of standard gauge was that it was now *standard*. Financially successful narrow gauge railroads were soon standard-gauged, unless the cargo carried would have to be transloaded anyway or the terrain made the cost of standard-gauging greater than any benefits of through operation.

Railroad empires and regulation

In the late 1800s, the United States was fast becoming an industrial nation, and ambitious, and often ruthless, men built industrial empires. Jay Gould, E. H. Harriman, Cornelius Vanderbilt, Henry Plant, and others assembled railroad systems, buying connecting lines to extend their systems, buying parallel lines to control competition, and sometimes just buying up railroads for the parts. The privately owned railroads were unregulated, which created natural monopolies that allowed them to set prices and control the market. The amount of publicity accorded these titans of industry (or robber barons) is due to the fact that railroads were larger, more conspicuous businesses than anything else.

These industrial empires and their leaders were featured prominently in newspapers and magazines.

Regulation had its roots in the Midwest and West, where farmers were more dependent on railroads to move their products to market than in the East. The farmers complained that railroad rates were unfair. Favored shippers received rebates, and rates were often higher where one railroad had a monopoly.

Illinois passed legislation in 1871 and 1873 that regulated freight rates and passenger fares, and Minnesota did likewise in 1874. By 1880, pressure for regulation, particularly from the Grange (the National Grange of the Patrons of Husbandry), had shifted to the national level, which resulted in the Interstate Commerce Act of 1887. The act created the Interstate Commerce Commission, and its purpose was to require the railroads to offer reasonable shipping rates and prevent unfair business practices.

At first, stagecoaches and canal and river boats were the railroads' only competition. Then, in 1888, the first practical electric streetcars appeared, and soon, electric interurban railways evolved. They employed rolling stock with smaller dimensions, operated on track in streets and on private rights of way, and emphasized local service. Suddenly, steam railroads were being paralleled by competing electric railways. A few roads recognized that the electric lines were going after local traffic, the service steam roads found most expensive to operate, and encouraged neighboring electric lines, but for the most part, hostility existed between the two types of railroads.

In 1916, railroad mileage in the United States hit its all-time peak of 254,037 miles. With the advent of mass-produced automobiles and paved highways after World War I, the interurban era was over by the 1930s. The expanding trucking industry also began eating into the traffic of the steam railroads. Many railroads responded by forming bus and truck lines, and a few even offered air service.

World War I, USRA control, and the Roaring Twenties

The United States entered World War I on April 6, 1917. Five days later, a group of railroad executives pledged their cooperation in the war effort and created the

Railroad War Board. Among the problems the board had to deal with were labor difficulties, a patriotic rush of employees joining the Army, and a glut of supplies for the war effort choking East Coast yards and ports.

The efforts of the board were not enough for the government. On Dec. 26, 1917, President Woodrow Wilson placed U. S. railroads under the jurisdiction of the United States Railroad Administration (USRA). The government guaranteed the railroads a rental based on their net operating income for the previous three years. Essentially, the government was renting the railroads as one would rent a house, with responsibility for anything lost or damaged. Measures taken by the USRA included the discharge of all railroad presidents, elimination of all rail competition, and a flat $20 wage increase for all employees earning less than $46 a month. The USRA ordered and assigned to railroads more than 2,000 locomotives and 50,000 freight cars of standardized design.

USRA control ended March 1, 1920. The USRA's net operating income for the 26 months of control fell short of the guaranteed payments by $714 million; damage claims were an additional $677 million. One happy legacy of the USRA was its set of 12 standardized locomotive designs, to which locomotives were built as late as 1944.

In 1920, Congress asked the ICC to prepare a plan for merging U. S. railroads into a limited number of systems that would preserve competition and existing routes of trade and, where possible, group the railroads so the cost of transportation on competing routes would be the same. In 1929, the ICC published its recommendations, which created 19 systems. Generally, subsidiaries would stay with their parents, short lines would be assigned to the connecting trunk line, and affiliates of the Canadian roads would stay with Canadian National and Canadian Pacific. A few railroads were assigned jointly to more than one system. The plan caused great discussion, and no one, not even the creators of the plan, was happy with all facets of it. In 1940, Congress withdrew the matter.

From Depression to dieselization

The Great Depression was no easier for the railroads than for anyone else. As business

The Electro-Motive FT was the first successful mass-production freight diesel locomotive, and it (and its successor F units) were largely responsible for the demise of the steam locomotive. Here Santa Fe 110 climbs the grade at Tehachapi, Calif., in the 1940s. *Linn Westcott*

declined, railroads had less freight and fewer passengers to carry. Locomotives and cars were stored or scrapped. Dozens of railroads declared bankruptcy, including such major lines as Frisco, Missouri Pacific, Milwaukee Road, and New Haven. Only the strongest survived unscathed.

During the 1920s, some railroads and locomotive builders had experimented with internal combustion engines in gas-electric passenger cars and diesel-electric switch engines. In both, an internal combustion engine (gasoline or diesel) drove a generator, which in turn produced electric current for traction motors that drove the wheels. The passenger cars could replace a two- or three-car local passenger train and be operated with fewer men. The switch engines were cleaner than steam engines and provided instant availability, being able to be turned on and off as needed.

By 1934, two internal-combustion streamlined trains emerged: Union Pacific's aluminum M-10000, built by Pullman-Standard, and Burlington's stainless steel *Zephyr*, built by Budd. Both trains toured the country, and the *Zephyr* made a non-stop dawn-to-dark run from Denver to Chicago. These trains captured the attention of the public as well as the railroad industry.

UP and Burlington quickly acquired fleets of diesel streamliners, and so did other railroads. In 1935, Baltimore & Ohio and Santa Fe bought diesels from Electro-Motive to pull conventional trains, and EMC passenger diesels became the usual power for the new streamliners.

In 1939, Electro-Motive produced a four-unit, 5400-horsepower freight diesel demonstrator, No. 103, which more than any other locomotive, was responsible for the dieselization of American railroads.

Decline after World War II

During World War II, U. S. railroads remained in control of their affairs. Freight traffic doubled and passenger business quadrupled. After the war, Detroit set out to satisfy a populace that hadn't seen a new automobile in four years, and the railroads tried to erase the memory of wartime travel conditions with new trains and innovations like the Vista-Dome.

By 1950, there were 2 million miles of hard-surfaced roads in the United States. By the mid-1950s the automobile had killed the local passenger train, and the Interstate highway system and jet airliners would soon start the decline of the long-distance train. Losses from passenger trains caused the railroads to cut back services and discontinue trains, while the public responded by riding less and less. The decline accelerated in the late 1960s when the Post Office withdrew mail from most

passenger trains in favor of trucks, planes, and a new sorting system. By 1970, train riding was only for the most determined.

On May 1, 1971, the National Railroad Passenger Corporation, doing business under the name Amtrak, took over most of the nation's passenger trains. The government company immediately discontinued approximately two-thirds of the remaining passenger trains and set out to beef up business on those that remained.

The Interstate highway system was as beneficial for trucks as it was for cars. The railroads soon lost their less-than-carload merchandise traffic, although much of that was picked up by freight forwarders who filled trailers and towed them across town to the railroad's trailer-on-flat-car terminal. Perishable and livestock traffic declined.

Innovative equipment, though, increased other categories of freight business. The railroads had long since lost the new-automobile business, but they brought it back, using bilevel and trilevel rack cars twice as long and half again as high as the automobile box cars they replaced. Boxcars the same size as the rack cars were developed for auto parts, many of which are light but bulky. Grain began to move in huge covered hopper cars, easier to load and unload than boxcars, and like coal, it moved in unit trains, solid trains moved intact from origin to destination.

The Southern Pacific used piggyback trailers on its Overnight LCL trains operating between Los Angeles and San Francisco in the 1950s. The service was a precurser to modern-day trailer-on-flatcar (TOFC) service. *Southern Pacific*

Piggyback traffic, trailers and containers on flat cars, became the hottest commodity the railroads moved.

Merger era

Some date the modern merger era from the spring of 1947, when three mergers occurred: Gulf, Mobile & Ohio with Alton; Denver & Rio Grande Western with Denver & Salt Lake; and Chesapeake & Ohio with Pere Marquette. Others choose Aug. 30, 1957, as the kickoff date when Louisville & Nashville merged with Nashville, Chattanooga & St. Louis.

At first, it seemed only the smaller regional roads were disappearing. Then in 1963, Chesapeake & Ohio acquired control of Baltimore & Ohio. C&O had traditionally been associated with Erie and Nickel Plate. A year later, the Norfolk & Western merged with the Nickel Plate, leased the Wabash and the Pittsburgh & West Virginia, and acquired control of the Akron, Canton & Youngstown. N&W and Wabash had long been affiliates of the Pennsylvania.

In 1964, Union Pacific, which had relied on Chicago & North Western and

later Milwaukee Road to forward its streamliners to and from Chicago, proposed a merger with the Rock Island. The ICC proceedings on the merger were the longest in history, and by the time they were done, the Rock Island was in such poor shape that UP didn't want it.

Rivals Pennsylvania and New York Central merged in 1968 to form Penn Central. Penn Central lasted little more than two years before becoming the biggest single bankruptcy in U. S. history. From its wreckage and that of several smaller roads, the federal government formed Consolidated Rail Corporation (Conrail) in 1976. Other major mergers included

- Southern and Norfolk & Western to form Norfolk Southern
- Seaboard System and Chessie System (themselves both products of mergers) to form CSX Transportation
- Burlington Northern and Santa Fe
- Union Pacific, which merged Western Pacific, Missouri Pacific, Missouri-Kansas-Texas, Chicago & North Western, and Southern Pacific (which included Denver & Rio Grande Western)

Spinoffs and regionals

Conrail did not include all the lines of its predecessors. Many branch and secondary lines were sold to become locally operated short lines. The demise of the Rock Island and the shrinkage of the Milwaukee Road similarly fostered the creation of several new short lines. In the early 1980s, it appeared that the U. S. would soon have a handful of huge railroads and a great many short lines.

Then Illinois Central Gulf began to turn itself into a lean north-south railroad by spinning off secondary lines and east-west routes to form regional railroads, those in the 100- to 1000-mile range. Soo Line in effect bought the Milwaukee Road, moved in, and sold its own lines east of the Twin Cities to form the Wisconsin Central. Most of the large railroads spun off branch and secondary lines to form regional railroads (of a size that used to be considered Class 1) and short lines.

Deregulation and renaissance

On October 14, 1980, President Jimmy Carter signed into law the Staggers Rail Act (named for Rep. Harley O. Staggers

A double-stack container train rolls near Cochise, Ariz., on the Union Pacific in September 2008. The locomotive at the rear of the train is an SD70ACe serving as a DPU (distributed power unit) and is controlled by the engineer in the lead locomotive. *Steve Schmollinger*

of West Virginia). It was a massive deregulation of the railroads, which included provisions to raise any rate that fell below 160 percent of out-of-pocket costs (later 180 percent) and to enter into contracts with shippers to set prices and service, without ICC approval.

Although by 1980 the railroads' share of the overall intercity freight business had dropped since 1930 from three-quarters to a bit more than one-third, ton-miles doubled at this time. Railroads carried the same amount of cargo twice as far (or twice the amount the same distance) with fewer employees, locomotives, and freight cars. Statistics (at right) comparing U. S. Class 1 railroads in 1930, 1980, and 2008 shed light on these changes.

1990s to 2013

Mergers continued, as Canadian Pacific swallowed Soo Line; Canadian National absorbed Illinois Central, Wisconsin Central, Chicago Central & Pacific, and several other roads; and CSX and Norfolk Southern divided Conrail. Kansas City Southern acquired substantial lines in Mexico.

In 1960, there were 106 Class 1 railroads. By 1978, that number had dropped to 48; by 2013, there were seven: BNSF, CN, CP, CSX, KCS, NS, and UP.

Although total route miles have continued to decline since the 1980s, railroads carry more freight today than ever before, as shown by the increase in ton-miles. New equipment has spurred efficiency. Modern locomotives from EMD and GE, typically 4,000 to 4,400 horsepower, allow two or three locomotives to haul 10,000-plus-ton trains, meaning railroads need fewer

locomotives to haul bigger trains. Rail cars have likewise increased in size and capacity, with 286,000-pound GRL (gross rail load) cars becoming standard (110 tons nominal capacity), compared to 100-ton cars of just a decade ago.

With the increase in traffic among the U. S., Canada, and Mexico, the evolution and expansion of unit trains, and the growth of international traffic traveling in containers, there's no doubt that the North American rail system will continue to evolve and grow.

FACTS & FIGURES

Year	1930	1980	2008
Trackage operated (route miles)	249,000	190,000	140,000
Number of employees	1,660,850	480,410	164,439
Locomotives in service	56,582	28,094	24,003
Freight cars in service	2,276,867	1,710,827	1,392,972
Average freight car capacity (tons)	46.6	80.4	100.5
Loaded freight cars moved	45,877,974	21,613,063	30,624,773
Revenue ton-miles (millions)	383,450	918,621	1,777,236
Passenger cars in service	52,130	4,347	1,177
Revenue passenger miles (millions)	26,815	11,500	6,179

Canada

To avoid the steep 4.5 percent grade through Kicking Horse Pass, in 1909, the Canadian Pacific developed the Spiral Tunnels as an alternative route, which reduced the grade to 2.2 percent. *Canadian Pacific Archives*

Canada's first railroad was the Champlain & St. Lawrence Railroad, opened in 1836 between the south bank of the St. Lawrence at Laprairie and St. Johns, Quebec, head of open-water navigation on the Richelieu River, which drains Lake Champlain. Railroads soon spread down the St. Lawrence River Valley into the Maritime Provinces and westward into Ontario.

When British Columbia joined the confederation in 1871, the Canadian government promised a railroad to link the new province with the rest of the country. The principal railroad in Quebec and Ontario, the Grand Trunk, was not interested in a western extension, so the Canadian Pacific Railway was incorporated in 1881 to build from Callander, Ontario, near North Bay, to the Pacific at what is now Vancouver. The builders of the railroad were faced with 1,300 miles of wilderness

across northern Ontario, 1,000 miles of prairie, and 500 miles of rugged mountains. Construction of the line along the north shore of Lake Superior was extremely difficult, but nationalistic feeling precluded a detour through the United States. The crossing of the Rockies called for 4.5 percent grades, replaced later by a pair of spiral tunnels. The line was completed on Nov. 7, 1885.

Even while it was constructing its line to the west, the CPR was extending eastward to Ottawa and Montreal. By 1890, the road's eastern lines stretched from Windsor, opposite Detroit, through Montreal, and across the state of Maine to Saint John, New Brunswick.

CPR spread an extensive network of branches across the wheat lands between Winnipeg and Calgary after 1900, and in 1916, opened a secondary main line through the Kootenay region of southern

British Columbia. Part of that line was financed by the government in exchange for a permanent reduction in grain shipping rates—the Crows Nest Pass Agreement of 1897.

Most of eastern Canada's railroads were part of one predecessor or another of Canadian National Railways. Financial difficulty brought these roads under government control between 1915 and 1923. The 3'-6" gauge Newfoundland Railway was added to CNR in 1949 when Newfoundland joined the confederation.

The provinces of Ontario and British Columbia are in the railroad business through ownership of the Ontario Northland Railway and BC Rail. The province of Alberta owned several railroads that were purchased by CNR and CPR jointly in 1929 to form Northern Alberta Railways, now part of CNR.

Mexico

Ferrocarril Mexicano 32, an 0-6-6-0 named *Orizava*, was built in 1872. The Fairlie articulated, a pair of swiveling engine units beneath a double-ended center-firebox boiler, tackled the grades of the Maltrata Incline. *Gerald M. Best Collection*

As with the United States and Canada, topography played a major factor in the development of railroads in Mexico. Short and steep rivers do not offer easy routes for railroads to follow, high mountains crisscross the country, and most major cities are at high altitudes.

Ownership and operational philosophy also affected the development of the railroads. Until 1996, Mexican railroads were largely in the hands of the government, dating to the 1907 incorporation of National Railways of Mexico.

Mexican Railway (Ferrocarril Mexicano)

The country's first major railroad connected Mexico City with Veracruz. Construction began in 1857, but French intervention and financial difficulty delayed its progress. Work began again in 1864, and the 264-mile line opened in 1873.

The line was notable for its engineering. In the 48 miles from Veracruz to Paso del Macho, the line climbed from sea level to 1,560 feet, and its maximum grade was 1.7 percent. From Mexico City east to Esperanza (elevation 8,045 feet) the line lay across a plateau, with grades of no more than 1.5 percent. The 64 miles between Esperanza and Paso del Macho included a difference in elevation of 6,485 feet. The steepest part of the line, the Maltrata Incline, had ruling grades of 4.7 percent and curves of 16.5 degrees. This segment was electrified in 1924-1928 and then discontinued in 1974.

The Mexicano had five principal branch lines with four different gauges. The Mexicano was purchased by the Mexican government in 1946. In 1959, it ceased to exist as a separate company and its operations were merged with National Railways of Mexico.

Expansion

In the years after the Mexican Railway was completed, President Sebastián Lerdo de Tejada and his successor, Porfirio Díaz, encouraged further rail development. They offered generous concessions and government subsidies for companies constructing railroads. By 1910, when the Mexican Revolution began, more than 15,000 miles of track were in operation.

Pacific Railroad (Ferrocarril del Pacifico)

The Ferrocarril del Pacífico was built by the Santa Fe in 1881 and 1882 as the Sonora Railway from Guaymas, the principal Gulf of California port in Sonora, to Nogales on the U.S. border.

In 1897, Santa Fe traded the railroad to the Southern Pacific for the SP line between Mojave and Needles, Calif. SP saw in the Sonora Railway access to

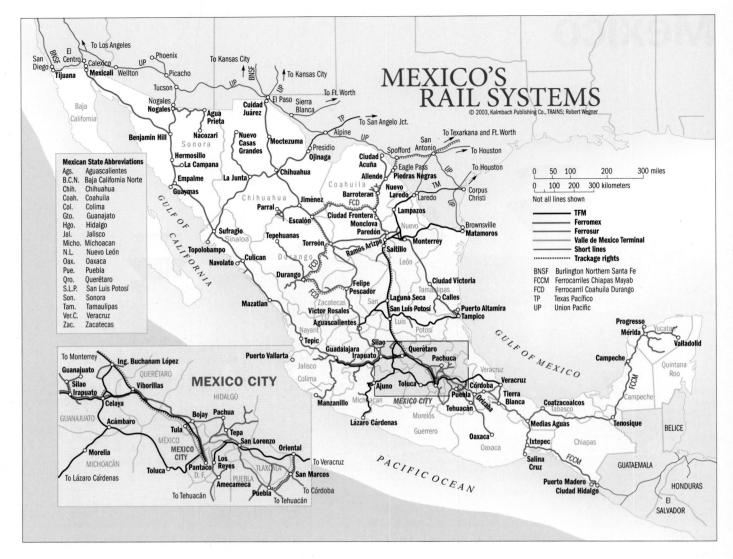

MEXICO'S RAIL SYSTEMS

© 2003, Kalmbach Publishing Co.; TRAINS; Robert Wegner

Mexican State Abbreviations
Ags.   Aguascalientes
B.C.N. Baja California Norte
Chih.   Chihuahua
Coah.   Coahuila
Col.   Colima
Gto.   Guanajato
Hgo.   Hidalgo
Jal.   Jalisco
Micho. Michoacan
N.L.   Nuevo León
Oax.   Oaxaca
Pue.   Puebla
Qro.   Querétaro
S.L.P. San Luis Potosí
Son.   Sonora
Tam.   Tamaulipas
Ver.C. Veracruz
Zac.   Zacatecas

Not all lines shown
TFM
Ferromex
Ferrosur
Valle de Mexico Terminal
Short lines
Trackage rights

BNSF   Burlington Northern Santa Fe
FCCM   Ferrocarriles Chiapas Mayab
FCD   Ferrocarril Coahuila Durango
TP   Texas Pacífico
UP   Union Pacific

Mexico, leasing it in 1898 and purchasing it outright at the end of 1911.

A new SP subsidiary, Cananea, Rio Yaqui & Pacific, extended the railroad south from Guaymas and built branches east of Nogales. The Southern Pacific Railroad of Mexico (Sud Pacifico de México) was incorporated in 1909, and it acquired the CRY&P in 1909 and the Sonora Railway in 1912.

Construction southeast along the coast was hampered by Indian uprisings and the Mexican Revolution. By the time those situations settled down, the railhead was in the wild, rough barranca country southeast of Tepic. The SPdeM finally reached a connection with the National Railways of Mexico at Orendain Junction, 24 miles from Guadalajara in 1927. Further revolutionary activity in 1929 destroyed bridges and interrupted service.

The SPdeM was a consistent money-loser for its parent, and at the beginning of 1940 Southern Pacific withdrew support,

forcing the SPdeM to live on its own income. Losses continued, partly because of labor laws and partly because tariffs imposed by the U. S. on Mexican produce stifled traffic. Mexican authorities operated the line during a strike in 1947 and 1948. The status of foreign-owned holdings in Mexico became questionable, and there was a possibility of expropriation. In December 1951, SP sold the railroad to the Mexican government, and it was renamed the Ferrocarril del Pacifico.

The railroad developed a considerable business in fruits and vegetables moving northward, in later years in solid piggyback trains at passenger-train speeds, and it teamed up with National of Mexico to operate first-class passenger service from the U. S. border at Nogales to Mexico City.

When the Mexican government unified its railroad as National Railways of Mexico., the FCP became the Pacific Region of the National Railways of Mexico in 1987.

In February 1998, Union Pacific and two Mexican partners completed privatization of Mexico's Pacific-North Line, taking control of the line from Nogales to Mexico City, including the former Ferrocarril del Pacífico as far as Guadalajara and the National Railways of Mexico line beyond.

Origins of NdeM

National Railways of Mexico (Ferrocarriles Nacionales de Mexico, NdeM) had is origins in several early railroads that were constructed during the 1880s by companies receiving concessions from the government. Mexican National and Mexican Central were combined Feb. 1, 1909, as National Railways of Mexico.

Mexican Central. Built by Santa Fe interests, the Mexican Central (Ferrocarril Central Méxicano) was completed in 1884. It ran south from Ciudad Juarez, across the Rio Grande from El Paso, through

NdeM's Mexico-Puebla narrow gauge route traverses terrain that includes hot, desert country as well as snow-capped mountains. The lowest point on the route is Puente del Muerto (Bridge of the Dead) shown here. *Frank Barry*

Chihuahua, Torreon, Aguascalientes, and Queretaro to Mexico City. The Mexican Central opened a branch from Irapuato to Guadalajara in 1888, one from Chicalote to Tampico in 1890, and another from Guadalajara to Manzanillo in 1908.

Mexican National. A line from Laredo was begun in 1881 by William Jackson Palmer, builder of the Denver & Rio Grande. The 3-foot gauge Mexican National (Ferrocarril Nacional Mexicano) was completed to Mexico City in 1888 via Monterrey, Saltillo, San Luis Potosi, Acambaro, and Toluca. It constructed a branch from Monterrey to Matamoros and another from Acambaro to Uruapan.

The company was reincorporated in 1902 as the National Railroad of Mexico, a company in which the Mexican government held a majority interest. The main line became standard-gauged as far south as Escobedo in 1903, and a new line was built through Queretaro to Mexico City, roughly parallel to the Mexican Central.

The Mexico City-Veracruz line, opened in 1892, was originally 3-foot-gauge Interoceanic Railway (Ferrocarril Interoceanico). The original main line ran via Oriental and Puebla. Interoceanic leased the narrow-gauge Mexican Eastern in 1903,

gaining a more direct route between Mexico City and Oriental. Both Interoceanic and Mexican Eastern were controlled by the Mexican National in 1903, purchased by the Mexican government in 1946, and converted to standard gauge in 1948.

United Railways of Yucatan (Ferrocarriles Unidos de Yucatán)

The first railroad in Mexico's state of Yucatan was the standard gauge Ferrocarril Progreso a Mérida (Progreso to Merida Railway), authorized in 1874 and opened in 1881 between the city of Merida and the port at Progreso, 24 miles north. Most of the railroad's business was in carrying sisal, a fiber from which rope is made. The road developed a system of standard and narrow gauge lines linking much of the state of Yucatan with its capital, Merida, and extending southwest into the neighboring state of Campeche.

Two other railroads were begun about the same time, the Ferrocarril Mérida a Valladolid and the Ferrocarril Peninsular, which completed a line to Campeche in the state of the same name in 1898. Both these railroads were 3-foot gauge. The three railroads were combined in 1902 as

the United Railways of Yucatan, and a fourth railroad, the 3-foot gauge Ferrocarril de Mérida a Peto, was added in 1909. A third rail for narrow gauge trains was added to the Merida–Progreso line between 1958 and 1960.

The UdeY was isolated until 1950, when the Southeastern Railway (Ferrocarril del Sureste) was completed from Allende, Veracruz, on the Rio Coatzacoalcos, to Campeche. The UdeY line from Campeche to Merida was standard-gauged in 1962.

Mexico's Southeastern Railway was constructed by the Ministry of Communications and Public Works (Secretaria de Comunicaciones y Obras Públicas). It was completed in 1950 from Allende, Veracruz, on the Rio Coatzacoalcos, to Campeche, where it connected with the United Railways of Yucatan. The railroad opened a bridge across the Rio Coatzacoalcos in 1962, forming an all-rail route to the southeastern part of Mexico.

In 1969, Southeastern Railway (Ferrocarril del Sureste) and United Railways of Yucatan (Ferrocarriles Unidos de Yucatán) were merged to form the United South Eastern Railways. The railroad consisted of a main line from Coatzacoalcos, in the state of Veracruz, the junction with the

National Railways of Mexico, east through Palenque, then northeast through Campeche to Merida, and branches radiating from Merida to Progreso, Valladolid, Tizimin, Peto, and Sotuta. In 1987, the FUS became part of the National Railways of Mexico.

Chihuahua Pacific (Ferrocarril de Chihuahua al Pacifico)

The Ferrocarril Chihuahua al Pacifico, a railroad to run from the city of Chihuahua to the Pacific coast, was incorporated in 1897 by Enrique Creel, governor of the Mexican state of Chihuahua. On March 31, 1900, the first section of the railroad, 124 miles from Chihuahua to Minaca, was opened.

The Rio Grande, Sierra Madre & Pacific Railroad was incorporated on June 11, 1897, to build a line between Ciudad Juarez (across the Rio Grande from El Paso) to the Pacific Ocean at Tijuana. The railroad travelled southwest through Casas Grandes into timber country and stopped at Madera, just west of the Continental Divide. The Chihuahua al Pacifico built a branch north from La Junta to Temosachic, and the ChP and the RGSM&P teamed up to organize the Sierra Madre & Pacific to construct the 54-mile line between Madera and Temosachic.

In 1909, the Sierra Madre & Pacific, the Rio Grande, Sierra Madre & Pacific, and the Chihuahua al Pacifico were consolidated as the Ferrocarril Nor-Oeste de Mexico (Mexico North-Western Railway). The entire route from Ciudad Juarez to Chihuahua was open by 1912.

In 1899, Arthur Stilwell proposed a railroad from Kansas City to Topolobampo, the nearest Pacific port. The rail distance would be less than 1,700 miles. Creel granted Stilwell trackage rights from Chihuahua to Minaca, 122 miles, and also the federal concessions of the Chihuahua al Pacifico. Stilwell then secured the rights and lands of the Texas, Topolobampo & Pacific.

Stilwell incorporated the Kansas City, Mexico & Orient Railway (Ferrocarril Kansas City, Mexico y Oriente) on April 30, 1900. By mid-1903, lines were open from Milton, Kan. to Carmen, Okla.; from Chihuahua to a point 34 miles east; and from Topolobampo to El Fuerte. By early 1912, the U.S. portion of the line reached from Wichita to Girvin, Texas, on the

Pecos River, traversing a barren, uninhabited area for much of its length.

Also by 1912, Mexico was deeply involved in a revolution. Neither the desolate topography in the U. S. nor the situation in Mexico was conducive to revenue, and the road entered receivership in March 1912.

The newly organized Kansas City, Mexico & Orient Railroad purchased the KCM&O on July 6, 1914. The first reorganization plan was rejected, and a second receiver, William Kemper, was appointed in 1917. The Orient scraped along, building an extension to Alpine, Texas, where it connected with Southern Pacific. During World War I, the USRA at first rejected the KCM&O but later took over its operation at Kemper's request.

In 1924, a U. S. government loan came due. The KCM&O was unable to repay it, and the government directed that the railroad be sold at auction. Kemper was the successful bidder, and he organized the Kansas City, Mexico & Orient Railway, the second company of that name. However, pipelines had begun to cut into the Orient's oil traffic, and Kemper realized he could never afford to extend the line from Wichita to Kansas City, much less connect the three disjointed Mexican portions of the railroad. He sought a buyer, first in the Missouri Pacific, which had financial difficulties of its own and then the Santa Fe.

On Sept. 24, 1928, the Santa Fe purchased the Orient (merger came on June 30, 1941, except for the Texas portion, which was merged in 1964). Santa Fe then sold the three Mexican portions of the road to B.F. Johnston and the United Sugar Co. of Los Mochis. Johnston combined the operations of the Mexican portion of the KCM&O with those of the Mexico North-Western, which ran from Chihuahua to Ciudad Juarez in long loop that reached west to the mountains, in the process linking the two segments of the Orient.

In October 1930, the eastern portion of the line was opened to Ojinaga. The Santa Fe extended a line from Alpine to Presidio and bridged the Rio Grande that same year, opening a new gateway for traffic between the U.S. and Mexico.

In 1940, the Mexican government purchased the KCM&O and announced the line would be completed—across some of

the roughest and wildest country in North America, Mexico's Sierra Madre. Some surveying and construction ensued.

In 1952, the government took over the North-Western and in 1955 merged it with the KCM&O to form the Ferrocarril de Chihuahua al Pacifico. Construction resumed, and on Nov. 23, 1961, the line was opened, completing the railroad Arthur Stilwell proposed in 1900.

Topolobampo never developed into a major port, and the rails of the Chihuahua Pacific carried little cargo from the heartland of the United States to waiting ships there, but the railroad opened the Copper Canyon area of northwest Mexico to tourism.

In 1987, the ChP was absorbed by the National Railways of Mexico.

Sonora-Baja California Railway (Ferrocarril Sonora-Baja California)

The Sonora-Baja California had its beginning in 1923 when a 43-mile line was constructed under the aegis of the Department of Communications and Public Works southeastward from Mexicali, the capital of the state of Baja California. No further work was done on the railroad until 1936, when construction resumed across the hot, dry, unpopulated Altar Desert. The line was opened as far east as Puerto Peñasco on the Gulf of California in 1940.

Construction resumed again in 1946. On Dec. 16, 1947, the line was completed to a connection with the Southern Pacific of Mexico (later the Ferrocarril del Pacifico) at Benjamin Hill, Sonora, creating an all-Mexican rail link between the state of Baja California and the rest of the country.

Although the Sonora-Baja California name was applied in 1948, at least until 1956, the railroad was operated by the Department of Communications and Public Works. The Sonora-Baja California developed a respectable passenger business and purchased much of its rolling stock in Europe: German coaches and British-built, Rolls-Royce-powered diesel cars (the latter were abject failures).

In 1970, the Mexican government purchased the Tijuana & Tecate Railway, the Mexican portion of the former San Diego & Arizona Eastern line from San Diego to El Centro. Later, its ownership was transferred to the S-BC, but because the T&T was connected only to the former

A southbound auto rack train on Kansas City Southern de Mexico crosses the arid terrain south of Saltillo. *Kansas City Southern*

SD&AE, it continued to be operated by the U. S. operator of that line—first the San Diego & Arizona Eastern Transportation Co., then the San Diego & Imperial Valley Railroad.

On April 2, 1987, the Sonora-Baja California became the Baja California Division of the National Railways of Mexico.

Revolution and Nationalization

While Porfirio Díaz ruled Mexico, railroads and other industries were modernized. While most of country's wealth was controlled by a few families, the majority of the people were repressed. In 1910, several leaders, including Emiliano Zapata, sought to reform the government through armed rebellion. The Mexican Revolution lasted for a decade, with periods of violence that continued into the 1920s. During this time, the rail system deteriorated greatly from neglect.

In 1937, the rail system became nationalized as the NdeM. Four additional government-owned railroads retained separate identities until consolidated in the late 1980s as FNM to distinguish it from its predecessor. By the late 1990s, freight customers were abandoning FNM for trucks, and the railroad suffered financial problems.

Privatization

In 1995, the Mexican government decided to privatize FNM, which split it into three principal railroads: TFM, Ferromex, and Ferrosur. Each was auctioned as a 50-year operating concession (renewable for another 50 years), with the winner committing to a specified level of capital investment and maintenance. The winner received title to locomotives and cars transferred from FNM; ownership of track and real estate remained with the Mexican government.

In 1996, Kansas City Southern, in a joint venture with Transportacion Maritima Mexicana (TMM), purchased the northeast railroad concession, which linked Mexico City, Monterrey, the Pacific port at Lázaro Cárdenas and the border crossing at Laredo. The company was called Transportación Ferroviaria Mexicana (TFM) but became Kansas City Southern de México (KCSM) in 2005 when KCS bought out TMM. The line has 2,661 route miles.

The northwest railroad concession connected Mexico City and Guadalajara with the Pacific port of Manzanillo and crossings along the U. S. border. In 1998, it was bought by a joint venture between UP and mining company Grupo Mexico. The company operates as Ferrocarril Mexicano or Ferromex (FXE). The line has 5,375 route miles.

Ferrocarril del Sureste, or Ferrosur, was the smallest private railroad with 972 route miles. It was formed in 2000 when the two southern concessions merged. The line ran between Mexico City and the port of Veracruz on the Gulf of Mexico. In 2011, Ferrosur merged with Ferromex.

Several short lines and regionals were also developed as a result of privatization including Ferrocarril y Terminal del Valle de México and Línea Coahuila Durango.

The two Class I railroads upgraded their trackage and opened new terminals, which increased traffic. The most prevalent commodities are auto traffic (auto parts and vehicles) and containers. Agricultural (grain) and industrial products (minerals, metals, cement) also make up a significant portion of commodities carried.

Akron, Canton & Youngstown

The Akron, Canton & Youngstown Railway was incorporated in 1907 and completed a line from Mogadore to Akron, Ohio, 8 miles, in 1913. In 1920 the AC&Y obtained control of the Northern Ohio Railway from the Lake Erie & Western. The Northern Ohio had a 161-mile route from Akron west to Delphos, Ohio. AC&Y also purchased outright a 9-mile portion of the Northern Ohio from Akron to Copley Junction.

Akron was noted for the manufacture of tires, and over the years tires and inner tubes moving from Akron to Detroit via the Detroit, Toledo & Ironton interchange at Columbus Grove constituted a significant part of AC&Y's freight traffic.

On Jan. 14, 1944, the AC&Y and the Northern Ohio were consolidated as the Akron, Canton & Youngstown Railroad. In 1947 AC&Y considered extending its line east to Youngstown for access to the steel industry there and also to serve as a route around the congestion of Cleveland, but nothing came of it.

In 1949 AC&Y's president proposed a 130-mile Ohio River-to-Lake Erie two-way

FACTS & FIGURES

Year	1929	1964
Miles operated	171	171
Locomotives	25	18
Passenger cars	5	—
Freight cars	223	1,799

Reporting marks: ACY

Historical society: acyhs.org

Akron, Canton & Youngstown No. 503, a Fairbanks-Morse H20-44, crosses the Big Four main line at New London, Ohio, in 1949. AC&Y painted its diesels yellow. *Vaughn K. Neel*

conveyor belt. AC&Y was, understandably, the only railroad to support the proposal or to advocate passage of bills by the Ohio legislature granting right of eminent domain to the conveyor belt company.

Norfolk & Western purchased the AC&Y in 1964 at the time it merged with the Nickel Plate and leased the Wabash. The N&W dissolved the AC&Y on Jan. 1, 1982. The Wheeling & Lake Erie Railway (the 1990 company) purchased the remaining portion of the AC&Y in 1990.

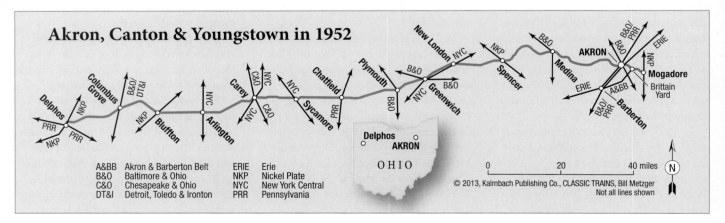

Akron, Canton & Youngstown in 1952

A&BB	Akron & Barberton Belt	ERIE	Erie
B&O	Baltimore & Ohio	NKP	Nickel Plate
C&O	Chesapeake & Ohio	NYC	New York Central
DT&I	Detroit, Toledo & Ironton	PRR	Pennsylvania

© 2013, Kalmbach Publishing Co., CLASSIC TRAINS, Bill Metzger
Not all lines shown

Alabama, Tennessee & Northern

Alabama, Tennessee & Northern No. 11, a General Electric 45-ton center-cab diesel, switches a cut of high-pressure tank cars at a refinery on Blakely Island at Mobile. The AT&N operated a car ferry and docks to reach this trackage. *David P. Morgan Library collection*

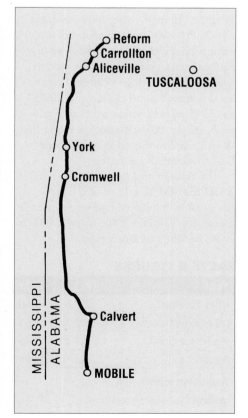

The Carrollton Short Line Railway was chartered in 1897. By 1906, when its name was changed to the Alabama, Tennessee & Northern Railroad, it had built a line from Reform, Ala., through Carrollton to Aliceville and was pushing slowly down the western edge of Alabama toward the Gulf of Mexico. The company underwent foreclosure and reorganization in 1918, and by 1920, the road reached south to Calvert, Ala., where the Southern Railway offered a connection to Mobile.

In 1928 AT&N completed its own line from Calvert to Mobile and that same year entered into an agreement with the St. Louis-San Francisco Railway (which had just built a line from Aberdeen, Miss., to Pensacola, Fla., making a connection with the AT&N at Aliceville) for joint handling of through traffic between the Port of Mobile and points on the Frisco.

The AT&N's finances were again reorganized in October 1944. On Dec. 28, 1948, Frisco purchased 97.2 percent of AT&N's common stock (later increasing its holdings to 100 percent) and unified AT&N's operations with its own. The Alabama, Tennessee & Northern was merged with the Frisco on January 1, 1971. Frisco itself became part of Burlington Northern on September 21, 1980. The line was abandoned in the 1980s in favor of trackage rights to Mobile on Norfolk Southern rails. AT&N's terminal trackage in Mobile is still in operation.

FACTS & FIGURES

Year	1929	1970
Miles operated	224	214
Locomotives	19	7
Passenger cars	14	—
Freight cars	419	—
Reporting marks: AT&N		

Alaska

The Alaska Railroad is descended from two short lines: the Alaska Northern Railway and the Tanana Valley Railroad. The Alaska Northern was reorganized in 1909 from the Alaska Central Railroad, a standard gauge line incorporated in 1902. It had a 72-mile line extending inland from Seward when it was purchased by the U. S. government in 1915. The Tanana Valley was a narrow gauge line connecting Fairbanks to the head of navigation on the Tanana River and to a gold-mining area 35 miles to the northeast. It began operation in 1904, was purchased by the U. S. government in 1917, and was converted to standard gauge in 1923.

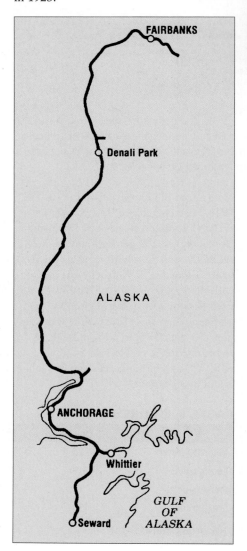

Passenger traffic is still important on the Alaska Railroad. In the 1980s, two of the railroad's F7s lead a train south of Healy in the Nenana River Canyon. *Jonathan C. Fischer*

There was pressure to build a tidewater-to-interior railroad to unlock the treasure chest which Alaska was considered at the time, but the lack of population in the territory made it clear that such a line would have to be built by the government. In 1912 President Taft asked Congress for such a measure; Congress provided it later that year as a rider on a bill granting Alaska self-government. The Alaska Central and the Tanana Valley were taken over by the Alaska Engineering Commission, which then built a railroad connecting the two lines, no small task. The line was renamed the Alaska Railroad in 1923, the year of its completion. The last spike was driven by President Harding.

The railroad was operated by the Department of the Interior until 1967, when it came under the Federal Railroad Administration, part of the new Department of Transportation. Ownership of the railroad was transferred to the State of Alaska on January 6, 1985.

Today's ARR is a Class II railroad with a main line extending from Anchorage to Fairbanks, 356 miles. Other routes reach south from Anchorage to Seward and Whittier. All main routes have passenger service. Privately operated tour cars supplement regular equipment on the Anchorage-Fairbanks run. Auto-ferry trains used to operate on the Portage-Whittier branch because there was no highway. The ARR has no direct connection with other railroads, relying on car barges (operating from Whittier to Seattle and Prince Rupert, B.C.) for interchange traffic.

The main motive power is a fleet of 28 EMD SD70MACs, 12 of which are equipped with head-end power for passenger service. Several GP40-2s and GP38-2s round out the mainline power.

FACTS & FIGURES

Year	1931	2012
Miles operated	559	656
Locomotives	23	51
Passenger cars	37	45
Freight cars	844	1,254

Reporting marks: ARR

Website: alaskarailroad.com

Algoma Central

Trees are showing their fall colors as Algoma Central's popular "Agawa Canyon Tour Train" rolls past Hubert Lake in October 1990. Lead unit 201 is a GM GP38-2, painted in the road's distinctive maroon, gray, and yellow scheme; older GP9s are also in the diesel consist. *Josh Madden*

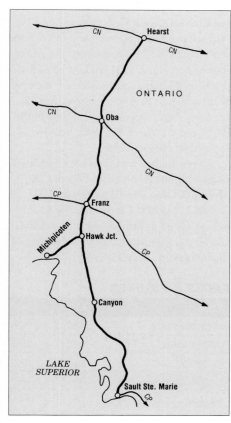

The Algoma Central Railway was chartered in 1899 to build into the Ontario wilderness north of Sault Ste. Marie. Its purpose was to bring out pulpwood and iron ore. In 1901 the ambitions of its founder added "& Hudson Bay" to the corporate title. The line reached Hawk Junction, 165 miles north of Sault Ste. Marie, in 1912. From there, a branch ran west through an iron-mining district to Michipicoten Harbor on Lake Superior. In 1914 the railroad was completed to a junction with the National Transcontinental Railway (a predecessor of Canadian National Railways) at Hearst, 297 miles from Sault Ste. Marie.

An early affiliate of the Algoma Central was the Algoma Eastern Railway, which ran west from Sudbury, Ont., through Drury and Espanola to Little Current, on Manitoulin Island, 86.9 miles. For nearly 50 miles it paralleled Canadian Pacific's Sudbury–Sault Ste. Marie line. Canadian Pacific leased the Algoma Eastern in 1930.

In recent decades the Algoma Central became known for its excursion trains from Sault Ste. Marie to the Agawa River canyon, where the railroad developed a park. The name of the company reverted to Algoma Central Railway in 1965, and in 1990, the company was renamed Algoma Central Corporation, with the railway as a subsidiary. The company also had shipping, trucking, real estate, and land and forest subsidiaries.

The Wisconsin Central purchased the Algoma Central in January 1995, and the WC was subsequently purchased by Canadian National in 2001. The CN operates the former Algoma Central line as part of its eastern division.

FACTS & FIGURES

Year	1929	1994
Miles operated	324	322
Locomotives	22	23
Passenger cars	12	45
Freight cars	1,133	947

Reporting marks: AC

Historical society: sooline.org

Alton

T he Alton & Sangamon Railroad was chartered in 1847 to build a railroad connecting the agricultural area centered on Springfield, Ill., with Alton, on the east bank of the Mississippi River 20 miles north of St. Louis. The railroad opened in 1851. During the ensuing decade it built a line north through Bloomington to Joliet and was renamed the St. Louis, Alton & Chicago Railroad. The Chicago & Alton Railroad was organized in 1861 to purchase the StLA&C.

In 1864 the Chicago & Alton leased the Joliet & Chicago Railroad to gain access to Chicago. Timothy B. Blackstone, president of the Joliet & Chicago, became president of the C&A. In 1870 the C&A leased the Louisiana & Missouri River Railroad (Louisiana, Mo., to the north bank of the Missouri River opposite Jefferson City) and in 1878 it leased the Kansas City, St. Louis & Chicago Railroad (Mexico, Mo.-Kansas City), creating the shortest Chicago-Kansas City route. (In 1888 the Santa Fe completed a Chicago-Kansas City route that was 32 miles shorter.)

By the end of the nineteenth century the Chicago & Alton had attracted the notice of Gould, Rockefeller, and Harriman, each of whom could find a place in his rail empire for the road. Harriman formed a syndicate of railroad financiers who were able to meet Blackstone's terms (basically $175 per $100 share of common stock and $200 per share for preferred; Blackstone controlled one-third of the stock), and in 1899 the syndicate

Alton's E7s, pictured at the Chicago station yard, were built in 1945, two years before the railroad was officially merged with the Gulf, Mobile & Ohio. *Al Chione collection*

purchased 95 percent of the stock. The Chicago & Alton then issued bonds, which the stockholders bought cheap and resold dear to the public, and the railroad used the proceeds of the bond sale to issue a 30 percent cash dividend on its stock.

The Chicago & Alton Railway was incorporated April 2, 1900, to take over a line from Springfield to Peoria, and on the following day, it leased the Chicago & Alton Railroad. The two companies were consolidated as the Chicago & Alton Railroad in 1906. In 1904 control passed to the Union Pacific and the Rock Island, and in 1907 to the Toledo, St. Louis & Western (the Clover Leaf, later part of the Nickel Plate).

In 1912 the Chicago & Alton began a string of deficit years that continued almost unbroken to 1941. It lost much of

the coal traffic it had carried to Chicago, and the cattle trade from Kansas City disappeared (Blackstone had been one of the developers of the Chicago Union Stockyards). In 1922 the Chicago & Alton entered receivership.

The Baltimore & Ohio, perhaps in an expansionist mood brought on by the Interstate Commerce Commission's proposal to consolidate U. S. railroads into 19 systems, purchased the road at a foreclosure sale in 1929. B&O incorporated the Alton Railroad on Jan. 7, 1931, and on July 18 of that year, the Alton purchased the property of the Chicago & Alton Railroad. For 12 years the Alton was operated as part of the B&O, but on March 10, 1943, B&O restored its independence.

Several midwestern railroads considered purchasing the Alton but declined; Gulf, Mobile & Ohio offered merger. In 1945 GM&O paid B&O approximately $1.2 million for all its claims against the Alton and all its Alton stock. The effective date of the merger was May 31, 1947.

FACTS & FIGURES

Year	1929	1945
Miles operated	1,028	959
Locomotives	292	193
Passenger cars	232	112
Freight cars	13,066	5,362
Reporting marks: C&A, A		

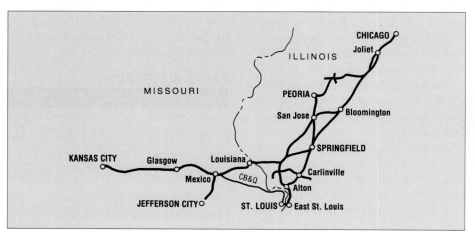

Ann Arbor

The Ann Arbor began when two companies organized in 1869 and 1872 to build a railroad between Toledo, Ohio, and Ann Arbor, Mich. It took another 20 years and 12 companies, most named Toledo, Ann Arbor & something, for the railroad to reach the eastern shore of Lake Michigan at Frankfort, Mich. From Elberta, across a small inlet from Frankfort, the Ann Arbor operated car ferries to Kewaunee and Manitowoc, Wis., and Menominee and Manistique, Mich.

The Ann Arbor Railroad was incorporated in 1895 as a reorganization of the Toledo, Ann Arbor & North Michigan Railroad. The Detroit, Toledo & Ironton obtained control of the Ann Arbor in 1905 but sold its interests in 1910. In 1911 the Ann Arbor purchased all the capital stock of the Manistique & Lake Superior Railroad, which extended north from Manistique, Mich., to connections with the Duluth, South Shore & Atlantic and the Lake Superior & Ishpeming.

In 1925 the Wabash acquired control of the Ann Arbor. By 1930 it held more than

Ann Arbor freight TF-1, led by Alco FAs in the blue, white, and gray of parent Wabash, crosses the Grand Trunk Western at Durand, Mich. *Rail Photo Service; David P. Morgan Library collection*

97 percent of Ann Arbor's stock. In 1963 Wabash sold the Ann Arbor to the DT&I (which was owned by the Wabash and the Pennsy). The M&LS and the connecting ferry route were abandoned in 1968. In 1970 the ICC authorized abandonment of the ferry to Menominee.

On Oct. 16, 1973, Ann Arbor declared bankruptcy. On April 1, 1976, Conrail took over its operation. The state of Michigan then purchased the railroad from the DT&I and arranged for its operation by Michigan Interstate Railway. The remaining car ferry lines from Frankfort to Manitowoc (79 miles) and Kewaunee (60 miles) ceased operation in April 1982.

In 1983, operation of the former Ann Arbor was split among three railroads: Michigan Interstate, Tuscola & Saginaw Bay, and Michigan Northern. In 1984 T&SB took over MN's portion of the Ann Arbor; the T&SB became the Great Lakes Central in 2006. A new Ann Arbor Railroad, an independent short line, was incorporated in 1988 to operate the line between Toledo and Ann Arbor; in 2013 this version of the AA was purchased by the Watco companies, a major operator of U.S. shortline railroads.

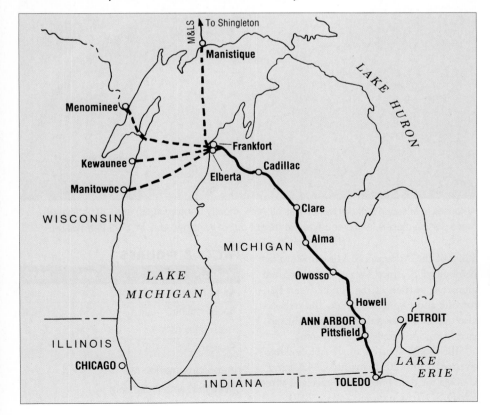

FACTS & FIGURES

Year	1929	1972
Miles operated	294	300
Locomotives	50	15
Passenger cars	25	—
Freight cars	2,082	397
Reporting marks: AA		
Historical society: trainweb.org/annarbor		

Arkansas & Missouri

Arkansas & Missouri's route from Monett, Missouri, south to Fort Smith, Arkansas, was built between 1880 and 1882 by the St. Louis, Arkansas & Texas Railway, an affiliate of the St. Louis-San Francisco. The route served as the Frisco's principal route to and from Texas from its completion to Paris, Texas, in 1887, until 1902, when Frisco opened a route through Tulsa. The Frisco became part of Burlington Northern on Nov. 21, 1980.

Not long afterward, a segment of the Monett-Fort Smith-Paris route in southeast Oklahoma was abandoned. What had been a secondary through route was now two stub branches, from Monett to Fort Smith and from Antlers, Okla., to Paris, Texas (the latter is now part of the Kiamichi Railroad).

In 1986 the group of investors that had developed the Maryland & Delaware Railroad looked west. They purchased the Monett-Fort Smith line from BN and formed the Arkansas & Missouri Railroad.

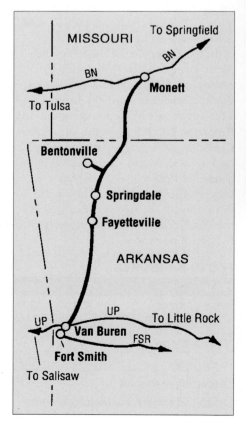

Arkansas & Missouri's diesel roster was all-Alco (mostly Century 420s) until 2013. Five of these classic diesels lead a southbound freight out of Winslow, Ark., in 1995. *Jeff Wilson*

Most of the Arkansas & Missouri's traffic is inbound, destined for customers located along the portion of the line between Bentonville and Fayetteville, Ark. The railroad also operates seasonal passenger train service from Springdale to Van Buren.

The A&M sported an all-Alco locomotive roster into 2013 (mainly C-420s and C-424s for road power), but received three EMD SD70ACe diesels in late 2013.

FACTS & FIGURES

Year	1985	2013
Miles operated	139	139
Locomotives	16	31
Passenger cars	8	8
Freight cars	88	383

Reporting marks: AM

Website: amrailroad.com

Atchison, Topeka & Santa Fe

Atchison, Topeka & Santa Fe train 19, the *Chief*, accelerates out of Chillicothe, Ill.,behind an A-B-B-B set of F units in early 1968, shortly before the train was discontinued. The Fs wear the Santa Fe's famous red-and-silver warbonnet paint scheme. *J. David Ingles*

By the mid-1600s the city of Santa Fe was established as the seat of government of the Spanish colony of New Mexico and as a trading center. Trade between the United States and New Mexico began in 1822, and a trail was established between Independence, Mo., just east of Kansas City, and Santa Fe. It ran west to what is now La Junta, Colo. south over Raton Pass, then west over the Sangre de Cristo Mountains to Santa Fe.

The Atchison & Topeka Railroad was chartered in 1859 to join the towns of its title and continue southwest toward Santa Fe. "Santa Fe" was added to the corporate name in 1863. Construction started in 1869; by the end of 1872 the railroad extended to the Kansas-Colorado border, opening much of Kansas to settlement and carrying wheat and cattle east to markets. The railroad temporarily set aside its goal

of Santa Fe and continued building west, reaching Pueblo, Colo., in 1876, just in time for the silver rush at Leadville.

In 1878 the railroad resumed construction toward Santa Fe, building southwest from La Junta to Trinidad, then south over Raton Pass. It chose that route instead of an easier route south across the plains from Dodge City because of hostile Indians and a lack of water on the southerly route and coal deposits near Trinidad, Colo., and Raton, N. M.

The Denver & Rio Grande was also aiming at Raton Pass, but Santa Fe crews arose early one morning in 1878 and were hard at work with picks and shovels when the Rio Grande crews showed up after breakfast. At the same time the two railroads skirmished over occupancy of the Royal Gorge of the Arkansas River west of Canon City, Colo.; the Rio Grande won that battle.

The Santa Fe reached Albuquerque in 1880 (because of geography the city of Santa Fe found itself at the end of a short branch from Lamy, N. M.) and connected with the Southern Pacific at Deming, N.M., in 1881. The Santa Fe then built southwest from Benson, Ariz., to Nogales, on the Mexican border. There it connected with the Sonora Railway, which Santa Fe interests had constructed north from the Mexican port of Guaymas.

Atlantic & Pacific

The Atlantic & Pacific Railroad was chartered in 1866 to build west from Springfield, Mo., through Amarillo, Texas, and Albuquerque, N. M., to a junction with the Southern Pacific at the Colorado River. The infant A&P had no rail connections. The line that was to become the St. Louis-San Francisco Railway (the Frisco) wouldn't reach Springfield for another four

Santa Fe 2-10-2 No. 3895 works hard as it pulls its train up Cajon Pass in 1949. The rear of the train can be seen in the distance at left. The 2-10-2 wheel arrangement became known as a "Santa Fe." *Donald Sims*

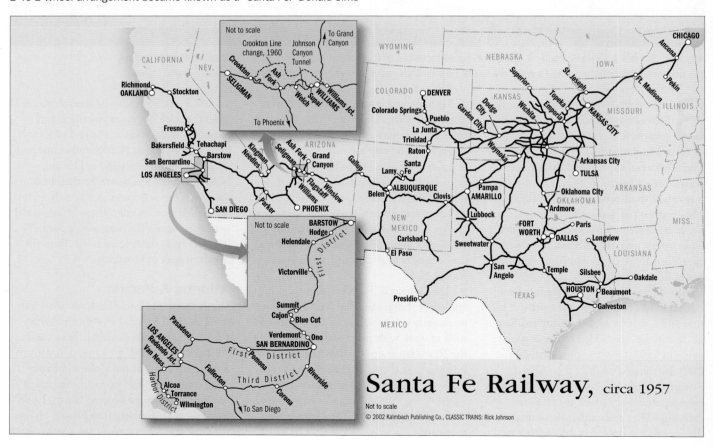

Santa Fe Railway, circa 1957

Not to scale

© 2002 Kalmbach Publishing Co., CLASSIC TRAINS: Rick Johnson

Railroad publicity photos were common in the early days of diesel streamliners. This 1937 view shows one of the initial E1 diesels (A-B set Nos. 2 and 2A) built for service with the original streamlined *Super Chief*. *Atchison, Topeka & Santa Fe*

years, and SP did not build east from Mojave to the Colorado River until 1883. The A&P started construction in 1868, built southwest into what would become Oklahoma, and entered receivership. As an operating railroad, the A&P dropped out of sight briefly, but not as a charter and corporate structure.

In 1879 the A&P struck a deal with the Santa Fe and the Frisco: Those railroads would jointly build and own the A&P west of Albuquerque. Construction began at Albuquerque, and in 1883 the A&P reached Needles, Calif., and a connection with the SP. Construction still hadn't begun on the Tulsa-Albuquerque portion of the Atlantic & Pacific.

Expansion

The Santa Fe began to expand:
- a line from Barstow, Calif., to San Diego

in 1885 and to Los Angeles in 1887
- control of the Gulf, Colorado & Santa Fe (Galveston to Fort Worth) in 1886 and construction of a line between Wichita and Fort Worth in 1887
- lines from Kansas City to Chicago, from Kiowa, Kan., to Amarillo, Texas, and from Pueblo to Denver (paralleling the Denver & Rio Grande) in 1888
- purchase of the Frisco and the Colorado Midland in 1890

The depression of 1893 had the same effect on the Santa Fe that it had on many other railroads: financial problems and subsequent reorganization. In 1895 Santa Fe sold the Frisco and the Colorado Midland and wrote off the losses, but it retained control of the Atlantic & Pacific, and purchased it in 1898.

The Santa Fe still wanted to reach California on its own rails (it leased the Southern

Pacific line from Needles through Barstow to Mojave), and the state of California eagerly courted the Santa Fe in order to break SP's monopoly. In 1897 the Santa Fe traded the Sonora Railway to Southern Pacific for the SP line between Barstow and Mojave, giving the Santa Fe its own line from Chicago to the Pacific—Santa Fe all the way.

Subsequent expansion of the Santa Fe encompassed:
- a line from Amarillo to Pecos in 1899
- a line from Ash Fork, Ariz., to Phoenix in 1901
- the Belen Cutoff from the Pecos line at Texico to Isleta, south of Albuquerque, bypassing the grades of Raton Pass in 1907
- the Coleman Cutoff, from Texico to Coleman, Texas, near Brownwood in 1912

In 1907 Santa Fe and Southern Pacific jointly formed the Northwestern Pacific

The Santa Fe's transcontinental double-track main line became a racetrack for hotshot intermodal trains. Here, SD75M No. 234 leads a double-stack train westward acros Illinois in August 1995, shortly before the Burlington Northern Santa Fe merger. *Jeff Wilson*

Railroad, which took over several short railroads and built new lines connecting them to form a route from San Francisco north to Eureka. In 1928 Santa Fe sold its half of the NWP to Southern Pacific.

Also in 1928 the Santa Fe purchased the U. S. portion of the Kansas City, Mexico & Orient Railway as a way to reach the oilfields of west Texas. Post-World War II construction projects included an entrance to Dallas from the north and relocation of the main line across northern Arizona.

Because long stretches of its main line traversed areas without water, Santa Fe was one of the first purchasers of diesel locomotives for road freight service. The road was known for its passenger trains, notably the Chicago-Los Angeles *Super Chief*, and for the on-line eating houses and dining cars operated by Fred Harvey.

Mergers

In 1960 the Santa Fe bought the Toledo, Peoria & Western Railroad, then sold a half interest to the Pennsylvania Railroad.

The TP&W cut straight east across Illinois from near Fort Madison, Iowa, to a connection with the Pennsy at Effner, Ind., forming a bypass around Chicago for traffic moving between the two lines. The TP&W route didn't mesh with the traffic pattern Conrail developed after 1976, so Santa Fe bought back the other half, merged the TP&W in 1983, then sold it back into independence in 1989.

During the 1960s the Santa Fe explored merger with the Frisco and the Missouri Pacific with no success. By 1980 Santa Fe, which had been the top railroad in route mileage in the 1950s, was surrounded by larger railroads. It was well managed and profitable, and it had the best route between the Midwest and Southern California, but its neighbors were larger, and friendly connections had been taken over by rival railroads. Southern Pacific was in the same situation. In 1980 Santa Fe and SP proposed merger. Approval seemed certain, but in 1986 the Interstate Commerce Commission denied permission because

the merger would create a railroad monopoly in New Mexico, Arizona, and California.

The Santa Fe, suddenly the smallest of the Super Seven freight railroads, began spinning off branches and secondary lines and became primarily a conduit for containers and trailers moving between the Midwest and Southern California. In June 1994 Santa Fe and Burlington Northern announced their intention to merge—BN would buy Santa Fe. The deal was consummated in 1995, forming the Burlington Northern Santa Fe.

FACTS & FIGURES

Year	1929	1994
Miles operated	13,157	7,800
Locomotives	1,993	1,696
Passenger cars	1,511	510
Freight cars	87,060	29,947

Reporting marks: ATSF, SFRD

Historical society: atsfrr.com

Atlanta & West Point

The Atlanta & West Point and the Western Railway of Alabama were together known as the West Point Route. They were affiliated with the Georgia Railroad, which was the representative of the Louisville & Nashville and the Atlantic Coast Line as lessees of the railroad properties of the Georgia Railroad & Banking Co., which held substantial interests in the two West Point Route railroads.

Ownership and control of these three railroads was particularly convoluted; for most purposes it is sufficient to say they were in the Atlantic Coast Line family. The West Point Route and the Georgia shared officers and *Official Guide* pages and were for most purposes considered a single entity.

Georgia Railroad

The Georgia Railroad was chartered in 1833 and amended its name to include "& Banking Company" in 1836. Its charter specified exemption from state and local taxation except for a small tax on net earnings. Construction was begun at Augusta, Ga., in 1835, and the 171-mile 5-foot-gauge main line was completed to Atlanta in 1845. In 1878 the Georgia Railroad absorbed the Macon & Augusta, which formed a branch from Camak to Macon.

The Georgia Railroad acquired stock in

An REA express reefer is tucked behind blue-and-silver Atlanta & West Point FP7 No. 552 as it gets ready to lead a passenger train in October 1960. *D. Schmidt*

the Atlanta & West Point and in 1875 purchased the Western of Alabama jointly with the Central Railroad & Banking Co. of Georgia. In May 1881 William Wadley leased the Georgia Railroad and its holdings in the West Point Route. He assigned the lease jointly to the Louisville & Nashville and the Central of Georgia. The CofG's interest later passed to the L&N, which assigned it to Atlantic Coast Line.

Atlanta & West Point

The Atlanta & La Grange Rail Road was chartered in 1847. In 1854 it opened a 5-foot-gauge line from East Point, Ga., six miles from Atlanta, through La Grange to West Point, Ga. It had trackage rights into Atlanta on the Macon & Western. In 1857 it was renamed Atlanta & West Point.

In 1889 the A&WP built its own line from East Point to Atlanta, and in 1909 made an agreement with Central of Georgia, successor to the Macon & Western, to operate Atlanta & West Point's and Central of Georgia's East Point-Atlanta lines as paired track.

Western Railway of Alabama

The Montgomery Rail Road was organized in 1834 to build from Montgomery, Ala., east to West Point, Ga. It built 32 miles of

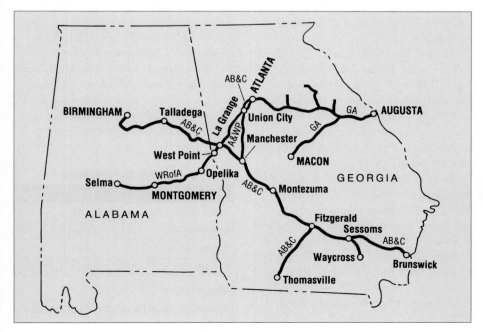

A&WP FACTS & FIGURES

Year	1929	1981
Miles operated	91	91
Locomotives	21	11
Passenger cars	26	4
Freight cars	581	400

Reporting marks: AWP

Historical society: railga.com/atlwp.html

The *Crescent Limited* steams eastward out of Montgomery, Ala., behind Western Railway of Alabama No. 186 in November 1941. The big 4-8-2 was built in 1924 for the Florida East Coast. *A. C. Kalmbach*

standard gauge track (rather than 5-foot gauge, which was almost universal in the South) before running into financial problems. It was taken over in 1843 by the Montgomery & West Point Rail Road. The remainder of the 88-mile route between was constructed by slave labor and opened in 1851. A branch from Opelika to Columbus, Ga., was opened in 1854.

During the Civil War the track gauge kept the road's rolling stock at home. An attack by Union forces in 1864 did not put the road out of business, but another in 1865, a few days after Lee's surrender, destroyed enough equipment to shut down the railroad. Reconstruction began, and the road converted to 5-foot gauge in 1866. In

1870 the company was taken over by the Western Rail Road of Alabama.

The Western of Alabama had opened a line from Montgomery west to Selma, 44 miles, and acquisition of the line to West Point more than tripled its size. In 1875 the road was sold under foreclosure jointly to the Georgia Railroad & Banking Co. and the Central Railroad & Banking Co. of Georgia.

In 1881 the WofA came under control of the Central Railroad and Banking Co. when William Wadley leased the Georgia Railroad and its interests in the A&WP and WofA. That same year the Opelika-Columbus branch was leased to the Columbus & Western; it later became part of the Central of Georgia.

In 1883 the Western Rail Road of Alabama was reorganized as the Western Railway of Alabama to untangle the various leases. During the 1890s the Central Railroad & Banking Co. interests in the Wadley lease passed to the L&N, which assigned them to ACL, but CofG retained ownership of some WofA stock until 1944.

The roads were standard-gauged in 1886, as were most railroads in the South.

By the turn of the century they were firmly in the ACL-L&N family, serving a rich agricultural area and working as a bridge route.

For many years Southern Railway's premier passenger train, the New York–New Orleans *Crescent Limited*, ran between Atlanta and New Orleans not on Southern's own rails but over those of the West Point Route between Atlanta and Montgomery and L&N between Montgomery and New Orleans. Georgia Railroad's passenger service was plebian, but its mixed trains lasted until 1983, when the newly formed Seaboard System bought the Georgia Railroad from the bank and merged it.

GEORGIA RR FACTS & FIGURES

Year	1929	1981
Miles operated	329	329
Locomotives	68	31
Passenger cars	72	—
Freight cars	1,512	810

Reporting marks: GA

Historical society: railga.com/atlwp.html

W of A FACTS & FIGURES

Year	1929	1981
Miles operated	133	133
Locomotives	29	14
Passenger cars	21	—
Freight cars	852	298

Reporting marks: WofA, WA

Historical society: railga.com/atlwp.html

Atlantic & Danville

The Atlantic & Danville had an all-Alco diesel roster: six RS-2s and an RS-3, two RS-36s rebuilt from earlier RS-2s, and a couple of RS-11s arriving after the Norfolk, Franklin & Danville reorganization. Number 104 is an RS-2 built in 1947. *American Locomotive Co.*

The Atlantic & Danville Railway was chartered in 1882 and completed its line from Portsmouth to Danville, Va., in 1890. Short branches from the main line led to West Norfolk, Hitchcock Mills, and Buffalo Lithia Springs, Va., and a 50-mile narrow gauge line ran from Emporia, junction with the Atlantic Coast Line, northeast to Claremont on the James River.

In 1899 the Southern Railway leased the Atlantic & Danville for 50 years. The A&D provided a good connection from Southern's Washington-Atlanta main line at Danville to the port area of Norfolk and Portsmouth. The narrow gauge branch was abandoned in 1934, and the Hitchcock Mills and Buffalo Lithia Springs branches were taken up in the early 1940s, but the main line and the West Norfolk branch remained intact.

When the lease expired in 1949, Southern weighed the cost of operating the A&D and the limitations of its track, mostly 60- and 85-pound rail, against the cost of trackage rights over Atlantic Coast Line from Selma, N. C., to Norfolk, and chose not to renew the lease. Atlantic & Danville resumed operation on its own Aug. 1, 1949. It filed for bankruptcy on Jan. 19, 1960, after the ICC turned down its request to guarantee a loan for capital expenditures and the purchase of freight cars.

On Oct. 31, 1962, the railroad was purchased at auction by the Norfolk & Western, which organized the Norfolk, Franklin & Danville Railway, a wholly owned subsidiary, to operate it. The merger of Norfolk & Western and Southern rendered the Norfolk-Danville route redundant. The western third of the NF&D was abandoned in early 1983, and the remainder was absorbed by the N&W on Dec. 30, 1983.

FACTS & FIGURES

Year	1949	1961
Miles operated	203	203
Locomotives	8	7
Passenger cars	—	—
Freight cars	139	271
Reporting marks: AD		

Atlantic & East Carolina

The newness of green-and-yellow EMD F2 No. 401 contrasts with the antiquity of the wood-sided passenger cars as Atlantic & East Carolina's daily train crosses the Trent River at New Bern, N. C., in 1946. *Atlantic & East Carolina*

The Atlantic & North Carolina Railroad was organized at New Bern, N. C., in 1854. It was to be the eastern portion of a state-owned system of three railroads that would cross North Carolina from west to east, tapping the commerce and agriculture of the state for the port of Morehead City—trade that the rivers of the area were taking to Norfolk, Va., and Charleston, S. C.

Morehead City never became the rival of New York, Baltimore, and Norfolk that its boosters predicted, and the three railroads continued as separate entities. The North Carolina Railroad and the Western North Carolina Railroad both became part of the Southern Railway family, and in 1904 the Atlantic & North Carolina was leased to the original Norfolk Southern.

The lease was forfeited in 1934 for nonpayment of rent and the A&NC began operating on its own in November 1935. On April 20, 1939, the stockholders voted to lease the road to H. P. Edwards, who organized the Atlantic & East Carolina Railway to operate the railroad. Within two years the A&EC was making a profit. The road dieselized in 1946 with two Electro-Motive F2s, an SW1, and a General Electric 44-ton switcher.

In February 1957 the Interstate Commerce Commission authorized the Southern Railway to purchase all the capital stock of the A&EC. By January 1958 the A&EC was listed under the Southern Railway in the *Official Guide*, and it still exists as a subsidiary of Norfolk Southern. The Atlantic & North Carolina also still exists; 70 percent of its stock is held by the state of North Carolina. The Beaufort & Morehead Railroad, an independent short line at one time in the fold of the old Norfolk Southern, is essentially a 3-mile extension of the A&EC from Morehead City to Beaufort.

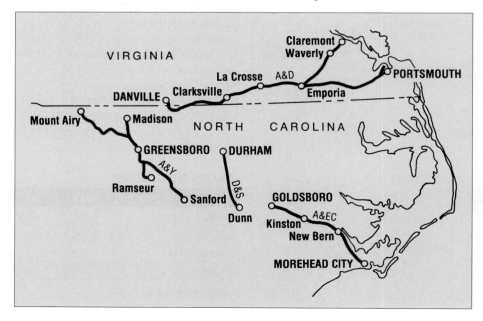

FACTS & FIGURES

Year	1939	1956
Miles operated	96	96
Locomotives	11	7
Passenger cars	10	9
Freight cars	41	128
Reporting marks: AEC		

Atlantic Coast Line

A northbound freight rolls near Vienna, Ga., behind double-headed steam locomotives in 1947. The lead engine is 2-8-2 No. 7230 and the trailing locomotive is 4-8-2 No. 7372. Both are former Atlanta, Birmingham & Coast locomotives. *David W. Salter*

The Atlantic Coast Line's history begins in 1830 with the organization of the Petersburg Railroad, which opened in 1833 between its namesake city in Virginia and the north bank of the Roanoke River opposite Weldon, N. C. In 1838 it made a rail connection with the newly opened Richmond & Petersburg Railroad.

In 1840 the Wilmington & Raleigh Railroad was opened from Wilmington, N. C., north 161 miles to Weldon. Its destination had been Raleigh initially, but the citizens of the state capital were not interested in the project.

The railroad was renamed Wilmington & Weldon in 1855. The Wilmington & Manchester Railroad from Wilmington west into South Carolina opened in 1853. The North Eastern Railroad opened in 1857 from Florence, S. C., south to Charleston.

After the Civil War William T. Walters of Baltimore acquired control of the Richmond & Petersburg, Wilmington & Weldon, Wilmington & Manchester, Petersburg, and North Eastern railroads, forming a route from Richmond to Charleston known as the Atlantic Coast Line—an association of more or less independent railroads.

The five railroads acquired a number of smaller railroads and the Wilmington & Weldon undertook a major piece of construction between 1885 and 1892, the Fayetteville Cutoff between Wilson, N. C., and Pee Dee, S. C. Sixty-two miles shorter than the line through Wilmington, it became the main route of the Atlantic Coast Line. In 1889 Walters formed a holding company to control them; it was renamed the Atlantic Coast Line Company in 1893.

In 1898 the Richmond & Petersburg

merged the Petersburg and was renamed the Atlantic Coast Line Railroad of Virginia. In April 1900 it merged the Norfolk & Carolina (Norfolk, Va.-Tarboro, N. C.), the Wilmington & Weldon, and the ACL of South Carolina (a group of five railroads between Wilmington and Charleston) and was renamed the Atlantic Coast Line Railroad. The new railroad stretched from Richmond and Norfolk, Va., to Charleston, S. C., and Augusta, Ga.

ACL FACTS & FIGURES

Year	1929	1966
Miles operated	5,155	5,743
Locomotives	1,007	629
Passenger cars	786	361
Freight cars	32,644	31,284
Reporting marks: ACL		
Historical society: aclsal.org		

The Atlantic Coast Line had a significant passenger train fleet, and in the diesel era relied on purple and silver EMD E units like this E7 A-B set. *Atlantic Coast Line*

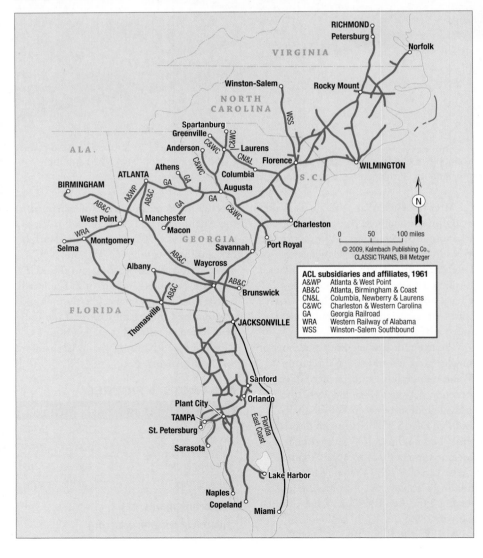

The Plant System

The ACL's lines south and west of Charleston, S. C., were part of the Plant System, which ACL purchased in 1902. Henry B. Plant had been superintendent of Adams Express at the beginning of the Civil War. In 1861 he organized Southern Express (it became a component of American Railway Express during World War I). In 1879 Plant acquired the Atlantic & Gulf Railroad, which had a main line from Savannah southwest to Bainbridge, Ga., and a branch to Live Oak, Fla. He reorganized the company as the Savannah, Florida & Western Railway and constructed several lines: west from near Bainbridge to Chattahoochee, Fla., to connect with a Louisville & Nashville predecessor; southeast from Waycross, Ga., to Jacksonville, Fla.; and south from Live Oak to Gainesville.

In 1893 the Plant System absorbed the South Florida Railroad (Sanford–Port Tampa) and in 1899, the Jacksonville, Tampa & Key West (Jacksonville–Sanford). It merged three more railroads, the Charleston & Savannah, the Brunswick & Western (Brunswick through Waycross to Albany, Ga.), and the Alabama Midland (Bainbridge to Montgomery, Alabama) in 1901. That same year the Plant System built a cutoff from Jesup to Folkston, Ga., bypassing Waycross.

Charleston & Western Carolina

Another member of ACL's family was the Charleston & Western Carolina (Port Royal, S. C., through Augusta, Ga., to Anderson, Greenville, and Spartanburg, S. C., connecting with the Clinchfield at Spartanburg). The first portion of the road, between Augusta and the coast, was financed by the Georgia Railroad & Banking Co. However, the Central Railroad & Banking Co. (Central of Georgia) gained control in 1881 to tap inland South Carolina for the port of Savannah. Central of Georgia lost the C&WC in 1894; ACL gained control in 1897.

By 1930 the C&WC shared officers with parent ACL. The ACL attempted to merge the C&WC in 1930, but neighboring roads protested. Although the C&WC was operated independently, it looked like Atlantic Coast Line—secondhand ACL steam locomotives, including Pacifics for freight service, and silver-and-purple diesels.

ACL finally merged the Charleston & Western Carolina in 1959. Connecting with the C&WC at Laurens, S. C., was another ACL family member, the Columbia, Newberry & Laurens Railroad, a 75-mile line joining the three cities of its name.

Interlocking relationships

In 1902 ACL acquired control of the Louisville & Nashville Railroad, which in turn controlled the Nashville, Chattanooga & St. Louis Railway. Later ACL and L&N jointly leased the Carolina, Clinchfield & Ohio Railway and formed the Clinchfield Railroad to operate it. The ACL and L&N also leased the railroad property of the Georgia Railroad & Banking Company (closely affiliated with the Atlanta & West Point and the Western Railway of Alabama) and formed the Georgia Railroad to operate it.

In 1926 ACL formed Atlanta, Birmingham & Coast Railroad to acquire the Atlanta, Birmingham & Atlantic. The AB&C had lines from Waycross to Atlanta and Birmingham, where it connected with L&N. (More on the Atlanta, Birmingham & Coast in a bit.)

Atlantic Coast Line was considered one of the three strong roads of the South (the other two were the Louisville & Nashville and the Southern). It carried the majority of Florida-bound passengers, turning Miami passengers over to Florida East Coast at Jacksonville but carrying west-coast passengers all the way—to Tampa, St. Petersburg, Sarasota, Fort Myers, and Naples. The ACL also participated in most of the Midwest-to-Florida passenger routes. The opening of ACL's Perry Cutoff in 1928 between Thomasville, Ga., and Dunellon, Fla., shortened considerably the route between the Midwest and west coast points.

Atlantic Coast Line advertised itself as the Standard Railroad of the South, and its route between Richmond and Jacksonville was fully signalled and mostly double track, much more than parallel Seaboard Air Line could boast. As with the Pennsylvania, which advertised itself as the standard railroad of the world, there were some nonstandard items. Two are notable: ACL was one of few railroads to consider the Pacific a dual-purpose engine, but the profile of its main line was such that a 4-6-2 could move freight at good speed. The

Brand-new Alco Century 628 diesels 2001 and 2002 pose for a publicity photograph shortly after delivery in December 1963. *Atlantic Coast Line*

ACL was particularly taken with the USRA light Pacific, which was the equal of a mid-size 2-8-0 in tractive effort and considerably better in the matter of speed. The other was the color choice for its diesels—purple (president Champion McDowell Davis liked purple). The 4-6-2s yielded to Es for passengers and Fs for freight, and purple on the diesels eventually gave way to black.

In 1958 Atlantic Coast Line and Seaboard Air Line announced they were considering merger, and in 1960 they petitioned to merge as the Seaboard Coast Line Railroad. The two roads served much the same territory, and they had 75 common points. The principal argument for merger was the elimination of duplicate lines and facilities. The merger was approved and took effect on July 1, 1967.

Atlanta, Birmingham & Coast

The Waycross Air Line Railroad was incorporated as a logging railroad in 1887. By the end of 1904 it had become the Atlanta & Birmingham Railway, a common carrier with a line from Brunswick to Montezuma, Georgia, and branches to Thomasville and Waycross, Ga. At Montezuma the Central of Georgia offered connections to Macon, Atlanta, and Birmingham.

In 1906 the newly created Atlanta, Birmingham & Atlantic Railroad absorbed the Atlantic & Birmingham. The new road built westward to Manchester, Ga., and from there to Atlanta and to Birmingham, reaching Atlanta in 1908 and Birmingham in 1910. By then the AB&A was in receivership, largely because of the cost of the marine terminal it had built at Brunswick.

The Atlanta, Birmingham & Atlantic Railway took over the operation at the beginning of 1916, but it fared little better financially. It was in receivership by 1921. The Atlanta, Birmingham & Coast Railroad was incorporated November 22, 1926, to acquire the Atlanta, Birmingham & Atlantic. The Atlantic Coast Line was firmly in control. AB&C offered ACL entries to Atlanta and Birmingham and a chance to participate more fully in Midwest-to-Florida traffic. ACL merged the AB&C on December 31, 1945.

AB&C FACTS & FIGURES

Year	1929	1945
Miles operated	640	639
Locomotives	30	59
Passenger cars	51	39
Freight cars	1,948	908
Reporting marks: AB&C		

Baltimore & Ohio

A Baltimore & Ohio Class S-1 2-10-2 lays down sand as it powers west through the Cumberland Narrows near Cumberland, Md., on Oct. 16, 1955. Sand Patch grade—for which the locomotives were designed—is next. *William P. Price*

The most important U. S. seaports in the early 1800s were Boston, New York, Philadelphia, Baltimore, and Charleston. Baltimore had an advantage in being farther inland than the others, almost at the head of navigation on Chesapeake Bay, the estuary of the Susquehanna River. New York gained an advantage in 1825 with the opening of the Erie Canal, permitting navigation all the way to Lake Erie, and in 1826 the commonwealth of Pennsylvania chartered a system of canals to link Philadelphia with Pittsburgh. Baltimore responded to the competition of the other cities by chartering the Baltimore & Ohio Railroad on Feb. 28, 1827.

The B&O was to build a railroad from Baltimore to a suitable point on the Ohio River. It was to be the first common carrier railroad in the U. S., the first to offer scheduled freight and passenger service to the public. Such a project would be

challenging today—and we know where the Ohio River is, we know something about the intervening territory, and we know what a railroad is. Today's equivalent of the chartering of the B&O might be the establishment of a company to operate scheduled freight and passenger service to the moon. Baltimore's only alternative was a canal, and the only route for that was south to Washington and up the Potomac, where the Chesapeake & Ohio canal was already under construction. Such a canal, too, would lead quickly to the Allegheny Mountains, where construction and operation of a canal would be difficult.

Ground was broken for the railroad with great celebration on July 4, 1828. The first stone was laid by 90-year-old Charles Carroll of Carrollton, Md., the last signer of the Declaration of Independence then still living. A route was laid out to follow the Patapsco and Monocacy rivers to the

Potomac, and work began.

The line was opened for scheduled service to Ellicott's Mills on May 24, 1830. On Dec. 1, 1831, the road was opened to Frederick, 60 miles. The B&O opened a branch from Relay (then called Washington Junction) to Washington in August 1835. Two years later a bridge was completed across the Potomac to Harpers Ferry, W. Va. (The separation of the western portion of Virginia did not occur until 1863, but for clarity we'll use present state names.) At Harpers Ferry the B&O connected with the Winchester & Potomac, forming the first junction of two railroad companies in the U. S.

B&O's line continued west through Cumberland, Md., to Grafton, W. Va., where it turned northwest to reach the goal of its charter at Wheeling, W. Va., 379 miles from Baltimore, on Jan. 1, 1853, almost 25 years after commencing

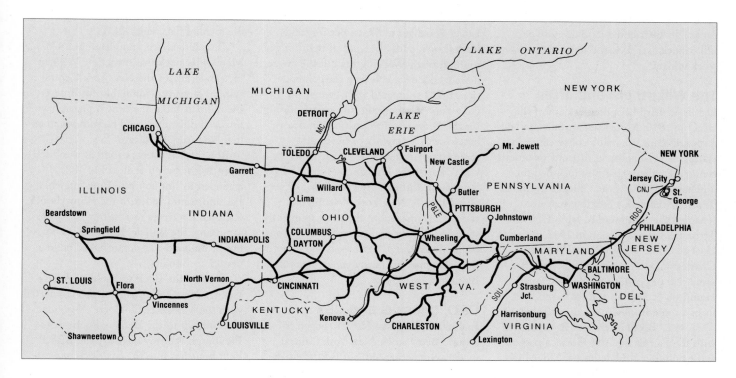

construction. Another line was pushed west from Grafton to reach the Ohio at Parkersburg, W. Va., in 1856.

The railroad continued westward in 1866 by leasing the Central Ohio Railroad, a line from Bellaire, Ohio, across the Ohio River from Wheeling, through Newark to Columbus, and in 1869 by leasing a line from Newark to Sandusky, Ohio. From a point on that line called Chicago Junction (now Willard) a subsidiary company, the Baltimore & Ohio & Chicago, built west to Chicago between 1872 and 1874.

Battle with the Pennsylvania

Under the leadership of John W. Garrett the B&O continued to expand. In 1871 the Pittsburgh & Connellsville Railroad completed a line from Cumberland to Pittsburgh and leased it to the B&O the following year. B&O opened the Metropolitan Branch, from Washington northwest to a connection with the main line at Point of Rocks, Md., in 1873.

The Pennsylvania Railroad considered Pittsburgh its exclusive territory. B&O's Cumberland-Pittsburgh route eventually resulted in another B&O incursion into Pennsy territory, a line from Baltimore to Philadelphia. New York-Washington trains in the 1870s were operated jointly by the Pennsylvania Railroad (Jersey City-Philadelphia), the Philadelphia, Wilmington & Baltimore (Philadelphia to Baltimore), and the B&O (Baltimore to Washington). The

B&O was less than cooperative in the matter of through ticketing of passengers and through billing of freight. Moreover, B&O had a monopoly on Washington, and its charter protected its monopoly status. In 1872 the Pennsylvania built a slightly roundabout but legal line from Baltimore to Washington. B&O moved its New York trains off the Pennsy and onto the Philadelphia & Reading/Central of New Jersey route east of Philadelphia.

The Philadelphia, Wilmington & Baltimore was figuratively and literally in the middle. Both the B&O and the Pennsy wanted it, and in 1881 the Pennsylvania secured control. In retaliation B&O proposed its own line from Baltimore to Philadelphia and its own terminal facilities on Staten Island. The Pennsy responded in 1884 by refusing to handle B&O trains east of Baltimore. B&O completed its own line from Baltimore to Philadelphia, parallel to the PB&W and no more than a few miles from it, in 1886.

Garrett died in 1884 and was succeeded by his son Robert for two years, Samuel Spencer for one, and then Charles F. Mayer. Mayer undertook to improve the road and at the same time keep its financial situation from crumbling. The most significant improvements were control of the Pittsburgh & Western (Pittsburgh-Akron), construction of a line from Akron, Ohio, to Chicago Junction; control of a route from Parkersburg, W. Va., through

Cincinnati to St. Louis (the Baltimore & Ohio Southwestern, which included the former Ohio & Mississippi, completed in 1857); construction of the Baltimore Belt line through, around, and under Baltimore to connect the Philadelphia route with the rest of the B&O; and electrification of the Baltimore Belt, the first mainline electrification in North America.

The financial situation was more difficult. B&O had a large debt. Freight and passenger rates were low and revenues were dropping—in 1889 B&O handled 31 percent of the country's tidewater soft coal traffic; by 1896, that had dropped to just 4 percent because of competition from other railroads. The B&O cut back on expenditures for maintenance and quickly acquired a reputation for unreliability. B&O entered receivership in 1896.

Baltimore & Ohio came out of receivership in 1899 still under its original charter, which included tax exemption privileges. In 1901 the Pennsylvania bought a large block of B&O stock and appointed Leonor F. Loree president of the road. He undertook a line improvement program that reduced grades and curves and added many miles of double track, and he secured for B&O a large interest in the Reading, which in turn controlled the Central Railroad of New Jersey. The Pennsylvania sold some of its B&O stock to Union Pacific in 1906 and traded the remainder to UP for Southern Pacific stock in 1913. The UP eventually distributed its Baltimore & Ohio stock as a dividend to its own stockholders.

The Willard era and after

Daniel Willard became president of the B&O in 1910. More than anyone else he is responsible for the road's conservative, courteous personality in the mid-twentieth century. Further expansion included the purchase in 1910 of the Chicago Terminal Transfer Railroad, a belt line that was renamed the Baltimore & Ohio Chicago Terminal; the acquisition in 1917 of the Coal & Coke Railway from Elkins to Charleston, W. Va.; and acquisition that same year of portions of the Cincinnati, Hamilton & Dayton and its leased lines to form a route from Cincinnati to Toledo.

In 1927 B&O celebrated its centennial with the Fair of the Iron Horse, a pageant and exhibition at Halethorpe, Md. Much of the rolling stock exhibited there was from B&O's museum collection, which formed the nucleus of the B&O Museum in Baltimore, one of the earliest and best railroad museums.

The Interstate Commerce Commission merger plan of the 1920s put B&O into an expansionist mood. In 1926 B&O purchased the Cincinnati, Indianapolis & Western's line from Hamilton, Ohio, to Springfield, Ill. In 1927 it acquired an 18 percent interest in the Wheeling & Lake Erie and began to purchase Western Maryland stock. In 1929 B&O bought the Chicago & Alton Railroad, reorganized it as the Alton Railroad, and operated it as part of the B&O. (Alton regained independence in 1943 and merged with Gulf, Mobile & Ohio in 1947.) In 1932 B&O acquired the Buffalo, Rochester & Pittsburgh from the Van Sweringens in exchange for B&O's interest in the W&LE and also purchased the Buffalo & Susquehanna.

In 1934 B&O arranged for trackage rights on Pittsburgh & Lake Erie's water-level route between McKeesport and New Castle, Pa., bypassing the curves and grades of its own route (which remained in service for local business). B&O's through passenger trains moved to P&LE's Pittsburgh station across the Monongahela River from the B&O station.

For many years B&O competed with Pennsylvania and New York Central in the New York-Chicago and New York-St.

Louis passenger markets. B&O's trains were slower, partly because of their longer route through Washington, but they were dieselized a decade before the competition. B&O competed with Pennsy on the New York-Washington run, compensating for the Pennsylvania's terminal in Manhattan with a network of buses that received passengers at trainside in Jersey City, crossed the Hudson by ferry, and fanned out through New York. Many preferred B&O's New York-Washington trains to Pennsy's, but the most frequently stated reason for preferring B&O—"You could always get a seat"—was the reason B&O dropped its passenger service east of Baltimore in 1958.

C&O, Chessie, and CSX

In 1960 Chesapeake & Ohio began to acquire B&O stock. New York Central made a competing bid, but B&O's stockholders approved C&O control, and on May 1, 1962, so did the ICC. By early 1964 C&O owned 90 percent of B&O's stock. In 1967 the ICC authorized C&O and B&O to control Western Maryland; B&O's WM stock had long been held in a nonvoting trust.

On June 15, 1973, B&O, C&O, and WM were made subsidiaries of the newly created Chessie System. There was no great surge of track abandonment, because in most areas B&O and C&O were complementary rather than competitive. In 1981 B&O leased the former Rock Island track from Blue Island to Henry, Ill.

B&O continued to exist within Chessie System. On May 1, 1983, B&O took over operation of the Western Maryland. Four years later, on April 30, 1987, C&O merged B&O, and four months after that, CSX Transportation merged C&O.

Buffalo, Rochester & Pittsburgh

Rochester, New York, had a well-developed flour-milling industry in 1869. The Genesee River furnished power to drive the mills, and wheat came from the fertile Genesee Valley south of Rochester in boats on the Genesee Valley Canal. To provide better grain transportation and, more important, to bring coal from Pennsylvania, the Rochester & State Line Railroad was incorporated in 1869. It was to build south up the valley of Genesee to the Pennsylvania state line—the destination was later changed to

the town of Salamanca, N. Y.

The railroad was completed in 1878. Most of its stock was owned by William H. Vanderbilt, of the New York Central system. However, Vanderbilt lost interest in the railroad about the time it began having financial difficulties, and he sold his stock to a New York syndicate.

The road was reorganized as the Rochester & Pittsburgh Railroad in 1881. It extended its line south to Punxsutawney, Pa., and contracted with the Pennsylvania Railroad for access to Pittsburgh. At the same time the Buffalo, Rochester & Pittsburgh Railroad was organized to build a branch to Buffalo.

In 1884 the R&P was sold to Adrian Iselin, a New York financier also connected with the Mobile & Ohio. He consolidated the railroads as the Buffalo, Rochester & Pittsburgh Railway in 1887. The BR&P built branches into the coalfields of western Pennsylvania and constructed a line north from Rochester to the shore of Lake Ontario to connect with a car ferry to Cobourg, Ont.

In 1893 BR&P opened a branch to Clearfield, Pa., and a connection with the New York Central and, via NYC, the Reading. In 1898 the Allegheny & Western Railroad was incorporated to extend the BR&P from Punxsutawney west to Butler, Pa., and a connection with the Pittsburgh & Western (Baltimore & Ohio). Trackage rights from Butler to New Castle and Pittsburgh were included in the deal with the B&O. The new line opened in 1899.

BR&P developed into a well-run coal hauler. After the Interstate Commerce Commission merger plan of the 1920s was published, both Delaware & Hudson and Baltimore & Ohio petitioned for control of the BR&P. The ICC approved B&O's application in 1930, but in the meantime the Van Sweringen brothers (who owned the Nickel Plate and controlled the Chesapeake & Ohio) had bought the BR&P. B&O still wanted it, and the Van Sweringens wanted the Wheeling & Lake Erie, in which B&O held a minority interest. They traded on January 1, 1932. Baltimore & Ohio wanted to assemble a Chicago–New York shortcut that would use BR&P from Butler to Du Bois, Buffalo & Susquehanna to Sinnemahoning, and a new line connecting with the Reading west of Williamsport (a railroad equivalent of Interstate 80). The Great Depression was not an auspicious time for railroad construction, and the project was shelved.

Chessie System sold the Rochester branch to the Genesee & Wyoming Railroad in 1986 to become the Rochester & Southern Railroad, and in April 1988 the remainder of the BR&P became the Buffalo & Pittsburgh Railroad, also a G&W subsidiary. The Rochester line has been abandoned between Machias and Silver Lake Junction, but most of the rest of the BR&P is still in service.

Buffalo & Susquehanna

In 1885 Frank Goodyear, a fuel and lumber dealer in Buffalo, New York, bought a large tract of timberland in northwest Pennsylvania. He organized the Sinnemahoning Valley Railroad to build a line from Keating Summit (on what later became the Pennsylvania Railroad line to Buffalo) to Austin, Pa., where he had a sawmill. Goodyear formed a partnership with his brother Charles in 1887 and began to expand their empire. By 1893 their railroad system reached east to Galeton and Ansonia, and the various railroad companies were consolidated as the Buffalo & Susquehanna Railroad. At the beginning of 1896 the B&S had a line northwest from Galeton to Wellsville, N. Y., In 1898 the Goodyears purchased the Addison & Pennsylvania, a former narrow gauge line from Galeton northeast to Addison, N. Y.

The Goodyears pushed their railroad southwest through Du Bois to Sagamore, Pa., with the thought of continuing to Pittsburgh. Coal became the mainstay of the south end of the railroad, and lumber and leather (many tanneries were located on the line) were the principal commodities carried at the north end. The Goodyear lumber and railroad empire prospered, and by the early 1900s it included lumber mills in the South and the New Orleans Great Northern Railroad.

In 1906 the Goodyears built the Buffalo & Susquehanna Railway from Wellsville to Buffalo, nearly 90 miles. A year later Frank Goodyear died; Charles died in 1911, and the Goodyear empire began to fall apart. The expense of constructing the line to Buffalo began to cause financial difficulty, and the road laid aside plans to extend its line to Pittsburgh and to relocate its line to eliminate the four switchbacks over the mountains between Galeton and Wharton. The Buffalo & Susquehanna Railway leased the

Coal was a major source of traffic on the B&O. Here, 2-8-8-4 No. 7609 lugs a coal train to the summit at Altamont, W. Va., in June 1945. *H. W. Pontin; David P. Morgan Library collection*

Buffalo & Susquehanna Railroad, but that didn't forestall receivership. After a brief period of operation as the Wellsville & Buffalo, the Buffalo extension was scrapped in 1916. The remainder of the system was reorganized as the Buffalo & Susquehanna Railroad Corporation.

In 1932 the B&O purchased the B&S to use the Du Bois–Sinnemahoning portion as part of a new freight line across Pennsylvania. In July 1942 a flood washed out much of the line south of Galeton. B&O abandoned the line between Sinnemahoning and Burrows, just south of Galeton, isolating the Wellsville–Galeton–Addison portion from the rest of the B&O.

Because of the problems of isolation and declining traffic, B&O considered selling or abandoning the northern part of the B&S, and to simplify sale, in 1954 B&O merged the B&S and two smaller roads it had leased since the turn of the century.

On Jan. 1, 1956, B&O sold the northern portion of the former Buffalo & Susquehanna to Murray M. Salzberg, who organized the Wellsville, Addison & Galeton Railroad to operate it. The WA&G was abandoned in stages, with the last piece going in 1979. The last portion of the south end of the B&S, B&O's branch from Du Bois to Weedville, disappeared from B&O's map in the 1970s.

Cincinnati, Indianapolis & Western

The Cincinnati, Hamilton & Dayton Railroad existed long before the period this

book covers, but a brief description is necessary as a prelude to describing the Cincinnati, Indianapolis & Western, and also to distinguish it from an electric railway that used the same name in the same territory from 1926 to 1929.

The CH&D built north from Cincinnati to Dayton in 1851 and 1852 to connect with the Mad River & Lake Erie. Relations between the two railroads were not comfortable, and the CH&D leased the Dayton & Michigan Railroad, which was under construction from Dayton north to Toledo. By 1858 it had reached Lima and was already arranging trackage rights from Toledo to Detroit over a predecessor of the Pere Marquette. Between Cincinnati and Dayton the CH&D laid a third rail for the broad gauge trains of the Atlantic & Great Western, the southwestern extension of the Erie, and it acquired branches, among them lines from Dayton northwest through Delphos, from Findlay west through Ottawa to Fort Wayne, and from Dayton southeast through the coalfields to the Ohio River at Ironton. It also acquired the Cincinnati, Hamilton & Indianapolis and the Indianapolis, Decatur & Springfield railroads.

Around the turn of the century the CH&D fell on hard times. It acquired and leased the Pere Marquette in 1904. J. P. Morgan & Company purchased the two roads in 1905 and offered them to the Erie. Word got about that the Erie accepted them. F. D. Underwood, president of the Erie, hurried home from Europe, inspected

The B&O dieselized its name passenger trains with six sets of Electro-Motive EA-EB passenger diesels in 1937 and 1938. Here, two of the sets rest in Chicago between runs. *Baltimore & Ohio*

the CH&D and PM, and rejected them. Morgan himself took them back, placed them in receivership, and offered them to the Baltimore & Ohio. B&O took them in 1909 on a 7-year trial basis.

Floods in Ohio in 1913 threw the CH&D back into financial trouble and receivership. It cast off the Pere Marquette and tore up some of its branches in western Ohio. It spun off the Hamilton–Springfield, Ill., line as the Cincinnati, Indianapolis & Western Railway. CH&D reorganized in 1916 as the Toledo & Cincinnati Railroad, and B&O acquired it in 1917.

Independence for the CI&W

The Cincinnati, Indianapolis & Western Railway was sold at foreclosure on Sept. 9, 1915. The Cincinnati, Indianapolis & Western Railroad was incorporated on Oct. 30 as its successor, effective Dec. 1, 1915. The new company took over the Hamilton, Ohio–Springfield, Illinois line plus trackage rights but spun off the line from Sidell to Olney, Ill., as the Sidell & Olney Railroad, owned by the CI&W but operated separately. In 1919 that line was sold to become the Kansas & Sidell Railroad plus two short-lived companies that briefly operated the line from Kansas to Casey and from Casey to Yale.

At the beginning of 1922 the CI&W purchased the West Melcher–Brazil, Indiana, line of the Chicago & Indiana Coal Railway (the rest of the Coal Road became the Chicago, Attica & Southern). Baltimore & Ohio acquired control of the CI&W on June 1, 1927, and thereafter the CI&W was operated as part of B&O.

The major role of the Cincinnati, Indianapolis & Western had been to serve as the Cincinnati extension of the Monon's Chicago–Indianapolis line. The B&O could move Chicago–Cincinnati traffic on its own rails all the way—east to Deshler, Ohio, on the Chicago–Pittsburgh main line, then south on the former CH&D. The route was about 80 miles longer than the direct routes—no passenger would choose that route unless he was trying to set a slow-play record. B&O acquisition of the CI&W had the effect of accelerating the Monon's decline and taking traffic off the CI&W. By 1941 passenger service on the line consisted of Hamilton–Indianapolis and Indianapolis–Decatur motor trains.

Staten Island Rapid Transit

Geographically, Staten Island is much closer to New Jersey than to New York, and until the completion of the Verrazano Bridge in 1964, it was connected to the rest of New York—city and state—by ferries from St. George, at the north end of the island.

In 1885 B&O purchased the Staten Island Rapid Transit Railway, which had a short line of its own between Tompkinsville and Clifton on the northeast shore of Staten Island and leased the Staten Island Railway, a line from Clifton to Tottenville, at its southern tip. B&O's intention was to build freight and passenger terminals on Staten Island; purchase of SIRT gave B&O

waterfront property on New York Bay.

SIRT built a line west to the Arthur Kill Bridge in 1889 at the same time the Baltimore & New York, another B&O subsidiary, built a connecting line from Cranford Junction on the Central of New Jersey. SIRT built a short line from Clifton to South Beach in 1892.

In anticipation of a tunnel under the Narrows to Brooklyn and a connection there with the New York subway system, SIRT electrified its lines in 1925 using third-rail power and cars similar to those of the Brooklyn-Manhattan Transit Co. The electrification brought no big increase in traffic, and the tunnel was never built.

In 1944 SIRT purchased the property of the Baltimore & New York and merged the Staten Island Railway. In 1948 the road discontinued its ferry service between Tottenville and Perth Amboy, N. J. The terminal at St. George was destroyed by fire in 1946; a modern replacement was opened in 1951. SIRT discontinued passenger service on the lines to Arlington and South Beach in March 1953 because of city-operated bus competition.

On Jan. 1, 1970, New York City's lease of the St. George–Tottenville line was terminated. After that date the city reimbursed the railroad for its passenger deficits. On July 1, 1971, operation of the Tottenville line was turned over to the Staten Island Rapid Transit Operating Authority, a division of the state's Metropolitan Transportation Authority, and the line itself was purchased by the city of New York. Later that year the name of the railroad was changed to Staten Island Railroad Corporation.

In 1985 the Staten Island Railroad was purchased by the Delaware Otsego System. By 1991 freight service had ceased, but the Kill bridge, which connects Staten Island to New Jersey, was reopened in 2007. That, along with track renovations, allowed freight service to resume by agreement with CSX and Norfolk Southern.

FACTS & FIGURES

Year	1929	1972
Miles operated	5,658	5,491
Locomotives	2,364	995
Passenger cars	1,732	23
Freight cars	102,072	58,132
Reporting marks: B&O, BO		
Website: borhs.org		

Bangor & Aroostook

Maine's northernmost county is Aroostook. In area it is somewhat larger than Connecticut and Rhode Island combined; the population even today is less than 75,000. Much of the county is forested wilderness, and the region is best known for growing potatoes. As late as 1891 Aroostook County was connected to the rest of the state only by some primitive wagon roads.

In 1871 a rail route had been opened from Bangor, Maine, north and east to the Canadian border at Vanceboro, forming part of a route from Boston through Portland and Bangor to Saint John, New Brunswick. In 1889 Canadian Pacific completed a line east from Montreal that cut across the state, meeting the Boston-Saint John route at Mattawamkeag, Maine. The CP had branches that penetrated the state of Maine from the east as far as Houlton and Presque Isle, but otherwise northern Maine was devoid of railroads.

The Bangor & Aroostook Railroad was incorporated in 1891 to build north from

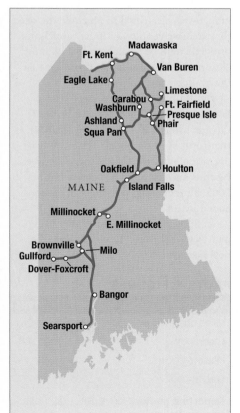

Two GP38s and a GP7 in Bangor & Aroostook's orange, gray, and black livery head a southbound freight at Chapman in September 1985. *Jim Shaw*

Brownville, Maine, on the CPR line, to Caribou, Ashland, and Fort Fairfield. In 1892 it purchased the Bangor & Piscataquis Railroad and the Bangor & Katahdin Iron Works Railway to achieve a connection with the U. S. railroad network. The first BAR train rolled into Houlton in December 1893; in December 1894 the road reached Caribou. The railroad continued to extend lines through much of Aroostook County. In 1905 the BAR built a line south from South LaGrange to a new connection with the Maine Central at Northern Maine Junction, six miles west of Bangor, and on south to tidewater at Searsport. By 1910 the road had reached its greatest extent, except for a bridge opened in 1915 between Van Buren, Maine, and St. Leonard, N. B.

In 1922 the first abandonment took place, and since then a number of branches and duplicate lines have been trimmed. BAR discontinued rail passenger service in 1961 but operated buses between Bangor and Aroostook County points until 1983.

In the 1950s the railroad achieved recognition out of proportion to its size and remoteness: for a fleet of red, white, and blue boxcars blazoned "State of Maine

Products;" for purchasing sufficient diesels to cover peak traffic and then leasing them during most of the year to the Pennsylvania Railroad; and for working a similar arrangement with Pacific Fruit Express to keep its fleet of potato-carrying refrigerator cars moving and thus earning money.

The Bangor & Aroostook was purchased by holding company Iron Road Railways in 1995. Following Iron Road's 2003 bankruptcy, the line was acquired by Rail World, Inc., which made the remaining BAR line part of its Montreal, Maine & Atlantic. After the MM&A petitioned to abandon the line from Millinocket to the Canadian border in 2010, the state of Maine purchased the route, and the segment is operated by the Maine Northern Railway.

FACTS & FIGURES

Year	1929	1983
Miles operated	614	422
Locomotives	81	38
Passenger cars	83	—
Freight cars	3,435	2,835
Reporting marks: BAR		

BC Rail
(Pacific Great Eastern)

Pacific Great Eastern owned six GE 70-tonners, purchased in 1949 and 1950. Two are shown on a mixed train in the early '50s. *Linn Westcott*

B C Rail began its existence in 1912 as the Pacific Great Eastern Railway. It constructed a 12-mile line

© 2014, Kalmbach Publishing Co., CLASSIC TRAINS, Bill Metzger
Not all lines shown

from North Vancouver westward to Horseshoe Bay and took over a bankrupt line that had built a few miles north from Squamish, which was 28 miles west of Horseshoe Bay. In 1918 the government of the province of British Columbia acquired the remaining capital stock of the railway. The PGE reached Quesnel in 1921 and stopped. In 1928 it abandoned its initial line between North Vancouver and Horseshoe Bay.

The PGE was known as the railroad that "ran from nowhere to nowhere," and other than a barge connection at Squa-mish (to North Vancouver) didn't have an interchange with another railroad until 1952. At that time the line was pushed north from Quesnel to a junction with Canadian National's Jasper-Prince Rupert Line at Prince George. It was PGE's first rail connection with the outside world.

In 1956 the PGE constructed a line east from Squamish to North Vancouver, replacing the 12 miles of track that it had built in 1912 and abandoned in 1928. It built extensions north from Prince George to Dawson Creek and Fort Nelson in 1958 and 1971, respectively. Traffic included coal, ore (including gold concentrate), heavy equipment, and general freight.

The railroad changed its name to Brit-ish Columbia Railway in 1972 and, amidst

a restructuring, to BC Rail in late 1984. Construction of an extension to Dease Lake in northwestern British Columbia was halted in 1977.

The 80-mile Tumbler Ridge Branch, begun in 1981, was completed in 1983. The branch was electrified to preclude the need for extensive ventilation in its tunnels; its principal item of traffic was coal. A mine closure in 2010 resulted in operations on the branch being suspended.

BC Rail operated passenger service between North Vancouver and Prince George using Rail Diesel Cars (RDCs); the Royal Hudson Steam Train, a tourist operation, ran on BC Rail tracks between North Vancouver and Squamish until 2001; all remaining passenger operations ended in 2002.

In 2003 it was announced that Cana-dian National would lease BC Rail; the deal became official in July 2004.

FACTS & FIGURES

Year	1929	1984
Miles operated	348	1,261
Locomotives	12	126
Passenger cars	28	6
Freight cars	309	9,793
Reporting marks: BCIT, BCOL, PGE, PGER		

Belt Railway of Chicago

The Belt Railway of Chicago was built between 1880 and 1882 as the Belt Division of the Chicago & Western Indiana, a terminal road owned by the predecessors of the Chicago & Eastern Illinois, Monon, Erie, Wabash, and Grand Trunk Western railroads (eventual components, respectively, of Union Pacific, CSX, Conrail, Norfolk Southern, and Canadian National). The railroad was reincorporated in 1882 as the Belt Railway Company of Chicago, and control passed from the C&WI to its owners.

The purpose of the belt line was to provide connections away from the congestion of downtown Chicago between line-haul railroads. The BRC was to have a large yard that could serve as a freight car clearinghouse in Chicago (hence the name Clearing Yard). A circular design for the yard was proposed by A. B. Stickney of the

Belt Railway of Chicago operated six C-424s in transfer and coal service. The Alcos, ballasted with extra weight, lasted in service until 1999. *Harold A. Edmonson.*

Chicago Great Western. Although only a small portion of that design was built (and of more-or-less conventional layout), when

Clearing Yard opened in 1902 it was the largest freight yard in the world and one of the first three hump yards in the U. S. (The other two were the Pennsylvania's East Altoona, Pa., yard and New York Central's DeWitt Yard at Syracuse, N. Y.)

In 1911 the Lowrey Agreement resulted in flat-rate switching charges for Chicago, and in 1912 the Belt Operating Agreement brought several more railroads into the ownership and operation of the BRC: Atchison, Topeka & Santa Fe; Chesapeake & Ohio; Chicago, Burlington & Quincy; Illinois Central; Pennsylvania; Rock Island; and Soo Line. Pere Marquette became an owner in 1923. Clearing Yard was extensively rebuilt in 1912, and in 1938 retarders were added, eliminating the need for men to ride and brake each car as it rolled down the hump.

BRC is currently owned by BNSF, Canadian National, Canadian Pacific, CSX, Norfolk Southern, and Union Pacific. It connects with all line-haul roads serving Chicago.

FACTS & FIGURES

Year	1929	1983
Miles operated	25	43
Locomotives	96	46
Passenger cars	—	—
Freight cars	346	—
Reporting marks: BRC		

Bessemer & Lake Erie

A brand-new A-B-B-A set of orange-and-black EMD F7 diesels pose on the State Route 358 bridge near Greenville, Pa., shortly after delivery to the Bessemer & Lake Erie in 1951. *Bessemer & Lake Erie*

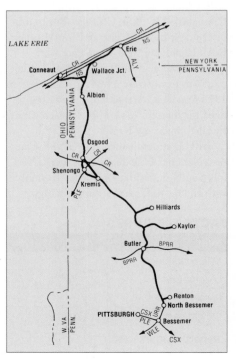

The Bessemer & Lake Erie began life around 1865 as the Bear Creek Railroad, which was built to serve the coalfields southeast of Greenville, Penn. It was renamed the Shenango & Allegheny Railroad in 1867 and reorganized as the Pittsburgh, Shenango & Lake Erie Railroad in 1888. By then it consisted of a main line from Osgood to Hilliards plus several branches, and its operations included the West Penn & Shenango Connecting Railroad south to Butler. The railroad was extended north, reaching the city of Erie in 1891 and Conneaut, Ohio, in 1892.

In 1896 the railroad joined in a three-way agreement with the Union Railroad and the Carnegie Steel Co. to build a line from Butler to East Pittsburgh. Carnegie already controlled the Mesabi Range iron mines in Minnesota, the railroads from the mines to the docks on Lake Superior, and the Union Railroad, a terminal railroad serving the steel mills in Pittsburgh. By financing the construction of the line from Butler to the connection with the Union Railroad, Carnegie gained control over all the companies involved in transporting ore to his mills.

In 1897 the railroad was renamed the Pittsburg, Bessemer & Lake Erie Railroad, and in 1900 Carnegie Steel chartered the Bessemer & Lake Erie Railroad, which then leased the PB&LE. In 1901 Carnegie Steel became part of the new United States Steel Corporation.

The Bessemer embarked on a series of projects to improve its line, and by the mid-1950s it had relocated or reduced the grade of approximately half the route between Pittsburgh and Conneaut. The topography of the area through which the Bessemer runs is hilly and lacks convenient watercourses to follow. The B&LE is noted for its bridges; two of the largest are a 1,724-foot-long viaduct near Osgood, Pa., and the 2,327-foot bridge over the Allegheny River northeast of Pittsburgh, adjacent to the Pennsylvania Turnpike (I-76) bridge.

The B&LE purchased the Western Allegheny Railroad from the Pennsylvania Railroad at the end of 1967. B&LE operates over trackage of the Unity Railways Co., a 3.9-mile line between Unity Junction and Renton, Pa. The railroad was owned by U. S. Steel until 1988, when it was acquired by Transtar, Inc.

Canadian National purchased B&LE's holding company, Great Lakes Transportation, from Transtar in 2004, but the railroad still operates as the Bessemer & Lake Erie.

FACTS & FIGURES

Year	1929	1983
Miles operated	209	205
Locomotives	140	51
Passenger cars	46	—
Freight cars	12,707	5,127
Reporting marks: BLE		

Boston & Maine

The Boston & Maine grew for the most part by acquisition, not by construction. The oldest component of the B&M was the line between Boston and Lowell, Massachusetts, 25 miles, opened by the Boston & Lowell Railroad on June 24, 1835, but not acquired until much later. It is easiest to deal with B&M's nineteenth-century history route by route (using early-1950s names).

Portland Division

The Boston & Maine's earliest corporate predecessor was the Andover & Wilmington Railroad, opened in August 1836 from Andover, Mass., south to a junction with the Boston & Lowell at Wilmington, about 7 miles. The line was extended north 10 miles to Bradford, on the south bank of the Merrimac River opposite Haverhill, the next year. Construction continued north, reaching North Berwick, Maine, in 1843, by which time the three companies involved (one for each state) had been consolidated using the name of the New Hampshire company, Boston & Maine Railroad. At North Berwick, the B&M connected with the Portland, Saco & Portsmouth Railroad, which was leased in 1847 jointly by the B&M and the Eastern Railroad (Boston to Portsmouth, N. H., opened in 1840).

B&M was dissatisfied with using the Boston & Lowell and in 1845 opened its own line from North Wilmington through Reading to Boston. The three major companies, B&M, Boston & Lowell, and Eastern, each bought up smaller railroads as they were built to keep the other two from getting them.

Competition between the B&M and the Eastern for Boston–Portland traffic was fierce. The Eastern route was shorter but reached Boston by a ferry from East Boston until 1854, when the Eastern built a line into Boston from the north. The B&M carried most of the traffic. In 1869 the Eastern and the Maine Central cahooted up to control the traffic, with the upshot that the Portland, Saco & Portsmouth canceled the joint lease and leased itself to the Eastern. The Eastern in turn obtained

Train No. 58, the eastbound *Minuteman*, approaches North Pownal, Vt., in August 1940. The 4-8-2 has a couple of milk cars tucked behind its tender. *John P. Ahrens*

control of the Maine Central. Just about that same time B&M built a line of its own line from South Berwick to Portland.

The new lease of the PS&P, the cost of control of the Maine Central, and several accidents nearly exhausted the Eastern. In the early 1870s the Eastern made merger overtures to the B&M, which was unwilling to assume the Eastern's debt. The two roads agreed in 1874 to end the worst of the competition, and in 1883 B&M leased the Eastern, acquiring control of the MEC.

The Worcester, Nashua & Rochester had an inland route northeast from Worcester to Rochester, N. H., a backdoor route to Maine. Several railroads wanted it, and B&M, which already controlled the Portland & Rochester, leased the Worcester, Nashua & Rochester in 1886 and became the dominant (and only) railroad in southern Maine.

New Hampshire Division

Lowell, Mass., was one of America's first industrial cities, combining falls on the Merrimac River with power textile loom technology. It began its rise in 1822 and needed year-round transportation to Boston. The Middlesex Canal, opened in 1803 to connect Boston with the Merrimac River, froze in the winter, and roads were

inadequate. The Boston & Lowell Railroad was built parallel to the canal and soon took its business.

In 1838, three years after the B&L opened, the Nashua & Lowell Railroad began operating from Lowell north alongside the Merrimac River to Nashua, N. H., 18 miles. By 1850 the N&L included branches west to Ayer, Mass., and Wilton, N. H., both intended primarily to block construction by the Fitchburg Railroad. In 1857 the Boston & Lowell and the Nashua & Lowell agreed to operate as a unit.

By then another textile mill city, Manchester, was growing on the banks of the Merrimac north of Nashua. The Manchester & Lawrence Railroad linked Manchester with Lawrence, Mass., on the Boston & Maine, competing with the Concord Railroad-Nashua & Lowell-Boston & Lowell route to Boston. The five railroads involved formed a pooling agreement, but then the Concord leased the Manchester & Lawrence. The B&L proposed consolidation with the Nashua & Lowell and the Concord; the B&M, of course, opposed such a move. In 1869 the Great Northern Railroad was chartered. It was to include the three roads plus the Northern (Concord, N. H., to White River Junction, Vermont). It required the approval of the New

Hampshire legislature, which it did not get. The B&L was equally unsuccessful with a proposal to consolidate with the Fitchburg and had a falling out with N&L.

In 1880 the B&L leased the Nashua & Lowell and gained control of the Massachusetts Central, being built from Boston to Northampton, Mass., on the Connecticut River. In 1884 it leased the Northern and the Boston, Concord & Montreal, acquired control of the St. Johnsbury & Lake Champlain, and came head to head with the Concord Railroad (Nashua to Concord, N. H.), kicking off a railroad war in the legislature and courts of New Hampshire. B&L leased itself to the B&M in 1887, and let the B&M do battle with the Concord Railroad.

The B&M and the Concord eventually reached accord. In 1895 the B&M, which by then had acquired control of the Concord & Montreal (the consolidation of the Concord and the Boston, Concord & Montreal), leased the C&M and became the dominant railroad in New Hampshire.

Fitchburg Division

B&M's line to the West was built by several firms over 30 years. The Fitchburg Railroad was opened from Boston to Fitchburg, Mass., 50 miles northwest, in 1845. The Vermont & Massachusetts built west from Fitchburg over a range of hills to the Connecticut River at Grout's Corner (later Millers Falls), near Greenfield, then turned north, reaching Brattleboro, Vt., in 1850.

As early as 1819 there was a proposal for a canal across northern Massachusetts, using a tunnel to penetrate Hoosac Mountain, which stood between the valleys of the Deerfield and Hoosic rivers. This became a proposal for a railroad from Boston to the Great Lakes at Oswego or Buffalo, N. Y. The tunnel was begun in 1851 by the Commonwealth of Massachusetts.

The state also built the Troy & Greenfield Railroad west from Greenfield to the Hoosac Tunnel and leased it to the Fitchburg and the Vermont & Massachusetts in 1868. In 1870 the Vermont & Massachusetts sold its Grout's Corner–Brattleboro line to the Rutland; the line later became part of the Central Vermont.

The Troy & Boston Railroad was opened in the early 1850s from Troy, N. Y., north to the Hoosic River, then east and south to connections at Eagle Bridge and White Creek with two railroads north to Rutland, Vt. By 1859 the Troy & Boston, the Southern Vermont (8 miles across the southwest corner of Vermont), and the 7-mile-long western portion of the Troy & Greenfield formed a route from Troy to North Adams, Mass.

Two petitions came before the Massachusetts legislature in 1873, one to allow consolidation of the Fitchburg, Vermont & Massachusetts, Troy & Greenfield, and Troy & Boston railroads and the Hoosac Tunnel, and the other to consolidate the Boston & Lowell with the Fitchburg. A legislative committee proposed consolidating all the railroads in both petitions; the railroads rejected the idea. The sole result was that the Fitchburg leased the Vermont & Massachusetts.

As the Hoosac Tunnel neared completion in 1875 two other railroads were started: the Massachusetts Central and the Boston, Hoosac Tunnel & Western. The Massachusetts Central was projected west from Boston to a connection with the Troy & Greenfield near the Hoosac Tunnel; the Boston, Hoosac Tunnel & Western Railroad was to run west from the tunnel to Oswego, N. Y.

The Massachusetts Central built west from Boston through sparsely populated territory about halfway between the lines of the Fitchburg and the Boston & Albany and crossing nine other railroads along the way. It ran out of breath when it reached the Connecticut River at Northampton. The BHT&W was built from the Vermont-Massachusetts state line near Williamstown, Mass., parallel to the Troy & Boston and crossing it several times, then west from Johnsonville, N. Y., to Mechanicville and Rotterdam.

In spite of the financial problems of both roads, the combination of the Massachusetts Central and the Boston, Hoosac Tunnel & Western constituted a competitive threat to the Fitchburg. The solution was control of the state-owned Hoosac Tunnel. The state would allow that only if the Fitchburg had its own route to the Hudson River. Accordingly, in 1887 the Fitchburg consolidated with Troy & Boston and the state-owned Troy & Greenfield and in 1892 with the Boston, Hoosac Tunnel & Western.

In 1899 the New York Central was seeking access to Boston and considered leasing either the Boston & Albany or the Fitchburg—or both. The B&A served larger cities; the Fitchburg had the easier crossing of the mountains of western Massachusetts. NYC chose the B&A; the Boston & Maine leased the Fitchburg in 1900.

Connecticut River line

The Connecticut River line connected with all the routes running west and northwest from Boston. It consisted of six railroad companies: Connecticut River Railroad from Springfield to East Northfield; Vermont & Massachusetts to Brattleboro; Vermont Valley to Bellows Falls; Sullivan County to Windsor; Central Vermont to White River Junction; and Connecticut & Passumpsic Rivers Railroad from White River Junction to the Canadian border at Newport, Vt. They were all under the control of the Connecticut River Railroad (except for the Central Vermont), as was the St. Johnsbury & Lake Champlain.

By 1893 the lines north of White River Junction had been leased to the B&M, and the New Haven was ready to lease what remained, but during the few months of control of the B&M by the Philadelphia & Reading, A. A. MacLeod, president of the P&R, secured control of the Connecticut River Railroad, leased it to the B&M, and signed an agreement with the New Haven to divide New England along the line of the Boston & Albany.

Twentieth century

The New Haven acquired control of the B&M in 1907. In 1914 the New Haven's B&M stock was placed in the hands of trustees for eventual sale, and that same year B&M sold its Maine Central stock. B&M was placed in receivership in 1916.

In 1919 B&M simplified its corporate structure by consolidating with itself the Fitchburg, Boston & Lowell, Connecticut River, and Concord & Montreal railroads. B&M returned to independent operation several roads it had been operating: Suncook Valley in 1924, St. Johnsbury & Lake Champlain in 1925, and Montpelier & Wells River in 1926. Also in 1926 B&M leased its lines north of Wells River, Vt., to the Canadian Pacific and CPR subsidiary Quebec Central. About that same time B&M abandoned some of the weakest of its redundant branch lines.

B&M opened a new North Station in Boston in 1928, replacing the adjacent

B&M, Boston & Lowell, and Fitchburg stations, which had been operated as a unit. In 1930 B&M acquired control of the Springfield Terminal Railway, an electric line between Charlestown, N. H., and Springfield, Vt., 6 miles.

From 1932 to 1952 B&M shared officers with Maine Central in a voluntary arrangement that provided many of the benefits of consolidation or merger. Floods in 1936 and a hurricane in 1938 caused the abandonment of several branches. In 1939 B&M disposed of its interest in the Mount Washington Cog Railway. In 1946 B&M purchased the Connecticut & Passumpsic Rivers Railroad south of Wells River, Vt.; Canadian Pacific and its subsidiaries purchased the line north of Wells River. Samuel M. Pinsly bought several branches to form short lines: the branch from Mechanicville to Saratoga, N. Y., became the Saratoga & Schuylerville in 1945; the Rochester, N. H.–Westbrook, Maine, line became the Sanford & Eastern in 1949; and the Concord–Claremont, N. H., branch became the Claremont & Concord Railroad in 1954.

B&M dieselized quickly, except for suburban passenger trains, and it was an early user of Centralized Traffic Control. In 1950 it was a well-run, progressive railroad—in a region that was losing its heavy industry and beginning to build superhighways. In 1956 Patrick B. McGinnis became president of the B&M, bringing in a new image—not just blue replacing maroon on the locomotives and cars but a new way of doing things, including deficits and deferred maintenance.

B&M amassed the world's largest fleet of Budd Rail Diesel Cars, using them for all passenger service except the New York–Montreal trains operated with the New Haven and the Central Vermont. By the mid-1960s only suburban passenger service remained, operated for the Massachusetts Bay Transportation Authority.

In 1958 B&M posted a deficit for the first of many years. B&M asked to be included in Norfolk & Western, but N&W was reluctant to take on the B&M. On March 23, 1970, B&M declared bankruptcy. By the end of the year, B&M's trustees had chosen John W. Barriger III to be chief executive officer. Barriger retired at the end of 1972.

Rather than split the B&M among its connections or ask for its inclusion in

Conrail, B&M's trustees decided to reorganize independently. Under Alan Dustin, the B&M bought new engines, rebuilt track, went after new business, and expanded operations. It sold the tracks and rolling stock of its commuter operations to MBTA in 1975, but retained freight rights on those lines and continued to operate the trains for MBTA. In 1977 it took over the operation of commuter trains on the former New Haven and Boston & Albany lines out of Boston's South Station, and in 1982 it purchased several lines in Massachusetts and Connecticut from Conrail.

Guilford, then Pan Am

A revived Boston & Maine was purchased in 1983 by Timothy Mellon's Guilford Transportation Industries, which had bought the Maine Central in 1981 and in 1984 would buy the Delaware & Hudson. Guilford began operating the three railroads as a unified system, selling unprofitable lines, closing redundant yards and shops, and eliminating jobs. Employees went on strike. Guilford leased most of the B&M and the Maine Central to the Springfield Terminal to take advantage of work rules. Track degenerated to the point that Amtrak discontinued the *Montrealer*, which operated on B&M rails between Springfield, Mass., and Windsor, Vt. (Central Vermont acquired and rebuilt the Brattleboro–Windsor line, and Amtrak restored the *Montrealer*, rerouting it on CV south of Brattleboro.)

In 1990 the principal point of interchange with Conrail was shifted from Rotterdam Junction, N. Y., west of Schenectady, to Ayer, Mass., removing all through freight traffic from the former Fitchburg Division line through Hoosac Tunnel. B&M's problem for years had been that its routes were so short that its share of revenue on a freight move was small; those routes became 173 miles shorter. Guilford renamed itself Pan Am Railways in 2006.

FACTS & FIGURES

Year	1929	1982
Miles operated	2,077	1,508
Locomotives	787	151
Passenger cars	1,275	—
Freight cars	11,062	3,112
Reporting marks: BM		
Historical society: bmrrhs.org		

Burlington Northern

A pair of SD40-2s lead a Chicago-bound intermodal train along Burlington Northern's Mississippi River line in September 1993. The track is the former Chicago, Burlington & Quincy route between the Twin Cities and Chicago. *Jeff Wilson*

When created, Burlington Northern had a greater extent than any other U. S. railroad: Vancouver, British Columbia, to Pensacola, Fla. If you crossed North America from east to west, you had to cross BN rails or get your feet wet in the Gulf of Mexico or find your way around the north side of the city of Winnipeg. It was created on March 2, 1970, by the merger of the Northern Pacific Railway, the Great Northern Railway, the Chicago, Burlington & Quincy Railroad, and the Spokane, Portland & Seattle Railway. It was during most of its existence the longest railroad in North America, edging past the previous title-holder, Canadian National Railways.

Great Northern and Northern Pacific covered most of Minnesota north and west of the Twin Cities and the eastern third of North Dakota. West of there, the main lines of the two roads were as much as 200 miles apart, coming together at Spokane but separating again to cross Washington. The two roads were instrumental in

settling much of the northern Great Plains, and they pretty much divided the northern tier of the country from the Mississippi River to Puget Sound between them (as the Milwaukee Road eventually learned).

The Chicago, Burlington & Quincy's main axis was its Chicago–Denver route. Branch lines covered much of western Illinois, southern Iowa, northern Missouri, and southern Nebraska, and long branch-less lines reached to Paducah, Kentucky, St. Paul, Minnesota, and Billings, Montana. Despite its image of diesels and stainless-steel *Zephyrs*, it was a very conservative railroad. The Spokane, Portland & Seattle was built to give the Great Northern and the Northern Pacific access to Portland, Oregon, from the east. It was owned equally by GN and NP, which acted more like stingy uncles than loving parents.

Burlington Northern existed in a way long before the merger formalities of 1970. In 1901 Great Northern and Northern Pacific each acquired almost 49 percent of

the stock of the Chicago, Burlington & Quincy, assuring a connection to Chicago from St. Paul, the eastern terminus of GN and NP. At the same time NP came under the control of GN. In 1905 GN and NP organized and constructed the Spokane, Portland & Seattle Railway. In 1927 the Great Northern Pacific Railway was organized to consolidate GN and NP and lease the CB&Q and the SP&S, but the Interstate Commerce Commission would approve it only without the inclusion of the CB&Q. The companies resumed merger studies in 1956, and in 1960 the

FACTS & FIGURES

Year	1970	1994
Miles operated	23,609	28,937
Locomotives	1,973	2,957
Passenger cars	1,171	—
Freight cars	116,491	88,858
Reporting marks: BN		
Website: fobnr.org		

directors of GN and NP approved the terms. Government approval and actual merger took another decade.

BN merged the St. Louis-San Francisco Railway (the Frisco) in 1980. At the end of 1981 BN absorbed the Colorado & Southern, which had been a CB&Q subsidiary, and transferred C&S's Denver-Texline route to the Fort Worth & Denver, a C&S subsidiary. On January 1, 1983, FW&D was also merged into BN.

BN developed into the nation's top coal-hauler because of the development of the coalfields in the Powder River Basin of eastern Wyoming. It slimmed down by spinning off several large chunks of its network, including strategic segments of the former Northern Pacific main line.

Meanwhile, BN's neighbor to the south, Union Pacific, was expanding, acquiring Western Pacific, Missouri Pacific, Missouri-Kansas-Texas, and partial ownership of Chicago & North Western. By 1990 UP was almost as big as BN.

The proposed Southern Pacific-Santa Fe merger would have created a three-railroad situation between the Midwest and the Pacific—SPSF across the south, Union

An eastbound freight with lots of covered hoppers rolls out of Skykomish, Wash., on the Burlington Northern's ex-Great Northern line in 1980. *Reg Hearn*

Pacific across the middle, and BN across the north. After the ICC ruled against SP-Santa Fe, the Denver & Rio Grande Western acquired SP, leaving Santa Fe on its own.

Gradually the western railroad situation shook out and settled down. In June 1994, after some months of denying rumors of impending merger, Santa Fe and Burlington Northern announced their intention to merge—BN would buy Santa Fe. The deal was consummated in 1995, creating the Burlington Northern & Santa Fe. The name officially became BNSF Railway Company in 2005.

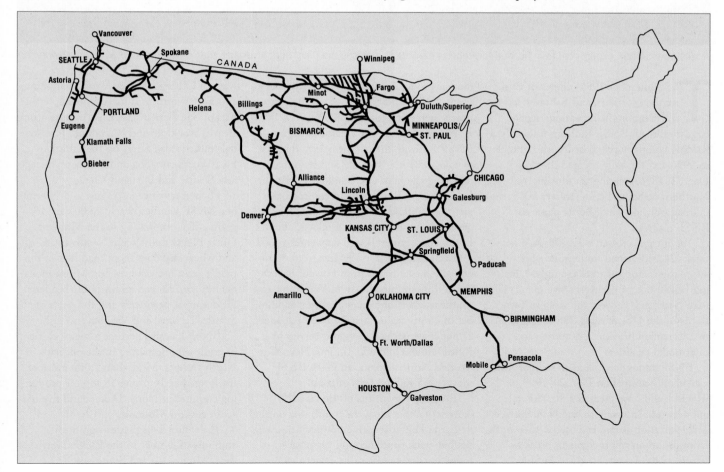

BNSF

A westbound BNSF export coal train headed for Roberts Bank, B. C., crosses the Clark Fork River just west of Noxon, Montana. *Tom Danneman*

The September 1995 merger of Burlington Northern and Santa Fe led to the creation of the nation's second largest railroad, BNSF Railway. Officially, a holding company purchased both railroads in 1996 and formally merged them on Dec. 31, 1996, creating the Burlington Northern & Santa Fe. In January 2005, the railroad officially changed its name to BNSF Railway.

The merger created a 32,000-mile network (24,000 owned route miles plus 8,000 route miles of trackage rights), making BNSF one of the west's two giant railroad systems. Its covers the western two-thirds of the U.S., serving 28 states and two Canadian provinces, 40 ports, and 30 intermodal facilities.

BNSF announced plans to merge with Canadian National on Dec. 20, 1999, which would have created a 50,000-mile rail network. In response, the U. S. Surface Transportation Board imposed a 15-month moratorium on rail mergers in order to rethink the rules under which future

merger proposals would be evaluated. As a result, BNSF and CN called off their proposed merger on July 20, 2000.

Along with the 2005 name change to BNSF Railway, the company introduced a new logo, with a "swoosh" and its initials replacing the first "circle and cross" Santa Fe-style logo. BNSF's main commodities are intermodal containers, coal, crude oil, grain, automobiles, forest products, chemicals, metals, minerals, and consumer goods.

Each day, BNSF originates from 40 to 60 loaded coal trains from Powder River Basin mines in northeastern Wyoming and southeastern Montana, with an equal number of empty trains arriving to be reloaded. Other coal-producing regions served by BNSF are in Colorado, Illinois, New Mexico, and North Dakota. In 2004, BNSF moved 255 million tons of coal.

Roughly two-thirds of the 70 to 90 daily trains that cross the Southwest on the ex-Santa Fe transcontinental main line are double-stack container and piggyback trains moving between the eastern gate

ways of Chicago, Kansas City, Memphis and Fort Worth, and the California terminals of San Bernardino, Los Angeles, Long Beach, Stockton, and Richmond. Intermodal traffic is also heavy on the Chicago-Fort Worth corridor, and between Chicago and Seattle and Portland, Ore.

Each year between August and November, BNSF handles nearly 2,000 cars of grain a day, originating in the Midwest, Great Plains, and Pacific Northwest. Corn and wheat make up more than half of the road's grain movements. The Minneapolis-Seattle corridor sees grain traffic headed for domestic producers and the ports of Seattle, Tacoma, and Vancouver, Wash.

BNSF has also become a major carrier of crude oil originating in the oil fields of North Dakota. More than 1,000 miles of track touches 16 of the 19 top oil-producing counties in North Dakota and five of six in eastern Montana.

The railroad originates significant amounts of lumber in the Pacific Northwest, Minnesota, and Southwest.

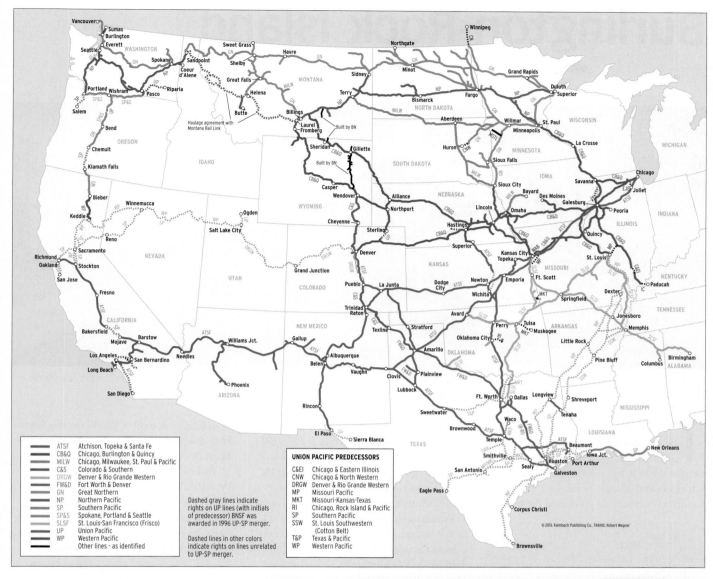

Legend:

ATSF	Atchison, Topeka & Santa Fe
CB&Q	Chicago, Burlington & Quincy
MILW	Chicago, Milwaukee, St. Paul & Pacific
C&S	Colorado & Southern
DRGW	Denver & Rio Grande Western
FW&D	Fort Worth & Denver
GN	Great Northern
NP	Northern Pacific
SP	Southern Pacific
SP&S	Spokane, Portland & Seattle
SLSF	St. Louis-San Francisco (Frisco)
UP	Union Pacific
WP	Western Pacific
	Other lines - as identified

UNION PACIFIC PREDECESSORS

C&EI	Chicago & Eastern Illinois
CNW	Chicago & North Western
DRGW	Denver & Rio Grande Western
MP	Missouri Pacific
MKT	Missouri-Kansas-Texas
RI	Chicago, Rock Island & Pacific
SP	Southern Pacific
SSW	St. Louis Southwestern (Cotton Belt)
T&P	Texas & Pacific
WP	Western Pacific

Dashed gray lines indicate rights on UP lines (with initials of predecessor) BNSF was awarded in 1996 UP-SP merger.

Dashed lines in other colors indicate rights on lines unrelated to UP-SP merger.

© 2013, Kalmbach Publishing Co. TRAINS: Robert Wegner

In 2009, billionaire businessman Warren Buffett announced his intent to purchase BNSF, and on Feb. 12, 2010, the railroad became the largest privately owned railway, as a subsidiary of Buffett's Berkshire Hathaway Inc. As of 2012, BNSF's 32,514-mile system included more than 9,000 miles of trackage rights, an amount so vast it enabled BNSF to eclipse Union Pacific's 31,868-mile system.

FACTS & FIGURES

Year	1996	2012
Miles operated	32,000	32,514
Locomotives	4,653	6,700
Passenger cars	—	—
Freight cars	118,000	82,300

Reporting marks: BNSF

Website: bnsf.com

An eastbound coal train on BNSF's Jamestown Subdivision, the former Northern Pacific main line, rolls by the old elevators in Cleveland, N. D. *Tom Danneman*

Burlington-Rock Island

Looking in this view like a purely Burlington Route operation, the *Sam Houston Zephyr* arrives at Fort Worth from Houston behind No. 9909, one of the unique-to-Burlington Lines E5s. *R. S. Plummer*

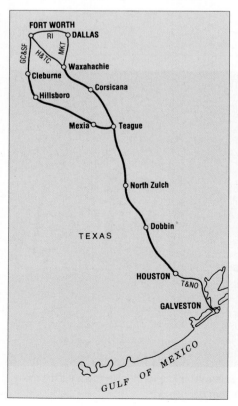

The Trinity & Brazos Valley Railway was chartered by the state of Texas on October 17, 1902. By the beginning of 1904 it had a line open between Cleburne and Mexia, Texas. In 1905 the Colorado & Southern purchased control of the T&BV, and in 1906 it sold a half interest in the road to the Rock Island. The T&BV filled out its map in 1907: Mexia to Houston; trackage rights over Gulf, Colorado & Santa Fe from Houston to Galveston and from Cleburne north to Fort Worth; Teague to Waxahachie; trackage rights from Waxahachie to Fort Worth on Houston & Texas Central (Southern Pacific); and trackage rights from Waxahachie to Dallas on the Missouri-Kansas-Texas.

The T&BV purchased a quarter interest in the Houston Belt & Terminal Railway, and T&BV's parents, C&S and Rock Island, jointly built the Galveston Terminal Railway. The T&BV constituted a Fort Worth-Houston-Galveston extension of the Burlington system and the Rock Island.

Texas in those days was not a booming petrochemical complex. Business did not meet expectations, and the T&BV entered receivership in 1914. During the receivership it lost its Santa Fe and Katy trackage rights; only the Fort Worth-Houston line via Waxahachie survived.

The Trinity & Brazos Valley emerged from receivership in July 1930 with a new name: Burlington-Rock Island Railroad (Chicago, Burlington & Quincy had gained control of the Colorado & Southern in 1908). It re-established trackage rights from Waxahachie to Dallas over the Katy and from Cleburne to Fort Worth on the Santa Fe and acquired rights to Galveston over the Texas & New Orleans (Southern Pacific).

In 1931 the Rock Island and the Fort Worth & Denver City (C&S) jointly leased the Dallas-Teague segment of the railroad and began operating it in alternate five-year periods. In 1932 B-RI abandoned its line from Hillsboro to Cleburne and dropped the Santa Fe trackage rights to Fort Worth. By 1942 the branch, the original T&BV line, was cut back to Mexia.

On June 1, 1950, B-RI ceased operation and its two parents made a new joint lease of the entire line with alternate 5-year operating periods. The Fort Worth & Denver and the Rock Island purchased the property of the B-RI in April 1964, and the corporation was dissolved in April 1965. Upon the demise of the Rock Island in 1980, the Burlington Northern assumed sole operation.

FACTS & FIGURES

Year	1929	1949
Miles operated	367	228
Locomotives	37	—
Passenger cars	20	3
Freight cars	721	34
Reporting marks: BRI		

Butte, Anaconda & Pacific

The Butte, Anaconda & Pacific was incorporated in 1892 and opened in 1893. It connected copper mines at Butte, Montana, with a smelter at Anaconda. The mines, the smelter, and the railroad were all owned by Marcus Daly.

By 1911 the Anaconda Copper Mining Co., Daly's company, had acquired considerable expertise using electric motors to drain and ventilate its mines. The BA&P electrified its line to take advantage of the economies that would result from electric operation of that aspect of the business as well. The BA&P was the first road to electrify for purely economic reasons; moreover, the electrification project would demonstrate uses of the copper produced by its parent. The road was the first to use General Electric's 2,400-volt DC system. Electric locomotives started hauling trains in 1913.

In 1957 two electric locomotives were added to the original fleet of 28; a few years earlier BA&P had replaced its few remaining steam locomotives with diesels for service on non-electrified track. In 1958 BA&P began operation over the Northern Pacific between Butte and Durant under a joint trackage agreement. Electric operation continued until 1967, when the installation of a new ore

General Electric built two new 125-ton, black-and-yellow hood-style electric locomotives for BA&P in 1957, Nos. 201 and 202. They were BA&P's last electrics. *General Electric*

concentrator at Butte changed the road's traffic pattern. The seven GP7s and GP9s that had been working the non-electrified trackage took over all of BA&P's operation.

The 1980 closing of Anaconda's smelter in Anaconda again changed the road's traffic pattern—indeed, eliminated most of it—and BA&P's operations changed from daily to "as required." The mines themselves closed in 1983, and the railroad all but ceased operation. In 1984 owner Anaconda Minerals petitioned for abandonment and in March 1985 agreed to sell and donate the railroad properties to the state of Montana for operation by the Rarus Railway Co., a new short line. Patriot Rail Corporation acquired Rarus in 2007 and changed the railroad's name back to the Butte, Anaconda & Pacific Railway.

FACTS & FIGURES

Year	1929	1982
Miles operated	69	43
Locomotives	35	8
Passenger cars	8	—
Freight cars	1,422	674
Reporting marks: BAP		

Canadian National

Four unique-to-CN cowl-body SD50Fs lead a coal train along Lake Abraham near Windy Point, Alberta, in the early 2000s. *Canadian National*

The two principal railroads in Canada today are Canadian National Railways, formerly government owned and then privatized, and privately owned Canadian Pacific Railway. A few paragraphs on Canadian Pacific are a necessary preface to the history of Canadian National—and a few sentences on Canadian history are necessary to explain Canadian Pacific.

The Dominion of Canada was created on July 1, 1867, by the union of the provinces of New Brunswick, Nova Scotia, and Canada (whose two parts, Upper and Lower Canada, became present-day Ontario and Quebec, respectively). Canada's population was anything but homogeneous: Immigrants came from England, Scotland, Ireland, France, Germany, and the United States, and they settled along

the seacoast, the St. Lawrence River, and the shores of Lake Ontario and Lake Erie. North and west of Toronto lay a thousand miles of rocky forested wilderness, and beyond that were the prairies and the Rockies.

In 1871 when British Columbia joined the confederation (it included Manitoba by then), the Canadian government promised a railway to link British Columbia with the rest of Canada. The Canadian Pacific Railway was incorporated in 1881 to build from Callander, Ont., near North Bay, to the Pacific at what is now Vancouver. The company received extensive land grants and subsidies from the Canadian government in exchange for unifying Canada.

CPR completed its main line on Nov. 7, 1885, and then began to spread an extensive network of branches across

the wheatlands between Winnipeg and Calgary. It became the dominant railroad on the prairies. In eastern Canada, though, Canadian Pacific was the minority railroad, with little more than a line east through Montreal and across Maine to Saint John, N. B., and another route southwest through Toronto to Windsor, Ont.

Canadian National Railways was not built—it was gathered and assembled. Its five major components were Intercolonial Railway, National Transcontinental Railway, Canadian Northern Railway, Grand Trunk Pacific Railway, and Grand Trunk Railway. All five were brought into CNR because they were in financial difficulty.

Intercolonial Railway

The maritime provinces had far more communication and commerce with New

England than with Quebec and Ontario. The government deemed a rail link necessary to tie the Maritimes to the rest of Canada and was willing to finance that railroad. A commission headed by Sandford Fleming surveyed a route from Moncton, N. B., northwest to Mont Joli, Que., and then southwest along the south bank of the St. Lawrence to a connection with the Grand Trunk at Riviere du Loup, Que. For military reasons Fleming chose a route as far as possible from the U. S. border.

The Intercolonial began operation between Halifax and Riviere du Loup in 1876, and in 1879 it assumed operation of Grand Trunk's line from Riviere du Loup to just west of Levis, across the St. Lawrence from Quebec City. Canadian Government Railways took over operation of the Intercolonial in 1913.

Canadian Northern Railway

In the late 1890s William Mackenzie and Donald Mann began assembling the Canadian Northern system. It included a new line across the prairies from Winnipeg through Edmonton to Vancouver (not completed until 1915), several lines in Manitoba leased from the Northern Pacific, and lines in Ontario, Quebec, and Nova Scotia. By 1916 Canadian Northern had a main line from Toronto west to Vancouver via Sudbury, Capreol, and Port Arthur-Fort William (now Thunder Bay), Ont.; Warroad, Minn.; Winnipeg and Dauphin, Man.; Canora (named for the railroad), Warman, and North Battleford, Sask.; Edmonton and Jasper, Alb.; and the canyons of the Thompson and Fraser rivers. Another main line ran from Toronto to Quebec City via Napanee and Ottawa, Ont., and Joliette and Garneau, Que. A Capreol–Ottawa line was completed in 1917, and a line into Montreal via the Mount Royal Tunnel in 1918.

The Canadian Northern system included two orphan lines in Nova Scotia (the Halifax & Southwestern along the south shore, and a line to Inverness on Cape Breton Island); a tentacle north to Chicoutimi, Que.; an extensive network of branches covering the prairies between Winnipeg and the Rockies; and the Duluth, Winnipeg & Pacific Railway from Fort Frances, Ont., to Duluth, Minn.

Canadian Northern ran out of money. The mother country couldn't help—World War I had stopped the export of capital

from Britain. Because of loans and land grants the Canadian government found itself CNoR's major creditor. On Sept. 6, 1917, CNoR management resigned and a new board appointed by the government took over. On Dec. 20, 1918, all government-owned railways were brought under the new CNoR management, to be known as "Canadian National Railways."

National Transcontinental Railway

In the first few years of the twentieth century the Grand Trunk Railway, prompted by a spirit of expansionism, tried to team up first with Canadian Pacific and then with Canadian Northern. Neither attempt succeeded, so GT proposed constructing a rail line from Callander, Ont., to Winnipeg well north of the Canadian Pacific line, then continuing west to the Pacific.

The Canadian Pacific was a product of Canada's Conservative Party. The Liberals, who came into power in 1896, decided to make their reputation with another transcontinental railroad. They seized GT's proposal, extended it east to Moncton, N. B., and laid out as direct a route as possible to Winnipeg, passing far to the north of Montreal, Ottawa, and Toronto. Except near Quebec City there was neither settlement nor population along the route (there is little more now), and the terrain was largely swamps and bare rock. The major engineering work on the NTR was the St. Lawrence River bridge at Quebec City, which collapsed twice during construction.

The line was to be constructed by Grand Trunk Pacific, a subsidiary of Grand Trunk, on behalf of the government. GTP would lease it from the government upon completion. The rental was to be based on the cost of construction—and that proved to be more than twice the estimate. Grand Trunk Pacific, already in financial trouble because of the cost of its own line west of Winnipeg, refused to take over the National Transcontinental upon its completion. Canadian Government Railways, which was already operating the Intercolonial, took over the National Transcontinental in 1915.

Grand Trunk Pacific

The Grand Trunk Pacific Railway was incorporated in 1903 to build from Winnipeg to the Pacific at Prince Rupert, B. C., the Canadian port nearest the Orient.

GTP's route through Saskatoon to Edmonton lay between the Canadian Pacific and the Canadian Northern lines. From Edmonton to Yellowhead Pass, 250 miles, GTP and CNoR were parallel. During World War I part of GTP's line west of Edmonton was dismantled so the rails could be used in France. GTP was given running rights on CNoR's track, portions of which were later relocated on the GTP roadbed. From Yellowhead Pass GTP's line reached 700 miles northwest to Prince Rupert. The line was completed in 1914.

Prince Rupert never developed into a major seaport. Land transportation rates were higher than those to and from Vancouver, and there was almost no population to provide local business in the area between Prince Rupert and the Rockies. On the prairies GTP was as deficient in branches as Canadian Northern was prolific. GTP entered receivership in 1919 and came under the Canadian National umbrella in 1920.

Grand Trunk Railway

The Grand Trunk (whose lines included the former Champlain & St. Lawrence, Canada's first railway—1836) was the last major addition to Canadian National Railways. It was conceived as a Canadian main line from Montreal through Toronto to Sarnia, Ont., where it would connect with a railroad to Chicago and in Chicago with a railroad to the Canadian West. At the time it was believed that the terrain north of Lake Superior would force any route to western Canada through Michigan. The project included two lines east from Montreal, one to the year-round port of Portland, Maine, and the other down the St. Lawrence to connect with a line from Halifax.

The Grand Trunk Railway was incorporated in 1852. By 1856 it was in operation between Quebec City (more accurately, Levis, on the south bank of the St. Lawrence River) and Windsor, Ont. In 1859 GT opened the Victoria Bridge across the St. Lawrence at Montreal—at a cost which sent GT to the government for funds.

At the time of confederation in 1867 it was proposed to extend the Grand Trunk west to the Pacific and east to New Brunswick and Nova Scotia at public expense. Public feeling was against the idea because of GT's debt and mismanagement. Nor was GT interested, because it could

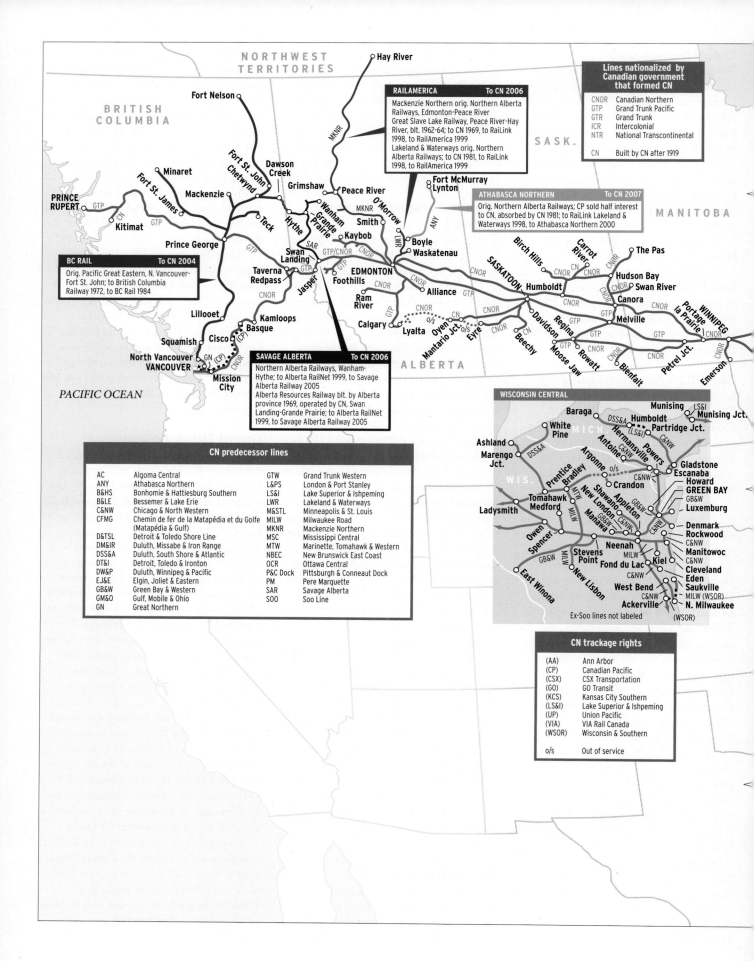

NORTHWEST TERRITORIES

Hay River

BRITISH COLUMBIA

Fort Nelson

Minaret
Fort St. John
Chetwynd
Dawson Creek
Fort St. James
Mackenzie
Grimshaw
Peace River
Teck
Hythe
Wanham
Grande Prairie
Smith
Kaybob
Swan Landing
Taverna
Redpass
Jasper
Ram River
Foothills
EDMONTON
Calgary
Lyalta
Oyen
Mantario Jct.
Eyre
Beechy
Davidson
Regina
Moose Jaw
Rowatt
Bienfait
Petrel Jct.
Emerson

Fort McMurray
Lynton
O'Morrow
Boyle
Waskatenau
Alliance

Birch Hills
Carrot River
Humboldt
SASKATOON
Canora
Melville
WINNIPEG
Portage la Prairie
Petrel Jct.
The Pas
Hudson Bay
Swan River

SASK.

MANITOBA

ALBERTA

Prince George
Kamloops
Basque
Cisco
Squamish
North Vancouver
VANCOUVER
Mission City
Lillooet

PRINCE RUPERT
Kitimat

PACIFIC OCEAN

Lines nationalized by Canadian government that formed CN

CNOR	Canadian Northern
GTP	Grand Trunk Pacific
GTR	Grand Trunk
ICR	Intercolonial
NTR	National Transcontinental
CN	Built by CN after 1919

RAILAMERICA To CN 2006

Mackenzie Northern orig. Northern Alberta Railways, Edmonton-Peace River
Great Slave Lake Railway, Peace River-Hay River, blt. 1962-64; to CN 1969, to RailLink 1998, to RailAmerica 1999
Lakeland & Waterways orig. Northern Alberta Railways; to CN 1981, to RailLink 1998, to RailAmerica 1999

ATHABASCA NORTHERN To CN 2007

Orig. Northern Alberta Railways; CP sold half interest to CN, absorbed by CN 1981; to RailLink Lakeland & Waterways 1998, to Athabasca Northern 2000

BC RAIL To CN 2004

Orig. Pacific Great Eastern, N. Vancouver-Fort St. John; to British Columbia Railway 1972, to BC Rail 1984

SAVAGE ALBERTA To CN 2006

Northern Alberta Railways, Wanham-Hythe; to Alberta RailNet 1999, to Savage Alberta Railway 2005
Alberta Resources Railway blt. by Alberta province 1969, operated by CN, Swan Landing-Grande Prairie; to Alberta RailNet 1999, to Savage Alberta Railway 2005

CN predecessor lines

AC	Algoma Central		GTW	Grand Trunk Western
ANY	Athabasca Northern		L&PS	London & Port Stanley
B&HS	Bonhomie & Hattiesburg Southern		LS&I	Lake Superior & Ishpeming
B&LE	Bessemer & Lake Erie		LWR	Lakeland & Waterways
C&NW	Chicago & North Western		M&STL	Minneapolis & St. Louis
CFMG	Chemin de fer de la Matapédia et du Golfe (Matapédia & Gulf)		MILW	Milwaukee Road
			MKNR	Mackenzie Northern
D&TSL	Detroit & Toledo Shore Line		MSC	Mississippi Central
DM&IR	Duluth, Missabe & Iron Range		MTW	Marinette, Tomahawk & Western
DSS&A	Duluth, South Shore & Atlantic		NBEC	New Brunswick East Coast
DT&I	Detroit, Toledo & Ironton		OCR	Ottawa Central
DW&P	Duluth, Winnipeg & Pacific		P&C Dock	Pittsburgh & Conneaut Dock
EJ&E	Elgin, Joliet & Eastern		PM	Pere Marquette
GB&W	Green Bay & Western		SAR	Savage Alberta
GM&O	Gulf, Mobile & Ohio		SOO	Soo Line
GN	Great Northern			

WISCONSIN CENTRAL

Munising
Munising Jct.
Baraga
White Pine
Humboldt
Partridge Jct.
Ashland
Marengo Jct.
Hermansville
Powers
Antoine
Gladstone
Escanaba
Argonne
Bradley
Prentice
Crandon
Howard
GREEN BAY
Luxemburg
Tomahawk
Medford
Shawano
Appleton
New London
Manawa
Denmark
Rockwood
Ladysmith
Owen
Spencer
Neenah
Manitowoc
Stevens Point
Kiel
Cleveland
Eden
Saukville
Fond du Lac
East Winona
New Lisbon
West Bend
N. Milwaukee
Ackerville
(WSOR)

Ex-Soo lines not labeled

CN trackage rights

(AA)	Ann Arbor
(CP)	Canadian Pacific
(CSX)	CSX Transportation
(GO)	GO Transit
(KCS)	Kansas City Southern
(LS&I)	Lake Superior & Ishpeming
(UP)	Union Pacific
(VIA)	VIA Rail Canada
(WSOR)	Wisconsin & Southern
o/s	Out of service

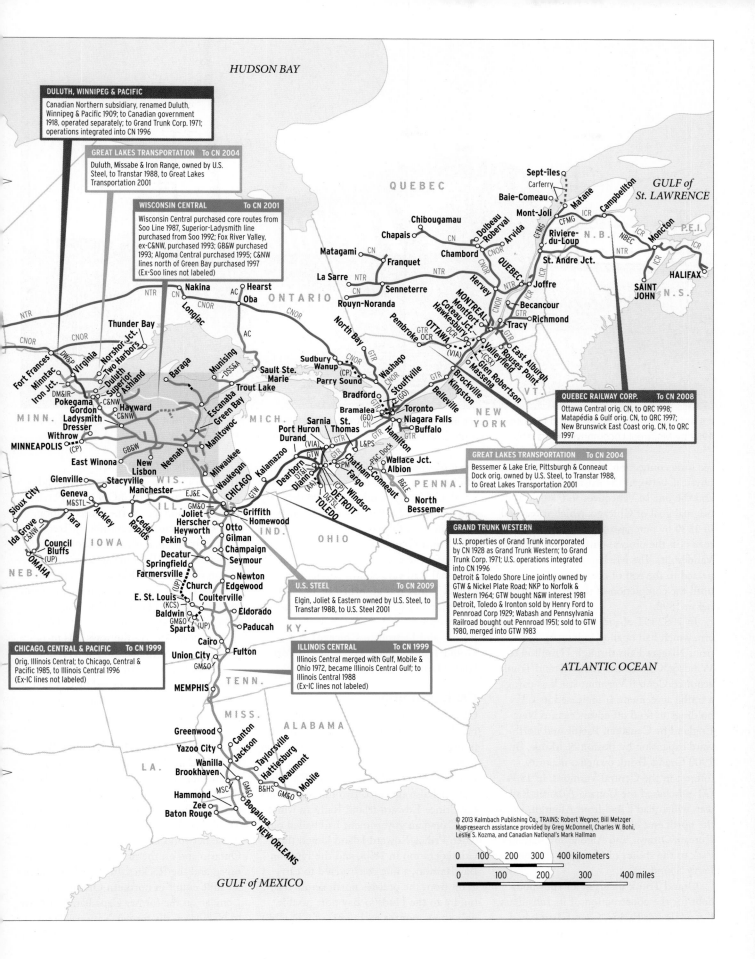

It's April 1974, and train 61 bound for Toronto glides into the Dorval (Montreal) station behind an FPA-4/F9B/FPB-4 combo. Built in 1958 and 1959 by Montreal Locomotive Works under Alco license, some FPA-4s lasted in service into the 1990s. *George W. Hamlin*

see little connection, either figurative or physical, between the existing GT system and the line to Vancouver. GT stuck to its original goal of Chicago, which it reached in 1880 by purchasing several short railroads (in the process outfoxing William H. Vanderbilt). The Michigan lines were connected to the rest of the system by ferry until the completion of the St. Clair Tunnel in 1890.

In 1882 GT absorbed the Great Western, which had opened in January 1854 from Niagara Falls through Hamilton to Windsor, Ont. In the 1880s Grand Trunk acquired Central Vermont stock as part of a traffic agreement. It increased its CV holdings to fend off advances into New England by Canadian Pacific and northward expansion by Boston & Maine. By 1900 Grand Trunk owned a majority interest in the Central Vermont. In 1904 GT purchased the Canada Atlantic Railway, which had a line from Alburgh, Vt., at the north end of Lake Champlain, through Coteau, Ottawa, and Algonquin National Park to the shores of Georgian Bay near Parry Sound.

Grand Trunk incurred an enormous debt for the construction of its subsidiary, Grand Trunk Pacific. Grand Trunk had an opportunity to turn over the GTP to the government, but GT's British board of directors rejected the government proposal. GT badly botched its own defense, and on May 21, 1920, the Canadian government took formal possession of Grand Trunk and Grand Trunk Pacific. Grand Trunk Pacific became part of Canadian National Railways almost immediately; Grand Trunk was absorbed in 1923. At that time GT's U. S. lines became separate companies: Grand Trunk Western (Port Huron and Detroit to Chicago) and Grand Trunk (Island Pond, Vt., to Portland, Maine).

CN beginnings

Canadian National Railways was incorporated on June 6, 1919; the name had been in use for six months to conveniently refer to the combined Canadian Northern and Canadian Government railways. Canadian National also included two minor railways, the Prince Edward Island Railway, which the Canadian government had bailed out when Prince Edward Island joined the Confederation in 1873, and the Hudson Bay Railway, a line constructed to carry grain from the prairies north across the tundra to the Hudson Bay port (usable only three months each year) of Churchill, Man.

Other CN properties

The 3 foot 6 inch-gauge Newfoundland Railway became part of CN in 1949 when Newfoundland joined the confederation. In 1979 CN created a subsidiary, Terra Transport, to operate all CN services in Newfoundland. The railway ceased operating on Oct. 1, 1988. Rail service on Prince Edward Island was discontinued at the end of 1989, and in March 1990 CN abandoned its operations on Vancouver Island.

Northern Alberta Railways was incorporated in 1929 to take over several lines owned and operated by the province of Alberta. It was jointly owned by CN and Canadian Pacific until CP sold its half to CN in 1980.

Evolution and privatization

In 1923 Canadian National had two transcontinental routes from Moncton, N. B., to the Pacific (the ex-Canadian Northern route to Vancouver and the ex-Grand Trunk Pacific route to Prince Rupert) plus dense networks of lines in Quebec and Ontario and on the prairies between Winnipeg and the Rockies. In 1923 CN built a 30-mile cutoff in northern Ontario, from Longlac on the former Canadian Northern to Nakina on the former National Transcontinental. The new line shortened CN's

Canadian National Ten-Wheeler No. 1357, pulling an express reefer and heavyweight baggage car and coach, has just arrived at the Fort Rouge yard from the downtown Winnipeg station in September 1958. *Franklin A. King*

Toronto-Winnipeg route by 102 miles.

In the 1960s CN pushed lines into the subarctic area north of the prairies to tap mineral deposits. Notable among these is the Great Slave Lake Railway, from Grimshaw, Alb., to its namesake lake at Hay River, N. T., and a nearby mine. CN sold this line (and the connected former Northern Alberta line) in the late 1990s to Rail-Link Canada, which renamed the combined lines the Mackenzie Northern Railway. RailLink Canada was later purchased by shortline holding company RailAmerica, which sold the line back to CN in 2006. CN also acquired BC Rail in 2003.

In 1961 CN underwent an image change, replacing the maple leaf with a modern logo (the connected CN "noodle" mark), and replacing olive green paint on passenger cars and locomotives with black and off-white.

Two years later CN kicked off a passenger renaissance with incentive fares, refurbished cars, fast intercity trains, and cars—even domes—purchased secondhand from U. S. railroads. Canadian National's passenger trains carried respectable numbers of passengers and served as the basis

for the establishment of VIA Rail Canada in 1977.

Canadian National went through a recapitalization in 1978, and from that point was run as a for-profit corporation, albeit still owned by the the Canadian government. At the same time it began spinning off other non-rail subsidiaries, including Air Canada and its marine and trucking operations, and it abandoned many unprofitable branch lines.

The movement toward privatization intensified in the early 1990s, and Canadian National was privatized following the CN Commercialization Act, which became law in July 1995. By November an IPO (initial public offering of stock) had placed CN in the hands of private investors. A restriction exists that no individual or corporate shareholder may own more than 15 percent of CN stock.

U. S. Subsidiaries

Grand Trunk Corporation was incorporated in 1970 to consolidate CN's U. S. subsidiaries: Grand Trunk Western; Central Vermont; and Duluth, Winnipeg & Pacific. The portion of the original Grand

Trunk route from Island Pond, Vt., to Portland, Maine, (which was operated as part of CN proper, not part of Grand Trunk Corporation) was sold in 1989 to become the St. Lawrence & Atlantic Railroad.

Since that time, CN has acquired additional U. S. lines, including Illinois Central in 1998, Wisconsin Central Ltd. in 2001, Great Lakes Transportation (Bessemer & Lake Erie and Duluth, Missabe & Iron Range) in 2003, and Elgin, Joliet & Eastern in 2008. Although some still exist on paper, these railroads have lost their individual identities within the CN system (more details can be found in each of those railroads' entries throughout this book).

FACTS & FIGURES

Year	1929	2012
Miles operated	19,571	20,600
Locomotives	3,096	1,965
Passenger cars	3,765	—
Freight cars	123,164	36,937
Reporting marks: CN, Can, CNIS, CNQ		
Historical society: cnlines.ca		

Canadian Pacific

Canadian Pacific's Laggan Subdivision follows the Trans-Canada Highway near Canmore, Alberta. This view includes the amazing Three Sisters peaks in the background, with snow still visible in the upper elevations in May 2012. *Stefan Loeb*

The history of CP Rail is intimately tied to Canadian politics. British Columbia joined the Canadian confederation in 1871 on the condition that a railroad would link the province to the rest of the country within 10 years. The geographic barriers to such a railroad were formidable, including the wilderness of northern Ontario, the vast emptiness of the prairies, and the Rocky Mountains.

The financial barrier was also formidable. The principal railroad in Canada, the Grand Trunk Railway, was not interested in the project, so in 1881 the Canadian

Pacific Railway was incorporated to build a railroad to the Pacific at what is now Vancouver. The starting point of the new railway was Callander, Ont., near North Bay, at the end of a Grand Trunk line from Toronto. Construction started at several points, and the line across the prairie was completed before the more difficult sections east and west.

In 1881 CP absorbed the Canada Central Railway, which was building northwest toward Callander from Brockville and Ottawa. In 1882 CP purchased the Western Division of the Quebec, Montreal,

Ottawa & Occidental Railway, a line from Montreal to Ottawa along the north bank of the Ottawa River. The acquisitions ensured that CP would have a route to Ottawa and Montreal, even if at the time there was still a gap of several hundred miles between those lines and the new railroad CP was building. Construction along the north shore of Lake Superior was extremely difficult, but nationalistic feelings precluded an easier route south of Lake Superior through the United States. The crossing of the Rockies at Kicking Horse Pass was accomplished only by

Royal Hudson 2841 awaits its next assignment in the 1950s. This was one of a group of 30 class H1c 4-8-4s (2820-2849) operated by Canadian Pacific; another 15 H1d and H1e locomotives were also semi-streamlined and known as Royal Hudsons. *Linn Westcott*

resorting to 4.5 percent grades as an interim solution and later a pair of spiral tunnels. The last spike was driven at Craigellachie, B. C., on Nov. 7, 1885.

In 1884 Canadian Pacific leased the Ontario & Quebec Railway, gaining a line from Toronto to Perth, Ont. In 1887 that line was extended east to Montreal and west to Windsor, Ont., on the Detroit River. By 1890 the CP had built eastward from Montreal across Maine to Saint John, New Brunswick, creating a true transcontinental railroad from the Atlantic to the Pacific.

Southeastern British Columbia was geographically and economically much closer to the U. S. (and to James J. Hill's Great Northern Railway) than to Canada. The discovery there of silver in 1887 sparked an outbreak of railroad fever. CP built a line from Medicine Hat, Alberta, west across Crows Nest Pass into the Kootenay region. The Canadian government provided a cash grant for its construction in exchange for a permanent reduction in grain rates—the Crows Nest Pass

Agreement of 1897. In 1916 the Kettle Valley Railway, a CP subsidiary, extended that route west to a connection with CP's main line at Hope, B. C., creating a secondary main line across the southern tier of British Columbia and part of Alberta. The line ran across the mountains rather than along the valleys and was expensive to build and operate. Much of the western portion of the Kettle Valley line has been abandoned in recent years.

Rogers Pass in the Selkirk Mountains of British Columbia had long been a bottleneck on CP's main line, not only because of 2.2-percent grades against westbound traffic, but also because of snow in the winter. Much of the traffic moving over Rogers Pass was export grain moving to Vancouver. Because the Crows Nest Pass Agreement kept rates artificially low, CP calculated that it lost $200 million a year on grain traffic. It couldn't reconcile such losses against the $600 million needed to improve the Rogers Pass line. In 1983 the Canadian parliament passed the Western Grain Transportation Act, which established

subsidies to the railways from grain producers and the federal government, giving CP the encouragement it needed to undertake the Rogers Pass project.

In May 1989, CP completed a new line for westbound traffic through Rogers Pass. The keystone of the project is the 9.1-mile Mount Macdonald Tunnel, the longest railroad tunnel in the western hemisphere. The new line reduced the westbound grade from 2.2 percent to 1 percent. Eastbound traffic continues to use the 5-mile Connaught Tunnel, opened in 1916.

Through the years the Canadian Pacific Railway grew to become, in its own words, "the world's greatest travel system." Its properties included ships, hotels, and an airline. In 1968 Canadian Pacific revised its image, much as Canadian National had done in 1961. Wine-red and gray locomotives gave way to bright red; the CP shield, sometimes surmounted by a beaver, was replaced by the "multimark," a black triangle on a white semicircle, and "Canadian Pacific Railway" became CP Rail, a unit of Canadian Pacific Limited.

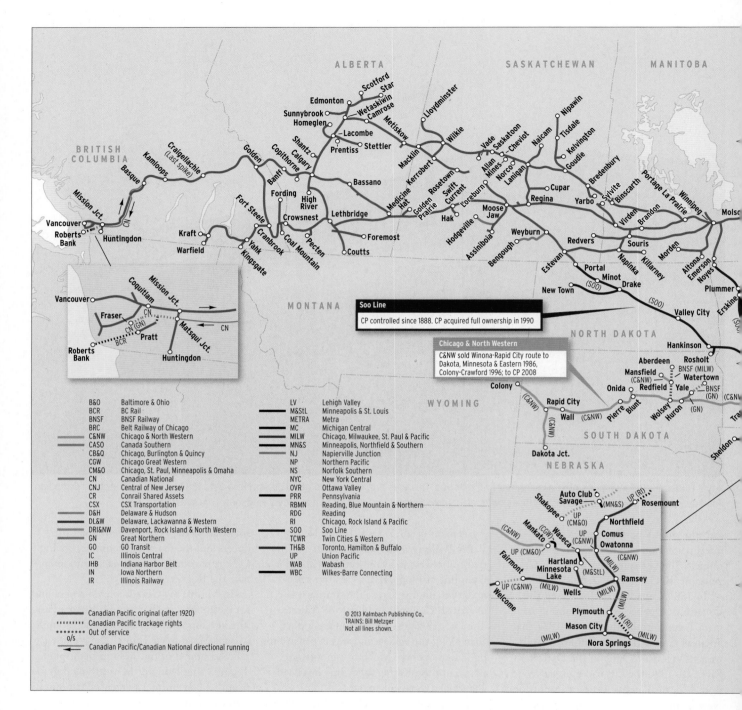

In 1996 the railroad name reverted to Canadian Pacific Railway, and in 2001, Canadian Pacific Limited spun off its subsidiaries, including the railroad, into separate entities. The railroad informally dropped the "Railway" in 2007.

Canadian subsidiaries

In 1912 Canadian Pacific leased three railroads: the Dominion Atlantic Railway (Halifax-Yarmouth, Nova Scotia); the Quebec Central Railway (Quebec City-Newport, Vermont); and the Esquimault & Nanaimo Railway (Victoria-Courtenay, B. C., on Vancouver Island). The DAR was sold in 1994 to Iron Road Railways, the QC was sold in 1999 and abandoned in 2004, and the E&N was sold to RailAmerica in 1998.

On Jan. 1, 1987, CP Rail absorbed the Toronto, Hamilton & Buffalo Railway, a wholly owned subsidiary. The TH&B's main line connected Hamilton and Welland, Ont., and was the middle third of a Buffalo-Toronto route operated in conjunction with CP and New York Central. In 1895 TH&B was purchased by four railroads: 27 percent by CP and 73 percent by New York Central and two subsidiaries. NYC's majority interest passed to Penn Central; CP Rail purchased PC's interest in 1977.

On Sept. 1, 1988, Canadian Pacific created the Canadian Atlantic Railway, a wholly owned subsidiary consisting of CP's lines east of Megantic, Que.: light-traffic branches in New Brunswick, the Dominion Atlantic Railway, and the main line across Maine to Saint John, N. B. (Halifax and Montreal are Canada's major Atlantic seaports). These lines were sold or abandoned by 1994.

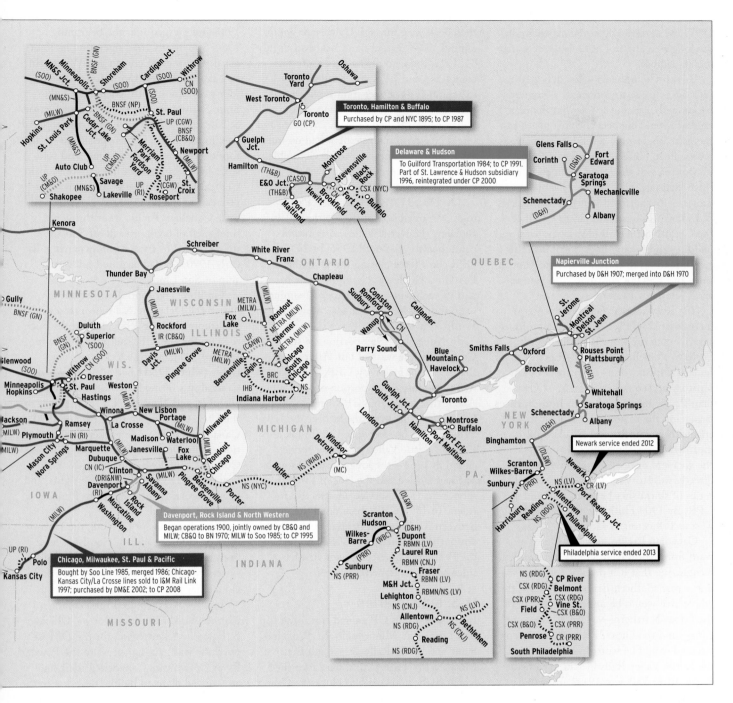

Kettle Valley

The Canadian Pacific main line across the prairies of Manitoba, Saskatchewan, and Alberta lies about 50 to 100 miles north of the U. S. border. The line turns northwest at Medicine Hat, Alberta, to cross the Rockies and the Selkirks, runs generally westward, then turns sharply to follow the Thompson and Fraser rivers almost due south for about 100 miles. On a map it looks like a detour—and it is. The Kootenay district of southern British Columbia is an area of rugged mountain ranges running north and south, and

watercourses useful to an east-west railroad are scarce.

In the late 1800s southern British Columbia was geographically and economically closer to the United States than to the rest of Canada. The discovery of silver near Nelson in 1887 and a desire to keep the region tied to Canada sparked the idea of a railroad across the southern part of British Columbia. Rails working north from Spokane, Washington, soon penetrated the area, adding impetus to the proposal; the Depression of 1893 and the repeal of the Silver Purchase Act in the

U. S. made it unlikely the proposal would become reality.

Prosperity returned within a few years, and there were further incursions by U. S. railroads. It became more and more necessary to build a Canadian railroad into the area. The CPR already reached west from Medicine Hat to Lethbridge, Alta. In 1898 it was extended west across the Rockies to Cranbrook, B. C. The Canadian government provided a cash grant for construction of the line in exchange for a permanent reduction in the rates for carrying grain—the Crows Nest Pass Agreement of

1897 (the agreement proved expensive in the long run, and not until 1983 were matters remedied).

British Columbians who advocated the railroad as a way to connect the Kootenay region with Vancouver saw that the new railroad would connect the area instead to the East. There were several immediate proposals to build a railroad east from Vancouver, and the forces grouped into three factions: the Canadian Pacific, the provincially chartered Vancouver, Victoria & Eastern Railway, and James J. Hill of the Great Northern Railway, who was building and buying lines north into the area intending to continue west to Vancouver—and Hill got control of the Vancouver, Victoria & Eastern.

The Kettle River Valley Railway was incorporated in 1901 as part of a project to carry copper ore from Republic, Wash., north to a smelter in Grand Forks, B. C. James J. Hill saw it as an intrusion of his territory and squashed it. In 1907 Canadian Pacific opened a branch from Spences Bridge on the main line southeast to the coalfields at Merritt and Nicola. Hill meanwhile was expanding his presence in the area and once again proposed a line directly west to Vancouver. There ensued a series of skirmishes between Hill and the CPR. By 1909 Hill's line reached as far west as Princeton, B. C.

Canadian Pacific surveyed routes westward from Midway, where its track ended, recognizing that if it did not complete a line across southern British Columbia, the whole area would be under the control of the Great Northern—an American company—and the lines CPR had already constructed would be worthless. It met with the Kettle Valley Railway (the renamed Kettle River Valley in 1911) and worked out an arrangement in which Kettle Valley would build the required line, including an extremely difficult stretch from Merritt southwest over Coquihalla Pass to Hope. Hill's Vancouver, Victoria & Eastern was also aiming at Coquihalla Pass—and the topography would barely permit one railroad, let alone two. In 1913 the two railroads agreed to share a single line.

In October 1914 the two railroads had built enough track to create a rail route from the Kootenay area to a connection with the CPR main line at Spences Bridge—a roundabout route but not nearly as roundabout as going east to Lethbridge then back west through Calgary or going around via Wenatchee and Seattle. On July 31, 1916, the Coquihalla Pass route was completed and CPR and Kettle Valley inaugurated passenger train service between Vancouver and Nelson.

James J. Hill died on May 29, 1916, and Great Northern management had no interest at all in rail lines in British Columbia. GN ran one inspection train over the Coquihalla Pass line and that was all.

On Dec. 31, 1930, Canadian Pacific took over operation of the Kettle Valley Railway. The Kettle Valley corporation continued to exist until 1956. In 1938 CPR considered closing the Coquihalla Pass line, which was closed by snow for part of each winter, but changed its mind scant months before Canada entered World War II.

In November 1959 portions of the Coquihalla line washed out. After more than a year of inactivity, CPR announced it was abandoning that portion of the route. About that same time CPR began routing Kootenay–Vancouver freight over the Lake Windermere line between Cranbrook and Golden. Kettle Valley passenger service ended in 1964—the longer route through Spences Bridge and the lack of through service made the service unattractive to riders. In 1978 CPR abandoned the line between Midway and Penticton, the eastern portion of the Kettle Valley proper, and the Penticton–Spences Bridge line has since been abandoned.

U. S. subsidiaries

In the late 1880s CP gained control of the Soo Line—the Minneapolis, St. Paul, and Sault Ste. Marie Railway—(Sault Ste. Marie to the Twin Cities) partly for the wheat traffic and partly to block the Grand Trunk Railway from doing so. The latter was also the primary reason for acquiring the Duluth, South Shore & Atlantic Railway (Sault Ste. Marie to Duluth) in 1888. The Soo Line leased the Wisconsin Central Railway in 1909, gaining access to Chicago, and by 1930 the Soo and the DSS&A had the same officers.

DSS&A declared bankruptcy in 1937 and was reorganized in 1949. In 1961 the DSS&A, Wisconsin Central, and the Soo Line merged to form the Soo Line Railroad (making "Soo Line" the official name and not just a nickname). Soo Line purchased the bankrupt Milwaukee Road in 1985 and merged it at the beginning of 1986. Soo briefly tried operating its light-density lines in Michigan and Wisconsin as Lake States Transportation Division (don't confuse it with Michigan's Lake State Railway, which is the former Detroit & Mackinac). Then Soo Line consolidated its Chicago-Twin Cities operations on the former Milwaukee Road route and sold what had been its own lines to Wisconsin Central Limited in 1987 (in many ways re-creating the pre-1909 Wisconsin Central). Canadian Pacific went through a brief spell of trying to sell off Soo Line, then decided to try for full ownership. By early 1990 CP had acquired full ownership of Soo Line's stock.

Guilford Transportation Industries placed the Delaware & Hudson Railway in bankruptcy in June 1988 and put the railroad up for sale. CP Rail purchased it in January 1991, eyeing D&H's trackage rights (which D&H had acquired when Conrail was formed) to Washington, Philadelphia, and Newark, N. J., in the light of the U. S.-Canada free trade pact of 1990. Canadian Pacific undertook a rehabilitation of the Delaware & Hudson, purchased Conrail's Buffalo-Binghamton, N. Y., line, over which D&H had trackage rights, and began regular freight service to Philadelphia and Newark.

The operations of CP Rail, the Delaware & Hudson, and the Soo Line have been integrated into the Canadian Pacific system, with the lines all losing their individual identities.

In 2009, CP acquired the Dakota, Minnesota & Eastern and Iowa, Chicago & Eastern. A key reason for the DM&E purchase was gaining access to the Powder River Coal Basin. Canadian Pacific had announced plans to build a new line to the area; however, in 2012 CP announced it had dropped those plans and wanted to sell the western end of the former DM&E.

FACTS & FIGURES

Year	1929	2012
Miles operated	20,780	14,800
Locomotives	2,145	1,800
Passenger cars	3,002	—
Freight cars	92,113	26,591

Reporting marks: CP, CPAA, CPI, CPT
Historical society: cptracks.ca

Central of Georgia

In the summer of 1947 the CofG inaugurated two coach streamliners. Here, four miles south of Atlanta, the *Nancy Hanks II* (left) is on its way to Savannah while the *Man o' War* (right) heads toward Atlanta. *Central of Georgia*

The opening in 1830 of the South Carolina Railroad between Charleston, S. C., and Augusta, Ga., diverted traffic from the port of Savannah, Ga., to Charleston. To recapture that business, the citizens of Savannah organized the Central Rail Road & Canal Company in 1833 to build a railroad toward Macon. Routes were surveyed and construction began in December 1835, about the same time the company's name was changed to Central Rail Road & Banking Company of Georgia. The railroad reached Macon, 191 miles from Savannah, in October 1843. By the Civil War the road had purchased or leased lines to Augusta and Eatonton.

In 1869 the CofG leased the South Western Railroad, which it had earlier helped finance, gaining lines from Macon to Columbus, Fort Gaines, and Albany, Ga., and Eufala, Alabama. In 1872 the road acquired a Savannah–New York steamship line and in 1875 purchased the Western Rail Road of Alabama jointly

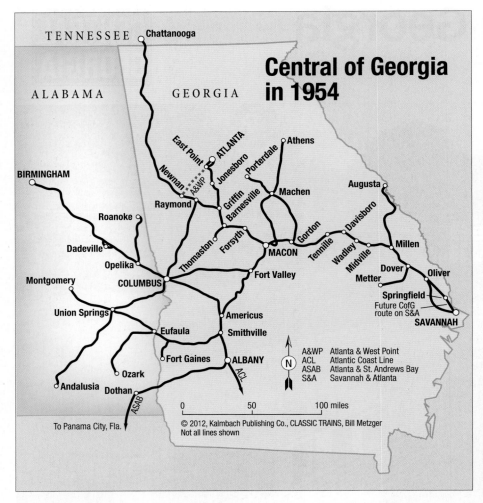

Central of Georgia in 1954

TENNESSEE
Chattanooga

ALABAMA
GEORGIA

BIRMINGHAM
East Point ATLANTA
Newnan A&WP Athens
Roanoke Jonesboro Porterdale
Raymond Griffin Machen Augusta
Dadeville Barnesville Davisboro
Opelika Thomaston Forsyth Gordon Millen
Montgomery MACON Tennille Wadley Midville Dover
COLUMBUS Fort Valley Metter Oliver
Union Springs Springfield
Eufaula Americus Future CofG route on S&A
Fort Gaines Smithville SAVANNAH
Ozark ALBANY
Andalusia Dothan ACL
To Panama City, Fla. ASAB

A&WP	Atlanta & West Point
ACL	Atlantic Coast Line
ASAB	Atlanta & St. Andrews Bay
S&A	Savannah & Atlanta

N

0   50   100 miles

© 2012, Kalmbach Publishing Co., CLASSIC TRAINS, Bill Metzger
Not all lines shown

E. H. Harriman and the Illinois Central

In 1907 E. H. Harriman gained control of the Central of Georgia. His system already included Union Pacific, Southern Pacific, and Illinois Central. None of those railroads connected directly with the CofG, so Harriman assembled a Jackson, Tenn.-Birmingham line for IC from 129 miles of trackage rights over Mobile & Ohio, Southern, and Frisco and 80 miles of new construction. In 1909 Harriman sold his interest in the CofG to the Illinois Central.

The Depression cut into CofG's traffic, and the relocation of textile mills from New England to the South eliminated much of the business in cotton moving through the port of Savannah. The road entered receivership at the end of 1932 and was reorganized in 1948, out from under IC control. In 1951 CofG purchased the Savannah & Atlanta, and in 1962, it consolidated operations with the S&A between Savannah and Waynesboro, Ga., to allow abandonment of part of each road's line between those points.

Southern Railway ownership

The Central of Georgia was a desirable and strategic property. In 1956 the Frisco purchased control, subject to Interstate Commerce Commission approval—but the ICC disapproved and ordered the Frisco to sell its interest in 1961. The ICC approved of Southern Railway's acquisition of CofG, and on June 17, 1963, the Central of Georgia Railway became a subsidiary of the Southern. The Central of Georgia Railroad was incorporated June 1, 1971, and immediately merged the Central of Georgia Railway and three smaller lines: the Georgia & Florida, the Savannah & Atlanta, and the Wrightsville & Tennille. The new CofG quickly lost its identity in the Southern system, but it survives on paper as part of the Norfolk Southern.

FACTS & FIGURES

Year	1929	1970
Miles operated	1,944	1,729
Locomotives	331	131
Passenger cars	262	30
Freight cars	9,693	7,381
Reporting marks: CG		
Historical Society: cofg.org		

with the Georgia Railroad. The year 1879 saw the CofG enter Montgomery, Ala., through purchase of a controlling interest in the Montgomery & Eufala.

In 1881 the Georgia Railroad and its interests in the Western of Alabama and the Atlanta & West Point were leased to William Wadley, president of the Central of Georgia. Wadley assigned half the lease to the CofG and half to the Louisville & Nashville. At the same time, CofG gained control of the Port Royal & Augusta and began development of a system to reach into western South Carolina, but encountered hostility from the government of the state of South Carolina. In that same era the CofG extended lines northwest from Columbus to Birmingham, Ala., and north through Rome to Chattanooga, Tennessee.

In 1888 the 2,600-mile CofG came under control of the Richmond Terminal and was leased to the Georgia Pacific Railway, a subsidiary of the Richmond & Danville (a predecessor of the Southern Railway). In 1892 CofG entered receivership. It lost the Port Royal system (which

became the Charleston & Western Carolina, a member of the Atlantic Coast Line family) and the Georgia Railroad and its affiliates.

Reorganization

Sold at foreclosure and reorganized as the Central of Georgia Railway, the new CofG included several former subsidiary companies, two leased railroads, the South Western and the Augusta & Savannah, and what was called the Auxiliary System—a land company, the steamship line, and several short lines. In 1900 the company opened a line southwest through Dothan and Hartford to Florala, Ala.; spurs of this line reached into Florida. In 1901 CofG regained its Chattanooga line, which had operated independently since the foreclosure sale, and acquired a branch from Dover west to Brewton, Ga. In 1905 the line from Columbus to Greenville, Ga., was widened from 3-foot gauge to standard and extended to Newnan, forming a direct Columbus-Atlanta route in conjunction with the Atlanta & West Point.

Central of New Jersey

The earliest railroad ancestor of the Central of New Jersey was the Elizabethtown & Somerville Railroad, incorporated in 1831 and opened from Elizabethport to Elizabeth, N. J., in 1836. Horses gave way to steam in 1839, and the road was extended west, reaching Somerville at the beginning of 1842. The Somerville & Easton Railroad was incorporated in 1847 and began building westward. In 1849 it purchased the Elizabethtown & Somerville and adopted a new name: Central Railroad Company of New Jersey. The line reached Phillipsburg, on the east bank of the Delaware River, in 1852. It was extended east across Newark Bay to Jersey City in 1864, and it acquired branches to Flemington, Newark, Perth Amboy, Chester, and Wharton.

The New Jersey Southern began construction in 1860 at Port Monmouth. The railroad worked its way southwest across lower New Jersey and reached Bayside, on the Delaware River west of Bridgeton, N. J., in 1871. The NJS came under the control of the CNJ in 1879. CNJ's influence briefly extended across the Delaware River in the form of the Baltimore & Delaware Bay Railroad from Bombay Hook, Del., east of Townsend, to Chestertown, Md. That line became part of the Pennsylvania Railroad family in 1901.

The New Jersey Southern was connected to the CNJ by the New York & Long Branch Railroad, which was completed in 1881 between Perth Amboy and Bay Head Junction. The NY&LB, at least in modern times, had no equipment of its own; CNJ and the Pennsylvania, joint owners of the Long Branch, both operated on it by trackage rights.

CNJ's lines in Pennsylvania were built by the Lehigh Coal & Navigation Co. as the Lehigh & Susquehanna Railroad. The main line was completed from Phillipsburg, N. J., to Wilkes-Barre in 1866. A notable feature of the line was the Ashley Planes, a steep stretch of line (maximum grade, 14.65 percent) operated by cables driven by stationary engines. The Ashley Planes remained in service until after World War II.

The Central of New Jersey had the only double-cab diesels in the U. S., six 2,000-hp Baldwins. Here, No. 2005 leads a train through Elizabeth. *Bob Krone*

B&O   Baltimore & Ohio
LV   Lehigh Valley
NY&LB   New York & Long Branch
PRR   Pennsylvania
PRSL   Pennsylvania-Reading Seashore Lines
RDG   Reading

© 2010, Kalmbach Publishing Co., CLASSIC TRAINS, Bill Metzger
Not all lines shown

Camelback locomotives, such as this 4-6-0 (note the mid-boiler cab), were designed with wide fireboxes for slow-burning anthracite. The CNJ had an extensive fleet. *William R. Frutchey*

Central of New Jersey leased the Lehigh & Susquehanna in 1871. The line was extended to Scranton in 1888 by a subsidiary of the L&S, the Wilkes-Barre & Scranton. Most of the traffic on the Pennsylvania lines was anthracite coal, much of it from mines owned by subsidiaries of the railroad, until the Commodities Clause of the Interstate Commerce Act of 1920 forbade railroads to haul freight in which they had an interest.

Reading control

From 1883 to 1887 the CNJ was leased to and operated by the Philadelphia & Reading, with which it formed a Jersey City–Philadelphia route. CNJ resumed its own management after a reorganization in 1887. In 1901 the Reading Company, successor to Philadelphia & Reading, acquired control of the CNJ through purchase of a majority of its stock, and at about that same time Baltimore & Ohio acquired control of the Reading.

CNJ's *Blue Comet*, inaugurated in 1929, was the forerunner of the coach streamliners that blossomed nationwide in the late 1930s and the 1940s. It was a deluxe coach train operating twice daily between Jersey City and Atlantic City, and its refurbished cars offered more comfort than the usual day coach of the era. It was painted blue

from the pilot of its 4-6-2 to the rear of its observation car. It succumbed to automobile competition in 1941.

In 1929 CNJ purchased a 30 percent interest in the Raritan River Railroad, a short line from Perth Amboy to New Brunswick. In 1931 it acquired total ownership of the Wharton & Northern and a partial interest in the Mount Hope Mineral Railroad from Warren Foundry & Pipe Corp.

CNJ maintained a small carfloat terminal in the Bronx. It was the site of the first successful Class 1 railroad diesel operation.

Postwar woes

The years after World War II were not kind to the Central of New Jersey. Passenger traffic was almost entirely commuter business, requiring great amounts of rolling stock for two short periods five days a week. Three-fourths of CNJ's freight traffic terminated on line—the road was essentially a terminal carrier. In addition, heavy taxes levied by the state of New Jersey ate up much of CNJ's revenue.

Between 1946 and 1952 CNJ's lines in Pennsylvania were operated as the Central Railroad of Pennsylvania in an effort to escape taxation by the state of New Jersey. CNJ resumed its own operation of the Pennsylvania lines at the end of 1952.

When the Lehigh & New England Railroad was abandoned in 1961, CNJ acquired a few of its branches and organized them as the Lehigh & New England Railway. In 1963 Lehigh Coal & Navigation sold its railroad properties to the Reading, but the lease to the CNJ continued. In 1965 CNJ and Lehigh Valley consolidated their lines along the Lehigh River in Pennsylvania and portions of each road's line were abandoned; the anthracite traffic that had supported both roads had largely disappeared. CNJ operations in Pennsylvania ended March 31, 1972.

Over the years CNJ maintained an extensive marine operation on New York Bay, including a steamer line to Sandy Hook. CNJ's last marine service, the ferry line between Manhattan and CNJ's rail terminal at Jersey City, made its final run on April 30, 1967. It was also the last day for the terminal itself; the next day CNJ passenger trains began originating and terminating at the Pennsylvania Railroad station in Newark, where New York passengers could transfer to either PRR or Port Authority Trans-Hudson trains.

Although the state of New Jersey began subsidizing commuter service in 1964 and the tax situation changed in 1966, CNJ entered bankruptcy proceedings on March 22, 1967. The merger between Chesapeake & Ohio and Norfolk & Western that was proposed in 1965 to counter the impending Pennsylvania-New York Central merger was to have included CNJ, but the bankruptcy of Penn Central killed that prospect.

CNJ drafted elaborate plans for reorganization; they came to naught as neighboring railroads collapsed. Conrail took over the railroad properties and freight operations of the Central of New Jersey on April 1, 1976; New Jersey Transit purchased the lines over which it now operates commuter service.

FACTS & FIGURES

Year	1929	1974
Miles operated	693	526
Locomotives	535	101
Passenger cars	917	157
Freight cars	22,978	2,232
Reporting marks: CNJ		
Historical society: jcrhs.org		

Central Vermont

T he Vermont Central Railroad was opened in 1849 between Windsor and Burlington, Vermont. Its builders found a relatively easy route over the divide between the Connecticut River and Lake Champlain by following the valleys of the White and Winooski rivers. Like many New England railroads of the time, it aimed to capture traffic moving between Boston and the Great Lakes. By 1850 connections were in place at each end, creating a through route from Boston to Ogdensburg, New York, on the St. Lawrence River.

By 1871 the Vermont Central rail system reached from New London, Conn., north to Montreal and west to Ogdensburg. It included the Rutland Railroad and steamship lines from New London to New York and from Ogdensburg to Chicago. In 1873 the Vermont Central was reorganized as the Central Vermont Railroad.

After the financial panic of 1893 the Central Vermont surrendered its leases of the Rutland and the Ogdensburg & Lake Champlain. The company was reorganized again in 1898 as the Central Vermont Railway, with Canada's Grand Trunk Railway as its majority stockholder. Control passed from Grand Trunk to Canadian National Railways in 1923. A flood in 1927 wiped out almost all of CV's main line across the

A northbound local freight behind 2-8-0 No. 469 rolls into Bolton, Vt., on a sunny October day in 1953. *Mert Leet*

middle of Vermont; Canadian National funded the rebuilding of the line.

CV was in receivership between 1927 and 1929. It trimmed back several branch lines during the Depression, and it discontinued its New London–New York steamship service after World War II. In the mid-1950s it abandoned its own line to Montreal in favor of trackage rights on parent CN. The railroad dieselized relatively late, in 1957.

In 1971 CN placed all its U. S. subsidiaries under the control of the Grand Trunk Corporation, headquartered in Detroit. Later in the 1970s CV regained a measure of independence and local control. However, traffic and revenues diminished—most of CV's traffic was received from CN and Conrail and terminated on line.

In 1983 the CV was briefly offered for sale, but there were no buyers. CV made several attempts to build business: a piggyback train, a unit train carrying wood chips to a power plant, a unit train carrying lumber and building materials, and a Tank-Train (linked tank cars). None of those attempts were outstandingly successful.

The middle portion of CV's main line, between Windsor and Brattleboro, Vt., consisted of trackage rights on Boston &

Maine's Connecticut River line. B&M's track deteriorated in the 1980s to such an extent that in 1987 Amtrak suspended the operation of its Washington–Montreal *Montrealer* and used its condemnation powers to take ownership of the Brattleboro–Windsor route. Amtrak transferred the line to CV, which rehabilitated the track, and the *Montrealer* resumed operation in 1989 on a new route—the entire length of CV's main line, from New London, Conn., to East Alburgh, Vt.

In the early 1990s CV was purchased by RailTex, Inc., which took over operations on Feb. 4, 1995 as the New England Central Railroad. In 2000 RailTex was merged into RailAmerica, which was acquired by shortline holding company Genesee & Wyoming in late 2012.

FACTS & FIGURES

Year	1929	1992
Miles operated	469	366
Locomotives	68	20
Passenger cars	128	—
Freight cars	3,350	223
Reporting marks: CV		
Historical society: cvrs.com		

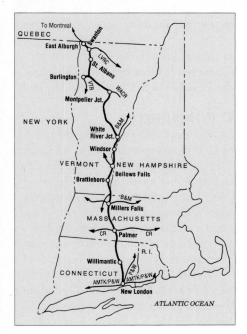

Chesapeake & Ohio

Two C&O passenger E units, an E7 and an E8, await their departures from Detroit's Fort Street Union Depot in the early 1960s. *J. David Ingles*

The rivers and the ocean were the primary avenues of transportation in Virginia in the 1830s. The few early railroads in the state connected the coast with inland points. One of these was the Louisa Railroad, chartered in 1836 to run from Taylorsville, on the Richmond, Fredericksburg & Potomac just south of what is now Doswell, to points in Louisa County. At first the RF&P operated the railroad, but in 1847 the Louisa Railroad acquired its own rolling stock and took over its own affairs. By 1850 the railroad had been extended west to Charlottesville. That year it became the Virginia Central Railroad, and in 1851 over the protests of the RF&P, it built its own line from Taylorsville to Richmond.

The state of Virginia undertook construction of the Blue Ridge Railroad west from Charlottesville and on completion leased it to the Virginia Central (which later purchased it). Meanwhile, the Virginia Central leapfrogged its rails ahead to Clifton Forge. In 1853 the state chartered the Covington & Ohio Railroad to connect the Virginia Central Railroad and the James River & Kanawha Canal at Covington with the Ohio River.

The Civil War halted the westward expansion of the railroad, even though the line would have been valuable to the Confederacy. During the latter part of the war the Virginia Central pulled up parts of its line for supplies to maintain other parts. However, by 1865 the entire line was back

in service. The Virginia Central and the Covington & Ohio were consolidated as the Chesapeake & Ohio Railroad in 1868.

C. P. Huntington

In 1869 the C&O came under the control of C. P. Huntington, builder of the Central Pacific and the Southern Pacific. The C&O had run out of money, and its officers asked Huntington if he could finance the westward construction of the road. Huntington and his associates subscribed to mortgage bonds, and the C&O was reorganized with Huntington as its president.

On Jan. 29, 1873, the C&O was completed from Richmond to the Ohio River a few miles east of its confluence with the Big Sandy (which forms the border between West Virginia and Kentucky). The western terminus of the road was the new city of Huntington, W. Va. In 1875 C&O entered receivership and was foreclosed and reorganized as the Chesapeake & Ohio Railway; another reorganization followed in 1888.

Huntington envisioned the C&O as the eastern portion of a transcontinental system. He organized the Chesapeake, Ohio & Southwestern Railroad in 1877 to take over the Memphis, Paducah & Northern Railroad, a line from Elizabethtown and Louisville through Paducah, Ky., to Memphis. Huntington's Louisville, New Orleans & Texas Railway provided the connection between Memphis and New Orleans, the eastern terminus of the Southern Pacific. In 1884 Huntington formed the Newport News & Mississippi Valley Co. to hold the C&O, the CO&SW, and the Elizabethtown, Lexington & Big Sandy (opened in 1872 from the Big Sandy River to Lexington, Ky., with trackage rights on the Louisville & Nashville to Louisville).

C&O's line along the Ohio River to Cincinnati opened in 1888 with the completion of the Maysville & Big Sandy Railroad from Ashland to Covington, Ky., opposite Cincinnati (the second Covington on C&O's main line), and the Covington & Cincinnati Elevated Railroad

& Transfer & Bridge Co.—one of few three-ampersand railroads in the U. S. Both the M&BS and the C&CER&T&B were proprietary companies of the C&O.

The Vanderbilt years

Huntington's empire fell apart in 1888. The C&O was taken over and reorganized by Vanderbilt interests. It soon acquired the Elizabethtown, Lexington & Big Sandy and its Lexington–Louisville trackage rights. Illinois Central, by then under the control of E. H. Harriman, purchased the Chesapeake, Ohio & Southwestern and the Louisville, New Orleans & Texas, consolidating the latter with the Yazoo & Mississippi Valley.

During the presidency of Melville Ingalls (also president of the Cleveland, Cincinnati, Chicago & St. Louis), C&O undertook expansion at its eastern end. In 1882 it constructed a line east from Richmond to a new tidewater terminal at Newport News. In 1888 it leased (and later purchased) the Richmond & Allegheny Railroad, which followed the towpath of the James River & Kanawha Canal from Richmond through Lynchburg to Clifton Forge. Two years later the road arranged for access to Washington over the Virginia Midland Railway (later Southern Railway) from Gordonsville.

Expansion into Ohio and Indiana

By the turn of the century C&O had become a major coal hauler, and the Midwest was becoming a better market for coal than the East. In 1903 the majority of the stock of the Hocking Valley Railroad (Toledo–Columbus–Athens and Gallipolis, Ohio) was purchased jointly by the C&O, Baltimore & Ohio, Erie, Lake Shore & Michigan Southern (New York Central), and Pennsylvania railroads. In addition, C&O and LS&MS jointly acquired the Kanawha & Michigan from the Hocking Valley (the K&M ran from Charleston, W. Va., through Gallipolis and Athens, Ohio, to Columbus), and LS&MS purchased most of the stock of the Toledo & Ohio Central (Toledo-Columbus-Corning). By 1911 C&O had acquired control of the Hocking Valley. (More on the Hocking Valley in a bit.)

In 1910 C&O purchased the Chicago, Cincinnati & Louisville Railroad, a line from Cincinnati to Hammond, Ind., and reorganized it as the Chesapeake & Ohio Railway of Indiana. About that same time C&O bought a one-sixth interest in the Richmond-Washington Co., operator of the Richmond, Fredericksburg & Potomac. In 1918 C&O bought White Sulphur Springs, Inc.—C&O had controlled the

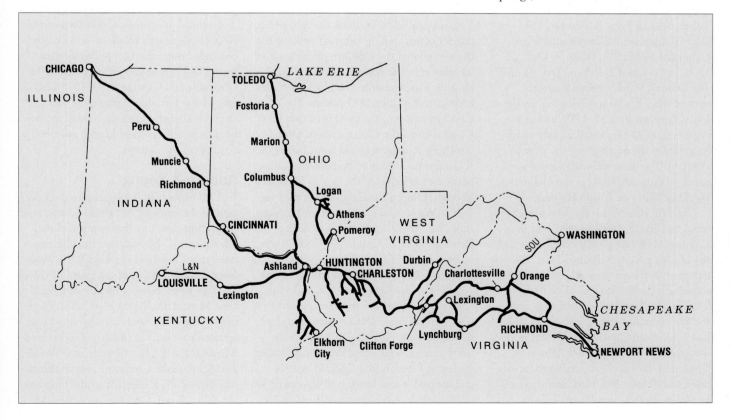

Chesapeake & Ohio's first Kanawha (2-8-4), built in 1943, leads a westbound coal train near Catlettsburg, Ky., on May 30, 1952. *Ed Theisinger*

company since 1910—operator of the Greenbrier, a resort hotel at White Sulphur Springs, W. Va.

Hocking Valley

The Columbus & Hocking Valley Railroad built a line from Columbus, Ohio, 50 miles southeast to Logan between 1869 and 1871. The lower half of the route followed the Hocking River. The line was extended first northwest, then southeast into the coalfields. In 1872 the Columbus & Toledo Railroad was incorporated by C&HV interests. Its line opened from Columbus to Marion, Ohio, on Oct. 15, 1876, and reached Toledo on Jan. 10, 1877. The Ohio & West Virginia Railway opened from Logan to Gallipolis, on the Ohio River, on Oct. 15, 1880, and at the beginning of 1881 opened an extension from Gallipolis north along the river to Pomeroy. The three railroads were consolidated on Aug. 20, 1881, as the Columbus, Hocking Valley & Toledo Railway.

The Hocking Valley Railway was chartered on Feb. 25, 1899, to take over the Columbus, Hocking Valley & Toledo and the Hocking Coal & Railroad Co. The new company conveyed the coal properties to a subsidiary, the Buckeye Coal & Railway Co. The Hocking Valley came to control the Kanawha & Michigan Railway, which had a line from Charleston, W. Va., northwest through Gallipolis and Athens to Columbus, more or less parallel to its own lines, and Toledo & Ohio Central, which had a line from Columbus to Toledo.

In June 1903 a majority block of Hocking Valley stock was acquired by five railroads: Pittsburgh, Cincinnati, Chicago & St. Louis (Pennsylvania Railroad), Baltimore & Ohio, Chesapeake & Ohio, Lake Shore & Michigan Southern (New York Central), and Erie. The PCC&StL acquired one-third of the stock and the other roads, one-sixth each.

The Hocking Valley and the Kanawha & Michigan gave the C&O a good route to the Midwest for coal from the West Virginia coalfields. In 1914, though, a U. S. district court, sniffing antitrust problems in the air, ordered the C&O to divest itself of its interest in the Kanawha & Michigan, creating a gap between the Hocking Valley and the rest of the C&O system. The C&O moved quickly. In May of that year C&O formed the Chesapeake & Ohio Northern Railway to build from Limeville, Ky., a few miles east of Portsmouth, Ohio, north up the valley of the Scioto River to Waverly, Ohio, a connection with the Norfolk & Western, and arranged for trackage rights on N&W for 62 miles to Valley Crossng, south of Columbus. C&ON was opened in 1917.

Soon C&O ran into limitations on the N&W: the number of trains it could run and the grades, which were steeper than on C&O's main line. C&O constructed the Chesapeake & Hocking Valley Railway north from Greggs, near Waverly, to Valley Crossing. C&O leased C&HV in 1926 and merged it and Hocking Valley in 1930. The effect of constructing the C&ON

and the C&HV was to remove through traffic from the portion of the Hocking Valley southeast of Columbus. In the mid-1970s C&O began to abandon that line bit by bit from the south end.

The Van Sweringen era

In 1923 Orris Paxton Van Sweringen and his brother Mantis James Van Sweringen, Cleveland real estate developers, purchased 30 percent of C&O's stock. The principal item in the Van Sweringens' empire was the Nickel Plate (formally, the New York, Chicago & St. Louis Railroad), and they drafted proposals to merge C&O, NKP, Erie, Hocking Valley, and Pere Marquette to form a fourth eastern system of the magnitude of New York Central, Pennsylvania, and Baltimore & Ohio.

By 1929 the Van Sweringens also hoped to include the Wheeling & Lake Erie, the Lackawanna, and the Chicago & Eastern Illinois, the last to furnish a connection with the Missouri Pacific, in which they held a sizable interest. Later that year the Van Sweringens withdrew their applications as their empire began to collapse. Meanwhile, in 1928 C&O had received permission to control the Pere Marquette. In 1930 C&O and PM unified their operations; they would merge on June 6, 1947. (The map on the previous page depicts the pre-Pere Marquette-era C&O system.)

In the depths of the Great Depression C&O inaugurated an all-air-conditioned passenger train, the *George Washington*, from Washington and Newport News to Louisville and Cincinnati. In 1933 C&O's advertising introduced the figure of a sleeping kitten—"Chessie," which quickly became one of the best-known advertising symbols in the country.

Robert R. Young

In 1937 Robert R. Young acquired 43 percent of the stock of Alleghany Corporation (a holding company that controlled the Chesapeake Corporation, a holding company that controlled the C&O). By 1942 Young was chairman of the board of C&O. In 1945 he proposed a merger of C&O, Pere Marquette, Nickel Plate, and Wheeling & Lake Erie, with the idea of adding western connections (likely prospects were Missouri Pacific, Rio Grande, and Western Pacific) to make a coast-to-coast railroad. The Nickel Plate objected to the proposal.

As it fell out, C&O merged the PM,

Chesapeake & Ohio H-8 Allegheny No. 1603 has a long string of loaded coal hoppers in tow in this early 1940s view. The C&O rostered 60 of the big 2-6-6-6s, built from 1941-1948, for hauling coal over the mountains for which they are named. *David P. Morgan Library collection*

Nickel Plate bought C&O's Wheeling & Lake Erie shares about the same time, and C&O distributed its NKP shares to C&O stockholders as a dividend later in 1947.

Young also proposed takeovers of the Association of American Railroads and the Pullman Company. He pushed for coast-to-coast through sleeping-car service with his famous ad headed, "A hog can cross America without changing trains—but you can't!"

Young intended to make C&O the top passenger railroad in the country. To this end he ordered a steam-turbine-powered Vista-Dome streamliner, the *Chessie*, for daylight service between Washington and Cincinnati, and he sent an order to Pullman-Standard for 289 passenger cars, enough to completely re-equip all of C&O's other trains. By the time the *Chessie* arrived from the Budd Company, C&O had discovered (possibly by counting the passengers on Baltimore & Ohio's new *Cincinnatian*) that there was no market for a daytime Washington–Cincinnati train. Most of the *Chessie* cars were sold to other U. S. railroads; a dozen went to Argentina.

Nearly half of the Pullman-Standard order was canceled or diverted to other railroads.

While all that was happening, in 1947 C&O became NYC's largest stockholder. Young proposed a merger of C&O, NYC, and the Virginian Railway. Young left the C&O in 1954 to take over management of the New York Central.

B&O, Western Maryland, and Chessie System

In 1960 C&O turned attention to neighbor Baltimore & Ohio and offered to purchase its stock. The Interstate Commerce Commission approved C&O control of B&O at the end of 1962, and the actual exchange of C&O stock for B&O took place in February 1963. By 1973 C&O owned more than 90 percent of B&O stock. B&O in turn owned nearly half the stock of Western Maryland and controlled the Reading Company; Reading controlled the Central Railroad of New Jersey. In 1966 the ICC approved C&O control of the Chicago South Shore & South Bend, a freight and commuter carrier with tracks through the industrial area just south of Lake Michigan.

Chessie System was incorporated in 1973 to own the C&O, B&O, and WM. The three did not merge immediately but became Chessie System Railroads, trading their identities for a new image whose emblem had an outline of C&O's cat, Chessie. In turn, Chessie System merged with Seaboard Coast Line Industries to form CSX. The South Shore Line did not become a Chessie System component but remained a stray in the alley behind her house until 1984, when it was purchased by the Venango River Corp.; this ownership lasted until 1989. (See South Shore's entry on page 104 for more details.)

FACTS & FIGURES

Year	1929	1972
Miles operated	2,740	4,994
Locomotives	946	1,030
Passenger cars	427	92
Freight cars	53,518	74,962
Reporting marks: C&O		
Historical society: cohs.org		

Chessie System

When formed in 1973, Chessie System adopted a system-wide paint scheme with a new logo, but locomotives and rolling stock remained lettered for their respective owners. This is Raleigh, W. Va., in September 1985. *George Hamlin*

The Chessie System was incorporated on Feb. 26, 1973. At that time, the Chesapeake & Ohio Railway controlled the Baltimore & Ohio, and C&O and B&O between them held more than 90 percent of Western Maryland's stock. On June 15, 1973, B&O, C&O, and WM were made subsidiaries of the Chessie System. A new image appeared using C&O's cat, Chessie, as the emblem, but the individual railroads continued in existence and rolling stock continued to carry the initials of the railroads. (The Chicago South Shore & South Bend, controlled by Chesapeake & Ohio since 1967, remained an orphan outside the Chessie System. Venango River Corporation purchased it in 1984.)

On Nov. 1, 1980, Chessie System and Seaboard Coast Line Industries, the parent of the Seaboard Coast Line Railroad, merged to form CSX Corporation. At the time the intention was for the subsidiary railroads to maintain their identities.

On May 1, 1983, B&O took over operation of the Western Maryland, reducing Chessie System to two railroads. Four years later, on April 30, 1987, Chesapeake & Ohio merged B&O, becoming the sole Chessie System Railroad. On Aug. 31, 1987, CSX Transportation, a subsidiary of CSX Corporation, merged C&O.

FACTS & FIGURES

Year	1973	1985
Miles operated	11,289	10,920
Locomotives	2,093	1,759
Passenger cars	—	—
Freight cars	135,513	84,957

Reporting marks: B&O, C&O, WM

Historical society: trainweb.org/CSHS

Chicago & Eastern Illinois

The earliest ancestor of the Chicago & Eastern Illinois was the Evansville & Illinois, chartered in 1849 to build north from Evansville, Ind., on the Ohio River. Its line reached Vincennes in 1853 and Terre Haute in 1854. By 1877 it had gone through several identities and was named the Evansville & Terre Haute Railway. That railroad controlled the Evansville & Indianapolis, a consolidation of several lines forming a second Evansville–Terre Haute route through Washington and Worthington, Ind., to the east of E&TH's own line.

Lines north and west of Terre Haute

The Evansville, Terre Haute & Chicago Railroad was chartered in 1869 and opened its line from Terre Haute to Danville, Illinois, in 1871. The Chicago, Danville & Vincennes Railroad, chartered in 1865, built south from Dolton, Ill., just south of Chicago, to Danville, completing the line in 1872. In 1873 it defaulted and in 1877 was sold at foreclosure to become the Chicago & Eastern Illinois Railroad. In 1880 the C&EI leased the Evansville, Terre Haute & Chicago and began to build southwest from Danville. By the turn of the century C&EI had by construction and purchase put together a line from Chicago to the Mississippi River at Thebes, Ill.

A new Chicago & Eastern Illinois Railroad was incorporated June 6, 1894, as a consolidation of the previous C&EI and the Chicago & Indiana Coal Railway. The latter road had a line from Momence, Ill., on C&EI's main line, to Brazil, Ind., with a branch from Percy Junction to La Crosse, Ind. The C&IC leased the Chicago & West Michigan (later Pere Marquette) line from La Crosse to New Buffalo, Mich.

In the next five years Chicago & Eastern Illinois purchased the Evansville, Terre Haute & Chicago, which it had previously leased; the Chicago, Paducah & Memphis Railroad (Mt. Vernon to Marion, Ill., about 40 miles); the Eastern Illinois & Missouri River Railroad (Marion to Thebes); and the Indiana Block Coal Railroad (Terre Haute to Brazil).

An FP7-E7 duo roll out of Chicago's Dearborn Station in April 1957 with C&EI train No. 1 en route to Evansville, Ind. *Dan Pope collection*

Frisco control

In 1902 the St. Louis & San Francisco acquired control of the C&EI. To connect with the Frisco at its closest point, the C&EI built a 20-mile line from Findlay Junction to Pana, Ill., and arranged for trackage rights on the Cleveland, Cincinnati, Chicago & St. Louis Railway (the Big Four, part of the New York Central System) from Pana to St. Louis. The C&EI also built a 62-mile line from Woodland Junction on the main line to Villa Grove, Ill., cutting off a dogleg through Danville for trains between Chicago and St. Louis.

In 1911 the C&EI absorbed the Evansville & Terre Haute and the Evansville Belt Railway, extending itself south from Terre Haute to the Ohio River. In 1913 the C&EI and its parent, the Frisco, entered receivership.

The Chicago & Eastern Illinois Railway was organized on Dec. 13, 1920, to acquire the properties and franchises of the Chicago & Eastern Illinois Railroad, except for the coal properties and the following lines: the former Evansville & Indianapolis (which became the Evansville, Indianapolis & Terre Haute and eventually part of the New York Central), the Evansville & Richmond (which became part of

Milwaukee Road's Chicago, Terre Haute & Southeastern); and the former Chicago & Indiana Coal Railway (which was incorporated as the Chicago, Attica & Southern). A coal strike in 1922 resulted in southern Illinois coal pricing itself out of a shrinking market, and C&EI's traffic, largely based on coal, began to fall off. In 1927 the C&EI purchased the Chicago Heights Terminal Transfer Railroad, a switching line at Chicago Heights.

In 1928 the Van Sweringen brothers of Cleveland acquired control of C&EI through their Chesapeake & Ohio, but did little to integrate it with the remainder of their empire (Chesapeake & Ohio, Missouri Pacific, Nickel Plate, Erie, Pere Marquette, and Wheeling & Lake Erie). By 1933 the C&EI was in reorganization.

The Chicago & Eastern Illinois Railroad took over the assets of the C&EI on Dec. 31, 1940. In 1952 the CE&I acquired the Jefferson Southwestern, a 12-mile line at Mt. Vernon, Ill., and later transferred one-third of the shares to Missouri Pacific and one-third to Illinois Central. Through a lease agreement it acquired the abandoned St. Louis & O'Fallon in October 1954 for access to East St. Louis.

Missouri Pacific began merger discussions with C&EI in 1959. In 1961 both

Mopac and Louisville & Nashville acquired C&EI stock and petitioned the ICC for permission to control the road; Illinois Central also petitioned for control. In 1963 the ICC ruled in favor of Mopac with the condition that MP negotiate in good faith for sale of the Evansville line to L&N. The Woodland Junction–Evansville line became L&N property in 1969. L&N purchased a half interest in the C&EI main line from there to Dolton Junction (Chicago) and half of C&EI's interests in the Chicago & Western Indiana and the Belt Railway of Chicago. L&N bought 48 diesel locomotives and 1,495 freight cars and cabooses from C&EI. Chicago & Eastern Illinois was merged with Missouri Pacific on Oct. 15, 1976.

Passenger traffic

For years, C&EI carried the majority of Florida-bound passengers out of Chicago on what was essentially a northern extension of L&N's passenger service—trains such as the *Dixie Flyer*, *Dixie Limited*, and *Dixie Flagler*. C&EI's own passenger trains included two of the earliest postwar streamliners, the *Whippoorwill* and the *Meadowlark*. C&EI's Chicago–St. Louis service succumbed shortly after World War II to the competition of Wabash, Illinois Central, and Gulf, Mobile & Ohio. Service to southern Illinois—ACF motorcars in the 1930s and an RDC in the 1950s—endured into the 1960s. C&EI discontinued passenger service south of Danville—the Evansville–Chicago portion of L&N's *Humming Bird* and *Georgian*—in 1968, shortly before L&N purchased the Evansville line. The last train, a Chicago–Danville local (briefly the *Danville Flyer*), remained in service until the start of Amtrak in 1971, though as an L&N train.

Chicago, Attica & Southern

The Chicago, Attica & Southern was a descendant of the grandly named Chicago & Great Southern, which by the

mid-1880s had put together a line in northwestern Indiana from Fair Oaks, on the Monon between Rensselaer and Shelby, to Brazil, between Indianapolis and Terre Haute.

The Chicago & Great Southern was reorganized as the Chicago & Indiana Coal Railway. The C&IC extended itself north to Wilder and La Crosse to connect with what in later years became the Erie, the Chesapeake & Ohio, and the Pennsylvania, and acquired trackage rights north to New Buffalo, Michigan.

The proprietor of the C&IC, Henry H. Porter, acquired control of the Chicago & Eastern Illinois and in 1888 constructed a connection between his two roads from Percy Junction, near Goodland, Ind., northwest to Momence, Ill., on the C&EI main line. The C&EI leased and in 1894 merged the Chicago & Indiana Coal Railway.

In 1921 as part of its reorganization C&EI offered the Coal Road for sale. The Brazil–West Melcher portion went to the Cincinnati, Indianapolis & Western and the remainder of the line to Charles F. Propst. Propst organized the Chicago, Attica & Southern Railroad, which began operation on Dec. 7, 1922. However, the CA&S faced formidable competition and had no money

to rehabilitate its track. The CA&S entered receivership on August 5, 1931.

In June 1942 C&EI abandoned the portion of the connecting line from Momence to the Illinois-Indiana state line, and in 1943 the Interstate Commerce Commission authorized abandonment of CA&S's portion of the connector plus the line from Percy Junction to La Crosse and the line south of Veedersburg. In April 1946 the ICC granted permission to abandon the remains of the CA&S.

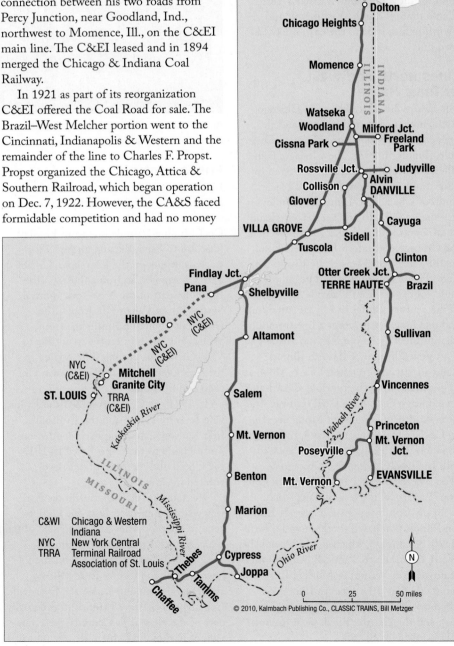

C&EI FACTS & FIGURES

Year	1929	1975
Miles operated	946	644
Locomotives	334	49
Passenger cars	284	—
Freight cars	14,818	6,937
Reporting marks: CEI		

Chicago & Illinois Midland

Chicago & Illinois Midland 2-10-2 No. 751 leads a coal train at Springfield, Ill., in the 1950s. The locomotive was one of nine former Atlantic Coast Line 2-10-2, each of which was fitted with a former New York Central tender. *Walter A. Peters; R.R. Wallin collection*

In 1888 the Pawnee Railroad was chartered to build west from Pawnee, Ill., a few miles south of Springfield, to a connection with the St. Louis & Chicago (later Illinois Central), a distance of 4 miles. In 1892 the road more than doubled its mileage with an extension west to the Chicago & Alton (later Southern Pacific) at Auburn.

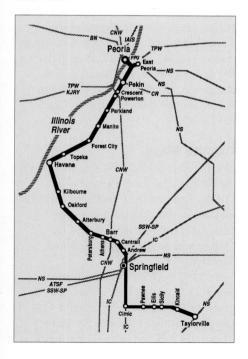

The Illinois Midland Coal Co., owned jointly by Peabody Coal Co. and Samuel Insull's Chicago Edison and Commonwealth Electric companies, had mines in the area. In 1905 the coal company purchased the railroad and organized it as the Central Illinois Railway. Later that year the railroad's name was changed to Chicago & Illinois Midland to avoid confusion with the neighboring Illinois Central. During the teens the railroad was extended east to Taylorville to connect with the Baltimore & Ohio and the Wabash and west to a connection with the Chicago & North Western. In 1926 the railroad purchased the Springfield-Peoria trackage of the defunct Chicago, Peoria & St. Louis and obtained trackage rights from Illinois Central from Pawnee Junction (now Cimic) to Springfield. As a result the coal traffic pattern changed. Instead of moving to connecting roads for rail haulage north to Chicago, it moved to the Illinois River at Havana, then north by barge.

Passenger trains were handled by a trio of 4-4-0s built in 1927 and 1928 by Baldwin, the last of their type built for a Class 1 railroad. In the 1940s and early 1950s C&IM purchased a number of Wabash and Atlantic Coast Line 2-10-2s. The road dieselized relatively late, in 1955.

Construction of a mine-mouth generating plant in the 1960s and later the restrictions against burning high-sulfur Illinois coal again altered the railroad's traffic pattern. Into the 1980s, much of C&IM's traffic was unit coal trains of low-sulfur Western coal off the Burlington Northern and Chicago & North Western at Peoria for delivery to Edison's generating station near Pekin, and to Havana for shipment by barge to generating stations near Chicago.

Commonwealth Edison, which was formed in 1907 by the merger of Chicago Edison and Commonwealth Electric, owned the Chicago & Illinois Midland until 1987. ComEd sold the C&IM to a group of investors; it remained privately held until 1996, when it was purchased by shortline holding company Genesee & Wyoming, which renamed it the Illinois & Midland Railroad.

FACTS & FIGURES

Year	1929	1983
Miles operated	135	121
Locomotives	24	20
Passenger cars	14	—
Freight cars	1,589	1,198
Reporting marks: CIM		

Chicago & North Western

For years the Chicago & North West-ern operated Chicago's most extensive commuter service. Its three routes were designated West, Northwest, and North. Those names also serve well to group C&NW's lines west, northwest, and north from Chicago.

West

The railroad capital of the United States, Chicago, saw its first locomotive in 1848: the Pioneer of the Galena & Chicago Union Rail Road. The G&CU, chartered in 1836, lay dormant for 12 years before construction began. By 1850, though, its rails reached west to the Fox River valley at Elgin and in 1853 to Freeport, where it connected with the Illinois Central Railroad.

In 1855 the Galena & Chicago Union completed a second line westward, from what is now West Chicago, reaching Fulton, Illinois, on the Mississippi River. By 1867 the Chicago, Iowa & Nebraska had built from Clinton, Iowa, to Cedar Rapids, and the Cedar Rapids & Missouri River Railroad had extended that line west across Iowa to a connection with the Union Pacific at Council Bluffs, on the east bank of the Missouri River (Chicago & North Western purchased those two companies in 1884).

That line was extended farther west, making a second connection with the Union Pacific at Fremont, Neb., and eventually reached Rapid City, S. D., and Casper, Wyo. A dispute with the Union Pacific caused the North Western to project an extension from Casper over South Pass toward Salt Lake City and Ogden, Utah. By the time the railhead reached Lander, Wyo., the C&NW had come to an agreement with UP and construction stopped.

North

Railroads were chartered in Illinois and Wisconsin in 1855 to connect Chicago with Milwaukee. The line was completed in 1855, and in 1863 the two companies were consolidated as the Chicago & Milwaukee Railway. The company was leased

A late-running Train No. 6, heavy with mail and express, speeds eastward near DeKalb, Ill., in 1949. The engine is H-1 4-8-4 No. 3014. *David P. Morgan Library collection*

by the Chicago & North Western in 1866 and was merged in 1883.

Two lines reached north from Milwaukee to Green Bay—one along the shore of Lake Michigan, a continuation of the line from Chicago, and the other northwest through the valley of the Fox River. (There are two Fox Rivers in eastern Wisconsin. One rises near Waukesha and flows south into the Illinois River. The other rises near Portage and flows north and northeast through several lakes into Lake Michigan at Green Bay.) The C&NW developed a dense network of branches in eastern Wisconsin and built lines into the mining area of Michigan's upper peninsula.

About 1906 C&NW constructed a second line from Chicago to Milwaukee for freight trains, a belt line around Milwaukee, and a long main line diagonally across Wisconsin from Milwaukee to a connection with the older Chicago–Twin Cities route at Wyeville.

Northwest

In 1855 the Chicago, St. Paul & Fond du Lac Rail Road was incorporated to extend an existing road northwest from Cary, Ill.,

through Madison and La Crosse, Wis., to St. Paul, Minn., and north through Fond du Lac, Wis., to the iron and copper country south of Lake Superior. The company was reorganized in 1859 as the Chicago & North Western Railway. In 1864 the C&NW was consolidated with the Galena & Chicago Union. At that point the C&CU consisted of lines from Chicago to Freeport and to Fulton, Ill., from Belvidere, Ill., to Beloit, Wis., and from Elgin to Richmond, Ill., plus the east-west route across Chicago known as the St. Charles Air Line.

Omaha Road

Notable among C&NW's acquisitions was the Chicago, St. Paul, Minneapolis & Omaha Railway. The Omaha Road reached from west-central Wisconsin to the Twin Cities, and from there southwest to Omaha and northeast to Duluth and Superior.

In 1857 the Minnesota legislature passed a bill vesting U. S. government land grants in four railroad corporations. One of them was the Root River & Southern Minnesota Railroad (later simply Southern

Minnesota). Work on that line began in 1858, and the company was reorganized in 1862—still having only roadbed, no rail. In 1864 St. Paul businessmen incorporated the Minnesota Valley Railroad to take over the Southern Minnesota. It was renamed the St. Paul & Sioux City Railroad in 1869.

The Chicago, St. Paul, Minneapolis & Omaha was formed in 1880 by the consolidation of the Northern Wisconsin Railway, which reached north to Bayfield and Superior, Wis., and the Chicago, St. Paul & Minneapolis Railway, which had started out as a railroad chartered to build from Tomah, Wis. to Lake St. Croix. The CStPM&O was headquartered in Hudson, Wis., a few miles east of St. Paul, Minn. It intersected with the Chicago & North Western at 17 points.

C&NW bought a majority of the Omaha Road's stock in 1882. The CStPM&O operated separately until January 1957 when the C&NW leased the CStPM&O; the North Western officially merged the Omaha Road in 1972.

Chicago & North Western

In 1901 C&NW built a long line south from the Chicago–Council Bluffs line at Nelson, Illinois, through Peoria toward St. Louis. The primary purpose of the line was to carry coal from southern Illinois, but the line also carried Chicago–St. Louis merchandise traffic in cooperation with the Litchfield & Madison Railway, a 44-mile terminal road in the industrial area across the Mississippi River from St. Louis.

Two EMD E8s lead the North Western's *400* out of Eau Claire, Wis., on subsidiary Chicago, St. Paul, Minneapolis & Omaha. *A. Robert Johnston; C&NW Historical Society collection*

The Chicago & North Western was one of a very few railroads in North America whose trains kept to the left on double track. Reasons given for the practice range from a preponderance of British stockholders to (more likely) the position of the station buildings on the lines around Chicago—generally on the left for trains heading toward Chicago. When C&NW double-tracked its lines through the suburbs, it assumed that Chicago-bound passengers would be more likely to use the depot buildings than homeward-bound suburbanites and made the track nearest the station the inbound line.

The North Western became Union Pacific's preferred connection at Council Bluffs. Until 1955 UP's yellow streamliners continued to Chicago on the C&NW. In 1955 Union Pacific surprised the railroad industry by switching its trains to the Milwaukee Road for the trip to Chicago. The North Western fell into a decline.

In the 1980s, the North Western once again became UP's favored connection, partly because C&NW thoroughly rebuilt its line between Chicago and Council Bluffs and partly by default—most of the competing routes had been abandoned.

Latter-day expansion

In the late 1950s and 1960s C&NW merged several smaller railroads: Litchfield & Madison in 1958; Minneapolis & St. Louis in 1960; Chicago Great Western in 1968; and Des Moines & Central Iowa (which owned the Fort Dodge, Des Moines & Southern) in 1968. C&NW gradually dismantled the lines of most of these railroads, keeping only a few strategic segments in service. In 1972 C&NW joined with Missouri Pacific to purchase the Alton & Southern from Alcoa, but a year later sold its half to St. Louis Southwestern.

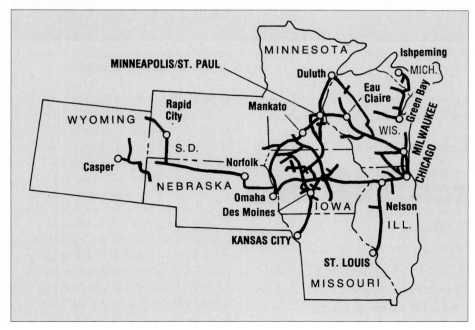

There was also a change in corporate structure in 1972. The Chicago & North Western Transportation Company was incorporated in 1970 as the North Western Employees Transportation Co., owned by nearly 1,000 C&NW employees. In 1972 it purchased the transportation assets of the Chicago & North Western Railway and changed its name to Chicago & North Western Transportation Co. For some time thereafter the road's herald carried the words "Employee Owned." In 1989 Chicago & North Western Holdings Corp., which owns the transportation company, was formed by Blackstone Capital Partners. It was privately held until 1992.

After the 1980 demise of the Rock Island the C&NW acquired Rock's Minneapolis–Kansas City "spine line," and by the mid-1980s abandoned the somewhat longer Chicago Great Western route between those cities.

The North Western's other major expansion was into the Powder River Basin of northeastern Wyoming. C&NW (through a subsidiary, Western Railroad Properties) and Burlington Northern jointly operated a line north into the coal-fields from Orin and Shawnee, Wyoming (the line was constructed by BN between 1976 and 1979). In 1984 C&NW opened a new line along the Wyoming-Nebraska state line to a connection with Union Pacific's line along the North Platte River rather than rebuild more than 500 miles of its line across northern Nebraska.

The North Western spun off two major groups of lines to form regional railroads:
• Dakota, Minnesota & Eastern Railroad: Winona, Minn., to Rapid City, S. D., plus branches, 965 miles in all (September 1986)
• Fox River Valley Railroad: two lines from Green Bay to Granville and Cleveland, Wis., plus branches, 214 miles (December 1988). Sale of the two main lines south of Green Bay had the effect of

Running on the left-hand main, as was customary on the C&NW, Mikado No. 2524 brings a train of refrigerator cars through West Chicago in September 1945. *Henry J. McCord*

isolating C&NW's lines in northern Wisconsin and Michigan's Upper Peninsula from the rest of the system. Wisconsin Central later purchased those lines as well

as the Fox River Valley Railroad.

By the 1990s most of Chicago & North Western's traffic was concentrated on two lines: Chicago to Council Bluffs, essentially an eastern extension of Union Pacific's transcontinental main line, and the Wyoming and Nebraska coal lines.

During the late 1980s the C&NW was the target of several hostile takeover attempts. Union Pacific was concerned about these—by then C&NW was its principal eastern connection. On March 17, 1995, Union Pacific announced its intention to buy the 70 percent of the C&NW that it did not already own.

C&NW FACTS & FIGURES

Year	1929	1993
Miles operated	8,459	8,243
Locomotives	1,805	1,040
Passenger cars	2,117	—
Freight cars	69,418	36,086
Reporting marks: CNW		
Historical society: cnwhs.org		

CStPM&O FACTS & FIGURES

Year	1929	1955
Miles operated	1,747	1,616
Locomotives	325	135
Passenger cars	258	100
Freight cars	10,507	4,119
Reporting marks: CMO		
Historical society: cnwhs.org		

Chicago Aurora & Elgin

The Aurora, Elgin & Chicago Railway was incorporated in March 1901. By 1902 it had built a line from Aurora, Ill., to Laramie Avenue in Chicago and a branch to Batavia. In May 1903 it opened a branch from Wheaton to Elgin. The AE&C used a third rail rather than overhead wire, except in streets, yards, and terminals. In 1905 the AE&C extended its service over the rails of the Metropolitan West Side Elevated (the "L") to a terminal on Chicago's Loop at Wells Street.

The company was consolidated with several streetcar lines in the Fox River Valley in 1906 to form the Aurora, Elgin & Chicago Railroad. In 1910 a subsidiary then built a line to West Chicago and Geneva; interurban cars continued from Geneva to St. Charles on streetcar tracks.

The AE&C entered receivership in 1919. In 1922 the company's properties were separated into two parts: the Fox River Division, encompassing the streetcar lines in the Fox Valley between Aurora and Elgin, and the Third Rail Division, the four-pronged line from Chicago to Aurora, Batavia, Geneva, and Elgin. The latter was sold to the Chicago Aurora & Elgin Railroad, which took over July 1, 1922.

Samuel Insull acquired control of the CA&E in 1926, and the road entered another receivership in 1932. The West Chicago–Geneva–St. Charles line was abandoned in 1937. Private right of way and a new terminal in Aurora in 1939

A Chicago local prepares to leave the Wheaton station. The head car is one of ten built by St. Louis Car Co. in 1945, the last new cars the CA&E purchased. *William D. Middleton*

replaced street running there, the last on the CA&E. By World War II, the physical plant was in poor condition and the road lacked the resources to rebuild it. Even with a reorganization as the Chicago Aurora & Elgin Railway in 1946, abandonment was inevitable.

The customary operating pattern was interesting. Originally local trains served Aurora and Elgin alternately; in the 1930s the service changed to alternate local trains to Wheaton and express trains with cars for Aurora, Elgin, and St. Charles—the expresses were divided and assembled at

Wheaton. Shuttle cars operated between Batavia and Batavia Junction on the Aurora line. The road's business was primarily passengers—there was little freight traffic.

A plan emerged to build an expressway along the route of the "L" and move Chicago Transit Authority tracks to its median strip. In 1953 temporary track replaced the "L" so construction could begin. CA&E and CTA set up an interchange station at Des Plaines Avenue. The loss of one-seat service to downtown Chicago aggravated the loss of passengers. Half of CA&E's riders switched to parallel railroads or autos by December 1953, and the opening of the new highway made the situation worse.

CA&E applied to discontinue passenger service in 1955, and passenger service ceased on July 3, 1957. Freight service continued until June 9, 1959, and legal abandonment occurred on June 10, 1961.

FACTS & FIGURES

Year	1929	1956
Miles operated	66	54
Locomotives	9	7
Passenger cars	87	89
Freight cars	—	—
Historical society: shore-line.org		

© 2002, Kalmbach Publishing Co., CLASSIC TRAINS; Robert Wegner

Chicago, Burlington & Quincy

Burlington Route

A GP20 and GP30 lead a freight westward out of Chicago on Burlington's three-track "speedway." The year is 1965, the scene is Brookfield, Ill., and merger with Great Northern and Northern Pacific is still five years away. *Ed DeRouin*

The Aurora Branch Railroad was chartered on Feb. 12, 1849, to build a line from Aurora, Ill., to a connection with the Galena & Chicago Union (forerunner of the Chicago & North Western) at Turner Junction (West Chicago). Service began with G&CU's first locomotive, the *Pioneer.*

In 1852 the road was renamed the Chicago & Aurora Railroad and received authority to build to Mendota, Ill., where it would connect with the Illinois Central. On Feb. 14, 1855, it was again renamed, becoming the Chicago, Burlington & Quincy Railroad.

That same year a railroad was opened between Galesburg and the east bank of the Mississippi opposite Burlington, Iowa; a year later a string of railroads, including the CB&Q, linked Chicago with Quincy, Ill., via Galesburg. A Galesburg–Peoria line was opened in 1857. By 1865 the CB&Q had acquired all these lines, built its own line from Aurora to Chicago, and had undergone several consolidations to become the corporation

that would endure until the Burlington Northern merger in 1970.

Beyond the Mississippi

West of the Mississippi expansion proceeded on two fronts. The Hannibal & St. Joseph, chartered in 1847, began operation between its namesake cities in 1859. A short spur to a point opposite Quincy and a steamboat across the Mississippi created the first railroad from Chicago to the Missouri River. The Burlington & Missouri River Railroad began construction in 1855 at Burlington, Iowa, and followed an old Indian trail (later U. S. 34) straight across Iowa—very slowly. Not until Nov. 26, 1869, did it reach the east bank of the Missouri River opposite Plattsmouth, Nebraska (Chicago & North Western reached Council Bluffs in 1867 and the Rock Island got there on May 11, 1869). By then CB&Q had bridged the Mississippi at Burlington and Quincy, both in 1868, and the Missouri in 1869 at Kansas City, as part of a line from Cameron, on the Hannibal & St. Joseph, to Kansas City.

The Burlington, in the form of the Burlington & Missouri River Rail Road In Nebraska, pushed beyond the Missouri River to Lincoln, Neb., in 1870. It acquired the Omaha & South Western for access to Omaha and built west from Lincoln to a junction with the Union Pacific at Kearney. The road began a colonization program to increase the population along its lines and to sell off the lands it had been granted. CB&Q provided financial backing for the two B&MR (Iowa and Nebraska) companies and directors for their boards. Meanwhile the CB&Q was acquiring branch lines in Illinois and upgrading its plant: double track, steel rail to replace iron, and iron bridges to replace wood.

Jay Gould acquired control of the Hannibal & St. Joseph in 1871, and friction began to develop among the railroads in the Burlington family over such matters as routing of connecting traffic to and from the Union Pacific. To begin unifying the system, CB&Q leased the B&MR in 1872 and merged it in 1875. Gould gained control of Union Pacific in 1875 and then in quick succession got the Kansas Pacific (Kansas City–Denver), the Wabash (and extended it to Council Bluffs), and the Missouri Pacific. Burlington's Nebraska lines were surrounded by Gould lines, and the Wabash would be likely to get the largest share of eastbound traffic from the UP. In the summer of 1880 the CB&Q consolidated with the B&MR, acquired the Kansas City, St. Joseph & Council Bluffs, opened a bridge over the Missouri at Plattsmouth, and began an extension west to Denver, completed in May 1882.

In May 1883 the Q regained control of the Hannibal & St. Joseph and soon found itself with increased competition in the Chicago–Kansas City market: Milwaukee Road in 1887 and Santa Fe in 1888.

North to St. Paul and Minneapolis

In 1882 the growth of the Pacific Northwest and the construction of the Northern Pacific and the St. Paul, Minneapolis & Manitoba (later the Great Northern) prompted the Burlington to consider building a line up the east bank of the Mississippi River to St. Paul. The line would be 25 miles longer than the Milwaukee Road and Chicago & North Western lines between Chicago and the St. Paul, but the grades would be easier. The Q extended its Chicago & Iowa line west to Savanna; the Chicago, Burlington & Northern (the Q owned one-third of its stock) built the line along the river. It was

opened in 1886. Considerable friction ensued between parent and child: The CB&N wanted to cut rates to secure business, and the CB&Q knew that retaliation by the Milwaukee and the North Western would be directed at CB&Q systemwide, not just at the CB&N. The matter was eventually settled when CB&Q increased its CB&N holdings in 1890 and absorbed the road in 1899.

Extensions and potential merger

Over the years the Burlington considered extension to the Pacific coast and merger with nearly every other railroad. Between 1883 and 1886 it made surveys west of Denver but did no construction. The arrival at Pueblo of the Missouri Pacific in 1887 and the Rock Island in 1888 (on trackage rights from Colorado Springs) put the Burlington at a competitive disadvantage. The Rio Grande received the same amount for moving freight from Salt Lake City to Pueblo as it did from Salt Lake City through Pueblo to Denver (the Dotsero Cutoff was still nearly five decades in the future). Naturally Rio Grande preferred to interchange at Pueblo—it received nothing additional for the 119-mile haul from Pueblo to Denver.

There was thought of the Burlington's acquiring James J. Hill's St. Paul, Minneapolis & Manitoba and vice versa. The CB&Q considered merger with the Pennsylvania; the two roads purchased interests

in the Toledo, Peoria & Western. In 1893 the Burlington looked eagerly at the Oregon Short Line and Oregon Railway & Navigation Co. when their parent, Union Pacific, was in receivership. Other merger partners considered were Northern Pacific, Yazoo & Mississippi Valley, Missouri-Kansas-Texas, Chicago Great Western, Denver & Rio Grande, Kansas City Southern, Minneapolis & St. Louis, Chicago & Eastern Illinois, and St. Louis-San Francisco. With one exception the Q was content for a while to stay within its boundaries, marked by corner stakes at Chicago, St. Louis, Kansas City, Denver, Omaha, Galesburg, and St. Paul. That exception was a line opened in 1894 from Alliance, Nebr., northwest through the coalfields of eastern Wyoming to Billings, Mont.

Merger—eventually

Perhaps the most important event in the Burlington's history was the purchase effective July 1, 1901, of nearly 98 percent of its stock jointly by the Great Northern and the Northern Pacific. James J. Hill, builder of the Great Northern, saw in the Burlington the connection he needed from St. Paul to Chicago—the Chicago & North Western was largely held by the New York Central, and the Milwaukee Road refused to consider the matter. At the same time Edward H. Harriman realized that the Burlington could bring his Union Pacific to Chicago from Omaha.

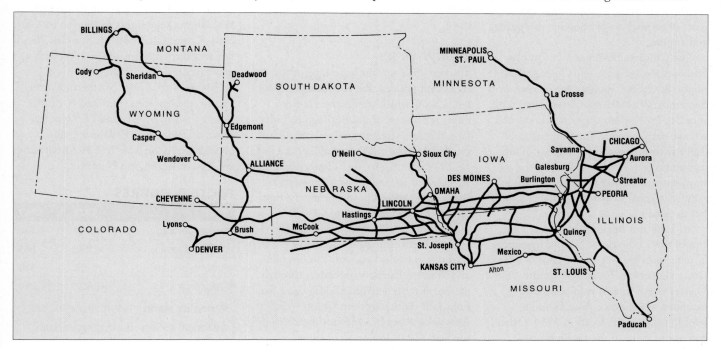

The Burlington hauled a fair share of coal on its southern Illinois lines. Here, an M-2A 2-10-2 pulls a string of coal gons northbound at Bushnell, Ill. *Chicago, Burlington & Quincy*

Burlington recognized it would be better off with the northern lines because of their on-line resources of coal and lumber, both lacking on the Union Pacific-Southern Pacific route to San Francisco. The battle for control was brief and intense. Control of the Burlington essentially moved from Boston to St. Paul. That same year, Hill, with the backing of J. P. Morgan, his banker, acquired control of Northern Pacific. The next logical step was merger of the three railroads, a process that took 69 years of off-and-on petitioning, protesting, and arguing.

The Chicago, Burlington & Quincy Railroad was leased to the Chicago, Burlington & Quincy Railway for 99 years on September 30, 1901; that lease lasted until June 30, 1907, when the railroad resumed its own management. The Railroad and Railway companies had a number of officers and directors in common. Of the railway company during those years Moody's railroad manual simply says "The company has decided not to issue a report."

In 1908 the Burlington acquired control of the Colorado & Southern, gaining a route from Denver to the Gulf of Mexico at Galveston, Texas, and a route from Denver north into Wyoming. CB&Q extended a line down from Billings, Mont., to meet the C&S in 1914. Other extensions were to the coalfields of southern Illinois and on across the Ohio River to Paducah, Kentucky, and a line from Ashland, Nebr., north to a connection with the Great Northern at Sioux City, Iowa, in 1916.

The Burlington's growth leveled off during the 1920s. In 1930 the ICC authorized merger of Great Northern and Northern Pacific on the condition that they relinquish control of the Burlington; GN and NP withdrew their merger application in 1931 in favor of retaining joint control of the Q.

Zephyr years

The year 1932 saw the beginning of two significant projects: the Rio Grande's Dotsero Cutoff, which would give Denver a direct rail line west, and Burlington's order for a stainless-steel streamlined train from the Budd Company. The cutoff opened June 16, 1934. The *Zephyr*, the country's first diesel-powered streamliner, was delivered in April 1934 and was prophetically the first train to traverse the Dotsero Cutoff.

A whole family of *Zephyrs* soon appeared on Burlington rails. In 1939 the Burlington teamed up with Rio Grande and Western Pacific to operate a through passenger train between Chicago and San Francisco via the Dotsero Cutoff—the *Exposition Flyer*. In 1945 Burlington built the first Vista-Dome coach. These elements achieved their ultimate synthesis in 1949 with the inauguration of the Vista-Dome-equipped *California Zephyr*, operated between Chicago and San Francisco by the Burlington, the Rio Grande, and the Western Pacific. The route was longer and slower than that of the competition, but the schedule took advantage of the scenery. The train was an immediate success and remained so through its life.

The Q was still aware of the shortcomings of its Chicago–Kansas City route across northern Missouri (the 1902 purchase of the Quincy, Omaha & Kansas City Railroad, a circuitous secondary line between Quincy and Kansas City, largely abandoned in 1939, appears to have been an act of mercy on the Burlington's part). The Burlington first proposed a four-way deal that would give Santa Fe a route to St. Louis; Gulf, Mobile & Ohio a route of its own to Chicago (Q president Ralph Budd had been a member of the board of directors of GM&O predecessor Gulf, Mobile & Northern); and the foundering Alton a good home. GM&O would get the Alton, less its St. Louis–Kansas City line, which didn't fit into GM&O's north-south pattern; Burlington would take that line and swap trackage rights into St. Louis to the Santa Fe for a shortcut across Missouri on Santa Fe's main line.

The other roads serving St. Louis protested. GM&O merged the Alton, but the rest of the plan did not come to fruition. In the early 1950s Burlington built a new line across Missouri and coupled it with Wabash trackage rights to shorten its Chicago–Kansas City route by 22 miles. The line was further improved in 1960 with a new bridge at Quincy.

Merger with Great Northern, Northern Pacific, and Spokane, Portland & Seattle (jointly owned by GN and NP) was proposed once again in 1960 and finally became reality on March 2, 1970, with the creation of Burlington Northern.

FACTS & FIGURES

Year	1929	1969
Miles operated	9,367	8,430
Locomotives	1,575	665
Passenger cars	1,225	624
Freight cars	62,225	36,264

Reporting marks: CBQ, RBBQ, RBBX, BREX
Historical society: burlingtonroute.com

Chicago, Central & Pacific

CHICAGO CENTRAL

The original route of the Illinois Central Railroad was from Cairo, at the southern tip of Illinois, north to Galena, in the northwest corner of the state. That line was completed in 1856, but the road's Centralia–Chicago branch proved to be more important than the main line to Galena. Nonetheless, the IC pushed the line west to the Mississippi River and across it into Iowa. In 1867 the Illinois Central leased the Dubuque & Sioux City Railroad; by 1870 that railroad had reached Sioux City. In the 1880s IC began serious expansion westward. It built branches to Cedar Rapids, Iowa, Sioux Falls, S. D., and Omaha, Nebr., and a line from Chicago west to Freeport, Ill., connecting the Iowa lines with Chicago.

In the early 1980s the Illinois Central Gulf (the product of the 1972 merger of IC and Gulf, Mobile & Ohio) decided to concentrate on its north-south main line and spin off its east-west routes. The first to be sold was the route to Omaha and Sioux City.

In December 1985 Jack Haley's Chicago, Central & Pacific Railroad purchased ICG's Chicago–Omaha line and its branches to Sioux City and Cedar Rapids, Iowa, for $75 million. Haley had started his railroad empire in 1984 by purchasing ICG's Cedar Falls, Iowa–Albert Lea, Minnesota, branch and operating it as the Cedar Valley Railroad. In 1986 the road later bought Chicago & North Western's line between Wall Lake and Ida Grove, Iowa, 24 miles.

Red-and-white GP10 No. 1705, a former Illinois Central engine, heads a Chicago Central freight at New Hartford, Iowa, on September 5, 1991. *Jim Shaw*

The Chicago Central got off to a good start, but in 1987 General Electric Credit Corporation, which had provided the financing, became anxious when Haley fell behind in loan payments. Haley took the Chicago Central into bankruptcy on Sept. 1, 1987, so he could retain control. The Chicago Central was released from bankruptcy in October under the leadership of Don Wood, former executive vice-president for operations of Burlington Northern. Wood trimmed the road's car fleet, reduced train miles, and lowered speed limits to save fuel and wear on the track. The CC undertook several track repair projects to recover from ICG's policy of deferred maintenance.

The Cedar Valley Railroad ceased operation on May 22, 1991, and the Interstate Commerce Commission let Chicago Central serve customers on the line. At the end of 1991 CC bought the Cedar Valley through a subsidiary, the Cedar River Railroad.

The Chicago Central became profitable in 1988. The Burlington Northern considered acquiring the road for its line between Chicago and the Mississippi River at Portage Junction—it would relieve congestion on BN's single-track line west from Aurora. However, after its period of shrinkage, the Illinois Central decided to grow again. It saw the Chicago Central as a source of Iowa grain traffic and perhaps get some of the traffic moving east from the coalfields of Wyoming. In June 1996 IC purchased the Chicago Central for $157 million. Part of the deal was trackage rights for Burlington Northern & Santa Fe between Chicago and Portage Junction.

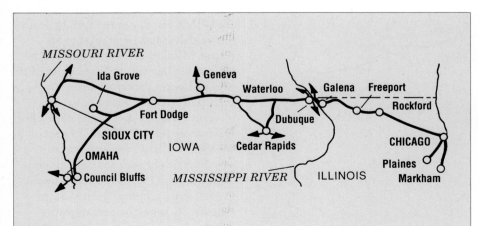

FACTS & FIGURES

Year	1987	1995
Miles operated	798	707
Locomotives	98	88
Passenger cars	—	—
Freight cars	2,043	2,390
Reporting marks: CC		

Chicago Great Western

By the late 1870s the Upper Midwest was spiderwebbed with the lines of four major railroads: the Burlington, the Milwaukee Road, the Chicago & North Western, and the Rock Island. Even so, people thought there was room for more. One of them was A. B. Stickney, who had been construction superintendent of the St. Paul, Minnesota, & Manitoba (forerunner of the Great Northern), general superintendent of the western portion of the Canadian Pacific, and an official of the Minneapolis & St. Louis. Stickney decided to build a railroad from St. Paul to Chicago. He acquired the franchise and outstanding stock of the Minnesota & Northwestern Railroad, which had been chartered in 1854 to build a line from Lake Superior through St. Paul toward Dubuque, Iowa. The charter was particularly enticing to Stickney because of a tax limitation clause it contained.

Construction of the road started at St. Paul in September 1884, and a year later the line was open to the Iowa state line, where it connected with a road the Illinois Central had leased. Stickney, however, was intent on having his own line, so even before the Minnesota & Northwestern was completed he acquired and merged with it

The CGW was a pioneer in trailer-on-flatcar operations, and in the diesel era, it was known for running long, heavy freight trains. Here, three F units in the original maroon-and-red scheme lead a freight across the Des Moines River at Fort Dodge, Iowa. *Robert J. Yanosey collection*

the Dubuque & Northwestern. That railroad had been incorporated in 1883 to build from Dubuque to Vancouver, British Columbia, or at least to a connection with the Northern Pacific. The M&NW met the Dubuque & Northwestern near Oneida, Iowa, in October 1886.

Meanwhile the Minnesota & Northwestern of Illinois was building west from what is now Forest Park, Ill. Completed in early 1888, the engineering feat of the line

was the longest tunnel in Illinois, the half-mile-long Winston Tunnel, named for the construction company that built the line.

Chicago, St. Paul & Kansas City

Stickney recognized that Minnesota & Northwestern was hardly an appropriate name for a railroad that began at St. Paul and went to Chicago. He renamed it the Chicago, St. Paul & Kansas City and set out for Kansas City. He acquired the Dubuque & Dakota Railroad, a short line from Sumner, Iowa, through Waverly to Hampton, and the Wisconsin, Iowa & Nebraska Railway, a line from Waterloo, Iowa, to Des Moines. The WI&N was nicknamed "The Diagonal" for its direction across the state of Iowa. Stickney extended the WI&N east to connect with his main line at Oelwein and southwest to St. Joseph, Missouri, and Leavenworth, Kansas, arriving there in 1891. Trackage rights over a Missouri Pacific subsidiary carried CStP&KC trains to Kansas City.

Construction costs and rate wars began to adversely affect CStP&KC's financial situation—Stickney was an advocate of simplified freight rates and a practitioner of rate cutting. The road was reorganized in 1892 as the Chicago Great Western Railway. Stickney took advantage of depressed prices during the Panic of 1893

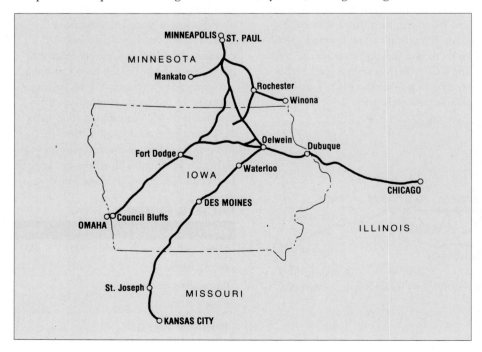

to rebuild the road and erect new shops at Oelwein, the hub of the railroad.

In 1901 the CGW leased the Wisconsin, Minnesota & Pacific Railroad, which had lines west out of Winona and Red Wing, Minn., and the Mason City & Fort Dodge Rail Road. The latter road (which had been controlled by James J. Hill since the late 1880s) served as a springboard for CGW's extension to Omaha. The route to Omaha, opened in 1903, led through largely unpopulated territory. A CGW subsidiary planned, developed, and sold towns at regular intervals along the line. About this same time the road planned and surveyed an extension to Sioux City but dropped the idea in 1906 because of the expense. CGW even set its sights briefly on Denver before turning its attention to a policy of encouraging the short lines, both steam and electric, with which it connected.

The Felton era

The CGW entered receivership in 1908. J. P. Morgan purchased it and reorganized it as the Chicago Great Western Railroad in August 1909. Samuel M. Felton, well known as a rehabilitator of weak railroads, replaced Stickney as president. During World War I, USRA control diverted much business from the CGW, but government payment for damages helped finance postwar improvements.

To cut passenger expenses, CGW replaced steam trains with motor cars. CGW had purchased several McKeen gasoline cars in the early 1900s, and it continued the motorization of its passenger trains with the purchase of Electro-Motive's first gas-electric car. In the mid-1920s CGW teamed up with Santa Fe to offer through Pullman car service from the Twin Cities to Texas and Los Angeles. In 1929 CGW converted three old McKeen cars to a deluxe gas-electric train, the *Blue Bird*, for service between Minneapolis and Rochester, Minn.

Felton retired in 1929 when a syndicate of industrial traffic managers led by Patrick H. Joyce acquired control of the CGW. The new management completely revised the operational structure of the railroad, closed facilities, and discharged employees. The Joyce administration got involved in a stock manipulation scheme—it included the Van Sweringen brothers of Cleveland and the Kansas City Southern—that resulted in CGW's bankruptcy in February

Merger with the Chicago & North Western is three years away as a set of four GP30s head northward from Des Moines on a cold January day in 1965. *J. David Ingles*

1935. More noteworthy fruits of the Joyce era were three dozen 2-10-4s for freight service and the inauguration in 1936 of piggyback service.

A 1941 reorganization created the Chicago Great Western Railway, which included a number of previously separate subsidiaries. Immediately after World War II the road began to dieselize; dieselization was complete by 1950.

The Deramus era

In 1948 a group of Kansas City businessmen began to invest heavily in the CGW. Among them were William N. Deramus, president of Kansas City Southern, and his son, William N., III. Within a few months the younger Deramus was president of the CGW. Under his direction the road caught up on deferred maintenance and improved its physical plant.

Passenger service was reduced to a single coach-only train each way between the Twin Cities and Kansas City, the Twin Cities and Omaha, and Chicago and Oelwein. With the intent of reducing train-miles, CGW began to run enormously long freight trains behind sets of six or more F-units. Service suffered as trains were held to reach maximum tonnage and through trains performed local work. The road consolidated its offices at Oelwein and Kansas City and closed its Chicago

general offices. The last passenger trains, between the Twin Cities and Omaha, made their last runs on Sept. 29, 1965. They lasted this long because of mail and express traffic inherited when Chicago & North Western dropped its Twin Cities–Omaha trains.

Chicago Great Western did reasonably well during the 1950s and 1960s, but it became clear that it would have to merge to survive. As early as 1946 there had been a proposal to merge CGW with Chicago & Eastern Illinois and Missouri-Kansas-Texas, and during the Deramus era it was generally thought that Kansas City Southern and CGW would team up. CGW investigated merger with Rock Island, Soo Line, and Frisco, but it was with the rapidly expanding Chicago & North Western that CGW merged on July 1, 1968. The North Western subsequently abandoned most of the CGW.

FACTS & FIGURES

Year	1929	1967
Miles operated	1,495	1,411
Locomotives	237	139
Passenger cars	185	—
Freight cars	7,363	3,540
Reporting marks: CGW Historical society: cnwhs.org		

Chicago, Indianapolis & Louisville (Monon)

THE HOOSIER LINE

A black-and-gold F3 leads the *Thoroughbred* through Smiths, Ind., in October 1963. *Tom Smart; Dan Pope collection*

The New Albany & Salem Rail Road was organized in 1847 to build a railroad from New Albany, Indiana, on the north bank of the Ohio River opposite Louisville, Kentucky, to the shore of Lake Michigan. The line's founder, James Brooks, chose Salem, Ind., for the destination in the road's title to provide an appearance of conservatism to attract investors. The line was opened to Salem in 1851, to Bedford and Bloomington in 1853, and to Gosport in early 1854. A branch was begun from Gosport toward Indianapolis, but financial problems stopped work on it before the grading was completed. (It was eventually built as part of the Pennsylvania Railroad system.) Finances also halted progress on the main line.

Meanwhile the Michigan Central was stymied at Michigan City in its effort to build west from Detroit to Chicago. The charter of the New Albany & Salem allowed construction anywhere in Indiana, and Brooks did some trading. Michigan Central built its line to the Illinois border using NA&S's franchise and bought a block of NA&S stock, providing the capital Brooks needed to finish the NA&S between Gosport and Crawfordsville.

In 1852 NA&S took over the Crawfordsville & Wabash, which had a line from Crawfordsville to Lafayette, and in 1853 opened a line between Lafayette and Michigan City. The line was as level and straight (including a 65-mile tangent) as the south end of the NA&S was crooked and hilly.

A drought in 1856 adversely affected farming along the railroad and the Ohio River steamboats with which the railroad connected. The New Albany & Salem defaulted on its interest payments and entered receivership in 1858. It was reorganized in 1869 as the Louisville, New Albany & Chicago Railway under the leadership of John Jacob Astor, but the reorganization was declared illegal. There was another foreclosure sale to the same group of investors, and in 1873 the road made a second start as the Louisville, New Albany & Chicago Railway.

The road had lost any claim it might have had to Michigan Central's line into Chicago. The Indianapolis, Delphi & Chicago Railway was incorporated in 1865, then reincorporated in 1872 with the same name as part of a proposed railroad, the Chicago & South Atlantic, between Chicago and Charleston, South Carolina. It began construction in 1877 of a narrow gauge railroad. The first portion was opened a year later from Bradford (renamed Monon in 1879) to Rensselaer.

A new company, the Chicago & Indianapolis Air Line Railway, took over in 1881, and it was merged with the LNA&C in 1883. The line was converted to standard gauge in 1881, and Chicago–Indianapolis trains began operating in 1883. Access to Chicago was over the rails of the Chicago & Western Indiana and entrance to Indianapolis was on the Indianapolis Union Railway. About the same time LNA&C gained access to Louisville from New Albany over the rails of the Pennsylvania and the Louisville & Nashville.

The Monon Route

The LNA&C map now resembled an elongated X, with the Chicago–Indianapolis and Michigan City–Louisville lines crossing at the town of Monon. The "Monon Route" slogan was first used in 1882, and the nickname quickly eclipsed the official title of the road. The map showed few branch lines. In the 1880s the road acquired two, one from Orleans west to French Lick and the other from Bedford west toward (but not to) the western Indiana coalfields. In 1898 the Indiana Stone Railroad was incorporated to build a water-level bypass of the severe grades north of Harrodsburg—the old main line remained in service as a branch. A branch was constructed from Wallace Junction to

Victoria to reach the coalfields that the branch from Bedford had stopped short of. It was built by the Indianapolis & Louisville Railroad as part of a proposed Indianapolis-Evansville line, but Wallace Junction-Victoria was all that was built.

In 1889 and 1890 the Monon made an agreement to use the Kentucky & Indiana bridge over the Ohio River between New Albany and Louisville, facilitating connections with the Louisville Southern, which extended east from Louisville to the Cincinnati, New Orleans & Texas Pacific (Southern Railway System). The Monon built a branch of the LS to Lexington and also built the Richmond, Nicholasville, Irvine & Beattyville east toward the coalfields of eastern Kentucky.

Early in 1890 Astor died. Dr. William L. Breyfogle of New Albany pulled a shareholder coup, unseated the management, and aborted the extension into Kentucky. The Louisville Southern became part of the Southern system, and the RNI&B became part of the L&N. The Monon was reorganized as the Chicago, Indianapolis & Louisville Railway in 1897, and J. P. Morgan acquired control in 1899.

In 1902 the Southern and the Louisville & Nashville acquired most of the Monon's common stock and more than three-quarters of the preferred. At that time the road was doing well enough to consider double-tracking the line between Monon and Chicago. To that end it acquired the Chicago & Wabash Valley, a short line parallel to and east of the main line across northwestern Indiana. Nothing came of the project. In 1916 the Monon merged that line and two other roads that formed Monon branches, the Indiana Stone Railroad and the Indianapolis & Louisville.

Decline

By the 1920s the Monon had begun to stagnate. The road served little of the industrial area of Indianapolis, and the through business on the route was largely in conjunction with the ne'er-do-well Cincinnati, Hamilton & Dayton and its successor, the Cincinnati, Indianapolis & Western. Baltimore & Ohio acquired the CI&W in 1927, drying up connecting traffic—B&O could move Cincinnati–Chicago traffic on its own rails all the way via Deshler, Ohio.

The Indiana coalfields were at a competitive disadvantage with the Appalachian

ones. The demand for building stone, which at times constituted nearly a quarter of Monon's freight traffic, diminished as construction activity dropped during the Depression. Both the railroads with which the Monon connected at Louisville, Southern and L&N, had more expeditious connections for Chicago business and did not particularly favor the Monon, even though they controlled it.

In an effort to avert bankruptcy, Monon applied to the Reconstruction Finance Corp. for a loan in December 1933. John W. Barriger III, head of the agency, recognized that the road's finances needed reorganization and refused the loan. The Monon filed for bankruptcy on Dec. 30, 1933. It cut passenger service to the minimum and abandoned the branch west of Bedford and the former Chicago & Wabash Valley. The trustees even considered total abandonment—the Monon had the longest route between an Ohio River crossing and Chicago and was the hardest to operate—but the road struggled through World War II.

The Barriger era

On May 1, 1946, a new Chicago, Indianapolis & Louisville Railway took over, with John W. Barriger III as president. Barriger was an advocate of the Super Railroad—flat, straight, fast, multiple track,

heavy duty—and the Monon was its antithesis. Nonetheless, Barriger replaced steam with diesel, purchased war-surplus hospital cars to convert to streamlined passenger cars (cheaper and quicker than ordering new cars), restored passenger trains, solicited freight business, bought freight cars by the hundreds, and caught up on 20 years of deferred maintenance.

Concluding that the south end of the railroad needed to be totally relocated, which was impossible, he limited relocation efforts to replacement of the Wabash River bridge at Delphi and a bypass of a bottomless bog at Cedar Lake. He was unable to relocate the Monon out of city streets at New Albany, Bedford, Lafayette, and Monticello. Nonetheless, when Barriger departed at the end of 1952 to assume a vice-presidency of the New Haven he left behind a well-maintained and well-operated railroad with black ink on its ledgers.

Barriger was succeeded by Warren Brown, during whose tenure the railroad changed its official name to Monon Railroad. In 1959 the Monon dropped its Indianapolis passenger trains; the Chicago–Louisville train lasted until 1967, largely because of business generated by Purdue University at Lafayette and Indiana University at Bloomington.

When the Louisville & Nashville purchased the eastern half of the Chicago & Eastern Illinois in 1969, the Monon approached the Southern Railway on the matter of merger. Southern had just upgraded its line into Cincinnati and was content to interchange Chicago business there rather than acquire its own line north from the Ohio River. Louisville & Nashville was much more receptive to merger, seeing the Monon as a useful alternate route and also eyeing Monon's interests in Chicago & Western Indiana, Belt Railway of Chicago, and Kentucky & Indiana Terminal. The Louisville & Nashville merged the Monon on July 31, 1971.

FACTS & FIGURES

Year	1929	1970
Miles operated	648	541
Locomotives	174	44
Passenger cars	91	27
Freight cars	6,356	3,078
Reporting marks: CIL, MON		
Historical society: www.monon.org		

Chicago, Milwaukee, St. Paul & Pacific

A Milwaukee Road F7-class 4-6-4 leads an eastbound *Hiawatha* over the C&NW diamonds at Mayfair in northern Chicago in 1941. *E. T. Harley*

The Milwaukee & Waukesha Rail Road was chartered in 1847. Even before it laid its first rails in 1850, its name was changed to the Milwaukee & Mississippi. In 1851 it reached Waukesha, Wis., 20 miles west of Milwaukee. Its rails reached Madison in 1854 and Prairie du Chien, on the Mississippi River, in 1857.

In 1858 the La Crosse & Milwaukee Rail Road was completed between the cities of its name, forming a second route across Wisconsin between Lake Michigan and the Mississippi River. It was reorganized in 1863 as the Milwaukee & St. Paul, and in 1867 it purchased the Milwaukee & Prairie du Chien, successor to the Milwaukee & Mississippi.

The Milwaukee & St. Paul acquired in 1872 the St. Paul & Chicago, which had just completed a route down the west bank of the Mississippi from St. Paul to La Crescent, opposite La Crosse. In 1873 the M&StP completed a line from Milwaukee south to Chicago and a year later added "Chicago" to its name.

In the next few years the road built or bought lines from Racine, Wis., to Moline, Ill.; from Chicago to Savanna, Ill., and two lines west across southern Minnesota. The road reached Council Bluffs, Iowa, across the Missouri River from Omaha, in 1882, and reached Kansas City in 1887. In 1893 the CM&StP acquired the Milwaukee & Northern, which reached from Milwaukee into Michigan's upper peninsula.

In 1900 the Chicago, Milwaukee & St. Paul was considered one of the most prosperous, progressive, and enterprising railroads in the U. S. Its lines reached from Chicago to Minneapolis, Omaha, and Kansas City. Secondary lines and branches covered most of the area between the Omaha and Minneapolis lines in Wisconsin, Iowa, and Minnesota. Lines covered much of eastern South Dakota and reached the Missouri River at three places in that state: Running Water, Chamberlain, and Evarts. Except for the last few miles into Kansas City and operation over Union Pacific rails from Council Bluffs to Omaha, the Missouri River formed the western boundary of the CM&StP. ("Milwaukee Road" as a name or nickname did not come into use until the late 1920s; "St. Paul Road" was sometimes used as a nickname, but the railroad's advertising used the full name).

Pacific extension

The battle over control of the Northern Pacific and the Burlington in 1901 made the Milwaukee Road aware that without its own route to the Pacific it would be at its competitors' mercy—a commodity the railroad industry was singularly short of. At the same time the Milwaukee Road was experiencing a change in its traffic from dominance by wheat to a more balanced mix of agricultural and industrial products. Arguments against extension westward included the possibility of the construction of the Panama Canal and the presence of strong competing railroads: Union Pacific, Northern Pacific, and Great Northern. Arguments for the extension banked heavily on the growth of traffic to and from the Pacific Northwest.

In 1901 the president of the Milwaukee Road dispatched an engineer west to estimate the cost of duplicating Northern Pacific's line. His figure was $45 million. Such an expenditure required considerable thought; not until November 1905 did Milwaukee's board of directors authorize construction of a line west to Tacoma and Seattle.

In 1905 and 1906 the Milwaukee Road incorporated subsidiaries in South Dakota, Montana, Idaho, and Washington. The Washington company was renamed the Chicago, Milwaukee & Puget Sound Railway, and it took over the other three companies in 1908. It was absorbed by the CM&StP in 1912.

The extension began with a bridge across the Missouri River at Mobridge, three miles upstream from Evarts, S. D. Roadbed and rails pushed out from several points into unpopulated territory. The work went quickly, and the road was open to Butte, Mont., in August 1908.

The route from Harlowton to Lombard was that of the Montana Railroad, the "Jawbone." Its mortgage was held by James J. Hill and the Great Northern Railway. Taking advantage of Hill's absence on a trip to England, the Milwaukee Road advanced the owner the funds required to pay off the mortgage and bought the railroad through the CM&PS.

Construction was also under way eastward from Seattle. The last spike on the line was driven near Garrison, Mont., on May 14, 1909. Local passenger service was established later that year; through passenger service was inaugurated in May 1911.

In 1912 the Milwaukee Road decided to electrify much of the new line. The terrain (the Belt, Rocky, Bitter Root, Saddle, and Cascade mountain ranges), the possibility of hydroelectric power, the difficulties associated with operating steam locomotives through tunnels and in severe winter weather, and an increase in traffic all suggested electrification. The section from Harlowton, Mont., to Avery, Idaho, was completely turned over to electric operation in late 1916. Early in 1917 the road decided to electrify the portion of the line from Othello, Wash., to Tacoma. Electric operation on the Coast Division began in 1919, and overhead wires reached Seattle, on a 10-mile branch off the main line, in 1927. The electrification cost $23 million, but in 1925 the road reported that the savings over steam operation had already amounted to more than half that sum.

Financial difficulty

The cost of the Pacific Extension, $234 million, greatly exceeded estimates. Traffic on the new route came nowhere near the projections: The boom in the Pacific Northwest

Two Milwaukee Road Little Joes team up with a diesel in the rugged territory of the electrified district on the Rocky Mountain Division. *David P. Morgan Library collection*

ended about 1910, and the Panama Canal opened in 1914. The debt incurred in building the Pacific Extension remained.

On top of that, in 1921 the Milwaukee leased the Chicago, Terre Haute & Southeastern and in 1922 acquired the Chicago, Milwaukee & Gary to gain access to the coalfields of southern Indiana. Both those roads were heavily in debt. The Milwaukee Road entered bankruptcy in 1925.

The company emerged from reorganization in 1928 as the Chicago, Milwaukee, St. Paul & Pacific Railroad. On June 29, 1935, it declared bankruptcy again. Despite the financial problems, the late 1930s and early 1940s were interesting times for Milwaukee Road. In May 1935 the road introduced the *Hiawatha*, a fast steam-powered streamlined train between Chicago and the Twin Cities. It was an immediate and

overwhelming success. In the next few years the train was re-equipped, service was doubled, and *Hiawathas* appeared on other Milwaukee routes. The cars of the *Hiawatha*, like most of Milwaukee Road's freight and passenger cars and many of its steam locomotives, were products of the road's shops in Milwaukee.

The postwar boom brought the Milwaukee Road out of bankruptcy, and the road remained reasonably healthy into the 1960s. In 1955 Union Pacific moved its streamliners from the Chicago & North Western to Milwaukee's Chicago–Council Bluffs, Iowa, route, and in the early 1960s Milwaukee Road modernized its Chicago suburban service and built a new station in Milwaukee. The road discussed merger with the Chicago & North Western and with the Rock Island. As a condition of the creation of Burlington Northern the Milwaukee Road was granted trackage rights on BN into Portland, Ore.; and as a condition of Louisville & Nashville's merger of the Monon, it received trackage rights over the former Monon line from Bedford, Ind., to Louisville, Ky.

The longest branch line

Through this period there was little change in Milwaukee's lines west of the Missouri River. North America's longest electrification continued unchanged—in the same two disconnected portions, with steam and later diesel power hauling trains over the 212 miles of nonelectrified track between Avery, Idaho, and Othello, Wash. With dieselization of the Milwaukee Road after World War II, it appeared that the electrification, by then 30 years old, would be dismantled, but the road purchased 12 electric locomotives that had been built by General Electric for Russia and embargoed because of international tensions. Milwaukee Road re-gauged the "Little Joes" (nicknamed for Joseph Stalin) from 5 feet to standard and equipped two with steam generators for passenger service. They went into service between Harlowton and Avery.

The electrification soldiered on for another two decades, but diesels showed up under the wires more and more often, sometimes running in multiple with the electrics. By the early 1970s passenger service had long since been discontinued, many of the original electric locomotives had been scrapped, and much of the hardware of the electrification needed replacement. Traffic on the line was insufficient to justify rebuilding the electric plant—and the road did not have the funds to do so anyway. The Milwaukee Road de-energized the catenary over the Coast Division in 1972 and ended electric operation on the Rocky Mountain Division on June 16, 1974.

Financial difficulties again

Except for its double-track Chicago–Twin Cities main line, the Milwaukee Road was secondary railroading. It was not the first railroad you thought of between, say, Chicago and Kansas City or St. Paul and Seattle. Traffic on the Pacific Extension barely supported one freight train a day each way. The lightly constructed branch lines that spider-webbed across Wisconsin,

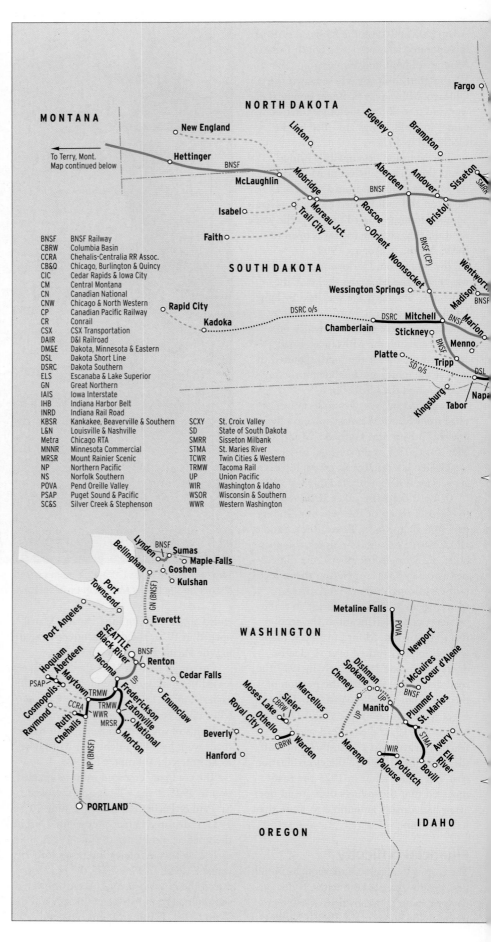

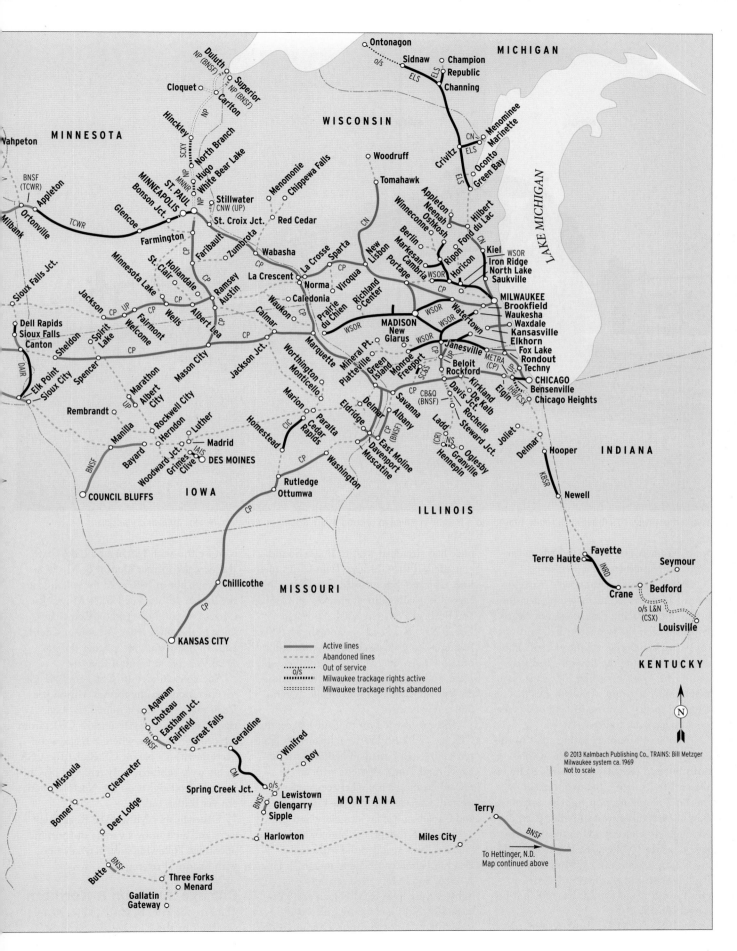

© 2013 Kalmbach Publishing Co., TRAINS: Bill Metzger
Milwaukee system ca. 1969
Not to scale

Active lines
Abandoned lines
o/s Out of service
Milwaukee trackage rights active
Milwaukee trackage rights abandoned

Two almost-new F7s (built in October 1949) lead a freight in Chicago around 1950. *Robert A. Caflisch; Helen Caflisch collection*

Iowa, Minnesota, and South Dakota carried mostly products of agriculture.

Over the decades, the road's management had made too many wrong decisions: building the Pacific Extension, not electrifying between the two electrified portions (or perhaps undertaking the electrification at all), purchasing the line into Indiana, and in the 1960s choosing Flexivans (containers with separate wheels/bogies that required special flatcars) instead of conventional piggyback trailers.

After several money-losing years in the early 1970s, the Milwaukee Road voluntarily entered reorganization once again on December 19, 1977. The major result of the 1977 reorganization was the amputation of everything west of Miles City, Montana, to concentrate on what became known as the "Milwaukee II" system linking Chicago, Kansas City, Minneapolis-St. Paul, Duluth (on Burlington Northern rails from St. Paul), and Louisville (but no longer Omaha).

By 1983 the Milwaukee's system, which

once had stretched west to Puget Sound, consisted of the Chicago–Twin Cities main line; Chicago–Savanna–Kansas City; Chicago–Louisville (almost entirely on Conrail and Seaboard System rails), Milwaukee–Green Bay; New Lisbon–Tomahawk, Wis.; Savanna–La Crosse, along the west bank of the Mississippi; Marquette to Sheldon, Iowa, and Jackson, Minn.; Austin, Minn.–St. Paul; and St. Paul–Ortonville, Minn., plus a few branches.

Three roads vied for the Milwaukee: the Chicago & North Western, financially none too solid itself; Canadian National subsidiary Grand Trunk Western, with an eye toward creating a route between eastern and western Canada south of the Great Lakes; and Canadian Pacific subsidiary Soo Line.

Soo Line, though not high bidder in the "auction," was awarded the Milwaukee Road in February 1985 and merged it Jan. 1, 1986. Soo briefly tried operating its light-density lines in Michigan and Wisconsin with different work-rules as its Lake States Transportation Division (don't

confuse this with Michigan's Lake State Railway, the former Detroit & Mackinac Railway), but in 1987 sold those lines, plus the former Milwaukee Road's Milwaukee–Green Bay and New Lisbon–Tomahawk lines, to the new carrier Wisconsin Central Ltd., in many ways re-creating the pre-1909 Wisconsin Central Railway.

Soo consolidated its Chicago-Twin Cities operations on the former Milwaukee Road main line and acquired trackage rights on Chessie System (now CSX) from Chicago to Detroit, where it made a connection with its parent CP Rail. (The CSX rights were subsequently replaced by Chicago–Detroit rights on the Norfolk Southern via Butler, Ind.).

Other former Milwaukee Road lines were and are run by a variety of shortline operators. Following are a few key lines with historical references.

Chicago, Madison & Northern

The Freeport, Ill.–Madison, Wis., route was built by the Chicago, Madison &

Northern Railroad, an Illinois Central subsidiary, as part of IC's expansion program of the late 1880s. Nearly a century later, in 1978, Illinois Central Gulf abandoned the line. A new company, the Chicago, Madison & Northern Railway, began operation in February 1978. In 1980 it extended its operations to the former Milwaukee Road branch line from Janesville, Wis., west through Monroe to Mineral Point. For a short period the CM&N also operated the state-owned former Milwaukee Road branch between Sparta and Viroqua, Wis.

Central Wisconsin

The Waukesha–Prairie du Chien route was built by the Milwaukee & Mississippi Rail Road between 1850 and 1857. It was purchased by the Milwaukee & St. Paul in 1868 and became part of the first Chicago–Milwaukee–St. Paul rail route. The line west of Madison was later part of Milwaukee Road's Chicago–Rapid City, S. D., route and retained secondary mainline status and passenger service until 1960, including a "pontoon" bridge over the Mississippi River at Prairie du Chien.

The line southeast from Janesville, Wis., to Fox Lake and Rondout, Ill.—known by employees as the "J Line"—was built in 1900 as a shortcut for Chicago–Madison trains. The Janesville–Monroe line was built in 1877 and extended west in 1881 to connect with lines to Platteville and Mineral Point, Wis.

Milwaukee Road abandoned its Waukesha–Milton Junction line in 1978. To preserve rail access to an agricultural chemical plant at Whitewater, the line was purchased by the state of Wisconsin, which conveyed it to the city of Whitewater. Operation was begun by the Central Wisconsin Railroad in 1980.

Upon the demise of the Chicago, Madison & Northern in 1982, the Central Wisconsin took over operation of its lines. Central Wisconsin established two subsidiaries to operate other ex-Milwaukee Road lines in the area: In 1982 the Wisconsin & Western began working the Madison–Prairie du Chien line from Middleton, a few miles west of Madison, as far as Lone Rock; the Elkhorn & Walworth operated from Janesville to Elkhorn via Bardwell, and from Milton Junction northwest to Madison. Central Wisconsin's parent company entered bankruptcy at the end of 1984.

Milwaukee Road train 222, led by SD40-2 No. 161, rolls past St. Croix Tower at Hastings, Minn., in September 1984. In the following year, Milwaukee was taken over by Soo. *Steve Glischinski*

Wisconsin & Calumet

The Wisconsin & Calumet Railroad (WICT reporting marks, nicknamed "Wicket"), began operation in January 1985 on the former IC line from Freeport, Ill., north through Monroe, Wis., to Madison, and on the Janesville–Monroe route. It woud add the routes from Waukesha through Milton Junction and Madison to Prairie du Chien; from Milton Junction through Janesville to Monroe; and from Janesville southeast to Fox Lake, Ill., and by trackage rights on Metra and Belt Railway of Chicago to BRC's Clearing Yard in Chicago.

The WICT had authority to continue west of Monroe to Mineral Point, but Central Wisconsin had embargoed that line in 1984. It was laster dismantled. The Milwaukee Road had ceased operating the Madison–Prairie du Chien line west of Lone Rock in 1980, but Wisconsin & Calumet reopened it in 1986.

Wisconsin & Calumet was a subsidiary of Chicago West Pullman Transportation Corp. (which owned switching line Chicago, West Pullman & Southern in Chicago's Calumet region, hence the name) until Aug. 21, 1992, when it was purchased by Railroad Acquisition Corp., owner of the Wisconsin & Southern Railroad (reporting marks WSOR). WICT was operated independently until WSOR merged it in 1997.

Wisconsin & Southern

To briefly summarize the Wisconsin & Southern Railroad (WSOR, commonly "Wisser"), it stems from the Milwaukee Road in 1978 considering abandonment of several branches northwest of Milwaukee. With the help of state and federal aid, the railroad instead sold the lines to FSC Corp. of Pittsburgh, which organized the Wisconsin & Southern and began operation July 1, 1980. WSOR's own entry in this book has more details.

Dakota Southern Railway

Dakota Southern Railway operates former Milwaukee trackage, owned by the South Dakota Department of Transportation, from Mitchell, S. D., west to Chamberlain and Kadoka, part of the former route from Madison, Wis., west through Marquette and Mason City, Iowa, to Rapid City, S. D. It was built between 1880 and 1907.

FACTS & FIGURES

Year	1929	1984
Miles operated	11,248	3,023
Locomotives	1,801	323
Passenger cars	1,330	—
Freight cars	73,184	11,411
Reporting marks: MILW		
Historical society: mrha.com		

Chicago North Shore & Milwaukee

The North Shore became famous for its high-speed *Electroliner* trainsets, which were delivered in 1939. Here, one of the two sets speeds southward on the Skokie Valley route in 1949. *George Krambles; Krambles-Peterson Archive*

In 1891 the Waukegan & North Shore Rapid Transit Co. was incorporated—a trolley line for the city of Waukegan, Ill., on the shore of Lake Michigan, 36 miles north of Chicago. In 1897, by which time it reached 6 miles south to Lake Bluff, it was sold and reorganized as the Chicago & Milwaukee Electric Railway. The line was extended south through the towns along the lake to Evanston, where it connected with a branch of the Milwaukee Road to Chicago. It also built a line west

from Lake Bluff to Libertyville in 1903 and to what is now Mundelein in 1905.

Construction northward from Lake Bluff began in 1904 following steam-railroad standards of grade and curvature—the line to Evanston was typical of suburban trolley line construction. In December 1905 the line reached Kenosha, Wis., where it connected with the Milwaukee Light, Heat & Traction Co. At the same time the Milwaukee Road connection at Evanston was replaced by the

Northwestern Elevated Railroad. This meant an all-electric Chicago to Milwaukee trip was now possible. It took five hours, considerably more than on the parallel Chicago & North Western or Milwaukee Road, but the fare was less. The Chicago & Milwaukee pushed its own rails north, reaching Milwaukee (and bankruptcy) in 1908. Operation began, nonetheless, and immediately included limited-stop express trains with parlor car and dining service.

Enter Samuel Insull

In 1916 the Insull interests purchased the railroad, reorganized it as the Chicago North Shore & Milwaukee Railroad, and immediately began a modernization program. Business nearly doubled during the first year of new management. In 1919 the North Shore made arrangements to operate to the Loop in downtown Chicago over the rails of the elevated (the "L") and constructed new terminals in Chicago and Milwaukee. Business flourished on the 85-mile route, even with the competition of two very healthy steam roads. The North Shore quickly developed into the definitive interurban.

In the early 1920s traffic between Waukegan and Evanston reached the saturation point of the line, which was handicapped by stretches of street running. The railroad saw that a new line a few miles west along the right of way of one of Insull's power companies would be cheaper than just the construction of temporary track needed to rebuild the existing line. The first 5-mile portion of the new Skokie Valley Line was opened in 1925 and was operated by Chicago Rapid Transit, which continued to operate local service until 1948. The entire line opened in 1926 and became the new main route. The Shore Line, as the original route was termed, was relegated to local service. The new route was much faster, materially helping the North Shore compete with the steam roads. North Shore quickly became America's fastest interurban. In addition the North Shore emphasized its parlor and dining service—it was perhaps the only interurban to have much success with such operations.

Electroliners and abandonment

In 1931 the Great Depression finally got a grip on the North Shore. The line declared bankruptcy in September 1932. Even so, the road continued to operate fast, frequent trains. It cooperated with parallel Chicago & North Western and public agencies in a line relocation project through Glencoe, Winnetka, and Kenilworth, eliminating grade crossings and street running. In 1939 the North Shore ordered a pair of streamliners from St. Louis Car Co.: the *Electroliners*. No other trains of the streamliner era had such disparate elements in their specifications: 85-mph top speed (North Shore's schedules called for start-to-stop averages of 70 mph) and the ability to

operate around the 90-foot radius curves of the Chicago "L." World War II brought increased traffic, and the North Shore emerged from bankruptcy in 1946—just as competition from automobiles and strikes by employees began to cut into the road's business. Waukegan and North Chicago streetcar services were taken over by buses in 1947, dining car service on trains other than the *Electroliners* was dropped in 1949, local streetcar service in Milwaukee was discontinued in 1951, and the Shore Line was abandoned in 1955.

By then the North Shore was owned by the Susquehanna Corporation, a holding company that found the road's losses useful for tax purposes—ditto for tax credits from abandonment. In 1959 an Interstate Commerce Commission examiner recommended abandonment, and the 1960 completion of the Edens Expressway took passengers away by the thousands. Protests and renewed petitions prolonged the struggles of the line until Jan. 21, 1963.

North Shore's freight business consisted of less-than-carload traffic carried in merchandise despatch cars (motor baggage cars) and intermediate traffic, received from one steam road and delivered to another. North Shore inaugurated piggyback service in 1926, but improved parallel highways led to its discontinuance in 1947.

Remnants of the North Shore exist. Many of its standard steel passenger cars are in trolley museums across the country, and the two *Electroliners* are at Illinois Railway Museum at Union, Ill., and Shade Gap Electric Railway, Orbisonia, Pennsylvania, after several years of service on the Philadelphia & Western. North Shore's right of way is still visible, and part of the Shore Line has become a bicycle path. Chicago Transit Authority restored service to the south end of the Skokie Valley Route in 1964—the *Skokie Swift*, a nonstop service between Howard Street in Chicago and Dempster Street in Skokie.

FACTS & FIGURES

Year	1929	1962
Miles operated	138	107
Locomotives	7	8
Passenger cars	214	135
Freight cars	211	17
Reporting marks: CNS&M		
Historical society: shore-line.org		

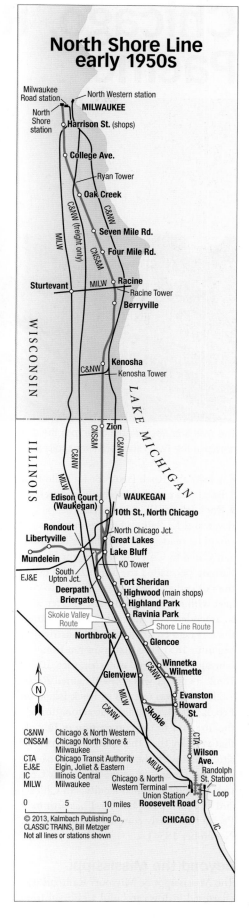

North Shore Line early 1950s

Milwaukee Road station
North Western station
MILWAUKEE
North Shore station
Harrison St. (shops)
College Ave.
Ryan Tower
Oak Creek
Seven Mile Rd.
Four Mile Rd.
Racine
Racine Tower
Berryville
Sturtevant
WISCONSIN
ILLINOIS
LAKE MICHIGAN
Kenosha
Kenosha Tower
Zion
Edison Court (Waukegan)
WAUKEGAN
10th St., North Chicago
Rondout
North Chicago Jct.
Libertyville
Great Lakes
Lake Bluff
Mundelein
KO Tower
South Upton Jct.
EJ&E
Fort Sheridan
Deerpath
Highwood (main shops)
Briergate
Highland Park
Ravinia Park
Skokie Valley Route
Shore Line Route
Northbrook
Glencoe
Winnetka
Glenview
Wilmette
Skokie
Evanston
Howard St.
N
Wilson Ave.
Randolph St. Station
Chicago & North Western Terminal
Union Station
Loop
Roosevelt Road
CHICAGO

C&NW	Chicago & North Western
CNS&M	Chicago North Shore & Milwaukee
CTA	Chicago Transit Authority
EJ&E	Elgin, Joliet & Eastern
IC	Illinois Central
MILW	Milwaukee

0   5   10 miles

© 2013, Kalmbach Publishing Co., CLASSIC TRAINS, Bill Metzger
Not all lines or stations shown

Chicago, Rock Island & Pacific

The *Twin Star Rocket* pounds across the diamonds of the Wabash and Burlington at Birmingham, Mo., on July 14, 1963. The train operated between the Twin Cities of Minneapolis and St. Paul, Minn. and Houston, Texas. *Frank Tatnall*

In 1847 the Rock Island & La Salle Rail Road was chartered to build between Rock Island, Ill., on the Mississippi River, and La Salle, where connections would be made with the Illinois & Michigan Canal to Chicago. Contractor Henry Farnam persuaded the organizers to extend the railroad all the way to Chicago to connect with other railroads. The charter was so amended, and the railroad was renamed the Chicago & Rock Island. Construction began in 1851. The first train ran from Chicago to Joliet, 40 miles, on Oct. 10, 1852. Its power was a 4-4-0 named *Rocket*.

The line was opened to Rock Island on Feb. 22, 1854, and the contractors turned the line over to the corporation in July of that year. By then the railroad had an agreement with the Northern Indiana Railroad (later part of the New York Central) for joint terminal facilities in Chicago, and a branch from Bureau, Ill., south to Peoria was nearly complete (it opened in November 1854).

Beyond the Mississippi

The Mississippi & Missouri Railroad was chartered in Iowa to build a railroad from Davenport, across the Mississippi River from Rock Island, to Council Bluffs, with branches south through Muscatine and north through Cedar Rapids. Money to finance construction of the Mississippi & Missouri was hard to come by. Both Iowa City, then the state capital, and Muscatine wanted the railroad first. Iowa City offered a bonus if a train arrived by midnight, Dec. 31, 1855. Muscatine got its railroad first, on Nov. 20, 1855, but (if we are to believe contemporary accounts) a frozen locomotive was pushed over hastily laid and barely spiked rails into Iowa City as church bells rang in the New Year, securing the bonus and providing a perfect scenario for a multitude of grade-B novels and movies.

A bridge across the Mississippi was necessary to connect the Chicago & Rock Island and Mississippi & Missouri railroads. The Mississippi had not yet been spanned, and the immediate reaction to the proposed railroad bridge was that it would be a hazard to navigation. However, the bridge was built, and it was officially opened on April 21, 1856. On the evening of May 6 the steamboat *Effie Afton*, which usually plied the New Orleans–Louisville run, cleared the open draw span then veered aside, turned around, rammed one of the piers, and suddenly and suspiciously burst into flames. The case of the bridge soon became one of railroad advocates versus steamboat advocates. The latter felt that even a single bridge would set an unfortunate precedent and soon there would be bridges every 40 or 50 miles along the length of the river. The railroad's case, argued by Abraham Lincoln, went one way and then the other in successive courts, but in 1866 the U. S. Supreme Court held for the railroad. Several other railroads immediately applied to bridge the Mississippi at other locations.

The Mississippi & Missouri, far behind its construction schedule, was sold to the newly incorporated Chicago, Rock Island & Pacific on July 9, 1866. On Aug. 20 that company consolidated with the Chicago & Rock Island to form a successor Chicago, Rock Island & Pacific Railroad. The line reached Des Moines a year later and arrived at Council Bluffs on May 11, 1869—one day after the completion of the Union Pacific and Central Pacific railroads from Council Bluffs to the West Coast.

The Rock Island was not the first railroad into Council Bluffs; the Cedar Rapids & Missouri (later part of the Chicago & North Western) had reached there more than two years earlier and established ties with the Union Pacific.

To Missouri, Kansas, and beyond

In the 1870s the road extended its Muscatine line southwest across Iowa and northwestern Missouri to Leavenworth, Kansas, and later negotiated trackage rights over the Hannibal & St. Joseph from Cameron, Mo., to Kansas City. Also during the 1870s the road acquired a couple of "firsts"—the first dining cars and Jesse James's first train holdup.

The 1880s saw some corporate simplification, the acquisition of the Keokuk & Des Moines and the St. Joseph & Iowa, and control of the Burlington, Cedar Rapids & Northern, which had a line from Burlington, Iowa, through Cedar Rapids and Cedar Falls to Plymouth, near Mason City, with a branch through Iowa Falls and Estherville to Watertown, South Dakota. The BCR&N later acquired lines west out of Davenport and Clinton, Iowa, and lines to Decorah, Iowa, Worthington, Minn., and Sioux Falls, S. D.

On Dec. 5, 1883, the Rock Island made a tripartite agreement with Union Pacific and the Milwaukee Road for interchange of business at Omaha. The Chicago & North Western, which had been UP's preferred connection, quickly became a party to the agreement, as did the Wabash, St. Louis & Pacific (a predecessor of the Wabash). The Burlington & Missouri River in Nebraska (part of the Burlington) protested the agreement.

Union Pacific suddenly found itself in financial difficulties, and Rock Island decided to build its own extensions west rather than rely on interchange traffic with UP. Two years later the Chicago, Kansas & Nebraska Railroad was chartered to build from St. Joseph and Atchison southwest across Kansas to Wichita, and another railroad of the same name was incorporated in Nebraska to build from the southeast tip of the state to Kearney. The two companies merged and were leased to the St. Joseph & Iowa Railroad, a subsidiary of the Rock Island. A charter was approved for the extension of the southwest line from Wichita to Galveston, Texas, and from

Liberal, Kans., to El Paso, Tex. By the end of 1887 rails reached to Caldwell, on the southern border of Kansas, and in February 1888 they reached Liberal. A year later the Rock Island had built west across northern Kansas and Colorado to Colorado Springs. RI made arrangements to use Denver & Rio Grande track north to Denver and south to Pueblo; in 1889 RI began using Union Pacific tracks from Limon, Colo. to Denver.

Rock Island's Chicago–Colorado route via St. Joseph was circuitous. To assemble a route through Omaha, RI constructed a line from Omaha to Lincoln and in 1890 traded the trackage rights from McPherson to Hutchinson, Kans. to Union Pacific for trackage rights on UP between Lincoln and Beatrice and use of UP's Missouri River bridge between Council Bluffs and Omaha. RI began Chicago–Colorado service via Omaha on August 16, 1891, and later built its own line west of Lincoln. Also in 1891 Rock Island acquired the property of the Chicago, Kansas & Nebraska. Subsidiary Chicago, Rock Island & Texas reached Fort Worth in 1893.

The Reid-Moore era

In 1901 control of the Rock Island was taken over by the Reid-Moore syndicate: Daniel G. Reed, William H. Moore, his brother James H. Moore, and William

Leeds, men who had put together the National Biscuit, Diamond Match, and American Can companies. The road continued to burgeon. It acquired the Choctaw, Oklahoma & Gulf Railroad, a line from Memphis, Tennessee, through Little Rock, Arkansas, and Oklahoma City to Elk City in western Oklahoma, and the 70-mile St. Louis, Kansas City & Colorado Railroad (which the Santa Fe at one point had considered acquiring for an entrance to St. Louis). Expansion continued:

- 1902—lease of the Burlington, Cedar Rapids & Northern for 999 years, and extension of the southwestern line from Liberal to Santa Rosa, New Mexico, to connect with the El Paso & Northeastern, a Southern Pacific predecessor (the new track included the second-longest stretch of straight track in the U. S., nearly 72 miles between Guymon, Okla., and Dalhart, Tex.)
- 1903—Chicago, Rock Island & Gulf completed a line between Fort Worth and Dallas
- 1904—the Choctaw line was extended west to Amarillo, Tex., and the Kansas City–St. Louis line was opened
- 1905—the road began assembling and constructing a line south from Little Rock to Eunice, Louisiana, with the intent of reaching New Orleans
- 1906—RI acquired a half interest in the Trinity & Brazos Valley Railway (Dallas–

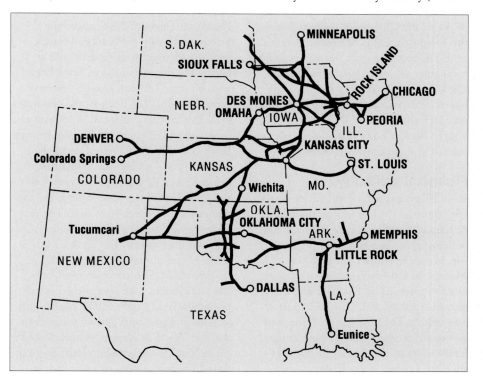

Rock Island had a fleet of 85 Northerns (4-8-4s), largest in the country. Here, No. 5058 leads a westbound freight near Lawrence, Kans., in January 1952. *Robert P. Olmsted Collection, American Heritage Center, University of Wyoming*

Houston–Galveston, later the Burlington-Rock Island Railroad) from the Colorado & Southern.

At the same time the controlling syndicate, which now included B. F. Yoakum, was busy acquiring control of the Chicago & Alton, the Chicago & Eastern Illinois, the Toledo, St. Louis & Western, and the St. Louis-San Francisco through holding companies and exchanges of stock. By 1909, though, the interest due on SLSF bonds far exceeded the dividends received on SLSF stock—none. B. F. Yoakum bought Rock Island's Frisco stock at a considerable loss to the Rock Island.

Financial difficulty

Rock Island created a Twin Cities–Kansas City route in 1913 by leasing the St. Paul & Kansas City Short Line Railroad and building a line between Allerton and Carlisle, Iowa, a few miles south of Des Moines. In 1914 red ink caused by debt interest appeared on Rock Island's ledgers, and on April 20, 1915, the road entered receivership. On June 22, 1917, the road was out of receivership and back in the hands of its stockholders. Shortly afterward the United States Railroad

Administration took over management for the duration of World War I.

New management took over in the 1920s and placed considerable emphasis on paying of stock dividends to the detriment of maintaining the property. Edward N. Brown, chairman of the board of the Frisco, began to buy Rock Island stock with the thought of using dividends to bolster the Frisco's situation. Soon Brown was chairman of Rock Island's executive committee. In 1927 Rock Island declared a stock dividend of 5 percent; in 1928, 6 percent; and in 1929, 7 percent—even though Rock Island's annual interest on its debt was nearly $14 million. In 1930 Brown began to secretly acquire Frisco stock for the Rock Island. Revenues dropped as the depression deepened. Then Rock Island's territory was struck with wheat crop failures and dust storms. The Rock Island declared bankruptcy on June 7, 1933.

Edward M. Durham, vice-president of Missouri Pacific, took over as chief executive officer in December 1935. He brought in John D. Farrington, general manager of the Fort Worth & Denver, as operating officer in May 1936. Farrington started a scrap drive to finance a rail relay program and

purchased ten diesel switchers and six diesel-powered *Rocket* streamliners. His program included line relocations between Davenport and Kansas City and a new bridge over the Cimarron River just east of Liberal, Kans. The road turned a profit in 1941. Durham retired in July 1942, and Farrington took over as CEO.

The Chicago, Rock Island & Pacific Railroad emerged from a long and acrimonious reorganization on January 1, 1948. Farrington was still leading the company and pursuing a program of dieselization, line improvement, and industrial development. Rock Island rolled on through the 1950s and into the 1960s doing decently although surrounded by stronger railroads. Its freight traffic was largely agricultural. Its passenger trains for the most part would take you anywhere the Burlington or the Santa Fe could, but not as quickly nor with quite as much style.

The fight over the Rock Island

In 1964 Ben Heineman, chairman of the Chicago & North Western, proposed merging the C&NW, the Rock Island, and the Milwaukee Road into an Upper Midwest system and selling the lines south of Kansas City to Santa Fe. Union Pacific made a counterproposal: merger, which would put the UP into Chicago. That year, 1964, was Rock Island's last year of profitability.

The proposal turned into the longest, most complicated merger case ever handled by the Interstate Commerce Commission. The other railroads west of Chicago protested one aspect or another of the merger, petitioned for inclusion, or asked for a piece of the Rock Island. In 1970 the Milwaukee Road, which had fallen on hard times, entered the case, asking for inclusion in Union Pacific or Southern Pacific. In 1973 the ICC proposed restructuring the railroads of the West into four systems: Union Pacific, Southern Pacific, Burlington Northern, and Santa Fe. The railroads involved in the merger case other than the two principals petitioned the ICC to dismiss the case and start over.

The ICC finally approved the merger on Nov. 8, 1974, with several conditions: Southern Pacific would be allowed to purchase the Kansas City–Tucumcari line (that had been part of the UP merger proposal from the beginning); the Omaha–Colorado Springs line would be sold to the Denver & Rio Grande Western; and Santa Fe would

Rock Island's early EMD Geeps were delivered in an eye-catching red-and-black scheme with "Route of the *Rockets*" lettering on the long hood. Here GP7 No. 1287 works at St. Paul in 1961. *J. David Ingles*

be permitted to buy the Choctaw Route (Memphis–Amarillo) only if it would absorb the bankrupt and decrepit Missouri-Kansas-Texas. Union Pacific said it would have to re-evaluate the merger, since the Rock Island of 1974 wasn't the Rock Island of 1964. Rock Island filed for bankruptcy on March 17, 1975, and on August 4 of that year UP withdrew its merger offer. The ICC dismissed the case on July 10, 1976.

Slow death

By then the Rock Island was in terrible shape. A new management headed by John W. Ingram did its best, introducing a new image of sky-blue and white and appointing John W. Barriger III, then 76 years old, as Senior Traveling Freight Agent (Barriger's own title) and consultant.

Rock Island's clerks walked off their jobs on Aug. 28, 1979, over a pay dispute, and United Transportation Union members followed the next day. President Jimmy Carter issued an order Sept. 20 creating an emergency board to settle the dispute. The UTU members then returned to their jobs, but members of the Brotherhood of Railway and Airline Clerks

stayed off. On Sept. 26 the Kansas City Terminal was ordered by the ICC to operate the railroad. KCT's owners plus Denver & Rio Grande Western and Southern Pacific began operating the Rock Island. On March 2, 1980, the ICC refused to extend its directed service order, and the Rock Island ceased operation March 31, 1980.

The railroad industry had never before seen an abandonment of the magnitude of Rock Island. Other railroads had been abandoned in their entirety, but they were roads like the New York, Ontario & Western (541 miles, 1957; it had always been sickly and shouldn't have been built), Fort Smith & Western (250 miles, 1939; it didn't go anywhere and shouldn't have been built), and the Colorado Midland (338 miles, 1918; it had steep grades and shouldn't have been built—and 1918 was ancient history anyway).

The 7,000-mile Rock Island connected big cities like Chicago, Denver, Minneapolis, Houston, and Kansas City. It had no major operating handicaps, like mountains. It had long routes, so it wasn't another Reading or Central of New Jersey. Industry

reaction to the abandonment ranged from "Someone has to take it over and run it" to "Can I have the Kansas City–Minneapolis line?"

When the dust settled it turned out that what was abandoned was the operating company and financial structure, not the physical plant. Rock Island's sky-blue freight cars showed up with reporting marks like C&NW and BM underneath the slogan "The Rock," and the fixed plant of the railroad was parceled out to other railroads, including Southern Pacific, Cotton Belt, Burlington Northern, Chessie System, and Missouri Pacific. Other lines became regional railroads, including Iowa Interstate and Kyle.

FACTS & FIGURES

Year	1929	1978
Miles operated	8,158	7,021
Locomotives	1,453	660
Passenger cars	1,075	79
Freight cars	43,751	26,592
Reporting marks: RI, ROCK		
Historical society: rits.org		

Chicago South Shore & South Bend

Late in 1901 the Chicago & Indiana Air Line Railway was incorporated. Nearly two years later it opened a 3.4-mile streetcar line between East Chicago and Indiana Harbor, Ind. In 1904 the name of the company was changed to the Chicago, Lake Shore & South Bend. The pace of construction accelerated, and in 1908 the entire line was in service from Hammond to South Bend, 76 miles. A year later the line was extended west across the state line to a connection with the Illinois Central at Kensington, Ill.

The line was electrified at 6,600 volts AC, unusual for an interurban, and the grades were gentler and curves broader than most interurbans, making the line resemble more a heavy steam railroad than a light electric railway.

Samuel Insull acquired control of the company in 1925, reorganized it as the Chicago South Shore & South Bend, and undertook a reconstruction that changed it from an interurban to a heavy electric railroad. The modernization included steel cars, a change of power system to 1,500 volts DC, and operation through to Chicago over Illinois Central's newly electrified suburban line.

Insull's control ended in 1932 and the company entered bankruptcy. New management continued to improve the road, though, and moved it further into the steam-road category—interurbans were dying off faster than they had been built a few decades earlier—with interline passenger ticketing, off-line freight solicitation, rebuilt passenger cars, and in 1956 a bypass around the city streets of East Chicago on

A westbound local with a caboose and single boxcar runs down 11th Street in Michigan City, Ind., in August 1972. Number 71 is a Class R-2 boxcab. South Shore electric freight operations ended in 1981. *Robert Jordan*

a right of way shared with the Indiana Toll Road.

Chesapeake & Ohio acquired control of the South Shore in 1967. Electric freight operation ended in 1981 (but continued with diesels), but passenger service continued under the wires, and the arrival in 1982 of new cars purchased by the Northern Indiana Commuter Transportation

District permitted the retirement of the Insull-era cars, which had begun to show their age in the early 1960s.

The line entered bankruptcy again in 1989, at which time passenger operation and dispatching were taken over by the NICTD and operated as the South Shore Line. A new iteration of the CSS&SB, owned by shortline holding firm Anacostia and Pacific, took over all freight service on the line.

FACTS & FIGURES

Year	1929	1984
Miles operated	77	76
Locomotives	13	10
Passenger cars	71	73
Freight cars	44	—

Reporting marks: CSS

Historical society: southshore.railfan.net

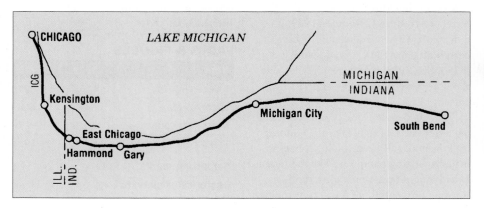

Cincinnati & Lake Erie

The Ohio Electric Railway was formed in 1907 as a confederation of several companies. The main trunk of the system was a line from Cincinnati north through Dayton, Springfield, and Lima to Toledo; branches reached from Dayton to Richmond, Ind., and Union City, Ohio, from Springfield through Columbus to Zanesville, and from Lima to Fort Wayne, Ind., and Defiance, Ohio. In 1918 the Cincinnati, Dayton & Toledo Railway pulled out of Ohio Electric and reorganized as the Cincinnati & Dayton Traction Co. Ohio Electric went bankrupt in 1921, and its other components resumed their own identities: Indiana, Columbus & Eastern; Dayton & Western; Columbus, Newark & Zanesville; Lima & Toledo, and Fort Wayne, Van Wert & Lima.

In 1922, Dr. Thomas Conway, a professor of finance at Penn's Wharton School of Finance, took over the Chicago Aurora & Elgin and in 1926 purchased the Cincinnati & Dayton Traction Co. and reorganized it as the Cincinnati, Hamilton & Dayton Railway (not to be confused with the steam railroad of the same name that became part of the Baltimore & Ohio).

Running as the *Golden Eagle* to Columbus, C&LE "Red Devil" No. 125 pauses to receive passengers at Osborn, Ohio, on Aug. 2, 1936. *George Krambles*

Conway began rebuilding the railroad, buying ten new interurban cars and ten new suburban cars. Conway acquired control of the Indiana, Columbus & Eastern Traction Co. and the Lima-Toledo Railroad, both remnants of Ohio Electric, and he coordinated their operation with CH&D. In the summer of 1929 CH&D ordered 20 passenger cars of a new low-slung, lightweight design and within a short time ordered 15 new freight motors.

At the end of 1929 CH&D was reorganized as the Cincinnati & Lake Erie Railroad and acquired the Indiana, Columbus & Eastern and the Lima-Toledo. The new railroad consisted of a main line from Cincinnati to Toledo and a branch from Springfield to Columbus.

The railroad began through service to Detroit in late 1930, but the connecting Eastern Michigan-Toledo Railway was abandoned in October 1932.

As the Depression was deepening, ridership and freight traffic dropped. Connecting interurban lines were dying, and to protect one of its connections, C&LE took over operation of the bankrupt Dayton & Western in 1931. Conway instituted cuts in executive salaries and one-man train crews. The company entered receivership in 1932 with Conway as receiver.

Automobile competition increased. C&LE was unable to take up the slack with freight because of franchise restrictions on street trackage. Several fatal accidents in 1935 and 1936 drove away timid riders. In 1936 operation of the Dayton & Western was turned over to the Indiana Railroad. In November 1937 C&LE abandoned its line between Springfield and Toledo. A road-widening project in 1938 caused the south end of the line to be cut back. In October of that year service ceased between Columbus and Springfield. The high-speed lightweights were sold to Lehigh Valley Transit and the Cedar Rapids & Iowa City. In May 1939 more service was abandoned, leaving only a suburban line in Dayton—and that was abandoned in September 1941. The company's bus affiliate continued in service and was purchased by Greyhound in 1947.

FACTS & FIGURES

Year	1930
Miles operated	270
Locomotives	46
Passenger cars	106
Freight cars	175
Reporting marks: C&LE, CH&D, LT	

Clinchfield

A railroad running north and south across the Blue Ridge Mountains in eastern Tennessee and western North Carolina had been proposed early in the railroad era, but until the end of the 1800s only bits and pieces of such a railroad were built. In 1900 the only piece of the future Clinchfield in existence was the Ohio River & Charleston, which meandered a few miles south from a connection with the Southern Railway at Johnson City, Tenn.

The South & Western Railroad was incorporated in 1905 and was almost immediately purchased by a syndicate as part of a plan to mine coal in western Virginia and eastern Tennessee. In 1908 it opened between Johnson City, Tenn. and Marion, N. C., and was renamed the Carolina, Clinchfield & Ohio Railway. By the end of 1909 the CC&O had been extended north from Johnson City to Dante, Va., and south from Marion to Spartanburg, S. C. In 1915 the road opened an extension north from Dante to a connection with the Chesapeake & Ohio at Elkhorn City, Ky.

In 1924 the Atlantic Coast Line and Louisville & Nashville railroads jointly leased the properties of the CC&O. The two lessees named the Clinchfield Railroad

Clinchfield's main traffic source was coal, and here a 4-6-6-4 gets underway with a long string of northbound hoppers at Ridge, N. C. in August 1952. *Floyd A. Bruner*

Company, an unincorporated entity, as the operating organization.

The Clinchfield's original mission was to haul coal. Its strategic location and relatively easy grades and curves—the result of construction late enough to take advantage of modern construction machinery and methods—led to Clinchfield's development into a fast freight route between the

Midwest and the Piedmont. At Spartanburg it connected with the Southern Railway and Atlantic Coast Line's Charleston & Western Carolina subsidiary, and at Elkhorn City, Ky., it connected with C&O. The Clinchfield was unusual in that it had no significant branches, just the single main stem.

The creation of the Seaboard System Railroad on Dec. 29, 1982, by the merger of Seaboard Coast Line and Louisville & Nashville rendered unnecessary a separate company to operate the Clinchfield. On Jan. 1, 1983, the Clinchfield Railroad became the Clinchfield Division of the Seaboard System Railroad.

On March 1, 1984, the Clinchfield Division was abolished and the former Clinchfield Railroad split between the Corbin and Florence divisions of the Seaboard. The entire line is still in service.

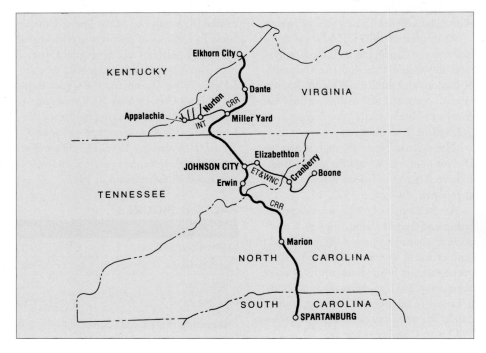

FACTS & FIGURES

Year	1929	1982
Miles operated	309	296
Locomotives	86	98
Passenger cars	38	—
Freight cars	7,562	5,291
Reporting marks: CRR		

Colorado & Southern (Fort Worth & Denver)

The Colorado & Southern was an amalgamation of standard gauge and narrow gauge lines radiating in almost every direction from Denver. After 1908 it was controlled by the Chicago, Burlington & Quincy; in its early years, it had no relation at all with the Burlington.

Lines west of Denver

The earliest part of the Colorado & Southern was the standard gauge line from Denver to Golden, which was opened in 1870 as the Colorado Central Railroad. From Golden it pushed a 3-foot-gauge line up Clear Creek Canyon to Georgetown (1877) and Central City. To allow its narrow gauge trains access to Denver, the road three-railed the Denver–Golden line in 1879. In 1881 the road made plans to continue west to Leadville. The few miles from Georgetown to Silver Plume required a complete loop—a much-publicized feat of engineering—in order to gain altitude.

Lines north of Denver

Meanwhile, with financial help from Union Pacific the road built a line north from Golden through Boulder. Although the goal of the line was Julesburg on the Union Pacific main line in the northeast corner of the state, construction halted at Longmont when the Panic of 1873 caused financial difficulty for the UP.

In 1877 UP resumed construction of the Colorado Central, this time with a line south from Cheyenne, and in 1879 leased the CC. In 1882 Colorado Central completed a line southwest from Julesburg to La Salle, where it connected with the Denver Pacific (UP's Denver–Cheyenne line). The Julesburg line gave UP a short route into Denver from the east, necessary to compete with the Burlington, whose rails reached Denver in May 1882.

The UP built a connecting line between Greeley and Fort Collins in 1882, and in 1886 CC built a direct line between Denver and Boulder. Two portions of the CC that were considered redundant were abandoned in 1889: the Colorado Central north of Fort Collins and most of the old Golden–Boulder line.

The *Texas Zephyr* kicks up a cloud of dust as it speeds southward through Colorado foothill country on July 5, 1965. The train will cross a corner of New Mexico and then move to Fort Worth & Denver rails at Texline on the Texas/New Mexico border. *Roger Meade*

Cheyenne interests began building the Cheyenne & Northern Railway in 1886 to head off a Chicago & North Western subsidiary at Douglas. The North Western line reached Douglas the next year, and the C&N stopped at Wendover, Wyo. It was extended north to a connection with the C&NW at Orin Junction a few years later.

Lines southwest of Denver

In 1873 the Denver, South Park & Pacific began constructing a 3-foot-gauge line southwest from Denver. Progress was slowed by the Panic of 1873, and not until 1880 did the line reach the Arkansas River at Buena Vista. By then Jay Gould had gained control of Union Pacific and a half interest in the Denver & Rio Grande. He acquired control of the South Park in 1880 and sold it to Union Pacific.

The DSP&P bored Alpine Tunnel under the Continental Divide in 1881 to extend its line to Gunnison. Neither the South Park nor the Rio Grande was happy with the DSP&P's trackage rights over Rio Grande from Buena Vista to Leadville, so in 1884 the South Park completed a Como–Leadville line that crossed the Continental Divide twice over Boreas and Fremont passes. The South Park entered

receivership in 1889 and was reorganized as the Denver, Leadville & Gunnison Railway, still under UP control. Union Pacific itself entered receivership in 1893. DL&G regained independence as part of the UP reorganization in 1894.

Lines southeast of Denver

In 1881 John Evans incorporated the Denver & New Orleans Railroad to build a line to Fort Worth, Texas. The goal was later changed to a connection with Fort Worth & Denver City Railway, which had started construction northwest from Fort Worth. Evans's line built southeast from Denver through Parker, Elizabeth, and Fountain to Pueblo, with a spur west to Colorado Springs from Manitou Junction.

The Denver, Texas & Fort Worth was organized to build south from Pueblo using trackage rights on the Denver & Rio Grande as far as Trinidad. In 1888 it met with the FW&DC. Soon afterward the DT&FW, itself having come under UP control, acquired control of the FW&DC and the Denver, Texas & Gulf, a reorganization of the Denver & New Orleans.

The north-south roads were brought together in 1890, when the UP formed the Union Pacific, Denver & Gulf to

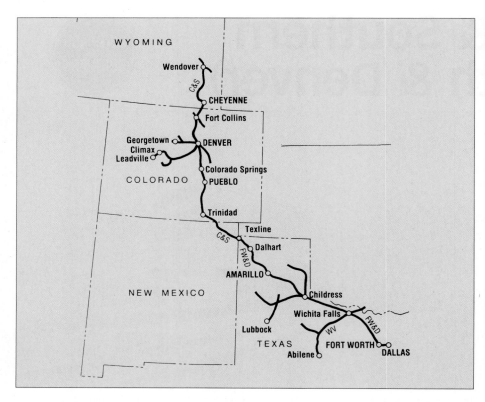

consolidate the Colorado Central, the Cheyenne & Northern, the Denver, Texas & Gulf, the Denver, Texas & Fort Worth, and several short lines. When the UP entered receivership in 1893, a separate receiver was appointed for these lines, Frank Trumbull, who was also to become receiver of the Denver, Leadville & Gunnison.

Colorado & Southern

The reorganization committees of the DL&G and the UPD&G (which by then owned the FW&DC) arranged for the sale of their roads at foreclosure in 1898, and they were consolidated as the Colorado & Southern Railway. The only portion of the predecessors that was not included was the Julesburg–La Salle line, which was sold to Union Pacific. C&S made agreements with Santa Fe for joint use of terminal facilities in Denver, Colorado Springs, and Pueblo, and for trackage rights between Denver and Pueblo, abandoning its own line from Manitou Junction to Pueblo.

C&S had its corporate eye on the boom town of Cripple Creek. Its plan was to extend the former South Park line south to a connection with the Colorado Midland, and to that end C&S acquired control of CM jointly with Rio Grande Western in 1900. In 1905 C&S purchased control of the Colorado Springs & Cripple Creek District Railway. Then the mining boom

declined. C&S sold its CM interest in 1912 (it was abandoned in 1921), and the CS&CCD was abandoned in 1922.

In the same era C&S organized an electric subsidiary, the Denver & Interurban, which built a line between Denver and Boulder and a streetcar system in Fort Collins. D&I entered receivership in 1918. The Denver–Boulder line was abandoned in 1926. The Fort Collins system was sold to the city; when service ended in 1951 it was the last city streetcar system in Colorado and the last in the U. S. to operate four-wheel Birney cars.

Control by the Burlington

In 1901 Great Northern and Northern Pacific acquired joint control of the Chicago, Burlington & Quincy. The three roads saw the C&S as an outlet to the Gulf of Mexico. In 1905 C&S bought control of the Trinity & Brazos Valley, gaining access to the port of Galveston (see the entry for Burlington-Rock Island), and in 1908 CB&Q bought nearly two-thirds of the common stock of the C&S. In the ensuing years, though, C&S and Fort Worth & Denver maintained a degree of independence, even if their image soon became that of the Burlington.

In 1911 C&S restored the abandoned Fort Collins–Cheyenne link and teamed up with the Denver & Rio Grande to

build a new double-track line between Pueblo and Walsenburg. That same year C&S abandoned the former South Park line west of Buena Vista. The last major portion of the South Park, between Denver and Climax, was abandoned in 1937. The Clear Creek lines to Idaho Springs and Black Hawk were torn up in 1941. The Leadville–Climax line, orphaned in 1937, was standard-gauged in 1943. Floods in May 1935 destroyed much of the original Denver & New Orleans line from Denver to Falcon, east of Colorado Springs, and that line was stubbed off outside Denver.

Fort Worth & Denver

The Fort Worth & Denver City Railway was chartered in 1873, and construction began in 1881. The line reached Wichita Falls in 1882 and met up with the line from Colorado on March 14, 1888.

The Wichita Valley Railway was chartered in 1890 to build southwest from Wichita Falls. It developed into a Wichita Falls–Abilene main stem with several branches owned by different railroads, all operated as Wichita Valley Lines.

In 1939 the Burlington proposed leasing the Fort Worth & Denver City to the C&S and closing its offices and shops in favor of C&S's facilities in Denver. There was loud protest in Fort Worth and Childress, and the ICC denied the request.

The Fort Worth & Denver ("City" was dropped in 1951) and Rock Island purchased the Burlington-Rock Island in 1964; FW&D took over its operation upon the demise of the Rock Island.

Burlington Northern

Ownership of C&S was transferred to Burlington Northern when it was created in 1970; by 1981 BN owned more than 92 percent of C&S stock. BN merged C&S on Dec. 31, 1981, and C&S's line south of Denver was transferred to the FW&D. A year later BN merged the FW&D.

FACTS & FIGURES

Year	1929	1980
Miles operated	2,004	678
Locomotives	255	235
Passenger cars	164	—
Freight cars	10,093	2,329

Reporting marks: C&S, RBCS, FW&D, FWDX
Historical society: burlingtonroute.com

Conrail

Penn Central's bankruptcy in 1970 upset the entire railroad industry. Something had to be done—Penn Central could not simply be liquidated. It operated one-third of the nation's passenger trains and was the principal freight carrier in the Northeast. Without PC, the industries of the area would die. Penn Central's management proposed reorganizing under certain conditions—abandonment of 45 per cent of its track, reduction of its work force, and increased payment for operating Amtrak trains—but there was no confidence in PC management.

Carving up PC and parceling it out to its neighbors was out of the question. PC's western neighbors wanted nothing to do with the railroad, and its eastern neighbors had problems of their own.

The Central Railroad of New Jersey had been bankrupt since 1967. Neither Chesapeake & Ohio nor Norfolk & Western wanted the Lehigh Valley. It entered bankruptcy on June 4, 1970, three days after Penn Central. The Reading entered bankruptcy Nov. 23, 1971.

The creation of Erie Lackawanna and Penn Central changed traffic patterns, leaving the Lehigh & Hudson River with almost no business. It declared bankruptcy April 18, 1972. Although a Norfolk & Western subsidiary purchased the Erie Lackawanna (and also the Delaware & Hudson) in 1968, N&W offered no

A matched pair of blue GP35s, led by No. 2358, pulls a long string of hopper cars at Euclid, Ohio in October 1980. *John C. Benson*

assistance when the EL suffered $9 million worth of damage in a hurricane in June 1972. EL entered bankruptcy on June 26, 1972. There were proposals to merge and reorganize the other bankrupt railroads to compete with PC, but those railroads, like Penn Central, had no money for much-needed repairs to track and rolling stock.

A new USRA

United States Railway Association, a federal government corporation, was formed to attempt a rescue. The USRA planned to

parcel out portions of the Reading and Erie Lackawanna to Chessie System and Penn Central's lines along the DelMarVa Peninsula to the Southern Railway. A new railroad, Consolidated Rail Corporation, would acquire the rest. Neither Chessie nor Southern could reach agreement with the labor unions, so Consolidated Rail Corporation (first ConRail, then Conrail), took over the railroad properties and operations of Penn Central, Central of New Jersey, Erie Lackawanna, Lehigh & Hudson River, Lehigh Valley, Reading, and Pennsylvania-Reading Seashore Lines on April 1, 1976. PRSL alone among the seven railroads was not bankrupt, but it had almost no traffic and was on the verge of physical collapse. (Those railroads and a number of their predecessors are also described in this book.)

FACTS & FIGURES

Year	1977	1994
Miles operated	17,000	12,828
Locomotives	4,594	2,583
Passenger cars	—	—
Freight cars	140,458	89,128
Reporting marks: CR		
Historical society: thecrhs.org		

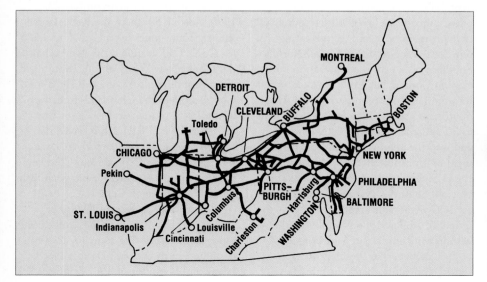

Conrail's early days of operation often featured an eclectic mix of diesels in various repainted and relettered schemes. This is Brookfield, Mass. in June 1982. *Scott A. Hartley*

Conrail started out with $2.1 billion from the U. S. government, which purchased Conrail debentures and preferred stock. The new railroad operated 5,000 locomotives on 17,000 route-miles of railroad; it had 162,000 freight cars, 95,000 employees, and 278 different labor agreements. It had excess plant; it had labor-protection agreements; and it had extensive commuter train operations serving Boston, New York, and Philadelphia.

Conrail identified 6,000 miles of railroad it did not need and abandoned those lines or sold them to short lines and state and local operating authorities. Conrail transferred ownership of the Northeast Corridor (Boston–New York–Washington, Springfield–New Haven, and Philadelphia–Harrisburg) to Amtrak. It began to catch up on years of deferred maintenance, rebuilding track and buying new locomotives and rebuilding old ones. It eliminated duplicate facilities and won a few minor concessions from labor unions.

In the second quarter of 1979 Conrail posted a modest net income, but an economic recession wiped out any chance of another quarter of profitability. Meanwhile, the USRA continued to consider Conrail's future.

In October 1980 U. S. president Jimmy Carter signed into law the Staggers Rail Act, which gave railroad companies freedom to set prices. Not long afterward the United States received a new president, Ronald Reagan, who intended to dismantle Conrail. Congress, however, allowed Conrail to discharge redundant employees and transfer its commuter services to state and regional authorities, giving Conrail a two-year reprieve.

Profit!

Freed of commuter services and able to set its own rates and abandon track it no longer needed, Conrail started to become a profitable freight railroad. L. Stanley Crane assumed the presidency of Conrail at the beginning of 1981, about the time the Reagan administration proposed selling the railroad. Crane continued to trim Conrail's physical plant and payroll. He took advantage of deregulation; he improved the quality of Conrail's service; he sharpened Conrail's image.

Conrail posted a profit for 1981, and kept doing better, even as almost every other railroad was (a) bidding to purchase it at a bargain price and (b) protesting anyone else's doing so. Santa Fe and Norfolk Southern both expressed interest in purchasing Conrail, but Santa Fe soon turned its attention to its proposed merger with Southern Pacific (which was denied). Norfolk Southern continued as the favorite and won the approval of the U. S. Department of Transportation. In February 1986 the U. S. Senate voted to sell Conrail to Norfolk Southern. Numerous other railroads, CSX notable among them, protested. In August 1986 Norfolk Southern withdrew its bid to purchase Conrail.

In October 1986 President Reagan signed a bill authorizing the sale of Conrail stock to the public. It went on sale March 25, 1987, at $28 a share, the largest single initial public stock offering in the history of the New York Stock Exchange. It netted the government $1.6 billion, plus $300 million of Conrail cash and a return of $2 billion worth of tax credits. Conrail settled down to a stable existence as one of America's "Super Seven" freight railroads.

During the recession of 1990 and 1991 Conrail reacted quickly to the anticipated drop in revenue by cutting expenses, storing locomotives and cars, and restructuring its services, with the result that it was still able to declare a stock dividend. In 1990 Conrail bought back about one third of its common stock as part of a restructuring to thwart possible takeover bids. By the end of 1991 the price of Conrail stock had risen to $84.50 a share—an indicator of the company's robust health.

By 1995 the Super Seven had become five: Burlington Northern & Santa Fe and Union Pacific west of Chicago, CSX and Norfolk Southern in the Southeast, Conrail in the Northeast—and CR, CSX, and NS between the Allegheny Mountains and Chicago. In 1995 NS again expressed an interest in purchasing Conrail, but nothing came of it. Then came a surprising announcement on Oct. 15, 1996, that Conrail and CSX planned to merge. Norfolk Southern immediately made a counter-offer. In January 1997 Conrail stockholders voted to reject CSX's offer in favor of NS's. Then the executives of the three railroads met to discuss compromises.

The result was that CSX and NS together together acquired Conrail by a joint stock purchase, approved by the Surface Transportation Board on July 23, 1998. Norfolk Southern received a larger share of route-miles (about 7,200 to 3,800 for CSX). CSX acquired the eastern half of the former New York Central (Boston and New York through Albany and Buffalo to Cleveland) and the Cleveland–Indianapolis–St. Louis route (part NYC—or Big Four—and part PRR). NS received the eastern portion of the Pennsylvania, the former New York Central from Cleveland through Toledo to Chicago, and what little remains of Michigan Central.

Conrail Shared Assets Operations, owned jointly by CSX and NS, still exists as a terminal operating company to serve customers in three areas: Detroit, North Jersey, and South Jersey/Philadelphia.

CSX Transportation

On Nov. 1, 1980, Chessie System Inc. (Baltimore & Ohio, Chesapeake & Ohio, and Western Maryland) and Seaboard Coast Line Industries, Inc. (Seaboard Coast Line and Louisville & Nashville, Clinchfield, and Georgia Group) merged to become the new CSX Corporation. The two components initially maintained separate identities.

SCL Indutries organized its railroads and marketed them as The Family Lines to show unity but collaboration starting in the late 1970s. This led to the 1982 creation of a railroad with a single name, Seaboard System, which lasted only four years.

On July 1, 1986, CSX Transportation was formed, combining the two lines (and all their predecessors) as a single unified railroad. The "C" is from Chessie and the "S" from Seaboard, with the "X" supposedly tying them together as a multiplier, indicating that they are much more together.

The result was a 25,000-mile railroad stretching from Chicago and St. Louis in the Midwest south to New Orleans and Miami in the South to Philadelphia and Buffalo in the Northeast. The railroad included heavy tonnage coal lines of the former Chessie System railroads as well as the Louisville & Nashville and Clinchfield. The fast eastern seaboard routes between Washington, D. C., and Florida added intermodal lanes.

Following deregulation of the railroad industry in 1980, the company aggressively sold or abandoned branches, secondary routes, and parallel main lines. Little changed until 1997, when, following a heated battle for control of the northeastern railroad Conrail, CSX and Norfolk Southern agreed to joinly acquire the railroad.

As it ended up, NS got about 58 percent of Conrail (mostly former Pennsylvania Railroad) or about 6,000 route miles while CSX got about 3,600 route miles of former Conrail lines, most of them former New York Central routes. Among the gems acquired by CSX were the famous Water Level Route into New York City

CSX AC4400CW No. 514 leads unit coal train U120 southbound at Folkston, Ga., in 2009. *Clint Renegar*

and the former Boston & Albany into New England.

With this newly expanded system, CSX started referring to itself as a triangular network with the I-90 corridor at the top (New York Central and Baltimore & Ohio), the I-95 corridor on the right (Richmond, Fredericksburg & Potomac and Atlantic Coast Line), and the Southeastern Corridor forming the left side of the triangle (L&N and ACL). In the middle the railroad's coal business flourished.

Sadly, the Appalachian coal boom of the 1970s and 1980s came to an abrupt halt in the early 2010s after declining natural gas prices, increased envrionmental regulations, and the lack of easily mined coal collided. Miles of former C&O and L&N tracks that were busy railroads just a few years ago are now dormant.

But the news was not all bad. The railroad completed a $175 million intermodal terminal in North Baltimore, Ohio in 2011 to expedite container traffic.

In 2013 CSX completed an $850

million double-stack clearance project called the National Gateway. This work focused on rebuilding the former Baltimore & Ohio main line from Baltimore to Greenwich, Ohio to expedite traffic between east coast ports and Chicago. Begun in 2011, the project's first phase included changes at 40 locations in four states, eight overhead bridges, and 10 tunnels, measuring 15,595 linear feet. Several tunnels were daylighted or bypassed. The next phase will rebuild routes leading to shipping terminals in Portsmouth, Va., and Wilmington, N. C.

FACTS & FIGURES

Year	1986	2013
Miles operated	25,000	21,000
Locomotives	2,093	4,000
Passenger cars	—	—
Freight cars	92,457	66,026
Reporting marks: CSXT		
Website: csx.com		

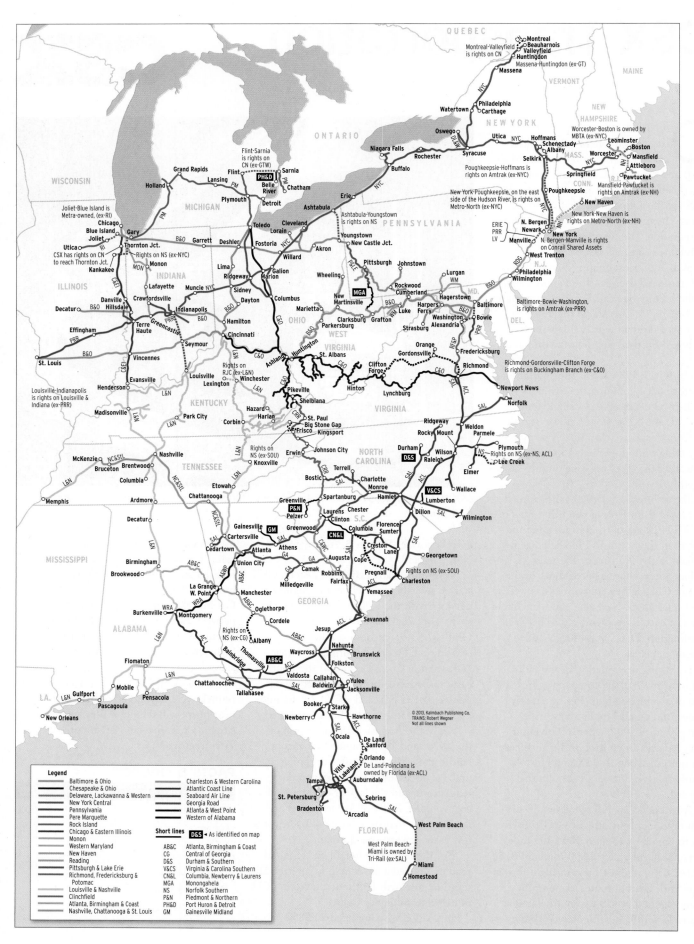

Legend

	Baltimore & Ohio	
	Chesapeake & Ohio	
	Delaware, Lackawanna & Western	
	New York Central	
	Pennsylvania	
	Pere Marquette	
	Rock Island	
	Chicago & Eastern Illinois	
	Monon	
	Western Maryland	
	New Haven	
	Reading	
	Pittsburgh & Lake Erie	
	Richmond, Fredericksburg & Potomac	
	Louisville & Nashville	
	Clinchfield	
	Atlanta, Birmingham & Coast	
	Nashville, Chattanooga & St. Louis	

	Charleston & Western Carolina
	Atlantic Coast Line
	Seaboard Air Line
	Georgia Road
	Atlanta & West Point
	Western of Alabama

Short lines   D&S ◄ As identified on map

AB&C Atlanta, Birmingham & Coast
CG Central of Georgia
D&S Durham & Southern
V&CS Virginia & Carolina Southern
CN&L Columbia, Newberry & Laurens
MGA Monongahela
NS Norfolk Southern
P&N Piedmont & Northern
PH&D Port Huron & Detroit
GM Gainesville Midland

© 2013, Kalmbach Publishing Co.
TRAINS; Robert Wegner
Not all lines shown

Dakota, Minnesota & Eastern

Chicago & North Western's line from the Mississippi River at Winona, Minn. west to Pierre, S. D., was built between 1864 and 1880. In 1906 and 1907 it was extended west to Rapid City. The line was instrumental in settling the South Dakota prairie, and it became a grain gatherer and carrier. The line achieved minor notoriety among rail enthusiasts in the 1970s as the home territory for C&NW's Alco diesels.

In late 1985 the C&NW applied to abandon its light-density line between Pierre and Rapid City. It was the only rail route connecting the eastern and western parts of the state (the Milwaukee Road's line to Rapid City was already gone; part of it is still operated by Dakota Southern, DSRC). The state protested, even while agreeing that C&NW would not have to operate the line at a loss. The solution was to sell it.

The North Western worked with the Railroad Management Services Venture Team, a division of L. B. Foster, a railroad supply firm in Pittsburgh, to put together a package that might attract a buyer. No one jumped to buy the Pierre-Rapid City segment, so the property offered was extended east to Huron, S. D., then Mankato, Minn., and finally all the way to Winona, Minn. The Foster group liked the final package enough to purchase it along with several branches on Sept. 4, 1986, for operation as Dakota, Minnesota & Eastern Railroad.

The DM&E's primary commodity was wheat, usually moving to midwestern flour mills or to a rail-barge transfer at Winona. Corn and soybeans moved in unit trains

Grain was a key commodity for Dakota, Minnesota & Eastern and Iowa, Chicago & Eastern. Here four SD40-2s, led by IC&E No. 6443, pull a long eastbound grain train on the original DM&E main line at Cavour, S. D., east of Huron, on Aug. 26, 2007. *Craig Williams*

bound for the Northwest, but agricultural products were less than half the traffic.

In 1997 the railroad announced plans to build a line into Wyoming's Powder River Basin to tap coal traffic. After much legal wrangling the Surface Transportation Board approved the plan in 2001, but the railroad could not secure financing and the line was not built.

Iowa, Chicago & Eastern

In 2002 DM&E puchased the I&M Rail Link from the Washington Companies, renaming it the Iowa, Chicago & Eastern. The 1,400-mile IC&E comprised mainly

former Milwaukee lines from Chicago west to Savanna, Ill., with routes from there to Kansas City, northwest Iowa, and southwest Minnesota. DM&E used a holding company, Cedar American Rail Holdings, to combine management and dispatching functions for both railroads.

In 2007 Canadian Pacific announced its intent to acquire the DM&E, with the intent of using the DM&E to build the planned line into the Powder River Basin. The STB approved the purchase in September 2008 and Canadian Pacific merged the DM&E and IC&E on Oct. 30, 2008. In December 2012, CP announced it no longer intended to build into the Powder River Basin, and stated it planned to sell the western end of the former DM&E (west of Tracy, Minn.), about 700 miles.

FACTS & FIGURES

Year	1987	2007
Miles operated	965	1,100
Locomotives	46	66
Passenger cars	—	—
Freight cars	—	4,444
Reporting marks: DME		

Delaware & Hudson

The D&H dates from 1823, when the Delaware & Hudson Canal Co. was chartered to build a canal from Honesdale, Pa., to Rondout, N. Y., on the Hudson River. The canal would carry anthracite coal from mines near Carbondale, Pa., to New York City. The mines would be served by a gravity railroad with stationary engines and cables for the uphill runs.

D&H imported four steam locomotives from England in 1829. They proved too heavy, but one, the *Stourbridge Lion*, earned D&H the distinction of operating the first steam locomotive in America.

D&H increased its coal holdings as the demand for anthracite grew. In 1863 the company proposed a railroad north from Carbondale to a connection with the Erie Railroad at Lanesboro. The Erie built the Carbondale–Lanesboro line in 1868, and three years later, the D&H extended it north to a connection with the Albany & Susquehanna at Nineveh, N. Y. D&H leased the A&S for access to Albany and to keep it from falling into the hands of Jay Gould and Jim Fisk.

About that same time, D&H built south to Scranton from Carbondale and found itself more a railroad than a canal company—a railroad with three track gauges. The gravity lines had a 4'-3" gauge, the Albany & Susquehanna was built to the Erie's 6-foot gauge, and the Carbondale–Scranton line was standard gauge.

Rensselaer & Saratoga

The Rensselaer & Saratoga Rail Road was chartered in 1832 to build a line from Troy, New York, north to a connection with the Saratoga & Schenectady, which was under construction from Schenectady north to Saratoga Springs. The R&S obtained control of the S&S in 1835.

Construction of the Saratoga & Washington Rail-Road began in 1836, but the railroad did not reach Whitehall, at the south end of Lake Champlain, until 1848. An eastward extension reached Rutland, Vt., in 1850. The company endured some financial difficulty before being leased by the Rensselaer & Saratoga in 1865, the

The Delaware & Hudson gained fame in the 1960s and early '70s with the purchase of four ex-Santa Fe PAs. Here two of them lead an inspection train across the Mohawk River at Cohoes, N. Y., in March 1974. *Jim Shaughnessy*

same year the R&S also leased the Troy & Rutland and Rutland & Washington railroads, which formed a route from Troy north along the New York-Vermont state line to Rutland.

North to Canada

The Hudson River and Lake Champlain formed a natural route from New York to Montreal, but it was unusable in winter. A rail route through Vermont was in place by 1849, but there was none on the New York shore of Lake Champlain. In 1852 the Plattsburgh & Montreal Rail Road and two Canadian roads were completed from Plattsburgh, almost at the north end of the lake, to Montreal. There was little local business to support it.

In 1866 the Whitehall & Plattsburgh Rail Road was chartered to join Whitehall and Plattsburgh. Two disconnected pieces of line were built, and the company was leased by the Rutland, which sought a route to northern New York and Canada that bypassed the Vermont Central. Soon afterward the VC leased the Rutland.

New York residents knew that power struggles by the two Vermont railroads would not get a railroad built through their area, and the Vermont roads would funnel commerce to Boston, not New York City. The D&H backed local residents in organizing the New York & Canada Railroad,

which absorbed the Whitehall & Plattsburgh and the Montreal & Plattsburgh (successor to the Plattsburgh & Montreal) in 1873. The line was opened between Whitehall and Plattsburgh in 1875, completing an Albany–Montreal route.

In the 1880s the D&H built west from Plattsburgh to an iron-mining area at Lyon Mountain, then south to Lake Placid. By 1900 D&H's interests included hotels and steamboat lines on Lake Champlain and Lake George and a network of electric railways around Albany. In 1898 D&H sold its interests in the Rutland, sold the canal, and converted the gravity railroad to standard gauge.

Two railroads in Canada came into the Delaware & Hudson family. In 1906 D&H purchased the Quebec, Montreal & Southern, which extended from the border to St. Lambert, opposite Montreal, then northeast to Pierreville, Que. More important was the 28-mile Napierville Junction Railway, opened in 1907 from Rouses Point, N. Y., on the border, north to Delson and connections with Canadian Pacific and Canadian National (to use modern-era names).

The Loree era

Leonor F. Loree became president of the D&H in 1907 after working on the Pennsylvania and the Baltimore & Ohio. He

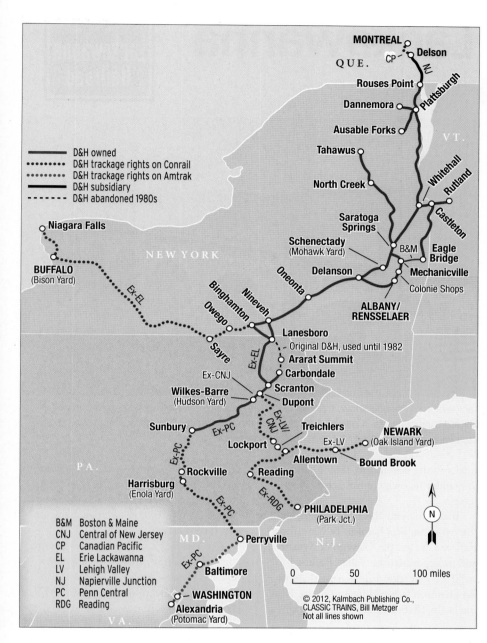

Legend:
— D&H owned
•••• D&H trackage rights on Conrail
•••• D&H trackage rights on Amtrak
— D&H subsidiary
---- D&H abandoned 1980s

B&M   Boston & Maine
CNJ   Central of New Jersey
CP   Canadian Pacific
EL   Erie Lackawanna
LV   Lehigh Valley
NJ   Napierville Junction
PC   Penn Central
RDG   Reading

© 2012, Kalmbach Publishing Co.,
CLASSIC TRAINS, Bill Metzger
Not all lines shown

undertook an upgrading of the D&H, but he had definite ideas about locomotives. He shunned most advances in steam locomotive technology—the initial demonstration of Lima's Super-Power concept took place practically under his nose—and pushed the Consolidation type to its limit. The road's traffic was primarily coal—not a time-sensitive commodity—and speed was secondary to tractive effort.

By the time Loree retired in 1938, oil had begun to replace coal for heating, so D&H turned its attention to developing bridge traffic (traffic received from one railroad and passed to another) from the Midwest to New England and Canada. To accelerate its trains, D&H bought two groups of modern locomotives: 4-6-6-4s

for freight and 4-8-4s for dual service. They arrived on the property just in time for the traffic increases of World War II.

D&H sold its hotels and steamboats in 1939, and abandoned its circuitous route to Lake Placid in 1946. In 1943 it merged the Rensselaer & Saratoga and the Albany & Susquehanna. D&H dieselized quickly in the early 1950s with utilitarian road-switchers instead of streamlined cab diesels.

Search for a merger partner

In 1957 D&H studied merger with Erie and Delaware, Lackawanna & Western, but was deterred by the long-term debt of those roads. D&H sold off its coal interests and asked to be included in the 1964 Norfolk & Western merger because the

impending merger of the Pennsylvania and the New York Central would surround it.

Frederick Dumaine Jr. became president of the D&H in 1966. He upgraded the road's passenger trains for traffic to the 1967 world's fair at Montreal. He proposed two alternate courses for D&H: independence or inclusion in a merger of the major roads of New England. New management took over in 1968 after a proxy fight. Dereco, a subsidiary of N&W, acquired control of D&H, but it was never considered part of the N&W system. D&H entered a period of joint management with Erie Lackawanna, also owned by Dereco.

With the 1976 formation of Conrail, D&H was given trackage rights to Buffalo, N. Y., Newark, N. J., Philadelphia, and Alexandria, Va., via Harrisburg, Pa. (reflected on the map at left). It sought loans from the United States Railway Association to compete with Conrail, yet USRA's mission was to ensure that Conrail succeeded. D&H's parent N&W provided no help. Management changed frequently, but D&H lost more money.

On Jan. 4, 1984, Guilford Transportation Industries purchased the D&H and began to consolidate its operations with Boston & Maine and Maine Central. D&H entered bankruptcy in June 1988, and New York, Susquehanna & Western was designated to operate it while Guilford put it up for sale. CP Rail purchased the D&H in January 1991, eyeing D&H's trackage rights to Washington, Philadelphia, and Newark, in the light of the U. S.-Canada free trade pact of 1990. CP rehabbed the D&H and began regular freight service to Philadelphia and Newark.

The office functions of the D&H were combined with those of parent CP Rail in Montreal, then moved to Calgary, Alberta. D&H's identity, like that of CP's other U. S. subsidiary, Soo Line, gave way to that of CP Rail System—and CP formally absorbed D&H in 2010.

FACTS & FIGURES

Year	1929	1983
Miles operated	898	1,581
Locomotives	445	134
Passenger cars	374	—
Freight cars	15,735	4,341

Reporting marks: D&H

Historical society: bridge-line.org

Delaware, Lackawanna & Western

The Lackawanna's history, like that of many Eastern railroads, is one of mergers, consolidations, and leases. The oldest portion was the Cayuga & Susquehanna Railroad, completed in 1834 between Owego and Ithaca, N.Y. Lackawanna's corporate structure dates from the incorporation of the Liggett's Gap Railroad in 1849. That line was built north from Scranton, Pa., to the Susquehanna River and a connection with the Erie at Great Bend, Pa. It was renamed the Lackawanna & Western in 1851, and it opened later that year.

Also incorporated in 1849 was the Delaware & Cobb's Gap Railroad, to build a line from the Delaware River over the Pocono Mountains to Cobb's Gap, near Scranton. It was consolidated with the Lackawanna & Western in 1853 to form the Delaware, Lackawanna & Western Railroad. It was completed in 1856 and almost immediately made a connection with the Central Railroad of New Jersey at Hampton, N.J., through the Warren Railroad, which was leased by the DL&W in 1857.

The Morris & Essex Railroad was chartered in 1835 to construct a line from Morristown, N.J., to New York Harbor. By 1860 the line extended west to the Delaware River at Phillipsburg, N.J. The

Lackawanna's *Phoebe Snow*, train No. 3, heads west across the Delaware River viaduct at Slateford Junction, Pa. A pair of EMD E8s lead the train, painted in maroon, gray, and yellow.
Stanwood K. Bolton; David P. Morgan Library collection

Lackawanna leased it in 1869 to acquire a line under its own control across New Jersey.

That same year the Lackawanna bought the Syracuse, Binghamton & New York Railroad, leased the Oswego & Syracuse, and incorporated the Valley Railroad to build a connection from Great Bend to Binghamton to avoid having to use Erie tracks. In 1870 DL&W leased the Utica,

Chenango & Susquehanna Valley and the Greene Railroad. Thus in the space of a couple of years the Lackawanna grew to extend from tidewater to Utica, Syracuse, and Lake Ontario.

On March 15, 1876, the Lackawanna converted its lines from 6-foot gauge (chosen because of the Liggett's Gap Railroad's connection with the Erie) to standard gauge. That year also marked the beginning of a short period of financial difficulty—not enough to cause reorganization, receivership, or bankruptcy, but enough for suspension of dividend payments.

In 1880 Jay Gould began buying Lackawanna stock. His empire reached as far east as Buffalo, east end of the Wabash, and he saw that the Lackawanna would be an ideal route to New York if the gap between Binghamton and Buffalo could be closed. Lackawanna management prevented Gould from acquiring control of the road, but Gould's proposed extension to Buffalo was built: The New York, Lackawanna & Western was incorporated in 1880 and leased to the DL&W in 1882, changing the DL&W from a regional railroad to a New York–Buffalo trunk line.

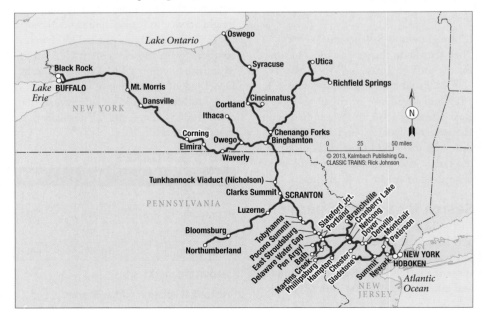

An A-B-A set of Electro-Motive F3s leads Train No. 47 through Stroudsburg, Pa., in May 1954. Several milk cars are at the head end, tucked behind the diesels. *Jack Emerick*

Diversification and upgrading

The 1880s brought diversification in Lackawanna's traffic. Anthracite coal, much of it from railroad-owned mines, had been the reason for the Lackawanna's existence. During the 1880s the coal traffic increased one-third, but Lackawanna's general merchandise traffic increased five times that amount. Meanwhile the DL&W was rapidly becoming a commuter carrier at its east end.

William H. Truesdale became president of the Lackawanna in 1899 and embarked on a rebuilding and upgrading program for the railroad. The two major items were a new line north of Scranton and a 28-mile cutoff straight across western New Jersey between Slateford and Port Morris that bypassed some 40 miles of slow, curvy, hilly track. Both new lines were characterized by massive cuts and fills and long, graceful reinforced-concrete viaducts—Paulins Kill, Tunkhannock, Delaware River, and Martins Creek. Lackawanna's suburban territory came in for track elevation, grade-crossing elimination, and new stations, all as prelude to the 1930 electrification of lines to Dover, Gladstone, and Montclair.

Merger, eventually

By the late 1930s the New York Central had purchased 25 percent of DL&W stock, giving it working—but unexercised—control of the DL&W. During World War II the Lackawanna merged a number of its subsidiaries and leased lines for tax purposes. After the war the Lackawanna began to purchase Nickel Plate stock with an eye to possible merger, but Nickel Plate and New York Central were both opposed to it.

In 1949, *Phoebe Snow* returned to the Lackawanna. Early in the century she had been Lackawanna's symbol with a gown that stayed white from morn till night upon the Road of Anthracite—anthracite was much cleaner-burning than the bituminous coal used by other roads. *Phoebe Snow*'s return to the road was in the form of a diesel-powered maroon-and-gray streamliner for daytime service between Hoboken and Buffalo.

In 1954 the Lackawanna and parallel rival Erie began to explore the idea of cooperation. The first results were the elimination of duplicate freight facilities at Binghamton and Elmira, and then in 1956 and 1957 the Erie moved its passenger trains from its old Jersey City terminal to Lackawanna's somewhat newer one at Hoboken. The two roads eliminated some duplicate track in western New York. The discussions of cooperation turned into merger talks, at first including the Delaware & Hudson.

Meanwhile DL&W's financial situation took a turn for the worse. Hurricanes in 1955 damaged Lackawanna's line through the Poconos. The cost of repairs no doubt contributed to the deficits of 1958 and 1959. DL&W threatened to discontinue all suburban passenger service if the state of New Jersey would not alleviate the losses and rectify the tax situation. The state responded with a minimal subsidy.

DL&W and Erie merged as the Erie-Lackawanna on Oct. 17, 1960.

FACTS & FIGURES

Year	1929	1983
Miles operated	898	1,581
Locomotives	445	134
Passenger cars	374	—
Freight cars	15,735	4,341
Reporting marks: DLW		
Historical society: dlwrrs.com		

Denver & Rio Grande Western

An eastbound Denver & Rio Grande Western *Rail Blazer* passes through the Denver suburb of Arvada, Colo., about to conclude its overnight run from Salt Lake City on Aug. 8, 1986. GP40-2 No. 3093 leads the hotshot intermodal train. *Steve Patterson*

The Denver & Rio Grande Railway was incorporated by William Jackson Palmer in 1870 to build a railroad from Denver south along the eastern edge of the Rockies to El Paso, Texas. Palmer, who had risen to the rank of brigadier general during the Civil War, chose a track gauge of 3 feet for reasons of economy. The line was completed to the new town of Colorado Springs in 1871. In 1872 it was extended south to Pueblo, then west to tap coal deposits near Canon City, Colo. There the railroad remained for a few years.

In 1878 the Rio Grande engaged in two railroad wars with the Santa Fe—perhaps "skirmishes" is more accurate than "wars." Palmer's forces narrowly lost Raton Pass in southern Colorado, but won occupancy of the Royal Gorge of the Arkansas River west of Canon City. Shortly afterward the D&RG was leased to the Santa Fe for a year. In 1879 the Rio Grande was

on its own again under the management of Palmer and Jay Gould. It made an agreement with the Santa Fe a year later to head in different directions: the Santa Fe south into New Mexico and the D&RG west into the Rockies. In 1881 the Rio Grande reached Gunnison and Durango, and foreshadowing changes to come, it added a third rail for standard gauge trains to its tracks between Denver and Pueblo.

In 1882 D&RG leased the affiliated Denver & Rio Grande Western Railway, which was building and consolidating lines southeastward from Salt Lake City. In 1883 the two railroads met near Green River, Utah, forming a narrow gauge route from Denver to Salt Lake City via Pueblo and Marshall Pass. In the early 1880s the D&RG built a new route from Leadville north over Tennessee Pass (10,239 feet, the highest point reached by a standard gauge main line in North America), then along

the Eagle and Grand rivers, reaching Glenwood Springs in 1887. Two years later it was extended west to Rifle. The line from there to Grand Junction was built by the Rio Grande Junction Railway, which was jointly owned with the standard gauge Colorado Midland Railway—which in 1890 came under the control of the Santa Fe. Meanwhile, D&RG had been adding a third rail to its line east of Leadville. The lines west of Grand Junction were converted to standard gauge, and by 1890 D&RG had standard gauge track all the way from Denver to Ogden, Utah.

At the same time, D&RG's narrow gauge network continued to expand south and west of the Pueblo-Grand Junction main line. In 1880 a line was extended south from Antonito, Colo., to Espanola, N. M. Rails reached Silverton from Durango in 1882, and in 1890 a line was built north from Alamosa to connect with

The *San Juan*, which ran between Alamosa and Durango, was the last narrow gauge train in the U. S. to offer first-class service and the last narrow gauge passenger train west of the Mississippi. Here the west- and eastbound *San Juans* meet at Carracas, Colo., in 1952. *Robert F. Collins*

existing lines southwest of Salida. In 1886 the Texas, Santa Fe & Northern Railroad constructed a line north from Santa Fe to Espanola. The company was reorganized as the Santa Fe Southern in 1888, and the Rio Grande acquired it in 1895.

The Rio Grande was deeply involved in financing the construction of the Western Pacific Railway between Salt Lake City and San Francisco, completed in 1910. When WP entered bankruptcy in 1915, it pulled the Rio Grande in after it. The Rio Grande was sold in 1920 to interests affiliated with the WP. The new company was the Denver & Rio Grande Western Railroad. It entered receivership in 1921 and emerged in 1924 under the joint ownership of Western Pacific and Missouri Pacific, and encumbered with debt that put it back in trusteeship again in 1935. There was a difference this time. The trustees were not East Coast bankers but local men: Wilson McCarthy of Salt Lake City and Henry Swan of Denver.

The Moffat Tunnel and Dotsero Cutoff

David Moffat's Denver, Northwestern & Pacific Railway had built westward from

Denver over Rollins Pass. In 1912 it was reorganized as the Denver & Salt Lake Railroad (see page 122), but it got no closer to the goal in its name than Craig, in northwestern Colorado. The city of Denver, which for decades had wanted a direct rail route to the west, constructed the six-mile Moffat Tunnel under James Peak for the D&SL (and also to bring Western Slope water to Denver). The tunnel, opened in 1928, let Denver & Salt Lake avoid the steep and often snowy climb over Rollins Pass, but D&SL had little traffic to send through the tunnel.

At Bond, the D&SL was about 40 miles up the Colorado River from D&RGW's main line at what became Dotsero. Both railroads wanted to build a cutoff connecting the routes; the Interstate Commerce Commission gave the nod to the Rio Grande. The Dotsero Cutoff was opened in 1934 and the Rio Grande acquired trackage rights on the D&SL between Denver and Bond. Denver finally was on a transcontinental main line, and D&RGW's route between Denver and Salt Lake City was 175 miles shorter. The D&RGW came out of trusteeship and merged the D&SL on April 11, 1947.

The *California Zephyr*

In 1939 the D&RGW, Western Pacific, and Chicago, Burlington & Quincy teamed up to operate a through passenger train, the *Exposition Flyer*, between Chicago and Oakland via Denver and the Moffat Tunnel. The *Flyer* did not set the world on fire with its speed, but westbound it offered magnificent views of the Rockies west of Denver and California's Feather River Canyon.

In 1949 the train became the *California Zephyr*. The *CZ* was slower than its competition, but it was scheduled and equipped—five Vista-Domes per train—to take advantage of the scenery it traversed. The *CZ* was more than a train—it was a long-distance land cruise. It was an immediate success, and its passenger count remained high even into the late 1960s. In 1970 the Western Pacific managed to disencumber itself of the passenger business, and the *CZ* degenerated into a triweekly Chicago-Salt Lake City-Ogden operation designated "California service." When Amtrak took over the nation's passenger trains in 1971, the Rio Grande elected to continue operating its sole passenger train, the Denver-Salt Lake City *Rio Grande*

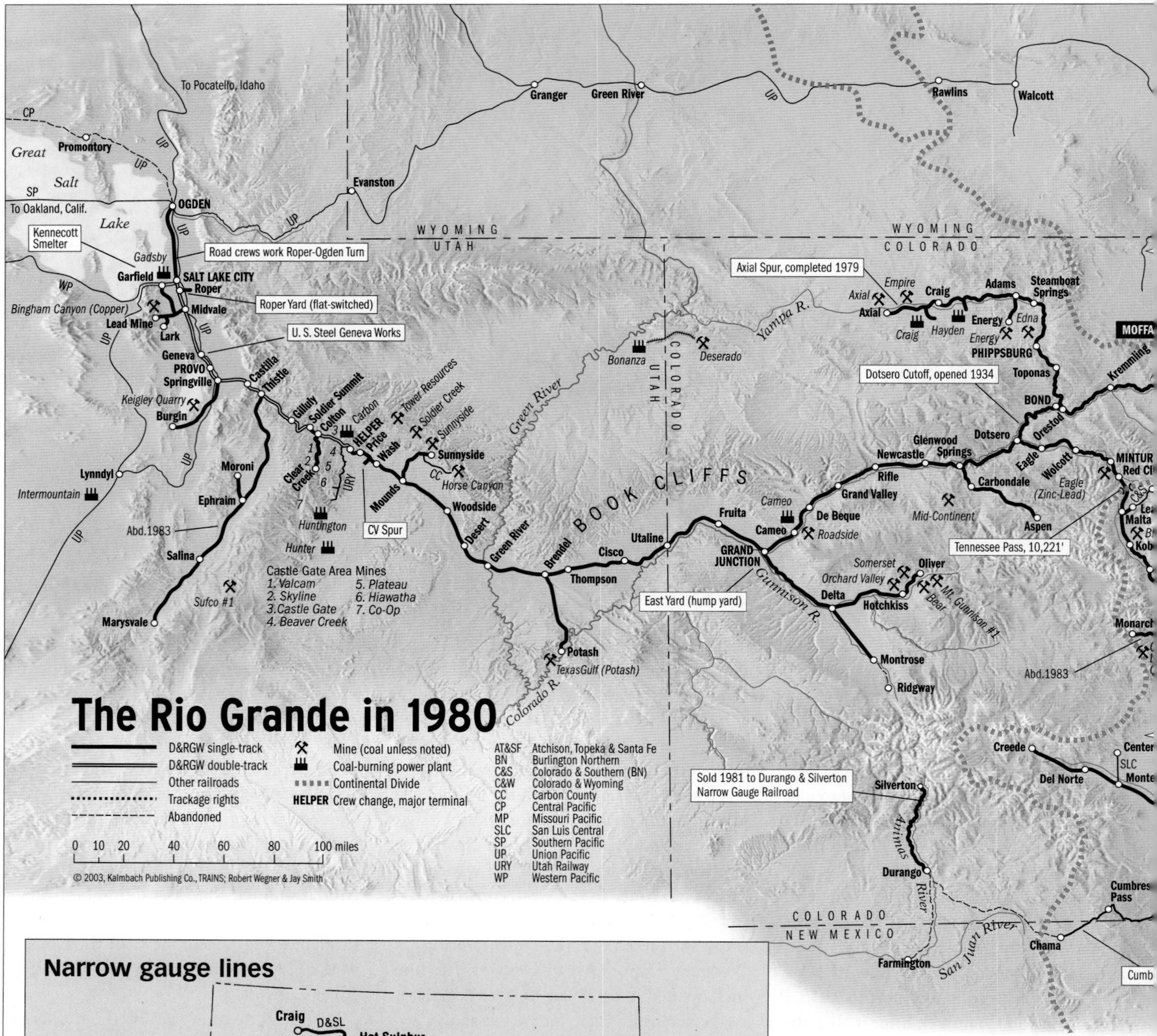

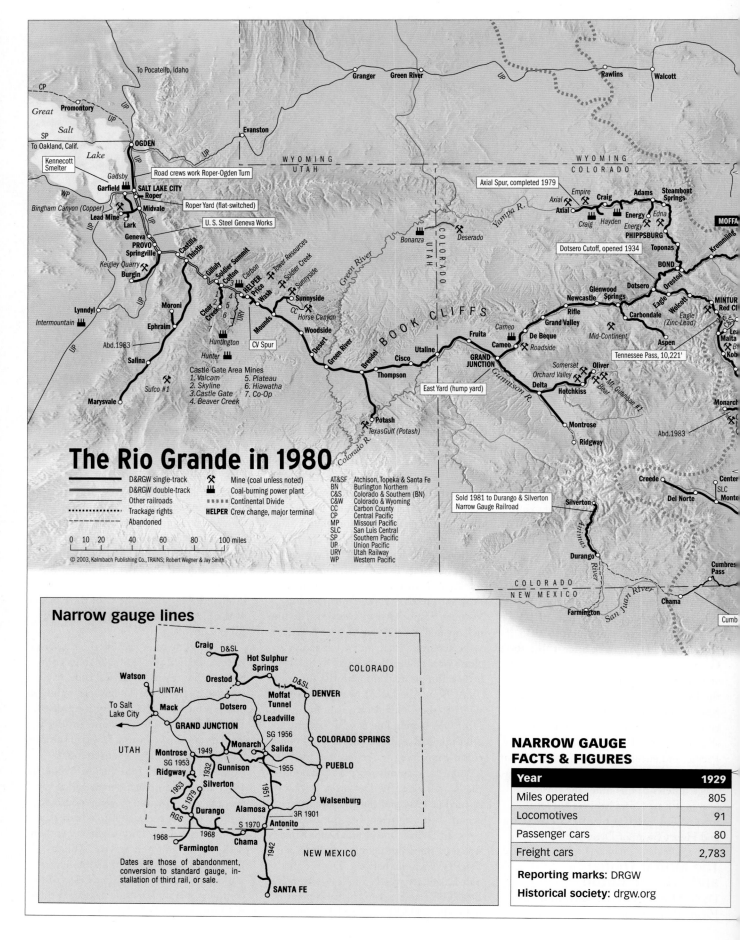

The Rio Grande in 1980
D&RGW single-track
D&RGW double-track
Other railroads
Trackage rights
Abandoned
Mine (coal unless noted)
Coal-burning power plant
Continental Divide
HELPER Crew change, major terminal
AT&SF Atchison, Topeka & Santa Fe
BN Burlington Northern
C&S Colorado & Southern (BN)
C&W Colorado & Wyoming
CC Carbon County
CP Central Pacific
MP Missouri Pacific
SLC San Luis Central
SP Southern Pacific
UP Union Pacific
URY Utah Railway
WP Western Pacific
0 10 20 40 60 80 100 miles
© 2003, Kalmbach Publishing Co., TRAINS; Robert Wegner & Jay Smith
To Pocatello, Idaho
Great Salt Lake
Promontory
To Oakland, Calif.
OGDEN
Kennecott Smelter
Gadsby
Garfield
SALT LAKE CITY
Roper
Bingham Canyon (Copper)
Lead Mine
Midvale
Lark
Geneva
PROVO
Springville
Keigley Quarry
Burgin
Castilla
Thistle
Road crews work Roper-Ogden Turn
Roper Yard (flat-switched)
U. S. Steel Geneva Works
Evanston
Granger
Green River
Rawlins
Walcott
WYOMING
UTAH
COLORADO
Gilluly
Soldier Summit
Colton
Carbon
HELPER
Price
Wash
Tower Resources
Soldier Creek
Sunnyside
Horse Canyon
Clear Creek
Huntington
Hunter
CV Spur
Mounds
Woodside
Desert
Green River
Brendel
Thompson
Cisco
Utaline
BOOK CLIFFS
Castle Gate Area Mines
1. Valcam
2. Skyline
3. Castle Gate
4. Beaver Creek
5. Plateau
6. Hiawatha
7. Co-Op
Lynndyl
Intermountain
Moroni
Ephraim
Abd.1983
Salina
Sufco #1
Marysvale
Potash
TexasGulf (Potash)
Colorado R.
Green River
Bonanza
Deserado
Yampa R.
Axial Spur, completed 1979
Axial
Empire
Craig
Hayden
Adams
Steamboat Springs
Energy
Edna
PHIPPSBURG
Toponas
MOFFA
Kremmling
Dotsero Cutoff, opened 1934
BOND
Orestod
Dotsero
Glenwood Springs
Newcastle
Rifle
Grand Valley
Eagle
Wolcott
Eagle (Zinc-Lead)
MINTUR
Carbondale
Aspen
Mid-Continent
Cameo
De Beque
Roadside
Fruita
GRAND JUNCTION
East Yard (hump yard)
Gunnison R.
Somerset
Orchard Valley
Oliver
Bear
Mt. Gunnison #1
Delta
Hotchkiss
Montrose
Ridgway
Tennessee Pass, 10,221'
Abd.1983
Monarch
Creede
Del Norte
Center
Sold 1981 to Durango & Silverton Narrow Gauge Railroad
Silverton
Animas River
Durango
Farmington
San Juan River
Cumbres Pass
Chama
NEW MEXICO

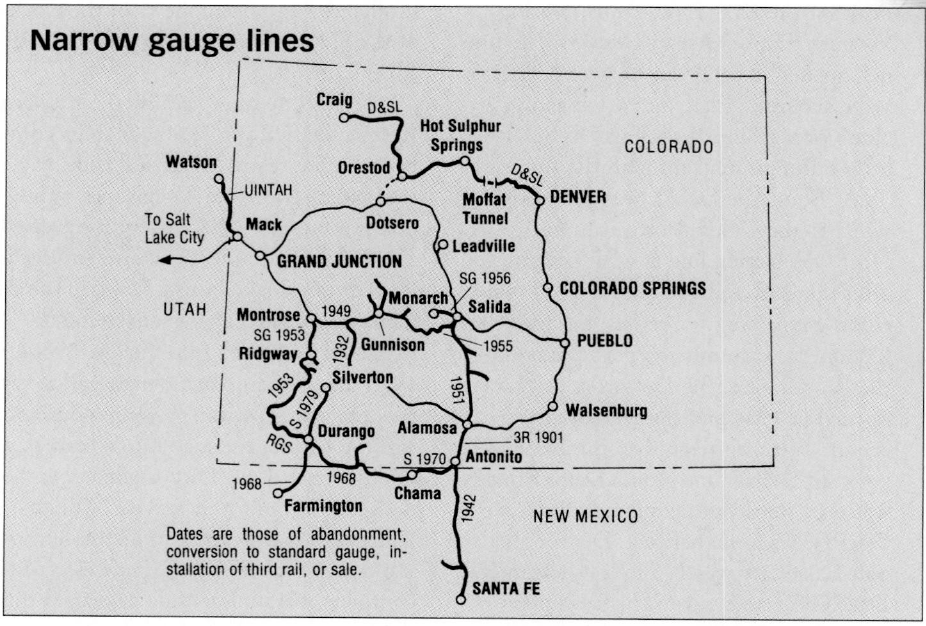

Narrow gauge lines
Craig
D&SL
Hot Sulphur Springs
COLORADO
Orestod
Watson
UINTAH
Moffat Tunnel
DENVER
To Salt Lake City
Mack
Dotsero
Leadville
GRAND JUNCTION
SG 1956
COLORADO SPRINGS
UTAH
Monarch
Salida
Montrose
1949
SG 1953
1932
Gunnison
1955
PUEBLO
Ridgway
1953
Silverton
1951
S 1979
Walsenburg
Durango
Alamosa
RGS
3R 1901
S 1970
Antonito
1968
1968
Farmington
Chama
1942
NEW MEXICO
SANTA FE
Dates are those of abandonment, conversion to standard gauge, installation of third rail, or sale.

NARROW GAUGE FACTS & FIGURES

Year	1929
Miles operated	805
Locomotives	91
Passenger cars	80
Freight cars	2,783

Reporting marks: DRGW

Historical society: drgw.org

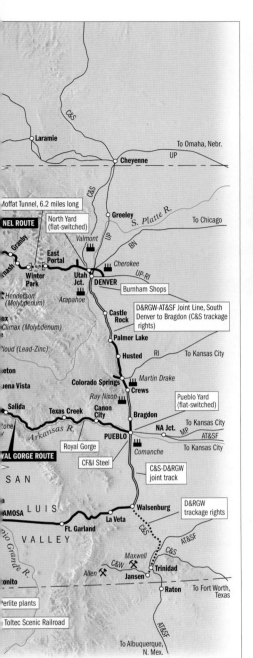

The westbound Vista-Dome *California Zephyr* leaves Denver Union Station behind an Alco PA and PB and an EMD F booster unit in July 1952. *Donald Sims*

Zephyr, a remnant of the *CZ*. D&RGW joined Amtrak in 1983, and the triweekly *RGZ* was replaced by the daily operation of Amtrak's three-pronged service from Chicago to San Francisco, Los Angeles, and Seattle. A seasonal ski train between Denver and Winter Park operated until 2009.

Narrow gauge lines

By the 1920s Rio Grande had worked its narrow gauge lines down to two routes: from Salida west to Montrose via Marshall Pass, the original main line, then south to Ridgway and a connection with the Rio Grande Southern Railroad, which D&RG had controlled since 1893; and from Alamosa west to Durango. From Antonito the "Chili Line" ran south to Santa Fe, N. M.; at Durango there were branches to Farmington, N. M., and Silverton, and another connection with the Rio Grande Southern. A narrow gauge line between Salida and Alamosa connected the two routes. It was possible to ride a complete circle on narrow gauge lines, until a bus replaced the passenger trains on the Salida-Alamosa branch in the mid-1920s.

The Chili Line was abandoned in 1942 for lack of traffic, and the narrow gauge circle was broken at Cerro Summit on the Marshall Pass route in 1949. The pace of narrow gauge abandonments accelerated (a few short segments were standard gauged), so that by the mid-1950s only the Alamosa-Durango-Farmington-Silverton line was left, and it remained operational until

1967. Two segments of that route, from Antonito to Chama and from Durango to Silverton, survive as tourist carriers.

Merger with Southern Pacific

Even though coal from mines in northwestern Colorado became increasingly important to the D&RGW, the road's principal role was that of a fast-freight bridge route between Denver and Pueblo on the east and Salt Lake City and Ogden on the west. Mergers and abandonments changed the railroad map in the 1980s. The Rock Island, a good source of interchange traffic at Denver, ceased operation. The Union Pacific acquired Rio Grande's principal eastern connection, the Missouri Pacific, and principal western connection, Western Pacific. D&RGW acquired trackage rights east over the former MP route to Kansas City as a condition of the UP-MP merger. Then Rio Grande's other western connection, Southern Pacific, began talking merger with Santa Fe. Had the SP-SF merger occurred, D&RGW would have gotten an exclusive lease of SP's line from Ogden west to Roseville, Calif., and Klamath Falls, Ore., plus trackage rights to Bakersfield, Oakland, and Ogden.

Philip Anschutz, a Denver businessman, acquired control of D&RGW in 1984. When the Interstate Commerce Commission rejected the SP-Santa Fe merger, Anschutz submitted an offer to purchase SP, and the ICC approved it on Aug. 9, 1988.

STANDARD GAUGE FACTS & FIGURES

Year	1929	1987
Miles operated	1,720	2,247
Locomotives	375	314
Passenger cars	188	—
Freight cars	13,098	11,361

Reporting marks: DRGW

Historical society: drgw.org

Denver & Salt Lake

When the Union Pacific pushed westward in the 1860s the city of Denver was the largest center of population between the Missouri River and the Pacific. The railroad did not pass through Denver, though, because the Rocky Mountains immediately west constituted an almost insurmountable barrier.

The Denver Pacific Railroad was organized to connect Denver with Cheyenne, Wyo., on the UP line; treasurer of the enterprise was David H. Moffat, a Denver businessman and banker. Its first train arrived in Denver on June 24, 1870, drawn by a locomotive named for Moffat. For the next 30 years Moffat tried to plan and build a railroad directly west from Denver.

Denver, Northwestern & Pacific

In 1902 Moffat decided to build a railroad west from Denver to serve as a connection from the Burlington and the Rock Island at Denver to the San Pedro, Los Angeles & Salt Lake at Salt Lake City. Construction of the Denver, Northwestern & Pacific Railway began almost immediately. The line was, and is, one of the most spectacular in North America.

In June 1904 the DNW&P began operating trains to Tolland—and was ousted from Denver Union Station, which was controlled by the UP and Denver & Rio Grande. By September 1904 rails had reached the top of Rollins Pass on what was intended to be a temporary line until a tunnel could be bored under the divide. The summit of the pass was 11,680 feet above sea level, and it was reached by 4 percent grades and tight curves. The road was shut down for much of that winter.

Late in the summer of 1905 DNW&P rails reached Hot Sulphur Springs, and soon afterward Moffat ran out of money. In 1907 a group of Denver men formed a company to extend the road to Steamboat Springs, completed in December 1908. A more important goal was the coalfields near Oak Creek.

In July 1912 the Moffat Road was reorganized as the Denver & Salt Lake Railroad. The new company entered receivership in January 1913. In November 1913 D&SL rails reached Craig, in northwestern

Ten-Wheeler No. 302 leads train 1, the Denver-Craig local, at Tolland, a few miles east of Moffat Tunnel, in November 1939. *R. H. Kindig*

Colorado. The D&SL struggled along and entered receivership again in 1917. In 1918 the employees went on strike for seven months. A tunnel fire and the subsequent collapse of the tunnel in South Boulder Canyon in March 1922 threatened to shut down the road permanently.

Moffat Tunnel

The city of Denver recognized the importance of the road and pressed for the construction of a tunnel under the Continental Divide. The state legislature in 1922 provided funds for the 6-mile tunnel.

The D&SL made a profit for the first time in 1925, and capital was becoming less scarce. The road emerged from reorganization as the Denver & Salt Lake Railway in 1926. The Moffat Tunnel opened on February 26, 1928, vastly improving the operation of the railroad and shortening the route by approximately 23 miles. The line over the pass was abandoned. (For D&SL routes, see D&RG map on page 120.)

Thought was given to the road's goal of Salt Lake City. A more practical route than one west from Craig was to follow the Colorado River 38 miles downstream to a connection with the Denver & Rio Grande Western at Dotsero, where the Eagle River joins the Colorado. The

D&SL incorporated the project in 1924 as the Denver & Salt Lake Western, but the Rio Grande fought for the right to build the new cutoff, knowing that the owner of the cutoff would control the route.

The Interstate Commerce Commission, after considering the financial condition of both roads, granted the right to the Rio Grande. Construction began in late 1932, and in June 1934 the route was opened, cutting 175 miles out of D&RGW's Denver–Salt Lake City route. The east end of the cutoff was at Orestod (Dotsero spelled backwards), and a new station named Bond was designated on the cutoff just west of Orestod. The Rio Grande acquired trackage rights on the D&SL from Denver to Orestod. D&RGW began to acquire D&SL stock and merged the D&SL on April 11, 1947.

FACTS & FIGURES

Year	1929	1945
Miles operated	238	232
Locomotives	58	39
Passenger cars	25	9
Freight cars	1,020	590

Reporting marks: D&SL
Historical society: moffatroad.org

Detroit & Toledo Shore Line

Two of Detroit & Toledo Shore Line's 10 EMD GP7s, wearing a paint scheme inspired by former half-owner Nickel Plate, roll a train led by a high-cube auto-parts boxcar into Toledo's Lang Yard in January 1978. *Eric Hirsimaki*

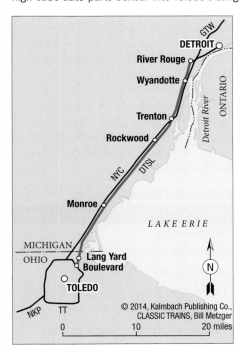

The Pleasant Bay Railway was incorporated in Toledo, Ohio, on March 29, 1898. A year later it purchased the Toledo & Ottawa Beach Railway, acquiring a substantial debt along with it, and was renamed Detroit & Toledo Shore Line Railroad. Plans were to create a fast electric line between Detroit and Toledo.

The track reached from Toledo north to Trenton, Mich., about three-fourths of the distance to Detroit, when the stockholders sold the line jointly to the Grand Trunk and the Toledo, St. Louis & Western (the Clover Leaf) in 1902. The acquisition was a logical one for both roads, giving Grand Trunk a connection to Toledo and the Clover Leaf a connection to Detroit. The road was opened in 1903.

Detroit & Toledo Shore Line carried no passengers and originated little freight—it was principally a bridge route for its owners. The two principal commodities it carried were automobiles and coal to fuel Detroit's automobile factories.

The Clover Leaf half interest passed to the Nickel Plate in 1923 and then to Norfolk & Western when N&W merged NKP in 1964. In April 1981 Grand Trunk Western purchased Norfolk & Western's half interest in the D&TSL, merged the road, and integrated D&TSL operations with its own.

FACTS & FIGURES

Year	1929	1980
Miles operated	50	50
Locomotives	31	16
Passenger cars	—	—
Freight cars	402	565
Reporting marks: D&TS		

Detroit, Toledo & Ironton

In May 1905 two bankrupt railroads, the Detroit Southern and the Ohio Southern, merged to form the Detroit, Toledo & Ironton Railway. The Detroit Southern, previously the Detroit & Lima Northern, extended southwest from Detroit to Lima, Ohio. Ohio Southern's antecedents included the Springfield, Jackson & Pomeroy, a 3-foot-gauge coal hauler that was intended to become part of a narrow gauge system stretching from Toledo, Ohio, to Mexico City. The new railroad then took control of the Ann Arbor to gain entry to Toledo. Ann Arbor regained independence in 1910, and the DT&I was reorganized in 1914 as the Detroit, Toledo & Ironton Railroad.

Detroit, Toledo & Ironton diesels began receiving a modernized version of the compass logo in 1979. Here GP40-2 No. 424 leads train DC-9 at Springfield, Ohio, in 1980. *Jim Hediger*

In 1920 Henry Ford wanted to straighten the shipping channel through which Great Lakes freighters reached his new River Rouge plant at Dearborn, Michigan. The project included a new bridge for DT&I, and the railroad suggested that Ford lend them the money in exchange for DT&I bonds. Ford decided instead to purchase the railroad.

He rebuilt it, instituted some unusual labor practices (wages considerably higher than average, white caps and clean overalls required, beards and mustaches not allowed, and no trains on Sundays), electrified a 17-mile portion between the Rouge Plant and Flat Rock, Mich., and built a 46-mile cutoff between Dundee, Mich., and Malinta, Ohio. In 1929 Ford sold the railroad to the Pennroad Corporation, which was closely associated with the Pennsylvania Railroad. The 1930s saw the end of passenger service, except for a Springfield–Jackson, Ohio, mixed train that lasted until 1955. Dieselization began in the late 1940s and was complete by the end of 1955.

In 1951 the Pennsylvania Company, a subsidiary of the Pennsylvania Railroad, and the Wabash Railroad purchased Pennroad's stock in DT&I. In 1965 Wabash sold its share, 18 percent, to the Pennsylvania Company (which held 87 percent of the stock of the Wabash). In 1963 DT&I purchased the Ann Arbor Railroad from the Wabash. Ann Arbor went bankrupt in 1973, and portions of its line were sold to the state of Michigan; DT&I retained trackage rights from Diann, Mich., to Toledo.

With the formation of Conrail in 1976 DT&I acquired trackage rights over Conrail from Springfield, Ohio, to Cincinnati. The Pennsylvania Company, by then a subsidiary of Penn Central, put the DT&I up for sale. Grand Trunk Western, a subsidiary of Canadian National Railways, offered to purchase the DT&I, and Chessie System and Norfolk & Western offered a joint counterproposal. The ICC approved the sale to Grand Trunk; the sale was consummated on June 24, 1980.

The south end of the DT&I, from Jackson to Ironton, Ohio, was abandoned in 1982, and the line was dismantled. That same year the line from Washington Court House to Waverly was abandoned in favor of trackage rights on former Baltimore & Ohio and Chesapeake & Ohio lines; two year later the line was abandoned south of Washington Court House, including the recently acquired trackage rights.

In 1990 GTW sold the DT&I line between Springfield and Washington Court House to the Indiana & Ohio, and in 1997 sold the Diann-Springfield portion to the I&O.

FACTS & FIGURES

Year	1929	1981
Miles operated	517	623
Locomotives	67	72
Passenger cars	11	—
Freight cars	2,746	3,778
Reporting marks: DTI		
Historical society: cg-tower.com/dti/		

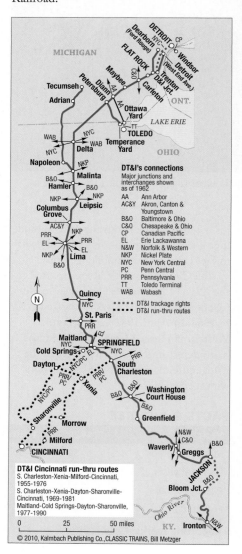

MICHIGAN

DETROIT
Dearborn
(Ford Rouge)
FLAT ROCK
Maybee
Diann
Petersburg
Tecumseh
Adrian
Ottawa Yard
LAKE ERIE
TOLEDO
Temperance Yard
WAB
NYC
Delta
Napoleon
NKP
Malinta
B&O
Hamler
NKP
Columbus Grove
Leipsic
AC&Y
PRR
EL
NKP
Lima
B&O
Quincy
NYC
St. Paris
PRR
Maitland
NYC
Cold Springs
Dayton
Xenia
SPRINGFIELD
South Charleston
Washington Court House
Greenfield
Sharonville
Morrow
Milford
CINCINNATI
Waverly
Greggs
JACKSON
Bloom Jct.
Ohio River
Ironton
KY.
Windsor
Detroit
CP
ONT.
Trenton
DT&I Jct.
Carleton
OHIO
N&W
C&O
B&O
N&W

DT&I's connections
Major junctions and interchanges shown as of 1962

AA	Ann Arbor
AC&Y	Akron, Canton & Youngstown
B&O	Baltimore & Ohio
C&O	Chesapeake & Ohio
CP	Canadian Pacific
EL	Erie Lackawanna
N&W	Norfolk & Western
NKP	Nickel Plate
NYC	New York Central
PC	Penn Central
PRR	Pennsylvania
TT	Toledo Terminal
WAB	Wabash

••••• DT&I trackage rights
- - - - DT&I run-thru routes

N

DT&I Cincinnati run-thru routes
S. Charleston-Xenia-Milford-Cincinnati, 1955-1976
S. Charleston-Xenia-Dayton-Sharonville-Cincinnati, 1969-1981
Maitland-Cold Springs-Dayton-Sharonville, 1977-1990

0   25   50 miles

© 2010, Kalmbach Publishing Co., CLASSIC TRAINS, Bill Metzger

Duluth, Missabe & Iron Range

The Duluth & Iron Range Rail Road was chartered in 1874 to bring iron ore from the Vermilion Range of northeastern Minnesota down to the Lake Superior ore docks at Two Harbors. The Duluth, Missabe & Northern Railway was incorporated in 1891 to link the open-pit iron mines of the Mesabi Range with docks at Duluth. Both railroads came under the ownership of U. S. Steel in 1901.

Duluth & Iron Range

In the late 1860s gold was discovered—so reports said—at Vermilion Lake in the wilderness north of Duluth, Minn. The gold turned out to be iron pyrites, often called fool's gold, but it led to a more important discovery—an immense deposit of high-grade iron ore, the Vermilion Range.

The Duluth & Iron Range Rail Road was chartered on December 21, 1874, to build a line from Duluth to Babbitt. The Minnesota legislature granted the company land through the wilderness, but the railroad remained no more than a charter.

The iron ore interested two Philadelphians, Charlemagne Tower and George C. Stone. Stone acquired ore lands from the public domain for Tower's Minnesota Iron Co., and Tower formed the Duluth & Iron Mountain Railroad in 1881. Tower was unable to get a land grant for his railroad, so he acquired control of the D&IR and vested its ownership in the Minnesota Iron Co.

Surveys and construction got under way, and the company built an ore dock at Agate Bay (now Two Harbors). The first trainload of iron ore rolled down to the docks at Two Harbors on July 31, 1884. In 1886 the road constructed a 26-mile extension southwest along the shore of Lake Superior to Duluth.

Illinois Steel Co. developed a mine at Ely, 20 miles northeast of the Minnesota Iron Co. operation, and proposed to build a railroad from Duluth. Tower sold Minnesota Iron and the D&IR to Illinois Steel, whose backers included Henry H. Porter, Marshall Field, Cyrus McCormick, and John D. Rockefeller. (Porter had built the

Big Yellowstone (2-8-8-4) No. 230 hauls an ore extra through Alborn, Minn., in 1959. The locomotives were simply known as "Mallets" on the Missabe. *Franklin A. King*

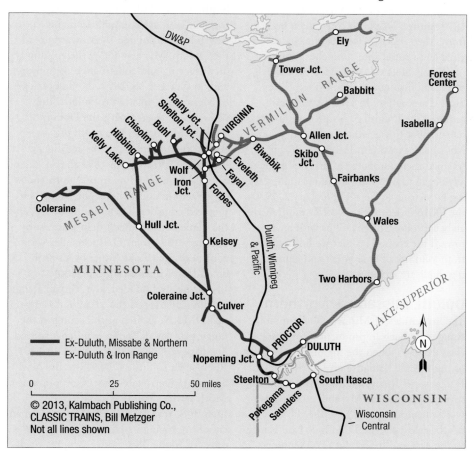

Missabe SD38AC No. 204 and SD9 No. 163, decked out in the railroad's standard maroon, lead a long string of loaded ore cars at Keenan Junction, Minn., in the 1970s. *Howard Patrick*

Chicago & Illinois Coal Railway and acquired control of the Chicago & Eastern Illinois for Illinois Steel.) The discovery of iron ore deposits of the Mesabi Range in 1890 spurred D&IR to construct a branch from Allen Junction west to the city of Virginia and several short branches to mines.

Illinois Steel was succeeded by Federal Steel, and Federal Steel by United States Steel Corporation. In 1901 U. S. Steel acquired the Duluth & Iron Range and also its neighbor to the west, the Duluth, Missabe & Northern. The two railroads retained their autonomy at first but gradually began to move toward unification, starting by sharing officers. On January 1, 1930, the DM&N leased the D&IR and immediately consolidated operations with an eye toward the economies that would result from joint use of equipment and eliminating duplicate facilities.

Duluth, Missabe & Northern

The iron mines of Minnesota's Vermilion Range had been in production for more than 20 years when the mammoth deposits of high-grade hematite ores of the Mesabi Range were discovered in 1890. (There are several spellings of "Mesabi," a Chippewa word meaning "giant.") Neither of the nearby railroads, the Duluth & Iron Range to the east and the Duluth & Winnipeg

(later Great Northern) to the southwest, was interested in extending to the Mesabi Range, so on June 3, 1891, the Merritt brothers of Duluth, who had acquired tracts of land at Mountain Iron and Biwabik, incorporated their own railroad, the Duluth, Missabe & Northern Railway.

Surveying and construction soon began, and on October 18, 1892, the first carload of Mesabi ore rolled into Duluth. The Merritts contracted with the Duluth & Winnipeg to use its line south of Brookston and its ore docks at Allouez (Superior), Wis., but in 1893 they decided to build their own line into Duluth and construct ore docks there. The Merritts incurred considerable debt in doing so, and the Panic of 1893 didn't help matters. By February 1894 John D. Rockefeller was in control of their Lake Superior Consolidated Iron Mines and the DM&N.

Business rebounded. The Mesabi Range quickly outstripped the Vermilion Range, and DM&N, located at the center of the range, prospered. Traffic required a second ore dock at Duluth, then a third. In 1901 Rockefeller sold the DM&N to the newly formed United States Steel Corporation, which in the same year acquired the Duluth & Iron Range. DM&N entered an era of improving its physical plant: steel ore cars, Mallet locomotives, double track,

and extensions to other mines.

At first U. S. Steel made no moves to consolidate its two railroads, but after tentative steps in that direction, on Jan. 1, 1930, DM&N leased the D&IR and integrated the operations of the two roads.

Merger

On July 1, 1937, the DM&N consolidated with the Spirit Lake Transfer Railway, part of a short connecting line from Adolph, Minn., to Itasca, Wis., to form the Duluth, Missabe & Iron Range Railway (DM&N had leased the Spirit Lake line since 1915). On March 22, 1938, DM&IR acquired the assets and property of the Duluth & Iron Range and the Interstate Transfer Railway (the other portion of the connecting line, also leased by DM&N since 1915). The names of the two predecessors survived as designations for the two divisions of the DM&IR, Iron Range and Missabe.

The Missabe Road was the country's largest carrier of iron ore. The DM&IR's peak year for hauling ore was 1953, when it carried more than 49 million tons to Lake Superior docks. Production began to decline after that as high-grade ore was mined out. Several mines closed in the 1960s, and the railroad's docks at Two Harbors closed from 1963 to 1965. A switch to taconite pellets, begun in the mid-1960s, brought traffic up again. Taconite is a lower-grade ore, but it is processed into round pellets—which have a lower density than iron ore—prior to loading on ships.

The DM&IR was owned by U. S. Steel until 1988, when it was acquired by Transtar, Inc., controlled by Blackstone Capital Partners. In 2001 the railroad was spun off to Great Lakes Trnasportation, which was wholly owned by Blackstone. In May 2004, Blackstone sold GLT to Canadian National, which in 2011 merged the DM&IR along with another of its subsidiaries, Wisconsin Central Ltd. The CN now operates the former DM&IR lines.

FACTS & FIGURES

Year	1938	2004
Miles operated	540	206
Locomotives	131	42
Passenger cars	22	—
Freight cars	13,783	3,279
Reporting marks: DMIR		
Historical society: missabe.com		

Duluth, South Shore & Atlantic

The backers of the Duluth, South Shore & Atlantic Railway proposed to build a railroad from Duluth, Minn., east through the iron ore country of Wisconsin and the Upper Peninsula of Michigan to Sault Ste. Marie, with branches to St. Ignace, Mich., on the Straits of Mackinac, and Houghton, Mich., in the copper-mining country of the Keweenaw Peninsula. The DSS&A was incorporated in 1887 as a consolidation of several railroads serving the iron ore region of Michigan's Upper Peninsula: Mackinaw & Marquette, Sault Ste. Marie & Marquette; Wisconsin, Sault Ste. Marie & Mackinac; and Duluth, Superior & Michigan. The first-named, the Mackinaw & Marquette, was successor to the Detroit, Mackinac & Marquette, which opened a line in 1881 between St. Ignace and Marquette.

The DSS&A reached Sault Ste. Marie in September 1887 and Duluth in September 1888, the latter by using Northern Pacific tracks west of Iron River, Wis. About the same time it acquired control of the Mineral Range Railroad, which reached north from Hancock to Calumet and Lake Linden. Canadian Pacific acquired control of the DSS&A in 1888.

DSS&A extended its own rails west from Iron River to Superior in 1892. When the Lake Superior & Ishpeming arrived in the iron-mining area in 1896 it took much of the ore business away from the South Shore, leaving it largely dependent upon forest products. The road carried

Duluth, South Shore & Atlantic train No. 1 is created at St. Ignace in September 1951, its cars ferried across the Straits of Mackinac on the vessel *Chief Wawatam* from connections NYC and PRR. The yellow-and-green RS-1 will pull the train on west to Marquette. *A. C. Kalmbach*

on—several issues of *Moody's Railroads* refer to it as "one of the least prosperous of the Canadian Pacific Railway's subsidiaries." By 1930 the road was sharing officers with Soo Line, also a CPR subsidiary.

South Shore filed for bankruptcy in 1937, emerging in 1949 as the Duluth, South Shore & Atlantic Railroad, which included the old South Shore and the Mineral Range Railroad (which ran from Houghton to Calumet and Lake Linden). In the late 1930s the South Shore abandoned its main line west of Marengo,

Wis., in favor of trackage rights from there to Ashland on Soo Line and from Ashland to Superior on Northern Pacific. Passenger service dwindled to a St. Ignace–Marquette round trip, operated with an RDC, discontinued in 1958, and the north end of the Chicago–Calumet *Copper Country Limited*, operated in conjunction with the Milwaukee Road.

On Jan. 1, 1961, the Soo Line Railroad was created by the merger of the DSS&A, the Minneapolis, St. Paul, & Sault Ste. Marie (the old Soo Line), and the Wisconsin Central Railway, which had long been operated by the Soo Line. The new railroad used DSS&A's corporate structure.

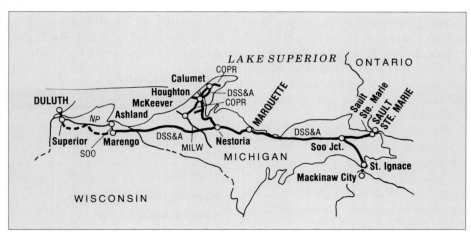

FACTS & FIGURES

Year	1929	1960
Miles operated	574	544
Locomotives	62	24
Passenger cars	58	—
Freight cars	2,709	1,720
Reporting marks: DSS&A, DSA		
Historical society: sooline.org		

Duluth, Winnipeg & Pacific

Two of Duluth, Winnipeg & Pacific's five remaining Alco RS-11s are ready to take a transfer from Burlington Northern's Bridge Yard. Downtown Duluth is in the background, with Interstate 35 next to the locomotives. It's a cold December day in 1982, two years before the railroad left downtown Duluth for a new facility in Superior, Wis. *David C. Schauer*

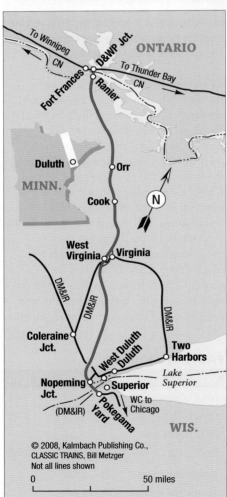

© 2008, Kalmbach Publishing Co., CLASSIC TRAINS, Bill Metzger
Not all lines shown

0   50 miles

The first portion of the Duluth, Winnipeg & Pacific was the middle of a logging railroad, the Duluth, Virginia & Rainy Lake Railway, which opened in 1901 from Virginia, Minn., to nearby Silver Lake. The road was soon purchased by Canadian Northern Railway interests and its name changed to Duluth, Rainy Lake & Winnipeg Railway. In 1908 the line was extended north to a connection with Canadian Northern (a predecessor of Canadian National Railways) at Fort Frances, Ontario.

In 1909 the line was renamed the Duluth, Winnipeg & Pacific Railway. The railroad extended its line southward to Duluth, reaching its namesake city in 1912. In 1918 control of Canadian Northern passed to the Canadian government and the DW&P became part of Canadian National Railways.

"The 'Peg" was continually upgraded as it became a vital piece of CN's route for western traffic to the U. S. The DW&P was known for its fleet of 15 Alco RS-11 diesels, Nos. 3600-3614, built in 1956, and the railroad adopted its "Delivered With Pride" slogan and logo in 1961.

In November 1984 the road abandoned its long, twisting descent into its West Duluth yard and opened Pokegama Yard in Superior, Wis. The DW&P reached the yard by trackage rights on Duluth, Missabe & Iron Range's Spirit Lake branch. The reason for the move was highway construction in downtown Duluth.

Traffic on the DW&P increased in the 1990s with the Canada-U. S. Free Trade Agreement. The railroad lost its own identity in the early 1990s with the "CN North America" branding, and paint schemes on CN subsidiaries were largely replaced with CN's own scheme. The DW&P was officially merged into CN's Wisconsin Central subsidiary in December 2011.

FACTS & FIGURES

Year	1929	1983
Miles operated	169	167
Locomotives	1	13
Passenger cars	—	—
Freight cars	1,905	2,428

Reporting marks: DWC, DWP
Historical society: cnlines.ca

Durham & Southern

Two freshly painted dark green and white Baldwin road-switchers, acquired from Norfolk Southern Railway and re-trucked from A1A-A1A to B-B, are running wide open as they lug the 27 cars of train 47 uphill from Durham toward Dunn, N. C., in August 1967. *Curt Tillotson Jr.*

The Durham & Southern was incorporated in 1906 as a reorganization and extension of the Cape Fear & Northern Railway. A lumber company had built the CF&N between Apex and Dunn, North Carolina, and the D&S would extend the line north to Durham. The purpose of the road was to connect Durham with the main lines of Atlantic Coast Line and Seaboard Air Line.

The Duke family was associated with the railroad from the beginning, and in 1930 control passed to the Duke Power Co., which also owned the Piedmont & Northern. The two roads were put under the same management, and a connection between the two was proposed, but it was rejected by the Interstate Commerce Commission. In 1954 management of the two roads was separated, and Durham & Southern came under the control of the Nello Teer Co., a Durham construction company.

The Durham & Southern was noteworthy from the standpoint of motive power: an assortment of Decapods, including one of only two common-carrier steam locomotives built in the U. S. during 1933, and an ex-Norfolk & Western Twelve-Wheeler in steam days; an array of seven Baldwin diesel road-switchers; and finally orthodoxy in the form of four GP38-2s.

Seaboard Coast Line bought the railroad in 1976 and dissolved the corporation on Sept. 15, 1981.

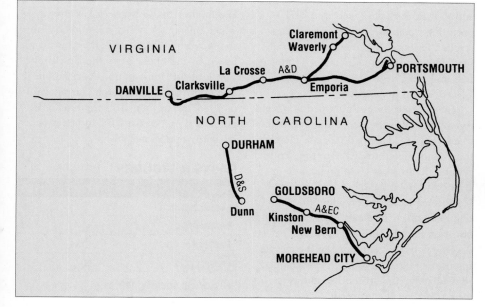

FACTS & FIGURES

Year	1929	1980
Miles operated	59	59
Locomotives	9	4
Passenger cars	—	—
Freight cars	1	50
Reporting marks: DS		

East Broad Top

The East Broad Top was the last narrow gauge common carrier in the U. S. east of the Mississippi. It was better known than most other roads of its size and remoteness.

The East Broad Top Railroad & Coal Company was chartered in 1856 to mine and transport coal from Broad Top Mountain, a plateau in Pennsylvania south of the Juniata River about halfway between Philadelphia and Pittsburgh. Construction did not begin until 1872, after the road's directors had chosen a track gauge of 3 feet. The line was opened from Mount Union, on the main line of the Pennsylvania Railroad, south to Orbisonia in 1873 and extended farther south to Robertsdale in 1874. By then the Rockhill Iron & Coal Company had been organized by the same management.

The Shade Gap Railroad was incorporated in 1884 to handle business that was sure to result from the construction of the South Pennsylvania Railroad, a line across the state backed by New York Central interests. A year later the Pennsylvania Railroad and the New York Central called a truce, and the half-dug tunnels of the South Penn were abandoned for the next 50 years.

The East Broad Top had a long career of carrying mostly coal but also limestone, lumber, and bark; its history is peppered with strikes by mine workers and flooding rivers and creeks. The EBT hit on hard times in the 1890s and was rehabilitated in the early 1900s. In 1919 the road was purchased by Madeira, Hill & Co., a coal mining firm. The chief improvements

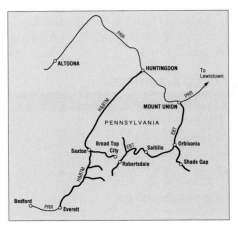

Loaded and empty East Broad Top coal trains meet at Kimmel, Pa., between Saltillo and Robertsdale, in March 1956, shortly before the line was abandoned. *John Krause*

under that management were a coal-cleaning plant at Mount Union and facilities for changing the trucks of standard gauge cars so they could move on the EBT. In 1934 Madeira, Hill underwent voluntary bankruptcy and in 1937 went bankrupt again.

In 1938 the road's bondholders bought the East Broad Top and the mining company and reorganized them as the Rockhill Coal Company. The Shade Gap branch finally got the traffic for which it had been built when the long-abandoned roadbed of the South Penn was used as the foundation for the Pennsylvania Turnpike, construction of which began in 1939.

After World War II, rising labor costs and shorter work days increased EBT's operating expenses, and frequent strikes resulted in less coal moving over the railroad. However, the road remained in business and went so far as to ask General Electric about diesel power.

The demand for coal dropped as oil and gas took its place in homes and industries. The Rockhill Coal Co. decided to close its mines and offered the EBT to the Pennsylvania Railroad at scrap prices, but Pennsy declined the offer. The Interstate Commerce Commission approved abandonment effective March 31, 1956, and the last train ran on April 13, 1956, just three days short of the centennial of the chartering of the railroad. Nothing was scrapped immediately; the locomotives and cars were stored on the property.

The railroad and the coal company were purchased by Kovalchick Salvage Co., a scrap dealer. Nick Kovalchick, its president, petitioned to postpone dismantling the railroad and the mine facilities, and mining activity resumed in 1957, but the coal moved in trucks. In 1960 Kovalchick was asked if the railroad could be reactivated for the celebration of the bicentennial of Orbisonia. It could, and the East Broad Top reopened on Aug. 13, 1960.

From then into the 2000s, EBT operated as a tourist railroad during the summer season. In 1963 standard gauge tracks were laid on a short portion of the Shade Gap branch by Railways to Yesterday, which operates a trolley museum at Orbisonia. From 2009 to 2011, the railroad was leased to and operated by the East Broad Top Railroad Preservation Association. The railroad did not operate during 2012 or 2013, but in June 2013 the EBTRPA purchased part of the EBT in hopes of resuming operation.

FACTS & FIGURES

Year	1929	1955
Miles operated	51	38
Locomotives	12	8
Passenger cars	18	4
Freight cars	402	311
Historical society: febt.org		

East Tennessee & Western North Carolina

E.T.&W.N.C.

The East Tennessee & Western North Carolina Railroad was chartered in 1866 and built a few miles of 5-foot gauge track (then standard for the South) before stopping for breath and refinancing. In 1879 a group of investors led by Ario Pardee (who was connected with the East Broad Top Railroad) bought the line and resumed construction with a track gauge of 3 feet. The line was opened in 1882 between Johnson City, Tenn., and Cranberry, N. C. At Cranberry were mines that produced high-grade ore used in the production of tool steel.

In 1913 the ET&WNC purchased the Linville River Railway, a logging railroad with which it connected at Cranberry. The line reached Boone, 33 miles from Cranberry, in 1918. In the 1930s ET&WNC turned to tourism to fill its trains—the mountains had been logged off, the mines were running out, and highways were taking passengers away. The mountains and the Doe River Gorge attracted excursionists, and during that era the road received its nickname, "Tweetsie." In 1940 rains washed out much of the Linville River line, and it was abandoned in 1941.

The ET&WNC kept busy during World War II because of the increased demand for steel and because of gasoline

Ten-Wheeler No. 11 leads a train across the Doe River after emerging from a tunnel on Aug. 5, 1941, nine years before the end of "Tweetsie" narrow-gauge operations. *Robert B. Adams*

and tire rationing. At the end of the war the mines were depleted, and without the ore traffic there was little need for the narrow gauge railroad. The last narrow gauge train ran on Oct. 16, 1950.

The railroad had installed a third rail for standard gauge traffic between Johnson City and Elizabethton in 1906. That portion of the railroad remained in service after the narrow gauge line was abandoned and was operated with steam locomotives until 1967, when the last two Consolidations, Nos. 207 and 208, were replaced with diesels. The two Consolidations returned to the Southern, their former owner, and given their old numbers, 630 and 722, for Southern's steam excursion service.

In September 1983 the East Tennessee Railway took over operation of the line between Johnson City and Elizabethton. The line to Elizabethton was abandoned in 2003, although the ETRY still serves customers in Johnson City. The Genesee & Wyoming purchased the ETRY in 2005.

FACTS & FIGURES

Year	1929	1949
Miles operated	36	34
Locomotives	7	6
Passenger cars	18	—
Freight cars	278	—
Website: tweetsie.com		

© 2014, Kalmbach Publishing Co., CLASSIC TRAINS, Bill Metzger

Elgin, Joliet & Eastern

In 1884 a group of Joliet, Ill., business-men incorporated a railroad that would run from the Indiana-Illinois state line west through Joliet and Aurora to the Mississippi River opposite Dubuque, Iowa. It would afford Joliet's steel mills and stone quarries connections to railroads that didn't serve Joliet directly. In 1886 the Joliet, Aurora & Northern Railway began operation between Joliet and Aurora. The anticipated traffic was slow to develop, and JA&N's builders got the idea of making the road into a belt line around Chicago.

The proposal attracted the attention of financier J. P. Morgan. A syndicate purchased the JA&N and chartered the Elgin, Joliet & Eastern Railway to extend the JA&N north to Elgin and east into Indiana. Even while the road was under construction it backed two other railroads: the Gardner, Coal City & Northern, which built a line south from Plainfield into a coal-mining area, and the Waukegan & Southwestern, which extended the EJ&E northeast to Waukegan, Ill., on the shore of Lake Michigan just south of the Wisconsin state line (the EJ&E absorbed both roads in 1891). In 1893 the EJ&E pushed its line east to Porter, Ind., a few miles east of the south end of Lake Michigan. The completed main line formed an arc 30 to 40 miles from the center of Chicago, intersecting with every railroad entering Chicago, giving the "J" its other nickname, Chicago Outer Belt.

Elgin, Joliet & Eastern SD38-2 Nos. 667 and 664 pull several cars to the Canadian Pacific interchange at Rondout, Ill., in October 2007. *Craig Williams*

In 1898 the EJ&E, Illinois Steel, and Minnesota Iron were all brought under the ownership of a new company, Federal Steel, presided over by Elbert H. Gary. In 1901 Federal Steel and Carnegie Steel merged to form U. S. Steel. The new company chose as the site for a huge new steel mill a tract of sand dunes at the south end of Lake Michigan; it also laid out and incorporated a city nearby and named it for Gary.

From one of its predecessors, the EJ&E inherited trackage rights on the Chicago & Eastern Illinois Railroad south to coalfields near Danville, Ill.—but only for trains carrying coal and limestone northbound. The EJ&E continued to exercise those trackage rights until 1947. For two months in 1980 the "J" found itself in a similar situation, as designated operator of the former Rock Island between Joliet and Peoria. The "J" abandoned part of its Aurora branch in 1976 and the rest in 1985; also in 1985 it abandoned the easternmost 20 miles of its line, between Griffith and Porter.

The "J" was the first railroad to install welded rail on its main line, and its Kirk Yard at Gary had the world's first electrically operated automatic car retarders. The road dieselized in 1949.

The railroad was owned by U. S. Steel until 1988, when it was acquired by Transtar Corporation (owned by U. S. Steel and the Blackstone Group). Canadian National purchased most of the EJ&E in February 2009 (except for a portion in Gary, Ind., which remains owned by Transtar as the Gary Railway) and officially merged it with CN subsidiary Wisconsin Central on Jan. 1, 2013.

FACTS & FIGURES

Year	1929	1983
Miles operated	231	231
Locomotives	58	100
Passenger cars	—	—
Freight cars	5,009	10,193
Reporting marks: EJE		

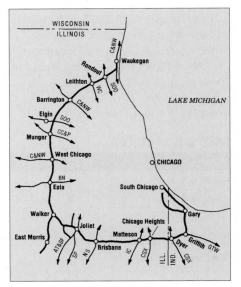

Erie

When the Erie Canal was built across upstate New York between Albany and Buffalo, DeWitt Clinton, governor of New York, promised the people of the Southern Tier of the state some kind of avenue of commerce by way of appeasement. William Redfield proposed a direct route from the mouth of the Hudson to the Great Lakes, but it was Eleazar Lord who was instrumental in the chartering of the New York & Erie Railroad by the New York state legislature in April 1832.

Among the conditions of the charter were that the railroad lie wholly within New York and that it not connect with any railroads in New Jersey or Pennsylvania without permission of the legislature. A track gauge of 6 feet ensured that even if it did connect, its cars and locomotives would not stray onto foreign rails.

The terminals were fixed: The town of Dunkirk offered land for a terminal on Lake Erie, and Lord lived at Piermont, on the Hudson River just north of the New Jersey state line. The New York & Harlem was willing to extend a line north to a point opposite Piermont, which would have given the New York & Erie an entrance to Manhattan, but the new road refused the offer. The surveyed route included two detours into Pennsylvania, one because the Delaware & Hudson Canal had already occupied the New York side of the Delaware River above Port Jervis, and the other to follow the Susquehanna River to maintain an easy grade.

Ground was broken on Nov. 7, 1835, near Deposit, N. Y. Shortly afterward fire destroyed much of New York and wiped out the fortunes of many of the road's supporters; then a business panic struck the nation.

Construction got under way in 1838, and the first train ran in 1841. Much of the railroad was built on low trestlework rather than directly on the ground; the resulting construction and maintenance costs drove the railroad into bankruptcy soon after it opened. Construction continued, however. The line that had been built east a few miles from Dunkirk was taken

A pair of Erie Alco RS-3s, Nos. 915 and 1016, lead an eastbound freight out of Owego, N. Y., on June 2, 1951. *S. K. Bolton, Rail Photo Service; David P. Morgan Library collection*

up to provide rails for the extension from Goshen, N. Y., to Middletown. Standard-gauging the line was proposed while it would still be relatively inexpensive to do so, but the road chose to stay with its broad gauge.

The New York & Erie reached Port Jervis, N. Y., on the Delaware River 74 miles from Piermont, on Dec. 31, 1847; just a year later it was into Binghamton. The whole road from Piermont to Dunkirk was opened in May 1851 with an inspection trip for dignitaries from U. S. President Millard Fillmore and Secretary of State Daniel Webster on down that included the customary eating, drinking, and speechifying.

The road acquired branches: at the east end to Newburgh, N. Y., on the Hudson, and at the west end to Rochester and to Buffalo, which soon replaced Dunkirk as the principal western terminal of the road.

In 1833 the Paterson & Hudson River Rail Road was chartered to build between Paterson, N. J., and Jersey City, and the Paterson & Ramapo Railroad north to the New York state line at Suffern. The two lines provided a shortcut between New York City and the New York & Erie at Suffern, even though they did not connect directly—passengers walked the mile between the two. The New York & Erie fought the situation until 1852, when it

leased the two railroads, built a connecting track, and made it the main route, supplanting the original line to Piermont.

Hard times

The New York & Erie came upon hard times in the 1850s. Cornelius Vanderbilt and Daniel Drew both lent the road money. In 1859 it entered receivership and was reorganized as the Erie Railway. Drew and two associates, James Fisk and Jay Gould, engaged in some machinations, with the result that in the summer of 1868 Drew, Fisk, and Vanderbilt were out and Gould was in as president of the Erie.

In 1874 the Erie leased the Atlantic & Great Western, which had been opened 10 years earlier between Salamanca, N. Y., on the Erie, and Dayton, Ohio. The A&GW entered Cincinnati over the Cincinnati, Hamilton & Dayton, which laid a third rail to accommodate A&GW's broad-gauge equipment. At Cincinnati the A&GW connected with the broad-gauge Ohio & Mississippi to St. Louis. (The CH&D and the Ohio & Mississippi later became part of Baltimore & Ohio.)

The lease to the Erie did not last long. A&GW entered receivership and was reorganized as the New York, Pennsylvania & Ohio. To obtain access to Cleveland and Youngstown, the NYP&O leased the Cleveland & Mahoning Valley in 1880.

A 2-8-2 lugs westbound way freight No. 95 up the steep grade near Alfred, N. Y., in 1950.
R. G. Nugent, Rail Photo Service; David P. Morgan Library collection

The Erie leased the Nypano (as it was known) in 1883, acquired all its capital stock in 1896, and acquired its properties in 1941.

Hugh Jewett became president of the Erie in 1874. His first task was to lead the road through reorganization; it became the New York, Lake Erie & Western Railroad. On June 22, 1880, the entire system was converted to standard gauge. That same year the Chicago & Atlantic was completed between Hammond, Indiana, and Marion, Ohio, where it connected with the Atlantic & Great Western. Access to Chicago was over the rails of the Chicago & Western Indiana, a terminal road. Jewett also double-tracked the Erie from Jersey City to Buffalo. The road was bankrupt again by 1893 and reorganized in 1895 as the Erie Railroad.

The Underwood era

In 1899 Frederick Underwood began a 25-year term as president of the Erie. He had been associated with James J. Hill, and he was a friend of E. H. Harriman. Both Hill and Harriman had considered the

Erie as a possible eastern extension of their respective systems. Neither man did much toward acquiring it, although Harriman became a member of Erie's board of directors and arranged financing for it. In 1905 the Erie briefly acquired the Cincinnati, Hamilton & Dayton and the affiliated Pere Marquette from J. P. Morgan, Erie's banker. Investigation revealed that CH&D's financial condition was not as advertised, so Underwood asked Morgan to take the two roads back—which he did. Two days later the CH&D and the PM entered receivership.

Underwood is remembered for rebuilding the Erie. His projects included double-tracking the remainder of the main line and building several freight bypasses with lower grades, making the line east of Meadville, Pa., largely a water-level route. In 1907 Erie electrified passenger operations on its branch between Rochester and Mount Morris, N. Y. Electric operation lasted until 1934.

In the 1920s the Van Sweringen brothers began buying Erie stock, seeing the road as a logical eastern extension of their

Nickel Plate Road. By the time they were done, they owned more than 55 percent of Erie's stock along with their interests in Chesapeake & Ohio, Pere Marquette, and Hocking Valley.

The Erie family included several short lines. The Erie began to buy New York, Susquehanna & Western stock in 1898 and leased the line that same year. The Susquehanna entered bankruptcy in 1937 and resumed life on its own in 1940. Bath & Hammondsport was controlled by the Erie from 1903 to 1936, when it was sold to local businessmen. Much of Erie's commuter business out of Jersey City was over subsidiary lines that Erie operated as part of its own system: New York & Greenwood Lake, Northern Railroad of New Jersey, and New Jersey & New York.

The Erie held its own against the Great Depression until January 18, 1938, when it entered bankruptcy. Its reorganization, accomplished in December 1941, included purchase of the leased Cleveland & Mahoning Valley, swapping high rent for lower interest payments, and purchase of subsidiaries and leased lines. To the surprise of many, Erie began paying dividends. Prosperity continued until the mid-1950s, but then began to decline. Erie's 1957 income was less than half that for 1956; in 1958 and 1959 the road posted deficits.

The business recession of the 1950s prompted Erie to explore the idea of cooperation with Delaware, Lackawanna & Western. The first results were the elimination of duplicate freight facilities at Binghamton and Elmira, and in 1956 and 1957 Erie moved its passenger trains from its old Jersey City terminal to Lackawanna's newer one at Hoboken. The discussions of cooperation turned into merger talks, at first including the Delaware & Hudson. An agreement was worked out with the Lackawanna, and the two roads merged as the Erie-Lackawanna on Oct. 17, 1960.

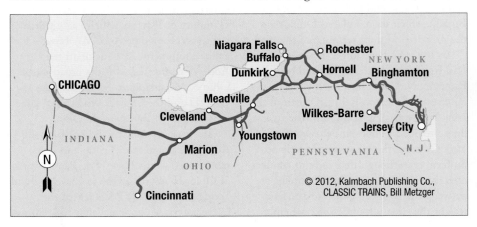
© 2012, Kalmbach Publishing Co., CLASSIC TRAINS, Bill Metzger

FACTS & FIGURES

Year	1929	1959
Miles operated	2,316	2,215
Locomotives	1,122	484
Passenger cars	1,368	535
Freight cars	44,916	20,028

Reporting marks: ERIE
Historical society: erielackhs.org

Erie Lackawanna

The Erie-Lackawanna Railroad was formed by the merger of the Erie Railroad with the Delaware, Lackawanna & Western on Oct. 17, 1960. (The hyphen was dropped in late 1963.) Both of EL's parents entered the merger with recent deficits on their books, and EL continued, except for 1965 and 1966.

EL quickly consolidated its passenger services, with most trains following the ex-Lackawanna route east of Binghamton and the ex-Erie route west. Long-distance passenger trains were gradually cut back during the 1960s, and the last Hoboken–Chicago train was discontinued in 1970, leaving EL with a single daily commuter round trip between Cleveland and Youngstown and its extensive New Jersey commuter services. In 1967 the state of New Jersey began subsidizing the commuter service and in 1970 began to acquire new cars and locomotives for the trains on the ex-Erie routes and the nonelectrified Lackawanna lines (Lackawanna electric cars ran until 1984). The Cleveland–Youngstown train lasted until 1977.

In 1960 Chesapeake & Ohio began acquiring Baltimore & Ohio stock, and in November 1961 New York Central and Pennsylvania announced their intention to merge. In 1964 Norfolk & Western teamed up with Nickel Plate, Wabash, Pittsburgh & West Virginia, and Akron, Canton & Youngstown. Erie Lackawanna was suddenly surrounded, or thought it would be, and asked to be included in the N&W system. In 1965 N&W and C&O

Erie Lackawanna's hottest freights, eastbound NE-74 (left, behind SD45s) and westbound CX-99, meet at Rood's Creek, N. Y., in the early 1970s. *J. J. Young*

announced their merger plan, to include EL and several other smaller eastern railroads, to be held by a wholly owned subsidiary holding company named Dereco.

The N&W-C&O merger didn't take place, but on March 1, 1968, Dereco and the Erie Lackawanna Railway were both incorporated. On April 1, 1968, the Erie Lackawanna Railway merged with the Erie Lackawanna Railroad. Stockholders of the Erie Lackawanna Railroad received Dereco shares. Put simply, the N&W bought the EL at arm's length.

Hurricane Agnes hit the East on June 22, 1972. After estimating that damage to the railroad, principally between Binghamton and Salamanca, N. Y., amounted to

$9.2 million, EL filed for bankruptcy on June 26, 1972. During the reorganization of the eastern railroads, it was thought that EL might be able to reorganize on its own, and there was a proposal by Chessie System to buy a portion of the EL. However, Chessie canceled the agreement and EL asked to be included in Conrail.

Consolidated Rail Corporation took over EL's operations on April 1, 1976. Conrail excluded most of the former Erie main line west of Marion, Ohio. The Erie Western was formed to operate the 152 miles from Decatur to Hammond, Ind., with subsidy from the state of Indiana. The EW operated briefly in 1978 and 1979, but the subsidy was withdrawn and on-line traffic couldn't support the operation. Other shortline operators have taken over various parts of EL with more success.

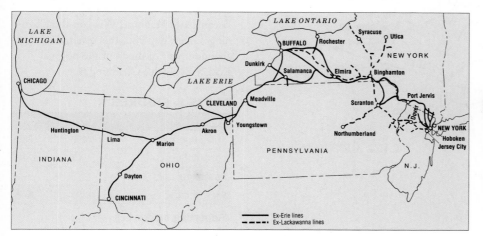

FACTS & FIGURES

Year	1960	1975
Miles operated	3,189	2,807
Locomotives	695	516
Passenger cars	1,098	407
Freight cars	29,905	19,162
Reporting marks: EL		
Historical society: erielackhs.org		

Escanaba & Lake Superior

In 1897 the I. Stephenson Co., through its Escanaba River Co., had built a logging railroad from Wells (Escanaba), on the shore of Lake Michigan, seven miles inland to tap an area of hardwood timber. To expand this line, the Escanaba & Lake Superior Railway was incorporated in 1898. The year it was chartered the E&LS continued the line to Watson, 26 miles, and eventually to Channing, Mich., where it connected with the Milwaukee Road. The railroad was reorganized in 1900 as the Escanaba & Lake Superior Railroad.

From 1900 through 1936 (before the Milwaukee Road/Chicago & North Western ore-pooling agreement of the 1930s) Milwaukee Road ore trains moved to ore docks at Escanaba over the E&LS.

Logging and iron ore were the railroad's initial primary sources of traffic, and over the years as the logging side of the business died out, the carrying of paper and lumber products increased, along with agricultural and other industrial products. Mixed-train service continued on the Wells to Channing line until 1960.

The E&LS was known for dieselizing (in the late 1940s) with Baldwin switchers and road switchers, and added several second-hand RS-12s and two Baldwin RF-16 Sharks in the 1970s and '80s. The road's current motive power includes

Escanaba & Lake Superior dieselized in the mid-1940s with Baldwin locomotives, including DS-4-4-660 No. 101, purchased new in November 1947. Number 101 was the second diesel on the property, and one of two of that model. *David P. Morgan Library collection*

EMD SD40-2s, GP38s, and SD9s.

In 1980 E&LS took over operation of (and eventually purchased, with financial aid for track rehabilitation from the states of Michigan and Wisconsin) several

Milwaukee Road lines: from Channing south to Green Bay, Wis., north to Republic, Mich., and northwest to Ontonagon, Mich. (The circa-1984 map also shows the Lake Superior & Ishpeming and some Soo Line and C&NW routes.) The E&LS also bought a couple of small former Soo and C&NW branches.

In 1992 the E&LS negotiated trackage rights over the Wisconsin Central (former Soo; now Canadian National) from Escanaba to Pembine, Wis., on the Channing-Green Bay line. This resulted in abandonment of much of the original E&LS Escanaba-Channing line.

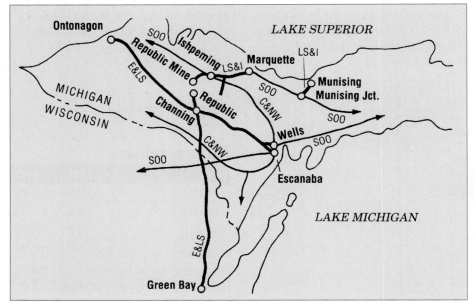

FACTS & FIGURES

Year	1929	2005
Miles operated	150	235
Locomotives	7	10
Passenger cars	5	—
Freight cars	394	877
Reporting marks: ELS		

Florida East Coast

Two biplanes joined Florida East Coast's *Henry M. Flagler* for the train's publicity photo in 1939. The *Flagler* ran from Jacksonville to Miami. The red-and-yellow E3, No. 1001, was FEC's first diesel locomotive. The road changed to solid blue for locomotves in the 1960s. *Florida East Coast*

In 1885 Henry M. Flagler took over the Jacksonville, St. Augustine & Halifax, a narrow gauge railroad extending 36 miles south from Jacksonville, Fla. He converted the line to standard gauge, built a bridge across the St. Johns River to connect with other railroads at Jacksonville, and pushed the line southward. Flagler purchased the St Johns Railroad, the St. Augustine & Palatka, and the St. Johns & Halifax River, extending his system to Daytona. The lines were incorporated as the Florida East Coast Railway in September 1895.

When the FEC reached Miami from the north in 1896, Flagler was not content to rest. The Florida Keys, a string of islands, reach more than 100 miles southwest from the southern tip of mainland Florida to the outermost island, Key West,

only 90 miles from Havana, Cuba. Until the 1950s there was a great deal of freight and passenger traffic between the U. S. and Cuba; in addition Key West was nearer the Panama Canal (then under construction) than any other U. S. port. In 1904 Flagler decided to extend his railroad to Key West.

The construction problems were formidable and labor turnover was high. On the portion of the line from Homestead to Key Largo, the dredging of canals to drain the swamp provided material for the roadbed. Along Key Largo the problem was not terrain but insects. Worse than terrain or insects was the weather: A hurricane in September 1906 destroyed the initial work on the Long Key Viaduct and killed more than 100 laborers. In 1907 the opening of Long Key Viaduct, more than 2 miles of

concrete arches (it became FEC's trademark), allowed service to Knights Key, where a marine terminal was built.

Hurricanes in 1909 and 1910 wiped out much of the completed railroad. After both hurricanes, work resumed at a faster pace—Flagler was getting old and wanted to ride all the way to Key West on his railroad. He did so on Jan. 22, 1912 (just over a year before his death in May 1913). Regular service began the next day, with through sleepers between New York and Key West and connections at Key West with passenger steamers and carferries for Havana.

The Florida land boom came in 1924, and FEC went whole hog: new cutoffs, branches, double track, signals, and 90 new 4-8-2 locomotives. The boom peaked and receded in 1926, the Seaboard Air Line

Florida East Coast intermodal train 226-17 rolls through St. Augustine, Fla., behind repainted SD40-2 No. 714, honoring the road's first diesel livery, in December 2011. *Eric Hendrickson*

Railway reached Miami in 1927—and then the Great Depression hit. FEC entered receivership in 1931.

A hurricane on Sept. 2, 1935, washed away 40 miles of the Key West Extension. The FEC was unwilling to repair a line that had never repaid its construction cost—an unknown figure only hinted at by the federal valuation of $12 million. The concrete viaducts survived to become the bridges of U. S. Highway 1, and the railroad was cut back to Florida City, 30 miles south of Miami. In recent years that line has been cut back to Miami. Twenty of the 4-8-2s were sold off to such roads as Cotton Belt and Western Pacific; eventually 30 more went to National Railways of Mexico.

In 1944 Atlantic Coast Line, whose streamliners FEC operated between Jacksonville and Miami, offered to purchase the FEC; later Seaboard Air Line and Southern Railway came up with a joint counterproposal. There was, however, considerable pressure to keep control of the railroad within the state of Florida.

The railroad was reorganized in 1960. Control was assumed by the St. Joe Paper Co., owned by the Alfred I. duPont estate.

In 1963 the nonoperating unions struck the railroad, which had refused to go along with an industry-wide pay increase. Within two weeks management personnel were operating freight service. The strike became increasingly bitter, with bombings and destruction. In spite of the strike, FEC was required to restore passenger service in 1965 to comply with provisions of its charter. The two-car Jacksonville-Miami train was discontinued in 1968. It was an odd end to the passenger service that in some years had contributed nearly half of FEC's revenues. The initial strike lasted until 1971; the strike by the operating unions was not settled until 1976. By then the railroad had instituted sweeping changes: two-man freight crews running trains the length of the railroad, where formerly three five-man crews had been required; extensive rebuilding of the railroad, including many miles of concrete ties; single track and CTC; several branches abandoned; and—a harbinger of an industry-wide development—no cabooses. Revenues and earnings began to climb, and in 1980 FEC broke its dividend record (none ever) by declaring a dividend on its common stock.

In 1984 FEC's corporate structure was revised to make the railroad a subsidiary of FEC Industries, a holding company that had been a subsidiary of the railroad. In July 2007, FEC Industries was purchased by Fortress Investment Group, which at the time also owned shortline rail operator RailAmerica. Fortress later sold RailAmerica, but retains ownership of the FEC.

Florida East Coast still maintains its high-speed main line, which now hosts intermodal traffic as well as a great deal of limestone traffic northbound from quarries near Miami.

FEC in 2010

FACTS & FIGURES

Year	1929	2012
Miles operated	863	351
Locomotives	248	91
Passenger cars	198	—
Freight cars	2,655	4,707

Reporting marks: FEC

Historical society: fecrs.com

Fort Dodge, Des Moines & Southern

THE FORT DODGE LINE

In 1893 the Boone Valley Coal & Railroad Company was formed to build a railroad from coalfields northwest of Des Moines, Iowa, to a connection with the Minneapolis & St. Louis Railway. Within a decade it was part of the Newton & Northwestern Railroad, a line from Newton, Iowa, northwest to Rockwell City. A notable feature of the line was a long, high trestle near Boone over Bass Point Creek, a tributary of the Des Moines River.

The Fort Dodge, Des Moines & Southern Railroad was incorporated in 1906 and built three lines branching off the Newton & Northwestern: from Hope north to Fort Dodge, from Midvale south to Des Moines, and from Kelly to Ames. The road purchased streetcar companies in Fort Dodge and Ames, and made a connection with the Inter-Urban Railway (later part of the Des Moines & Central Iowa) for access to downtown Des Moines. The Des Moines and Fort Dodge lines were electrified from the beginning, and trolley wires were erected over the Newton & Northwestern between Midvale and Hope.

The N&NW entered receivership in 1908 and was purchased in 1909 by the FDDM&S; a year later the FDDM&S also entered receivership, which lasted until 1913, when the road was sold at foreclosure to another company of the same

Car 72, operating as Fort Dodge–Des Moines train No. 2, crosses the Des Moines River south of Fort Dodge in April 1955. The interurban cars were painted yellow. *William D. Middleton*

name. The Rockwell City line was electrified, and the line from Midvale to Newton was dismantled in 1917 after several years of disuse. About that same time the FDDM&S built and acquired lines from Fort Dodge east to Webster City and Lehigh to tap coal and gypsum mines.

The railroad was primarily a freight carrier, and was built to heavier standards than most interurbans. Passenger service on the branches was discontinued in the 1920s, and by 1930 mainline passenger service was down to four trips a day in each direction. That was reduced to two each way from 1935 until the early 1940s, when four trips were again scheduled.

The Fort Dodge, Des Moines & Southern Railroad entered receivership again in 1930; the Fort Dodge, Des Moines & Southern Railway took over the property in 1943. The Iowa Commerce Commission permitted abandonment of passenger service in 1952, but trains continued to operate until 1955. Dieselization began in 1949, and the road was temporarily totally dieselized for three months in the summer of 1954 because of floods. Electric operation ended when passenger service ceased.

In 1954 control of the FDDM&S was acquired by the Des Moines & Central Iowa. Most of the Fort Dodge Line's branches were abandoned in the 1960s. C&NW leased the FDDM&S in 1971 and quickly took over its operations. In 1983 most of the main line was abandoned. Boone Railroad Historical Society bought 11 miles of the line from Boone north to Wolf Crossing, including a high trestle over a Des Moines River tributary, for operation as the Boone & Scenic Valley Railroad, a tourist carrier, which continues.

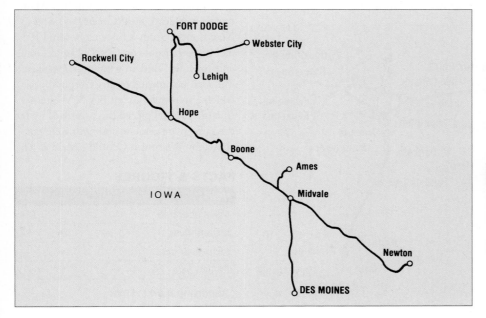

FACTS & FIGURES

Year	1929	1970
Miles operated	151	112
Locomotives	12	9
Passenger cars	19	—
Freight cars	683	202

Reporting marks: FtDDM&S

Historical society: scenic-valleyrr.com

Fox River Valley

An SD24/RSD-15/SD35 trio (ex-BN, LS&I, SOU) leads an FRV train north across the Fox River in Menasha, Wis., on May 13, 1990. *Tom Danneman*

Between 1854 and 1862 the Chicago & North Western Railway pushed a line north from Janesville, Wis., to the Fox River Valley towns of Fond du Lac, Oshkosh, Appleton, and Fort Howard (now Green Bay). In 1873 it opened a direct line from Milwaukee to Oshkosh and, through a subsidiary, began building a line north from Milwaukee along the shore of Lake Michigan. This route reached Manitowoc in 1873 and was extended northwest to Green Bay in 1906.

C&NW in 1988 sold lines in eastern Wisconsin to the new Fox River Valley Railroad, which began operating on Dec. 9, 1988. FRV ran from Granville (Milwaukee) through Fond du Lac and Appleton to Green Bay; from Cleveland, south of Manitowoc, to Duck Creek (Green Bay); and to New London from Kaukauna South. FRV had trackage rights on C&NW from Granville to Butler Yard, in western Milwaukee. The road was owned by Itel Corporation, which also owned Green Bay & Western. In late 1991 Itel placed the two roads under the same management, and both were purchased by Wisconsin Central Ltd. in 1993.

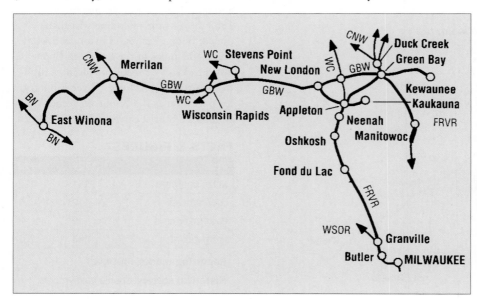

FACTS & FIGURES

Year	1989
Miles operated	214
Locomotives	28
Passenger cars	—
Freight cars	60
Reporting marks: FRVR	

Gateway Western

In 1878 the Chicago & Alton Railroad created a Chicago-Kansas City route by leasing the Kansas City, St. Louis & Chicago Railroad, a line between Kansas City and Mexico, Mo. The new route was shorter than the existing Chicago-Kansas City routes (Burlington, Rock Island, and Milwaukee Road), and the C&A developed a respectable Chicago-Kansas City business. An even shorter route was opened by the Santa Fe in 1888, and C&A's line began a long, slow descent into branchline status. It began losing money in 1912 and entered receivership in 1922. The Baltimore & Ohio purchased it in 1929 and reorganized it as the Alton Railroad. It operated as part of the B&O from 1931 to 1943.

The Gulf, Mobile & Ohio Railroad merged the Alton in 1947, becoming a Great-Lakes-to-Gulf railroad. GM&O, Burlington, and Santa Fe got together and proposed selling GM&O's Kansas City line to the Burlington, which would grant Kansas City-St. Louis trackage rights to the Santa Fe, which would in turn let Burlington use part of its Kansas City-Chicago line. Other railroads protested, and GM&O's Kansas City line remained an east-west route for an otherwise north-south carrier.

The Kansas City line gained some measure of fame among rail enthusiasts in the late 1950s when its Bloomington, Ill.-Kansas City trains qualified as the longest (and among the last) motor car runs in the country. (Careful definition is necessary

Gateway Western GP38s 2044 and 2025 wait for their next train at East St. Louis, Ill., in February 1991. Gateway's road motive power fleet was mainly ex-Conrail GP38s and former Western Pacific GP40s. *M. W. Blaszak*

here—"motor car" means an old gas-electric car repowered with a diesel engine—to keep from stumbling over Western Pacific's *Zephyrette*, a Budd Rail Diesel Car, which lasted a few months longer and covered almost three times the mileage.) Illinois Central merged the GM&O in 1972, creating Illinois Central Gulf.

In the 1980s ICG underwent a major restructuring, spinning off its east-west routes to form new regional railroads. Most of the old Alton was set loose and became the Chicago, Missouri & Western Railway in 1987. The CM&W entered bankruptcy less than a year after its

creation. Southern Pacific purchased the St. Louis-Joliet, Ill., main line to create SPCSL (Southern Pacific Chicago St. Louis). The Kansas City line was purchased by Wertheim Schroeder & Co. and became the Gateway Western Railway.

Gateway Western's main line ran from East St. Louis, Ill., to Kansas City. Short branches reached Fulton, Mo., Jacksonville, Ill., and Springfield, Ill. The line between East St. Louis and Godfrey, Ill., was owned jointly with SPCSL. The GWWR saw a lot of Santa Fe intermodal traffic to St. Louis until the BNSF merger in 1995, when much of that traffic began to move over former Burlington Northern lines.

Kansas City Southern purchased the Gateway Western in 1997 and operated it as a subsidiary until Oct. 1, 2001, when it merged the railroad.

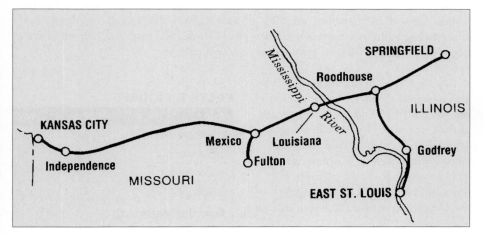

FACTS & FIGURES

Year	1991
Miles operated	408
Locomotives	22
Passenger cars	—
Freight cars	75
Reporting marks: CMNW, GWWR	

Georgia & Florida

John Skelton Williams, former president of the Seaboard Air Line, proposed in 1906 to assemble a railroad from Columbia, S. C., to a port to be developed on the Gulf of Mexico in Florida. To form the Georgia & Florida Railway he acquired four short lines: the Augusta & Florida Railway (Keysville–Swainsboro, Ga.); the Millen & Southwestern Railroad (Millen-Pendleton–Vidalia, Ga.), the Douglas, Augusta & Gulf Railway (Hazlehurst–Nashville–Sparks, Ga.); and the Valdosta Southern Railway (Valdosta, Ga.–Madison, Fla.). In addition the four roads included several branches and leased lines. He connected these by constructing four segments of track totaling 84 miles: Swainsboro–Pendleton, Vidalia–Hazlehurst, Garent–

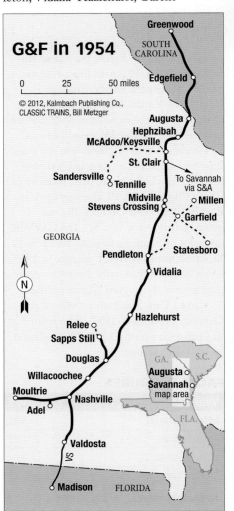

G&F in 1954

0   25   50 miles

© 2012, Kalmbach Publishing Co.,
CLASSIC TRAINS, Bill Metzger

Greenwood
SOUTH CAROLINA
Edgefield
Augusta
Hephzibah
McAdoo/Keysville
St. Clair
Sandersville
Tennille
Midville
Stevens Crossing
To Savannah via S&A
Millen
Garfield
GEORGIA
Statesboro
Pendleton
Vidalia
Hazlehurst
Relee
Sapps Still
Douglas
Willacoochee
Moultrie
Nashville
Adel
Valdosta
Madison   FLORIDA
GA.
S.C.
Augusta
Savannah
map area
FLA.
N

Georgia & Florida's largest steam locomotives were three 4-8-2s originally built for New Orleans Great Northern and purchased from Gulf, Mobile & Ohio in 1947. *T. Blasingame*

Douglas Junction, and Nashville–Valdosta. In addition, he secured trackage rights between Augusta and Keysville over the Augusta Southern.

By 1910 a line was complete between Augusta, Ga., and Madison, Fla. In 1911 the G&F reached Moultrie, Ga., by completion of a short branch and purchase of a few miles of trackage rights. In 1919 the road purchased the Augusta Southern at foreclosure, gaining a line to Sandersville and Tennille, Ga. In 1924 the road leased the Midland Railway of Georgia, which formed a branch to Statesboro (the Midland had begun life as a Savannah–Chattanooga proposal and had gone through several identities).

The Georgia & Florida entered receivership in 1915. Skelton became receiver of the G&F in 1921, and it was reorganized as the Georgia & Florida Railroad shortly after Skelton's death in 1926. The road began construction of an extension north to Greenwood, S. C., completed in 1929. The cost of construction and the effects of the Depression put the G&F into receivership again in 1929.

In March 1954 the road sold the Valdosta–Madison line to the Valdosta Southern Railroad—a new company, not the one acquired by Skelton. In February 1962 the Southern Railway formed the Georgia & Florida Railway to acquire the road and sell it to three other roads controlled by the Southern: Live Oak, Perry & Gulf; Carolina & North Western; and South Georgia. Transfer of the Georgia & Florida to the three roads occurred July 1, 1963.

On June 1, 1971, the Georgia & Florida Railway was merged into the Central of Georgia Railroad, another subsidiary of the Southern.

FACTS & FIGURES

Year	1929	1961
Miles operated	502	321
Locomotives	32	12
Passenger cars	29	—
Freight cars	635	513
Reporting marks: G&F		

Georgia Northern

In 1891 a private logging railroad that extended a few miles north from Pidcock, Ga., was organized as the Boston & Albany Railroad of Georgia. Within two years it had been extended north to Moultrie and the company had entered receivership. J. N. Pidcock, who owned lumber mills in the area, purchased the railroad and reorganized it as the Georgia Northern Railway. In 1905 the railroad relocated the line's southern 4 miles to terminate at Boston, east of Pidcock, and that same year completed the line north to Albany, 68 miles from Boston.

The Flint River & Northeastern was completed between Pelham and Ticknor, 23 miles, in 1904. By 1908 Pidcock had acquired an interest in the road and was operating it as part of the Georgia Northern. In 1922 Pidcock organized the Georgia, Ashburn, Sylvester & Camilla Railway to take over a 50-mile portion of a subsubsidiary of the Southern Railway between Ashburn and Camilla.

The Albany & Northern was organized in 1895 to take over a 35-mile line between Albany and Cordele. In 1910 the Georgia, Southwestern & Gulf, which had been incorporated to build a line from Albany southwest to St. Andrews Bay on the Gulf

Georgia Northern SW8 No. 13 rolls a Georgia, Ashburn, Sylvester & Camilla freight through a sea of dry grass between Camilla and Bridgeboro. *Jim Boyd*

of Mexico, purchased control of the Albany & Northern, leased it, and operated it as the Georgia, Southwestern & Gulf. (The line to the Gulf never became reality.) The GSW&G entered receivership in 1932, and Pidcock was appointed receiver in 1939. In 1942 the GSW&G was dissolved, the lease was canceled, and the Albany & Northern resumed its own operation.

The roads shared many officers. Georgia Northern, GAS&C, and FR&N were

listed together in *The Official Guide* and shared general offices at Moultrie. Offices of the Albany & Northern and the Georgia, Southwestern & Gulf were at Albany.

Back in the teens, the Georgia, Southwestern & Gulf and the Georgia Northern participated in operating a through passenger train, the *Hampton Springs Special*, which came down from Atlanta on the Atlanta, Birmingham & Atlantic and continued south of Moultrie on the Valdosta, Moultrie & Western and the South Georgia to Hampton, 6 miles west of Perry.

The Flint River & Northeastern was abandoned in 1946. Southern Railway acquired control of Georgia Northern, Albany & Northern, and GAS&C in 1966. The roads were merged on Jan. 1, 1972; Georgia Northern continued to exist as a subsidiary of the Southern Railway. The railroad was merged into the Georgia Southern & Florida Railway in December 1993; the GS&F remains a subsidiary of Norfolk Southern.

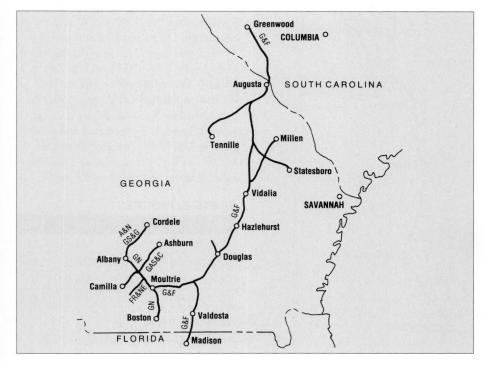

FACTS & FIGURES

Year	1929	1965
Miles operated	68	68
Locomotives	5	3
Passenger cars	7	1
Freight cars	10	1
Reporting marks: GANO		

Grand Trunk Western

GTW 4-8-4 No. 6317 nears South Bend (Ind.) Union Station on its way to Chicago in April 1948. Sister 4-8-4s ended U. S. regular mainline passenger steam usage in 1960. *B. Andrew Corsini*

The Grand Trunk Western's ancestor was Canada's Grand Trunk Railway, conceived in 1852 to connect Montreal and Toronto. To that was added a line from Montreal to the nearest seaport, Portland, Maine. Construction and acquisition to the west in 1858 put the Grand Trunk into Sarnia, Ontario, and across the St. Clair River into Port Huron, Mich., first by ferries and later by a tunnel. The line was extended through Flint, Lansing, and Battle Creek, Mich., and South Bend, Ind., reaching Chicago in 1880.

Grand Trunk stockholders guaranteed the bonds for construction of the Grand Trunk Pacific Railway from Winnipeg, Manitoba, to Prince Rupert, British Columbia. The GTP proved expensive, and GT's financial problems brought it under Canadian government ownership and absorption into the nationalized Canadian National Railways in 1923.

CN incorporated the Grand Trunk Western Railway in 1928 to consolidate the Grand Trunk properties in Michigan,

Indiana, and Illinois; it also owned a car ferry dock yard in Milwaukee, Wis.

In 1980 GTW bought the 580-mile Detroit, Toledo & Ironton, which ran from Detroit south to the Ohio River at Ironton, Ohio. DT&I's history included control by Henry Ford, an electrification experiment, ownership by subsidiaries of the Pennsylvania and its successor, Penn

Central, and ownership of the Ann Arbor.

In 1981 GTW purchased Norfolk & Western's half interest in the jointly owned Detroit & Toledo Shore Line (Detroit–Toledo, 50 miles). N&W had acquired its share of D&TSL when it merged the Nickel Plate Road in 1964.

GTW's main line from Port Huron to Chicago was augmented by secondary mains to Detroit from Durand and Port Huron. In 1987 GTW sold its line from Durand north to Bay City to the Central Michigan Railway. Most of the line west of Durand to Grand Rapids and Muskegon was abandoned. In 1990, GTW sold the remnant of DT&I south of Springfield to Washington Court House to the Indiana & Ohio, and in 1997 GTW sold the Diann (Mich.)–Springfield portion to the I&O.

The map depicts GTW circa 1991, the year Canadian National and its U. S. subsidiaries began to be marketed and publicized as CN North America. With this, GTW and the other subsidiaries lost their own identities and colors to the parent.

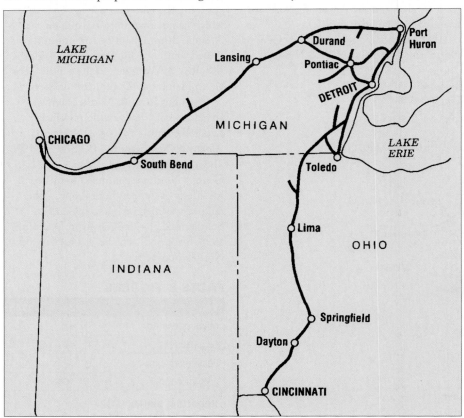

FACTS & FIGURES

Year	1929	1983
Miles operated	925	1,514
Locomotives	286	262
Passenger cars	n/a	—
Freight cars	7,441	11,867
Reporting marks: GTW		
Historical society: gtwhs.org		

Great Northern

Great Northern 2-8-4 No. 2526, with white extra flags posted, rolls a long string of red boxcars across the Minnesota prairie around 1950. The class P-2 locomotive was built by Baldwin in 1923. *Linn H. Westcott*

In 1857 the Minnesota & Pacific Railroad was chartered to build a line from Stillwater, Minn., on the St. Croix River, through St. Paul and St. Cloud to St. Vincent, in the northwest corner of the state. The company defaulted after completing a roadbed between St. Paul and St. Cloud, Minn., and its charter was taken over by the St. Paul & Pacific Railroad, which ran its first train between St. Paul and St. Anthony (now Minneapolis) in 1862.

For financial reasons the railroads were reorganized as the First Division of the St. Paul & Pacific. Both StP&P companies were soon in receivership, and Northern Pacific, with which the StP&P was allied, went bankrupt in the Panic of 1873.

In 1878 James J. Hill and an associate, George Stephen, acquired the two St. Paul & Pacific companies and reorganized them as the St. Paul, Minneapolis & Manitoba Railway (often referred to as "the Manitoba"). By 1885 the company had 1,470 miles of railroad and extended west to Devils Lake, N. D. In 1886 Hill organized the Montana Central Railway to build from Great Falls, Mont., through Helena to Butte, and in 1888 the line was opened, creating in conjunction with the StPM&M a railroad from St. Paul to Butte.

In 1881 Hill took over the 1856 charter of the Minneapolis & St. Cloud Railroad. He first used its franchises to build the Eastern Railway of Minnesota from Hinckley, Minn., to Superior, Wis., and Duluth. Its charter was liberal enough that he chose it as the vehicle for his line to the Pacific. He renamed the road the Great Northern Railway; it then leased the Manitoba and assumed its operation.

Over the mountains to Puget Sound

Hill decided to extend his railroad from Havre, Mont., west to the Pacific, specifically to Puget Sound at Seattle. He had briefly considered building to Portland, but it was already served by the Oregon-Washington Railroad & Navigation Co. and the Northern Pacific.

Hill's surveyors found an easy route through the Rockies over Marias Pass. Later there was considerable advocacy for creating a national park in the Rockies of northern Montana, and GN—in particular, Louis W. Hill, son of James J. and president of GN from 1907 to 1912 and 1914 to 1919—joined the forces urging the establishment of Glacier National Park. Great Northern developed the park, and for many years furnished the only transportation to it. The park, in turn, drew passengers to the railroad-owned hotels and provided the railroad with a herald, a Rocky Mountain goat (actually a species of antelope). GN sold its Glacier Park hotel properties in 1960.

The Cascade Range in the state of Washington was a far more formidable barrier to the Great Northern. The Northern Pacific had originally detoured to the south, using Oregon-Washington rails along the Columbia River. Hill, however, saw the vast stands of timber on the slopes of the mountains as a resource, and his engineer, John Stevens, found a pass (it now bears his name) that could afford a route from the interior of Washington to the tidewater of Puget Sound.

The Great Northern was opened through to Seattle in 1893 using a temporary line over Stevens Pass. In 1900 the first Cascade Tunnel, 2.63 miles long, provided relief from the switchbacks and the 4 percent grades of the temporary line and lowered the summit of the line from 4,068 feet to 3,383 feet.

The tunnel was electrified with a two-wire, three-phase system in 1909. The electrification was replaced with a more conventional system in 1927 as a prelude to the opening of the 7.79-mile second Cascade Tunnel in 1929. The new tunnel, the longest in the Western Hemisphere, lowered the maximum elevation of the line to 2,881 feet and eliminated 8 miles of snowsheds and more than five complete circles of curvature. The tunnel project included other line relocations in the area and the extension of the electrified portion of the line east to Wenatchee and west to Skykomish.

A new General Electric U33C in the Big Sky Blue scheme is paired with a couple of F units as it leads a freight through Index, Wash., in June 1969. *Jerrold F. Hilton*

Lines in Canada

Even before completion of the route from St. Paul, the Great Northern opened a line along the shore of Puget Sound between Seattle and Vancouver, British Columbia, in 1891. In the years that followed, Hill pushed a number of lines north across the international boundary into the mining area of southern British Columbia in a running battle with Canadian Pacific. In 1912 GN traded its line along the Fraser River east of Vancouver to Canadian Northern for trackage rights into Winnipeg.

Great Northern gradually withdrew from British Columbia after Hill's death. In 1909 the Manitoba Great Northern Railway purchased most of the property of the Midland Railway of Manitoba (lines from the U. S. border to Portage la Prairie

and to Morden), leaving the Midland, which was jointly controlled by GN and NP, with terminal properties in Winnipeg. The Manitoba Great Northern disposed of its rail lines in 1927. They were later abandoned.

Later expansion

In 1907 the Great Northern purchased the properties and assets of the St. Paul, Minneapolis & Manitoba and of a number of its proprietary companies, such as the Eastern Railway of Minnesota and the Montana Central. In 1928 there was another spate of such activity. The result was that GN was a large railroad with very few subsidiaries, unlike, for example, the Southern Railway.

Among the major branches and lines added to the system were the Surrey

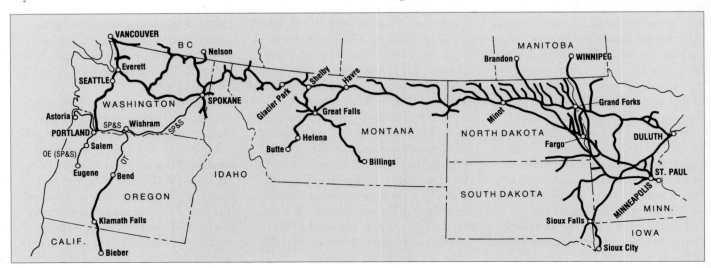

When Great Northern re-equipped its *Empire Builder* in 1951, only four years after the first sets of the train's green-and-orange streamlined equipment entered service, the 1947 equipment became the *Western Star*, which is shown in Glacier National Park. *Great Northern*

Cutoff between Fargo and Minot, N. D. (opened in 1912), which shortened the route between St. Paul and Seattle by about 50 miles.

Another acquisition was an interurban system, the Spokane, Coeur d'Alene & Palouse, which ran east and south from Spokane. This line was absorbed by GN in 1943.

Another addition was an extension of the Oregon Trunk from Bend, Ore., south to a connection with the Western Pacific at Bieber, Calif., completed in 1931 (from Chemult to Klamath Falls, Ore., on Southern Pacific rails).

The Great Northern changed little in the modern era—from the 1920s through the 1960s—apart from the industry-wide change from steam to diesel. A ventilating system allowed dieselization of the Cascade Tunnel in 1956 and eliminated the electrification. In November 1970 the Cascade Tunnel acquired a rival, the Flathead Tunnel, shorter by only 70 yards, as part of a line relocation necessitated by

construction of a dam at Libby, Mont. Most of the construction was done by GN; only the last portion and the actual opening of the tunnel were done by Burlington Northern.

The 69-year merger

On July 1, 1901, the Great Northern and the Northern Pacific jointly purchased more than 97 percent of the stock of the Chicago, Burlington & Quincy to ensure a connection between St. Paul and Chicago. GN and NP backed construction of the Spokane, Portland & Seattle Railway from Spokane, Wash., to Portland, Ore. SP&S, in turn, sponsored the construction of the Oregon Trunk Railway from Wishram, Wash., on the Columbia River, south to Bend, Ore. GN got another route to Portland by acquiring trackage rights on Northern Pacific from Seattle.

Hill soon acquired control of Northern Pacific with the intent of merging GN, NP, Burlington, and SP&S into a single railroad. As a start, he formed Northern

Securities as a holding company, but the Interstate Commerce Commission quickly ruled against such a merger.

In 1927 the Great Northern Pacific Railway was incorporated to merge GN and NP and lease SP&S and the Burlington. The ICC approved the merger upon the condition that GN and NP divest themselves of the Burlington—a condition the two Northerns were unwilling to meet. More than four decades passed before the merger went through on March 2, 1970—with the CB&Q included and providing half the name of the Burlington Northern.

FACTS & FIGURES

Year	1929	1969
Miles operated	8,368	8,274
Locomotives	1,164	609
Passenger cars	946	415
Freight cars	55,777	36,300
Reporting marks: GN		
Historical society: gnrhs.org		

Green Bay & Western

The Green Bay & Lake Pepin Railway was chartered in 1866 to build west from Green Bay, Wis., to the Mississippi River. The road was to provide a Lake Michigan port for Minnesota's wheat and serve the growing lumber industry of northern Wisconsin. The first spike was driven in 1871, and the road reached the Mississippi at East Winona, Wis., in 1873. After several name changes and a period of control by the Lackawanna Iron & Coal Co., an affiliate of the Delaware, Lackawanna & Western, the road was reorganized as the Green Bay & Western Railway in 1896.

The railroad's eastern extension to Lake Michigan was incorporated in 1890 as the Kewaunee, Green Bay & Western Railroad, and opened in 1891. At Kewaunee it connected with the carferries that crossed Lake Michigan to Frankfort and Ludington, Mich. The KGB&W came under GB&W control in 1897. GB&W merged it on Jan. 1, 1969.

Another subsidiary, the Ahnapee & Western, branched off the KGB&W at Casco Junction and ran 33 miles northeast to Sturgeon Bay. GB&W sold the short line in 1947.

The importance of GB&W's bridge traffic diminished in the late 1970s—Ann Arbor's ferries from Frankfort ceased running in 1982, and Chesapeake & Ohio was down to a single Ludington–Kewaunee run. At the same time the importance of Wisconsin's paper industry increased to the point that Burlington Northern expressed interest in acquiring the GB&W.

The Itel Corporation acquired the Green Bay & Western in 1977 primarily as

Westbound Green Bay & Western train No. 1 departs Green Bay for Winona, Minn., behind Alco C-430 No. 315 and C-424 No. 320 in July 1985. *Michael S. Murray*

a place to store its box car fleet, as traffic was down.

Fox River Valley

In its downsizing of the late 1980s, the Chicago & North Western sought to sell its lines between Milwaukee and Green Bay—more specifically, from Granville, in the northwest corner of the city of Milwaukee, north through Fond du Lac and Appleton to Green Bay; from Cleveland, north of Sheboygan, to Duck Creek (a junction on the north side of Green Bay); and from Kaukauna South to New London. The Itel Corporation purchased the lines to form the Fox River Valley Railroad. It began operation Dec. 9, 1988.

The new railroad was unable to earn enough money to pay the interest on the

purchase price, and the business surge as the 1990s began meant Itel no longer needed a place to store its box cars.

Wisconsin Central

In late 1991 Itel placed the GB&W and FRV under the same management and approached Wisconsin Central about buying the two railroads. In January 1992 WC announced it was forming a subsidiary, Fox Valley & Western Ltd., to acquire those railroads. There were loud protests from the C&NW (which had sold those lines), Soo Line (which had sold most of its Wisconsin routes to WC), and from labor unions. The Interstate Commerce Commission imposed conditions protecting the jobs of the employees affected. The ICC made its final ruling on Aug. 27, 1993, and Wisconsin Central took possession of the two roads that day.

FACTS & FIGURES

Year	1929	1992
Miles operated	234	254
Locomotives	31	25
Passenger cars	32	—
Freight cars	888	1,687

Reporting marks: GBW

Historical society: gbwhs.org

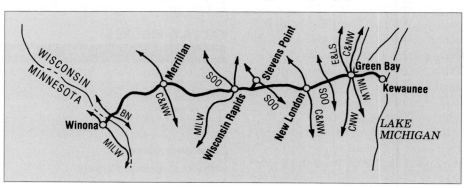

Gulf, Mobile & Northern

In 1890 the Mobile, Jackson & Kansas City Railroad was chartered to tap the longleaf-pine areas of southern Mississippi. In 1898 it opened the first 50 miles of line northwest from Mobile, Ala., to the new town of Merrill, Miss., named for one of the promoters of the railroad, and in 1902 reached Hattiesburg, Miss.

New promoters bought the line and also purchased the 62-mile narrow gauge Gulf & Chicago between Middleton, Tenn., and Pontotoc, Miss., then proceeded to fill in the 240 miles between the two railroads. The MJ&KC entered receivership in 1906 shortly after construction was completed; it emerged in 1909 as the New Orleans, Mobile & Chicago Railroad. In 1911 the Louisville & Nashville and the Frisco assumed joint control of the NOM&C with the thought of using the road as an entrance to New Orleans. In 1913 the railroad's finances collapsed again.

The Gulf, Mobile & Northern Railroad began operation on Jan. 1, 1917, as a reorganization of the NOM&C. One of the first items of business was to extend the road north 40 miles from Middleton, Tenn., to Jackson and connections with Illinois Central and Nashville, Chattanooga & St. Louis. (See the Gulf, Mobile & Ohio map on the next page).

In 1926 GM&N began operating freight trains from Jackson, Tenn., north to Paducah, Ky., on trackage rights over NC&StL. At Paducah GM&N connected with the Chicago, Burlington & Quincy, with which it made a preferential traffic agreement, forming a Chicago to Gulf route that did not require a competing road, such as Illinois Central, to short-haul itself in order to give traffic to GM&N. (IC had considered GM&N a friendly connection until GM&N extended itself to Jackson, Tenn.)

In 1928 GM&N merged with the 49-mile Birmingham & Northwestern, which ran from Jackson, Tenn., northwest to Dyersburg, Tenn. The GM&N had controlled it since 1924. In 1929 GM&N merged with the Meridian & Memphis (from Union, Miss., east to Meridian) and the Jackson & Eastern (from Union west

In 1934, Decapods (2-10-0s) made up one-third of Gulf, Mobile & Northern's steam roster. Number 261 is equipped with a Coffin feedwater heater. *C. W. Witbeck*

to Jackson, Miss.). Over the years the two Jacksons on GM&N's map, both of them important cities, must have created untold confusion for GM&N's ticket agents, traffic reps, and historians. On Dec. 30, 1929, GM&N acquired control of New Orleans Great Northern, which ran from Jackson, Miss., to New Orleans, and on July 1, 1933, GM&N leased the NOGN.

GM&N got through the Depression by reducing wages, services, and maintenance, but subsidiary New Orleans Great Northern defaulted on bond interest and had to reorganize. In 1935 GM&N upgraded its through passenger service with the *Rebel* trains, the first streamliners in the South. The *Rebels* and the various types of rail motor cars GM&N had been using gave the road an all-motorized passenger service. In 1936 GM&N organized Gulf Transport, a bus and truck subsidiary to supplement rail service and replace money-losing local passenger trains; GM&N had been operating highway services for several years under its own banner.

On June 1, 1933, GM&N moved its Jackson, Tenn.–Paducah freight trains from the NC&StL to Illinois Central rails on a route 34 miles shorter. In 1934 the road began to study acquisition of bankrupt Mobile & Ohio, whose line paralleled GM&N from Mobile to Jackson, Tenn., and continued north from Jackson to St. Louis. A line to St. Louis would bypass

the need for operating on the rails of competitor Illinois Central and would afford connections with railroads to the east, north, and west. Ralph Budd (who represented Burlington's stock interest, nearly 30 percent, on GM&N's board) objected, because Burlington would lose its exclusive connection with GM&N and also collect a smaller portion of the freight revenue because of its lesser mileage on a through move. M&O acquisition was given added impetus in 1936 when problems arose with GM&N crews operating over IC rails. On June 30, 1938, a decree was rendered— GM&N trains would have to use IC crews within 20 days. GM&N quickly executed a traffic agreement with Mobile & Ohio and ceased operating to Paducah.

Despite the objections of the CB&Q and the IC—IC said that one day it would buy GM&N and M&O—the merger of Gulf, Mobile & Northern and Mobile & Ohio took place on Sept. 13, 1940.

FACTS & FIGURES

Year	1929	1940
Miles operated	734	827
Locomotives	77	55
Passenger cars	39	31
Freight cars	1,573	1,647
Reporting marks: GM&N		
Historical society: gmohs.org		

Gulf, Mobile & Ohio

A Gulf, Mobile & Ohio Alco PA waits with its local train for a crew change at Bloomington, Ill., en route to St. Louis in 1950. *Richard K. Smith*

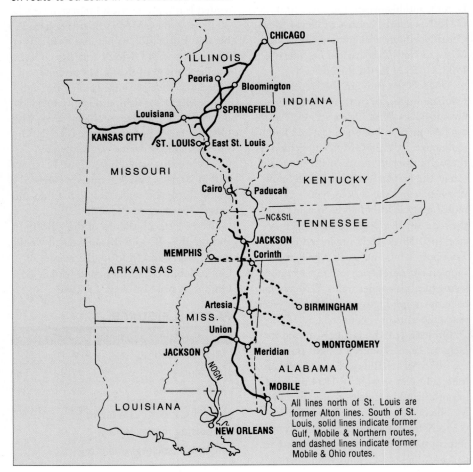

All lines north of St. Louis are former Alton lines. South of St. Louis, solid lines indicate former Gulf, Mobile & Northern routes, and dashed lines indicate former Mobile & Ohio routes.

The Gulf, Mobile & Ohio was incorporated in Mississippi on Nov. 10, 1938, to acquire the properties of the Mobile & Ohio and the Gulf, Mobile & Northern. It acquired the M&O through foreclosure sale on Aug. 1, 1940, and was consolidated with the GM&N on Sept. 13, 1940. The new railroad extended from New Orleans and Mobile and Montgomery, Ala., north to St. Louis.

During World War II GM&O trimmed a few branches from its system, consolidated shop facilities, and otherwise tightened up the organization. In 1944 the road began to investigate acquiring the bankrupt Alton Railroad, which extended from St. Louis to Chicago and from Springfield, Ill., west to Kansas City. On May 31, 1947, GM&O merged the Alton and became a Great Lakes-to-Gulf carrier.

At first GM&O planned to sell the Kansas City line, which was an east-west appendage to an otherwise north-south system. In 1948 GM&O, the Burlington, and the Santa Fe formulated a plan that would result in the sale of the Kansas City line to the Burlington, Santa Fe's use of that line and the connecting Burlington line at Mexico, Mo., for access to St. Louis, and Burlington trackage rights over Santa Fe into Kansas City from the northeast. Several railroads serving St. Louis protested Santa Fe's part in the plan. As it fell out, Burlington acquired trackage rights over GM&O between Mexico and Kansas City and in 1952 opened 71 miles of new line across northern Missouri to shorten its own Chicago to Kansas City route. Santa Fe never gained access to St. Louis.

FACTS & FIGURES

Year	1929	1971
Miles operated	1,808	2,734
Locomotives	180	258
Passenger cars	96	92
Freight cars	6,255	12,699

Reporting marks: GM&O
Historical society: gmohs.org

In 1949 and 1950 GM&O acquired the properties of three roads the Alton had leased: the Kansas City, St. Louis & Chicago Railroad; the Louisiana & Missouri River Railroad; and the Joliet & Chicago Railroad. GM&O inherited Mobile & Ohio's trackage rights on Southern and Illinois Central track between Memphis, Corinth, Miss., and Birmingham. In 1952 GM&O acquired trackage rights over Louisville & Nashville from Tuscaloosa to Birmingham and ceased use of the Corinth–Birmingham route.

GM&O was one of the first major railroads to dieselize completely. Its last steam operation was on Oct. 7, 1949. By 1947 GM&O's passenger service south of St. Louis consisted of the *Rebel* trains, the first streamliners in the South, between St. Louis and New Orleans and the St. Louis–Mobile *Gulf Coast Rebel*. In addition subsidiary Gulf Transport operated an extensive bus system between St. Louis and the Gulf Coast. Rail passenger service to New Orleans ended in 1954, and the St. Louis–Mobile train was discontinued in 1958.

North of St. Louis GM&O took over an intensive passenger service from the Alton: seven trains daily between Chicago and St. Louis, a pair of St. Louis–Kansas City trains operated jointly with the Burlington, and a few motor-train locals and mixed trains on branches. The Bloomington, Ill.–Kansas City motor train run endured until 1960.

When Amtrak took over the nation's passenger trains, GM&O was operating three Chicago–St. Louis trains and a Chicago–Joliet commuter train. Amtrak continued the operation of the two daytime Chicago–St. Louis trains. The Chicago–Joliet train survived the startup of Amtrak and the ICG merger. Metra now operates three Chicago–Joliet commuter trains on the former GM&O route.

GM&O merged with Illinois Central on Aug. 10, 1972, forming the Illinois Central Gulf Railroad. Successive events are properly part of ICG's history, but a summary here will not be amiss. ICG was trying hard to be a north-south railroad and realized it had eight east-west lines. In the 1980s it spun off those routes—indeed, spun off two-thirds of its mileage, including most of the former Gulf, Mobile & Ohio.

On July 10, 1985, Gulf & Mississippi purchased most of the former GM&O

Three GP30s and a GP35 lead a southbound freight through Scooba, Miss., in the late 1960s. The EMDs ride on AAR trucks from traded-in Alco FAs. *J. Parker Lamb*

routes in Alabama, Mississippi, and Louisiana. On April 14, 1988, a subsidiary of MidSouth Rail (which had purchased ICG's Meridian–Shreveport route) bought the Gulf & Mississippi. Kansas City Southern acquired MidSouth in 1993. (For a few months in 1994, Illinois Central was intent on purchasing KCS, which would have started the whole cycle over again.)

The Chicago, Missouri & Western bought the Joliet–St. Louis and Springfield–Kansas City routes on April 28, 1987, essentially re-creating the Alton Railroad. CM&W declared bankruptcy less than a year later.

On Sept. 30, 1989, Southern Pacific purchased the Joliet–East St. Louis route from the CM&W, extending its Cotton Belt subsidiary to Chicago. The new operation was titled SPCSL (for Southern Pacific Chicago St. Louis). Union Pacific acquired the line as part of its merger of Southern Pacific.

On Jan. 9, 1990, Gateway Western, an affiliate of the Santa Fe, purchased the Springfield–Kansas City and Godfrey–Roodhouse lines from CM&W. On May 5, 1997, Gateway Western became a subsidiary of the expanding Kansas City Southern.

Illinois Central (Illinois Central Gulf)

SD70 No.1005, one of 40 bought new from EMD in the 1990s, is at Coles, Ill., in July 2007. It displays the post-1988 "new Illinois Central" image, with the "AT&T-like" emblem on the solid black associated with IC's early diesels. The SD70s were IC's last new power. *Aaron Ryherd*

Illinois Central Railroad dated from 1851 when it was chartered by its home state to build a line from Cairo, at Illinois' southern tip—the confluence of the Ohio and Mississippi rivers—to Galena, in the northwestern corner of the state and at the time a mining center. Soon added was the "Chicago Branch" from Centralia (named for the railroad) northeast to the growing city on the Lake Michigan shore. The "branch" would soon become the railroad's more important route.

After its 19th-century growth, the IC had a stable system until its 1972 merger with the Gulf, Mobile & Ohio to form the Illinois Central Gulf. To summarize what then happened between 1972 and 1988 can be done in 23 words: Illinois Central got married, put on weight, had a bunch of kids, got divorced, slimmed way down, and took its old name back.

During the 1940s, '50s, and '60s the IC was as conservative and traditional a railroad as you could find. It stayed with steam power for freight service longer than most railroads, into 1960. It carried great quantities of coal north from the seams of southern Illinois, and it ran fast merchandise freight trains up and down the Mississippi Valley. Its passenger operations included an intense suburban service south from Chicago, electrified in 1926, as well as a glossy brown-and-orange fleet of streamliners south to St. Louis, and New Orleans, and west on its Iowa Division. During the passenger-train decline of the 1960s, many observers considered IC's Chicago–New Orleans *Panama Limited* to be the best train in the country.

As Illinois Central Gulf, the company bought some short lines in the 1970s, then in the mid-1980s sold off a large number of lines (including nearly all the former GM&O) to entrepreneurs who created shortline and regional railroads. IC shrank to about 40 percent of its pre-1970 size, then later bought back some of those new 1980s lines. ICG went back to being Illinois Central in 1988 and returned to black on its locomotives (but gray for cabooses) to replace the IC orange-and-white livery from the '60s, which ICG minimally modified before trying, briefly, solid orange and then an unattractive gray-and-orange.

Canadian National bought the IC on Feb. 11, 1998, and merged it in 1999.

Early history

When the IC was chartered in 1851, a previous undertaking had resulted in a few miles of grading north of Cairo, but nothing else. The IC was aided, however, by a land-grant act signed by President Millard Fillmore in 1850. Finished in 1856, the IC was a Y-shaped railroad with its junction just north of Centralia. With the "branch," the IC gave Chicago an outlet to the Mississippi River for north-south traffic, and the railroad operated a steamboat line between Cairo and New Orleans.

On the southern front, IC entered into a traffic agreement with the New Orleans, Jackson & Great Northern Railroad and the Mississippi Central Railway. The former had been opened in 1858 from New Orleans north through Jackson, Mississippi, to Canton, Miss.; the latter was completed in 1860 from Canton north to Jackson, Tenn. IC completed its own line between Jackson, Tenn., and Cairo in 1873. (Traffic had previously used the Mobile & Ohio Rail Road between Jackson and Columbus, Ky., and a riverboat between Columbus and Cairo.)

In 1874 the IC, principal bondholder of the NOJ&GN and Mississippi Central, took them over. The lines south of Cairo were built to the 5-foot track gauge that was standard in the South, and remained at that gauge until July 29, 1881.

Illinois Central No. 2619, last of 20 4-8-2s built in IC's Paducah, Ky., shops in 1942–1943 (considered the finest 4-8-2s among its 147) leads a train of mostly Louisville & Nashville two-bay hopper cars near Monee, Ill., Sept. 5, 1955. *George Krambles; Krambles-Peterson Archive*

In the 1870s railroads began to penetrate the fertile Yazoo Delta along the western edge of the state of Mississippi (eastern bank of the great river). IC's entry was the Yazoo & Mississippi Valley Railroad, incorporated in 1882 to build a railroad west from Jackson, Miss. Meanwhile, a north-south rival, the Louisville, New Orleans & Texas Railway, was under construction between Memphis and New Orleans via Vicksburg and Baton Rouge, west of IC's main line. That company obtained the backing of C. P. Huntington, who saw the route as a connection between his Southern Pacific at New Orleans and his Chesapeake, Ohio & Southwestern at Memphis.

Huntington's forces completed the LNO&T in 1884, then purchased the Mississippi & Tennessee Railroad, whose line from Memphis southeast to Grenada, Miss., funneled traffic to the IC. Saber-rattling ensued—in the form of canceled traffic agreements—but Huntington's empire was in financial trouble. IC purchased the LNO&T and the Mississippi & Tennessee and consolidated them with the Yazoo & Mississippi Valley. This all increased IC's mileage by 28 percent and greatly expanded its presence in the South.

IC's southern lines were connected by rail to the northern part of the system in 1889 with the completion of the Ohio River bridge at Cairo. In 1893 IC purchased the Chesapeake, Ohio & Southwestern (Louisville to Memphis) and in 1895 built a line into St. Louis from the southeast, near Carbondale, Ill.

Expansion west and east

IC's original line had been extended west from Galena, Ill., to the Mississippi River, then across Iowa by leasing the Dubuque & Sioux City Railroad, which reached Sioux City in 1870. In the late 1880s under the leadership of E. H. Harriman, the road undertook a westward expansion program. The Chicago, Madison & Northern was incorporated in 1886 to build from Chicago to a connection with the Centralia–Galena line at Freeport, Ill., then north to Madison, Wisconsin's capital, with a branch to Dodgeville, Wis., in another mining area. IC also built branches to Cedar Rapids, Iowa; Sioux Falls, S. D.; and Omaha, Neb.

In 1906 the IC completed a line from Effingham, Ill., east to Indianapolis, partly through new construction and partly through acquisition of narrow-gauge lines.

In 1908 it assembled a route from Fulton, Ky., to Birmingham, Ala., largely on trackage rights, and in 1909 it acquired control of the Central of Georgia. In 1928 IC built a cutoff line between Edgewood, Ill., south of Effingham, and Fulton, Ky., to bypass congestion at Cairo; modern engineering made this a preferred freight route over the hill-and-dale country south of Carbondale on the original route.

After World War II, IC began to simplify its corporate structure, absorbing the Yazoo & Mississippi Valley and the Gulf & Ship Island (in southeastern Mississippi), purchasing the Chicago, St. Louis & New Orleans, and acquiring control of the east-west Alabama & Vicksburg and Vicksburg, Shreveport & Pacific, which had been leased by the Y&MV.

In the 1950s and early '60s IC purchased several short lines: former interurban Waterloo, Cedar Falls & Northern (jointly with the Rock Island through a new subsidiary, Waterloo Railroad); Tremont & Gulf in Louisiana; Peabody Short Line, a coal-hauler at East St. Louis, Ill.; and Louisiana Midland.

In 1968 Illinois Central acquired the western third—Nashville to Hopkinsville, Ky.—of the Tennessee Central when that

Illinois Central equipped its Chicago-New Orleans *Panama Limited* with streamlined lightweight cars and new Electro-Motive E6 diesels in 1942. *Electro-Motive*

financially ailing line was split among IC, Louisville & Nashville, and Southern.

Illinois Central Gulf

Illinois Central and parallel Gulf, Mobile & Ohio "married" on Aug. 10, 1972, to create the Illinois Central Gulf Railroad, a wholly owned subsidiary of Illinois Central Industries. (This was when Class Is were diversifying away from just railroads.) As part of the merger, ICG took over three Mississippi lines: Bonhomie & Hattiesburg Southern; Columbus & Greenville; and Fernwood, Columbia & Gulf.

GM&O was itself the product of several mergers, being created in September 1940 by the merger of the Gulf, Mobile & Northern; Mobile & Ohio; and New Orleans Great Northern. In May 1947 GM&O bought the Alton Railroad, a triangular system linking Chicago, St. Louis, and Kansas City, and the premier Chicago–St. Louis passenger carrier.

GM&O was a likely merger partner for Illinois Central, as it was a north-south railroad through much the same area as IC. In the 1960s the management team that in its younger years had put together the GM&O was no longer young, and no replacements were being groomed.

The north-south lines of ICG's map resembled an hourglass. Driving across Mississippi or Illinois from east to west, you could encounter as many as eight ICG lines. The former IC system converged at Fulton, Ky., on the Tennessee border, and the former GM&O main line was less

than 10 miles west of Fulton at Cayce.

In addition, ICG had these routes that ran east and west:

- Chicago to Omaha, Nebraska, and Sioux City, Iowa (ex-IC)
- Springfield and Godfrey (Alton), Ill., to Kansas City, Missouri (ex-GM&O)
- Effingham, Ill., to Indianapolis (ex-IC)
- Paducah to Louisville, Ky. (ex-IC)
- Birmingham, Alabama, to Corinth, Miss. (ex-IC, mostly on trackage rights), and on from Corinth to Memphis, Tenn. (ex-GM&O, trackage rights on Southern)
- Montgomery, Ala., to Columbus, Miss. (ex-GM&O) and on to Greenville, Miss. (ex-Columbus & Greenville)
- Meridian, Miss., to Shreveport, Louisiana (ex-IC; previously Alabama & Vicksburg and Vicksburg, Shreveport & Pacific)
- Mobile, Ala., to Natchez, Miss. (a combination of former GM&O, Bonhomie & Hattiesburg Southern, and Mississippi Central lines).

Slimming down

ICG soon decided that the east-west lines did not fit with a north-south railroad. Its 515-mile Chicago–Council Bluffs route was the longest of the six post-World War II railroads connecting those cities (the others being Milwaukee Road; Chicago Great Western; Chicago & North Western; Burlington Route; and Rock Island. Wabash also did, but indirectly.) GM&O had tried to sell its Kansas City line to the Burlington in 1947, but it remained a long rural branch, as it had been with the Alton.

The Louisville line, once the Chesapeake, Ohio & Southwestern, ultimately proved more valuable for its route to Memphis from the north than for the line east to Louisville. The Mobile–Natchez route had a ferry, not a bridge, at its west end, and the connecting railroads west of the Mississippi River led mostly to junctions with the Meridian–Shreveport line. In most cases, use of one of ICG's east-west lines as a bridge route required one of the connecting roads to short-haul itself (get less than the maximum possible haul and revenue from a car of freight).

New regionals from ICG lines

In slimming down, ICG created several sizeable new regional lines:

- July 10, 1985: Gulf & Mississippi purchased most of the former GM&O routes south of Tennessee.
- December 24, 1985: Chicago, Central & Pacific purchased the line from Chicago to Omaha and its branches to Cedar Rapids and Sioux City, Iowa.
- March 31, 1986: MidSouth Rail Corp. purchased the Meridian–Shreveport line and the Hattiesburg–Gulfport, Miss., line (the southern half of the former Gulf & Ship Island).
- August 27, 1986: Paducah & Louisville purchased the Louisville–Paducah route, plus branches west and south of

IC FACTS & FIGURES

Year	1929	1971
Miles operated	6,712	6,760
Locomotives	1,762	766
Passenger cars	2,034	462
Freight cars	65,035	49,709

Reporting marks: IC

Historical society: icrrhistorical.org

ICG FACTS & FIGURES

Year	1972	1987
Miles operated	9,657	3,205
Locomotives	1,039	558
Passenger cars	371	—
Freight cars	58,882	17,172

Reporting marks: ICG

Historical society: icrrhistorical.org

Three E units in the classic IC orange-and-brown livery (with the 1967 "split-rail" emblem) cross above the electric suburban line at 23rd Street in departing Chicago with the *City of Miami* on April 25, 1971, six days before Amtrak. *James L. Jeffrey photo; Frank and Todd Novak collection*

Paducah, and the Paducah shops.
- April 28, 1987: Chicago, Missouri & Western purchased the Joliet–St. Louis and Springfield/Godfrey (Alton)–Kansas City routes, essentially re-creating the old Alton Railroad (CM&W declared bankruptcy on April 1, 1988).
- April 14, 1988: A MidSouth subsidiary, SouthRail, purchased the Gulf & Mississippi, which was also bankrupt.
- 1988: The Fulton, Ky.–Birmingham, Ala., route was sold to Norfolk Southern.
- September 30, 1989: ICC approved Southern Pacific's purchase of the Joliet–East St. Louis route from CM&W to operate as Southern Pacific–Chicago–St. Louis (SPCSL).
- January 9, 1990: Gateway Western, a Santa Fe affiliate, purchased the Springfield–Kansas City and Godfrey–Roodhouse, Ill., routes from the bankrupt CM&W. Kansas City Southern would ultimately buy and absorb the Gateway Western.

New short lines from ICG

Shorter new carriers also were created:
- March 28, 1974: ICG sold the Louisiana Midland, which it had purchased

Illinois Central Gulf GP38-2 No. 9631 pulls an extra freight northbound past the grain elevator at Tuscola, Ill., on the former IC Chicago–New Orleans main line, July 16, 1986. *Scott A. Hartley*

exactly seven years before.
- 1975: ICG sold the Columbus & Greenville, which it had acquired in September 1972.
- February 26, 1980: Chicago, Madison & Northern, re-using the original name, began operation between Freeport, Ill., and Madison, Wis. The line was later operated by the Central Wisconsin Railroad, then the Wisconsin & Calumet, which began operation Jan. 1,

1985. Ultimately this line woud be abandoned.
- March 1982: Tradewater Railway purchased two western Kentucky branches, from Waverly to Princeton and from Blackford to Providence.
- March 1, 1982: Natchez Trace Railroad began operation on the Grand Junction, Tenn.–Oxford, Miss., route (the ex-IC line southwest from Jackson, Tenn.)
- December 5, 1983: Tennken Railroad

began operation on the Dyersburg, Tenn.–Hickman, Ky., route (an ex-GM&O branch northwest of Jackson, Tenn.).

- August 1984: Gibson County Railroad Authority acquired 43 miles of the former Mobile & Ohio main line from Lawrence, Tenn., near Jackson, north to Kenton. It is operated by the West Tennessee Railroad, an affiliate of Tennken.
- September 20, 1984: Cedar Valley Railroad purchased the Waterloo, Iowa–Albert Lea, Minnesota, route.
- March 1986: Indiana Hi-Rail Corp. acquired the Henderson, Ky.–Evansville, Ind.–Browns, Ill., route.
- March 19, 1986: Indiana Rail Road began operation on the Indianapolis line between Indianapolis and Sullivan, Ind.
- 1990: Indiana Rail Road purchased the Sullivan, Ind.–Newton, Ill. (east of Effingham), and Newton-Browns, Ill.,

lines, and turned the latter over to Indiana Hi-Rail for operation. The Indianapolis–Newton line has enjoyed increased traffic, but Newton–Browns is abandoned.

ICG's slimming down included not only routes but track and rolling stock. More than half its Chicago–New Orleans main line was double track; IC reduced it to single track with a computerized CTC system. IC scrapped its surplus freight cars and sold its excess locomotives. It turned its attention to long-haul business between Chicago and the Gulf of Mexico.

Illinois Central again

On Feb. 29, 1988, the railroad changed its name back to Illinois Central, having divested itself of nearly all the former Gulf, Mobile & Ohio routes it acquired in 1972, when it added "Gulf" to its name. At the end of 1988 the Whitman Corp. (formerly IC Industries) spun off the railroad, which then dropped "Gulf" from the name, and in August 1989 control of the railroad was gained by the Prospect Group, which formerly controlled spinoff MidSouth Rail.

In late 1990 Illinois Central made an offer to purchase MidSouth, but MidSouth rejected the offer. Then as stock prices changed, IC withdrew the offer. Kansas City Southern purchased MidSouth (plus SouthRail and MidLouisiana Rail) in 1993. The next year IC proposed merger with the Kansas City Southern, but that did not occur.

IC then turned its eyes west, to the Chicago Central & Pacific, which it had sold for $75 million. It saw CC&P's route across northern Iowa as a source of grain traffic and perhaps a way to get some of the coal moving east from Wyoming. In June 1996 IC purchased the CC&P for $157 million. The line remains active.

In February 1998 Canadian National Railway Co., recently privatized after more than 80 years of government ownership, agreed to purchase the IC, creating a 19,000-mile railroad that would be the fifth-largest in North America in revenue. CN absorbed IC operations as of July 1999, and IC lost its own identity within the CN system. CN would ultimately go on to acquire other lines to strengthen itself in the central U.S., including Wisconsin Central Ltd.; Duluth, Missabe & Iron Range; Bessemer & Lake Erie; and Elgin, Joliet & Eastern.

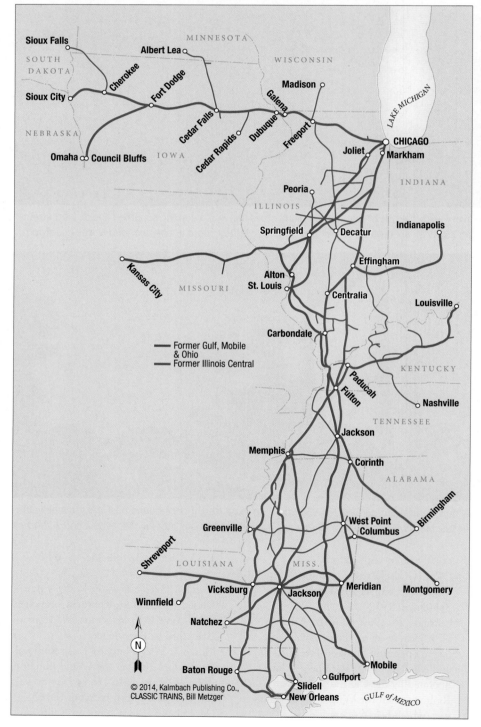

Illinois Terminal

The Illinois Terminal had its beginning in the 1890 purchase of a streetcar system serving the adjacent towns of Urbana and Champaign, Ill., by William B. McKinley, an Illinois congressman and utilities tycoon. He sold it in 1893, bought it again, and within two decades expanded it into an interurban system from Danville and Peoria through Springfield to East St. Louis and across the Mississippi River on its own bridge (which would bear his name) to St. Louis, Mo. His empire also included an interurban line between Joliet and Princeton, Ill., that was intended to form a Chicago extension of the system.

When McKinley was elected to Congress in 1904 the railway system was placed in the hands of Illinois Traction Co. The ITC early recognized the importance of freight service: It built bypasses around most of the major cities to avoid running freight trains on city streets, and in 1909 it established joint rates with Chicago & Eastern Illinois and St. Louis-San Francisco—similar arrangements with other steam roads soon followed.

In 1923 ITC formed a subsidiary, Illinois Power & Light, to hold the railroad properties, which were then consolidated as Illinois Traction System (the various parts of the system had been built by different companies, though all under the same ownership). Manager of the system was Clement Studebaker, of the South Bend, Indiana, automobile manufacturing family.

In 1925 Illinois Traction acquired two steam railroads serving the industrial area east of the Mississippi, the St. Louis & Illinois Belt and the St. Louis, Troy & Eastern. At the beginning of 1928 Illinois Power & Light Corporation acquired all the common stock of the Illinois Terminal Railroad, a line from Edwardsville to Alton. Illinois Terminal then leased the two steam roads and Illinois Traction. In 1930 the Alton & Eastern, a remnant of the steam road Chicago, Peoria & St. Louis, was brought into the family, which by then was known as the Illinois Terminal Railroad System.

Orange ITC interurban car 270 loads passengers in the street at Danville for the trip west to Springfield in May 1950. *Kalmbach Publishing Co.: David A. Strassman*

Reorganization, purchase

The company was reorganized in 1937 as the Illinois Terminal Railroad Co. Most railroad reorganizations involved minor changes of name, usually "Railroad" to "Railway" or vice versa. IT's history is different in the matter of names. The Purchaser Railroad was incorporated in 1945 to acquire Illinois Terminal Railroad Co. On Dec. 14, 1945, the old IT became the

Liquidating Railway, and Purchaser Railroad was renamed Illinois Terminal.

In 1954 the Illinois-Missouri Terminal Railway was incorporated by nine Class I railroads (the reason being the IT could furnish steam roads neutral access to the industrial area between East St. Louis and Alton): Baltimore & Ohio; Chicago & Eastern Illinois; Chicago, Burlington & Quincy; Gulf, Mobile & Ohio; Litchfield & Madison; Illinois Central; Nickel Plate; Frisco; and Wabash. The Illinois-Missouri Terminal purchased the IT in June 1956, whereupon Illinois-Missouri Terminal was renamed Illinois Terminal Railroad and the previous Illinois Terminal was renamed Liquidating Terminal. Later, Rock Island and the New York Central bought in to IT.

Passenger service

IT was one of the last interurbans to offer passenger service. The 1930s saw the abandonment of branchline passenger service and the routing of mainline passenger trains off the streets of the major cities (except Bloomington) and onto IT's freight belt lines. IT discontinued all of its city streetcar services in 1936, except for those in Peoria, which lasted another decade, and St. Louis's Illinois suburbs.

IT's interurban passenger service was notable for several features: sleeping cars, parlor cars, and streamliners. Only three interurbans operated sleeping cars: Interstate Public Service (Indianapolis–Louisville), Oregon Electric (Portland–Eugene), and IT. IT's service was much more extensive and longer-lived than the other two and was operated largely with private-room cars. The principal sleeper route was Peoria–St. Louis, a route with no steam-road competition. Peoria–St. Louis sleepers ran until 1940. For a short time a sleeper ran between Champaign and St. Louis, and a Springfield–St. Louis setout car lasted until 1934.

IT offered parlor-buffet car service on many of its day trains almost until the end of passenger service. After World War II the road purchased three streamliners (eight cars—three cab-baggage-coach cars, two coaches, and three buffet-parlor-observation cars) for St. Louis–Decatur and St. Louis–Peoria service. Streamliner service to Decatur was discontinued within two years, and the trains never reached Peoria because IT's track curvature into the depot could not handle them, so streamliner service was offered only into East Peoria. Moreover, the cars had to be uncoupled to be turned at East Peoria and St. Louis. The ill-advised streamliners lost their names and their parlor-buffet cars in 1951.

In 1955 passenger service was dropped north and east of Springfield. Less than a year later, Springfield–St. Louis passenger service was discontinued, leaving only the St. Louis–Granite City, Ill., suburban service, which lasted until June 1958.

Shrinkage

In 1950 the Illinois Terminal began eliminating unproductive track, beginning with the line through Bloomington and most of the Granite City–Wood River–Alton–Grafton route. At the same time IT began dieselizing its freight service, and by the end of 1955 only the passenger service—what little remained of it—was operated electrically. By 1980, IT's main lines were about two-thirds trackage rights on parallel railroads and one-third owned. The major portions of IT's own lines remaining in service were the former steam-powered lines in the East St. Louis area. To quit its line north of Lincoln, IT in 1976 purchased a former Pennsylvania branch between Maroa (north of Decatur) and Farmdale (near East Peoria).

Norfolk & Western purchased Illinois Terminal on Sept. 1, 1981, and IT's corporate existence ended on May 8, 1982.

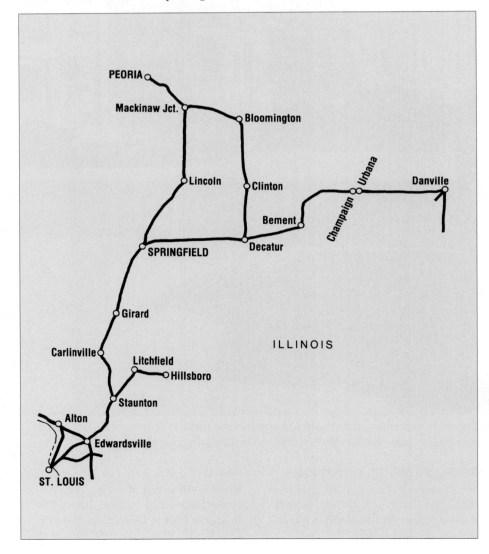

FACTS & FIGURES

Year	1929	1980
Miles operated	484	413
Locomotives	73	46
Passenger cars	124	—
Freight cars	—	2,624
Reporting marks: ITC		
Historical society: illinoistractionsociety.org		

Indiana Rail Road

In 1906 the Indianapolis Southern Railroad, a subsidiary of the Illinois Central, completed a line from Effingham, Ill., on IC's main line, east and north to Indianapolis. Part was new construction; the segment between Sullivan and Switz City, Ind., was the former narrow-gauge Illinois & Indiana Railroad—incorporated in 1880 and reorganized and renamed several times before it came under IC control in 1900. In 1977 Illinois Central Gulf petitioned to abandon 89 miles of the line from Switz City to Indianapolis. Much of it had a 10-mph speed limit because of track conditions. A year later the Federal Railroad Administration embargoed 56 miles of that segment, from Bloomington to Indianapolis, owing to the track condition.

In the late 1970s Thomas Hoback began negotiations with ICG to purchase the line. Negotiations ended when ICG obtained state and federal funds to repair the track to raise the speed limit to 25 mph, but in 1983 ICG changed its course and decided to sell the line. Hoback resumed negotiations, and in December 1985 he purchased the Sullivan-Indianapolis segment through a holding company, Indianapolis Terminal Corporation.

Indiana Rail Road (reporting marks INRD) began operations March 18, 1986. In August 1989 INRD acquired from Norfolk Southern a 40-mile line from Indianapolis north to Tipton, the south

An Indiana Rail Road freight rolls southbound behind SD90MAC No. 9001 at Shuffle Creek Viaduct, north of Unionville, Ind. (east of Bloomington), on Sept. 10, 2008. *Michael Stickel*

end of the former Nickel Plate's Indianapolis–Michigan City line. INRD abandoned the line in November 1991. Indiana Transportation Museum operates excursion service on it by agreement with NS.

In 1990 INRD purchased the Sullivan to Newton, Ill., segment of the IC line and also IC's Newton-Browns, Ill., branch, but sold the latter (since abandoned) to Indiana Hi-Rail in May 1992. In May 2006, INRD bought from Canadian Pacific the former Milwaukee Road line from Terre Haute to Bedford, Ind. (The map depicts INRD circa 1991, prior to this purchase.)

INRD remains a growing operation, its principal jobs being to carry coal to an Indianapolis Power & Light power plant at Indianapolis and to a Central Illinois Public Service plant west of Newton, and to serve Marathon Oil's refinery at Robinson, Ill.

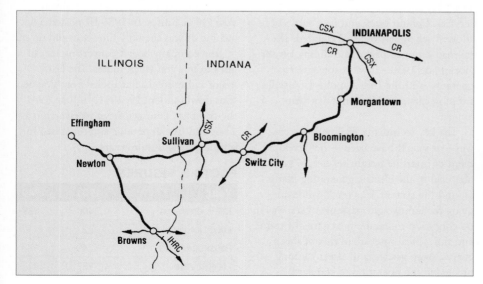

FACTS & FIGURES

Year	1986	2012
Miles operated	160	552
Locomotives	12	41
Passenger cars	—	—
Freight cars	71	208
Reporting marks: INRD		

Indiana Railroad

In the early 1920s Samuel Insull owned large interests in electric power companies and electric railways in Indiana. Among the companies controlled by his Midland United Corporation were:

- Interstate Public Service, which had an interurban line between Indianapolis and Louisville, Ky.
- Northern Indiana Public Service Company, whose rail lines centered on Kokomo, Ind.
- Winona Service Company, which had a single line connecting the interurbans of northern and central Indiana
- Gary Railways, which operated street-cars in Gary and interurban lines radiating from Gary, Ind.

In 1925 Insull added the Chicago, Lake Shore & South Bend (predecessor of the Chicago South Shore & South Bend) and the Indiana Service Corporation, which had rail lines centered on Fort Wayne. That same year Insull proposed consolidating these companies. The Indiana Public Service Commission rejected the proposal.

In 1930 Insull acquired the property of the bankrupt Union Traction Company, which had lines north, northeast, and east of Indianapolis. Insull reorganized the Union Traction system as the Indiana Railroad on Aug. 1, 1930, and coordinated its operations with the Northern Indiana,

Indiana Railroad car 375, built in 1926, was rebuilt in 1935 for the road's new Railway Post Office route. It's shown here at the Indianapolis terminal. *Wilbourne B. Cox collection*

Indiana Service, and Interstate lines. The new system covered almost 700 route miles.

Not included in the Indiana Railroad were the Winona, the only link with the northern tier of the state but a weak company; the Terre Haute, Indianapolis & Eastern, whose lines ran northwest, west, and southwest from Indianapolis (it was in receivership at the time the IR was formed); and the Fort Wayne-Lima Railroad.

The new railroad made a point of offering frequent, coordinated passenger train services and fast freight and package service, and it immediately ordered 35 high-speed lightweight cars to re-equip those services. Rebuilt track and new substations allowed schedules to be accelerated. The railroad dropped parlor and dining car service in late 1930—it was expensive to operate—and the Indianapolis–Louisville sleeping cars remained only two years longer.

The key to Indiana Railroad's success was—or would have been—the development of interline freight service, in particular coal to the electric generating plants around the system. IR's track, while adequate for lightweight passenger cars, was in no condition to handle heavy freight trains, and the typical interurban mix of sharp curves, steep grades, and street running precluded the operation of standard

steam-railroad freight cars over much of the system.

In June 1931 the Indiana Railroad acquired the bankrupt Terre Haute, Indianapolis & Eastern. It abandoned the weaker lines but retained the routes east to Richmond and west to Terre Haute and Paris, Illinois. Then IR began to abandon the weakest of its lines as the Depression took hold. Insull was forced out of the management of the company in 1932, and the company entered receivership in 1933. The company struggled to keep the business it had, emphasizing its package freight service and even acquiring two Railway Post Office routes. In 1936 IR posted a net income. It was the only time it would do so.

The company began converting its rail lines to bus and truck routes. The last major rail route, Indianapolis–Fort Wayne, shut down on Jan. 19, 1941. In June 1941 the company emerged from receivership as a bus and truck operator and remained in business several more years.

FACTS & FIGURES

Year	1931	1940
Miles operated	404	189
Locomotives	27	19
Passenger cars	240	138
Freight cars	253	113

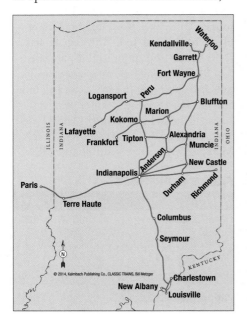

© 2014, Kalmbach Publishing Co., CLASSIC TRAINS, Bill Metzger

Interstate

One of the Interstate's ten Alco RS-3 diesels switches hopper cars at the railroad's yard at Andover, Va., on May 21, 1960. The diesels wore a colorful white, gray, orange, and silver scheme. *Steve Patterson*

The Interstate was incorporated in 1896 and completed in 1909 from Stonega to Norton, Virginia, 16 miles. In 1913 it absorbed the Wise Terminal Co., and in 1923 it constructed a branch line from Norton to a connection with the Clinchfield near St. Paul, Va. That branch soon became the main line. Interstate's chief business was hauling coal for its parent, Virginia Coal & Iron Co.

Whatever the goal implied by the name of the railroad, it never crossed the Virginia state line, though it got within a mile or two. The Southern Railway bought the Interstate in June 1961. Operations largely remained unchanged through the mid-1960s, when Interstate operations were absorbed by the Southern, and the railroad's ten colorful RS-3s were repainted in Southern colors.

FACTS & FIGURES

Year	1929	1960
Miles operated	83	88
Locomotives	12	10
Passenger cars	6	—
Freight cars	3,052	2,812

Reporting marks: INT

Historical society: interstaterailroad.net

© 2014, Kalmbach Publishing Co., CLASSIC TRAINS, Bill Metzger

Iowa Interstate

The Rock Island & La Salle Rail Road was chartered in 1847 to build a railroad between the Mississippi River at Rock Island, Ill., and the Illinois & Michigan Canal at La Salle. The charter was soon amended to extend the railroad all the way to Chicago and rename the company the Chicago & Rock Island Rail Road. Construction began in 1851, and the railroad was opened between Chicago and Rock Island in 1854. The railroad built the first bridge across the Mississippi in 1856 to join its rails with those of the Mississippi & Missouri Railroad. Through sale and consolidation the two railroad companies became the Chicago, Rock Island & Pacific Railroad. The rails reached the Missouri River at Council Bluffs, Iowa, opposite Omaha, on May 11, 1869.

When the bankrupt Rock Island ceased operation on March 31, 1980, several agencies took over operation on portions of the line. Chicago's Regional Transportation Authority purchased the Chicago-Joliet line so Rock Island's commuter service could continue. Freight service on that segment was operated by Chicago Rail Link. The Joliet-Bureau-Peoria portion was operated briefly by the Elgin, Joliet & Eastern, then equally briefly in part by Burlington Northern and in part by Winchester & Western. In August 1980 Baltimore & Ohio began operating the Joliet-Bureau portion of the main line and part of the Peoria branch, with trackage rights from Joliet east to Blue Island. Farther west, short segments of the main line were operated by Davenport, Rock Island & Northwestern; Milwaukee Road; and Chicago & North Western.

In November 1981 the Iowa Railroad

Iowa Interstate ES44AC No. 506 leads two other diesels on westbound freight BICB at Marengo, Iowa, on the Third Subdivision on January 12, 2011. *Craig Williams*

began operating the west end of the route from Council Bluffs to Dexter, Iowa, 97 miles, plus branches to Audubon and Oakland. In June 1982 the Iowa Railroad extended its operation east to Bureau, Illinois, in hopes of capturing traffic moving between Union Pacific at Council Bluffs and B&O at Bureau. An interesting quirk in Iowa's operations was a shared-track arrangement with the Milwaukee Road between Iowa City and West Davenport—Iowa Railroad used the track from 8 p.m. to 8 a.m., and Milwaukee Road used it from 8 a.m. to 8 p.m. Iowa Railroad's operation was not particularly successful.

Several industries along the route and the Cedar Rapids & Iowa City Railway formed Heartland Corporation, which purchased the railroad between Council

Bluffs and Bureau (except for a short piece at Des Moines that Chicago & North Western had bought) in October 1984. Included in the deal were branches to Oakland, Audubon, and Pella, Iowa, and Milan, Ill., and trackage rights from Bureau to Blue Island. Heartland established an operating subsidiary, the Iowa Interstate Railroad.

Iowa Interstate Railroad began operations on Nov. 2, 1984. The road's freight traffic is primarily agricultural products and ethanol.

Railroad Development Corporation purchased the railroad and infrastructure from Heartland in December 2003.

Early motive power consisted mainly of rebuilt GP7s and GP9s; today the railroad has 14 GE ES44ACs and a large group of second-hand GP38-2 and SD38-2 diesels.

FACTS & FIGURES

Year	1985	2013
Miles operated	598	580
Locomotives	37	45
Passenger cars	—	—
Freight cars	398	574
Reporting marks: IAIS		

© 2014, Kalmbach Publishing Co., CLASSIC TRAINS, Bill Metzger

Kansas City, Mexico & Orient

In the 1880s Albert Kimsey Owen proposed a railroad that would form a land bridge for traffic between Europe and the Far East, to connect Norfolk, Va., and Topolobampo, Mexico. Owen incorporated the Texas, Topolobampo & Pacific Railroad, but little more came of his proposal.

In 1897 Enrique Creel, governor of the Mexican state of Chihuahua, incorporated the Ferrocarril Chihuahua al Pacifico, a railroad to run from the city of Chihuahua to the Pacific coast. The railroad opened its first section, 124 miles from Chihuahua to Minaca, on March 31, 1900.

The Rio Grande, Sierra Madre & Pacific Railroad was incorporated on June 11, 1897, to build a line between Ciudad Juarez to the Pacific at Tijuana. The railroad worked southwest to Madera, just west of the Continental Divide. The Chihuahua al Pacifico built a branch north from La Junta to Temosachic, and the ChP and the RGSM&P teamed up to organize the Sierra Madre & Pacific to construct the line between Madera and Temosachic, 54 miles. In 1909 the Sierra Madre & Pacific, the Rio Grande, Sierra Madre & Pacific, and the Chihuahua al Pacifico were consolidated as the Ferrocarril Nor-Oeste de Mexico (Mexico North-Western Railway).

In 1899 Arthur E. Stilwell proposed a railroad from Kansas City to the nearest Pacific port, Topolobampo. Creel granted

Number 402, a former Santa Fe 2-8-0, leads an eastbound way freight at Pichachos, between Chihuahua and Ojinaga. *Edward C. Spalding*

Stilwell trackage rights from Chihuahua to Minaca, 122 miles, and also the federal concessions of the Chihuahua al Pacifico. Stilwell secured the rights and lands of the Texas, Topolobampo & Pacific.

On April 30, 1900, Stilwell incorporated the Kansas City, Mexico & Orient Railway. By mid-1903 lines were open from Milton, Kan., near Wichita, to Carmen, Okla.; from Chihuahua 34 miles eastward; and from Topolobampo to El Fuerte. By early 1912 the U. S. portion of the line reached from Wichita to Girvin, Tex. However, by 1912 Mexico was deep in a revolution. The road entered receivership in March 1912, and the newly organized Kansas City, Mexico & Orient Railroad purchased the KCM&O on July 6, 1914. The Orient built an extension to Alpine, Tex., where it connected with Southern Pacific.

In the early 1920s, the Mexican government said it would extend the line east from Chihuahua toward the border at Presidio, and oil was discovered in west Texas.

In 1924 a U. S. government loan came due. The KCM&O was unable to repay it, and the railroad was sold at auction and emerged as the Kansas City, Mexico & Orient Railway. Oil pipelines had begun to cut into the Orient's oil traffic. The extension to Kansas City was never built, nor were the three disjointed Mexican portions of the railroad connected.

On Sept. 24, 1928, the Santa Fe purchased the Orient (merger came on June 30, 1941, except for the Texas portion, which was merged in 1964). Santa Fe then sold the three Mexican portions of the road to B. F. Johnston and the United Sugar Co. of Los Mochis. Johnston combined the operations of the Mexican portion of the KCM&O with those of the Mexico North-Western, whose rails joined the eastern and middle portions of the KCM&O. In October 1930 the eastern portion of the line was opened to Ojinaga. The Santa Fe extended a line from Alpine to Presidio and bridged the Rio Grande that same year, opening a new gateway for traffic between the U. S. and Mexico.

FACTS & FIGURES

Year	1929	1954
Miles operated	349	384
Locomotives	11	15
Passenger cars	11	18
Freight cars	255	356
Reporting marks: KCM&O		

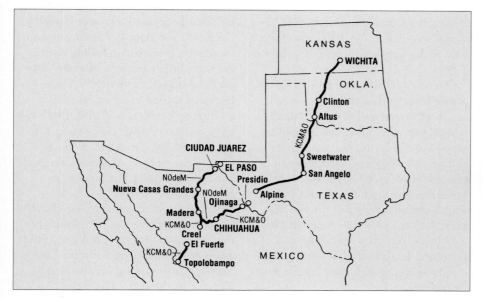

Kansas City Southern

Kansas City Southern 3936, an SD70MAC in the railroad's classic red, yellow, and black scheme, leads northbound train GHVKC-27 at Gentry, Ark., on the Heavener Subdivision on May 27, 2012. *Dan Kwarciany*

In 1889 Arthur Stilwell began building the Kansas City, Nevada & Fort Smith Railroad (the Nevada being Nevada, Mo.), the earliest antecedent of a trunk line that would one day extend from Kansas City to the Gulf of Mexico. (The railroad's name was changed to Kansas City, Pittsburg & Gulf in 1892.) Intended to facilitate the export of Midwestern grain, the railroad was built directly south from Kansas City, Mo., creating the shortest route from Kansas City to tidewater. In 1897 its rails reached the Gulf of Mexico at the new city of Port Arthur, Texas—which Stilwell built and named for himself.

The KCP&G fulfilled its purpose. Midwestern farmers saw immediate additional profits, the Kansas City Board of Trade thrived, and new timber stands in Louisiana and East Texas were tapped. But Stilwell was a promoter, not an operating man,

and he was unable to cope with the resulting traffic on his lightly-built line. In 1899 the railroad was forced into receivership. Stilwell was ousted (he turned his hand to building the Kansas City, Mexico & Orient Railway) and the KCP&G was reorganized as the Kansas City Southern Railway in 1900.

Discovery of the Spindletop oil field in eastern Texas the following year brought more northbound traffic. To build up the railroad, Leonor F. Loree was brought in, and he served as board chairman from 1906 to 1936. (For most of that period he was also president of Delaware & Hudson, explaining, perhaps, the similarity of the steam locomotive rosters of the two railroads. Both railroads were dominated by improbably large Alco-built 2-8-0s, all of them hand-fired, with a sprinkling of Mallet locomotives to assist drag freights over the mountains.)

Today's KCS also includes two railroads with Louisiana roots. Between 1896 and 1907 William Edenborn built a railroad between New Orleans and Shreveport, La.—the Louisiana Railway & Navigation Co. In 1923 he extended the line west to McKinney, Texas, within hailing distance of Dallas, by purchasing a Missouri-Kansas-Texas branch. Separately, William Buchanan started a logging railroad in southwestern Arkansas in 1896. By 1906 it was a common carrier: the Louisiana & Arkansas Railway, with a main line from Hope, Ark., south to Alexandria, La., and a short branch from Minden, La., to Shreveport.

Louisiana utility entrepreneur Harvey Couch became interested in railroads in the 1920s, acquiring the L&A and LR&N and consolidating them under the L&A banner. He then turned his attention to Kansas City Southern, acquiring a controlling interest in 1939, and merging L&A into it. For the first time, there was direct, single-line service from Kansas City to New Orleans, and KCS celebrated by christening a new daily streamliner, the *Southern Belle*. The marketing blitz associated with the train was a powerful statement of brand identity for the reborn KCS, serving notice to shippers and the traveling public that a new option was available.

Couch died in 1941, and leadership passed to William N. Deramus Jr., who had risen through the ranks at KCS since hiring on in 1909. Faced immediately with the demands of heavy World War II traffic (Texas crude was still a significant revenue generator, and the KCS service area was replete with military bases), Deramus rebuilt the railroad with heavier rail, new ties, Centralized Traffic Control, and diesel locomotives. He was succeeded in 1961 by his son, William N. Deramus III.

The post-war years were a dark period for much of the industry and for KCS. Over-regulation and publicly subsidized competition were eroding revenue, and with no end in sight, cost containment seemed to be the order of the day. The younger Deramus had previously kept M-K-T and Chicago Great Western afloat with aggressive economy measures, and he did the same at KCS.

Eventually, however, deferred maintenance began to take its toll, and by the late 1960s, KCS was in poor condition. It didn't help that the railroad's first-generation

The northbound *Southern Belle* is ready to depart New Orleans for Kansas City behind an Electro-Motive E6 in August 1950. *James G. La Vake*

diesels were wearing out at the same time, foreshadowing a significant capital spending need for motive power and track maintenance alike. Worse, management's attention was diverted during this time by a diversification scheme that was intended to cushion the losses from the railroad. Holding company Kansas City Southern Industries eventually owned more than 100 non-rail subsidiaries, while the railroad that had started it all languished.

In late 1972 KCS experienced a rash of derailments and a traffic surge at the same

time. Deramus was still focused largely on KCSI, but he tapped Thomas S. Carter, a civil engineer who had served under him at M-K-T, to address the problems at the railroad. Carter was named president in 1973, and he recognized that KCS had two major problems: undermaintained track and midtrain helper locomotives positioned so they were pushing more than pulling. The helper problem was easy to solve; the track required (and got) a $75 million rebuilding program.

While the rebuilding was in process, the road landed a contract to move coal to power plants in Arkansas, Louisiana, and Texas, further justifying reconstruction. Besides an improved physical plant, Carter is also credited with a change in operating philosophy—away from the lengthy, once-daily trains of the Deramus III era, and embracing scheduled operations with shorter trains and more efficient car handling.

The KCS renaissance of the past 20 years is often reckoned to have started with the 1994 acquisition of MidSouth Rail Corp. This former Illinois Central property provided KCS with a link between its legacy lines at Shreveport and a connection with Norfolk Southern at Meridian, Miss. (MidSouth also had branches to Birmingham, Ala. and central Tennessee.) Ironically, MidSouth was acquired to make KCS more attractive as a takeover candidate.

Kansas City Southern 2-10-4 No. 901 heads upgrade on Rich Mountain (Ark.) as it crosses the Ouachita Mountains in 1939. *Preston George; Louis A. Marre collection*

Mike Haverty thought he could make a going concern of KCS, however. He was named CEO of the railroad in 1995, following successful stints at the Santa Fe, where he had served as president, and Missouri Pacific. In the mid-1990s, Western railroads were consolidating into two mega-systems, BNSF and Union Pacific, and few believed that KCS could remain independent. But Haverty was an avid student of railroad history, and he understood that KCS had always been a north-south railroad in an east-west world: The way to remain independent was to double-down on that heritage.

Shortly after arriving at KCS, Haverty began discussions that would result in the acquisition of the Northeast rail franchise in Mexico, which had become available for privatization. (Haverty was also aware of Arthur Stilwell's dream of a railroad to Mexico's West Coast.) By 2005, KCS and the newly renamed Kansas City Southern de México were a single, integrated railroad, connecting the second-biggest rail center in the U. S. (Kansas City) with Mexico's principal industrial centers and ports on both of Mexico's coasts. Cross-border container and automotive traffic represent a significant share of the company's revenue base.

Also acquired on Haverty's watch were the Texas Mexican Railway and a former Southern Pacific line in Texas, which together closed the gap between KCS's legacy U. S. lines and KCSM. KCS also acquired the former Alton Route lines from Kansas City to East St. Louis, Ill. and Springfield, Ill., thus gaining new connections to the east. In addition, KCS holds a 50 percent interest in the Panama Canal Railway, which provides a faster and often less expensive alternative to the Canal for container traffic.

Kansas City Southern, left for dead more than once, is a modern railroad renaissance story.

FACTS & FIGURES

Year	1984	2012
Miles operated	1,663	6,200
Locomotives	284	900
Passenger cars	—	—
Freight cars	7,025	15,556
Reporting marks: KCS		
Historical society: kcshs.org		

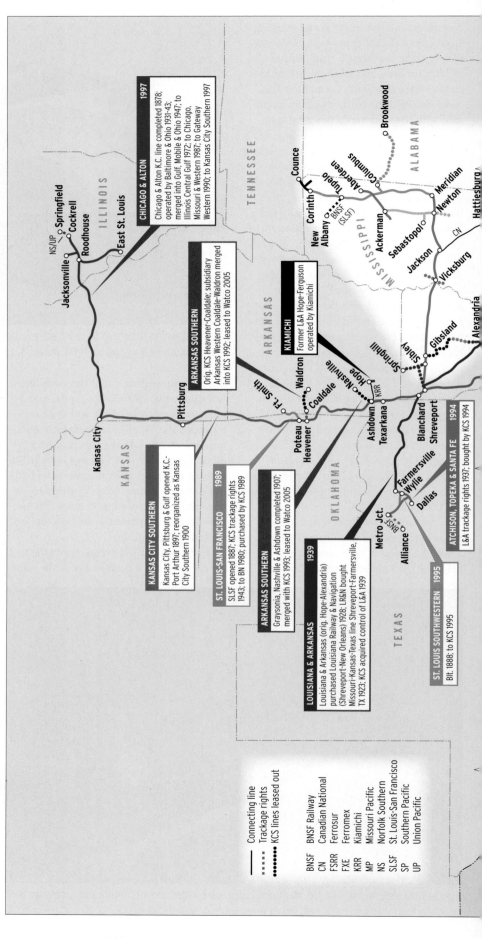

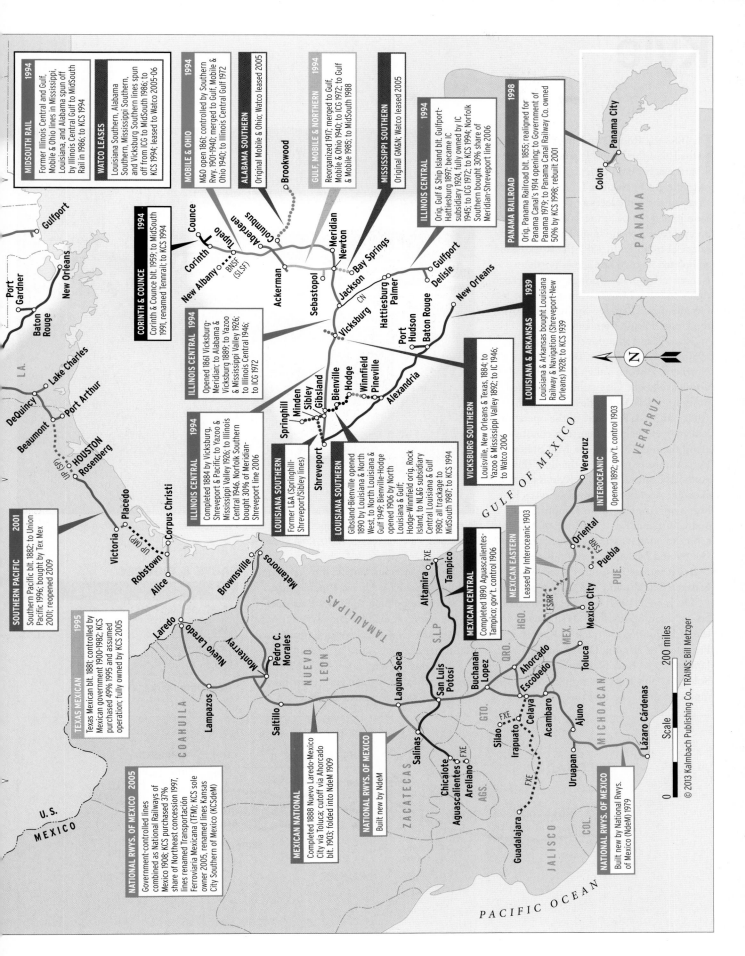

MIDSOUTH RAIL · 1994
Former Illinois Central and Gulf, Mobile & Ohio lines in Mississippi, Louisiana, and Alabama spun off by Illinois Central Gulf to MidSouth Rail in 1986; to KCS 1994

WATCO LEASES
Louisiana Southern, Alabama Southern, Mississippi Southern, and Vicksburg Southern lines spun off from ICG to MidSouth 1986; to KCS 1994; leased to Watco 2005-06

MOBILE & OHIO · 1994
M&O open 1861; controlled by Southern Rwy. 1901-1940; merged to Gulf, Mobile & Ohio 1940; to Illinois Central Gulf 1972

ALABAMA SOUTHERN
Original Mobile & Ohio; Watco leased 2005

GULF, MOBILE & NORTHERN · 1994
Reorganized 1917; merged to Gulf, Mobile & Ohio 1940; to ICG 1972; to Gulf & Mobile 1985; to MidSouth 1988

MISSISSIPPI SOUTHERN
Original GM&N; Watco leased 2005

ILLINOIS CENTRAL · 1994
Orig. Gulf & Ship Island blt. Gulfport-Hattiesburg 1897; became IC subsidiary 1924, fully owned by IC 1945; to ICG 1972; to KCS 1994; Norfolk Southern bought 30% share of Meridian-Shreveport line 2006

PANAMA RAILROAD · 1998
Orig. Panama Railroad blt. 1855; realigned for Panama Canal's 1914 opening; to Government of Panama 1979; to Panama Canal Railway Co. owned 50% by KCS 1998; rebuilt 2001

CORINTH & COUNCE · 1994
Corinth & Counce blt. 1959; to MidSouth 1991; renamed Tennrail; to KCS 1994

ILLINOIS CENTRAL · 1994
Opened 1861 Vicksburg-Meridian; to Alabama & Vicksburg 1889; to Yazoo & Mississippi Valley 1926; to Illinois Central 1946; to ICG 1972

ILLINOIS CENTRAL · 1994
Completed 1884 by Vicksburg, Shreveport & Pacific; to Yazoo & Mississippi Valley 1926; to Illinois Central 1946; Norfolk Southern bought 30% of Meridian-Shreveport line 2006

LOUISIANA SOUTHERN
Former L&A (Springhill-Shreveport/Sibley lines)

LOUISIANA SOUTHERN
Gibsland-Bienville opened 1890 by Louisiana & North West, to North Louisiana & Gulf 1949; Bienville-Hodge opened 1906 by North Louisiana & Gulf; Hodge-Winnfield orig. Rock Island, to NL&G subsidiary Central Louisiana & Gulf 1980; all trackage to MidSouth 1987; to KCS 1994

VICKSBURG SOUTHERN
Louisville, New Orleans & Texas, 1884; to Yazoo & Mississippi Valley 1892; to IC 1946; to Watco 2006

LOUISIANA & ARKANSAS · 1939
Louisiana & Arkansas bought Louisiana Railway & Navigation (Shreveport-New Orleans) 1928; to KCS 1939

MEXICAN EASTERN
Leased by Interoceanic 1903

MEXICAN CENTRAL
Completed 1890 Aguascalientes-Tampico; gov't. control 1906

INTEROCEANIC
Opened 1892; gov't. control 1903

SOUTHERN PACIFIC · 2001
Southern Pacific blt. 1882; to Union Pacific 1996; bought by Tex Mex 2001; reopened 2009

TEXAS MEXICAN · 1995
Texas Mexican blt. 1881; controlled by Mexican government 1900-1982; KCS purchased 49% 1995 and assumed operation; fully owned by KCS 2005

NATIONAL RWYS. OF MEXICO · 2005
Government-controlled lines combined as National Railways of Mexico 1908; KCS purchased 37% share of Northeast concession 1997, lines renamed Transportación Ferroviaria Mexicana (TFM); KCS sole owner 2005, renamed lines Kansas City Southern of Mexico (KCSdeM)

MEXICAN NATIONAL
Completed 1888 Nuevo Laredo-Mexico City via Toluca; cutoff via Ahorcado blt. 1903; folded into NdeM 1909

NATIONAL RWYS. OF MEXICO
Built new by NdeM

NATIONAL RWYS. OF MEXICO
Built new by National Rwys. of Mexico (NdeM) 1979

Gulfport
New Orleans
Port Gardner
Baton Rouge
Lake Charles
DeQuincy
Beaumont
Port Arthur
HOUSTON
Rosenberg
Placedo
Victoria
Robstown
Corpus Christi
Alice
Laredo
Nuevo Laredo
Brownsville
Matamoros
Monterrey
Pedro C. Morales
Lampazos
Saltillo
Salinas
Chicalote
Aguascalientes
Arellano
Guadalajara
Uruapan
Lázaro Cárdenas
Ajuno
Acámbaro
Celaya
Escobedo
Ahorcado
Toluca
Irapuato
Silao
Buchanan
Lopez
San Luis Potosí
Laguna Seca
Altamira
Tampico
Oriental
Puebla
Mexico City
Veracruz

Brookwood
Columbus
Aberdeen
Tupelo
Counce
Corinth
New Albany
Ackerman
Meridian
Newton
Bay Springs
Jackson
Sebastopol
Vicksburg
Hattiesburg
Palmer
Gulfport
Delisle
Port Hudson
Baton Rouge
New Orleans
Alexandria
Pineville
Winnfield
Hodge
Bienville
Gibsland
Minden
Sibley
Springhill
Shreveport

BNSF (SLSF)
CN

COAHUILA
NUEVO LEON
TAMAULIPAS
ZACATECAS
AGS.
JALISCO
MICHOACAN
GTO.
QRO.
HGO.
S.L.P.
MEX.
PUE.
COL.
VERACRUZ
LA.
U.S.
MEXICO

FXE
ESRR

GULF OF MEXICO
PACIFIC OCEAN
PANAMA
Panama City
Colon

N

Scale
0   100   200 miles

© 2013 Kalmbach Publishing Co., TRAINS: Bill Metzger

Kyle

In 1883 the Rock Island, the Milwaukee Road, and the Union Pacific made a tripartite agreement covering interchange of traffic at Omaha. The Chicago & North Western and a predecessor of the Wabash soon joined the pact; the Burlington, left out, protested, then Union Pacific fell into financial troubles. In 1889 the Rock Island completed its own line across northern Kansas to Colorado Springs, with trackage rights to reach Denver, at first over the Rio Grande from Colorado Springs, later over the Union Pacific from Limon, Colo.

Rock Island shut down on March 31, 1980. The Union Pacific, Burlington Northern, Wabash Valley, Brandon, and Cadillac & Lake City railroads operated portions of RI's Colorado main line in 1980 and 1981, but none of the operations had any permanence. Fourteen counties along the route formed the Mid States Port Authority to acquire the line. The Authority contracted with Kyle Railways, a shortline operator, to provide service. Kyle began operating between Limon, Colo., and Courtland, Kan., on Feb. 16, 1982, and soon extended its operations east to Clay Center and Mahaska. In 1986 Kyle purchased a former Missouri Pacific line between Scandia and Yuma Junction, Kan.

On June 2, 1991, Kyle began operation on its Solomon division: 347 miles of leased Union Pacific track in Kansas: Frankfort to Lenora, Downs to Stockton, Jamestown to Burr Oak, and Beloit to Solomon, plus trackage rights from Solomon to Salina. The first three segments

A pair of former Southern Pacific SD45T-2s lead a westbound grain train on the Kyle at Goodland, Kan., on Nov. 3, 2010. *Chip Sherman*

are former Missouri Pacific lines; Beloit-Solomon-Salina is Union Pacific proper.

Shortline holding company RailAmerica bought Kyle in 2002 and owned it until 2012, when Genesee & Wyoming acquired RailAmerica.

The principal reason for the line's existence is wheat, and the Kyle is at its busiest during the summer wheat harvest.

FACTS & FIGURES

Year	1986	2011
Miles operated	778	561
Locomotives	21	28
Passenger cars	—	—
Freight cars	696	906
Reporting marks: KYLE		

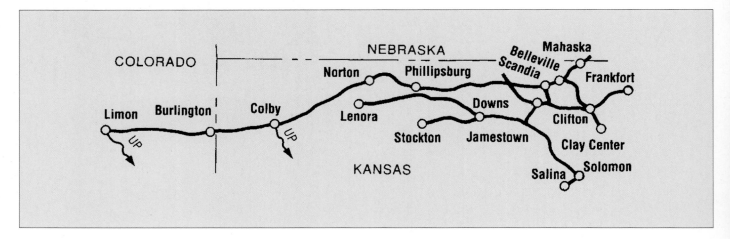

Lake Superior & Ishpeming

A U25C and two U23Cs, painted a bright red and an iron-ore red (or maroon), respectively, switch cars into the car dumper at Empire Mine in Palmer, Mich., in June 1987. LS&I was known for steaming its 2-8-0s into the 1960s, then for its Alco and GE diesels. *Eric Hirsimaki*

In 1896 the Cleveland Cliffs Iron Mining Co. opened the Lake Superior & Ishpeming Railway to transport iron ore from Cleveland Cliffs' mines in Michigan's Upper Peninsula to the Presque Isle docks on Lake Superior at Marquette, Mich.

Previously the ore had been handled by the Duluth, South Shore & Atlantic.

In 1927 the LS&I was merged with the Munising, Marquette & Southeastern Railway, also a Cleveland Cliffs operation and a product of a merger of two small roads between Marquette and Munising, Mich. The new road became the Lake Superior & Ishpeming Railroad. Between 1952 and 1974 the LS&I built branches to serve mines and pellet plants near Ishpeming. In 1963 it sold the Big Bay branch, which ran northwest from Marquette, to tourist line Marquette & Huron Mountain Railroad.

In 1979 LS&I abandoned its trackage east of Marquette, except for a 5-mile segment between Munising and the Soo Line at Munising Junction. That branch was sold to Wisconsin Central Ltd. in 1989. LS&I continues to haul iron, both as ore and as magnetite and hematite pellets for its owner, Cliffs Natural Resources.

FACTS & FIGURES

Year	1929	2012
Miles operated	103	44
Locomotives	33	15
Passenger cars	14	—
Freight cars	2,005	1,304
Reporting marks: LSI		

Lehigh & Hudson River

The Warwick Valley Railroad was chartered in 1860 to build from Warwick, N. Y., to Greycourt, on the New York & Erie. Until 1880, when it went from 6 feet to standard gauge, it was operated with Erie cars and locomotives.

The line was extended southwest to serve iron mines, then all the way to the Delaware River at Belvidere, N. J., as the Lehigh & Hudson River Railroad. The two railroads were consolidated as the Lehigh & Hudson River Railway in 1882.

The a 10-mile extension from Greycourt to Maybrook, N. Y., opened in 1890. At the other end of the line, the Delaware River was bridged.

Initially traffic was agricultural, but soon coal became predominant. The principal industry on the L&HR was a mine and crushing plant of the New Jersey Zinc Co. near Franklin. The purchase of the Central New England and its bridge at Poughkeepsie by the New Haven turned the L&HR into a bridge route. At the insistence of the New Haven, the L&HR was purchased in 1905 by several major railroads to ensure the New Haven's connections with those roads.

In the 1960s the Erie Lackawanna merger shifted traffic off the L&HR to the former Erie line, which connected directly with the New Haven. With the creation of Penn Central, traffic between New England and the South was rerouted through Selkirk, near Albany, via the ex-New York Central West Shore and Boston & Albany lines.

L&HR filed for bankruptcy in April 1972. What little traffic remained disappeared when the Poughkeepsie Bridge burned in 1974. L&HR's property was transferred to Conrail on April 1, 1976.

A Maybrook–Allentown freight rolls through Lake, N. Y., behind No. 94, a massive 2-8-0 with a wide firebox designed for burning anthracite. L&HR dieselized with Alco RS3s. *Donald W. Furler*

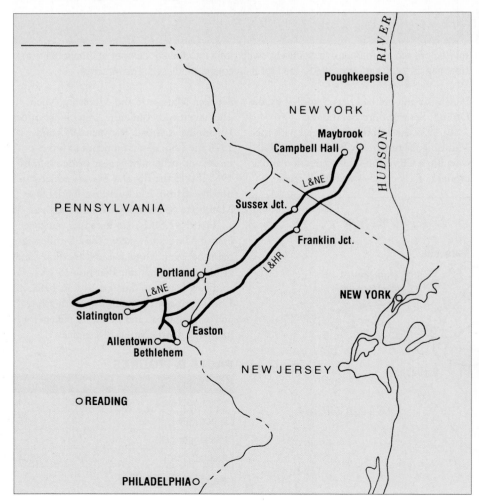

FACTS & FIGURES

Year	1929	1975
Miles operated	97	90
Locomotives	34	6
Passenger cars	14	—
Freight cars	398	2

Reporting marks: LHR

Historical society: anthraciterailroads.org

Lehigh & New England

A matched set of black-and-white Alco FAs leads a long string of coal hoppers through the Lehigh River Gorge circa 1950. *General Electric*

The Lehigh & New England's oldest ancestor was the South Mountain & Boston, chartered in 1873 to construct a railroad between Harrisburg, Pa., and Boston, Mass. Several reorganizations finally produced the Pennsylvania, Poughkeepsie & Boston, which completed a line from Slatington, Pa., on the Lehigh River, to Pine Island, N. Y., using the tracks of the New York, Susquehanna & Western between Hainesburg Junction and Swartswood Junction., N. J.

In 1891 the Philadelphia & Reading leased the road, but canceled the lease when the Pennsylvania, Poughkeepsie & Boston entered receivership in 1893. Yet another reorganization in 1895 produced the Lehigh & New England Railroad (see the map on the facing page). After 1904 most of the L&NE's stock was owned by the Lehigh Coal & Navigation Co.

In 1926 the L&NE and the Reading agreed to a lease of the L&NE by the Reading, but the Interstate Commerce Commission denied the application. In 1929 the Baltimore & Ohio and the Chesapeake & Ohio both asked for four-way control of the L&NE by B&O, C&O, New York Central, and Pennsylvania; that same year the Wabash asked to control the road. All three applications were withdrawn in 1930. The ICC's merger plan of 1929 assigned the road to the New Haven.

Declining traffic in cement and anthracite made the L&NE's fate obvious to its owner. In 1960 the still-solvent L&NE petitioned for abandonment. The Central of New Jersey organized the Lehigh & New England Railway to buy and operate the portions of the line between Hauto and Tamaqua, Pa., and from Bethlehem and Allentown through Bath to Martins Creek,

Pa., about 40 miles total. The remainder of the L&NE was abandoned in 1961.

In 1972 CNJ transferred its own Pennsylvania lines to the Lehigh Valley but continued to operate the L&NE remnants. In 1974 the ICC assigned operation of the line out of Bethlehem to the LV and the Hauto–Tamaqua line to the Reading. Two years later both of those railroads were taken over by Conrail.

FACTS & FIGURES

Year	1929	1960
Miles operated	217	177
Locomotives	61	32
Passenger cars	12	—
Freight cars	3,457	2,608
Reporting marks: LNE		
Historical society: anthraciterailroads.org		

Lehigh Valley

Anthracite coal was discovered at Mauch Chunk (later Jim Thorpe), Pa., in 1791. The only practical means to transport the coal to a sizable market was by boat down the often unnavigable Lehigh River. A canal was constructed, and by the 1820s the Lehigh Coal & Navigation Co. had a near-monopoly on the mining and transportation of coal in the region.

To break the monopoly and also to improve transportation, the Delaware, Lehigh, Schuylkill & Susquehanna Railroad was incorporated in 1846 to build a line from Mauch Chunk to Easton, Pa., where the Lehigh River flows into the Delaware. Construction began in 1851; then with the management and the financing of Asa Packer work began in earnest. The railroad was renamed the Lehigh Valley Railroad in 1853, and it was opened from Easton to Mauch Chunk in 1855.

The railroad began to grow both by new construction and by consolidating with existing railroads. In 1866, the year the Lehigh & Mahanoy merged with Lehigh Valley, Alexander Mitchell, master mechanic of the L&M, designed a freight locomotive with a 2-8-0 wheel arrangement and named it "Consolidation"—the name became the standard designation for that wheel arrangement.

The Lehigh Valley reached north into the Wyoming Valley to Wilkes-Barre in 1867, the same year that Lehigh Coal & Navigation's Lehigh & Susquehanna Railroad, originally a White Haven-to-Wilkes-Barre line, opened a line south along the Lehigh River to Easton, in places on the opposite bank from the LV and in other places sharing the same bank.

In 1865 Packer purchased a flood-damaged canal, renamed it the Pennsylvania & New York Canal & Railroad, and used its towpath as roadbed. The P&NY was completed to the New York & Erie at Waverly, N. Y., in 1869, giving the LV an outlet to the west. In 1876 LV furnished the material and the money necessary for Erie to lay a third rail to accommodate standard gauge trains on its line from Waverly to Buffalo, eliminating the need to transfer

In the late 1930s and early '40s LV streamlined several of its named passenger trains. This is the *John Wilkes*, decked in Cornell red, near Glen Onoko, Pa., in 1939. *Wayne Brumbaugh*

freight and passengers at Waverly. Lehigh Valley leased the P&NY in 1888.

To New York and to Buffalo

At its eastern end Lehigh Valley saw its connecting routes taken over by rival railroads: The Lackawanna acquired the Morris & Essex in 1868, and the Central of New Jersey, formerly considered friendly, leased the Lehigh & Susquehanna in 1871, getting a line parallel to the Lehigh Valley from Easton to Wilkes-Barre.

LV bought the Morris Canal across New Jersey chiefly for its property on New York Harbor at Jersey City. It assembled a line to Perth Amboy in 1875, but not until 1899 did LV reach its Jersey City property on its own rails.

Lehigh Valley's use of Erie rails to reach Buffalo was not completely satisfactory. In 1876 LV got control of the Geneva, Ithaca & Sayre Railroad, which put it into Geneva, N. Y. In the early 1880s LV built a terminal railroad and a station in Buffalo and established a Great Lakes shipping line (whose flag became the emblem of the railroad).

Construction of a line from Geneva to Buffalo and a freight bypass to avoid the steep grades on the GI&S began in 1889. In 1890 LV merged the companies involved in building the new line as the

Lehigh Valley Rail Way. The Buffalo extension was opened in September 1892.

LV lines in western New York included a branch from the new line to Rochester; the former Southern Central Railroad from Sayre to North Fair Haven on Lake Ontario; and the Elmira, Cortland & Northern Railroad, which meandered from Elmira through East Ithaca, Cortland, and Canastota to Camden. In 1896 LV opened a short bypass around Buffalo for traffic to and from Canada.

Alliance with the Reading

A few years earlier Archibald A. McLeod had started the Philadelphia & Reading on a course of expansion with the backing of financiers J. P. Morgan and Anthony Drexel. The Reading negotiated quietly with the Lehigh Valley, which had a Great Lakes outlet for Reading's anthracite as well as its own. The financial arrangement seemed beneficial to LV, too, which had just spent a lot of money getting to Buffalo and was noticing a decline in anthracite traffic. In February 1892 the Reading leased the Lehigh Valley (and also the Central of New Jersey). Morgan and Drexel were suddenly alarmed by the growth of the Reading (it was pursuing the Boston & Maine by then) and withdrew their support. The Reading collapsed into receivership. The lease of the Lehigh Valley was terminated in August 1893.

J. P. Morgan agreed to fund the LV and began rebuilding the road. The independent stockholders of the line protested the diversion of money from dividends into physical plant and regained control in 1902. Several other railroads bought blocks of LV stock—New York Central, Reading, Erie, Lackawanna, and CNJ—and the road became part of William H. Moore's short-lived Rock Island system. In 1913 LV's passenger trains were evicted from the Pennsylvania Railroad's Jersey City terminal and moved to the Central of New Jersey station; in 1918 under the direction of the USRA they were moved into Pennsylvania Station in New York. It remained LV's New York terminus until the end of passenger service.

Several events during the teens adversely affected LV's revenues: a munitions explosion on Black Tom Island on the Jersey City waterfront in 1916, the divestiture of the Great Lakes shipping operation in 1917 (required by the Panama Canal Act), the divestiture of the coal mining subsidiary (required by the Sherman Antitrust Act), and a drop in anthracite traffic as oil and gas became the dominant home-heating fuels.

The ICC merger proposal of the 1920s called for four major railroad systems in the East. The response of Leonor F. Loree, president of the Delaware & Hudson, was a proposal for a fifth system, to include D&H; LV; Wabash; Wheeling & Lake Erie; and Buffalo, Rochester & Pittsburgh. Loree purchased large amounts of LV stock but not enough to gain control. He was later able to sell his shares in Wabash and Lehigh Valley to the Pennsylvania Railroad, which suddenly found itself with 31 percent of LV's common stock, enough to keep LV from falling into the hands of the New York Central. However, the Pennsylvania Railroad exercised no noticeable influence on the policies and operations of the Lehigh Valley.

The Depression and aftermath

Lehigh Valley entered the Depression with its physical plant in good shape and with little debt of its own maturing in the next few years. However, the maturation of bonds of the Lehigh Valley Coal Co., New Jersey state taxes, and interest on debt soon had the railroad in debt to the

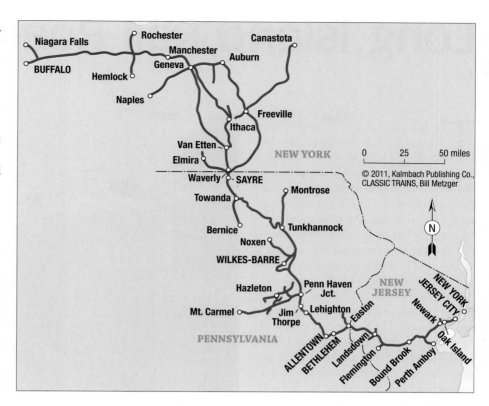

federal government for nearly $8 million. Highways were taking away passenger and freight business. LV began to prune its branches, starting with the former Elmira, Cortland & Northern.

In the late 1930s LV made a valiant effort to attract passenger business by hiring designer Otto Kuhler to streamline its old cars and locomotives. World War II brought a surge of business to on-line Army bases and LV's port facilities, but LV's decline resumed when the war was over.

The route chosen for the New York State Thruway in Buffalo lay along LV's right of way, so after first considering renting facilities from another railroad LV constructed and opened a new terminal in Buffalo in 1955. That same year Hurricane Diane inflicted severe damage on much of LV's line in Pennsylvania, with attendant costs of rebuilding. The next year, 1956, was to be LV's last profitable year.

On the New York–Buffalo run LV's passenger trains competed with the newer and faster trains of the Lackawanna and the New York Central—to say nothing of the new Thruway. In May 1959 LV discontinued all but two of its mainline passenger trains, and those two, the New York–Lehighton *John Wilkes* and the New York–Toronto *Maple Leaf*, lasted less than two years longer. LV was one of the first major railroads to offer only freight service.

Relief from passenger losses made no difference. LV's financial situation continued to worsen. In 1961 the Pennsylvania Railroad bought all the outstanding stock to protect its previous investment in the Lehigh Valley. LV continued to prune branches and reduce double track to single and teamed up with Central of New Jersey to eliminate duplicate lines between Easton and Wilkes-Barre. In 1972 Lehigh Valley took over all of Central of New Jersey's operations in Pennsylvania.

A condition of the creation of Penn Central was that Lehigh Valley be offered to Norfolk & Western and Chesapeake & Ohio; neither wanted it. Penn Central declared bankruptcy on June 21, 1970, and Lehigh Valley filed for bankruptcy protection three days later. LV's properties were taken over by Conrail on April 1, 1976. Most of the track west of Sayre, Pa., was considered redundant and abandoned.

FACTS & FIGURES

Year	1929	1974
Miles operated	1,362	988
Locomotives	725	149
Passenger cars	673	—
Freight cars	26,443	3,965
Reporting marks: LV		
Historical society: lvrrhs.org		

Long Island Rail Road

The Long Island Rail Road was chartered in 1834. It was intended to be one link in a complex New York-Boston route: ferry from Manhattan to Brooklyn; rail to Greenport, New York, at the northeastern tip of Long Island; steamer across Long Island Sound to Stonington, Connecticut; and rail to Boston. The line was completed to Greenport in 1844, but by 1850 the engineers who had assured LIRR backers that a railroad could never be built along the Connecticut shore had been proven wrong—an all-rail route between New York and Boston was capturing most of the business. The Long Island entered receivership and turned its attention away from Boston and toward local matters for several decades.

In 1880 Austin Corbin gained control of the railroad. He planned to make Montauk, N. Y., at the eastern tip of Long Island, a port for transatlantic shipping. His plans came to naught, but the capital he provided helped the railroad. The LIRR absorbed its competitors, including the New York & Flushing and the South Side Railway, and became the only railroad on the island. In 1885 LIRR began operating trains of flatcars to carry farmers' wagons into New York City—the first piggyback service. Under Alexander J. Cassatt the Pennsylvania acquired control of the Long Island in 1900 and included it in plans for Pennsylvania Station in New York City.

Because of its involvement in the Penn Station project, LIRR was able to boast of mainline electrification with 600-volt DC third rail (1905), the first steel passenger car (1905), and the first all-steel passenger

Long Island Rail Road train 233, behind a gray Fairbanks-Morse CPA-20-5, pauses at Mineola Station on its westbound run from Oyster Bay to Jamaica and Queens in 1950. *John Flood*

fleet (1927). The suburban boom on Long Island began in the early 1920s, and LIRR's access to a terminal in Manhattan was a decided asset in building its commuter business.

The LIRR found it difficult to make money in the commuter business, which required lots of rolling stock and large numbers of employees to run it for two short periods each day, plus the track and stations to handle large crowds. Nor was the railroad helped by a New York Public Service Commission freeze on commuter fares from 1918 to 1947. LIRR went into the red in 1935. Taxes, grade-crossing elimination projects, and the maintenance from heavy World War II traffic drove the railroad into bankruptcy.

New York State and LIRR's owner, the Pennsylvania Railroad, reached an agreement in 1954 calling for a 12-year rehabilitation period during which Pennsy would receive no dividends and fares could be increased to cover expenses. The plan also included relief from property taxes. Rehabilitation included modernization of cars and purchase of new ones, dieselization of the nonelectrified portion of the line, plant improvements, and increased service.

In 1965 the Metropolitan Commuter Transportation Authority was created; it purchased the railroad in 1966. In 1968 the Metropolitan Transportation Authority was formed; it now owns the LIRR.

The Long Island is the busiest passenger railroad in the U. S., carrying approximately 335,000 passengers on an average weekday. Freight accounts for only a tenth of LIRR's revenue.

FACTS & FIGURES

Year	1929	2012
Miles operated	404	701
Locomotives	170	45
Passenger cars	1,352	1,140
Freight cars	905	89
Reporting marks: LI		

© 2009, Kalmbach Publishing Co., CLASSIC TRAINS, Bill Metzger
Not all lines shown

Louisville & Nashville

A single Electro-Motive E6 diesel leads the Cincinnati-to-New Orleans *Humming Bird* through Turner, Ky., in 1948. A rebuilt heavyweight sleeper trails the original six lightweight cars of the streamliner. *Louisville & Nashville*

In the 1840s Louisville, Ky., was developing into a river port and distribution center—except during seasons of low water in the Ohio River. The growing city needed more dependable transportation. Tennessee was already building railroads from Memphis and Nashville to Chattanooga, and the Western & Atlantic Railroad opened from Chattanooga to Atlanta, Georgia, in 1850.

Nashville interests proposed a railroad north toward but not into Louisville to capture the trade that moved through Louisville. That proposal spurred Louisville to action: In 1850 the Kentucky legislature chartered the Louisville & Nashville Railroad to build between the cities of its name, with branches to Lebanon, Ky., and Memphis, Tenn. The state of Tennessee issued a charter for the southern portion of the line, with the condition that the railroad come no closer to Nashville than the north bank of the Cumberland River—any freight for Nashville would have to enter the city by wagon.

Work went slowly because of problems with financing, disputes over the route, and low water that kept materials from arriving at Louisville. In March 1850 the road was opened between Louisville and Lebanon. The segment between Nashville and

Bowling Green opened in August 1859, and two months later the line was completed, including a bridge across the Cumberland into Nashville and another over the Green River at Munfordville, Ky., that was the longest iron bridge in America at the time. The line to Memphis opened in April 1861. It was a joint effort by the L&N, the Memphis & Ohio, and the Memphis, Clarksville & Louisville railroads.

By then the Civil War had begun, with Kentucky on one side and Tennessee on the other. During the war Union and Confederate forces fought up and down the L&N, destroying as they went. By mid-1863 the major action of the war had moved to the Southeast. L&N began to pick up the pieces and get back to business—and there was enough business that L&N prospered.

Postwar expansion

With the war over, L&N began to find its territory invaded by competing railroads. On the west the Evansville, Henderson & Nashville was completed in 1872 and sold to the St. Louis & Southeastern Railway, and to the east the city of Cincinnati was busy planning and building the Cincinnati Southern Railway (now operated by the Norfolk Southern but still owned by the city).

To the south, though, L&N faced little competition. By 1860 several railroad companies had put together a line from Nashville to Decatur, Ala.—they were consolidated in 1866 as the Nashville & Decatur Railroad—and by 1870 a rail line was open from Montgomery, Ala., through Mobile to New Orleans. The Nashville & Decatur proposed a lease to the L&N if L&N would guarantee the completion of the South & North Alabama, which was under construction from Mobile north through the infant industrial center of Birmingham to Decatur. The Louisville–Montgomery route was completed in 1872. L&N also began extending its Lebanon branch southeastward toward Knoxville and Cumberland Gap.

In 1875, therefore, L&N had a main line from Louisville to Montgomery and branches from Lebanon Junction to Livingston, Ky., from Richmond Junction to Richmond, Ky., and from Bowling Green, Ky., to Memphis. L&N began expanding in earnest. It purchased the Evansville, Henderson & St. Louis at foreclosure in 1879, gaining a second route from the Ohio River to Nashville. EH&StL's owner, the St. Louis & Southeastern, had been in receivership since 1874; its line from East St. Louis to Evansville was purchased by

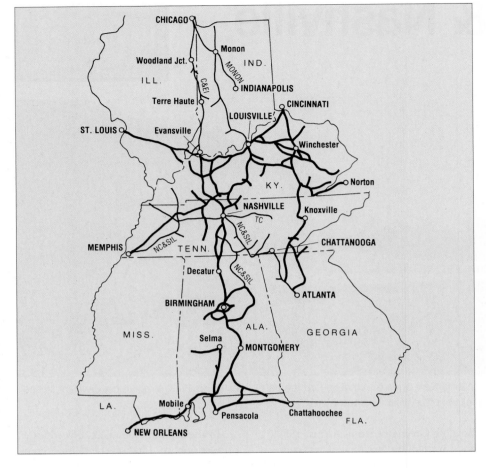

In 1902 L&N acquired the Knoxville Southern and the Marietta & North Georgia railroads, which formed a line from Knoxville to Marietta, Ga., 20 miles northwest of Atlanta on the Western & Atlantic. This line ran through an area rich in copper and marble—and through mountainous territory that required a pair of sharp curves between Whitestone and Talking Rock, Ga.—the "Hook"—and a complete loop between Farner and Appalachia, Tenn.—the Hiwassee Loop or "Eye." In 1906 L&N constructed a line with easier grades and curves between Etowah, Tenn., and Cartersville, Ga., west of the Hook & Eye line.

Affiliations

In 1898 L&N became the sole lessee of the Georgia Railroad and the affiliated Western Railway of Alabama and Atlanta & West Point but almost immediately assigned a half interest in the lease to Atlantic Coast Line.

In April 1902 Edwin Hawley and John W. Gates acquired a large block of L&N stock which they sold within a few weeks to J. P. Morgan & Co. Before the year was over Morgan sold his L&N interest—51 percent—to the Atlantic Coast Line Railroad. In May 1902 L&N and Southern, both under J. P. Morgan's control, jointly purchased the Chicago, Indianapolis & Louisville (Monon). Many pieces of the Seaboard System were in place 80 years before the creation of that railroad.

L&N was one of only a few railroads to build its own locomotives in any great numbers. Between 1905 and 1923 L&N's South Louisville Shops constructed more than 400 Consolidations, Pacifics, Mikados, and 0-8-0 switchers. Although L&N was the largest coal hauler south of Virginia it began dieselizing relatively early. At the beginning of World War II, L&N purchased 14 Berkshires for freight and passenger service and simultaneously began dieselizing passenger trains with a fleet of Electro-Motive E6s. L&N had already purchased its first road freight diesels, albeit for helper service, when 22 more 2-8-4s came from Lima in 1949 for service in the eastern Kentucky coalfields at a time when L&N was undertaking a great deal of branchline construction in that area. In 1950 L&N began to dieselize freight service in earnest, finishing the job by the end of 1956.

the Nashville, Chattanooga & St. Louis.

On the southern front, L&N purchased the Montgomery & Mobile and the New Orleans, Mobile & Texas, obtaining a route to New Orleans; along with the Montgomery & Mobile came routes into western Florida. L&N was alarmed at the sudden expansion of the NC&StL that promised a bridge over the Ohio, a link between Owensboro and Evansville, and leases of the Western & Atlantic and Central of Georgia. L&N began buying NC&StL stock, soon acquiring virtual control over its rival. L&N quickly took over NC&StL's East St. Louis–Evansville line and added it to its own system.

One of L&N's major acquisitions was the "Short Line" between Louisville and Cincinnati. The Louisville & Frankfort and Lexington & Frankfort railroads completed a line from Louisville to Lexington in 1851. There were proposals to extend that line from Lexington to Cincinnati and to build a new short, direct line from Louisville to Cincinnati. The latter was built in 1869 by the Louisville & Frankfort in the face of rivalry between the cities of Louisville and Cincinnati, debate over the gauge

(and thus over which city would have the freight transfer business), and even the route into Louisville—the city council advocated a route that the railroad said could be damaged by floods, and when the railroad knuckled under to the city and sent surveyors out, they found the proposed route deep under water. The two railroads consolidated in 1869 to form the Louisville, Cincinnati & Lexington Railroad, over the protests of the city of Frankfort that it would become simply a way station. L&N purchased the Louisville, Cincinnati & Lexington in 1881.

Another major acquisition was the Kentucky Central Railway, purchased from the C. P. Huntington interests in 1892. The road consisted of a main line from Covington, Ky., across the Ohio River from Cincinnati south to a junction with L&N's Lebanon Branch just north of Livingston, Ky., and a line from Lexington to Maysville, Ky., crossing the main line at Paris, Ky.

L&N had made a connection with the Southern Railway at Jellico, Tenn., for traffic to and from Knoxville, but shortly after the turn of the century decided to build its own line south to Knoxville and Atlanta.

The year and the engine number are the same—1954—as one of L&N's M-1-class ("Big Emma") Berkshires leads an Atlanta-bound freight out of Decoursey (Kentucky) Yard a few miles south of Cincinnati. *Louisville & Nashville*

Passenger trains

The upgrading of passenger service after World War II centered on two coach streamliners, the Cincinnati-New Orleans *Humming Bird* and the St. Louis-Atlanta *Georgian*, placed in service in 1946. Both trains soon acquired sleeping cars and through cars to Chicago via the Chicago & Eastern Illinois—Chicago traffic on the *Georgian* quickly outstripped that on its original route.

The L&N played a role in other railroads' trains as well. The New York–New Orleans *Crescent Limited*, considered the premier train of the Southern Railway, but operated between Montgomery and New Orleans by L&N, was streamlined in 1950. In 1949 L&N and Seaboard teamed up to offer the Jacksonville–New Orleans *Gulf Wind*. Louisville & Nashville provided a key link in the busiest Chicago–Florida passenger route, the "Dixie Route" (C&EI-L&N-NC&StL-ACL), and also forwarded the Pennsylvania Railroad's Chicago–Florida trains south of Louisville.

Mergers

L&N merged the Nashville, Chattanooga & St. Louis on Aug. 30, 1957—a date some consider the beginning of the modern railroad merger era (others say it began a decade earlier when Pere Marquette, Denver & Salt Lake, and Alton were merged into larger systems). In 1969 L&N purchased the Woodland, Ill.–Evansville, Ind., line of the Chicago & Eastern Illinois and acquired 140 miles of the abandoned Tennessee Central from Nashville to Crossville, Tenn. In 1971 L&N merged the Monon Railroad to obtain a second route from the Ohio River to Chicago. (L&N's financial interest in the Monon had been eliminated in Monon's 1946 reorganization.)

L&N's ownership by Atlantic Coast Line included a joint lease of the Carolina, Clinchfield & Ohio Railway (operated by the Clinchfield Railroad) and the railroad properties of the Georgia Railroad & Banking Co. (Georgia Railroad, Western Railway of Alabama, and Atlanta & West Point Rail Road). Atlantic Coast Line

merged with Seaboard Air Line in 1967 to form Seaboard Coast Line Railroad.

In the mid-1970s SCL began to refer to the "Family Lines" in its advertising, and the ad usually included a list of the members. It wasn't an official railroad name, but it indicated probable merger in the future. On Nov. 1, 1980, Seaboard Coast Line Industries, parent of Seaboard Coast Line Railroad, merged with Chessie System to form CSX Corporation. Then on Dec. 29, 1982, Seaboard Coast Line Railroad merged with L&N to form the Seaboard System Railroad.

FACTS & FIGURES

Year	1929	1982
Miles operated	5,250	10,396
Locomotives	1,350	1,086
Passenger cars	1,006	—
Freight cars	64,134	53,095
Reporting marks: LN		
Historical society: lnrr.org		

Maine Central

MEC GP7s lead a train bound for Dover-Foxcroft over the Kennebec River at Fairfield, Maine, near Waterville, on Feb. 14, 1976. *Ronald N. Johnson*

A recurring theme in the history of railroad development in Maine is the establishment of a year-round Atlantic seaport for Canada—the St. Lawrence River freezes over in winter. Numerous railroads were chartered in Maine with Montreal or Quebec as their destinations. Several more were proposed to build from the coast to the shore of Moosehead Lake, a large body of water about halfway between Bangor and Quebec.

Although the Maine Central didn't get caught up in the push to Canada, the first of the railroads that did, the Atlantic & St. Lawrence, provided the jumping-off place for two predecessors of the Maine Central. Construction of the A&StL began in 1846, but it went slowly. The line was completed from Portland to Montreal in 1853, and it was immediately leased by the Grand Trunk Railway of Canada.

From Danville, 27 miles north of Portland on the A&StL, the Androscoggin & Kennebec began construction of a line to Waterville. At the same time the Penobscot & Kennebec, which had the same backers, was under construction from Waterville to Bangor. Both of these railroads, like the Atlantic & St. Lawrence, were built with a track gauge of 5 feet 6 inches.

Meanwhile the standard gauge Kennebec & Portland was under construction from Yarmouth, 12 miles from Portland on the A&StL, east to Brunswick, then north along the Kennebec River to Augusta, the state capital, where it connected with (and operated and later leased) the Somerset & Kennebec to Waterville and Skowhegan. In 1850 the Kennebec & Portland built its own line into Portland from Yarmouth.

By the late 1850s there were four railroads in the area between Portland, Waterville, and Bangor, all with "Kennebec" in their names. Two were broad gauge and two were standard gauge. In the same territory was the broad gauge Androscoggin Railroad, opened in 1855 between Leeds Junction on the Androscoggin & Kennebec east of Lewiston, and Farmington. In 1861 after discussions with the A&K fell apart, the Androscoggin Railroad built an extension south to the Kennebec & Portland at Brunswick and narrowed its track to standard gauge. The Eastern Railroad added to the confusion by taking sides with the standard gauge lines in a dispute over through fares.

Maine Central gathers them in

The Maine Central was incorporated in 1862 to consolidate the Androscoggin & Kennebec and Penobscot & Kennebec railroads. In 1870 it leased the Portland & Kennebec (the reorganized Kennebec & Portland) and in 1871 leased the Androscoggin Railroad. That same year Maine

Central converted its own lines to standard gauge. It absorbed the leased lines soon after and came under the control of the Eastern Railroad. That control passed to the Boston & Maine in 1884.

With a monopoly established in the territory between Bangor and Portland, the Maine Central began expanding. In 1882 MEC leased the European & North American Railway. The E&NA had been conceived as a rail line to the farthest tip of Nova Scotia (cutting the steamship time to Europe to a minimum) and as part of a rail route between Montreal and the Maritime Provinces. It opened from Bangor to Vanceboro, on the New Brunswick border, in 1871; consolidated with its Canadian counterpart (Vanceboro to Saint John); leased the Bangor & Piscataquis and Bucksport & Bangor railroads; then slipped into receivership in 1875, losing most of its acquisitions. Construction in 1884 extended the Maine Central through Ellsworth to Mount Desert Ferry.

Maine Central leased the Portland & Ogdensburg in 1888. The P&O was the Maine and New Hampshire portion of a series of railroads from Portland to Lake Ontario. Control of the other segments by other railroads reduced the line to local status (the other pieces became the St. Johnsbury & Lake Champlain and the western portion of the Rutland).

In 1890 MEC leased the Upper Coos Railroad and the Hereford Railway, which together formed a route along the upper reaches of the Connecticut River and north across the Canadian border to a connection with the Quebec Central.

In 1891 MEC leased the Knox & Lincoln Railway, which ran from Woolwich, across the Kennebec River from Bath, east to Rockland. In 1904 it acquired control of the Washington County Railroad, built in 1893 from Ellsworth east to Calais and Eastport. In 1907 MEC acquired control of the Somerset Railroad, which stretched north along the Kennebec River from Oakland, west of Waterville, to Moosehead Lake. That same year, MEC leased the Portland & Rumford Falls Railway, which ran from Auburn west to Poland and Mechanic Falls, then north to Kennebago.

In 1911 the Portland Terminal Company was created as a wholly owned subsidiary of the MEC. It acquired MEC's and Boston & Maine's terminal properties in and around Portland.

Maine's most prosperous 2-foot-gauge railroads, the Sandy River & Rangeley Lakes and the Bridgton & Saco River, came under the control of the Maine Central in 1911 and 1912. The prosperity soon evaporated, and the narrow gauge lines regained their independence in 1923 and 1927, respectively.

Pruning the tree

The lease of the Hereford Railway was terminated in 1925. Part of its line was abandoned; part sold to Canadian Pacific. The Belfast & Moosehead Lake Railroad, which MEC had leased since its opening in 1871, began independent operation in 1926. In 1927 the state of Maine opened a rail and highway bridge across the Kennebec between Bath and Woolwich, replacing the ferry which had been the Rockland Branch's connection to the rest of the railroad.

Two long branches reaching northward were abandoned in the 1930s: the former Somerset Railroad from Austin Junction, near Bingham, to Kineo Station on the shore of Moosehead Lake, and the Portland & Rumford Falls north of Rumford in 1935 and 1936. Most of the remainder of the Portland & Rumford Falls was abandoned in 1952.

Control of the Maine Central by the Boston & Maine ended in 1914, but in

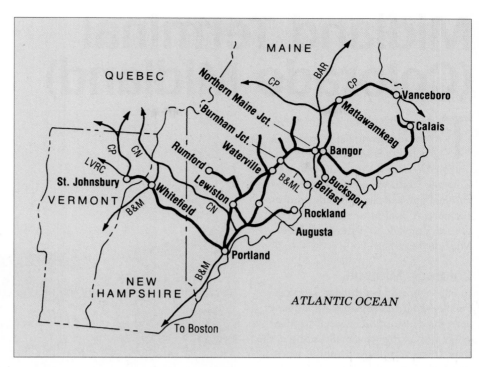

1933 MEC entered an agreement with the B&M for joint employment of some officers and personnel. The cooperative arrangement, which provided the benefits of merged operation, continued until 1952, when MEC took steps to resume its independence. Separation from B&M was completed on December 29, 1955.

Passenger service on the Maine Central ceased in 1960, though the trains remained in service for a while as mail and express carriers (handicapped somewhat by the decision of Boston & Maine, MEC's principal passenger connection, to drop all mail and express service and concentrate on carrying passengers).

In 1974 Maine Central sold the former European & North American line between Mattawamkeag and Vanceboro, 57 miles, to Canadian Pacific, retaining trackage rights—essentially swapping positions on that stretch of track, which was part of CPR's Montreal–Saint John line.

Two years later MEC sold its North Stratford, N. H.–Beecher Falls, Vt., line to the state of New Hampshire. The North Stratford Railroad began operating the line in 1977. In the late 1970s Maine Central upgraded the track on its Mountain Division, the former Portland & Ogdensburg line from Portland through the White Mountains to St. Johnsbury, Vt. Even though local business had decreased, traffic interchanged with Canadian Pacific at St. Johnsbury was still at a good level.

Purchase of the Maine Central

In December 1980 U. S. Filter Corporation purchased the railroad. Almost immediately Ashland Oil took over U. S. Filter and in June 1981 sold the railroad to Guilford Transportation Industries. Suddenly it made more sense to route traffic to and from the west via Boston & Maine and Delaware & Hudson, and the Mountain Division was out of a job. Through freight service ceased, and Mattawamkeag replaced St. Johnsbury as the interchange with CPR. By the mid-1980s the Portland–St. Johnsbury line was all but abandoned. MEC abandoned the Rockland and Calais branches about the same time and petitioned to abandon most of the "Lower Road," the Portland–Augusta–Waterville route, leaving the railroad with a main line from Portland through Lewiston, Waterville, and Bangor to Mattawamkeag and a few branches.

The MEC largely lost its own identity in Guilford; Guilford became Pan Am Railways in 2006.

FACTS & FIGURES

Year	1929	1981
Miles operated	1,121	818
Locomotives	201	73
Passenger cars	246	—
Freight cars	6,698	4,523
Reporting marks: MEC		

Midland Terminal (Colorado Midland)

The name "Midland Terminal" refers to the road's original purpose as a switching road between mines at Cripple Creek and a mainline railroad, the Colorado Midland—and also refers to the terminal phase of the Colorado Midland's existence. A brief history of the CM is a necessary prelude to discussion of the Midland Terminal.

Colorado Midland

In 1883 a line drawn through Denver, Pueblo, and Trinidad, Colo., would have been the demarcation between standard gauge and narrow gauge railroading in the state. It was surprising, therefore, when a standard gauge railroad from Colorado Springs over Ute Pass into the South Park was proposed and incorporated in November 1883—the Colorado Midland Railway, to build from Colorado Springs to Leadville and Salida. It was to be primarily a local railroad; the Rock Island's line into Colorado Springs from the east was still five years in the future.

Financial backing for the new railroad came from James J. Hagerman, who had been instructed by his physician to find a climate better for his health than that of Milwaukee. Hagerman owned mines near Aspen and Glenwood Springs, and he proposed building a western extension of the CM first because of the traffic those mines would furnish. When the two established roads in Colorado, the Denver & Rio Grande and the Union Pacific, doubled their rates on rails carried to Leadville,

Three Midland Terminal Moguls work an ore train near Bull Hill in October 1948. The engines were rebuilt from ex-U. S. Army 0-6-0s. *Donald Duke*

Hagerman decided to start from Colorado Springs. Construction of the hastily surveyed route over Ute Pass began in 1886, and the line was completed to Glenwood Springs in December 1887. It included the Hagerman Tunnel west of Leadville, 2,060 feet long at an elevation of 11,530 feet.

By then Grand Junction, Colo., and Ogden, Utah, were CM's goals. (The rail route west from Grand Junction was the independent Denver & Rio Grande Western Railway at the time.) CM continued its line down the south bank of the Grand River (the pre-1921 name of the Colorado River east of Grand Junction), reaching New Castle about the time the Denver &

Rio Grande on the north bank did. The two roads formed the Rio Grande Junction Railway to build the line to Grand Junction. In 1890 that line was completed, Denver & Rio Grande finished standard-gauging its main line, and Santa Fe purchased the Colorado Midland.

Midland Terminal Railway is born

Also in 1890 gold was discovered west of Pikes Peak. Colorado Midland proposed a branch south from the main line at the summit of Hayden Divide to Midland, which would connect with a new 2-foot-gauge line, the Midland Terminal Railway, to go the last few miles to Victor and Cripple Creek. The Midland Terminal built the whole line from Divide to Cripple Creek. The knowledge that the narrow gauge

FACTS & FIGURES

Year	1929	1948
Miles operated	56	56
Locomotives	9	7
Passenger cars	15	—
Freight cars	240	279

Historical society: nrhs.com/chapters/ colorado-midland

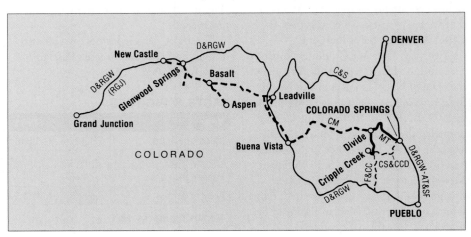

At Glenwood Springs, the Midland entered the Colorado Valley, with a clear path to Grand Junction. The 93-class Ten-Wheeler (4-6-0) was built by Schenectady in 1887. *T. J. Routh; Denver Public Library Western Collection*

Florence & Cripple Creek was building north from a connection with the narrow gauge Denver & Rio Grande caused a change to standard gauge, since MT's only connection would be the standard gauge CM. The line was opened to Victor in December 1894 and to Cripple Creek a year later. Traffic was outbound ore for processing in the mills at Colorado Springs and inbound merchandise and supplies.

The panic of 1893 was caused in part by the closing of the mints of India to silver coinage. The resulting silver glut was doubly hard on Colorado: The U. S. was on a bimetallic money standard (until silver was demonetized in late 1893), and silver mining was one of Colorado's major industries. CM's traffic fell off. The company defaulted on its bond interest and soon found itself in receivership. Reorganization occurred in 1897.

Also in 1893 the Busk-Ivanhoe Tunnel under Hagerman Pass was opened, eliminating 575 feet of elevation and more than five complete circles from CM's line. The tunnel was owned by a separate company, and after a dispute over tolls in 1897 CM reopened its old line over the pass. Blizzards in early 1899 tied up the Leadville-Glenwood end of the road for more than two months. CM purchased the Busk-Ivanhoe Tunnel in 1899.

Colorado Midland purchased

That same year the Colorado & Southern and the Rio Grande Western jointly purchased the Colorado Midland; two years later Denver & Rio Grande, CM's principal competitor, bought the RGW and with it RGW's half interest in the Colorado Midland. Initially CM's fears that its traffic would be diverted to the D&RG proved groundless. Rio Grande routed traffic over CM while rebuilding and upgrading its own line, but took the traffic itself once it had the capacity to move it. Colorado & Southern was purchased by the Burlington, which was in turn part of the Hill empire—of which the CM was an insignificant piece. CM defaulted on its Rio Grande Junction obligations, Rio Grande bought CM's half interest, and CM entered receivership again in 1912.

Colorado Midland abandoned

In 1917 Albert E. Carlton purchased the Colorado Midland at foreclosure. He proposed an extension to Utah, using the Uintah Railway as part of the new line (but bypassing the 7.5-percent grades and 66-degree curves of Baxter Pass). During World War I the USRA noted on its maps CM's short route across Colorado and routed a great deal of traffic over the line—until the road

choked up and the USRA withdrew all traffic. The road closed down in August 1918. Carlton delayed dismantling the line while the Santa Fe considered purchasing it, but scrapping began in 1921. Carlton gave the right of way to the state for highways, except for the Busk-Ivanhoe Tunnel, which became first a toll highway tunnel, then a conduit to bring western slope water into the Arkansas Valley for irrigation.

For a few years in the late teens all the railroads in Cripple Creek—the Midland Terminal, the Colorado Springs & Cripple Creek District, and the remains of the Florence & Cripple Creek—were united as the Cripple Creek & Colorado Springs under Carlton. Upon the demise of the Colorado Midland, the Midland Terminal took over the CM line from Divide to Colorado Springs. Within a few years it was the sole railroad serving the dying mining industry of Cripple Creek.

There was a brief revival in 1933 when the government revised gold prices, but for the most part the trend was just as much downhill as the journey the ore made from Cripple Creek and Victor to the mill at Colorado Springs. Finally a new mill near Victor removed the last reason for the existence of the railroad. The Midland Terminal ceased operation in February 1949.

Midland Valley

MIDLAND VALLEY RAILROAD CO.
KANSAS, OKLAHOMA & GULF RY. CO.
OKLAHOMA CITY-ADA-ATOKA RY. CO.

Three railroads were controlled by the Muskogee Company and were operated jointly: Midland Valley; Kansas, Oklahoma & Gulf; and Oklahoma City-Ada-Atoka. In later years, much rolling stock wore emblems with all three roads. Muskogee also owned the Foraker Co., which in turn owned the 18-mile Osage Railway, which connected with Midland Valley at Foraker in northern Oklahoma. The Osage was abandoned in 1953.

Two Midland Valley Geeps brings a train from Wichita into Fort Smith, Ark., on Frisco trackage rights on Nov. 21, 1958. The emblems listed all three "Muskogee Roads." *Robert Milner*

Midland Valley

The Midland Valley was incorporated in 1903 and completed its line from Hoye, Ark., south of Fort Smith, through Muskogee and Tulsa, Okla., to Wichita, Kan., in 1906. MV reached Fort Smith by exercising trackage rights over the Frisco; the road owned considerable coal land in that area of Arkansas and adjoining Oklahoma. In 1926 MV made a joint facility and operation agreement with the Kansas, Oklahoma & Gulf, and in 1930 did the same with the Oklahoma City-Ada-Atoka. The Muskogee Company acquired control of the MV in 1930.

Kansas, Oklahoma & Gulf

The Kansas, Oklahoma & Gulf was incorporated in 1918 as a successor to the Missouri, Oklahoma & Gulf. The MO&G was built between 1903 and 1913 from Muskogee northeast to Joplin, Mo., and southwest to Denison, Texas. The only major town it served was Muskogee, and at nearly every town it faced competition

from the long-established Frisco and Katy. It was proposed to extend the MO&G north to Pittsburg, Kan., then to Kansas City on trackage rights over Kansas City Southern to form a connection between the Union Pacific at Kansas City and the Houston & Texas Central (Southern Pacific) at Denison, but this was never built. The MO&G was sold at foreclosure and reorganized as the Kansas, Oklahoma & Gulf in July 1919.

KO&G entered receivership in 1924 and was acquired by Midland Valley interests in 1925. The KO&G and MV worked out joint facility agreements, and KO&G developed into a bridge route for Kansas–Texas traffic between the Missouri Pacific and the Texas & Pacific. About 1960 MP and T&P rerouted such traffic to remain on MP and T&P rails all the way, drying up much of KO&G's traffic. In 1962

KO&G abandoned the northern 105 miles of its line between Baxter Springs, Kan., and Okay (North Muskogee), Okla.

Oklahoma City-Ada-Atoka

The Oklahoma City-Ada-Atoka was incorporated in 1923 to acquire the Shawnee Division of the Missouri-Kansas-Texas, which was undergoing reorganization. The line ran from Oklahoma City to Atoka, Okla. In 1930 OCAA acquired the Oklahoma City–Shawnee Interurban Railway. Muskogee Co. acquired control in 1929.

Purchase by Texas & Pacific

In 1962 the Muskogee Co. authorized the sale of all its railroad stocks to the Texas & Pacific. In September 1964 T&P acquired control of the three Muskogee roads but immediately sold the OCAA to the Santa Fe, which merged OCAA on Dec. 1, 1967. Midland Valley was merged into T&P on April 1, 1967, and the same happened to KO&G exactly three years later. The Muskogee Company was dissolved in 1964 after its properties were sold.

FACTS & FIGURES (COMBINED)

Year	1929	1966
Miles operated	819	640
Locomotives	54	15
Passenger cars	29	—
Freight cars	550	—
Reporting marks: MV, KO&G		

MidSouth

As part of Illinois Central Gulf's slimming down in the 1980s, on March 31, 1986, MidSouth Rail Corporation purchased ICG's line from Meridian, Miss., to Shreveport, La., plus short branches north and south from Vicksburg (remnants of ICG's Memphis–Baton Rouge line) and a line not connected with the others extending from Hattiesburg to Gulfport, Miss., (once part of the Gulf & Ship Island Railroad).

ICG had operated a single daily train each way. MidSouth increased that to two trains a day over much of its main line, and scheduled those to minimize delay to cars delivered to the railroad. Pulpwood, paper, and chemicals constituted more than 60 percent of the road's traffic.

On Sept. 8, 1987, MidSouth purchased the 40-mile North Louisiana & Gulf Railroad, with which it connected at Gibsland, La. The NL&G was incorporated in 1906 and was owned by Continental Can Co., which had a large paper mill at Hodge, La. Along with the NL&G came a 25-mile

A MidSouth local freight returns to Vicksburg from a trip to a paper mill at Redwood, Miss. *Louis R. Saillard*

subsidiary, the Central Louisiana & Gulf, which in 1980 acquired a short segment of former Rock Island track between Hodge and Winnfield, La. MidSouth renamed its

acquisition MidLouisiana Rail Corp.

Gulf & Mississippi

Before MidSouth was created, ICG spun off most of its ex-Gulf, Mobile & Ohio lines in Mississippi and Alabama to the Gulf & Mississippi Railroad (GMSR) in July 1985. GMSR was facing bankruptcy when a MidSouth subsidiary, SouthRail Corp., acquired it on April 14, 1988. In late 1991 MidSouth purchased through a new subsidiary, TennRail, the Corinth & Counce Railroad.

In December 1990 Illinois Central offered to buy MidSouth, which objected. IC asked the Interstate Commerce Commission for approval, then almost immediately dropped its request. Kansas City Southern in September 1991 announced its offer to purchase MidSouth, and the ICC approved KCS's proposal on June 4, 1993.

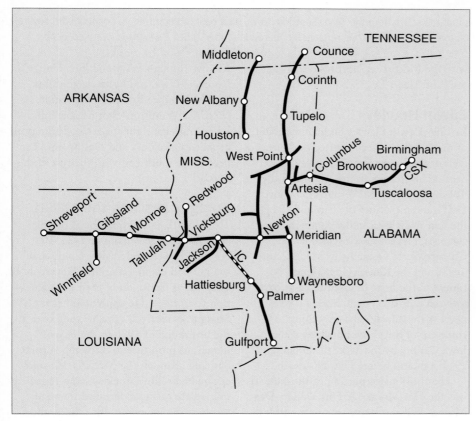

FACTS & FIGURES

Year	1986	1993
Miles operated	474	1,197
Locomotives	58	117
Passenger cars	—	—
Freight cars	1,571	4,694
Reporting marks: GMSR		

Minneapolis & St. Louis

Minneapolis & St. Louis was known for its freights that ran south from the Twin Cities into Iowa, then east to Peoria, Ill., to connect with several Class 1s. The green-and-yellow F2 set was manufactured in 1947, which is reflected in its road number. *David P. Morgan Library collection*

The Minneapolis & St. Louis began with the chartering of the Minnesota Western Railroad in 1853. The name was changed to Minneapolis & St. Louis Railway in 1870. The company built a line that reached from White Bear, Minn., south through Minneapolis to Albert Lea, and by 1881, to Fort Dodge, Iowa. By 1884 a tentacle stretched west from Minneapolis to Watertown, S. D., and in 1900, a line was opened from Winthrop, Minn., on the Watertown line, south to Storm Lake, Iowa. In 1905 the Minnesota, Dakota & Pacific Railway extended the Watertown line west to Leola and Le Beau, S. D., with the thought of eventual extension to the Pacific. M&StL purchased the MD&P in 1912.

Meanwhile the Iowa Central, after reorganizations and renamings, had assembled a railroad from Albia east through Oskaloosa to Peoria, Ill., and from Oskaloosa north across Iowa to a connection with the M&StL at Northwood, Iowa, south of Albert Lea.

Edwin Hawley

In 1896 Edwin Hawley became president of the M&StL and soon afterward president of the Iowa Central. Hawley also became involved with the Alton and the Toledo, St. Louis & Western (the Clover Leaf), and for a brief time around 1911, the four roads were under common management. Hawley also invested in the Chesapeake & Ohio, the Missouri-Kansas-Texas, and the Kansas City, Mexico & Orient in the hope of assembling a coast-to-coast railroad system. Such a system never materialized—the only thing to come out of it was the purchase of the Iowa Central by the M&StL on Jan. 1, 1912, a month before Hawley's death.

The third major portion of the M&StL was the Des Moines & Fort Dodge–Des Moines Valley system, a route from Des

Moines through Perry and Fort Dodge to Ruthven, Iowa, and by trackage rights over Milwaukee Road to Spencer, on M&StL's Winthrop–Storm Lake line. Later, trackage rights over the Burlington between Oskaloosa and Des Moines connected the south end with the rest of the M&StL.

Sprague rescues the M&StL

The M&StL ran into financial trouble and entered receivership in 1923. The bondholders elected Walter Colpitts, of the railroad engineering firm Coverdale & Colpitts, as chairman of their reorganization committee. He appointed Lucian Sprague as receiver. Sprague took over at the beginning of 1935 in the face of numerous proposals to dismember, parcel out, and abandon the M&StL. He sold antiquated rolling stock as scrap to realize immediate cash, modernized the road's locomotives, opened traffic offices, and

With white extra flags flying, Minneapolis & St. Louis Mikado No. 611 leads a sugar-beet extra out of Hopkins, Minn. (southwest of Minneapolis), in 1946. The 2-8-2 was built by Schenectady in 1918. In the Sprague era, M&StL kept its engines looking nice. *David P. Morgan Library collection*

began soliciting business at a time when other railroads were pulling back.

In 1942 the road was sold—after 42 previous efforts to auction it off—to Coverdale & Colpitts. The reorganized M&StL encompassed a new Railway Company (the main lines), a new Railroad Corporation (the branches), and the old Railroad Company, all titled Minneapolis & St. Louis. The separation of the branch lines was found unnecessary by 1944. The

M&StL began dieselization in 1938 and was fully dieselized by 1950.

Ben Heineman and the C&NW

In May 1954 a group of stockholders led by attorney Ben Heineman took over the M&StL, and Heineman replaced Sprague as chairman of the board. Heineman's only previous railroad experience was in representing a group of stockholders in a dividend case against the Chicago Great

Western. Heineman revived an old idea of a belt route around Chicago and began negotiating to purchase Toledo, Peoria & Western stock. His purchase of a block of Monon stock apparently alerted the Santa Fe and the Pennsylvania, which jointly purchased the TP&W to block Heineman.

In 1956 the M&StL acquired all the stock of the Minnesota Western Railway (Minneapolis to Gluek, Minn., 115 miles; a 1924 reorganization of the Electric Short Line Railway and a sometime affiliate of the Minneapolis, Northfield & Southern) and renamed it the Minneapolis Industrial Railway. It was abandoned in the early 1970s.

Heineman gave the M&StL a modern-thinking, aggressive management before he moved on to the Chicago & North Western in 1956. Chicago & North Western purchased the railroad assets of the M&StL on Nov. 1, 1960, and over the course of the next decade, abandoned much of the line.

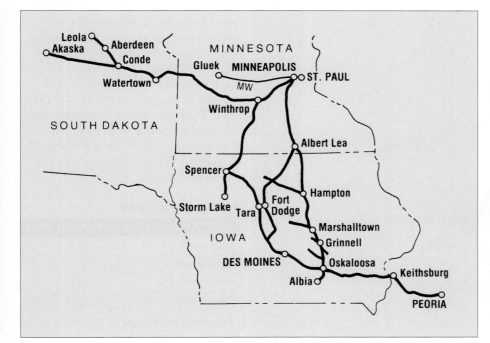

FACTS & FIGURES

Year	1929	1959
Miles operated	1,628	1,391
Locomotives	218	74
Passenger cars	122	10
Freight cars	6,581	4,178

Reporting marks: M&StL, MSTL
Historical society: cnwhs.org/ch_mstl.htm

Minneapolis, Northfield & Southern

The Minneapolis, Northfield & Southern was incorporated in 1907 as the Minneapolis, St. Paul, Rochester & Dubuque Electric Traction Company. One of its incorporators was Col. Marion W. Savage, a livestock feed tycoon who bought Dan Patch, one of the most famous race horses of all time. Savage had a farm a few miles south of Minneapolis and sought to improve the transportation system in the area.

The new railroad was known as the "Dan Patch Electric Line," and it was like other interurban lines of the era with one major difference: no trolley wire. Its passengers rode in General Electric gas-electric cars. The road inaugurated service between the outskirts of Minneapolis and Antlers Park on July 4, 1910, and the line was extended to Northfield, Minn., 37 miles from Minneapolis, later that year.

The MStPR&D inaugurated freight service in 1913 using a GE gas-electric locomotive, and was the first railroad in the world to operate freight and passenger service exclusively with internal-combustion power. It negotiated trackage rights over the Chicago Great Western from Northfield to Mankato and operated through service between Minneapolis and Mankato,

Minneapolis, Northfield & Southern favored Baldwins like this blue-and-silver DRS-6-6-1500, shown switching the yard at Auto Club Junction in September 1958. *William D. Middleton*

107 miles, using gas-electric cars. Additional local trains ran as far as Faribault and Randolph on the CGW. The railroad built a second route into Minneapolis and bought more locomotives (both gas-electric and steam) plus a large fleet of passenger and freight cars. Col. Savage purchased land for a suburban housing development. The road's listing in the June 1916 issue of

The Official Guide proudly advertised "Freight Handled by Steam Power."

The company was overextended, and in late 1916 it entered bankruptcy. In 1918 its properties were purchased by the newly organized Minneapolis, Northfield & Southern. The new company concentrated on freight, aided by a route map that constituted a belt line most of the way around Minneapolis. It developed a healthy business moving freight between other railroads, bypassing the congestion of downtown Minneapolis. It did so well that, in 1938, the Chicago Great Western and the Rock Island led a campaign to have all through freight rates via the MN&S canceled. There was considerable protest from labor and shippers, and the Interstate Commerce Commission ruled in favor of the MN&S. In June 1982 Soo Line purchased the MN&S.

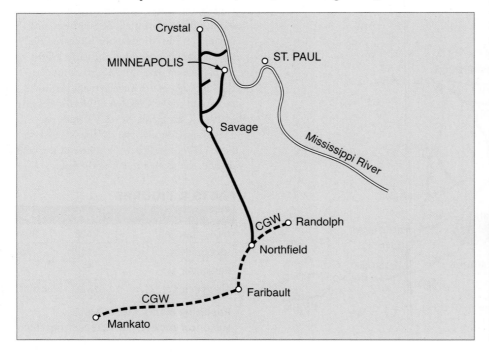

FACTS & FIGURES

Year	1929	1979
Miles operated	140	82
Locomotives	12	13
Passenger cars	8	—
Freight cars	53	716
Reporting marks: MNS		

Missisippi Central

In 1896 the Pearl & Leaf Rivers Railroad was incorporated. It was a logging road from Hattiesburg to Sumrall, Miss., 19 miles. The western goal of the railroad was Natchez, across the state on the Mississippi River. In 1905 after a reorganization the railroad was renamed the Mississippi Central Railroad, and the line was completed in 1908 (the western portion was built by the Natchez & Eastern Railway, absorbed by Mississippi Central in 1909).

The road's plans to extend its line to the Gulf of Mexico were never fulfilled, but in 1921 MSC leased a branch of the Gulf, Mobile & Northern from Hattiesburg to Beaumont and acquired trackage rights to Mobile over GM&N. In 1924 GM&N sold off the branch, which became the Bonhomie & Hattiesburg Southern, and MSC pulled back to Hattiesburg.

Mississippi Central ran its last passenger train in 1941. Just before World War II the Army announced it would reopen Camp Shelby, south of Hattiesburg. The MSC had torn up its branch to Camp Shelby some years previously, but hastily relaid 7 miles of track in the interests of national defense and freight revenue.

MSC's business held up well after the war, and the road participated in east-west bridge traffic with the Louisiana Midland, a new road created from a Louisiana & Arkansas branch west of the Mississippi River. The route was a joint Louisiana & Arkansas-Louisiana Midland-MSC project using the name "Natchez Route." Profits turned to deficits in the early 1960s and MSC looked for a buyer. At first Illinois Central rejected the offer, but the prospect of a new paper mill between Wanilla and Silver Creek changed the situation. IC purchased the MSC on March 29, 1967.

FACTS & FIGURES

Year	1929	1966
Miles operated	151	148
Locomotives	21	9
Passenger cars	19	—
Freight cars	698	165
Reporting marks: MSC		

Mississippi Central 2-8-2 No. 131 heads a work train assisting in the cleanup of a mishap at Cobbs, west of Brookhaven, Miss. The Mikado has two bells, a characteristic of the railroad's steam locomotives—and both are nicely polished. *C. W. Witbeck*

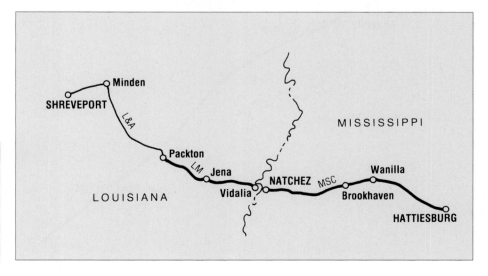

Missouri & North Arkansas

In 1882, to provide access to the northwest Arkansas resort town of Eureka Springs, the St. Louis & San Francisco chartered the Missouri & Arkansas Railroad to build from Seligman, Mo., to Beaver, Ark., on the White River, 13 miles. That same year the Eureka Springs Railway was chartered to build 5 miles of railroad from the M&A to Eureka Springs, and the two railroads were consolidated under the Eureka Springs name. The line was completed in February 1883.

In May 1899 the St. Louis & North Arkansas Railroad was chartered to purchase the Eureka Springs and extend it east to Harrison. It reached there in March 1901. In 1906 the road was reorganized as the Missouri & North Arkansas Railroad. It arranged for trackage rights on the Frisco between Seligman and Wayne, Mo., and on the Kansas City Southern between Neosho and Joplin, Mo. It built a line from Wayne to Neosho, 32 miles, and started construction southeast across Arkansas to Helena, on the Mississippi River.

The line was completed from Neosho to Helena in 1909. It soon became clear that the Missouri & North Arkansas would

ACF Motorailer No. 705, the *Thomas C. McRae*, pauses at Harrison, Ark., en route from Kensett, Ark., to Neosho, Mo. The Motorailer was built in 1938. *M. B. Cooke*

have to rely on local business, and there wasn't much of that. The road entered receivership in 1912.

The railroad was reorganized as the Missouri & North Arkansas Railway in 1922. It entered receivership in 1927 and was sold at foreclosure in 1935 to become

the Missouri & Arkansas Railway. In 1946 employees threatened a strike. Management retaliated with the threat of abandonment. The employees walked out on Sept. 6, 1946, and the Missouri & Arkansas was abandoned.

The Arkansas & Ozarks Railway was incorporated on March 4, 1949, to operate the line between Seligman, Mo., and Harrison, Ark. It began operations in February 1950 and was abandoned in April 1961.

The portion of the line from Cotton Plant, Ark., to Helena was revived as the Helena & Northwestern Railway. Operation began in September 1949; after a foreclosure suit the last train operated on Oct. 18, 1951. The Cotton Plant-Fargo Railway was chartered in February 1952 to operate the six miles of line between those two towns. It ceased operation in 1977.

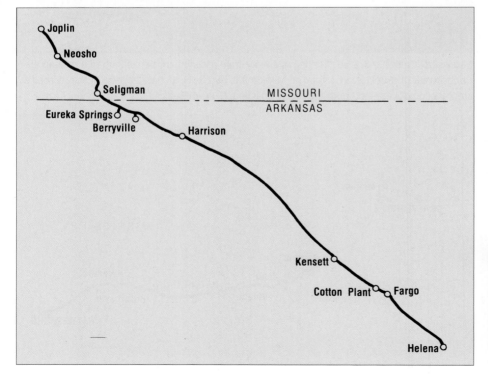

FACTS & FIGURES

Year	1929	1945
Miles operated	365	365
Locomotives	32	22
Passenger cars	14	11
Freight cars	394	53
Reporting marks: M&NA		

Missouri-Kansas-Texas (Katy)

A northbound freight, with a GP40 leading and a slug immediately behind, heads out of Texas City, Texas, along the sea wall. The tank farm is owned by Arco Pipeline (now BP). Note that the trailing locomotive is in Katy red in this July 1988 view. *Laurence Pearlman*

The Katy was incorporated in 1865 as the Union Pacific Railway, Southern Branch (although it had no corporate connection with the Union Pacific proper) to build south from Junction City, Kan., along the Neosho River through Emporia and Parsons to New Orleans. It received a land grant, and construction began in 1869.

The railroad changed its name to Missouri, Kansas & Texas Railway the following year. In late 1870, it reached the southern boundary of Kansas at Chetopa ahead of two rival lines, earning the right to build south through what is now Oklahoma. Also in 1870 the MK&T absorbed the Tebo & Neosho, a line from Sedalia, Missouri, southwest to Parsons, Kan.

Katy rails reached Denison, Texas, in 1872. Other significant events about that time were a battle with the Atlantic & Pacific (a Frisco predecessor) over a crossing at Vinita, Okla., in 1871; extension of the road from Sedalia to a junction with the Burlington at Hannibal, Mo., in 1873; and control of the road by Jay Gould, who saw it as a feeder to his Missouri Pacific system.

The Katy reached Dallas and Fort Worth in 1881, the latter on trackage rights over the Texas & Pacific from Whitesboro, Texas. That same year the Katy purchased the International & Great Northern (another Gould road). The lines of the MK&T, building south, and I&GN, building north, met at Taylor, Texas, in 1882. In 1883 the Katy purchased the Galveston, Houston & Henderson, which Gould leased to the I&GN.

In 1886 MK&T built north from Parsons, Kan., to Paola, and negotiated trackage rights from Paola to Kansas City over the Kansas City, Fort Scott & Gulf (later part of the Frisco). In 1888 Jay Gould lost financial control of the Katy. Missouri Pacific's lease of the Katy was canceled, and control of I&GN passed to Missouri Pacific. In 1891 the Missouri, Kansas &

Pacific 385 leads the *Katy Limited* south of Dallas in February 1948. Katy steam locomotives characteristically had lots of white trim along with enameled heralds on the tender sides. *C. W. Witbeck*

Texas of Texas was created to hold all the Katy's Texas properties to comply with a law the state of Texas had passed in 1886 requiring railroads operating in Texas to maintain general offices there.

Expansion and reorganization

The MK&T emerged from receivership in 1891 and began a period of expansion which put its rails into Houston (1893), St. Louis (1896), Shreveport (1900), San Antonio (1900), Tulsa (1903), and Oklahoma City (1904). In 1910 Katy acquired the Texas Central, which reached out toward Abilene from Waco, and in 1911 took over the Wichita Falls & Northwestern and the Wichita Falls & Southern. By 1915 the sprawling system had 3,865 miles of railroad that reached south from St. Louis, Hannibal, Kansas City, and Junction City to Galveston and San Antonio, east to Shreveport, and west into the Oklahoma panhandle.

In 1923 the Katy was reorganized as the Missouri-Kansas-Texas Railroad. It leased the Moberly–Hannibal portion of the Hannibal branch to the Wabash, sold the Shreveport line to the Louisiana Railway & Navigation Co. (now part of the Kansas City Southern), and sloughed off the Oklahoma City line to become the Oklahoma City-Ada-Atoka Railway (after 1929 part of the Muskogee group; later Santa Fe). In 1931 Katy purchased the Beaver, Meade & Englewood, which reached almost to the west end of the Oklahoma panhandle.

World War II and decline

Through the 1930s and into World War II Katy's image was one of classic American railroading tempered with individuality—red and white heralds on the tenders of its Pacifics and Mikados with bright yellow cabooses and boxcars. The war brought increased traffic to the Katy. Oil moving north became an exception to Katy's predominantly southbound traffic.

Not everything associated with the war was beneficial. The increased traffic was hard on the track, and in a three-month period in 1945 Katy's top three officers died. Dieselization helped the road briefly—it had not purchased new locomotives since 1925—but Katy's diesel maintenance program was insufficient. Track deterioration continued, and drought in the 1950s held traffic down. Suddenly in 1957 Katy was in the red. William N. Deramus III was brought in from the Chicago Great Western to become Katy's president. He rationalized the locomotive roster, repowering non-EMD units with EMD engines; abandoned the Junction City branch, Katy's original line; trimmed the payroll; consolidated offices at Denison, Texas (the St. Louis offices were moved over a weekend; employees received notice of the closure by encountering locked doors Monday morning); and cut most of the road's passenger service.

Barriger revives the Katy

Katy's decline resumed in a few years. In 1965 John W. Barriger III was brought in to save the railroad. In the 1940s he had rebuilt the Monon; more recently he had retired after several years as president of the Pittsburgh & Lake Erie. Barriger faced the same situation that he had on the Monon: almost complete deterioration of the physical plant and equally complete lack of employee morale. Barriger set to work as traveling freight agent and president (his own description of his job) and did what he had done before and would do again (for Boston & Maine and Rock Island). He reopened the railroad's office in St. Louis; discontinued the remaining passenger service (on June 30, 1965); and found money for a rehabilitation program by liquidating bonds, applying for loans that had been approved but not made, and even cleaning up scrap around the railroad. His program included rebuilding the track, purchasing new locomotives, and purchasing and leasing new freight cars. After a long period of economizing itself to death, Katy spent more than a year's gross receipts for new equipment.

The railroad embarked on a program of diversification in 1967 with the incorporation of Katy Industries, which acquired much of the stock of the railroad in exchange for its own stock. A lean, rejuvenated Katy returned to profitability in 1971 under the leadership of Reginald Whitman. Upon the demise of the Rock Island in 1980 a Katy subsidiary, the Oklahoma, Kansas & Texas Railway, acquired RI's line from Abilene, Kan., south through Herington, Wichita, and El Reno, Okla., to Dallas.

Merger

Much of Katy's business in the 1970s and 1980s was unit trains of grain and coal moving south from connections. Since more than 70 percent of Katy's traffic was

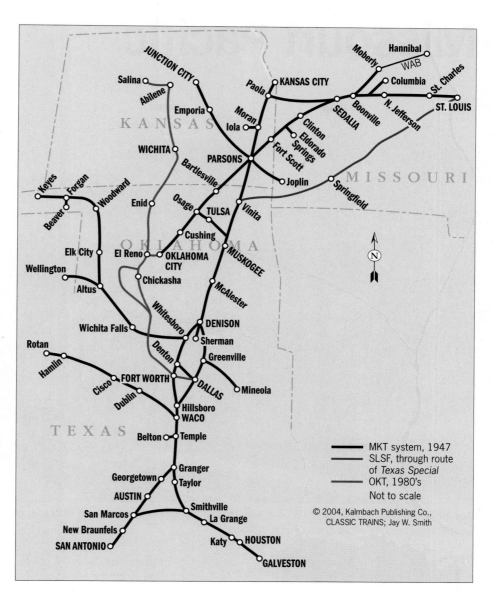

MKT system, 1947
SLSF, through route of *Texas Special*
OKT, 1980's
Not to scale

© 2004, Kalmbach Publishing Co., CLASSIC TRAINS; Jay W. Smith

interline, the mergers taking place around Katy (Missouri Pacific into Union Pacific and Frisco into Burlington Northern) were of great concern to Katy's management. The initial reaction to the UP-MP-WP merger was to protest it as unjustified. As a condition of that merger, Katy received trackage rights on UP to Omaha, Council Bluffs, Lincoln, and Topeka.

In early 1985 the Katy announced that it was receptive to merger or sale. In mid-1985 Union Pacific made a bid, which it soon withdrew, restructured, and resubmitted in mid-1986. Katy and UP already shared operations on several lines via trackage rights, the longest being from Wagoner, Okla., east of Tulsa, to San Marcos, Texas, northeast of San Antonio. Indeed, by 1987, 939 miles (32 percent) of Katy's operation was on tracks of other roads, and other roads used 598 miles of Katy track. As a

condition of the deal, the trackage rights between Kansas City and Omaha that Katy had used were granted to Kansas City Southern, apparently to preserve access to Omaha by a railroad otherwise terminating at Kansas City. The ICC approved the purchase of the Katy by the Missouri Pacific Railroad (a subsidiary of UP) on May 16, 1988. UP absorbed the Katy's operations on Aug. 12, 1988.

FACTS & FIGURES

Year	1929	1987
Miles operated	3,189	3,130
Locomotives	515	237
Passenger cars	411	—
Freight cars	20,140	3,566
Reporting marks: MKT, MKTT, BKTY, OKKT		
Historical society: katyrailroad.org		

Missouri Pacific

Two 4-8-4s, Baldwin products of 1943, lead a westbound freight with a long string of hopper cars through Sandy Hook, Mo., about 19 miles west of Jefferson City on the River Line. *C. T. Wood*

The history of the Missouri Pacific Railroad is easier to understand if the railroad is considered in three parts: the lines west of St. Louis, the lines south and southwest of St. Louis, and the lines in Texas and Louisiana.

Lines west of St. Louis

Ground was broken for the Pacific Railroad at St. Louis, Mo., on July 4, 1851, the nation's 75th birthday. The road had been chartered two years previously to build west from St. Louis through Jefferson City, Mo., to the Pacific. The first four miles of the railroad were opened in 1852, and its train was the first to operate west of the Mississippi River. The railroad reached Jefferson City in 1854, Tipton in 1858, and Sedalia, Mo., 185 miles from St. Louis, in 1860. It was completed to Kansas City, 94 miles farther, in 1865.

In 1866 the road leased the Kansas City, Leavenworth & Atchison Railway, and in 1869, leased the Leavenworth,

Atchison & Northwestern Railroad, reaching Atchison, Kan., with the intention of continuing to Omaha.

The Pacific Railroad was built with a state-decreed track gauge of 5 feet 6 inches. When it was begun, a bridge across the Mississippi was considered impossible, so interchange with railroads east of the river was not a consideration. The Rock Island bridged the Mississippi in 1856, and the Union Pacific and Central Pacific were built to standard gauge; construction of the Eads Bridge at St. Louis had just begun when the Pacific Railroad converted to standard gauge on July 18, 1869. In 1870 the railroad took a new name, Missouri Pacific Railroad, and it was reorganized as the Missouri Pacific Railway in 1876.

Lines south and southwest of St. Louis

Two early railroads formed the nucleus of the southern part of the Missouri Pacific. The St. Louis & Iron Mountain Railroad

was chartered in 1851 to build southwest from St. Louis. It was opened in 1858 from St. Louis to Pilot Knob. In 1869 it completed a line from Bismarck southeast to the Mississippi River and a connection by ferry with the Mobile & Ohio. The Iron Mountain was built, like the Pacific Railroad, with a gauge of 5 feet 6 inches, but the connection with the M&O was important enough that the road converted to 5-foot gauge, the standard in the South. The Iron Mountain continued building south through Poplar Bluff and reached the Arkansas state line in 1872.

The Cairo & Fulton Railroad was chartered in 1854 to build a railroad from Birds Point, Mo., across the Mississippi River from Cairo, Ill., to Fulton, Ark., near the Texas border. It reached a connection with the Texas & Pacific at Texarkana in 1873. In 1874 the Iron Mountain and the Cairo & Fulton were consolidated as the St. Louis, Iron Mountain & Southern Railway.

Lines in Texas and Louisiana

The Texas portion of the Missouri Pacific system consisted of several entities that at various times owned, controlled, or included each other. The two major ones are the International-Great Northern and Gulf Coast Lines.

The International & Great Northern Railroad was chartered in 1873 to consolidate the Houston & Great Northern Railroad, a railroad between Houston and Palestine, Texas, and the International Railroad, which ran from Longview, where it connected with the Texas & Pacific, through Palestine to Hearne, with the intention of continuing to Laredo to be part of a route to Mexico City. The I&GN underwent reorganization in 1879 and soon afterward was leased to the Missouri, Kansas & Texas (Katy), which had just become part of Jay Gould's empire. In 1883 the I&GN leased the Galveston, Houston & Henderson Railroad.

When the Katy ran into financial difficulties in 1888, the lease was canceled, and the I&GN resumed independence, though it remained in the Gould family. In 1895 it "adjusted its debt," in the words of Poor's *Manual of Railroads*, and it entered receivership in 1908. It was succeeded in 1911 by the International & Great Northern Railway. In 1914 the I&GN found itself unable to pay either the principal or the interest due on its bonds. The I&GN's creditors, the executors of the Jay Gould Estate, consented to extend the debt, but were unable to do so because of the unsettled financial situation resulting from the war in Europe and a poor cotton crop that year. The I&GN entered receivership in 1914.

The International-Great Northern Railroad was incorporated in 1922 as successor to the I&GN. The New Orleans, Texas & Mexico (Gulf Coast Lines) purchased the I-GN in 1924.

Gulf Coast Lines was a collection of railroads between New Orleans and Brownsville, Texas, which had been assembled by B. F. Yoakum when he was chairman of the board of the Rock Island and the Frisco. The principal component and parent of GCL was the New Orleans, Texas & Mexico; the biggest of the subsidiaries was the St. Louis, Brownsville & Mexico, a relative latecomer, opened in 1908 from Houston to Brownsville.

The NOT&M, StLB&M, and others

Blue had not yet given way to Union Pacific Armour Yellow as this train rolls by Pilot Knob, Mo., on Oct. 1, 1982. Merger with UP would come less than three months later. *Mark Bess*

were divorced from the Frisco in 1913, at which time they acquired the Gulf Coast Lines name. NOT&M purchased the International-Great Northern in 1924, and acquired control of the San Antonio, Uvalde & Gulf in 1925. Missouri Pacific purchased control of NOT&M in 1924.

The Gould era

Jay Gould bought control of Missouri Pacific in 1879. He soon added to his portfolio the St. Louis, Iron Mountain & Southern; Missouri, Kansas & Texas; International & Great Northern; Texas & Pacific; Galveston, Houston & Henderson; Wabash; and Central Branch, Union Pacific (a railroad running west from Atchison, Kan.).

Gould began an expansion program that extended MP to Omaha, Neb., and Pueblo, Colo.; I&GN to Laredo, Texas, on the Mexican border; Iron Mountain to Memphis, Tenn., Lake Charles, La., and Fort Smith, Ark.; and T&P west to a connection with Southern Pacific at Sierra Blanca, Texas.

Then his empire fell apart. Wabash entered receivership in 1884, T&P in 1885, MK&T in 1888, and I&GN in 1889. T&P and I&GN remained in the Missouri Pacific family; MK&T became independent; and Wabash eventually became part of the Pennsylvania Railroad family.

Twentieth century

In the early 1900s Missouri Pacific constructed several new lines along rivers to bypass stiff grades on its older routes. Among them were the Illinois Division along the Mississippi southeast of St. Louis and the Jefferson City–Kansas City line along the Missouri. In 1917 the Missouri Pacific Railroad was incorporated to consolidate the Missouri Pacific Railway and the Iron Mountain, which had entered receivership in 1915.

MoPac acquired control of the New Orleans, Texas & Mexico Railway (Gulf Coast Lines) in 1924, and by 1930 MP owned 92 percent of its stock. MP also owned a 69 percent interest in the T&P. The expanded system was known as Missouri Pacific Lines; at times the term included the Texas & Pacific.

Missouri Pacific owned half the common stock of the Denver & Rio Grande Western (Western Pacific had the other half). MoPac and WP lost their control of the Rio Grande when it was reorganized in 1947.

Mergers

In 1961 MoPac acquired an interest in the Chicago & Eastern Illinois. In 1967 MoPac took control of C&EI, in 1969 sold the Evansville line to Louisville & Nashville, and in 1976 merged C&EI.

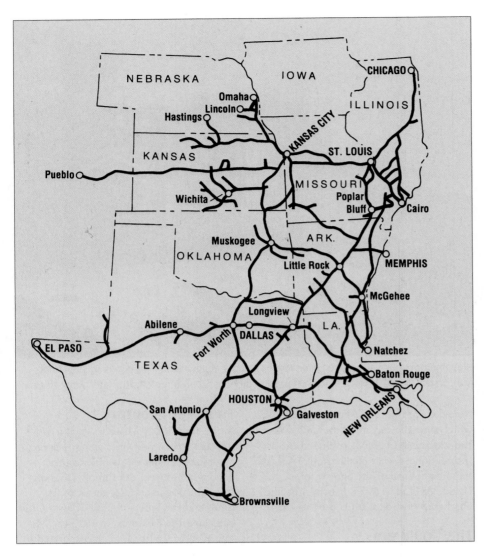

The Missouri-Illinois Railroad was incorporated in 1921 to acquire the Illinois Southern. Missouri Pacific acquired control of the M-I in 1929 by acquiring 51 percent of its stock from the lead companies that owned the M-I. At the same time the M-I leased the MR&BT, which it crossed at Derby, Mo. The Missouri-Illinois entered reorganization in 1933, emerged from bankruptcy in 1944, and merged the MR&BT in 1945. The M-I discontinued its ferry operation in 1961. In 1964 Missouri Pacific acquired nearly all the remaining stock of the M-I, and in 1974 acquired the final shares. MP merged the M-I in 1978.

Merger with Union Pacific

The creation of Burlington Northern in 1970 formalized long-established alliances, but Chicago, Burlington & Quincy's acquisition of Frisco stock in 1966 and the opening of merger discussions between BN and Frisco in 1977 in effect put BN in MoPac's back yard. Santa Fe and Union Pacific both considered MoPac as a merger partner in the early 1960s, and in 1966 MoPac purchased a large block of Santa Fe stock, filed an application to control the Santa Fe, then withdrew the application a year or two later.

In January 1980 Union Pacific announced an agreement to acquire Missouri Pacific—then two weeks later made an offer to acquire Western Pacific. The announcement constituted the first significant realignment of railroad alliances in the West since E. H. Harriman had put UP and Southern Pacific together 80 years before.

The merger of UP and MP was consummated on Dec. 22, 1982. Initially, the two railroads were to remain separate in name and image. A year later yellow paint began to replace blue on Missouri Pacific locomotives, and not long after that "Union" replaced "Missouri" in the lettering diagrams.

FACTS & FIGURES

Year	1929	1982
Miles operated	9,732	11,167
Locomotives	1,543	1,602
Passenger cars	1,119	17
Freight cars	55,197	47,825
Reporting marks: MP		
Historical society: mopac.org		

In 1923, T&P issued preferred stock to MP in exchange for mortgage bonds. By 1930 MP owned all T&P's preferred stock and more than half its common stock. MP merged Texas & Pacific on Oct. 15, 1976. With T&P came the remnants of the Midland Valley and the Kansas, Oklahoma & Gulf, which T&P had acquired in 1964.

In 1968 MP purchased a half interest in Alton & Southern from the Aluminum Corporation of America (Alcoa); Chicago & North Western purchased the other half interest but sold it to St. Louis Southwestern (Cotton Belt). In 1977 MP merged several smaller subsidiaries, among them the Fort Worth Belt and the Missouri-Illinois. That same year MP was reincorporated and became a wholly owned subsidiary of Missouri Pacific Corporation.

Missouri-Illinois Railroad

The predecessors of the Missouri-Illinois were the Mississippi River & Bonne Terre Railway and the Illinois Southern Railway. The MR&BT was incorporated in 1888 and opened in 1890 from a connection with the St. Louis & Iron Mountain at Riverside, about 30 miles south of St. Louis, south into the lead-mining area east of the Iron Mountain line. The MR&BT was owned by the St. Joseph Lead Co.

The Illinois Southern was incorporated in 1900 as successor to the Centralia & Chester, which had a line from Salem, Ill., southwest to Chester on the east bank of the Mississippi. The Illinois Southern planned to extend the line across the Mississippi and on to Kansas City, bypassing St. Louis. The line reached the Iron Mountain at Bismarck, Mo., in 1903, but the ferry crossing of the Mississippi near St. Genevieve, Mo., restricted any serious consideration of the road as a major route. The company underwent reorganization in 1911 and entered receivership in 1915.

Mobile & Ohio

The 2-8-2 was Mobile & Ohio's principal freight locomotive. Number 408, built by Baldwin in 1913, was one of 21 similar light Mikados on the roster. The railroad also had 37 heavier Mikes of USRA design. *R. J. Foster*

The original purpose of the Mobile & Ohio was to tap the trade of the Mississippi, Missouri, and Ohio rivers for the port of Mobile, Ala. It would do this by connecting the city with the Ohio and the Mississippi at their confluence at Cairo, Ill. Cities, counties, and states along the route bought stock and aided the project financially, and Congress passed a land grant bill in 1850 to aid the M&O (and also the Illinois Central).

The first 30 miles of the M&O, from Mobile to Citronelle, Ala., opened in 1852, and the line was completed to Columbus, Ky., on the east bank of the Mississippi a few miles south of Cairo, on April 22, 1861. River steamboats connected Columbus with the south end of the Illinois Central at Cairo, and the St. Louis & Iron Mountain planned to build a terminal at Belmont, Mo., across the river from Columbus.

The road was completed just 10 days after the Confederates fired on Fort Sumter. The Civil War negated any salutary effect the road might have had on the city of Mobile—in addition to pretty much

using up M&O's rolling stock and track. The cost of rebuilding the railroad combined with its previous debt sent the M&O into receivership in 1875.

The Iron Mountain did not reach Belmont until 1871, and by then M&O had decided to extend its line north to East Cairo, about 20 miles. Because of M&O's financial difficulties the extension was not completed until 1882. In 1886 M&O acquired the 3-foot gauge St. Louis & Cairo, which ran between East St. Louis and Cairo, and standard-gauged it. The importance of the terminal at Columbus, Ky., declined, and soon M&O abandoned the spur to the river there. In 1898 the road opened a line from Artesia and Columbus, Miss., to Montgomery, Ala. (See the Gulf, Mobile & Ohio map on page 150 for details on M&O routes.)

The M&O recognized that it was not as strong a railroad as the Illinois Central or the Louisville & Nashville and accepted Southern Railway's offer of an exchange of securities in 1901— Southern had its eye on M&O's route between Mobile and St. Louis. Merger of Southern and M&O nearly

occurred, but the bill allowing the merger was vetoed by the governor of Mississippi.

Southern control continued, however. In the late 1920s traffic fell off, and deficits appeared on M&O's ledgers in 1930. Southern was unable to provide financial assistance. M&O entered receivership on June 3, 1932.

Mobile & Ohio pursued its own course, but Southern ownership continued until 1938, when Southern had to sell its M&O bonds to meet other financial commitments. The Gulf, Mobile & Ohio purchased the Mobile & Ohio on Aug. 1, 1940, and was consolidated with Gulf, Mobile & Northern a month later.

FACTS & FIGURES

Year	1929	1940
Miles operated	1,159	1,180
Locomotives	231	119
Passenger cars	112	31
Freight cars	8,368	3,298

Reporting marks: M&O

Historical society: gmohs.org

Monongahela

THE
MONONGAHELA
RAILWAY

Baldwin RF-16s 1216 and 1205 lug a train of empty hopper cars alongside the Monongahela River at Alicia, Pa., in the late 1960s. The former New York Central sharknose diesels would later go to the Delaware & Hudson. *David H. Hamley*

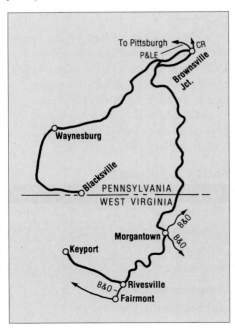

The Monongahela Railway extended southward from Brownsville, Pa., following its namesake river to Fairmont, W.Va.

The Monongahela Railroad was incorporated in 1900 by the Pennsylvania Railroad and Pittsburgh & Lake Erie to be a jointly owned subsidiary into the coalfields of southwest Pennsylvania and adjacent West Virginia. The Monongahela Railway was incorporated in 1915 as a consolidation of the Monongahela Railroad and the Buckhannon & Northern Railroad. In the 1920s and 1930s it absorbed several shorter railroads in the coal mining area of southwestern Pennsylvania and adjacent portions of West Virginia. On Jan. 1, 1927, the Baltimore & Ohio acquired a one-third interest (one-sixth each from PRR and P&LE) in exchange for some strategic trackage rights.

In 1952 the Monongahela replaced its USRA light Mikados (2-8-2s) with 27 Baldwin S-12 switchers to be operated singly and in multiple as needed. The Monongahela attracted the attention of rail enthusiasts in early 1968 when it bought eight Baldwin RF-16 freight diesels from the New York Central. They couldn't operate in multiple with Monongahela's fleet of Baldwin road-switchers, and their carbody configuration wasn't optimal for Monongahela's needs, but they were cheap and, quite importantly, Monongahela's shop forces understood Baldwin diesels. A year later the railroad ordered five specially ballasted GP38s, the heaviest examples of that model.

In 1968 the Waynesburg Southern Railroad opened to provide an easier route to coal mines that the Monongahela reached by a steep, curving branch that was unsuitable for long unit coal trains—the principal customer of those mines was Detroit Edison. Monongahela operated the Waynesburg Southern right from the beginning.

Conrail inherited the Pennsylvania's interest in the Monongahela. In 1989 Pittsburgh & Lake Erie sold its interest in the railroad to Conrail, and in 1990 CSX, successor to Baltimore & Ohio, did the same in exchange for trackage rights that would allow it to abandon its ex-B&O line from Morgantown, W. Va., to Uniontown, Pa. Conrail merged the Monongahela on May 1, 1993.

FACTS & FIGURES

Year	1929	1992
Miles operated	94	162
Locomotives	69	15
Passenger cars	9	—
Freight cars	51	—
Reporting marks: MGA		

Montana Rail Link

Montana Rail Link train M-LAUMIS1-18, behind two new SD70ACe diesels plus an older GP35, crawls up Bozeman Pass west of Livingston, Mont., en route to Logan and Helena. A large plume of smoke rises above the area from a forest fire south of Livingston. *Tom Danneman*

The last spike of the Northern Pacific Railroad was driven near Garrison, Mont., on Sept. 8, 1883, completing a line from Carlton, Minn., near Duluth, to Wallula Junction, Wash. Within a few years extensions were in place to St. Paul, Minn., and Seattle and Tacoma, Wash. In 1901 the NP came under the control of James J. Hill, who had built the parallel Great Northern Railway, and NP and GN jointly purchased the Chicago, Burlington & Quincy. All that was needed to bring what would become Burlington Northern into existence was a nod from the Interstate Commerce Commission—and that took almost 70 years.

Burlington Northern began operation March 2, 1970. It had two main lines all the way from St. Paul to Seattle, and alternate routes and cutoffs essentially made it

three or more routes for much of the distance. In the mid-1980s Burlington Northern began to prune its route structure. The former Great Northern line across Montana was 10 years newer than the ex-Northern Pacific line and had easier grades. BN thought it could easily concentrate its traffic on the GN line and looked to divest itself of some of the Northern Pacific route.

Montana Rail Link was formed in 1987 as a division of the Washington Companies, a transportation and industrial conglomerate controlled by Missoula businessman Dennis Washington. Under Washington's direction, MRL acquired the ex-Northern Pacific line from Huntley, Mont., east of Billings, through Helena to Sandpoint, Idaho, plus trackage rights from Sandpoint to Spokane, Wash. Montana

Rail Link leased the main line and purchased branches to Harrison, Alder, Phillipsburg, Darby, St. Regis, and Polson, Mont. Burlington Northern (and successor Burlington Northern Santa Fe, later officially BNSF) retained ownership of the line from Helena to Phosphate for access to the Montana Western Railway, a short line created from the Garrison-Butte segment of the former Northern Pacific line via Butte (the steep line over Homestake Pass east of Butte has been abandoned; the rest of the Montana Western reverted to BNSF in 2003). BNSF also kept trackage rights from Huntley through Billings to Laurel, Mont.

The start of Montana Rail Link operations on Oct. 31, 1987, occurred during contract negotiations between BN and the United Transportation Union (MRL's

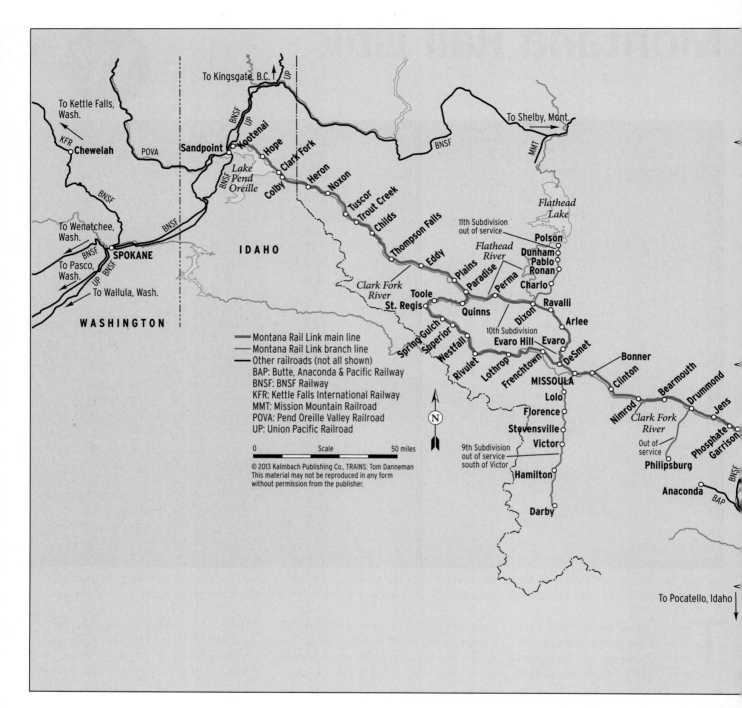

© 2013 Kalmbach Publishing Co., TRAINS: Tom Danneman
This material may not be reproduced in any form
without permission from the publisher.

operating employees are all members of the Brotherhood of Locomotive Engineers). There was picketing as well as vandalism at Livingston, Mont., the location of a major NP shop that had been closed by BN.

In 1988 the Washington Companies (which also owns the Southern Railway of British Columbia, or SRY Rail Link) reopened the Livingston shops as a contract repair shop, not only for its own locomotives but for those of other roads. The railroad's headquarters are in Missoula, with major classification yards and car

repair facilities at Laurel and Missoula. Dispatching is done (with Centralized Traffic Control) out of Missoula.

In 1991 MRL petitioned for and was granted exemption from the Interstate Commerce Commission's Class 1 status, citing the cost of the extra paperwork involved in being a Class 1 railroad, so MRL operates as a Class 2 (regional). In August 1992 MRL leased the Helena-Phosphate line, known as "The Gap." In mid-1992 the Phillipsburg and Alder lines were out of service.

Montana Rail Link's principal items of

traffic are paper, lumber and other forest products, grain, and BNSF trains moving between Spokane and Billings—the MRL route is 125 miles shorter, and BNSF's northern route was operating at capacity. Another MRL operation is the Gas Local, a tank train between Missoula and Thompson Falls, which bridges a gap in a gasoline pipeline.

Into the 2000s MRL's locomotive fleet was mainly second-hand SD40- and SD45-family diesels. In 2005 the railroad received its first new power, 16 EMD SD70ACe diesels.

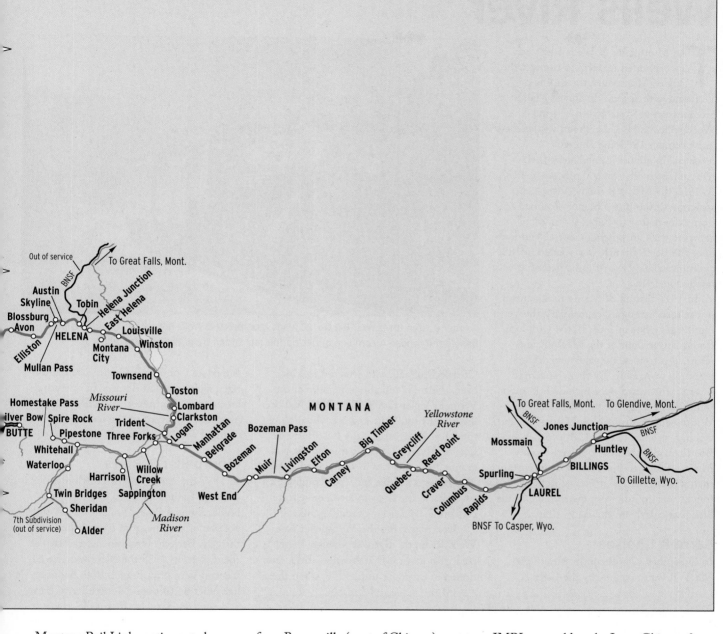

Montana Rail Link continues to be held by the Washington Companies, which also has subsidiaries in mining, aviation, environmental, and sea transportation.

I&M Rail Link

Although not connected physically to the MRL, another Washington Companies property was I&M Rail Link (IMRL), which operated about 1,400 miles of former Milwaukee Road trackage in Illinois, Iowa, Missouri, and Minnesota.

In April 1997 I&M Rail Link purchased from Canadian Pacific its lines from Bensenville (west of Chicago) west to the Mississippi River, with lines diverging and running southwest to Kansas City and northwest across northern Iowa and southern Minnesota, with trackage rights north to St. Paul, Minn. Soo Line had acquired the lines with its purchase of the Milwaukee; Canadian Pacific gained them when it acquired the Soo.

Washington Companies owned two-thirds of I&M Rail Link, with CP owning the remaining third. Initially, CP dispatched the line, but that task was eventually transferred to Montana Rail Link. The IMRL was sold to the Iowa, Chicago & Eastern (which was owned by the Dakota, Minnesota & Eastern) in July 2002.

FACTS & FIGURES

Year	1989	2012
Miles operated	939	937
Locomotives	88	96
Passenger cars	—	—
Freight cars	985	1,300
Reporting marks: MRL		
Website: montanarail.com		

ontpelier & Wells River

The Montpelier & Wells River was incorporated in 1867 to connect the city of Montpelier, the capital of Vermont, with several Boston & Maine predecessors at Wells River, Vt., and Woodsville, N. H. The railroad was opened in November 1873 and entered receivership almost immediately. It was reorganized by its original officers in 1877. In 1883 the M&WR financed the construction of the Barre Branch Railroad from Montpelier to Barre, six miles, to compete with an existing Central Vermont line. The Barre Branch was opened in 1889 and immediately leased to its parent; it was merged in 1913.

In 1911 Boston & Maine took control of the road through its subsidiary, the Vermont Valley, but in 1926 B&M withdrew from management of the M&WR and returned it to local management while retaining ownership. By then, passenger service, which had once included through trains between Burlington, Vt., and the White Mountains of New Hampshire and through sleepers between Montpelier and Boston, had dwindled to mixed trains. Mail and milk traffic were more important than passengers. The principal item of freight was granite from quarries along the line, particularly on the Barre Branch.

Barre & Chelsea

In December 1944 the properties of the M&WR were acquired by the Barre &

Former Boston & Maine 2-8-0 No. 20 leads Montpelier & Wells River train 1, with a milk car behind the tender. A combine brings up the rear of the train. *William Moedinger Jr.*

Chelsea Railroad, with which it had long been affiliated (and also a member of the Vermont Valley family). The B&C had been incorporated in 1913 as a consolidation of the Barre Railroad and the East Barre & Chelsea Railroad. B&C's chief traffic was granite from quarries in and around Barre. The line was notable for 5 percent grades, a switchback, and a steam locomotive roster consisting exclusively of saddle-tankers.

After absorbing the Montpelier & Wells River, the Barre & Chelsea dieselized with three GE 70-tonners. B&C continued in existence until 1956, when the

Interstate Commerce Commission authorized abandonment because of operating losses (the Montpelier–Wells River line produced 5 percent of the revenue but was charged with 40 percent of operating cost).

Montpelier & Barre

In 1957 the newly organized Montpelier & Barre Railroad, owned by short-line holder Samuel Pinsly, bought the 14-mile portion of the line from Montpelier through Barre to Graniteville, and two of the diesels. In 1958 the M&B purchased Central Vermont's branch from Montpelier Junction through Montpelier to Barre and combined it with its parallel track.

Montpelier & Barre received ICC permission to abandon in 1980. The state of Vermont purchased the tracks, and since then, the Washington County Railroad has operated the line.

FACTS & FIGURES

Year	1929	1944
Miles operated	44	44
Locomotives	9	6
Passenger cars	7	1
Freight cars	9	2
Reporting marks: M&WR		

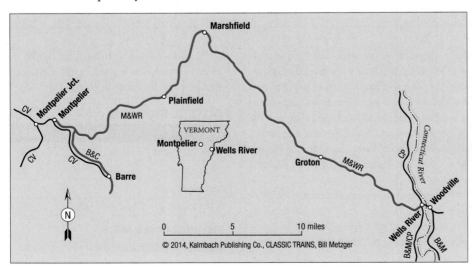

© 2014, Kalmbach Publishing Co., CLASSIC TRAINS, Bill Metzger

Nashville, Chattanooga & St. Louis

The Nashville & Chattanooga Railroad was incorporated in 1845. The first 9 miles out of Nashville were opened in 1851, and by 1853 it had crossed Cumberland Mountain and reached the Tennessee River at Bridgeport, Ala. The next year the N&C arrived in Chattanooga, where a connection to Atlanta was made with the Western & Atlantic, owned by the state of Georgia. Floods in 1862 destroyed much of the N&C before retreating Confederate and advancing Union forces could tear it up, but each army demolished one of the two Tennessee River bridges. In 1864 and 1865 the U. S. Military Railroad thoroughly rebuilt the road and returned it to its owners.

In 1870 the road leased the Nashville & Northwestern, a line from Nashville to Hickman, Ky., on the Mississippi River, and in 1873 N&C purchased the line. The N&C was renamed the Nashville, Chattanooga & St. Louis Railway in 1873. During the 1870s the road acquired several short lines which became branches off the N&C's main from Hickman to Chattanooga.

In 1879 the road's president, Edwin W. Cole, attempted to make the NC&StL a St. Louis–Atlanta route. He obtained control of the incomplete Owensboro & Nashville, which was building a line from Owensboro, on the Ohio River, toward Nashville, and purchased the Illinois and Indiana portion of the St. Louis & Southeastern, which had been in receivership since 1874. Evansville, Ind., the eastern terminus of the StL&SE, was about 30 miles west of Owensboro, Ky. Cole

All of Nashville, Chattanooga & St. Louis's F units, including F7 No. 817, had steam generators for use in passenger service, and were painted blue and aluminum (road-switchers were maroon and yellow). All went to Louisville & Nashville in the 1957 merger. *Linn Westcott*

initiated negotiations (but didn't complete them) to lease the Western & Atlantic and the Central of Georgia.

Louisville & Nashville reacted by buying 55 percent of NC&StL's stock and transferring the East St. Louis–Evansville line to its own system. In 1896 L&N acquired and leased to NC&StL the Paducah, Tennessee & Alabama (Paducah, Ky.–Bruceton–Lexington, Tenn.) and the Tennessee Midland Railway (Memphis–Lexington–Perryville, Tenn.). This gave NC&StL a route north to the Ohio River at Paducah and a route southwest to Memphis, a much more important

destination than Hickman, Ky., which was NC&StL's original western terminal.

In 1917 NC&StL and the Burlington built a bridge over the Ohio River between Paducah, Ky., and Metropolis, Ill., and a connecting railroad. In 1924 the two roads sold a one-third interest in the Paducah & Illinois Railroad to the Illinois Central, which used it to bypass its own congested Ohio River crossing at Cairo, Ill.

NC&StL was a link in several Midwest–Southeast routes, notably Chicago–Florida passenger trains operated with Chicago & Eastern Illinois and L&N north of Nashville and Atlanta, Birmingham & Coast or Central of Georgia, Atlantic Coast Line, and Florida East Coast south of Atlanta.

After nearly 60 years of control, L&N merged the NC&StL on Aug. 30, 1957.

FACTS & FIGURES

Year	1929	1956
Miles operated	1,223	1,043
Locomotives	249	132
Passenger cars	219	106
Freight cars	8,510	6,761
Reporting marks: NC, NC&StL		
Historical society: ncstl.com		

Nevada-California-Oregon

B y 1879 Wadsworth, Nev., east of Reno, was a major trans-shipment point for supplies going to area mines. John T. Davis formed the Western Nevada Railroad to build a line south from Wadsworth to Walker Lake.

Davis moved his base of operations to Reno and on June 1, 1880, organized the Nevada & Oregon Railroad to build south to Aurora (southwest of Hawthorne, almost on the California state line) and north to the California-Oregon state line at Goose Lake in the northeast corner of California. Davis quit in a dispute and returned to San Francisco.

New management decided to build northward first and broke ground on Dec. 22, 1880. The Nevada & Oregon was in financial trouble by the time it had graded

Southern Pacific moved several NCO engines to its California narrow gauge lines when the NCO converted to standard gauge. This is 2-8-0 No. 14 in 1906. *H. L. Broadbelt collection*

a mile of roadbed. A new Nevada & Oregon company took over in April 1881, and the first spike was driven in May. The 3-foot-gauge line started north from Reno.

In 1884, the Moran brothers bought the railroad, and by 1885 it had a new name—Nevada & California Railroad. Construction continued north, pretty much following present-day highway U. S. 395.

In 1893 the assets were transferred to a new company, the Nevada-California-Oregon Railway. Construction resumed in 1899. The line reached Madeline in 1902, Alturas in 1908, and Lakeview, Ore., in 1912, 238 miles from Reno.

The NCO operated profitably from 1899 to 1913. In 1901 NCO acquired the Sierra Valleys Railway (later Sierra Valley & Mohawk, consolidated with NCO in 1915), which ran from Beckwourth Pass west to Clio. Other railroads began to penetrate the area. The Western Pacific came up the Feather River Canyon from the west, paralleled the Sierra Valleys as far as Beckwourth Pass, then turned north and paralleled the NCO as far as Hackstaff (present-day Herlong) before turning east. The Southern Pacific built northwest from Wadsworth, crossed the NCO at Wendel, and continued west to Susanville and Westwood.

Western Pacific wanted a branch to Reno. It considered adding a third rail to the NCO from Beckwourth Pass to Reno, then bought the NCO property from Reno north to Hackstaff and the former Sierra Valleys line. The last NCO train departed Reno on Jan. 30, 1918, and the NCO moved its headquarters to Alturas.

Meanwhile, deficits had appeared on NCO's books. NCO management tried to sell the entire road to Western Pacific, without success. In 1921 NCO considered an extension northwest from Lakeview into a lumbering area. WP was involved to the point of providing rails, though there was some debate over that. NCO threatened to abandon the line south of Wendel, where it crossed SP's Westwood Branch, but WP invoked a clause in the sale agreement for the Reno line. A year later NCO abandoned the Hackstaff–Wendel part of the line.

Lumber shipments from the north end of the line began to increase, and NCO began to consider standard-gauging its line. Meanwhile Southern Pacific was planning to build a line to connect its Overland and Cascade routes, using part of the Westwood Branch and new construction southeast from Klamath Falls. SP offered to buy the NCO to use the Wendel–Alturas segment as part of that line. SP acquired control of the NCO in October 1926 and began standard-gauging in July 1927. Standard gauge service made it to Lakeview on May 27, 1928. SP leased the NCO on Sept. 1, 1929.

FACTS & FIGURES

Year	1916	1929
Miles operated	272	155
Locomotives	14	3
Passenger cars	18	—
Freight cars	257	63
Reporting marks: NCO		

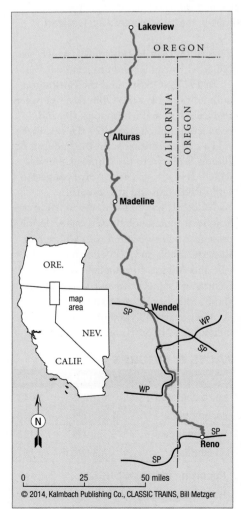

Lakeview

OREGON

CALIFORNIA | OREGON

Alturas

Madeline

ORE.

map area

NEV.

SP — Wendel

WP

SP

CALIF.

WP

SP

Reno

SP

0   25   50 miles

© 2014, Kalmbach Publishing Co., CLASSIC TRAINS, Bill Metzger

Nevada Northern

A three-car freight rolls northward toward the road's Western Pacific connection at Shafter behind Nevada Northern's only road locomotive, a bought-new SD7 painted yellow with a red top. The train is near Goshute in September 1976. *Ted Benson*

Mining in Nevada meant gold or silver—until the electrical industry began to grow toward the turn of the 20th century. Then copper, which had been treated almost as a waste material, became valuable. A large deposit of copper ore was discovered near Ely, in east-central Nevada many miles from the nearest railroad. One proposal for a railroad to Ely involved standard-gauging the Eureka & Palisade and extending it 75

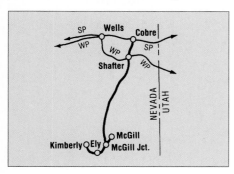

miles eastward from Eureka to Ely over four mountain ranges.

In 1905 the Nevada Consolidated Copper Co., which had been created the previous year by merger of several mining companies active in the area, incorporated the Nevada Northern Railway to build a line from Ely north through the Steptoe Valley to a connection with the Southern Pacific's line between Reno, Nev., and Ogden, Utah. NN's route was almost twice as long as the proposed line from Eureka, but the only obstacle was sagebrush. The railroad was completed in 1906.

Nevada Consolidated Copper Co. became a subsidiary of Utah Copper Co. in 1909; Kennecott Copper Corp. acquired control in 1923. In the Ely area the Nevada Northern was used by the mine trains of its parent, but the major portion of the road saw only a biweekly freight train. In mid-1983 Kennecott shut down

its smelter at McGill, Nev., and due to lack of traffic, NN suspended operation.

Kennecott donated the trackage around Ely and the railroad's yard and shop facilities in East Ely—now a National Historical Landmark—to the White Pine Historical Railroad Foundation. The foundation runs the facilities as the Nevada Northern Railway Museum, which operates steam and diesel passenger excursions. The line north to Shafter is owned by the city of Ely, but sees no traffic.

FACTS & FIGURES

Year	1929	1981
Miles operated	166	149
Locomotives	8	1
Passenger cars	13	—
Freight cars	37	58
Reporting marks: NN		

New York Central

The New York Central was a large railroad, and it had several subsidiaries whose identity remained strong, not so much in cars and locomotives carrying the old name but in local loyalties: If you lived in Detroit, you rode to Chicago on the Michigan Central, not the New York Central; through the Conrail era and even now under CSX, the line across Massachusetts is still known as "the Boston & Albany."

New York Central's history is easier to digest in small pieces: first New York Central followed by its two major leased lines, Boston & Albany and Toledo & Ohio Central; then Michigan Central and Big Four (Cleveland, Cincinnati, Chicago & St. Louis). By the mid-1960s NYC owned 99.8 percent of the stock of Michigan Central and more than 97 percent of the stock of the Big Four. NYC leased both on Feb. 1, 1930, but they remained separate companies to avoid the complexities of merger.

In broad geographic terms, the New York Central proper was everything east of

Buffalo plus a line from Buffalo through Cleveland and Toledo to Chicago (the former Lake Shore & Michigan Southern). NYC included the Ohio Central Lines (Toledo through Columbus to and beyond Charleston, W. Va.) and the Boston & Albany (neatly defined by its name). The Michigan Central was a Buffalo–Detroit–Chicago line and everything in Michigan north of that. The Big Four was everything south of NYC's Cleveland–Toledo–Chicago line other than the Ohio Central.

The New York Central System included several controlled railroads that did not accompany NYC into the Penn Central merger. The most important of these were (with the proportion of NYC ownership in the mid-1960s):

- Pittsburgh & Lake Erie (80 percent)
- Indiana Harbor Belt (NYC, 30 percent; Michigan Central, 30 percent; Chicago & North Western, 20 percent; and Milwaukee Road, 20 percent)
- Toronto, Hamilton & Buffalo (NYC, 37 percent; MC, 22 percent; Canada

Southern, 14 percent; and Canadian Pacific, 27 percent).

New York Central

The Erie Canal, opened in 1825 between Albany and Buffalo, New York, followed the Hudson and Mohawk rivers between Albany and Schenectady. The 40-mile water route included several locks and was extremely slow; in consequence, stagecoaches plied the 17-mile direct route between the cities. In 1826 the Mohawk & Hudson Rail Road was incorporated to replace the stages between Albany and Schenectady.

The railroad opened in 1831; its first locomotive was named *DeWitt Clinton* after the governor of the state when the M&H was incorporated. Within months there was a proposal for a railroad all the way from Albany to Buffalo, but the subject was touchy—the state was still deeply in debt for the construction of the Erie Canal.

One by one, railroads were incorporated, built, and opened westward from the

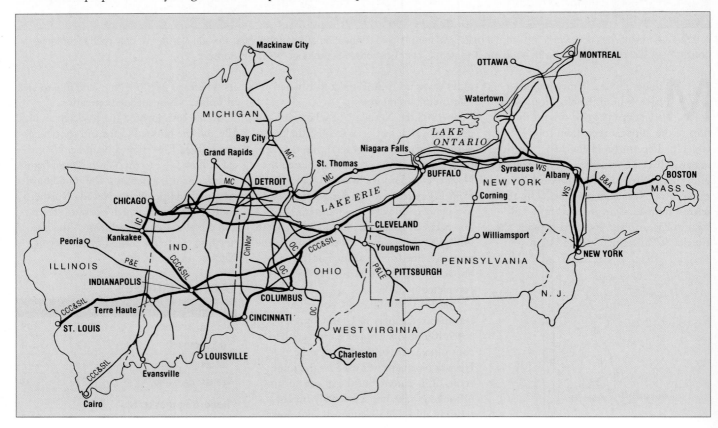

A pair of sparkling EMD E8s leads train 51, the westbound *Empire State Express*, through Rochester, N. Y., in 1953. *Linn H. Westcott*

end of the Mohawk & Hudson: Utica & Schenectady, Syracuse & Utica, Auburn & Syracuse, Auburn & Rochester, Tonawanda (Rochester to Attica via Batavia), and Attica & Buffalo. By 1841 it was possible to travel between Albany and Buffalo by train in just 25 hours, lightning speed compared with the canal packets. By 1851 the trip took a little over 12 hours. In 1851 the state passed an act freeing the railroads from the need to pay tolls to the Erie Canal, with which they competed. That same year the Hudson River Railroad opened from New York to East Albany and the New York & Erie (later the Erie Railroad) opened from Piermont, on the Hudson River, west to Dunkirk, N. Y., on Lake Erie.

From the beginning the railroads between Albany and Buffalo had cooperated in running through service. In 1853 they were consolidated as the New York Central Railroad—the roads mentioned above or their successors plus the Schenectady & Troy, the Buffalo & Lockport, the Rochester, Lockport & Niagara Falls, and two unbuilt roads, the Mohawk Valley and the Syracuse & Utica Direct.

The New York & Harlem Railroad was incorporated in 1831 to build a line in Manhattan from 23rd Street north to 129th Street between Third and Eighth avenues (the railroad chose to follow Fourth Avenue). At first the railroad was primarily a horsecar system, but in 1840 the road's charter was amended to allow it to build north toward Albany. In 1844 the rails reached White Plains and in January 1852 the New York & Harlem made connection with the Western Railroad (later Boston & Albany) at Chatham, N. Y., creating a New York–Albany rail route.

The Hudson was a busy river, and the towns along it felt no need of a railroad, except during the winter when ice prevented navigation. Poughkeepsie interests organized the Hudson River Railroad in 1847. In the autumn of 1851 the railroad opened from a terminal on Manhattan's west side all the way to East Albany. By then the road had leased the Troy & Greenbush, gaining access to a bridge over the Hudson at Troy. (A bridge at Albany was completed in 1866.)

By 1863 Cornelius Vanderbilt controlled the New York & Harlem and had a

substantial interest in the Hudson River Railroad. In 1867 he obtained control of the New York Central, consolidating it with the Hudson River in 1869 to form the New York Central & Hudson River Railroad. (For simplicity we'll refer to the NYC&HR as "NYC," "Central," or "New York Central.")

Vanderbilt wanted to build a magnificent terminal for the NYC&HR in New York. He chose as its site the corner of 42nd Street and Fourth Avenue on the New York & Harlem, the southerly limit of steam locomotive operation in Manhattan. Construction of Grand Central Depot began in 1869 and took two years. The new depot was actually three separate stations serving the NYC&HR, the New York & Harlem, and the New Haven. Trains of the Hudson River line reached the New York & Harlem by means of a connecting track completed in 1871 along Spuyten Duyvil Creek and the Harlem River (they have since become a single waterway). That was the first of three Grand Centrals.

The present station, Grand Central Terminal, was opened in 1913. Even in the space age Grand Central remains awesome. Superlatives are inadequate. GCT has a total of 48 platform tracks on two subterranean levels; the project included depressing and decking over the tracks along Park Avenue and electrifying NYC's lines north to Harmon and White Plains. (NYC had two other stretches of electrified line: the Detroit River Tunnel, opened in 1910, and Cleveland Union Terminal, opened in 1930. Diesels put an end to both those electrifications in 1953.)

The Watertown & Rome Railroad was chartered in 1832 to connect Watertown, N. Y., with the Syracuse & Utica (then only a proposal itself). The road opened in 1851, and in 1852 it was extended to Cape Vincent, where it connected with a ferry to Kingston, Ontario. In 1861 the W&R consolidated with the Potsdam & Watertown to form the Rome, Watertown & Ogdensburg. The RW&O built a line to Oswego and bought lines to Syracuse and Buffalo. The line to Buffalo was a mistake—it bypassed Rochester, had almost no local business, and was not part of any through route.

The RW&O came under Lackawanna control briefly before a rehabilitation in the 1880s. New management extended the RW&O north to connect with a Grand Trunk line to Montreal and added the Black River & Utica (Utica to Watertown and Ogdensburg) to the system. NYC leased the RW&O in 1893.

Meanwhile, NYC had built its own line north from Herkimer: the St. Lawrence & Adirondack (later Mohawk & Malone) of William Seward Webb, son-in-law of William H. Vanderbilt. NYC merged the Mohawk & Malone in 1911 and the RW&O in 1913.

Lake Shore & Michigan Southern

The Michigan Southern was chartered by the state of Michigan in 1837 to build from the head of navigation on the River Raisin west of Monroe across the southern tier of Michigan to Lake Michigan. Under state auspices it got as far west as Hillsdale, Mich. It was sold to private interests which combined it with the Erie & Kalamazoo (opened in 1837 from Toledo, Ohio, to Adrian, Mich.) and extended it west to meet the Northern Indiana Railroad, which was building east from La Porte, Ind. The line opened from Monroe

to South Bend in 1851; by February 1852 it reached Chicago, where it teamed up with the Rock Island to build terminal facilities. (Its successors shared a Chicago station, La Salle Street, with Rock Island until 1968). The roads were combined as the Michigan Southern & Northern Indiana in 1855. By then a direct line between Elkhart, Ind., and Toledo had been constructed.

The railroad situation along the south shore of Lake Erie was complicated by Ohio's insistence on a track gauge of 4 feet 10 inches, Pennsylvania's reluctance to let a railroad from another state cross its borders, and the desire of the city of Erie, Pa., to have the change of gauge within its limits in the hope that passengers would spend money while changing trains there.

The NYC controlled the Buffalo & State Line and the Erie & North East railroads by 1853; they were combined as the Buffalo & Erie in 1867. The Cleveland, Painesville & Ashtabula was opened between Cleveland and Erie in 1852. In 1868 the CP&A took its familiar name, Lake Shore, as its official name, and a year later it absorbed the Cleveland & Toledo and joined with the Michigan Southern & Northern Indiana to form the Lake Shore & Michigan Southern. During a business panic about that time, Cornelius Vanderbilt acquired control of the LS&MS.

In 1914 the New York Central & Hudson River, the Lake Shore & Michigan Southern, and several smaller roads were combined to form the New York Central Railroad—the second railroad of that name.

West Shore

In 1869 and 1870 several railroads were proposed and surveyed up the west bank of the Hudson River. In 1880 the New York, West Shore & Buffalo Railroad was formed to build a line from Jersey City to Albany and Buffalo, parallel to the New York Central. William Vanderbilt suspected (correctly) that the Pennsylvania Railroad was behind the project. The road opened to Albany and Syracuse in 1883 and reached Buffalo at the beginning of 1884. A rate war ensued. The West Shore entered bankruptcy, as did the construction company that built the line. The West Shore cut its rates to beat those of the NYC, hoping the Central, with its far greater volume of business, would lose a lot more money than the West Shore. The

Central, however, had resources to withstand a temporary loss.

In retaliation Vanderbilt decided to revive an old survey for a railroad across Pennsylvania that was considerably shorter than the Pennsylvania Railroad. He enlisted the support of Andrew Carnegie and John D. Rockefeller.

It took J. P. Morgan to work a compromise between the NYC and the Pennsylvania: The Central would lease the West Shore, and the Pennsy would get the South Pennsylvania and its partially excavated tunnels. In 1885 the West Shore was reorganized as the West Shore Railroad, wholly owned by the NYC and leased to it. (The roadbed of the South Pennsylvania was later used for the Pennsylvania Turnpike.) The Weehawken–Albany portion of the West Shore proved to be a valuable freight route for NYC and even more so for its successors Penn Central and Conrail. Most of the West Shore west of Albany has been abandoned. In 1952, NYC merged the West Shore.

Boston & Albany

The Boston & Worcester Railroad opened between the cities of its name in 1835. Its charter had a clause prohibiting the construction of a parallel railroad within 5 miles for 30 years. The Western Railroad opened in 1840 from Worcester west to Springfield and in 1841 across the Berkshires to Greenbush, N. Y., on the east bank of the Hudson opposite Albany. The two railroads shared some directors, but efforts at merging them were futile until 1863, when B&W's protection clause expired and the Western proposed building its own line from Worcester to Boston. The two roads were consolidated as the Boston & Albany Railroad in 1867.

The B&A had several minor branches and a few major ones: Palmer to Winchendon, Mass., Springfield to Athol, Mass., Pittsfield to North Adams, Mass.; and Chatham to Hudson, N. Y.—only short portions of them remain in service.

The B&A's principal connection was the New York Central at Albany, and in 1900 the NYC leased the B&A. The New York Central wanted a route to Boston. It had a choice of the B&A or the parallel Fitchburg Railroad (later Boston & Maine). If NYC chose the Fitchburg, the B&A would be left with only local business, so B&A willingly forsook independence. In

One of New York Central's 600 4-8-2 Mohawks leads a westbound freight past the depot at Waterloo, Ind., in 1948. *Robert A. Hadley*

1961 NYC merged the Boston & Albany.

B&A maintained more of its identity than other NYC subsidiaries. It had its own officers, and until 1951 its locomotives and cars were lettered "Boston & Albany" rather than "New York Central Lines," largely to appeal to local sensitivities. B&A's steam power was basically of NYC appearance but with a few distinctive features, such as square sand domes on the Hudsons and offset smokebox doors on Pacifics. The profile of the B&A, definitely not the water level route NYC was so proud of elsewhere, called for heavy power in the form of 2-6-6-2s and 2-8-4s (the latter named for the Berkshires over which the line ran). Nearer Boston, B&A ran an intense suburban service powered by 2-6-6Ts and 4-6-6Ts, the latter looking like condensed, solid-pack NYC Hudsons.

Ohio Central Lines

Ohio Central Lines included the Toledo & Ohio Central Railway and three leased lines (merged in 1938), the Zanesville & Western Railway, the Kanawha & Michigan Railway, and the Kanawha & West Virginia Railroad. They formed a route from Toledo southeast through Columbus, across the Ohio River, and through Charleston to Swiss and Hitop, W. Va. The Ohio Central began as the Atlantic & Lake Erie, chartered in 1869. After a series of receiverships and a name change to Ohio Central, the road managed to link Columbus with the Ohio River at Middleport in 1882. It then pushed into the coalfields along the Kanawha River in West Virginia and extended itself northwest toward Toledo. It was renamed the Toledo & Ohio Central in 1885.

The NYC acquired control of the T&OC by 1910 and began operating it as part of the New York Central System. NYC leased the road in 1922 and merged it in 1952. Penn Central briefly revived the road's identity with the "TOC" reporting marks.

Michigan Central

Michigan Central had its beginnings in the Detroit & St. Joseph Railroad, which was incorporated in 1832 to build a railroad across Michigan from Detroit to St. Joseph. Michigan attained statehood in 1837 and almost immediately chartered railroads to be constructed along three routes: the Northern, from Port Huron to the head of navigation on the Grand River; the Central, from Detroit to St. Joseph; and the Southern, from the head of navigation on the River Raisin to New Buffalo.

The state purchased the Detroit & St. Joseph to use as the basis for the Central Railroad. About the time the road reached Kalamazoo in 1846 it ran out of money. It was purchased from the state by Boston interests led by John W. Brooks and was reorganized as the Michigan Central Railroad. Construction resumed in the direction of New Buffalo rather than St. Joseph, and in 1849 the line reached Michigan City, Ind., about as far as its Michigan charter could take it.

To reach the Illinois border the Michigan Central used the charter of the New Albany & Salem (a predecessor of the Monon) in exchange for which it purchased a block of NA&S stock. The MC continued on Illinois Central rails to Chicago, reaching there in 1852.

Vanderbilt began buying Michigan Central stock in 1869. New York Central leased the Michigan Central in 1930.

The Great Western Railway opened in 1854 from Niagara Falls to Windsor, Ont., opposite Detroit. In March 1855 John Roebling's suspension bridge across the Niagara River was completed, creating with the New York Central a continuous line of rails from Albany to Windsor. The Great Western (which had a track gauge of 5 feet 6 inches) installed a third rail for standard gauge equipment between 1864 and 1866.

Vanderbilt tried without success to purchase the Great Western and turned his attention to the Canada Southern. It

FACTS & FIGURES

Year	1929	1967
Miles operated	6,915	9,696
Locomotives	3,472	1,917
Passenger cars	3,866	2,085
Freight cars	138,199	78,172
Reporting marks: NYC, B&A, CASO, CCC&StL, MCRR, P&E, P&LE		
Historical society: nycshs.org		

had been incorporated in 1868 as the Erie & Niagara Extension Railway to build a line along the north shore of Lake Erie and then across the Detroit River below the city of Detroit. He acquired the Canada Southern in 1876, and Michigan Central leased it in 1882. Conrail sold the Canada Southern to Canadian Pacific and Canadian National in 1985. New York Central leased the Michigan Central in 1930.

Cleveland, Cincinnati, Chicago & St. Louis (Big Four)

The oldest predecessor of the Big Four (and a comparatively late addition to it) was the Mad River & Lake Erie. Ground was broken in 1835, and the line opened from Sandusky to Dayton, Ohio, in 1851. It went through several renamings and became part of what later was the Peoria & Eastern before it was merged into the CCC&StL in 1890.

The Cleveland, Columbus & Cincinnati got its charter in 1836, broke ground in 1847, and opened in 1851 between Cleveland and Columbus. In 1852 it teamed up with the Little Miami and Columbus & Xenia railroads to form a Cleveland–Cincinnati route.

In 1848 the Indianapolis & Bellefontaine and the Bellefontaine & Indiana railroads were incorporated to build a line between Galion, Ohio, on the CC&C, and Indianapolis. The I&B and the B&I amalgamated and became known as "The Bee Line." They were absorbed by the CC&C when it reorganized as the Cleveland, Columbus, Cincinnati & Indianapolis in 1868.

The Cleveland, Columbus, Cincinnati & Indianapolis reached Cincinnati with its own rails in 1872. That same year it opened a line from Springfield to Columbus. By then the Vanderbilts owned a good portion of the road's stock.

The Terre Haute & Alton Railroad was organized in 1852. Its backers were certain that with a railroad to Indiana the Mississippi River town of Alton, Ill., could easily outstrip St. Louis a few miles south. It soon combined with the Belleville & Illinoistown Railroad (Illinoistown is now East St. Louis) as the Terre Haute, Alton & St. Louis. The Indianapolis & St. Louis was organized to build between Indianapolis and Terre Haute. It leased the St. Louis, Alton & Terre Haute, successor to the

Terre Haute, Alton & St. Louis, and came under control of the CCC&I in 1882.

In the late 1840s and early 1850s several railroads were completed forming a route from Cincinnati through Indianapolis and Lafayette, Ind., to Kankakee, Ill., connecting there with the Illinois Central north to Chicago. In 1880 these roads were united as the Cincinnati, Indianapolis, St. Louis & Chicago—which some consider the first "Big Four." Heading the company was Melville Ingalls, and on its board was C. P. Huntington, whose Chesapeake & Ohio formed a friendly connection at Cincinnati.

The Vanderbilts had invested in the first Big Four, and they were firmly in control of the second Big Four, the Cleveland, Cincinnati, Chicago & St. Louis, which was formed in 1889 by the consolidation of the old Big Four (Cincinnati, Indianapolis, St. Louis & Chicago) and the Bee Line (Cleveland, Columbus, Cincinnati & Indianapolis).

In the late 1880s Ingalls and the Vanderbilts gathered in a group of railroads between Cairo and Danville, Ill.; added to them the St. Louis, Alton & Terre Haute, then added them all to the Big Four. The line from Danville north to Indiana Harbor was a comparatively late addition to the system: It was built in 1906 and became part of the New York Central rather than the Big Four.

The Peoria & Eastern was formed in 1890 from several small roads. At one time its predecessor briefly included the former Mad River & Lake Erie and a line from Indianapolis east to Springfield, Ohio, before settling down to be simply a Peoria–Bloomington–Danville–Indianapolis route.

In 1902 the Big Four bought the Cincinnati Northern, a line that had been proposed in 1852 and finally constructed in the 1880s from Franklin, Ohio, between Dayton and Cincinnati, to Jackson, Mich.

In 1920 the Big Four acquired the Evansville, Indianapolis & Terre Haute, a castoff from the Chicago & Eastern Illinois in southwestern Indiana. The New York Central leased the Big Four in 1930.

New York Central System

The New York Central System was the largest of the eastern trunk systems from the standpoint of mileage and second only to the Pennsylvania in revenue. It served

Three Alco FAs in their as-delivered black-and gray scheme, with the gray band not filling the flanks, lift a westbound freight up Washington Mountain on the Boston & Albany line in western Massachusetts in September 1949. NYC led in FA ownership with almost 200. *R. E. Tobey*

most of the industrial part of the country, and its freight tonnage was exceeded only by the coal-carrying railroads. In addition it was a major passenger railroad, with perhaps two-thirds the number of passengers as the Pennsylvania, but NYC's average passenger traveled one-third again as far as Pennsy's. NYC did not share as fully in the postwar prosperity because of rising labor costs, material costs, and an expensive improvement program, especially for passenger service.

In 1946 and 1947 Chesapeake & Ohio purchased a block of NYC stock (6.4 percent), becoming the road's largest stockholder. Robert R. Young gained control of New York Central and became its chairman in 1954 as part of a maneuver to merge it with C&O. One of his first acts was to put Alfred E. Perlman in charge of the Central.

Under Perlman NYC slimmed its physical plant, reducing long stretches of four-track line to two tracks under Centralized Traffic Control, and developed an

aggressive freight marketing department. At the same time NYC's passenger operations were de-emphasized. On Dec. 3, 1967, just before NYC and Pennsy merged, the Central reduced its passenger service to a skeleton, combining its New York–Chicago, New York–Detroit, New York–Toronto, and Boston–Chicago services into a single train and dropping all train names (including that of the *Twentieth Century Limited*, once considered the world's finest train) except for, curiously, that of the Chicago–Cincinnati *James Whitcomb Riley*.

The Central's archrival was the Pennsylvania Railroad. West of Buffalo and Pittsburgh the two systems duplicated each other at almost every major point; east of those cities the two hardly touched. Both roads had physical plant not being used to capacity (NYC was in better shape); both had a heavy passenger business; neither was earning much money. In 1957 NYC and Pennsy announced merger talks.

The initial industry reaction was utter surprise. "Who? Why?" Every merger

proposal for decades had tried to balance the Central against the Pennsy and create two, three, or four more-or-less equal systems in the east. Traditionally Pennsy had been allied with Norfolk & Western and Wabash; New York Central with Baltimore & Ohio, Reading, and maybe the Lackawanna; and everyone else swept up with Erie and Nickel Plate. Tradition also favored end-to-end mergers rather than those of parallel roads.

Planning and justifying the merger took nearly ten years, during which time the eastern railroad scene changed radically, in large measure because of the impending merger of NYC and PRR: Erie merged with Lackawanna, Chesapeake & Ohio acquired control of Baltimore & Ohio, and Norfolk & Western took in Virginian, Wabash, Nickel Plate, Pittsburgh & West Virginia, and Akron, Canton & Youngstown.

Tradition aside, though, the New York Central and the Pennsylvania merged on Feb. 1, 1968 to form Penn Central.

New York, Chicago & St. Louis (Nickel Plate)

A westbound Nickel Plate freight rolls along the Lake Erie shore between Lorain and Vermilion, Ohio, in April 1957, behind a signature 2-8-4, of which NKP had 80 (plus 32 from W&LE). This one, No. 779, was the last steam locomotive built by Lima Locomotive Works, in 1949. *John A. Rehor*

In 1879 and 1880 a syndicate headed by George I. Seney, a New York banker, assembled the Lake Erie & Western Railway, a line from Fremont, Ohio, to Bloomington, Ill. After a dispute with the New York Central System about the routing of freight, Seney decided to build a line to connect the LE&W to Cleveland. He incorporated the New York, Chicago & St. Louis Railway in 1881 as a Buffalo–Chicago project.

About this time the railroad was referred to by a Norwalk, Ohio, newspaper as the "great double-track nickel-plated railroad" and the nickname stuck. (That's one theory about the name; another hinges on the pronunciation of "NYCL.") The line was completed in August 1882. William H. Vanderbilt offered to buy off Seney during its construction and then threatened to starve it of traffic—from Cleveland to Buffalo it was parallel to Vanderbilt's

Lake Shore & Michigan Southern. Jay Gould began to negotiate to purchase the road; to block Gould, Vanderbilt purchased it instead and installed his son William K. Vanderbilt as president in 1883. Then he wondered what to do with it—benign neglect is what happened. Even though it was no more than a secondary line in the Vanderbilt system, it gained a reputation for fast movement of perishables, particularly meat.

In 1916 Cleveland real estate developers Oris Paxton Van Sweringen and Mantis James Van Sweringen bought NYC's interest in the Nickel Plate. NYC recognized that the Clayton Antitrust Act would require selling NKP; selling it to the Van Sweringen brothers would keep it out of the clutches of the Lackawanna or the Pennsylvania. The Van Sweringens were suddenly in the railroad business, and to run their railroad they chose John Bernet

of the NYC. Bernet upgraded NKP's locomotives and track, with the result that by 1925 the road had doubled its freight tonnage and average speed, halved its fuel consumption per ton mile, and led all U. S. railroads in car miles per day.

The Interstate Commerce Commission merger plan of the 1920s grouped NKP with Lake Erie & Western; Toledo, St. Louis & Western; Wheeling & Lake Erie; Lehigh Valley; and Pittsburgh & West Virginia. In 1922 the Van Sweringens acquired both the LE&W, an unprofitable ward of the NYC, and the TStL&W (the Clover Leaf), which was in receivership because it had defaulted on bonds it issued to gain control of the Chicago & Alton.

Lake Erie & Western

The Lake Erie & Western Railway was formed in 1879 to consolidate smaller railroads between Fremont, Ohio, and

Westbound train NC-3 rolls through the east side of Cleveland in July 1959. The Nickel Plate dieselized its freights with road-switchers, and a mix of six Alcos and EMDs, led by Alco RS-11 No. 568 and EMD GP9 No. 532, powers the train. *Herbert H. Harwood Jr.*

Bloomington, Ill. In 1880 the LE&W extended its line east from Fremont to Sandusky to replace boats on the lower stretches of the Sandusky River and teamed up with the Lake Shore to offer through freight and passenger service. The Lake Shore's lack of cooperation in the matter of westbound traffic was the reason LE&W's backers built the Nickel Plate.

The LE&W nearly died during the 1880s, but the discovery of natural gas and oil along the line in Ohio and Indiana revived it. In 1887 it was reorganized and extended west to Peoria, Ill. That same year it acquired a Michigan City–Indianapolis line that crossed its main line at Tipton, Ind., and in 1890 it acquired a line from Fort Wayne to Connersville and Rushville, Ind., a line which crossed the Lake Erie & Western at Muncie. In 1895 the LE&W

proposed assembling a line to the East Coast by using the Reading, the Buffalo, Rochester & Pittsburgh, and the Pittsburgh, Akron & Western, a former narrow gauge line from Akron to Delphos, Ohio. The PA&W was reorganized that year as the Northern Ohio and leased to the LE&W.

In 1899 the LS&MS purchased a majority interest in the LE&W and proceeded to let it decline gently. In 1920 LE&W sold the Northern Ohio to the Akron, Canton & Youngstown.

Toledo, St. Louis & Western

The Toledo, Delphos & Indianapolis was organized in 1877 and that year opened a 3-foot gauge line a few miles north from Delphos, Ohio. Two years later it became part of the Toledo, Delphos & Burlington,

a consolidation of four railroads. The TD&B had as its goal a 3-foot gauge line from Toledo to Burlington, Iowa. The line was opened from Toledo to Kokomo, Ind., in 1880. It began extending south, buying up railroads to form a line south through Dayton to Cincinnati and Ironton, Ohio. Then it got caught up in a proposal to assemble a narrow gauge line all the way from Toledo to Mexico City.

The line was opened from Toledo to East St. Louis, Ill., in 1883 and the company collapsed soon afterwards. The lines south of Delphos to Cincinnati and Ironton were spun off to eventually become standard gauge pieces of the Cincinnati, Hamilton & Dayton, the Pennsylvania, and the Detroit, Toledo & Ironton. The Toledo–East St. Louis line was nearly dead when gas and oil were discovered along the line. It was reorganized as the Toledo, St. Louis & Kansas City Railroad, and it adopted a clover leaf as its emblem. Trackage east of Frankfort, Ind., was converted to standard gauge on June 25, 1887; the remainder of the line was converted two years later. The road developed a good freight business, particularly in eastbound livestock and perishables received from connections at East St. Louis.

The TStL&KC went bankrupt in 1893. The court proceedings included William Howard Taft as judge and Benjamin Harrison as counsel. The railroad was sold to its bondholders and became the Toledo, St. Louis & Western. It continued as a fast freight line, particularly in competition with the Wabash. In contrast to many Midwestern roads, the TStL&W got along well with neighboring interurbans, even filing joint passenger tariffs. In 1903 the Clover Leaf acquired a half interest in the Detroit & Toledo Shore Line. In 1907 it purchased control of the Alton. The TStL&W issued bonds to finance the purchase; however, interest on the bonds brought on another receivership in 1914.

Nickel Plate

In 1923 the Nickel Plate, the Lake Erie & Western, and the Clover Leaf were consolidated as a new New York, Chicago & St. Louis Railroad. On the recommendation of Alfred H. Smith, president of the NYC, the Van Sweringens went after the Chesapeake & Ohio, for its coal traffic, and the Pere Marquette, for its automobile business. In 1925 the New York, Chicago & St. Louis Railway was incorporated to lease and operate the Nickel Plate, C&O, PM, Erie, and Hocking Valley. The railroad industry was in favor of the merger, but a small group of C&O stockholders fought it. In 1926 the ICC rejected the petition on financial grounds—it was in favor of it from the standpoint of transportation. Then the Van Sweringens tried again in 1926—C&O applied to acquire PM, Erie, and Hocking Valley. The ICC rejected that in 1929.

The Van Sweringens moved Bernet to the Erie; taking his place was Walter Ross, who had been president of the Clover Leaf. He engineered an about-face for NKP's passenger service, which for years had been operated on the assumption there was no sense trying to compete with the NYC. Ross went after the long-haul passenger with comfort and personal service. The passenger renaissance lasted only until 1931, when the Depression occasioned cutbacks.

Nickel Plate came under Chesapeake & Ohio management in 1933, and Bernet was back in the presidency. He initiated a scrap drive to finance rebuilding of the Clover Leaf district, and he ordered the first 15 of a series of big 2-8-4 Berkshires that eventually numbered 80 to upgrade the road's freight power. The design of the new locomotives drew heavily on Chesapeake & Ohio's 2-10-4s. Other improvements of the late 1930s and the war years were strengthening the bridges east of Cleveland, introducing Centralized Traffic Control, and upgrading track and bridges on the Lake Erie & Western and the Clover Leaf to permit the Berkshires to work to Peoria and Madison (East St. Louis), Ill.

Nickel Plate resumed its own management in December 1942; Chesapeake & Ohio attempted merger in 1945, but NKP stockholders objected. Dieselization of passenger service began in the late 1940s, but freight continued to roll behind steam. In 1948 Nickel Plate tested a set of Electro-Motive F3s and immediately ordered 10 more Berkshires (they proved to be Lima's last steam locomotives). A four-unit set of F3s could outperform the 2-8-4s, but fuel costs were greater; a Berkshire developed greater horsepower at speed than a three-unit set—and at speed was where Nickel Plate used most of its horsepower.

NKP also tested General Electric's gas turbine-electric, and EMD painted a pair of F7s blue and gray, like the PAs, for a demonstration on the former LE&W. Freight diesels finally began to arrive in the form of GP7s in 1951, but steam dominated mainline freight service until the business recession of 1957 and 1958. Nickel Plate was one of the last U. S. railroads to operate steam, and two of the Berkshires, 759 and 765, remained active in excursion service.

In 1946 and 1947 NKP purchased about 80 percent of the stock of Wheeling & Lake Erie, and on Dec. 1, 1949, NKP leased the W&LE. The Wheeling served the steel-and-coal area of Ohio and originated much of its tonnage, in contrast to NKP, thus providing balance to the NKP's bridge-route freight business.

For years the NKP's principal freight competitors had been the Erie and the Wabash; after 1954 the New York Central under Alfred Perlman began to become a lean, fast railroad. The Lackawanna proposed merger with Nickel Plate; NKP management rejected the union. When Lackawanna merged with Erie, it disposed of a large block of NKP stock. Norfolk & Western merged the Virginian, and the New York Central and the Pennsylvania announced their engagement. Nickel Plate, suddenly unattached, looked around, set up through freight trains with Lehigh Valley, and began merger negotiations with Norfolk & Western. On Oct. 16, 1964, N&W merged the Nickel Plate.

© 2013, Kalmbach Publishing Co., CLASSIC TRAINS, Bill Metzger
No scale; not all lines shown

EL	Erie Lackawanna
GM&O	Gulf, Mobile & Ohio
LE&W	Lake Erie & Western
NKP	New York, Chicago & St. Louis
TStL&W	Clover Leaf Route
W&LE	Wheeling & Lake Erie

FACTS & FIGURES

Year	1929	1963
Miles operated	1,691	2170
Locomotives	465	408
Passenger cars	159	60
Freight cars	21,625	22,305
Reporting marks: NKP		
Historical society: nkphts.org		

New York, New Haven & Hartford

The New York, New Haven & Hartford eventually gathered in nearly all the railroads in Connecticut, Rhode Island, and southeastern Massachusetts. Its four principal predecessors were the Old Colony, the New York & New England, the Central New England, and the New York & New Haven (for simplicity, the "New Haven"), which was the dominant corporation.

Old Colony

The Old Colony Railroad was opened in 1845 between Boston and Plymouth, Mass. In 1854 it was consolidated with the Fall River Railroad, which had been formed in 1845 from three smaller roads to form a route from the port of Fall River, Mass., north to a junction with the Old Colony at South Braintree. In 1876 the Old Colony leased and in 1883 merged the Boston, Clinton, Fitchburg & New Bedford, which extended from New Bedford to Fitchburg, Mass., with a branch from Framingham to Lowell. The final addition to the Old Colony came in 1888 with the lease of the Boston & Providence. The B&P had been chartered in 1831 and completed in 1835 between the Massachusetts and Rhode Island cities of its name.

Most of the railroading in southeastern Massachusetts was now under the control of the Old Colony. The area was rich in industry, and the road's traffic included not only raw materials and finished goods but also coal distributed inland from the ports. The Old Colony had an intense passenger business, participating not only in an all-rail route to New York in conjunction with other lines beyond Providence but also connecting with steamers operating on Long Island Sound, principally between Fall River and New York.

New York & New England

Only fragments remain today of the New York & New England, which at its height reached from Boston and Providence through Hartford, Conn., to the Hudson River, with branches to Worcester and Springfield, Mass., and New London, Conn. Its oldest ancestor was the

Streamlined Hudson 1406 accelerates the 15 cars of the westbound *Yankee Clipper* out of New London, Conn., in March 1947. *Kent W. Cochrane*

Manchester Railroad, chartered in 1833 to build east from Hartford, Conn., through Manchester to Bolton. The charter lay dormant for some years until a group of Providence, R. I., businessmen sought to build a railroad to the industrial towns of western Rhode Island and eastern Connecticut. The project quickly expanded, first taking over the Manchester charter and then blossoming into a line from Providence to the Hudson River at Fishkill Landing (now Beacon), N. Y. The first part of the Hartford, Providence & Fishkill was opened in 1849, and by 1855 the line was in service between Providence and Waterbury, Conn.

Meanwhile two small railroads were building southwest out of Boston into the area between Providence and Worcester. A combination of the Charles River Branch, the Charles River Railroad, and the New York & Boston assembled a line from Brookline, Mass., on the Boston & Albany, to Woonsocket, R. I., with the intention of building on through Willimantic, Conn., to New Haven.

The Norfolk County Railroad opened a line through Walpole to Blackstone,

Mass., in 1849. It became the Boston & New York Central and also aimed for Willimantic, but to connect there with the Hartford, Providence & Fishkill. It reorganized and changed its name several times. Among its names were Midland and Boston, Hartford & Erie, and under the latter it consolidated with the New York & Boston and the Hartford, Providence & Fishkill in 1864, creating a line chartered all the way from Boston to the Hudson River and in service from Boston to Mechanicsville, Conn. (just north of Putnam), and from Providence to Waterbury.

The BH&E entered bankruptcy in 1870 after a short period of control by the Erie Railroad and emerged as the New York & New England Railroad. NY&NE closed the Mechanicsville-Willimantic gap in eastern Connecticut in 1872 and completed the line west to the Hudson in December 1881. In 1884 the NY&NE inaugurated the *New England Limited*, a Boston–New York express operated in conjunction with the New Haven, which handled the train southwest of Willimantic. The train achieved a place in railroad lore

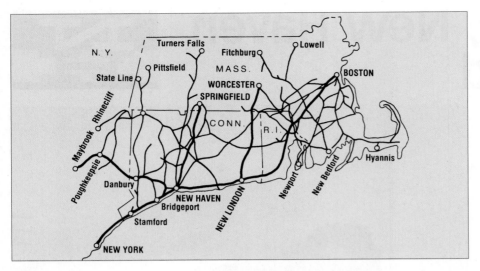

as the "Ghost Train" in 1891 when the cars were painted white (some accounts add that the coal in the tender was sprayed with whitewash before departure each afternoon).

Every few miles NY&NE's route crossed a railroad offering a connection to New York—but nearly all those connections depended on the New Haven. The New Haven, feeling some anxiety about competition from the NY&NE, began to choke off the connections. The NY&NE turned first to the Housatonic Railroad to form a route to New York that included a ferry across Long Island Sound from Wilson's Point (south of Norwalk) to Oyster Bay and a connection with the Long Island Rail Road. The New Haven took over the Housatonic.

The NY&NE then turned to the New York & Northern, which it met at Brewster, N. Y. The New Haven and the New York Central had previously agreed not to compete with each other, so at the New Haven's request the New York Central acquired the New York & Northern (it became NYC's Putnam Division) to put itself briefly into and out of competition with the New Haven for Boston–New York business. The New York & New England was squeezed out again.

In 1893 the Philadelphia & Reading acquired control of the NY&NE, which declared bankruptcy by the end of that year. The New Haven acquired control of the New York & New England through J. P. Morgan and in 1898 leased the road.

Central New England

Almost nothing remains of the Central New England. In the early 1890s under the presidency of A. A. McLeod, the Philadelphia & Reading put together a group of small railroads as the Central New England & Western to form a New England outlet for anthracite coal. The new road took over the Hartford & Connecticut Western, which had a line reaching from Hartford to the northwestern corner of the state, then consolidated with the Poughkeepsie Bridge & Railroad Co. to form the Philadelphia, Reading & New England. In October 1893, the PR&NE gained control of the New York & New England and the Boston & Maine, and even tried to grab the Old Colony. By the end of 1893, the Philadelphia & Reading was bankrupt.

The PR&NE was reorganized as the Central New England in 1899, still under Reading control. In 1904 the New Haven purchased the Central New England, thus acquiring the Poughkeepsie Bridge over the Hudson River (originally backed by the Pennsylvania; opened in 1888). The railroad was operated separately until 1927, when it was fully absorbed by the New Haven. Most of the Central New England, other than the portion that formed NH's freight route to Maybrook, N. Y., was abandoned in 1938.

New York & New Haven

The New York & New Haven Railroad was a relative latecomer because of the adequacy of road and water transportation along the Connecticut coast—early railroad activity aimed inland. The Hartford & New Haven Railroad was chartered in 1833 and opened in 1839; by 1844 it had been extended north to Springfield, Mass. The Housatonic Railroad was chartered in 1836 to build up the river of that name from Bridgeport to the Massachusetts state line. In 1842 it reached a connection with the Western Railroad (later Boston & Albany).

It was not until 1844 that the New York & New Haven Railroad was chartered in Connecticut; a New York charter was opposed by the New York & Harlem Railroad until arrangements were made to use the Harlem's tracks into New York City. The line was opened in 1848.

That same year the first portion of the New Haven & Northampton was opened from New Haven north to Plainville, Conn., along the route of a canal. The New York & New Haven promptly leased the Canal Line to use as a competitive weapon against the Hartford & New Haven.

The year 1848 also saw the chartering of the New Haven & New London Railroad. It opened in 1852 and was soon extended to Stonington, Conn., with ferries taking whole trains across the Connecticut River at Saybrook and across the Thames at New London. The NH&NL was reorganized in 1864 as the Shore Line Railway and leased to the New York & New Haven in 1870. The Connecticut and the Thames were bridged in 1870 and 1889, respectively.

Hartford & Connecticut Western

The Central New England had its beginnings in the Hartford & Connecticut Western Railroad, opened in 1871 from Hartford northwest to Millerton, N. Y. There it connected with the Harlem Division of the New York Central, giving Hartford a route to Albany and the West. The intention of the Hartford & Connecticut Western was to meet the Dutchess & Columbia Railroad, but the Boston, Hartford & Erie got control of the Dutchess & Columbia and blocked alliance with the HC&W.

The HC&W found two other outlets to the Hudson. The more northerly was the Rhinebeck & Connecticut, a 42-mile line from State Line north to Boston Corners, then southwest to Rhinecliff (airline distance, about 24 miles). In 1881 the H&CW bought the bankrupt Rhinebeck & Connecticut, creating a line under one management from Hartford to the Hudson—and more important, to the Hudson directly opposite the eastern terminal of the Delaware & Hudson Canal.

Symbol freight OB-6 is eastbound on the Maybrook line a half mile east of Berkshire Junction in March 1966. Three of the New Haven's General Electric U25Bs, led by No. 2505, are in charge of the train. *John P. Ahrens*

HC&W's other outlet to the Hudson was the Poughkeepsie & Eastern, from Poughkeepsie northeast 37 miles to Boston Corners. In the 1880s a bridge over the Hudson at Poughkeepsie was proposed by Philadelphia interests, who saw a market for Pennsylvania anthracite in New England. The Poughkeepsie & Eastern would have been the ideal connection between the bridge and the Hartford & Connecticut Western, but the owner of the Poughkeepsie & Eastern would have nothing to do with the idea. He changed the railroad's name to New York & Massachusetts and proposed to extend it east to a connection with the Central Massachusetts near Springfield. The bridge company built a parallel railroad, the Poughkeepsie & Connecticut, from Poughkeepsie to a connection with the HC&W.

The Poughkeepsie bridge opened in 1888, and soon afterward the Poughkeepsie & Connecticut and the Hudson Connecting Railroad (Poughkeepsie to Campbell Hall) were consolidated as the Central New England & Western Railroad. That company leased the HC&W and also the Dutchess County Railroad, from Poughkeepsie southeast to a connection with the New York & New England. In 1892 the CNE&W was consolidated with the Poughkeepsie Bridge & Railroad Company as the Philadelphia, Reading & New England Railroad, under the control of the Philadelphia & Reading. Within months the Philadelphia & Reading controlled the

New York & New England and the Boston & Maine, and within two months more, the bankruptcy of the Philadelphia & Reading caused the whole empire to collapse.

The PR&NE was reorganized as the Central New England Railway in 1898. In 1904 the New Haven bought control of the Central New England for the Poughkeepsie Bridge and the connections at Maybrook and Campbell Hall. The Central New England continued to exist until Jan. 1, 1927, when the New Haven merged it. Nearly all of the CNE east of the bridge was abandoned in 1938.

New York, New Haven & Hartford

On Aug. 6, 1872, the New York & New Haven and the Hartford & New Haven were consolidated as the New York, New Haven & Hartford Railroad. The new road had close affiliations with the Housatonic and Naugatuck lines (the latter followed the river of that name up to Waterbury and Winsted). It acquired control of the Canal Line in 1881 (the lease had ended in 1869), leased the Air Line (New Haven to Willimantic), and bought the Hartford & Connecticut Valley (Hartford to Saybrook) in 1882. In 1892 the New Haven leased the New York, Providence & Boston (which had leased the Providence & Worcester), and in 1893 leased the Old Colony, completing an all-rail route under one management between Boston and New York.

In 1893 the New York & New England collapsed and NYNH&H began acquisition of its former rival. The New Haven also looked covetously at the group of railroads that stretched up the Connecticut Valley from Springfield but was content with an agreement with Boston & Maine to split New England between them along the line of the Boston & Albany (B&M had no lines south of the B&A; NYNH&H had several tentacles reaching almost to the northern border of Massachusetts). By the turn of the century the New Haven had a virtual monopoly on the railroads and the steamboat lines in Connecticut, Rhode Island, and much of Massachusetts.

Enter Charles S. Mellen, a protege of J. P. Morgan. Mellen set out to gain control of all the railroads in New England. He bought the street and interurban railways in New Haven's territory, then bought control of Boston & Maine and Maine Central and, jointly with New York Central, the Rutland. He reached outside New England for control of the New York, Ontario & Western. He undertook the construction of the New York, Westchester & Boston, an interurban line parallel to New Haven's own line from New York to Port Chester, with a branch to White Plains.

A long battle ensued between the Mellen interests and Louis D. Brandeis, then a Boston lawyer, over what was basically a violation of the Sherman Antitrust Act. A series of wrecks in 1911 and 1912 turned public feeling against the New Haven.

The costs of electrifying the line between New York and New Haven and of constructing the New York Connecting Railroad and its Hell Gate Bridge to connect with the Pennsylvania Railroad would have helped push the road into bankruptcy had it not been taken over by the United States Railroad Administration during World War I.

New Haven's electrification deserves special mention. Before the turn of the century NH electrified several branch lines using low-voltage DC systems, but for its main line between Woodlawn, N. Y., and New Haven, the road chose the relatively unproven high-voltage AC system, even though the locomotives would have to be able to use New York Central's low-voltage DC system from Woodlawn to Grand Central Terminal.

The New Haven's situation improved in the late 1920s. The Pennsylvania acquired nearly one-fourth of New Haven's stock and an interest in the Boston & Maine, and New Haven also acquired B&M stock, effectively regaining control of B&M. The New Haven struggled through the Depression as long as it could and entered bankruptcy on Oct. 23, 1935.

In the ensuing reorganization NH pruned much of its branchline network, abandoned its steamship lines and the New York, Westchester & Boston, and upgraded the physical plant and rolling stock on its main lines. It inaugurated piggyback service in 1938 and dieselized many of its mainline trains with a fleet of Alco DL-109s. New Haven's traffic increased greatly during World War II. If the New Haven is remembered for nothing else it will be for a 1942 advertisement, "The Kid in Upper 4." The ad showed a young soldier lying awake in an upper berth on his way to war. The accompanying text, which told of his feelings, was a masterpiece.

The New Haven was heavy-duty, intense railroading as few other roads in North America have practiced it. The main passenger routes came from Pennsylvania Station and Grand Central Terminal to merge at New Rochelle, N. Y., forming a four-track electrified line as far east as New Haven. From there double-track lines continued east to Boston and north to Springfield. The principal freight route was the line east from Maybrook, N. Y., where New Haven connected with Erie, Lehigh

& Hudson River, Lehigh & New England, and New York, Ontario & Western; New Haven also interchanged a great deal of freight with the Pennsylvania via carfloats across New York harbor.

The New Haven experimented very early with electrification of branch lines and was the first railroad with a long-distance mainline electrification. The road had four major bridges: the high bridge that carried the Maybrook Line across the Hudson at Poughkeepsie, N. Y., the vertical lift bridge, until 1959 the longest in the world, over the Cape Cod Canal at Buzzards Bay, Mass., the Canton Viaduct across the Neponset River valley at Canton, Mass., and the Hell Gate Bridge (operated by New Haven, but owned by the New York Connecting Railroad, which was jointly owned by the New Haven and the Pennsylvania).

The Dumaines and McGinnis

New Haven's reorganization was completed on Sept. 18, 1947. Frederic C. Dumaine Sr. and others, including Patrick B. McGinnis, gained control in 1948. The experienced executives who had overseen the reorganization were dismissed, new management came in, and the road began another plunge into the depths. Frederic C. Dumaine Jr. took over upon his father's death in 1951 and immediately set about restoring the condition of the railroad and the morale of the employees.

In 1953 control passed from the preferred stockholders to the common stockholders. A proxy battle ensued and Patrick B. McGinnis won. He slashed maintenance and ordered experimental lightweight trains for Boston–New York service. Another McGinnis contribution was a new image of red-orange, black, and white. New paint or not, Connecticut commuters revolted at the imposition of parking charges at stations. Directors resigned. Hurricanes (not McGinnis's fault) in 1955 washed out a number of lines. Upon McGinnis's departure for the Boston & Maine in 1956, auditors found that New Haven's earnings for 1955 were less than half what McGinnis had been saying they were.

George Alpert became president just as the lightweight trains that McGinnis ordered arrived. One caught fire on the press run, then derailed later that day. The piggyback traffic disappeared as the railroads serving New York initiated their own

piggyback service and found that trailers could move into NH's territory by highway, especially the newly completed Connecticut Turnpike that paralleled NH from Greenwich to New London.

In 1956 the New Haven decided to buy 60 FL9s, diesel locomotives that could also draw power from third rail in the New York terminals, in order to phase out its electrification—for which it had just taken delivery of 10 new passenger locomotives and 100 new M. U. cars. A few years after the FL9s arrived, the New Haven purchased 11 nearly new electric freight locomotives from the Norfolk & Western.

Government loans guaranteed by the ICC kept the road afloat until July 7, 1961, when the New Haven went back into reorganization. The railroad sought local and state tax relief and petitioned for inclusion in the Pennsylvania-New York Central merger. The initial condition imposed by the two larger railroads was that NH be free of passenger service, but the ICC denied that request and on December 2, 1968, ordered Penn Central (which had come into being on Feb. 1 of that year) to take over the New Haven by the beginning of 1969. On Dec. 31, 1968, PC purchased New Haven's properties.

With all of its problems, the New Haven soldiered on. Freight business suffered as much from the change in New England's economy and the shift from heavy industry to high technology as it did from truck competition. Until its inclusion in Penn Central the New Haven offered hourly passenger service between Boston and New York, with parlor and dining cars on nearly all trains, and almost as frequent service between New York, Hartford, and Springfield. Only in the past few years and by virtue of extensive track work has Amtrak managed to equal New Haven's Boston–New York running time.

FACTS & FIGURES

Year	1929	1967
Miles operated	2,133	1,547
Locomotives	957	332
Passenger cars	2,110	855
Freight cars	24,033	3,563
Reporting marks: NH		
Historical society: nhrhta.org		

New York, Ontario & Western

Westbound symbol freight BC-3 rolls past the station at Summitville, N. Y., in early 1957. Between the gray-and-orange Electro-Motive FT diesels and the caboose are only 12 cars, illustrating one reason for the railroad's demise. *Jim Shaughnessy*

In 1866 the New York & Oswego Midland Railroad was incorporated to build a railroad from Oswego, N. Y., on the shore of Lake Ontario, to New York—or more specifically to the New Jersey state line, then to a point on the Hudson River opposite New York City.

The railroad's first problem was finance. Cities and towns that refused to issue bonds to finance the line found themselves bypassed by the new railroad, with the result that the line went through few established places of any size and made unnecessary contortions, both horizontal and vertical. The state of New Jersey refused to allow such bonding, so the NY&OM struck a deal with the Middletown, Unionville & Water Gap and the New Jersey Midland (forerunners of the Middletown & Unionville and the New York, Susquehanna & Western). One of the incorporators of the railroad boasted that the line would run at right angles to the mountains. After construction began, the railroad discovered just what that meant in terms of bridges and tunnels.

The NY&OM opened from Oswego to Norwich in 1869. In 1871 it opened a line known as the Auburn Branch—it straggled northwest, southwest, and northwest from Norwich through Cortland and Freeville to end at Scipio, about ten miles short of Auburn. In 1872 the NYO&M leased railroads to create branches to Utica and Rome. The first train ran all the way from Oswego to Jersey City in July 1883.

Within a few weeks the railroad declared bankruptcy. For a short period in early 1875 the NY&OM ceased operation entirely except for the portion from Sidney to Utica and Rome, which was operated by Delaware & Hudson, in much the same way as designated operators took over portions of the Rock Island a century later. While the line was idle, a number of local residents, fearing they would not be paid for their land, tore up the track and reclaimed their land.

Operation resumed, and the company was reorganized in 1879 as the New York, Ontario & Western Railway. Implicit in the new name was hope of a ferry connection across Lake Ontario and a continuation to the West. Missing from the map was the Auburn branch, dismantled except from Freeville through Cortland to De Ruyter, which became part of the Lehigh Valley.

Soon added to the map was a line from Middletown east to Cornwall, on the Hudson River. NYO&W made arrangements with the West Shore for trackage rights south from Cornwall to West Shore's terminal at Weehawken, N. J. The West Shore soon came under the control of New York Central. NYO&W found NYC amenable to continued use of the Weehawken–Cornwall portion of the West Shore, but NYC's presence put NYO&W firmly in the position of a feeder line, not part of a trunk route—and the through route that NYO&W participated in was hardly competitive with NYC: Rome, Watertown & Ogdensburg from Oswego to Buffalo, and Wabash from Buffalo to Chicago.

Anthracite carrier

More important to NYO&W's future was the opening in 1890 of a 54-mile branch from Cadosia, N. Y., to Scranton, Penn., to tap the anthracite regions. The road converted a number of its locomotives to anthracite-burners, in the process changing them from conventional configuration to Camelbacks. In 1904 the New Haven purchased control of the NYO&W for its coal business.

In 1912 the New York Central and the New Haven discussed trading their interests in Rutland and NYO&W, respectively; New Haven wound up with part of NYC's Rutland stock but retained its NYO&W control.

The 1920s saw a travel boom on the NYO&W as the Catskill Mountains became a resort area. The Depression killed much of that business. Coal from the Scranton Branch provided a greater and greater portion of the road's revenue, peaking in 1932. However, it was downhill from there. The coal mines in Scranton failed in 1937, and NYO&W filed for reorganization in May of that year.

Bridge route

The road's trustee, Frederic Lyford, recognized that any future the NYO&W had lay in general merchandise traffic, not coal, and began to change the road into a bridge route between the west end of the New Haven at Maybrook and connections at Scranton. By this time passenger traffic to the Catskills was growing again. NYO&W couldn't afford a streamliner but asked designer Otto Kuhler to do what he could for $10,000 for the 1937 summer season. The result was *The*

Mountaineer: streamstyling for a 4-8-2, slipcovers for the seats of the coaches, and maple armchairs replacing wicker in the parlor car, all painted maroon and black with orange trim—and matching uniforms for the crew.

In 1941 NYO&W sold its New Berlin branch to the Unadilla Valley. Dieselization of the NYO&W began in 1941 with five General Electric 44-ton switchers. Several sets of Electro-Motive FTs soon followed for freight service. One pair of FTs was financed by Standard Oil in exchange for detailed performance data over three years of operation.

Demise

The NYO&W enjoyed a brief postwar surge of business, but NYO&W's division of the revenue wasn't enough to keep the rest of the road in business. The originating carrier gets most of the revenue from a freight move. To make money as a bridge carrier you need lots of business and a long haul—longer than the 145 miles from Scranton to Campbell Hall. Passenger service was reduced to a single summer-only Weehawken–Roscoe round trip. A booster organization of shippers was formed but little of the road's freight originated on line.

In 1952 the New Haven offered to purchase the road but soon withdrew its offer (and had financial problems of its own). Abandonment was loudly protested by towns along the line, which considered unpaid back taxes as an investment in the railroad. The New York state legislature passed a $1 million aid bill, citing the road as essential for civil defense, but the state civil defense commission rejected it. The federal government recommended liquidation. Finally operation ceased on March 29, 1957. The assets were auctioned off—the diesels found new owners, but everything else was scrapped. None of the road's lines remain in operation.

FACTS & FIGURES

Year	1929	1956
Miles operated	569	541
Locomotives	177	46
Passenger cars	401	12
Freight cars	5,077	152
Reporting marks: OW		
Historical society: nyow.org		

New York, Susquehanna & Western

New York, Susquehanna & Western train SU99 crosses the Delaware River from New York to Pennsylvania at Mill Rift, Pa., a few miles west of Port Jervis, N.Y., on the former Erie main line, behind a pair of SD60s in September 2012. *David T. Horree*

In 1966 the New York Central abandoned the western end of its Ulster & Delaware branch. The Delaware Otsego Corporation purchased 2.6 miles of the line at Oneonta, N. Y., and operated it as a steam-powered tourist carrier. DO also offered freight service, but there was little market for it.

Five years later DO's Oneonta operation was in the path of highway construction, and Delaware & Hudson wanted to abandon its Cooperstown branch.

Delaware Otsego bought the D&H branch and operated it as the Cooperstown & Charlotte Valley Railway. Although the passenger operation was not a success, freight was and Delaware Otsego management saw potential in acquiring low-traffic branches that larger roads couldn't operate profitably.

Between 1973 and 1986 Delaware Otsego acquired other branches and short lines: the Richfield Springs branch of the Erie Lackawanna, EL's line between

Lackawaxen and Honesdale, Pa., the Fonda, Johnstown & Gloversville Railroad, the Staten Island Railway, and the Rahway Valley Railroad.

Delaware Otsego's major success, though, was the New York, Susquehanna & Western. The Susquehanna's original purpose was to be part of a route from New York to the Great Lakes. Its partner in this endeavor was the New York, Ontario & Western. The Susquehanna reached west to the Delaware River and leased the

Wilkes-Barre & Eastern for access to the coalfields of northeastern Pennsylvania. It was the weakest of the Pennsylvania-to-Hudson River coal roads, and it came under control of the Erie Railroad in 1898.

The Susquehanna (often, "Susie-Q") entered bankruptcy in 1937 (Erie was right behind it) and took charge of its own affairs in 1940. The railroad modernized its commuter service with ACF Motorailers and connecting bus service to New York, and dieselized its other operations by the end of World War II; then it upgraded its commuter service again in the early 1950s with RDCs and new coaches from Budd. The Susquehanna fell on hard times during the economic recession of 1957. It sold its modern passenger cars and replaced them

with third-hand coaches (and later offered its commuters $1,000 each to stop using the trains). Two of its connecting railroads, the NYO&W and the Lehigh & New England, ceased operation, and washouts cut off its other western connections.

The Susquehanna declared bankruptcy in 1976 but stayed out of Conrail, which had surrounded it. The bankruptcy court ordered that the road be abandoned and its assets sold. By then the road was down to a 43-mile line from Croxton and Edgewater through Paterson to Butler.

Enter Delaware Otsego

The state of New Jersey, aware of Delaware Otsego's reputation at rehabilitating short lines, asked DO to take over the

railroad. A new DO subsidiary, the New York, Susquehanna & Western Railway, began operation in September 1980 under a lease agreement. In 1982 DO purchased the NYS&W. In 1981 Conrail proposed abandonment of its former Erie Lackawanna line between Binghamton, N. Y., and Jamesville, just south of Syracuse, and the Utica branch of that line. Delaware Otsego purchased those lines and organized them as the Northern Division of NYS&W. To connect the two divisions, DO also purchased from Conrail a portion of the former Lehigh & Hudson River Railway between Warwick, N. Y., and Franklin, N. J., and secured trackage rights on Conrail from Binghamton to Warwick and from Franklin to Sparta Junction, to connect it all.

DO's management recognized the potential in coast-to-coast container traffic. Sea-Land leased property adjacent to NYS&W's yard at Little Ferry, N. J., and contracted with the railroad to operate container trains. Almost all their mileage west to Binghamton was on Conrail track by virtue of the trackage and haulage rights agreements. After a few years, Conrail, which operated container trains of its own, wanted to raise the rates it charged NYS&W for moving the trains. The process required renegotiating trackage rights and haulage agreements; as a result, NYS&W reopened its line west of Butler and got more favorable operating arrangements on Conrail track.

In 1997, NYS&W (and all of DO) was merged by DOCP Acquisition LLC, owned 40 percent by Norfolk Southern and 40 percent by CSX, and 20 percent by DO founder Walter G. Rich. The Susquehanna had been successful with its container trains and become a regional railroad. Delaware Otsego's shorter lines operated with some success during the 1980s but ceased operation around 1990.

FACTS & FIGURES

Year	1929	2012
Miles operated	219	403
Locomotives	2	15
Passenger cars	16	—
Freight cars	2,186	—
Reporting marks: NYSW		
Historical society: nyswths.org		

Norfolk & Western

Norfolk & Western has two distinct images. Before 1964, it was a coal hauler controlled by the Pennsylvania Railroad. It even looked like the Pennsy in places: Tuscan red coaches, position-light signals, and a short electrified district—but no Belpaire fireboxes. In 1964, possibly as a reaction to the proposed merger of the Pennsylvania and the New York Central, N&W merged, leased, or purchased four other railroads. Suddenly the N&W was a Midwestern railroad, with a multiplicity of routes from Buffalo to Chicago and St. Louis and terminals on the Missouri River at Kansas City and Omaha.

Norfolk & Western's oldest ancestor was a line from Petersburg, Va., to City Point, a few miles away on the James River. In 1850 the Norfolk & Petersburg Railroad was chartered to build a railroad between the cities of its name. It reached Petersburg in 1858 after crossing part of the Dismal Swamp on a roadbed laid on a mat of trees and logs. Other N&W forebears were the Southside Railroad, opened in 1854 from Petersburg to Lynchburg, Va., and the Virginia & Tennessee, completed in 1856 from Lynchburg to Bristol on the Virginia-Tennessee line.

Norfolk & Western streamlined J-class 4-8-4 No. 611, built in 1950 and later a steam-excursion star, rolls downgrade with train 45, the *Tennesseean*, near Bonsack, Va. *Bob Krone*

Consolidation and a new name

The Norfolk & Petersburg, Southside, and Virginia & Tennessee were consolidated in 1867 but retained their identities until 1870, when they were organized as the Atlantic, Mississippi & Ohio Railroad.

The AM&O was sold in 1881 to the Clark family, who ran a banking house in Philadelphia and owned the Shenandoah Valley Railroad. The Clarks moved the headquarters of their railroads to a place called Big Lick. The place was soon renamed Roanoke, and the AM&O was renamed the Norfolk & Western Railroad.

The N&W was extended northwest into the coalfields of West Virginia, and in 1890 it began building an extension to the Ohio River. It reached the river in 1892 and bridged it to connect with the Scioto Valley & New England Railroad, which ran north to Columbus, Ohio.

Purchase of the Cincinnati, Portsmouth & Virginia Railroad put the Norfolk & Western into Cincinnati in 1901. The Norfolk–Columbus/Cincinnati main line plus branches to Hagerstown, Md., and Winston-Salem and Durham, N. C., constituted the major part of the "old" Norfolk & Western, a coal carrier operating trains between the Ohio River and tidewater.

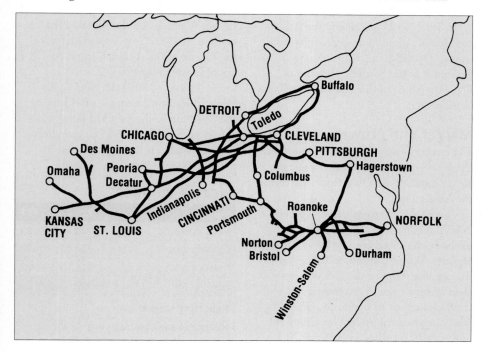

One of Norfolk & Western's 81 big Y6-class 2-8-8-2s handles a long coal drag at Blue Ridge, Va., in the mid-1950s. *Jim McClellan*

Pennsylvania Railroad control

The Pennsylvania Railroad began purchasing N&W stock in 1900, and by 1964 Pennsy owned about one-third of N&W's stock, either directly or through a subsidiary holding company. The Pennsy treated the N&W as an investment, not a fief, despite superficial resemblances—mostly those signals and the red paint.

Between 1915 and 1924 N&W electrified 56 route miles between Iaeger and Bluefield, W. Va., to increase the capacity of a line that included 2 percent grades and a 3,014-foot tunnel. A line relocation and a new tunnel in 1950 eliminated the need for the electrification, and the line reverted to steam power.

Less than a decade later N&W inherited Virginian's electrified operation; it fell victim to one-way traffic patterns.

Coal

The N&W was the acme of coal railroading, and longer than any other coal road— well into the late 1950s—it burned in its locomotives what it hauled in its hopper cars. N&W built many of its steam locomotives in its Roanoke Shops, experimented with a steam turbine-electric locomotive, and explored what modern servicing facilities could do for steam locomotive operating efficiency.

The tide of the coal movement was generally westward to the Great Lakes until the mid-1950s, when there was a demand for high-grade coal in Europe. That change in the direction of the flow may have precipitated the first in a long string of mergers. Eastbound coal on N&W had to cross several summits; on the parallel Virginian Railway it had a gentle descent most of the way. N&W had applied to lease the Virginian in 1925 and was denied permission by the Interstate Commerce Commission. In 1959 the situation was different. There was surprisingly little protest, and the ICC moved quickly. Merger took place on Dec. 1, 1959.

In 1962 N&W purchased the Atlantic & Danville, a line running from Norfolk west to Danville, Va., 211 miles, and reorganized it as the Norfolk, Franklin & Danville. Much of this line has since been abandoned.

Merger and growth

The merger plans of the Pennsylvania and the New York Central created a merger frenzy north of the Ohio River and east of the Mississippi.

Norfolk & Western moved quickly. N&W acquired the Nickel Plate, the Wabash, the Pittsburgh & West Virginia, and the Akron, Canton & Youngstown. To connect them to the N&W proper, it then acquired the Pennsylvania's line from Columbus to Sandusky, Ohio, which crossed the AC&Y at Chatfield and the Nickel Plate at Bellevue. The

merger, leases, and purchases took effect Oct. 16, 1964.

Less than a year later, on Aug. 31, 1965, N&W and Chesapeake & Ohio (plus Baltimore & Ohio and Western Maryland) announced merger plans, offering to include Reading, Central Railroad of New Jersey, Erie Lackawanna, Delaware & Hudson, and Boston & Maine. It would have created a system about the same size as Penn Central. N&W and C&O stockholders approved the merger, and by the end of 1969 there were only two opponents, Penn Central and the state of New York. N&W and C&O were confident that merger would take place within a year.

Ironically, Penn Central had its way. PC's bankruptcy on June 21, 1970, and the ensuing bankruptcies of several other Eastern railroads changed the situation. On April 22, 1971, the boards of N&W and C&O canceled the proposed merger. A residue was the ownership of Erie Lackawanna and Delaware & Hudson by an N&W subsidiary, a holding company named Dereco.

Further discussion of merger was delayed by the formation of Conrail and the question of its ultimate disposition. Spurred perhaps by the formation of the CSX Corporation in 1980, N&W turned to the Southern Railway. On June 1, 1982, N&W and Southern Railway became subsidiaries of Norfolk Southern Corporation, a newly formed holding company.

N&W purchased the Illinois Terminal on Sept. 1, 1981. Corporate existence of the IT and of the Akron, Canton & Youngstown ended in 1982.

At the end of 1990 the Norfolk & Western Railway became a subsidiary of the Southern Railway (it had been a subsidiary of Norfolk Soutern Corporation), and the Southern Railway changed its name to Norfolk Southern Railway.

FACTS & FIGURES

Year	1929	1981
Miles operated	2,240	7,803
Locomotives	788	1372
Passenger cars	476	23
Freight cars	30,222	87,903
Reporting marks: NW		
Historical society: nwhs.org		

Norfolk Southern (1942-1982)

Norfolk Southern 1501, a six-axle Baldwin DRS-6-4-1500, leads a freight train in the early 1950s. The NS had 32 Baldwin diesels, some of which lasted into the 1970s. *Robert A. Caflisch; Helen Caflisch collection*

Today's Norfolk Southern is quite a different railroad from the original Norfolk Southern that is the subject of this entry. Perhaps the problem is the Southern Railway's historical penchant for reusing names.

The Elizabeth City & Norfolk Railroad was chartered in 1870. In 1880 construction began on its line from Berkley, Va., now part of Norfolk, along the east edge of the Dismal Swamp to Elizabeth City, N. C. The line was opened to Elizabeth City in June 1881 and extended a few miles farther to Edenton, on the shore of Albemarle Sound, in December of that year. There, steamers connected with the trains for points up the rivers and along the coast of North Carolina. The road received a new name, Norfolk Southern Railroad, in 1883.

The Norfolk Southern entered receivership in 1889 and was reorganized as the Norfolk & Southern Railroad in 1891. Included in the N&S was the Albemarle & Pantego Railroad, which had been organized in 1887 by the John L. Roper Lumber Co. to build from Mackey's Ferry, across the sound from Edenton, to Belhaven, N. C.

In 1900 the N&S absorbed the Norfolk, Virginia Beach & Southern Railroad. The NVB&S had opened in 1883 as a 3-foot gauge line from Norfolk to Virginia Beach; in 1899 it was standard-gauged and acquired a branch to Munden, in the extreme southeast corner of Virginia. In 1902 Chesapeake Transit Co. opened an electric line from Norfolk to Cape Henry, Va. To meet the competition, N&S built a short branch from Virginia Beach to Cape

Henry, electrified its line from Norfolk to Virginia Beach, and bought Chesapeake Transit—and the former management of Chesapeake Transit wound up in control of N&S.

That same year N&S acquired the 3-foot gauge Washington & Plymouth, which connected the North Carolina towns of its name, widened it to standard gauge, built a 10-mile link between Plymouth and Mackey's Ferry, and installed the John W. Garrett, a ferry that had been on Baltimore & Ohio's roster, on the run between Edenton and Mackey's Ferry.

The Suffolk & Carolina Railway was chartered in 1873. By 1897 its 3 foot 6 inch gauge line reached from Suffolk, Va., to Ryland, N. C. In 1902 it was extended to Edenton; in 1904 it was standard-gauged and it built a branch to Elizabeth City. In

1906 the Suffolk & Carolina was taken over by the Virginia & Carolina Coast. The V&CC bought the Roper Lumber Co. and built a line east from Mackey's Ferry to Columbia, N. C. In 1903 the Raleigh & Pamlico Sound was organized to build lines from Raleigh and New Bern to Washington, N. C., and the Pamlico, Oriental & Western began a line from New Bern to Oriental.

Consolidation

In 1906 the Norfolk & Southern Railway was formed as a consolidation of the Norfolk & Southern Railroad, the Virginia & Carolina Coast Railroad, the Raleigh & Pamlico Sound Railroad, the Pamlico, Oriental & Western Railway, and the Beaufort & Western Railroad. It also held the lease of the Atlantic & North Carolina.

Expansion outpaced the railroad's finances in 1908. The road entered the hands of receivers that year and was reorganized as the Norfolk Southern Railroad in 1910. That same year a trestle was constructed across Albemarle Sound to replace the ferry that operated between Edenton and Mackey's Ferry. The expansion program continued. NS bought four railroads and undertook new construction, extending the main line from Raleigh to Charlotte with branches to Fayetteville, Aberdeen, and Asheboro. In 1920 the NS leased the Durham & South Carolina

Norfolk Southern received five light 2-8-4 Berkshires from Baldwin in 1940. They were sold in 1950 and later wound up on the National Railways of Mexico. *H. Reid*

Railroad, gaining access to Durham.

The Depression drove the NS into receivership yet again in 1932. The electric passenger service to Virginia Beach and Cape Henry, primarily suburban in character, was replaced by gasoline-powered cars in 1935 (it was discontinued in 1948). Also in 1935 the Atlantic & North Carolina withdrew its lease for nonpayment, and in 1937 the Beaufort & Western was sold to local interests to become the Beaufort & Morehead. In 1937, NS abandoned much of the Belhaven branch and, in 1940, all of

the former Virginia & Carolina Coast. The road was sold at foreclosure in 1941.

The Norfolk Southern Railway took over at the beginning of 1942. In 1947 a group of investors headed by Patrick B. McGinnis took control. The railroad acquired a pair of office cars, leased apartments or suites in New York, Washington, and Miami, lavishly entertained its shippers, and got investigated by the Interstate Commerce Commission. McGinnis resigned and moved on, eventually to the New York, New Haven & Hartford. New management took over in 1953. In the early 1960s NS constructed a branch to serve phosphate deposits between Washington and New Bern.

The Southern Railway purchased the Norfolk Southern in 1974. Southern merged the NS with the Carolina & Northwestern under the NS name. In 1981 the name was changed to Carolina & Northwestern so that the Norfolk Southern name could be used for a newly formed holding company as part of the Southern-Norfolk & Western merger.

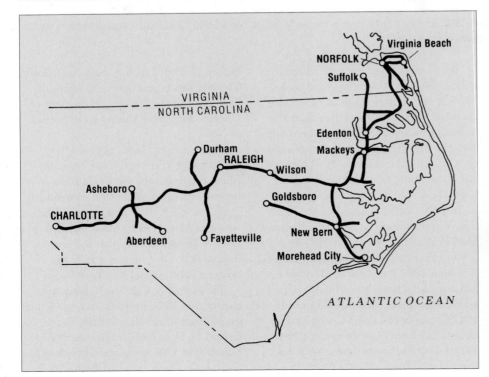

FACTS & FIGURES

Year	1929	1973
Miles operated	933	622
Locomotives	105	37
Passenger cars	108	—
Freight cars	3,282	2,245
Reporting marks: NS		
Historical society: norfolksouthernhs.org		

Norfolk Southern (1982-)

Norfolk Southern ES40DC No. 7553 leads an EMD mate on an eastbound coal train passing under a classic Pennsylvania Railroad signal bridge at Tipton, Pa., a few miles east of Altoona, in June 2009. In 1998, NS split Conrail with CSX on a 58-to-42 percent basis. *Alex Mayes*

Historians have argued that one key to the success of the June 1, 1982 consolidation of Norfolk & Western and Southern Railway was that the two Eastern railroads shared similar cultures: determined, forward-looking, and committed to success. This attitude served to douse the fires of early rivalries with a single-minded focus on making the unified system work, and work well.

It didn't hurt that each railroad also had a solid franchise—not always the shortest or fastest route, but track, locomotives, and rolling stock that were productive and well-maintained nonetheless.

In the 1960s, when most railroads were merging to eliminate parallel lines, including the giant Penn Central, N&W by force looked outward, acquiring the Nickel Plate Road, leasing the Wabash, and tying all three together with a Pennsylvania Railroad line from Columbus, Ohio, to Lake Erie. N&W's strategic play got it more than just track: It gained access to western

gateways and new traffic sources, such as Wabash's Detroit-area auto business that would reduce its dependence on coal.

Southern, meanwhile, went about consolidating regional connections (notably the Central of Georgia and the original Norfolk Southern Railway), improving major routes and laying welded rail from Alexandria, Va., to New Orleans. Chief among the improvements was rebuilding the Cincinnatti-Chattanooga, Tenn., main line, known as the "Rat Hole" for its many tunnels (formally the Cincinnati, New Orleans & Texas Pacific or CNO&TP).

Southern and N&W might not have been prominent on each other's radars before the CSX accretion of 1980. (In the 1970s, Southern had explored mergers with Illinois Central Gulf and Missouri Pacific and petitioned unsuccessfully for Monon's route to Chicago.) But each recognized the benefits of combining two strong Eastern railroads that shared common endpoints yet served different regions.

Initially, the merger produced few changes. A connection was built at Hurt, Va., to connect the Southern main line and the former Virginian main line, thus enabling through traffic between Roanoke, Va., and Southern's newest hump yard at Linwood, N. C. Overall, though, traffic patterns remained the same, and most of the diesel fleets remained stationed and deployed as they had been. The company launched a common paint scheme and brand, "the Thoroughbred of Transportation," in October 1983, thus slowly erasing the well-honed N&W and Southern identities.

Norfolk Southern had sought to buy Conrail in 1985, but gave up after opposition from Congress, labor unions, and competitors derailed that plan.

But traffic between Norfolk Southern and Conrail was always brisk, and NS continued to watch its northern neighbor's increasingly robust intermodal traffic as a charm.

Thus, buying 58 percent of Conrail in 1998 was an equally critical move that strategically positioned Norfolk Southern for handling today's growth commodity, intermodal traffic, which polished the rails of Conrail's high-volume traffic lanes between Chicago and the Eastern Seaboard.

Until recently, Norfolk Southern's component franchises had remained essentially independent operations: Coal moving on former N&W lines had nothing to do with the land-bridge containers rolling across the former Pennsylvania main line. Where the benefits of today's 20,023-mile system (which includes 4,271 miles of trackage rights) were seen most clearly were on key routes no other U. S. railroad either had or served nearly so well: Detroit to Kansas City on the Wabash, and the CNO&TP between the Great Lakes and the Sunbelt.

However, 30 years into the NS era, that historic traffic separation has begun to dissolve, driven first by the Heartland Corridor project, which cleared tunnels on the former N&W main line to handle double-stacked containers coming out of Virginia's ports, across the Appalachian Mountains, and into Columbus, Ohio. The route that was once best known as a coal conveyor now also handles container trains and auto racks.

NS in 2012 became focused on the Crescent Corridor, a project to add intermodal yards and capacity on its main routes from New Jersey and Pennsylvania south to Memphis and Mississippi, paving the way for double-stacked containers to flow north and south in the eastern United States. The principal route via Harrisburg, Pa., and Bristol, Tenn./Va., encompasses portions of both the N&W and Southern. This was one of the very same routes that was touted as an ideal corridor for freight when the railroad was put together in 1982. In 2014 it is becoming a reality, and the ultimate promise of the Norfolk Southern merger is being fulfilled.

FACTS & FIGURES

Year	1983	2013
Miles operated	18,252	20,023
Locomotives	2,905	4,011
Passenger cars	—	—
Freight cars	159,905	82,917
Reporting marks: NS		
Website: nscorp.com		

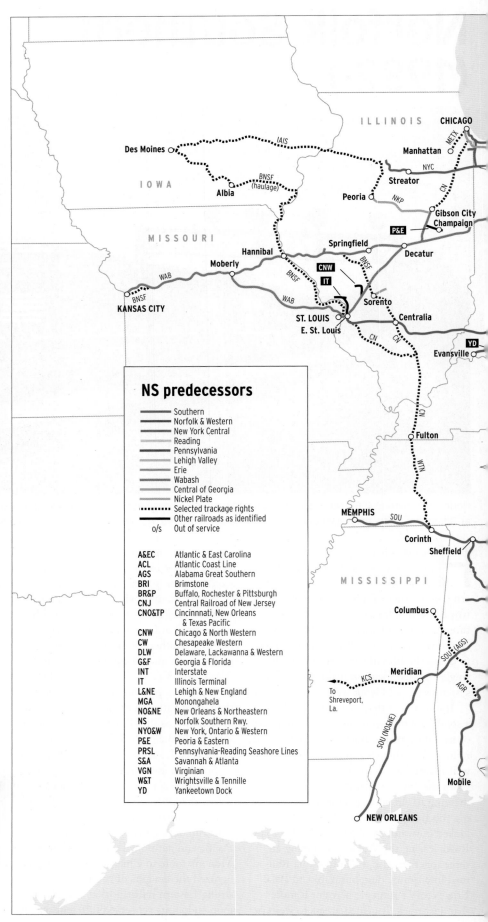

NS predecessors

— Southern
— Norfolk & Western
— New York Central
— Reading
— Pennsylvania
— Lehigh Valley
— Erie
— Wabash
— Central of Georgia
— Nickel Plate
···· Selected trackage rights
— Other railroads as identified
o/s Out of service

A&EC	Atlantic & East Carolina
ACL	Atlantic Coast Line
AGS	Alabama Great Southern
BRI	Brimstone
BR&P	Buffalo, Rochester & Pittsburgh
CNJ	Central Railroad of New Jersey
CNO&TP	Cincinnnati, New Orleans & Texas Pacific
CNW	Chicago & North Western
CW	Chesapeake Western
DLW	Delaware, Lackawanna & Western
G&F	Georgia & Florida
INT	Interstate
IT	Illinois Terminal
L&NE	Lehigh & New England
MGA	Monongahela
NO&NE	New Orleans & Northeastern
NS	Norfolk Southern Rwy.
NYO&W	New York, Ontario & Western
P&E	Peoria & Eastern
PRSL	Pennsylvania-Reading Seashore Lines
S&A	Savannah & Atlanta
VGN	Virginian
W&T	Wrightsville & Tennille
YD	Yankeetown Dock

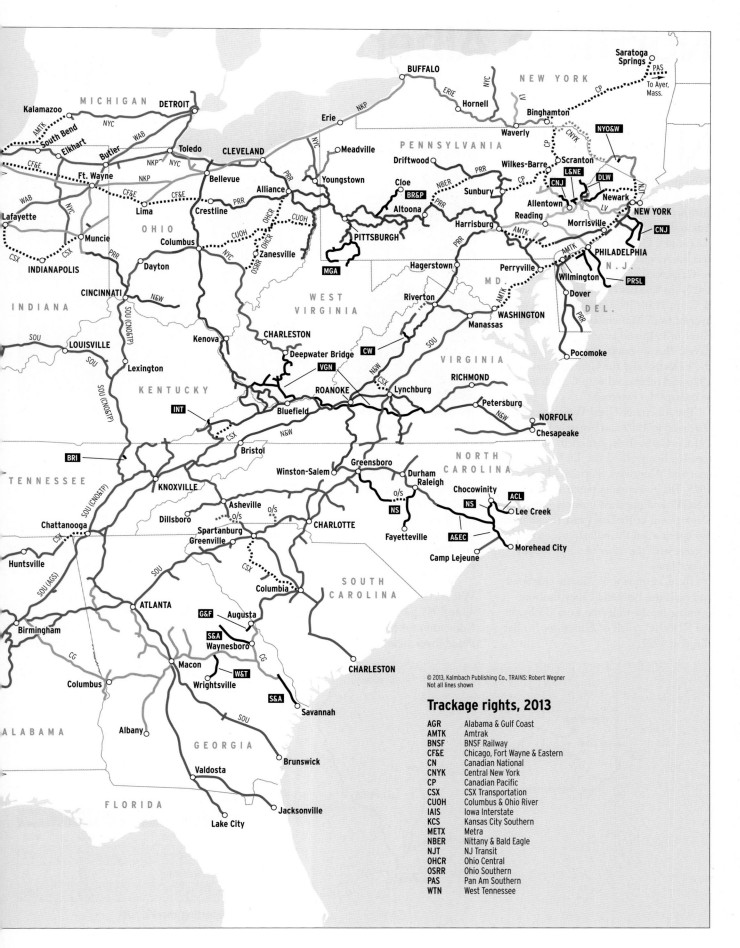

BUFFALO

NEW YORK

Saratoga Springs
PAS
To Ayer, Mass.

MICHIGAN
Kalamazoo
DETROIT
South Bend
Elkhart
Butler
Toledo
NYC
WAB
CLEVELAND
Erie
Hornell
Binghamton
Waverly
CP
CNYK
NYO&W
Scranton
Meadville
Driftwood
Wilkes-Barre
L&NE
CNJ
DLW
CF&E
Ft. Wayne
NKP
NKP
NYC
Bellevue
Youngstown
Cloe
BR&P
Sunbury
NBER
Allentown
Newark
Lafayette
WAB
Lima
CF&E
CF&E
Alliance
Crestline
PRR
Altoona
PRR
Reading
LV
NEW YORK
Muncie
NYC
Columbus
OHCR
CUOH
Harrisburg
AMTK
Morrisville
CNJ
CSX
CUOH
OSRR
Zanesville
PHILADELPHIA
INDIANAPOLIS
CSX
OHIO
PRR
Dayton
NYC
OSRR
PITTSBURGH
Hagerstown
PRR
Perryville
N.J.
AMTK
Wilmington
PRSL
CINCINNATI
N&W
MGA
MD.
Dover
INDIANA
Riverton
DEL.
SOU (CNO&TP)
WEST
VIRGINIA
AMTK
PRR
LOUISVILLE
SOU
Kenova
CHARLESTON
WASHINGTON
Manassas
Pocomoke
Lexington
SOU
Deepwater Bridge
CW
VGN
SOU
N&W
VIRGINIA
KENTUCKY
ROANOKE
N&W
CSX
Lynchburg
RICHMOND
Bluefield
INT
Petersburg
BRI
N&W
Bristol
N&W
NORFOLK
CSX
Chesapeake
Greensboro
NORTH
CAROLINA
TENNESSEE
Winston-Salem
Durham
KNOXVILLE
Asheville
o/s
Raleigh
Chocowinity
ACL
Chattanooga
Dillsboro
o/s
o/s
NS
NS
Lee Creek
CSX
Spartanburg
Greenville
CHARLOTTE
A&EC
Morehead City
Huntsville
SOU (AGS)
CSX
Fayetteville
Camp Lejeune
SOU
SOUTH
CAROLINA
Columbia
ATLANTA
SOU (CNO&TP)
G&F
Augusta
Birmingham
CG
S&A
Waynesboro
CG
Macon
W&T
Wrightsville
S&A
Columbus
Savannah
Albany
GEORGIA
Brunswick
Valdosta
FLORIDA
Jacksonville
ALABAMA
Lake City

© 2013, Kalmbach Publishing Co., TRAINS: Robert Wegner
Not all lines shown

Trackage rights, 2013

AGR — Alabama & Gulf Coast
AMTK — Amtrak
BNSF — BNSF Railway
CF&E — Chicago, Fort Wayne & Eastern
CN — Canadian National
CNYK — Central New York
CP — Canadian Pacific
CSX — CSX Transportation
CUOH — Columbus & Ohio River
IAIS — Iowa Interstate
KCS — Kansas City Southern
METX — Metra
NBER — Nittany & Bald Eagle
NJT — NJ Transit
OHCR — Ohio Central
OSRR — Ohio Southern
PAS — Pan Am Southern
WTN — West Tennessee

Northern Alberta

Northern Alberta Railways Co. was incorporated June 14, 1929, and was owned equally by Canadian Pacific Railway and Canadian National Railways. On July 1, 1929, NAR purchased from the province of Alberta four railways: the Edmonton, Dunvegan & British Columbia; the Central Canada; the Pembina Valley; and the Alberta & Great Waterways.

Construction of the ED&BC began in 1912. The line reached Dawson Creek, B. C., in 1930. The Central Canada was opened from McLennan north to Peace River in 1916 and later extended to Hines Creek. The provincial government leased the ED&BC and the Central Canada in 1920 and contracted with Canadian Pacific to operate the two roads.

The Alberta & Great Waterways was chartered in 1909 and began building in 1914 at Carbondale, just north of Edmonton. The line reached Lac La Biche a year later and Waterways (Fort McMurray) in 1925. The government purchased the A&GW and operated it through its Department of Railways and Telephones, but later turned the railroad over to CP to operate with the other two provincially owned lines.

The government of Alberta chartered and built the Pembina Valley Railway, opening the 26-mile line from Busby, on the ED&BC north of Edmonton, to Barrhead in 1927.

The conductor of Northern Alberta train 2 signals the engineer to back into the siding at Hythe to pick up the dining car from the rear of train 1. The trains traded the diner, which served evening to noon meals on one train and noon to evening meals on the other. *Donald E. Smith*

The provincial government in November 1926 took over operation from CP. In 1928 CP offered to purchase the railroads if CN would go halves. The arrangement was acceptable to the province, and Northern Alberta Railways, jointly owned by the two large roads, began operation.

Traffic remained brisk after World War II. The opening of provincial highway 43 in 1955 provided a shortcut from Edmonton to the Dawson Creek and Peace River areas, and in 1958 the Pacific Great Eastern Railway (now BC Rail) reached Dawson Creek from North Vancouver. Both the highway and BCR siphoned traffic from NAR.

In 1962 the Canadian government began construction of the Great Slave Lake Railway north from Roma Junction, west of Peace River. The line, operated by CN, was opened in 1964. It furnished much bridge revenue to NAR in the form of lead and zinc ores moving south to Trail, B. C., to supplement the grain that was NAR's principal commodity. Another provincially owned, CN-operated road, the Alberta Resources Railway, reached Grande Prairie from the south in 1969.

CP sold its share of NAR to CN in 1980. Northern Alberta's operations were absorbed into CN on January 1, 1981, as part of the Peace River Division.

FACTS & FIGURES

Year	1930	1980
Miles operated	862	923
Locomotives	27	21
Passenger cars	39	9
Freight cars	225	100
Reporting marks: NAR		

Northern Pacific

Northern Pacific A-2s-class 4-8-4 No. 2654 leads a westbound freight over the long (3,860-foot) steel viaduct spanning the Sheyenne River Valley at Valley City, N. D., in the early 1950s. *Linn Westcott*

In 1864 Abraham Lincoln signed the charter of a railroad to be built from the Great Lakes to Puget Sound—the Northern Pacific Railroad. The Philadelphia banking house of Jay Cooke & Co. undertook to sell the bonds, which were to yield 7.3 percent interest, and sold $30 million worth. Work began in 1870 at Carlton, Minn., 20 miles from Duluth on the Lake Superior & Mississippi Railroad. The LS&M had just been opened between St. Paul and Duluth, and in 1872 Northern

Pacific leased the road. By 1873 the NP was completed west to Bismarck, N. D., plus an isolated section from Kalama, Wash., on the Columbia River, to Tacoma. The Panic of 1873 wiped out Cooke and work ceased on the railroad.

NP reorganized by converting the bonds to stock, and the Lake Superior & Mississippi was reorganized as the St. Paul & Duluth. In 1881 control of the NP was purchased by Henry Villard, who also controlled the Oregon Railway & Navigation

Co. and the Oregon & California Railroad. On Sept. 8, 1883, NP drove a last spike at Gold Creek, Mont., near Garrison, completing a line from Duluth to Wallula Junction, Wash. Northern Pacific trains continued on the rails of the OR&N to Portland, where NP's own line to Tacoma resumed (it crossed the Columbia River by ferry from Goble, Ore., to Kalama, Wash.

Even before completing the line at Gold Creek, NP began constructing a direct line from Pasco, Wash., over the

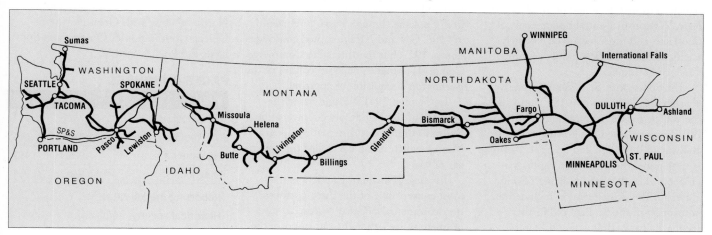

Five black and gold freight F units (passenger Fs were green) lift a freight up the west slope of the Continental Divide at Elliston, Mont., in the 1950s. The NP relied on EMD Fs for both passenger and freight service. *R. V. Nixon*

Cascade Range to Tacoma. The Puget Sound area was beginning to grow, and NP wanted to reach it with its own line rather than rely on OR&N. Indeed, soon after the last-spike ceremonies, Villard's empire collapsed and OR&N became part of Union Pacific (Southern Pacific got the Oregon & California). The Pasco–Tacoma line opened in 1887, with temporary switchbacks carrying trains over Stampede Pass until the opening of Stampede Tunnel in May 1888.

East to Chicago
In 1889 NP contracted with the Wisconsin Central to operate through service to Chicago from the Twin Cities, and in 1890 NP leased the WC. NP organized a terminal company, the Chicago & Northern Pacific, and leased it to the WC. NP entered receivership in 1893 and defaulted on lease payments to Wisconsin Central, which in turned defaulted on the C&NP lease. Wisconsin Central became part of Soo Line, and the Chicago & Northern Pacific became the Baltimore & Ohio Chicago Terminal.

The Superior & St. Croix Railroad, chartered in Wisconsin in 1870, provided the vehicle for the reorganization of the NP. It was renamed the Northern Pacific Railway in July 1896 and on Sept. 1 of that year acquired the properties, rights franchises, and lands of the Northern Pacific Railroad. The reorganization included the absorption of the St. Paul & Northern Pacific Railway (Brainerd and Staples,

Minn., to St. Paul). In 1900 NP acquired the properties of the St. Paul & Duluth, and in 1901, the Seattle & International Railway (Seattle to Sumas, Wash.). Also in 1901 NP leased its Manitoba lines (Emerson–Winnipeg–Portage-la-Prairie and Morris–Brandon) to the Province of Manitoba. (They were sold to Canadian National Railways in 1946.)

The beginnings of Burlington Northern
In 1901 Northern Pacific and Great Northern gained control of the Chicago, Burlington & Quincy by jointly purchasing approximately 98 percent of its capital stock. That same year James J. Hill and J. P. Morgan formed the Northern Securities Co. as a holding company for NP and Great Northern. The U. S. Supreme Court dissolved Northern Securities in 1904. In 1905 the two roads organized the Spokane, Portland & Seattle, which was completed from Spokane through Pasco to Portland in 1908. GN and NP attempted consolidation in 1927, but the Interstate Commerce Commission made giving up control of the Burlington a requisite for approval.

In October 1941 NP purchased the property of the Minnesota & International Railway (Brainerd to International Falls, Minn.), which it had controlled for a number of years.

In image, Northern Pacific was the most conservative of the three northern transcontinentals. (Great Northern was a prosperous, well-thought-out railroad; the

Milwaukee Road was a brash newcomer.) Bulking large in NP's freight traffic were wheat and lumber. In the 1920s and 1930s NP suffered from smaller than usual wheat crops and competition from ships for lumber moving to the East Coast. Ship competition decreased during World War II, and postwar prosperity brought an increase in building activity and population growth to the area NP served. NP was the oldest of the northern transcontinentals and had been instrumental in settling the northern plains. It served the populous areas of North Dakota, Montana, and Washington. Its slogan was "Main Street of the Northwest," and its secondary passenger train of the 1950s and 1960s was the *Mainstreeter*.

In 1956 NP and Great Northern again studied merger of the two roads, the Burlington, and the Spokane, Portland & Seattle. In 1960 the directors of both roads approved the merger terms. On March 2, 1970, NP was merged into Burlington Northern along with Great Northern; Chicago, Burlington & Quincy; and Spokane, Portland & Seattle.

FACTS & FIGURES

Year	1929	1969
Miles operated	6,784	6,771
Locomotives	1,087	604
Passenger cars	933	192
Freight cars	50,960	34,961
Reporting marks: NP, NPM		
Historical society: nprha.org		

Northwestern Pacific

Three months remain before the final steam operations on the NWP as train 3, the overnight to San Rafael, picks its way along the trestle at the base of Scotia Bluff, about 30 miles south of Eureka, on June 20, 1953. *Richard C. Brown*

The Northwestern Pacific was a subsidiary of Southern Pacific. It had no locomotives, passenger cars, or interchange freight cars of its own after 1960, and to the casual observer it appeared to be simply another piece of the far-flung SP.

NWP gradually lost its identity in that of its parent but until SP merged it in 1992, it existed as a "paper railroad," which is a railroad that exists only on paper and has no rolling stock of its own.

San Francisco & North Pacific

The earliest ancestor of the NWP was the Petaluma & Haystack Railroad, which in 1864 opened a three-mile line from Petaluma, Calif., to a landing on Petaluma Creek and a connection with boats for San Francisco. A boiler explosion destroyed its locomotive in 1866 and the line reverted to horse power.

In the 1860s there were several rival proposals for railroads in Sonoma County, some aimed north at the redwood country and some aimed south toward San Francisco Bay. The San Francisco & North Pacific was the successor to most of these. By 1870 construction was in progress from Petaluma north toward Santa Rosa. In 1871 the California Pacific, which had lines from Vallejo to Sacramento, Marysville, and Calistoga, purchased the SF&NP and completed it to Healdsburg—and then made noises about building a line up the Feather River Canyon and over Beckwourth Pass to connect with the Union Pacific at Ogden. Central Pacific, already smarting because upstart California Pacific had built a shorter, faster route between San Francisco and Sacramento, snapped up California Pacific and considered making Sausalito its San Francisco Bay terminal. The SF&NP was extended to Cloverdale in 1872. At the beginning of 1873 Central Pacific sold the SF&NP back to its builder, Peter Donahue.

In 1874 the Sonoma & Marin was organized to build a line from Petaluma south to San Rafael. It purchased the Petaluma & Haystack, surveyed a line to San Rafael, and was taken over by the SF&NP. The S&M opened and closed several times in 1878 and 1879. A tunnel cave-in was responsible for one closing, but the SF&NP was responsible for another—the new line in conjunction with the San Rafael & San Quentin and its ferry could provide a much faster trip to San Francisco than SF&NP's own steamer winding down

FACTS & FIGURES

Year	1929	1959
Miles operated	477	328
Locomotives	65	—
Passenger cars	207	—
Freight cars	1,234	—
Reporting marks: NWP		

Petaluma Creek. However, the growing commuter trade from San Rafael to San Francisco prompted SF&NP to extend the Sonoma & Marin south to Tiburon on San Francisco Bay. The SF&NP also gained a branch to Sonoma that had been started as a monorail, then converted to narrow gauge. In 1886 a line was completed across the marshes to connect it to the rest of the SF&NP at Ignacio.

In 1886 SP (successor to Central Pacific) built a line to Santa Rosa from Napa Junction, finally establishing a rail connection between the lines north of San Francisco and the rest of the country. Mervyn Donahue, Peter's son and his successor as head of the SF&NP, discovered that SP had an option on the Eel River & Eureka, which Donahue had anticipated using as the north end of the SF&NP. Donahue invoked the prospect of extending his system up the Feather River Canyon, and SP let its option drop. When the younger Donahue died in 1890, the road was sold to new owners who organized the California Northwestern and leased the SF&NP to it.

North Pacific Coast
In 1870 the standard gauge San Rafael & San Quentin Railroad opened from San Rafael to the San Quentin ferry landing,

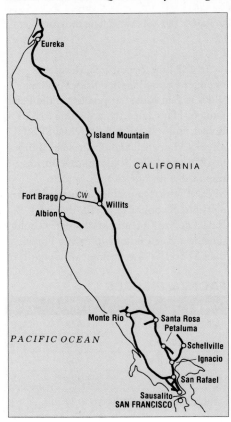

three miles to the southeast. In 1871 the North Pacific Coast Railroad was incorporated to build a line from Sausalito north through San Rafael to Tomales, on the coast, to serve a growing redwood lumber industry. The 3-foot-gauge line was was completed in 1875.

Since its line bypassed San Rafael by a couple of miles, the NPC built a branch from what is now San Anselmo to San Rafael. It leased the San Rafael & San Quentin, narrowed its gauge, and made that the main line rather than the route to Sausalito. In 1876 NPC rails reached the Russian River, and the road re-established Sausalito as its principal terminal after boring a tunnel at Corte Madera to replace a stiff climb over the hills. In 1877 the road extended its rails north of the Russian River to Duncan Mills.

New management took over the NPC in 1902. They renamed it the North Shore Railroad and standard-gauged, double-tracked, and electrified it from Sausalito to Mill Valley and San Rafael.

Northwestern Pacific
In 1903 the Santa Fe acquired the Eel River & Eureka and the Albion & Southeastern (an isolated line extending inland from the coast). Southern Pacific acquired the California Northwestern (by then its northern terminal was Willits) and the North Shore and started talking about building to Eureka. The battle lines were drawn. The principals, E. H. Harriman and Edward Ripley, soon recognized that the Eureka area could not support two railroads. They formed the jointly owned Northwestern Pacific Railway as a compromise; the Northwestern Pacific Railroad soon followed. Construction of a line along the Eel River canyon—inaccessible and prone to flood—was completed in 1914.

In 1929 SP assumed sole ownership of the NWP. The former NPC was standard-gauged as far as Point Reyes in 1920; the line from there north to the Russian River remained narrow gauge until its abandonment in 1930. The Manor–Point Reyes line was abandoned in 1933, and the Russian River branch was abandoned in 1935. The NWP bought the Petaluma & Santa Rosa, an interurban connecting the towns of its name, in 1932. P&SR discontinued its passenger service then and ended electric operation in 1947. NWP merged the P&SR in 1985.

NWP's electric suburban service was discontinued on March 1, 1941. Two San Rafael–Eureka trains remained; the day train was discontinued in May 1942. The overnight train was replaced by the tri-weekly daytime *Redwood* in 1956, and that was cut back to a Willits–Eureka run handled by SP's sole RDC in 1958.

During the 1930s NWP began to lease steam locomotives from parent SP. The last of these was returned to SP in August 1953, leaving just five active NWP steamers; the last steam run was Sept. 20, 1953. The diesels that took over were all SP property. NWP's last passenger cars left the roster in 1957, and the last interchange freight cars to carry NWP markings were gone by October 1958. A few cabooses carried NWP lettering until the 1970s.

A tunnel fire north of San Rafael in July 1961 cut off rail access to the south end of the NWP. Traffic was maintained by Santa Fe carfloat to the slip at Tiburon. The tunnel was repaired in 1967 after a long legal battle. Floods in December 1964 washed out more than 100 miles of the line in the Eel River Canyon; replacement took six months. A fire in a tunnel north of Island Mountain severed the line again in September 1978; it was reopened a year later. In January 1980 heavy rains washed out the interchange yard at Schellville, NWP's only rail connection.

SP closed the NWP north of Willits in April 1983, citing heavy expenses. In June of that year SP reopened the line but levied a $1200-per-car surcharge on each shipment. Another tunnel fire north of Willits in September 1983 again shut down the line—and SP threatened to make it permanent. A U. S. District Court ordered the line reopened, since it had been closed without ICC approval, and the line was reopened in March 1984.

On Nov. 1, 1984, the line north of Willits was sold to a new company, the Eureka Southern. The Eureka Southern declared bankruptcy, and operations were taken over by the North Coast Railroad Authority (operating as the North Coast Railroad) in April 1992. Southern Pacific continued to operate the NWP south of Willits and merged the NWP in 1992.

In 1993 SP leased the Schellville–Willits portion of the NWP to the California Northern Railroad. The SP sold the line in 1995. The NCR has operated the line sporadically since.

Oahu Railway & Land Co.

In September 1888 Benjamin F. Dillingham received a franchise from King Kalakaua to build a railroad from Honolulu to a sugar plantation at Ewa, about 20 miles west. Dillingham organized the Oahu Railway & Land Co. The 3-foot-gauge line opened Nov. 16, 1889, and the rails reached Ewa in May 1890. The railroad was extended up the west coast of Oahu, around Kaena Point and east to Kahuku, 71 miles by rail from Honolulu.

In 1906 the railroad constructed an 11-mile branch north from Waipahu to a pineapple plantation being developed by James B. Dole at Wahiawa, with a spur to the U. S. Army base at Schofield Barracks.

The road prospered. Between 1908 and 1916 it thoroughly modernized its roster of locomotives and cars and installed block signals along the double-track line between Honolulu and Waipahu. By 1927 the company was free of debt; the Depression merely reduced the dividend rate.

Passenger business dropped during the 1930s, but freight traffic held up. When World War II began, traffic to Army and Navy bases increased, but the bombing of Pearl Harbor on Dec. 7, 1941, brought a complete change of pace. The road found itself running 20-car commuter trains. To handle the traffic it acquired used cars and locomotives from the Pacific Coast Railway, the Nevada County Narrow Gauge, and the Boston, Revere Beach & Lynn.

Oahu Railway No. 70, a Mikado built by Alco in 1925, leads a Kahaku-bound freight along the edge of the Pacific Ocean east of Kaena Point. *Kent W. Cochrane*

By the end of 1946 the servicemen had gone home and passenger traffic dropped 50 percent. As plantation owners scrapped their railroads and turned to trucks, freight traffic on the Oahu Railway dropped. The railroad abandoned most of its line at the end of 1947. A short portion serving docks and canneries at Honolulu remained in operation until 1971.

The U. S. Navy purchased the main line from Pearl Harbor to Nanakuli and operated it until 1970 to serve ammunition dumps at Lualualei. Some of the locomotives and cars were sold to El Salvador.

Hawaii's other common-carrier railroads were:
- Koolau Railway (3-foot gauge) from Kahuku to Kahana, 11 miles
- Ahokini Terminal & Railway (30-inch gauge), 12 miles on Kauai's eastern shore
- Kauai Railway (30-inch gauge), 19 miles along the south shore of Kauai
- Hawaii Railway (3-foot gauge) on the island of Hawaii, 18 miles, abandoned 1945
- Hawaii Consolidated Railway (standard gauge), 77 miles along the eastern shore of Hawaii, wiped out by a tidal wave April 1, 1946
- Kahului Railroad (3-foot gauge), 16 miles along Maui's north shore.

The Lahaina, Kaanapali & Pacific Railroad along the west shore of Maui was built in 1970 as a tourist carrier; it is still in operation.

FACTS & FIGURES

Year	1929	1945
Miles operated	88	93
Locomotives	30	26
Passenger cars	64	83
Freight cars	1,033	1,308
Historical society: hawaiianrailway.com		

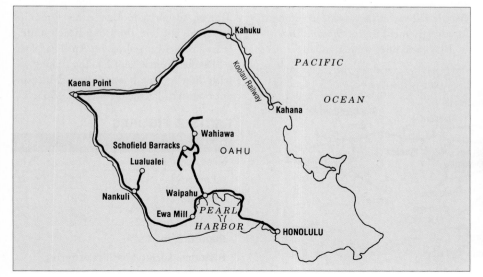

Pacific Electric

The 1900 census put the population of Los Angeles at 102,479—it had more than doubled in the previous decade and would more than triple in the next. During the 1890s the city acquired a local trolley system, and in 1895 the Los Angeles & Pasadena Railway opened from Los Angeles to Pasadena, 10 miles. Another line opened the next year, the Pasadena & Pacific, from Los Angeles to Santa Monica. Both companies were reorganized in 1898 as the Pasadena & Los Angeles and the Los Angeles Pacific, respectively. The Pasadena & Los Angeles was purchased (and along with it the Los Angeles Consolidated Electric Railway) by a group of investors headed by Henry E. Huntington (nephew of Collis P. Huntington, one of the builders of the Southern Pacific).

Huntington incorporated the Pacific Electric Railway in 1901 to build a high-speed interurban line from Los Angeles to Long Beach (20 miles), which opened in 1902. PE's tracks quickly spread throughout the Los Angeles area. E. H. Harriman was concerned about the effect the interurban would have on his Southern Pacific. He opposed Huntington at first and then purchased a 45 percent interest in the PE. Huntington, who was at the time a vice-president of SP, then incorporated the Los Angeles Inter-Urban Railway, entirely under his control. That company soon outgrew the PE. In 1908 Huntington leased the Los Angeles Inter-Urban to PE; in 1909 he sold several traction properties elsewhere in California to SP; and in 1910 he sold his Pacific Electric interests to

A Pacific Electric Los-Angeles-bound train of "Blimp" cars, led by No. 450, gets ready to move in the early 1950s. *Linn Westcott*

Southern Pacific. He retained his ownership of the Los Angeles Railway, the 3-foot-6-inch gauge local trolley system.

A new Pacific Electric Railway was incorporated in 1911 to consolidate the old PE, the Los Angeles Pacific, the Los Angeles Inter-Urban, and several other traction companies. It was the largest electric railway in the country. In addition to interurban lines stretching from Santa Monica east to Redlands and from San Fernando south to Balboa, PE operated local trolley service in most of the cities and towns. By 1918 PE was the largest electric railway in the world, according to its advertisement in *The Official Guide*.

PE's local lines were gradually abandoned or converted to bus operation, but the interurban lines remained strong into the 1940s, operating from terminals in Los Angeles at Sixth and Main streets and on Hill Street near Fourth at the end of a mile-long subway for trains to Hollywood, Burbank, and Van Nuys. After World War II, the interurban lines disappeared one by one. In 1953 PE sold the remaining passenger operations (to Bellflower, Long Beach, San Pedro, Burbank, and Hollywood) to Metropolitan Coach Lines. The Burbank and Hollywood lines were abandoned in 1955. Metropolitan Transit Authority took over the system in 1958; the last line, the Long Beach route, ceased passenger service on April 8, 1961.

Pacific Electric kept hauling freight with diesel power. It was merged with parent Southern Pacific on Aug. 13, 1965.

FACTS & FIGURES

Year	1929	1965
Miles operated	575	316
Locomotives	64	42
Passenger cars	822	—
Freight cars	2,296	29

Reporting marks: PE

Historical society: pacificelectric.org

Paducah & Louisville

Paducah & Louisville GP35 No. 2434—an ex-Gulf, Mobile & Ohio unit riding on Alco trucks—was typical of the railroad's motive power during its early years. The P&L later acquired several ex-CSX SD70MACs. *David P. Morgan Library collection.*

A railroad was opened between Elizabethtown and Paducah, Ky., by the Elizabethtown & Paducah Railroad in 1872. The railroad went through several reorganizations; in 1877 the route became part of the Chesapeake, Ohio & Southwestern Railroad, extending from Elizabethtown and Louisville through Paducah to Memphis, Tenn. It was to be a link in a transcontinental system that C. P. Huntington was trying to create, with the Southern Pacific and the Chesapeake & Ohio as the two ends.

In 1888 the Illinois Central Railroad purchased the Chesapeake, Ohio & Southwestern, gaining access to Louisville, the coalfields east of Paducah and, more important to IC in the long run, Memphis.

Following the 1972 Illinois Central Gulf merger, its owner, IC Industries, began to look for a buyer so it could get out of the railroad business. No one wanted the whole railroad. In 1981 IC Industries decided to sell pieces to trim ICG to a Chicago-New Orleans trunk line. It soon found buyers for ICG's east-west routes, and within a few years ICG's route mileage shrank by 70 percent.

In 1985 ICG approached two western Kentucky businessmen, Jim Smith and David Reed, who singly or jointly owned coal mines, a highway construction firm, a quarry, and a rail-to-barge transfer operation. ICG suggested that with the impending downsizing of the railroad, the best way for the men to preserve rail service would be to operate their own. On Aug. 27, 1986, the Paducah & Louisville took ownership of the Paducah-Louisville main line (there were two routes between Central City and Dawson Springs), branches to Elizabethtown, Kevil, and Clayburn, and ICG's shop complex at Paducah, which was spun off to a subsidiary, VMV Enterprises.

Most of P&L's traffic either originates or terminates on line, and more than 60 percent of it is coal. P&L motive power was mainly second-hand, second-generation EMD four- and six-axle diesels, but 16 former CSX SD70MACs arrived on the property in early 2013.

FACTS & FIGURES

Year	1986	2013
Miles operated	309	270
Locomotives	71	68
Passenger cars	—	—
Freight cars	1,183	448
Reporting marks: PAL		

Penn Central

Penn Central came into existence on Feb. 1, 1968. More accurately, it was incorporated in 1846 as the Pennsylvania Railroad; changed its name to Pennsylvania New York Central Transportation Co. on Feb. 1, 1968, when it merged the New York Central; and adopted the name Penn Central Company on May 8, 1968. On Oct. 1, 1969, it again changed its name, to Penn Central Transportation Company, and became a wholly owned subsidiary of a new Penn Central Company, a holding company.

The stockholders of the Pennsylvania and the New York Central approved merger of the two roads on May 8, 1962; nearly four years later the Interstate Commerce Commission approved the merger on the following conditions:

- The new company ("Penn Central" for convenience) had to take over the freight and passenger operations of the New York, New Haven & Hartford. That happened on Dec. 31, 1968.
- Penn Central had to absorb the New York, Susquehanna & Western. PC and the Susquehanna could not agree on

Train 111 is westbound at Trenton, N. J., behind former Pennsylvania Railroad GG1 No. 4918 on Aug. 10, 1970. *Krambles-Peterson Archive*

price, and NYS&W became part of the Delaware Otsego System.

- Penn Central had to make the Lehigh Valley available for merger by either Norfolk & Western or Chesapeake & Ohio or, if neither of those roads wanted it, merge it into PC. Lehigh Valley struggled along on its own and entered bankruptcy only three days after Penn Central did.

The beginnings of failure

The merger was not a success. Little thought had been given to unifying the two railroads, which had long been intense rivals with different styles of operation. In the previous decade New York Central had trimmed its physical plant and assembled a young, eager management group under the leadership of Alfred E. Perlman. The

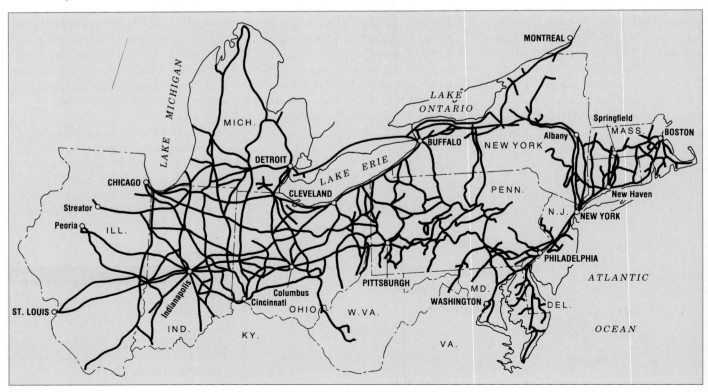

Pennsy was a more conservative and traditional operation. Many of NYC's management people (the "green team") saw that Pennsy (the "red team") was dominant in Penn Central management and soon left for other jobs.

In addition to the problems of unification, the industrial states of the Northeast and Midwest were fast becoming the "Rust Bowl." As industries shut down and moved away, railroads found themselves with excess capacity. The Pennsylvania was worse than practically anyone else in having four or six tracks where one or two would do—tracks that were no longer needed but were still on the tax rolls. West of the Alleghenies, Pennsy and Central duplicated each other's track nearly everywhere. The PC merger was like a late-in-life marriage to which each partner brings a house, a summer cottage, two cars, and several complete sets of china and glassware—plus car payments and mortgages on the houses.

Bankruptcy and reorganization

Pennsy and New York Central came into the merger in the black, but Penn Central's first year of operation yielded a deficit of $2.8 million. In 1969 the deficit was nearly $83 million. PC's net income for 1970 was a deficit of $325.8 million. By then the railroad had entered bankruptcy proceedings—specifically on June 21, 1970. The nation's sixth largest corporation had become the nation's largest bankruptcy.

The reorganization court decided in May 1974 that PC was not reorganizable on the basis of income. A U. S. government corporation, the United States Railway Association, was formed under the provisions of the Regional Rail Reorganization Act of 1973 to develop a plan to save Penn Central. The outcome was that Consolidated Rail Corporation, owned by the U. S. government, took over the railroad properties and operations of Penn Central and six other railroads—Central of New Jersey, Erie Lackawanna, Lehigh Valley, Reading, Lehigh & Hudson River, and Pennsylvania-Reading Seashore Lines—on April 1, 1976.

It was a major step toward nationalization of the railroads of the U. S. They had been nationalized briefly during World War I (through the agency of another

A mix of EMD and GE diesels power a westbound Penn Central freight on the former Pennsy Pittsburgh-St. Louis line at Mingo Junction, Ohio, in 1976. *Jay Potter*

USRA, the United States Railroad Administration), but the U. S. had held out against a world-wide trend toward nationalization of railroads until the creation of Amtrak, which nationalized the country's passenger trains, on May 1, 1971.

Metroliner and TurboTrain

PC participated in two passenger service experiments in cooperation with the U. S. Department of Transportation. Both were aimed at upgrading passenger service in the Northeast Corridor. Between New York and Washington PC inherited the Metroliner experiment that the Pennsy had begun—fast electric trains that were intended for a maximum speed of 160 mph. The inauguration of service was delayed several times, and when it did begin, it was not shown in *The Official Guide*. While not an absolute success, the Metroliners reversed a long decline in ridership on the New York–Washington run.

On the Boston–New York run PC operated a United Aircraft TurboTrain in an effort to beat the 3-hour, 55-minute running time of the New Haven's expresses of the early 1950s. Information about TurboTrain schedules was even more difficult for the public to obtain than Metroliner timetables.

The combination of untested equipment, track that had been allowed to deteriorate, and the general incongruity of

space-age technology and traditional railroad thinking made the services the butt of considerable satire.

Amtrak took over PC's intercity passenger service on May 1, 1971. The Metroliners were soon stored, and their schedules taken by Amfleet trains with accelerated timings. The TurboTrains were scrapped. The commuter service, already subsidized by local authorities, passed first to Conrail and then to other operating authorities.

Aftermath

The Penn Central bankruptcy was a cataclysmic event, both to the railroad industry and to the nation's business community. The PC and its problems were the subject of more words than almost anything else in the railroad industry, everything from diatribes on the passenger business to analyses of the reason for PC's collapse.

Few undertakings have had less auspicious beginnings than Conrail—and Conrail surprised everyone with its success.

FACTS & FIGURES

Year	1968	1975
Miles operated	20,530	19,300
Locomotives	4,411	4,033
Passenger cars	5,046	3,569
Freight cars	187,423	137,546
Reporting marks: PC		
Historical society: pcrrhs.org		

Pennsylvania

A Pennsylvania J1-class 2-10-4 lugs a freight upgrade on Horseshoe Curve, arguably the railroad's most-famous landmark, in 1955. Pennsy had 125 of the big Texas-type locomotives, more than any other railroad. *Bob's Photo*

The original Pennsylvania Railroad ran from Philadelphia to Pittsburgh. Much of the road's subsequent expansion was accomplished by leasing or purchasing other railroads: the Pittsburgh, Fort Wayne & Chicago, the Pittsburgh, Cincinnati, Chicago & St. Louis, the Little Miami Railroad (to Cincinnati); the Northern Central (Baltimore to Sunbury, Pa.); the Philadelphia, Baltimore & Washington; and the Philadelphia & Trenton and the United New Jersey Railroad & Canal Company (to New York).

The Main Line

Philadelphians were slow to recognize that the Erie Canal and the National Road (and later the Baltimore & Ohio Railroad) were funneling to New York and Baltimore commerce that might have come to Philadelphia. A canal opened in 1827 between the Schuylkill and Susquehanna rivers, and another was proposed along the Susquehanna, Juniata, Conemaugh, and Allegheny rivers (along with a 4-mile

tunnel under the summit of the Allegheny Mountains) to link Philadelphia and Pittsburgh. Parts of that project were declared impractical and it was modified to consist of alternate stretches of railroad and canal. In 1828 the Main Line of Public Works was chartered to build a railroad from Philadelphia to Columbia and another across the mountains, as well as canals from Columbia and Pittsburgh to the base of the mountains.

By 1832 canals were open from Columbia to Hollidaysburg and from Pittsburgh to Johnstown. In 1834 a railroad opened from Philadelphia to Columbia and a portage railroad started operation over the mountains. The latter was a series of rope-operated inclined planes; canal boats were designed to be taken apart and hauled over the mountains.

The Pennsylvania Railroad

The pace of the state's action increased when the Baltimore & Ohio requested a charter for a line to Pittsburgh. The B&O

line was chartered, but so was the Pennsylvania Railroad, on April 13, 1846—to build a railroad from Harrisburg to Pittsburgh with a branch to Erie. B&O's charter would be valid only if the Pennsylvania Railroad were not constructed.

The line was surveyed by J. Edgar Thomson, who had built the Georgia Railroad. His operating experience led him to lay out not a line with a steady grade all the way from Harrisburg to the summit of the mountains, but rather a nearly water-level line from Harrisburg to Altoona where a steeper grade (but still less than that of the Baltimore & Ohio) began for a comparatively short assault on the mountains. This arrangement concentrated the problems of a mountain railroad in one area.

Construction began in 1847. In 1849 the Pennsy made an operating contract with the Harrisburg, Portsmouth, Mountjoy & Lancaster (Harrisburg & Lancaster from here on), and by late 1852 rails ran from Philadelphia to Pittsburgh, via a connection with the Portage Railroad between Hollidaysburg and Johnstown. The summit tunnel was opened in February 1854, bypassing the inclined planes and creating a continuous railroad from Harrisburg to Pittsburgh. By then more than half the line had already been double-tracked.

The Main Line of Public Works was constructed with a much smaller loading gauge or clearance diagram than the Pennsylvania. Although the Pennsy was operating the Harrisburg & Lancaster, the road's own management was responsible for maintenance—and not doing much of it. In 1857 PRR bought the Main Line and in 1861 leased the Harrisburg & Lancaster, putting the entire Philadelphia–Pittsburgh line under one management.

To protect its canal the state included a tax on railroad tonnage in PRR's charter. When PRR purchased the Main Line, canals and all, it mounted a long battle to have the tax repealed. The charter was amended only to the point that the funds were used to aid short lines that connected with the Pennsy. Most of those railroads eventually became part of the PRR.

PRR also acquired interests in two major railroads, the Cumberland Valley and the Northern Central. The Cumberland Valley was opened in 1837 from Harrisburg to Chambersburg, and it was extended by another company in 1841 to Hagerstown, Maryland. The Baltimore & Susquehanna was incorporated in 1828 (not long after the Baltimore & Ohio got under way) to build north from Baltimore. Progress was slowed not by construction difficulties but because of the reluctance of Pennsylvania to charter a railroad that would carry commerce to Baltimore. The line reached Harrisburg in 1851 and Sunbury in 1858. By then the railroad companies that formed the route had been consolidated as the Northern Central Railway. A block of its stock that had been held by John Garrett, president of the B&O, was purchased by John Edgar Thomson, PRR's president, about 1860 and transferred to PRR ownership. Pennsy acquired majority ownership of the Northern Central in 1900.

The Pennsylvania Railroad expanded into the northwestern portion of the state by acquiring an interest in the Philadelphia & Erie Railroad in 1862 and assisting that road to complete its line from

Pennsy GG1 No. 4831 is at the head of the *Congressional* awaiting departure from Washington Union Station. *H. W. Pontin; David P. Morgan Library collection*

Sunbury to the city of Erie in 1864. The line to Erie was not particularly successful, but from Sunbury to Driftwood it could serve as part of a freight route with easy grades. The rest of that route was the Allegheny Valley Railroad, conceived as a feeder from Pittsburgh to the New York Central and Erie railroads. The Pennsylvania obtained control in 1868, and in 1874 opened a route with easy grades from Harrisburg to Pittsburgh via the valleys of the Susquehanna and Allegheny rivers. PRR leased the Allegheny Valley Railroad in 1900.

Pittsburgh, Fort Wayne & Chicago

By 1847 the directors of the Pennsylvania were looking west into Ohio. In 1851 they discussed assisting the Ohio & Pennsylvania Railroad which by then was open from Allegheny, Pa., across the Allegheny River from Pittsburgh, to Salem, Ohio. Projected west from the end of the O&P at Crestline, Ohio, was the Ohio & Indiana, which was building a line to Fort Wayne, with extensions to Burlington, Iowa, and, almost incidentally, Chicago.

In 1856 the Ohio & Pennsylvania, the Ohio & Indiana, and the Fort Wayne & Chicago were consolidated as the Pittsburgh, Fort Wayne & Chicago Rail Road. The Pennsylvania held an interest in the road, but not a controlling one. In 1858 the Fort Wayne connected its track with the Pennsylvania at Pittsburgh, and at the end of that year, its rails reached into

Chicago. In 1860 the Fort Wayne leased the Cleveland & Pittsburgh, a line from Cleveland through Alliance (where it crossed the Fort Wayne) to the Ohio River near Wellsville, Ohio, and then upstream to Rochester, Pa., where it again met the Fort Wayne.

In 1869 Jay Gould tried to get control of the Fort Wayne for the Erie, but the Fort Wayne evaded him and was leased by the Pennsy. The lease included the Grand Rapids & Indiana, a line from Richmond, Ind., north through Fort Wayne and Grand Rapids, Mich. In 1873 the Pennsylvania assembled a route into Toledo; about 50 years later it extended the line to Detroit, mostly on trackage rights.

Pittsburgh, Cincinnati, Chicago & St. Louis

West of Pittsburgh lay a string of railroads—Pittsburgh & Steubenville, Steubenville & Indiana, Central Ohio, Columbus & Xenia, and Little Miami—that formed a route through Columbus to Cincinnati. The Pittsburgh & Steubenville was the last to be opened because the state of Virginia, which held a large interest in the B&O, refused to permit a railroad to be built across its narrow strip of territory (now the panhandle of West Virginia) between Pennsylvania and the Ohio River. The Pittsburgh & Steubenville was sold at foreclosure and a new company, the Panhandle Railway, took over in January 1868. In May of that year the Pennsylvania consolidated the Panhandle and the

Alco RS-27 No. 2409 leads five diesels (from three builders) pulling a southbound transfer across the intricate trackwork of Chicago's 21st Street interlocking in the mid-1960s. *Jim Boyd*

Steubenville & Indiana as the Pittsburg, Cincinnati & St. Louis Railway, but the nickname "Panhandle" stuck with it and its successors.

West of Columbus, the Columbus, Chicago & Indiana Central Railway had a line from Columbus to Indianapolis and another from Columbus through Logansport, Ind., to Chicago. The Pennsy leased the CC&IC in February 1869, snatching it from the clutches of Jay Gould.

Beyond Indianapolis lay the Terre Haute & Indianapolis and the St. Louis, Alton & Terre Haute. Because several roads in the area could not agree about the division of traffic, the St. Louis, Vandalia & Terre Haute was constructed between 1868 and 1870 from East St. Louis to Terre Haute. It was leased by the Terre

Haute & Indianapolis, which then made traffic agreements with the Panhandle and the Columbus, Chicago & Indiana Central. (The St. Louis, Alton & Terre Haute wound up in the New York Central System.)

The Little Miami Railroad was incorporated in 1836. By 1846 it had a line from Cincinnati through Xenia to Springfield, Ohio, and it grew by purchasing and leasing lines to Columbus and Dayton. The Pennsylvania saw it as a route to Cincinnati. To force the issue, the Panhandle got control of the Cincinnati & Zanesville, a secondary line into Cincinnati. The Panhandle leased the Little Miami in 1869.

In 1890 the Pittsburg, Cincinnati & St. Louis and several other lines were consolidated as the Pittsburgh, Cincinnati,

Chicago & St. Louis Railway. In 1905 the Vandalia Railroad was incorporated to consolidate the lines west of Indianapolis. The PCC&StL, the Vandalia, and several others were consolidated in 1916 as the Pittsburgh, Cincinnati, Chicago & St. Louis Railroad. At the beginning of 1921 the PCC&StL was leased to the Pennsylvania Railroad.

Pennsylvania Company

With the leases of 1869 the Pennsylvania suddenly had more than 3,000 miles of line west of Pittsburgh. Rather than try to manage it all from Philadelphia, the PRR organized the Pennsylvania Company to hold and manage the lines west of Pittsburgh. The new company also operated the Fort Wayne and its affiliate roads.

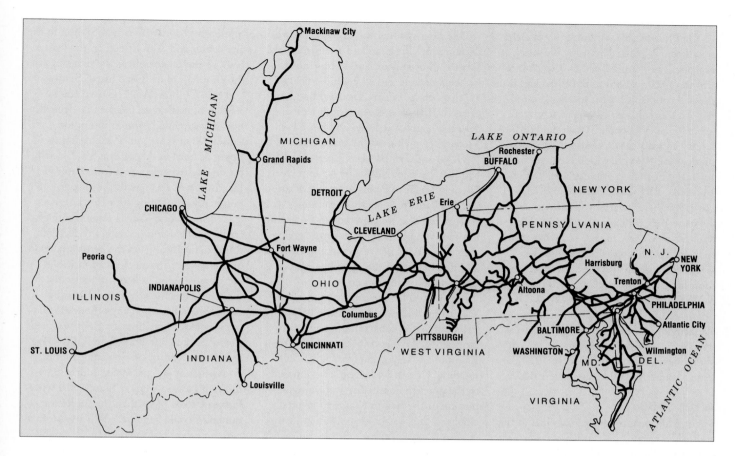

The division of the Pennsylvania system into several more or less autonomous divisions was not altogether successful, partly because the pieces all came together at Pittsburgh, where the yards and terminals were under three managements. In 1918 the Pennsylvania Company ceased to be an operating company and transferred its leases to the Pennsylvania Railroad.

Lines east of Philadelphia

Even with the loyalty to Philadelphia engendered by having its roots and headquarters there, the Pennsy could not ignore New York, both as a city and as a port. Any traffic from the west to New York had to be turned over to the Reading at Harrisburg because there was no through Philadelphia–New York route. In 1863 the PRR contracted with the Philadelphia & Trenton (which was built and opened in 1834), the Camden & Amboy (with lines from Camden to South Amboy and from Trenton to New Brunswick, New Jersey), and the Delaware & Raritan Canal Co. In 1871 it leased the properties of these companies and the United Canal & Railroad Companies of New Jersey, acquiring lines northeast to Jersey City, south to Cape May, and north along the Delaware River

to Belvidere. In the 1880s PRR constructed lines up the Schuylkill Valley into Reading territory and acquired lines from Philadelphia east across New Jersey to the shore. The latter were combined in 1933 with a parallel line owned by the Reading to form the Pennsylvania-Reading Seashore Lines.

The New York Central had long had an advantage in New York: It had a terminal, Grand Central, on Manhattan Island, and all the other roads (except the New Haven, which shared NYC's facilities) had to ferry their passengers to Manhattan. Pennsy's desire for a rail terminal in Manhattan was given added impetus by its acquisition of the Long Island Rail Road in 1900.

After studying proposals for bridges and tunnels, PRR began construction in 1904 of Pennsylvania Station, between Seventh and Eighth Avenues and 31st and 33rd Streets; two tunnels under the Hudson River; four tunnels under the East River; and a double-track line across the Jersey Meadows to connect it to the main line east of Newark—all electrified. The new station opened in 1910.

In 1917 the New York Connecting Railroad, including the Hell Gate Bridge, was opened, creating a rail route from Bay

Ridge in Brooklyn for freight service and from Penn Station for passenger service to a junction with the New Haven in the Bronx.

Lines south of Philadelphia

Baltimore & Ohio had a monopoly on traffic to and from Washington, D. C.— and protection of that monopoly in its charter. B&O refused to make arrangements with the Northern Central or the Philadelphia, Wilmington & Baltimore for through ticketing of passengers and through billing of freight. The Pennsy bought the charter of the Baltimore & Potomac. The B&P was to have built a railroad from Baltimore straight south to the Potomac River at Popes Creek, Md., but it had lain dormant since its chartering in 1853. B&P's charter allowed it to build branch lines no more than 20 miles long, and the PRR saw that a 16-mile branch from Bowie could reach Washington nicely. The resulting Baltimore–Washington route, opened in 1872, was only three miles longer than B&O's. Congress authorized the Pennsylvania to continue its line through Washington and across the Potomac to connect with railroads in Virginia.

The Philadelphia, Wilmington & Baltimore opened in 1838 between the cities of its name. The Pennsy was quick to connect it to the B&P in Baltimore (it had had no physical connection with the B&O), and in 1873 through service was inaugurated between Jersey City and Washington. Both Pennsy and B&O saw the strategic importance of the PW&B, which included lines down the Delmarva Peninsula—PRR got it in 1881. PRR soon extended the Delmarva lines southward by construction of the New York, Philadelphia & Norfolk Railroad to Cape Charles, Va., where they connected with a ferry to Norfolk, Va.

In 1902 the PW&B and the B&P were consolidated as the Philadelphia, Baltimore & Washington Railroad. PB&W and Baltimore & Ohio teamed up to form the Washington Terminal Co., which constructed a new Union Station in Washington, opened in 1907. In 1917 the Pennsylvania Railroad leased the PB&W.

After 1900

Major additions to the Pennsylvania at the end of the nineteenth century were extension of the Grand Rapids & Indiana north to Mackinaw City, Mich. (1882); construction of the Trenton Cutoff, a freight line bypassing Philadelphia (1892); control of the Toledo, Peoria & Western (1893; sold in 1927); and acquisition of the Western New York & Pennsylvania Railroad, which had lines from Oil City, Pa., to Buffalo, N. Y., and Emporium, Pa., and from Emporium to Buffalo and Rochester.

By 1910 the Pennsylvania had achieved full growth. The PRR has been described as a man with his head in Philadelphia, his hands in New York and Washington, and his feet in Chicago and St. Louis. The metaphor, which is unkind to Pittsburgh, requires for completeness a fishnet spread over the man with pins holding it down at Buffalo, Rochester, and Sodus Point, N. Y., Detroit and Mackinaw City, Mich., Marietta, Cincinnati, and Cleveland, Ohio, Madison, Ind., and Louisville, Ky. The hand in New York holds a large fish—Long Island—and resting on the other shoulder is another, the Delmarva Peninsula. Almost everywhere the Pennsy went it was the dominant railroad, the principal exception being the New York Central territory in upstate New York and along the south shore of Lake Erie.

The Pennsylvania was also, by its own declaration, "The Standard Railroad of the World." The standardization was internal. Passenger trains moved behind a fleet of 425 K4s-class Pacifics. The road had hundreds of P70-class coaches built to a single design. Freight was hauled by 579 Lls-class Mikados (which used the same boiler as the K4s) and 598 Ils-class Decapods; PRR had thousands of X29-class 40-foot steel boxcars. Much of Pennsy's standardization was different from nearly everything else in North America: Belpaire boilers on steam locomotives; position-light signals giving their indications with rows of amber lights at different angles; tuscan red passenger cars instead of olive green.

At the turn of the century under the leadership of Alexander Johnston Cassatt, PRR purchased substantial interests in Norfolk & Western, Chesapeake & Ohio, Baltimore & Ohio, and (through B&O) Reading. Cassatt was vigorously opposed to the practice of rebating (returning a portion of the freight charge to favored shippers) and was in favor of an industry-wide end to the practice. Strong railroads would be able to resist pressure to grant rebates, but weaker ones would not—unless they were controlled by strong railroads. In 1906 PRR sold its B&O and C&O interests but increased its Norfolk & Western holdings.

In 1929 the Pennroad Corporation was formed as a holding company owned principally by PRR stockholders. Pennroad purchased sizable interests in Detroit, Toledo & Ironton; Pittsburgh & West Virginia; New Haven; and Boston & Maine. While the Pennsylvania Railroad would have needed ICC approval to purchase interests in other railroads, it was not necessary for the holding company.

The biggest single improvement accomplished by the Pennsylvania Railroad in the 1920s and 1930s was the electrification of its lines from New York to Washington and from Philadelphia to Harrisburg. The nucleus of the project was the 1915 electrification between Philadelphia and Paoli, Pa. That was extended south to Wilmington in 1928. PRR decided to change the New York terminal third-rail electrification to high-voltage AC to match the Philadelphia electrification. The Philadelphia-New York electrification was completed in 1933.

At the same time the road opened two new stations in Philadelphia, Suburban

Station next to Broad Street Station in the city center and 30th Street, on the west bank of the Schuylkill, as the first steps in the elimination of Broad Street Station and the "Chinese Wall" elevated tracks leading to it. Two years later the electrification was extended from Wilmington through Baltimore and Washington to Potomac Yard in Alexandria, Va. Electrification was extended west from Paoli to Harrisburg in 1938, with the thought of eventually continuing it to Pittsburgh.

During World War II Pennsy's freight traffic doubled and passenger traffic quadrupled, much of it on the eastern portion of the system. The electrification was of inestimable value in keeping the traffic moving. After the war Pennsy had the same experiences as many other railroads but seemed slower to react. PRR was slower to dieselize, and when it did so it bought units from every manufacturer.

As freight and passenger traffic moved to the highways, Pennsy found itself with far more fixed plant than the traffic warranted or could support, and it was slow to take up excess trackage or replace double track with Centralized Traffic Control.

PRR was saddled with a heavy passenger business. It had extensive commuter services centered on New York, Philadelphia, and Pittsburgh and lesser ones at Chicago, Washington, Baltimore, and Camden, N. J. It had gone through the Depression without going bankrupt—and bankruptcy can have a salutary effect on old debt. (The Pennsylvania Railroad had to its credit, though, the longest history of dividend payment in U. S. business history.)

Pennsylvania and New York Central surprised the railroad industry by announcing merger plans in November 1957. The two had long been rivals, and the merger would be one of parallel roads rather than end-to-end. The merger took place on Feb. 1, 1968—and Penn Central fell apart faster than it went together.

FACTS & FIGURES

Year	1929	1967
Miles operated	10,512	9,538
Locomotives	6,152	2,211
Passenger cars	7,384	2,632
Freight cars	270,653	112,431
Reporting marks: PRR		
Historical society: prrths.com		

Pennsylvania-Reading Seashore Lines

The Philadelphia–Atlantic City, N. J., corridor was the setting for one of North America's most intense railroad rivalries—back long before the term "corridor" was applied to railroad routes. The two railroads were the Pennsylvania and the Reading—specifically Pennsy's West Jersey & Seashore Railroad and Reading's Atlantic City Railroad.

The West Jersey & Seashore was formed in 1896 by the consolidation of several Pennsylvania Railroad properties in New Jersey, among them the Camden & Atlantic, which had a direct route from Camden to Atlantic City via Haddonfield and Winslow Junction; the West Jersey Railroad (Camden to Cape May through Newfield and Millville plus several branches to towns west of that line); and the West Jersey & Atlantic, which ran from Newfield to Atlantic City. In 1906 the West Jersey & Seashore electrified the Camden–Newfield–Atlantic City route, which served a more heavily populated area and did more local business than the former Camden & Atlantic, with a 650-volt third-rail system. The Newfield–Atlantic City electrification was dismantled in 1931, but Camden–

A Budd Rail Diesel Car, one of 12 owned by Pennsylvania-Reading Seashore Lines, pauses at the Collingswood, N. J., station in September 1964. *William J. Coxey*

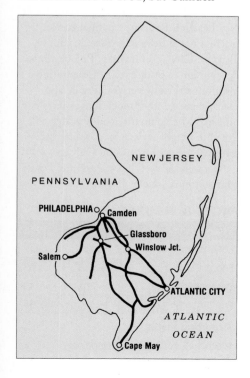

Millville electric trains lasted until 1949.

The Atlantic City Railroad was built as a narrow gauge line from Camden to Atlantic City through Haddon Heights and Winslow Junction, parallel to the Camden & Atlantic and no more than a few miles from it—indeed, within sight much of the way. The narrow gauge line went bankrupt and was acquired in 1883 by the Reading, which standard-gauged and double-tracked it. By the mid-1890s the Reading's subsidiary had reached Cape May, duplicating the West Jersey & Seashore route.

In the 1920s it was clear that the competition and duplication were ruinous, particularly for traffic that could easily be diverted to the highways. Moreover, the business was seasonal—two-thirds of the revenue came from the summer travel to and from the New Jersey shore.

The two railroads agreed in 1932 to consolidate the operations. The Pennsylvania bought two-thirds of Reading's Atlantic City stock for $1 (the AC was piling up deficits because of taxes, interest on debt, and equipment rentals), and assigned its lease of the West Jersey & Seashore to the Atlantic City. The consolidation was effective June 25, 1933, and the Atlantic City

Railroad was renamed Pennsylvania-Reading Seashore Lines on July 15 of that year. The initial rationalization of the lines resulted in the abandonment of the Reading line east of Winslow Junction and the Pennsylvania line route south of Woodbine. Most of the Newfield–Atlantic City line was abandoned in the early 1960s.

PRSL's business, largely passenger, dwindled to a handful of Camden–Atlantic City and Camden–Cape May RDC runs, which eventually terminated at Lindenwold, end of the PATCO rapid transit line, instead of Camden. (PRSL's Camden–Philadelphia ferries were discontinued in 1952.) On July 1, 1982, the last of those runs was replaced by buses because of a federally imposed track speed limit of 15 mph. PRSL's properties were conveyed to Conrail on April 1, 1976.

FACTS & FIGURES

Year	1933	1975
Miles operated	413	307
Locomotives	22	14
Passenger cars	216	—
Freight cars	—	—
Reporting marks: PRSL		

Pere Marquette

The Pere Marquette Railroad was formed on Jan. 1, 1900, by the consolidation of the Chicago & West Michigan Railway, the Detroit, Grand Rapids & Western Railroad, and the Flint & Pere Marquette Railroad.

The three railroads had been built to serve Michigan's lumber industry, and they were feeling the effects of the decline in lumber production as the forests were logged off. Consolidation would make them into one larger, more powerful road.

The Pere Marquette inherited substantial debt from its predecessors, and new management concentrated on absorbing short lines in the interior of Michigan rather than extending the line to Chicago.

New management in 1903 leased the Lake Erie & Detroit River Railway, which had lines from Walkerville (Windsor), Ontario, to St. Thomas and from Sarnia to Erieau and acquired trackage rights over the Michigan Central (ex-Canada Southern) from St. Thomas to Suspension Bridge, N. Y., and over New York Central from Suspension Bridge to Buffalo. The Pere Marquette of Indiana was chartered to build a line from New Buffalo, Mich., to Porter, Ind., 22 miles. That line was opened in 1903, and trackage rights on the Lake Shore & Michigan Southern (NYC) and Chicago Terminal Transfer Railroad (the predecessor of Baltimore & Ohio Chicago Terminal) brought the PM the remaining 52 miles to Chicago.

Pere Marquette Berkshire 1229 darkens the sky as it heads out of Plymouth, Mich., with a freight bound for Grand Rapids. *Robert A. Hadley*

In 1904 the Cincinnati, Hamilton & Dayton leased the PM, but in 1905 the CH&D annulled the lease. PM purchased the Chicago, Cincinnati & Louisville in 1904 and soon let it go—it become Chesapeake & Ohio's line across Indiana. B&O briefly controlled the PM through the CH&D, and the PM was briefly leased to the Erie. Meanwhile, PM had entered receivership, from which it emerged in 1907. It again went into receivership in 1912.

The Pere Marquette Railway was incorporated in 1917 to succeed the Pere Marquette Railroad. The auto industry was growing, and PM was in the right places to serve it. The Van Sweringen brothers acquired control of the road in 1924 to provide markets for coal from their Chesapeake & Ohio; PM's largest source of traffic soon was the interchange with the Hocking Valley (controlled by C&O) at Toledo. In 1928 the ICC approved control of PM by C&O.

In 1932 PM purchased the Manistee & Northeastern Railway, a lumber carrier that reached north from Manistee, Mich., to Traverse City and Grayling. PM began to develop into a bridge route. Despite the a ferry transfer between Walkerville and Detroit and another much longer ferry run on Lake Michigan, the road was able to expedite freight service by avoiding the terminal congestion around Chicago.

Chesapeake & Ohio merged the Pere Marquette on June 6, 1947.

FACTS & FIGURES

Year	1929	1945
Miles operated	2,241	1,949
Locomotives	388	283
Passenger cars	281	113
Freight cars	16,405	14,335
Reporting marks: PM		
Historical society: pmhistsoc.org		

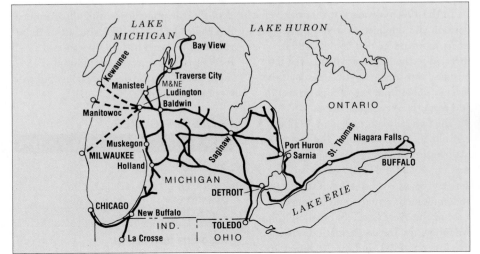

Piedmont & Northern

When the American Tobacco Trust was dissolved in 1910 by the U.S. government, its founder, James B. Duke, turned his attention to industry in the Piedmont area of North and South Carolina. Duke soon owned several power companies, which in turned owned streetcar systems in area cities.

In 1909 William S. Lee, vice-president of Southern Power & Utilities, proposed an interurban railroad system to connect the cities in the Piedmont area. Two companies were organized, the Piedmont Traction Company in North Carolina and the Greenville, Spartanburg & Anderson Railway in South Carolina, with Duke as president and Lee as vice-president. The railroads were planned for freight service from the outset and would use a 1500-volt DC system. The Piedmont Traction Co. was opened in 1912 as was the Greenwood–Greenville segment of the South Carolina company. The line to Spartanburg was opened in 1914, and in that year the two railroads were consolidated as the Piedmont & Northern Railway.

Even while the railroad was under construction, Duke proposed joining the two portions of the system with a 51-mile line between Spartanburg and Charlotte. He also proposed an extension to Norfolk, Virginia. Through the years there were other proposals for extensions to Raleigh, Winston-Salem, and Atlanta, and even to take over and electrify the Georgia & Florida Railroad.

A northbound train stops at Belton, S. C., on its run from Greenwood to Spartanburg in April 1951. *A. C. Kalmbach*

In the 1920s the P&N had rebuilt the line and begun a new emphasis on freight service. A connection between the two portions of the line was again proposed in 1924, but a Southern Railway protest and ICC ruling, backed by the Supreme Court, kept it from happening.

During the Depression the management of the P&N was combined with that of the Durham & Southern, also owned by Duke interests.

By 1950 the road was turning to diesel power. It dropped all passenger service in 1951 and ended electric operation in South Carolina that year. Mainline electric operation ended in North Carolina in 1954, but a short switching operation at Charlotte remained under wires until 1958.

In 1930 Charleston & Western Carolina and Clinchfield (both controlled by Atlantic Coast Line) and Piedmont & Northern proposed a tunnel under the Southern main line at Spartanburg to connect the Clinchfield directly with the other two without involving the Southern for a half-mile move. The 750-foot tunnel was opened in 1963.

In 1965 P&N constructed a branch north from Mount Holly, N. C., to a new Duke Power Co. plant at Terrell. That same year the Duke interests decided to divest their P&N holdings and looked for a buyer. Seaboard Air Line was interested; following the Seaboard Coast Line merger, the SCL merged the Piedmont & Northern July 1, 1969.

FACTS & FIGURES

Year	1929	1968
Miles operated	127	150
Locomotives	17	18
Passenger cars	30	—
Freight cars	340	23
Reporting marks: PN		

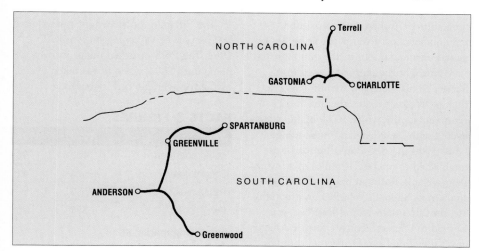

Pittsburg & Shawmut

Three yellow-and-red EMD SW9s bring a long cut of hopper cars from the coal-cleaning plant at Ringgold, Pa. Pittsburg & Shawmut dieselized in 1953 with a fleet of nine of these 1200-h.p. switchers. For the U.S. Bicentennial, they were repainted red-white-and-blue. *Richard J. Cook*

In 1903 the Brookville & Mahoning Railroad was incorporated by Edward Searles, who in 1882 had married the widow of Mark Hopkins (one of the four men who built the Central Pacific) and in 1891 had inherited her fortune. The first portion of the line was built south from Brookville, Pa., to Knoxdale, 9 miles; soon the railroad also had a line from Brookville east to Brockway. From 1908 to 1916 the railroad was leased and operated by the Pittsburg, Shawmut & Northern (for a P&S map, see next page). In 1910 the Brookville & Mahoning changed its name to Pittsburg & Shawmut. (Shawmut is said to be a reference to a Boston bank that had an interest in the railroad.)

The railroad prospered on coal traffic, some of which came from mines of the Allegheny River Mining Co., owned by the railroad.

The Shawmut dieselized in 1953 with nine SW9s. To celebrate the nation's bicentennial in 1976 these were repainted, renumbered, and given patriotic names or names of men famous in the gun industry.

Control of the railroad passed from Searles to his secretary, Arthur T. Walker, then to Walker's estate, then to the Dumaine family, which has long been connected with New England railroading.

In 1990 the Red Bank Railroad was established to operate 10 miles of a former Pennsylvania Railroad branch from Lawsonham to Sligo, Pa. In 1991 another affiliate, the Mountain Laurel Railroad, was formed to operate Pennsy's former Allegheny Valley line from Driftwood through

Brookville to Lawsonham, and a former New York Central branch from Brookville to Gretchen (later cut back to Reidsburg; no longer on the map).

The Pittsburg & Shawmut was acquired by Genesee & Wyoming on April 27, 1996. The P&S operated under its own name until 2004, when it was taken over by G&W's Buffalo & Pittsburgh.

FACTS & FIGURES

Year	1929	1994
Miles operated	103	96
Locomotives	24	11
Passenger cars	8	—
Freight cars	1,591	675
Reporting marks: PS		

Pittsburg, Shawmut & Northern

Number 71, a 2-8-0, leads a southbound freight between West Eldred and Corryville, Pa., in February 1947, just before the road was abandoned. *H. D. Runey*

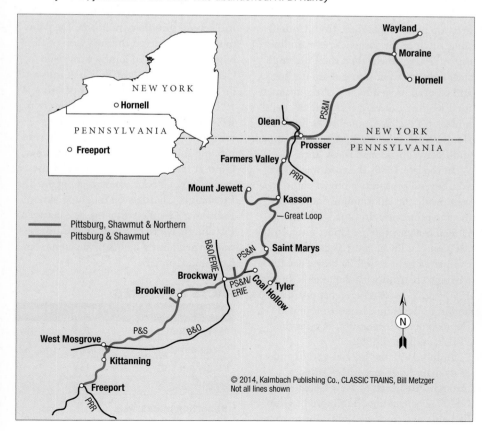

© 2014, Kalmbach Publishing Co., CLASSIC TRAINS, Bill Metzger
Not all lines shown

The Pittsburg, Shawmut & Northern was incorporated in 1899 to consolidate five small railroads, some standard gauge and some narrow, in southwestern New York and northwestern Pennsylvania. The road's immediate task was to join the five separate parts with new construction and standard-gauge the narrow ones to form a route from Wayland and Hornell, N. Y., to Hyde, Pa., north of Brockway in the Shawmut area (a tract of coal land which had been named by a group of Boston industrialists).

The PS&N then organized the Brookville & Mahoning (which later became the Pittsburg & Shawmut Railroad) to extend the line southwest toward Pittsburgh (at the time, spelled without the "h"). P&S was leased to and operated by the PS&N until 1916, when it gained independence.

No sooner had the PS&N assembled its railroad than it found it could not pay the interest on the money borrowed to finance construction. It entered receivership in 1905. The road earned a modest income most years, but it could not begin to repay its accrued debt, nor could it formulate an acceptable reorganization plan. The PS&N served no major industrial centers; the few large towns that it reached were well served by other roads. Coal and lumber formed the Shawmut's principal traffic, and both gradually disappeared as the mountains were logged off and the mines played out. In the mid-1940s the courts and the management decided that 40 years of receivership was enough, and the road was abandoned in its entirety in 1947.

Only PS&N's herald survived: In 1978 onetime affiliate Pittsburg & Shawmut began using, for a time, the diamond-shaped "Shawmut Line" emblem in its ads.

FACTS & FIGURES

Year	1929	1945
Miles operated	198	190
Locomotives	33	16
Passenger cars	18	—
Freight cars	416	220
Reporting marks: PS&N		

Pittsburgh & Lake Erie

The Pittsburgh & Lake Erie was chartered in 1875 and opened from Pittsburgh, Pa., to Youngstown, Ohio, in 1879. Cornelius Vanderbilt of the New York Central subscribed to 15 percent of the railroad's stock, because he saw the P&LE as the route by which his New York Central system could enter Pittsburgh to compete with the Pennsylvania Railroad to serve the steel industry. NYC gained control of P&LE in 1889, and from then on it was for all practical purposes a division of the NYC—and a highly profitable one.

The portion of the P&LE south of Pittsburgh was incorporated in 1881 as the Pittsburgh, McKeesport & Youghiogheny. It was jointly owned by P&LE and NYC and was operated as part of P&LE. In 1965 P&LE bought NYC's half interest in the PMcK&Y.

When Penn Central (successor to New York Central) went bankrupt in 1970, it owed P&LE $15 million and it owned 92.6 percent of P&LE's stock. Officials who held positions with both PC and P&LE were replaced with new management, and P&LE began to chart an independent course. Local congressmen were persuaded by P&LE management, labor, and shippers to amend the Regional Rail Reorganization Act of 1973 to allow

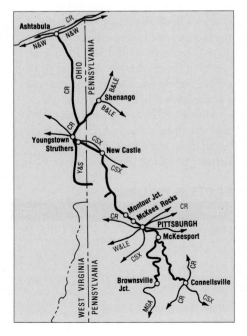

Pittsburgh & Lake Erie Berkshire No. 9401, among the last steam locomotives built by Alco (in 1948) leads a southbound freight at Beaver, Pa., on June 20, 1948. *Richard J. Cook*

solvent subsidiaries of Penn Central to stay out of Conrail. Later negotiations gave P&LE access to Norfolk & Western's ex-Nickel Plate line at Ashtabula, Ohio, via trackage rights on Conrail north from Youngstown. On Feb. 27, 1979, Penn Central sold the Pittsburgh & Lake Erie Railroad to the new Pittsburgh & Lake Erie Company, which subsequently became a private corporation.

The new P&LE made a good start. It drew up plans to purchase from Conrail some or all of the former Erie main line east of Youngstown. Then the Pittsburgh steel industry went into a sharp decline and Conrail proved to be a sharp competitor. Flooding caused the closure of coal mines on P&LE's Connellsville line and along P&LE subsidiary Montour Railroad, and P&LE abandoned those lines.

In the late 1980s the road was up for sale. Several prospective buyers came and went while the labor unions fought for income protection. In June 1989 the United States Supreme Court reversed the decision of a lower court and upheld a company's right to sell its business without having to bargain with the unions. In May 1990 P&LE reached agreement with its 14 unions on severance benefits. Railroad Development Corporation bought the P&LE on June 6, 1990.

In July 1991 the P&LE sold 61 miles of its main line—from McKeesport through Pittsburgh to New Castle—to CSX Transportation. Baltimore & Ohio had obtained trackage rights on the route

in 1934 to bypass the steep grades and sharp curves of its own line west of Pittsburgh. The sale reversed the owner-tenant relationship and generated some much-needed cash for P&LE.

P&LE continued to decline. P&LE's last day of operation was Sept. 11, 1992. The next day, the remaining rail lines and trackage rights were purchased by Three Rivers Railway, a CSX subsidiary.

P&LE operated few branch lines but had several subsidiary railroads. The Montour Railroad served the area west of Pittsburgh. It was owned jointly with Penn Central; P&LE bought PC's half interest in 1975. The Montour ceased operation in 1983, and abandonment was approved in 1986. The Montour owned the Youngstown & Southern Railway, a 35-mile road running south and east from Youngstown, Ohio. It remains in operation under the ownership of P&LE's parent company. The Pittsburgh, Chartiers & Youghiogheny Railway, a 12-mile switching line between Pittsburgh, McKees Rocks, and Carnegie, was owned jointly by P&LE's parent company and Conrail.

FACTS & FIGURES

Year	1929	1991
Miles operated	231	404
Locomotives	267	39
Passenger cars	158	—
Freight cars	33,265	3,174
Reporting marks: PLE		

Pittsburgh & West Virginia

In 1881 Jay Gould acquired control of the barely begun Wheeling & Lake Erie Rail Road. The Wheeling was to be a Toledo, Ohio–Wheeling, W. Va., link in a chain of railroads to connect the Wabash with the Central of New Jersey—and more than that, a link in the transcontinental system Gould sought to assemble. In the mid-1880s Gould lost much of his railroad empire, but he was able to pass the Missouri Pacific and the Wabash on to his son George.

George Gould saw that the Wheeling & Lake Erie put him within 60 miles of the industries of Pittsburgh. Spurred by a traffic agreement with Andrew Carnegie, who was feuding with the Pennsylvania Railroad, Gould built a railroad into Pittsburgh from the west to form an eastern extension of the Wheeling & Lake Erie and the Wabash. The easy locations for railroads had already been taken, so the new line was built from hilltop to hilltop and finally through Mount Washington in a tunnel, across the Monongahela on an immense cantilever bridge, and into an elaborate passenger terminal in downtown Pittsburgh. It was an expensive railroad.

It was completed in 1904 and the three companies that had built the lines were consolidated as the Wabash Pittsburgh Terminal Railway, though it and the West Side Belt (a coal-hauling line around the southern part of Pittsburgh) were operated as an integral part of the W&LE.

By 1904 George Gould had acquired control of the Western Maryland and was trying, as his father had tried, to assemble a transcontinental railroad system. Western Maryland planned to build an extension from Cumberland, Md., northwest to

One of P&WV's seven 2-6-6-4s leads a freight across the Monongahela River bridge at Belle Vernon, Pa. *Ralph E. Hallock*

Connellsville, Pa., and Wabash Pittsburgh Terminal projected a 40-mile extension southeast to Connellsville.

The Panic of 1907, the cost of building the WPT, and an accord between Andrew Carnegie and the Pennsylvania put an end to Gould's plans. Both WPT and the Wheeling & Lake Erie entered receivership in 1909.

The Pittsburgh & West Virginia Railway was incorporated as successor under foreclosure to the Wabash Pittsburgh Terminal Railway. In the 1920s Frank Taplin, president of the P&WV, made overtures to control the Wheeling & Lake Erie and the Western Maryland, but the ICC disapproved. In 1931 Taplin completed the extension to Connellsville, where the Western Maryland had been waiting since 1912. About that time, control of the P&WV was acquired by the Pennroad Corporation, a holding company that shared many officers with the Pennsylvania Railroad.

During the last 1930s the P&WV developed into a bridge railroad, part of

the "alphabet route" between the Midwest and the East (Nickel Plate, Wheeling & Lake Erie, P&WV, Western Maryland, and Reading). P&WV pulled out of downtown Pittsburgh after its freight house burned in 1946—the fire may well have sparked the redevelopment of downtown Pittsburgh. In 1949 the road tore down its nine-story office building (the passenger terminal in it had lain idle since 1931), dismantled its downtown Monongahela River bridge, and sealed the Mount Washington tunnel.

The Pittsburgh & West Virginia was a natural eastern extension of the Wheeling & Lake Erie (later Nickel Plate), providing access to the industries of Pittsburgh, as George Gould had intended years before. When Norfolk & Western merged the Nickel Plate in 1964 it leased the Pittsburgh & West Virginia.

In 1990 Norfolk Southern sold most of the former Wheeling & Lake Erie to form a new Wheeling & Lake Erie Railway. Included in the deal was the lease of the Pittsburgh & West Virginia.

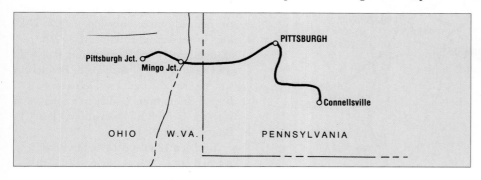

FACTS & FIGURES

Year	1929	1963
Miles operated	89	132
Locomotives	30	25
Passenger cars	5	—
Freight cars	5,589	1,334
Reporting marks: P&WV		

Reading

A Reading EMD F3A and an Alco FB-1 team up on a mixed freight in the 1960s. Reading bought cab units from both Electro-Motive (FTs, F3s, and F7s) as well as Alco (FA-1, FB-1), and only its cab units wore this attractive livery. *Jim McClellan*

The Philadelphia & Reading Railroad was chartered in 1833 and opened in 1842 from Philadelphia along the Schuylkill River through Reading to Pottsville, Pa. The purpose of the railroad was to carry anthracite to Philadelphia.

The Philadelphia & Reading grew by acquiring other roads. It assisted construction of the Lebanon Valley Railroad from Reading to Harrisburg; in 1858 the Lebanon Valley was merged into the Philadelphia & Reading. By 1869 the P&R had acquired the East Pennsylvania Railroad between Reading and Allentown. In 1870 the P&R leased the Philadelphia, Germantown & Norristown Railroad, which had been built between 1831 and 1835 from Philadelphia to Germantown and along the east bank of the Schuylkill to Norristown.

In 1869 Franklin B. Gowen became president of the P&R and began buying coal lands for the railroad. The Philadelphia & Reading Coal & Iron Co. acquired about 30 percent of the anthracite land in Pennsylvania, but the cost of the land put the railroad into receivership in 1880. During Gowen's administration, the P&R acquired the North Pennsylvania Railroad, which ran from Philadelphia to Bethlehem and Yardley, and built the Delaware & Bound Brook from Yardley to a connection with the Central Railroad of New Jersey at Bound Brook, N. J.

Between 1880 and 1890, the P&R reached out to Shippensburg, Pa., with a

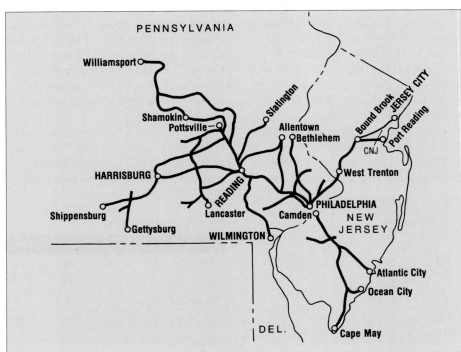

line that would eventually carry much of the road's bridge traffic, and extended a line from Bound Brook to a new port, Port Reading, on the New Jersey shore of Arthur Kill (the body of water that separates Staten Island from the mainland).

McLeod's brief empire

Archibald A. McLeod became president of the P&R in 1890. The P&R leased the Central Railroad of New Jersey (P&R had previously leased the CNJ between 1883 and 1887) and the Lehigh Valley; the three railroads transported more than half of the country's mined coal at the time. To get a better grip on the New England coal market, the P&R acquired control of the Poughkeepsie Bridge route, the Boston & Maine, and the New York & New England. The P&R was reaching out for the Old Colony when it collapsed once again into receivership.

Lines in New Jersey

The Philadelphia & Reading expanded into New Jersey in 1883 by purchasing the Atlantic City Railroad, a narrow gauge line from Camden to Atlantic City, N. J. P&R standard-gauged and double-tracked the line—Philadelphia–Atlantic City passenger traffic was growing—and extended it to Cape May.

By the 1930s traffic to the New Jersey seashore was declining on the Atlantic City Railroad and also on Pennsylvania Railroad's West Jersey & Seashore, which duplicated the Atlantic City Railroad at almost every point. In 1932 the Reading and the Pennsy agreed to consolidate operations. The Pennsylvania bought two-thirds of Reading's Atlantic City stock and assigned its lease of the West Jersey & Seashore to the Atlantic City, which was renamed Pennsylvania-Reading Seashore Lines. The consolidation took effect June 25, 1933.

The Reading Company

In the reorganization of 1896, the railroad and the coal company both became properties of the Reading Company, a holding company. In 1898 the Reading leased the Wilmington & Northern Railroad, a line from Reading to Wilmington, Del., and in 1901, the Reading acquired control of the Central of New Jersey. At that same time the Baltimore & Ohio Railroad purchased a controlling interest in the Reading.

Reading 2-10-2 No. 3012, a 1931 Baldwin product, leads a train of anthracite along the bank of the Schuylkill River at Tamaqua, Pa., in July 1953. *David P. Morgan Library collection*

At the end of 1923 the Reading Company merged several of its wholly owned subsidiary railroads (the Philadelphia & Reading chief among them) and became an operating company. Between 1929 and 1933, Reading electrified its Philadelphia suburban service.

Beginning in 1945 the Reading underwent a series of corporate simplifications, merging controlled and leased lines. In 1963 Reading acquired the Lehigh & Susquehanna Railroad from Lehigh Coal & Navigation—Central of New Jersey's lines in Pennsylvania—and in 1968 Reading acquired the Cornwall Railroad, a 12-mile line from Lebanon to Mount Hope, Pa., from Bethlehem Steel.

As the use of coal for domestic heating—especially anthracite—dwindled, the Reading supplemented its coal traffic with bridge traffic between the Western Maryland at Shippensburg and connections at Allentown for New York and New England. Reading became part of the "alphabet route" between the Midwest and the East Coast: NKP, W&LE, P&WV, WM, RDG, L&HR. The bridge traffic, though, could not compensate for the fact that the Reading's freight business looked more like that of a switching and terminal railroad than a long-haul, line-haul carrier.

In 1971 Reading's passenger trains were deemed commuter trains and therefore were not taken over by Amtrak. Service on Philadelphia-Reading-Pottsville and Philadelphia-Bethlehem routes continued to operate for another 10 years. Philadelphia–New York service, once part of the *Royal Blue* route operated in partnership with Baltimore & Ohio and Central of New Jersey, was down to a single Newark–West Trenton train when service ceased in November 1982.

The Reading entered bankruptcy proceedings on Nov. 23, 1971. The company's railroad operations were taken over by Conrail on April 1, 1976 (although the holding company existed until 2000). Southeastern Pennsylvania Transportation Authority subsequently took over operation of Reading's extensive Philadelphia-area commuter service.

FACTS & FIGURES

Year	1929	1975
Miles operated	1,460	1,149
Locomotives	988	225
Passenger cars	910	176
Freight cars	43,298	12,213

Reporting marks: RDG

Historical society: readingrailroad.org

Richmond, Fredericksburg & Potomac

The Richmond, Fredericksburg & Potomac was a strategic link in the chain of railroads along the east coast. The Atlantic Coast Line and Seaboard Air Line both terminated in Richmond, the Baltimore & Ohio reached as far south as Washington, and the Pennsylvania reached just beyond Washington to Alexandria, Va. RF&P tied them together and also carried the Southern Railway's trains the last few miles from Alexandria to Washington—Chesapeake & Ohio trains, too, which ran on Southern rails. It was a double-track main line without any branches. It did little local business, and through passenger and freight trains ran at pretty much the same speed along the line.

The RF&P was chartered in 1834 to build northward from Richmond, Va., to a point on the Potomac River, where it would connect with steamboats to Washington, D. C. The rail route from Richmond to Washington was opened in 1872

A northbound freight rolls into Alexandria, Va., almost at its destination of Potomac Yard, on Dec. 29, 1949. The A-B-A set of blue-and-gray F units is nearly brand new. *Charles Wales*

© 2014, Kalmbach Publishing Co., CLASSIC TRAINS, Bill Metzger

with the completion of the Alexandria & Fredericksburg, a subsidiary of the Pennsylvania, south to a connection with the RF&P at Quantico. The northernmost portion of the route was the Alexandria & Washington, also a PRR subsidiary. In 1890 the two Pennsy properties were consolidated as the Washington Southern, and in 1901 the Richmond-Washington Company was formed to operate the WS and the RF&P as a single railroad. In 1920 the RF&P absorbed the WS.

Richmond-Washington owned about three-fourths of RF&P's common stock; the remainder was owned by the Virginia Supplemental Retirement System and the public. The Richmond-Washington Company was equally owned until the 1960s by SAL, ACL, C&O, B&O, Southern, and Pennsylvania. Penn Central relinquished its ex-PRR share in 1978, and mergers brought ownership down to CSX (80 percent) and Norfolk Southern (20 percent). The RF&P became a link between two halves of CSX, the former Chessie System at Washington and the former Seaboard System at Richmond. Because CSX trains

ran straight through and much of NS's traffic had been shifted to the Shenandoah Valley line, RF&P's enormous Potomac Yard in Alexandria was no longer necessary—and it was valuable real estate.

CSX offered merger in 1990, but the Virginia legislature rejected the offer. Later that year, the Virginia Retirement System acquired a block of RF&P stock from Norfolk Southern and got together with CSX on another proposal: CSX would get the railroad and the retirement system would get CSX's shares in the RF&P and be free to develop the real estate. By the end of 1991 CSX had absorbed the RF&P's operation.

FACTS & FIGURES

Year	1929	1990
Miles operated	118	113
Locomotives	101	31
Passenger cars	117	—
Freight cars	1,319	1,876

Reporting marks: RFP

Historical society: rfandp.org

Rio Grande Southern

Galloping Goose No. 4—or more properly, Motor No. 4 of the Rio Grande Southern—rolls northward past Trout Lake, between Lizard Head Pass and Ophir. *Otto Perry*

In 1882 the Denver & Rio Grande completed its line from Durango to Silverton, Colo. In 1887, it pushed a line south from Montrose to Ouray, a silver-mining center about 15 miles north of Silverton—straight-line distance, ignoring Red Mountain. Otto Mears surveyed and built a wagon road from Silverton over Red Mountain Pass. He then built the Silverton Railroad on much the same alignment as far as Albany, about 8 miles short of Ouray. (See the map with the Denver & Rio Grande Western on page 120.) To descend from Albany to Ouray, the railroad would have to use stairs, not rails, or resort to extremely expensive construction to build a line that would be subject to rockslides part of the year and snowslides during the rest.

Mears knew that the ore-rich area west and northwest of Durango needed transportation, so he had a railroad surveyed from Dallas, north of Ridgway, to Durango by way of Telluride, Rico, and Dolores. The Rio Grande Southern Railroad was incorporated in 1889 and completed in 1891. The route crossed four major summits, highest of which was Lizard Head Pass

(10,250 feet), and included innumerable trestles and bridges.

The road basked briefly in the prosperity that resulted from the passage of the Silver Purchase Act in 1890. Repeal of the act in 1893, however, ended the prosperity, and the Rio Grande Southern entered receivership because of its construction debt. The Denver & Rio Grande gained control in 1893.

The RGS continued to exist as a separate entity on paper, but it was operated as a division of its parent, eking out an existence carrying ore and livestock while battling snow and slides. Even though it operated at a profit, it never earned enough to cover interest on its bonds or issue a stock dividend. In 1929 it was again placed in the care of a receiver, Victor Miller.

In 1931 RGS assembled a motor rail car from Buick parts. It was successful enough that the road built a fleet of motor cars from Pierce-Arrow parts. These cars, which acquired the nickname "Galloping Geese," replaced the mixed trains that had previously replaced the passenger trains. They became a symbol of the railroad.

In 1942 the property of the RGS was purchased by the Defense Supplies Corporation (one of the road's cargoes during World War II was uranium ore from mines at Vanadium). In spite of Galloping Geese and uranium, the Rio Grande Southern continued to decline. Its problems included floods and washouts, a fire that destroyed a large lumber mill, the explosion of the boiler of its rotary snowplow, a drop in zinc prices, and loss of the mail contract. The imposition of a surcharge on every car of freight drove away business. There were no formal protests to Rio Grande Southern's abandonment petition, and the last train ran on Dec. 27, 1951.

FACTS & FIGURES

Year	1929	1951
Miles operated	174	172
Locomotives	13	5
Passenger cars	5	—
Freight cars	9	—
Reporting marks: RGS		
Historical society: narrowgauge.org		

Rutland

GREEN MT
RUTLAND
GATEWAY

Two major themes in New England railroad history are the competition between railroads to build lines to the Great Lakes, and the consolidation of many small railroads into a few major ones. Rutland's development is easiest to understand considered route by route: the original Bellows Falls–Rutland–Burlington route diagonally across Vermont, the line south from Rutland through Bennington to Chatham, N. Y., and the tentacle from Burlington across the north end of Lake Champlain to Ogdensburg on the St. Lawrence River.

Bellows Falls–Rutland–Burlington

The Champlain & Connecticut River Rail Road Company was incorporated Nov. 1, 1843, to build a railroad between Bellows Falls and Burlington, Vt., as part of a route from Boston to Ogdensburg, N. Y. The enterprise was reorganized as the Rutland & Burlington Railroad in 1847, and was completed in December 1849. At Bellows Falls, there were connections southeast to Boston and south down the Connecticut River, but at Burlington, the railroad fought and feuded with the Vermont Central for traffic and for connections with the Vermont & Canada at nearby Essex Junction. In 1854 the Rutland & Burlington defaulted on interest payments. It was reorganized in 1867 as the Rutland Railroad.

The Vermont Central leased the Rutland on Dec. 30, 1870, partly to acquire Rutland's leases of the Vermont Valley (Bellows Falls south to Brattleboro, Vt.) and the Vermont & Massachusetts (Brattleboro to Millers Falls, Mass.), which gave Vermont Central a connection to the New London Northern and a water route from New London, Conn., to New York.

A more pressing reason for the lease was to forestall a move by the Rutland to construct a line around the south end of Lake Champlain and then north along the west shore of the lake to a connection west to Ogdensburg. The terms of the lease were particularly beneficial to the Rutland; the rental was better than the income the Rutland would earn operating independently.

In 1887 Delaware & Hudson gained

An eastbound milk train from Ogdensburg, N. Y., passes the Rutland/Central Vermont station at Alburgh, Vt., in October 1951, behind green-and-yellow RS3 No. 204. *Jim Shaughnessy*

control of the Rutland, which was still leased to the Central Vermont (the 1873 successor to the Vermont Central). The Rutland renewed its lease to the CV in 1890. CV entered receivership in 1896 and terminated the lease of the Rutland.

Rutland–Bennington–Chatham

The Western Vermont Railroad was chartered in 1845 to build south from Rutland to North Bennington and west to a connection with the Troy & Boston at White Creek, N. Y. The railroad opened in 1853 and was leased to the T&B in 1857, forming a route from Boston to the Hudson River in conjunction with the Rutland & Burlington, Cheshire, and Fitchburg railroads. The WV was renamed the Bennington & Rutland in 1865.

When the Hoosac Tunnel in western Massachusetts opened in 1875, the T&B gained a direct route to Boston and cast off the B&R. The B&R filed suit against the T&B. Then the B&R merged with the Lebanon Springs, a line that meandered north from Chatham, N. Y., to form the Harlem Extension Railroad. It was essentially a northward extension of the New York & Harlem. Vermont Central leased the Harlem Extension from 1873 to 1877. The Harlem Extension emerged from the

lease as two railroads, the Harlem Extension South (later the Lebanon Springs), then Chatham & Lebanon Valley, and the Bennington & Rutland. The Rutland purchased the Bennington & Rutland in 1900 and the Chatham & Lebanon Valley in 1901.

Burlington–Ogdensburg

Ogdensburg, N. Y., was at the eastern limit of Great Lakes and St. Lawrence River navigation. A railroad between Ogdensburg and Lake Champlain was discussed as early as 1830, but it was 1850 before the Northern Railroad (of New York) opened between Ogdensburg and Rouses Point. It was extended east to connect with the Vermont & Canada in 1852, and the company was eventually reorganized as the Ogdensburg & Lake Champlain in 1864. A subsidiary, the Ogdensburg Transportation Company, operated a fleet of lake boats between Ogdensburg and Chicago. The O&LC was leased to the Vermont Central in 1870. It resumed independent operation after CV entered receivership in 1896. In 1901 the Rutland purchased the road.

To connect the O&LC with its own line, the Rutland chartered the Rutland & Canadian Railroad, which quickly constructed a line from Burlington to Rouses

Point. The line used the islands at the north end of Lake Champlain as stepping stones; a 3-mile causeway connected the islands with the mainland north of Burlington. In 1901 the line opened and the company was consolidated with the Rutland.

By 1902 the Rutland participated in Boston–Montreal and New York–Montreal passenger traffic, and in conjunction with its navigation line on the Great Lakes, it offered freight service between New England and Chicago. It did a good business carrying Boston- and New York-bound milk out of Vermont.

New York Central control

Shortly after 1900 the New York Central & Hudson River, and William Seward Webb (son-in-law of William H. Vanderbilt of the NYC&HR), began to buy Rutland stock. Webb became president of the Rutland in 1902, and by 1904, NYC interests owned more than half the capital stock of the Rutland. The railroad entered a period of NYC control and prosperity.

About that same time, the New Haven acquired control of the New York, Ontario & Western. The New Haven regarded New England as its own territory and was concerned about New York Central's acquisitions of the Boston & Albany and the Rutland. NYC, for similar reasons, was wary of NH's interest in the NYO&W. There was discussion of an exchange of

subsidiaries. In 1911 the New Haven purchased half of the New York Central interest in the Rutland.

The Panama Canal Act of 1915 amended the Interstate Commerce Act to prohibit railroad ownership of a competing interstate water carrier. The Interstate Commerce Commission ruled that Rutland's Great Lakes boats competed with parent New York Central. The boats were discontinued, and their traffic, which formed a large part of Rutland's freight business, wound up on NYC trains.

Control by the United States Railroad Administration during World War I brought a great increase of traffic to the Rutland but at a considerable cost in deferred maintenance. Passenger traffic began to trickle away, and floods in 1927 washed out much of Rutland's line. The Rutland was strong enough financially to remain solvent through much of the Great Depression, but on May 5, 1938, the Rutland entered receivership.

Economy measures, wage cuts, tax reductions, and a "Save the Rutland" Club kept the railroad going. Symbolic of the effort was a new Bellows Falls-Norwood, N. Y., freight train, *The Whippet*, for which the road streamstyled and painted a 1913-vintage 2-8-0. It was more than 12 years before a new company emerged—the Rutland Railway, which came into existence on Nov. 1, 1950.

The revived Rutland

Heading the management committee of the new company was Gardner Caverly, a major bondholder. He scrapped 25 miles of sidings and branches, and used the scrap value of Rutland's roster of steam locomotives and the worst of the freight cars as a down payment on 15 diesels. He scrapped the Bennington-Chatham line to pay for 450 new boxcars, which wore yellow and green paint and a new herald, plus 70 gondolas and 27 covered hopper cars.

A short strike in the summer of 1953 had the beneficial effect of ridding the Rutland of its passenger trains, which were expensive to operate and ran almost empty. The physical plant of the railroad was modernized and the labor force thinned. In 1957 the Rutland paid a dividend on its preferred stock.

Rutland's employees were being paid less than the national standard, and in September 1960, they walked out. Traffic, particularly milk, was declining, and the company had no cash reserve. An injunction brought the employees back to work, but the cooling-off period ended on Sept. 25, 1961, and so did all service on the Rutland Railway. Neither management nor labor would compromise, and on Dec. 4, 1961, the Rutland petitioned for abandonment. Hearings went on for more than a year, but the Rutland was dead.

The state of Vermont bought the Burlington-Bennington-White Creek and Rutland-Bellows Falls lines. The Vermont Railway began operation on the former on January 6, 1964, and the Green Mountain Railroad began freight service between Bellows Falls and Rutland in April 1965 after a season of steam passenger operation on the line by the Steamtown museum at Bellows Falls. Service resumed on the Norwood-Ogdensburg portion of the former O&LC in 1967 following its acquisition by the Ogdensburg Bridge & Port Authority.

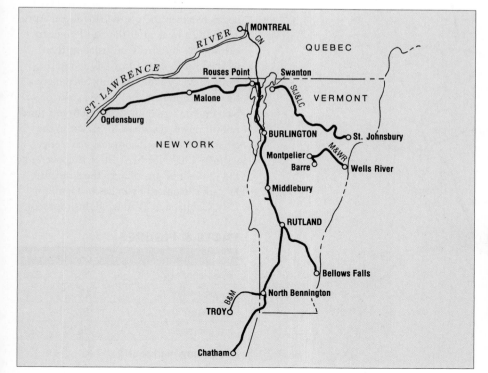

FACTS & FIGURES

Year	1929	1961
Miles operated	413	391
Locomotives	85	15
Passenger cars	138	—
Freight cars	1,778	465
Reporting marks: R, RUT		
Historical society: rutlandrr.org		

Sacramento Northern

At one time Sacramento Northern offered the longest interurban ride in the world, 183 miles from San Francisco to Chico, Calif. The ride included the Bay Bridge between San Francisco and Oakland, a tunnel through the Oakland hills, a train ferry across Suisun Bay just west of the confluence of the Sacramento and San Joaquin rivers, a fast ride across California's delta country, and a long look at the agricultural Sacramento Valley.

Sacramento Northern abandoned much of its main line, leaving odds and ends of track in the towns and cities it served, and it shared most of its officers with parent Western Pacific (or vice versa, to be more accurate). The Western Pacific was acquired by Union Pacific in 1982, and as a result, by 1984, SN no longer had interchange freight cars of its own and most of its officials were in Omaha.

Sacramento Northern Combine 1017 sits under a maze of overhead wires next to a bus bound for San Francisco in 1940. *Linn Westcott*

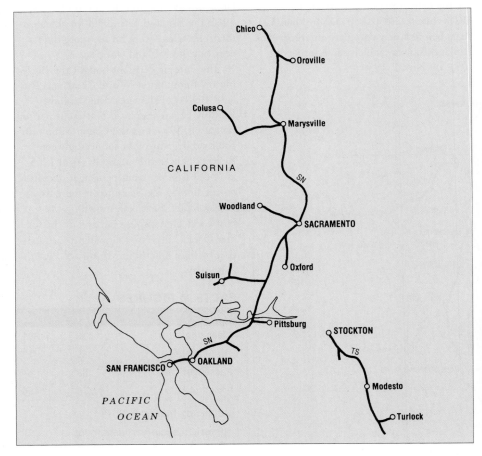

Northern Electric

The Northern Electric Company was incorporated in 1905 to build a railroad from Chico to Sacramento, 90 miles long. Construction began at Chico, and service began between there and Oroville on April 25, 1906, a week after the San Francisco earthquake and fire. Construction then worked south from Oroville Junction through Marysville, reaching Sacramento, the state capital, in 1907. The extension to Sacramento was built with a 600-volt third rail for power distribution, except in the cities, where it used conventional trolley wire. In 1909 Northern Electric converted the Oroville–Chico line to third rail. The line soon acquired branches to Hamilton City, Colusa, and Woodland. It proposed

FACTS & FIGURES

Year	1929	1971
Miles operated	261	336
Locomotives	24	8
Passenger cars	82	—
Freight cars	315	229
Reporting marks: SN		

an extension north to Redding, and a subsidiary built an isolated line between Vacaville and Suisun as part of a proposed extension from Woodland to Vallejo.

In 1914 Northern Electric entered receivership. The Hamilton branch, which had a pontoon bridge over the Sacramento River, was abandoned in 1915 after only eight years of operation. A new company, the Sacramento Northern Railroad, took over the properties and operations in 1918, and in 1921 Western Pacific acquired control of the SN.

Oakland, Antioch & Eastern

The Oakland, Antioch & Eastern was successor to the Oakland & Antioch Railway, which was incorporated in 1909. By early 1913 the line was open from Bay Point (now Port Chicago) south through the San Ramon Valley towns of Concord, Walnut Creek, and Lafayette to Oakland. The engineering feat of the line was a 3,600-foot tunnel through the Oakland hills. From 40th Street and Shafter Avenue in Oakland, the O&A used Key System rails to reach the Key System pier and a ferry connection to San Francisco.

In September of that year, the line to Sacramento was opened. Trains were ferried across Suisun Bay; the railroad obtained permission from the U. S. War Department to build a bridge, but specifications for height and clear channel put it beyond OA&E's means. From the north shore of Suisun Bay, the line made a straight shot through unpopulated country to Sacramento. A branch was constructed as far east as Pittsburg, but the line never reached Antioch. DA&E's cars were equipped with pantographs to draw current from Key System's 600-volt overhead wire and trolley poles for DA&E's 1,200-volt overhead.

In 1920 the OA&E was succeeded by the San Francisco-Sacramento Railroad. In 1927 the Western Pacific bought control of the San Francisco-Sacramento with the idea of using its line to save 50 miles between Oakland and Sacramento. (WP's own line headed south out of Oakland, then crossed the Coast Range and reached the Central Valley at a point well south of Stockton.)

On Dec. 31, 1928, Sacramento Northern acquired all the properties of the San Francisco-Sacramento, creating a single railroad between Oakland and Chico.

Motors 604 and 603 prepare to pull cars off the ferry *Ramon* at Mallard, on the south shore of Suisun Bay, in 1951. *Reginald McGovern*

Sacramento Northern

The Sacramento Northern Railway was incorporated in 1921. In 1925 it purchased the properties of the Sacramento Northern Railroad, and in 1928, it acquired the San Francisco-Sacramento. SN placed its emphasis on freight. For passengers, SN offered no time advantage over Southern Pacific between San Francisco and Sacramento, and the opening of SP's bridge across the Carquinez Strait put SP well ahead. Paved highways began to siphon off SN's passengers, and the Depression put an end to any thought of acquiring additional all-steel passenger cars. Dining car and parlor car service ended in 1936 and 1938, respectively.

The Bay Bridge opened between San Francisco and Oakland for motor vehicles in 1936 and for Key System, Interurban Electric (SP), and SN trains in 1939. San Francisco–Sacramento through service lasted little more than a year before discontinuance on Aug. 26, 1940. San Francisco–Pittsburg commuter service ran less than a year longer. Interurban service north of Sacramento ended Oct. 31, 1940. There was almost no opposition to SN's petitions to cease passenger service. Marysville–Yuba City streetcar service was discontinued in 1942. Streetcar service in Chico ended in December 1947—it was the last Birney car and the last nickel fare in California.

In 1929 SN opened a line south along the Sacramento River to Oxford, and the same year, SN connected its isolated Vacaville–Suisun line, by then freight-only, with the rest of the system by building a line from Vacaville Junction east to Creed (construction of Travis Air Force Base later required a relocation of the line and a new junction at Dozier).

In December 1937 floods damaged the Feather River bridge at Oroville, severing the branch line. SN's presence in Oroville changed to that of a switching road for its parent WP. The Oroville line was dieselized in 1954 and discontinued in 1957.

SN dieselized its operation between Sacramento and Marysville in 1946. In 1951 a low trestle at Lisbon collapsed under a train. Trains were rerouted over WP and Santa Fe between Sacramento and Pittsburg, an arrangement that became permanent when the ferry *Ramon* failed an inspection in 1954. When the trestle was repaired, the line was de-electrified.

Floods in 1955 washed out some of SN's line near Marysville and caused a rerouting to the WP line there. The Oakland–Walnut Creek line with its tunnel through the Oakland hills was abandoned in 1957, and the remaining Pittsburg–Walnut Creek segment was dieselized. SN's last electrified operation was at Marysville. As late as April 1965 it was possible to ride underneath live catenary in the domes of WP's *California Zephyr* and watch SN motors on the adjacent track.

Gradually SN was dismembered, leaving short stubs of its lines where it intersected other railroads. Eventually its affairs were all but indistinguishable from those of Western Pacific. The absorption of WP by Union Pacific spelled the end of any separate existence for Sacramento Northern.

St. Johnsbury & Lake Champlain

The Bridge Road

In 1869 ground was broken at St. Johnsbury, Vt., for the Vermont Division of the Portland & Ogdensburg Railroad. The destination was Lake Champlain; the railroad was to be part of a bridge route between Portland, Maine, and the Great Lakes. In 1875 the Portland & Ogdensburg Railroad, building northwest from Portland, met the independent Vermont Division at Lunenburg, Vt., east of St. Johnsbury on the New Hampshire state line. The line was pushed west to Swanton, Vt., almost to Lake Champlain, in 1877. Receivership followed within months.

The railroad was reorganized as the St. Johnsbury & Lake Champlain by its bondholders in 1880, and it built the last few miles to the shore of Lake Champlain at Maquam that year. In 1883, with the encouragement of the Ogdensburg & Lake Champlain, it built a short extension from Swanton to Rouses Point, New York, to connect with the O&LC, the westernmost link in the Portland-to-Ogdensburg route. In the meantime, the Central Vermont took over the O&LC and refused to interchange traffic with the StJ&LC at Rouses Point, prompting abandonment of the now-useless new extension.

In 1880 Maine Central acquired the Portland & Ogdensburg and leased the portion of the StJ&LC that lay east of St. Johnsbury. Boston & Lowell obtained control of the StJ&LC in 1885; that control passed to Boston & Maine in 1895.

Independence

Boston & Maine guaranteed StJ&LC's bonds, but in 1925 when the StJ failed to earn enough to pay the interest on them, B&M turned the line over to local management—the same management that later operated the Montpelier & Wells River—in an experiment to see if local management could run the road better than B&M could from its Boston headquarters. The road struggled on into bankruptcy in 1944, and it was reorganized in 1948 as the St. Johnsbury & Lamoille County Railroad. (See the Rutland map on page 255.)

Boston & Maine soon sold the railroad to local interests. They in turn sold it in

GE 70-tonners bring a mixed train into Cambridge Junction, Vt., on May 30, 1955. In the distance is the road's covered bridge over the Lamoille River. *Jim Shaughnessy*

1956 to the H. E. Salzberg Co.; it was sold again in 1967 to Samuel M. Pinsly, who like Salzberg was the owner of a group of short lines.

Pinsly's rehabilitation of the railroad included abandonment of the western end between Swanton and East Swanton (including the three-span covered bridge over the Missisquoi River at Swanton), purchase of a short piece of Central Vermont track from East Swanton to Fonda Junction, and replacement of two more covered bridges at Cambridge Junction and west of Wolcott with steel bridges. The Fisher Bridge east of Wolcott was preserved by adding concealed reinforcement, retaining its appearance as a covered bridge. It became the emblem of the railroad.

Pinsly had no more financial success with the road than had previous management. He petitioned for abandonment, embargoed the line, and proposed that the state of Vermont purchase it. In 1973 the state purchased the railroad from Pinsly and awarded the operating contract to Bruno Loati of Morrisville, Vt. The road began operation as the Lamoille County Railroad, then reassumed its former name. Because of a dispute with the state over track rehabilitation and a strike by maintenance-of-way employees, the state announced that Vermont Northern, a

subsidiary of Morrison-Knudsen, would take over in October 1976.

Vermont Northern took over, but the state was still not satisfied with the operation of the railroad and refused to provide long-term subsidy. A local group that included the line's major shippers formed the Northern Vermont Corporation, bid on the operation, and incorporated the Lamoille Valley Railroad, which took over the railroad on Jan. 1, 1978.

In 1980 the Lamoille Valley and the Central Vermont agreed to interchange traffic at St. Albans rather than Fonda Junction, with LVRC operating between Sheldon Junction and St. Albans on CV track and CV in turn serving the road's customers at Swanton and East Swanton. In the mid-1980s the Lamoille Valley briefly operated excursion trains. Floods in the mid-1990s damaged the line, forcing abandonment and conversion to a trail.

FACTS & FIGURES

Year	1929	1972
Miles operated	96	98
Locomotives	9	10
Passenger cars	5	—
Freight cars	7	47
Reporting marks: SJL		

St. Louis-San Francisco (Frisco)

Ground was broken on July 19, 1853, at Franklin (now Pacific), Mo., for the South-West Branch of the Pacific Railroad (now the Missouri Pacific). The line reached Rolla, Mo., 77 miles from Franklin, in 1860, but the Civil War brought a halt to construction. In 1866 the state of Missouri took over the railroad—separation from the parent road seemed desirable—and sold it to John C. Fremont, who reorganized it as the Southwest Pacific Railroad. Fremont was unable to keep up the payments, and the road was reorganized again as the South Pacific Railroad in 1868. The line continued to inch southwest. It reached Springfield in 1870 and was consolidated with the Atlantic & Pacific that same year.

Frisco's *Meteor* from St. Louis, behind a 4-8-2, swings through a reverse curve about 20 miles east of its destination of Oklahoma City on Oct. 12, 1946. *Preston George*

Atlantic & Pacific

The Atlantic & Pacific Railroad was chartered in 1866 to build a railroad from Springfield, Mo., to the Pacific. Its route lay roughly along the 35th parallel—west along the Canadian River to Albuquerque, then along the Little Colorado and Colorado rivers and west to the Pacific by a "practicable and eligible route," to quote the act of incorporation. Among the provisions of the act were that the U. S. government would clear up the matter of Indian lands being granted to the railroad, the

Southern Pacific Railroad would connect with it at the Colorado River, and the railroad had to be completed within 12 years to receive the land grant.

Financing was difficult to find, and the Atlantic & Pacific entered receivership in 1875. The portion of the Atlantic & Pacific within Missouri was sold to become the St. Louis & San Francisco Railway, and the 37-mile portion in Indian Territory (now Oklahoma) from the border to Vinita retained the Atlantic & Pacific name.

The St. Louis & San Francisco began expanding. Lines reached Wichita, Kan., in 1880, Fort Smith, Ark., and Tulsa in 1882, and St. Louis (to replace the use of Missouri Pacific track) in 1883. In 1887 an extension of the Fort Smith line reached Paris, Texas, and in 1888, a line was opened from Wichita to Ellsworth, Kan.

In 1879 Frisco, A&P, and Santa Fe signed an agreement under which Frisco and Santa Fe would jointly build and own the Atlantic & Pacific west of Albuquerque. At the time, Jay Gould was trying to gain control of the Frisco to head off its extension into Texas—and forestall competition with Gould's Texas & Pacific. Gould and C. P. Huntington acquired control of the Frisco in 1882. The A&P was completed in 1883 from Albuquerque to Needles, Calif., on the west bank of the Colorado River, where it connected with the SP.

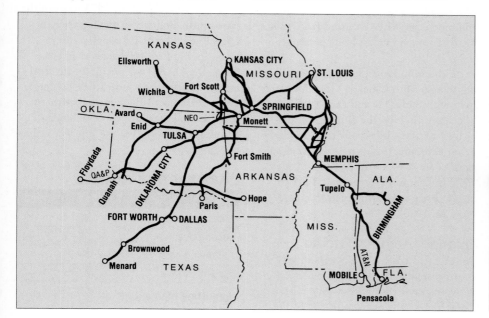

SLSF FACTS & FIGURES

Year	1929	1979
Miles operated	5,735	4,653
Locomotives	880	431
Passenger cars	669	—
Freight cars	34,009	17,392
Reporting marks: SLSF		
Historical society: frisco.org		

The Santa Fe would not allow earnings from the completed portion to finance the construction of the line from Sapulpa, near Tulsa, to Albuquerque. In 1886 Congress voided A&P's land grant for the unbuilt part of the line. The Santa Fe purchased the Frisco in 1890, briefly creating the largest railroad in North America (measured in route-miles). During the Panic of 1893, though, Santa Fe entered receivership.

Reorganization

A new St. Louis & San Francisco Railroad, organized in 1896, bought the old Frisco and the Oklahoma portion of the Atlantic & Pacifi, while the A&P from Albuquerque to Needles became part of Santa Fe. The new Frisco extended its main line from Tulsa to Oklahoma City in 1898, and a subsidiary, the Kansas City, Osceola & Southern, completed a Kansas City-Springfield route that same year. In 1901 Frisco put in service a line from Sapulpa, Okla., near Tulsa, to Denison, Texas. A year later, the line reached Carrollton, Texas, within striking distance of Dallas and Fort Worth. Also in 1901, Frisco leased the Kansas City, Fort Scott & Memphis, which with subsidiaries formed a route from Kansas City through Springfield, Mo., and Memphis, Tenn., to Birmingham, Ala.

Benjamin F. Yoakum acquired control of the Frisco right after the turn of the century. His holdings included the Rock Island, the Chicago & Eastern Illinois, and a group of railroads stretching from New Orleans through Houston to Brownsville, Texas (later known as Gulf Coast Lines). Yoakum's empire collapsed in 1913, and the Frisco was reorganized in 1916 as the St. Louis-San Francisco Railway.

The new Frisco settled down to become a regional railroad, an X-shaped system with lines from St. Louis through Oklahoma to Texas, including the Quanah, Acme & Pacific, the west Texas tail of the system, and from Kansas City to Birmingham. In 1925 the Frisco purchased the Muscle Shoals, Birmingham & Pensacola Railway (Kimbrough, Ala.–Pensacola, Fla., successor in 1922 to the Gulf, Florida & Alabama Railway), and constructed a new line from Aberdeen, Miss., to Kimbrough. In 1928 Frisco purchased and absorbed the Kansas City,

Four red-and-white GP40s lead fast freight train 33, the *Texas Special*, into Valley Park, Mo., on Nov. 25, 1980, four days after merger with Burlington Northern. *George A. Forero Jr.*

Fort Scott & Memphis and its subsidiaries.

The Frisco again entered receivership in 1932. In 1937 the road sold the Fort Worth & Rio Grande, a line from Fort Worth to Menard, Texas, to the Santa Fe. Revenues from increased traffic during World War II helped boost Frisco out of receivership in 1947. In 1948 SL-SF acquired control of the Alabama, Tennessee & Northern, gaining a second Gulf port, Mobile. (Merger with AT&N occurred Jan. 1, 1971.)

In 1956 Frisco purchased control of the Central of Georgia, but the ICC disapproved and Frisco sold its interest to the Southern Railway in 1961. In 1964 Frisco acquired control of the Northeast Oklahoma Railroad (a one-time interurban) and merger of NEO occurred Jan. 1, 1967. Frisco dropped the last of its passenger trains in 1967.

In the mid-1960s, Frisco began talking merger with Chicago Great Western, then with Santa Fe, and then with Southern. In 1966 the Burlington purchased a sizable block of Frisco stock. For about a decade, there was no further substantive news of a Frisco merger, but in 1977 Burlington Northern and Frisco began discussions which led to merger on Nov. 21, 1980.

Quanah, Acme & Pacific

The Acme, Red River & Northern was incorporated May 3, 1902, to build between Acme (five miles west of Quanah, Texas, the southwesternmost end of the

Frisco) and Floydada, Texas. The railroad was renamed the Quanah, Acme & Pacific on Jan. 28, 1909. QA&P projected a line west to El Paso, about 500 miles, and, although never built, the extension appeared on route maps as late as 1944.

The St. Louis-San Francisco guaranteed some QA&P bonds in 1911 and eventually acquired full control of the road. By the early 1960s the QA&P had no rolling stock of its own and relied on parent Frisco for its equipment, although three of Frisco's GP7s bore QA&P lettering when they were delivered.

The QA&P was a bridge line between the Frisco at Quanah (named for the last chief of the Comanches) and the Santa Fe at Floydada for traffic moving to and from the West Coast. In 1973 most of the transcontinental traffic moving over the QA&P was diverted through a direct Frisco-Santa Fe interchange at Avard, Okla. The QA&P was merged with Burlington Northern on June 8, 1981. Merger of the Frisco with Burlington Northern rendered the Quanah Route redundant, and the western half of the line was abandoned in 1982.

QA&P FACTS & FIGURES

Year	1929	1980
Miles operated	126	119
Locomotives	7	—
Passenger cars	—	—
Freight cars	47	—
Reporting marks: QAP		

St. Louis Southwestern (Cotton Belt)

The St. Louis Southwestern (usually called the Cotton Belt) was Southern Pacific's principal subsidiary. The reason it remained a separate railroad through more than half a century of SP control was that when the Interstate Commerce Commission approved control of Central Pacific by Southern Pacific in 1923, it imposed the condition that SP solicit freight traffic for movement via Ogden, Utah, and the Union Pacific in preference to its own route across Texas. Cotton Belt traffic offices were not governed by that agreement and could solicit traffic to move over SP and SSW rails all the way to East St. Louis.

The Cotton Belt began as the 3-foot-gauge Tyler Tap Railroad, chartered in 1871 and opened in 1877 between Tyler, Texas, and a junction with the Texas & Pacific at Big Sandy. It was rechartered as the Texas & St. Louis Railway in 1879 under the leadership of James Paramore, a St. Louis financier, who sought an

Big SD45 No. 8970 pauses with train MSE in the passing track at Big Sandy, Texas, in 1971. The diesel paint scheme matched parent SP but with "Cotton Belt" lettering. *Chuck Harris*

economical way to transport cotton from Texas to St. Louis. The road was extended to Texarkana and a connection with the

St. Louis, Iron Mountain & Southern in 1880. A year later the west end of the railroad was extended to Waco.

In 1881 Jay Gould purchased the Iron Mountain (he already owned the T&P), returning the Texas & St. Louis to one-connection status, and canceled the Iron Mountain's traffic agreements with the T&StL. The T&StL decided to fulfill its name. In 1882 it reached Birds Point, Mo., across the Mississippi River from Cairo, Ill. There it connected by barge with the narrow gauge St. Louis & Cairo. By 1885 a continuous line of 3-foot-gauge railroads reached from Toledo, Ohio, to Houston, Tex., with intentions of heading for Laredo and eventually Mexico City.

In 1886 the T&StL was reorganized as the St. Louis, Arkansas & Texas Railway. It converted its lines to standard gauge, built branches to Shreveport, La., and Fort

FACTS & FIGURES

Year	1929	1983
Miles operated	1,809	2,375
Locomotives	248	307
Passenger cars	168	—
Freight cars	8458	17,407
Reporting marks: SSW		

Cotton Belt's *Blue Streak* rolls west of Mount Pleasant, Texas, on Oct. 1, 1931. The train is led by Ten-Wheeler No. 659, built by Baldwin in 1913. *Harold K. Vollrath*

Worth in 1888, and then entered bankruptcy in 1889.

Jay Gould organized the St. Louis Southwestern Railway in 1891 and took over the StLA&T. Shortly thereafter, the road gained access to Memphis, Tenn., by way of trackage rights over the Iron Mountain. Cotton Belt acquired trackage rights over Missouri Pacific from Thebes, Ill., to St. Louis in exchange for letting MP operate over SSW between Illmo, Mo., and Paragould, Ark. It joined with MP in 1905 to construct a bridge over the Mississippi between Thebes and Illmo. Passenger trains to and from Memphis were moved to Rock Island's Brinkley, Ark.–Memphis line in 1912; freight trains made the change in 1921.

After World War I, overhead traffic (also called intermediate or bridge traffic—freight received from one railroad to be turned over to another) began to increase on the Cotton Belt. The Rock Island purchased a controlling interest in the road in

1925 and sold it almost immediately to Kansas City Southern. KCS proposed a regional system to include KCS, SSW, and the Missouri-Kansas-Texas, but the ICC refused approval. KCS lost interest in the Cotton Belt about the time Southern Pacific was looking for a connection to St. Louis from its Texas lines. SP applied for control and in 1932 took over.

Cotton Belt weathered receivership between 1935 and 1947. From the 1950s through the end of the SP, it was essentially a division of the SP, though its equipment was still lettered "Cotton Belt." The last diesels painted in Cotton Belt's yellow and gray were delivered in 1949; after that, they wore SP colors.

Cotton Belt was never a major passenger carrier. The Dallas–Memphis *Lone Star* was discontinued in 1953. All passenger service in Texas ended in 1956, and Cotton Belt's last passenger train, a St. Louis–Pine Bluff coach-only local, made its last run Nov. 30, 1959. As SSW's 4-8-4s had done,

the passenger diesels and ten streamlined coaches moved west for service on SP lines.

In 1973 Cotton Belt purchased a half interest in the Alton & Southern, a belt line serving East St. Louis, Ill., from the Chicago & North Western. In 1980 SSW acquired the former Rock Island line from St. Louis through Kansas City to Santa Rosa, New Mexico. (The Tucumcari–Santa Rosa portion of the RI had long been leased to SP.) The reason Cotton Belt purchased the line, not SP itself, is also rooted in the 1923 treaty with the UP. (The St. Louis–Kansas City track apparently was part of a package deal; even when Cotton Belt purchased it, it was in no condition for high-speed heavy freight service.) In 1982 SSW obtained another piece of the late Rock Island, the line from Brinkley, Ark., to the Mississippi River bridge west of Memphis.

Union Pacific's merger of Southern Pacific on Sept. 12, 1996, included the Cotton Belt.

San Diego & Arizona Eastern

Three former Union Pacific GP20s lead an 11-car San Diego & Arizona Eastern freight eastward across Campo Creek at Campo, Calif., in June 1982, in the Kyle era. The train is bound for the Southern Pacific interchange at Plaster City. The temperature: 105 degrees. *William T. Morgan*

In 1907 John D. Spreckels broke ground at San Diego, Calif., for a railroad that would give the city a direct route east. Financial backing for the San Diego & Arizona came from Spreckels and from E. H. Harriman of the Southern Pacific. The new railroad would bring SP into San Diego and break Santa Fe's monopoly there—a reversal of the usual situation in California in those days.

The route of the railroad was south across the Mexican border to Tijuana, east to Tecate via the subsidiary Tijuana & Tecate Railway, back into the U. S., north through awesome Carriso Gorge, and then east to a connection with SP at El Centro, the principal town in California's Imperial Valley. In spite of revolution in Mexico and

a ban on construction of new railroads during World War I, the last spike was driven in 1919.

In 1932 Spreckels sold his interest to SP, which formed the San Diego & Arizona Eastern Railway to take over operation on Feb. 1, 1933. In 1951 the SD&AE ran its last passenger train. The slow trip east to a connection with the secondary trains of SP's *Golden State* Route was no match for Santa Fe's frequent *San Diegans* to Los Angeles and the best of Santa Fe, Union Pacific, and Southern Pacific from there.

In 1970 SP sold the Tijuana & Tecate to the Mexican government, and it became an isolated part of the Sonora-Baja California Railway. (SP retained trackage rights for through traffic.) A hurricane in

September 1976 damaged a 40-mile stretch of the line, and Southern Pacific petitioned for abandonment of all but a few miles from El Centro to Plaster City.

In 1979 San Diego's Metropolitan Transit Development Board purchased three portions of the SD&AE: from Plaster City west to the border, from San Diego south to the border at San Ysidro, and from San Diego east to El Cajon. MTDB began construction of a 16-mile transit line from the Amtrak (ex-Santa Fe) station in San Diego to the border. Trolleys began operating in July 1981.

Freight trains were operated on the line first by San Diego & Arizona Eastern Transportation Co., a subsidiary of Kyle Railways, then by the San Diego & Imperial Valley Railway. They are currently run by Pacific Imperial Railroad and San Diego & Imperial Valley Railroad.

FACTS & FIGURES

Year	1929	1975
Miles operated	201	199
Locomotives	16	5
Passenger cars	34	—
Freight cars	175	3
Reporting marks: SDAE		

Sandy River & Rangeley Lakes

The Sandy River was the most extensive 2-foot gauge railroad in Maine. Its ancestry, like that of the state of Maine itself, lies in Massachusetts. In 1875 George Mansfield organized the Billerica & Bedford Railroad to build a 2-foot gauge railroad between the towns of its name. Mansfield had visited the Festiniog Railway, a 23½-inch gauge slate carrier in Wales, and he promoted the narrow gauge as economical. There was no traffic to support the B&B. It operated only from November 1877 through May 1878 and then was abandoned.

Mansfield went north to Franklin County, Maine, which was having an attack of railroad fever and also had a growing lumber industry. Standard gauge rails, later to become a branch of the Maine Central, had reached the county seat, Farmington, about 80 miles north of Portland, in 1865.

The Sandy River Railroad was organized in 1879 with Mansfield as its manager and a track gauge of 2 feet. Mansfield knew where he could get a complete 2-foot gauge train set, only slightly used, in exchange for Sandy River stock. The first train arrived in Phillips, 18 miles from Farmington, on Nov. 20, 1879—the town of Phillips had set that date as a deadline in order for the railroad to use the town's credit.

In 1883 the Franklin & Megantic railroad was incorporated to build from

A gasoline railcar and baggage trailer are ready to depart Strong in 1934. The local freight behind 2-6-2 No. 24 will follow it out of town. *Peter Cornwall collection*

Strong, 11 miles north of Farmington, to Kingfield, 15 miles. The line was completed in October 1884. Both the F&M and the Sandy River suddenly were busy hauling lumber. The Phillips & Rangeley Railroad was incorporated in 1890 to build north from Phillips to Rangeley, 28 miles. The P&R organized a subsidiary, the Madrid Railroad, to build a branch into the forests west of Madrid, and in 1903, the Eustis Railroad was chartered to build into the area northeast of Rangeley.

In 1894 the owners of the F&M organized the Kingfield & Dead River Railroad to extend their railroad north to Carrabasset and, in 1900, to Bigelow. In 1897 Josiah Maxcy, who had purchased the Sandy River in 1892, acquired control of the F&M and the K&DR and began operating the three roads as a single system.

Maxcy's system expanded in 1908. In January of that year, he organized the Sandy River & Rangeley Lakes Railroad, which took over the Sandy River, the F&M, and the K&DR. In June 1908 the SR&RL purchased the Phillips & Rangeley and the Madrid Railroad and leased the Eustis Railroad (purchasing it in 1911).

Maine Central gained control of the SR&RL in 1911. Traffic, chiefly pulpwood, was good on the narrow gauge through

World War I, but paved highways began to penetrate Franklin County. In the early 1920s the SR&RL's expenses began to outpace income—and a good portion of the expense was interest on the debt owed to the Maine Central for improvements. The SR&RL entered receivership in 1922. In July 1926 the former K&DR was cut back to Carrabasset, and in 1931, service was discontinued north of Phillips. On July 8, 1932, the SR&RL ceased operating and stored its equipment.

Operation resumed April 17, 1933, with the assurance of traffic from a plywood mill. Operations were briefly profitable at the expense of maintenance—cars and locomotives were simply run until they could run no more. In June 1935 the railroad was sold to railroad scrapper H. E. Salzberg & Co. The last day of operation was June 29, 1935.

FACTS & FIGURES

Year	1929	1933
Miles operated	96	43
Locomotives	31	10
Passenger cars	20	—
Freight cars	296	309
Historical society: srrl-rr.org		

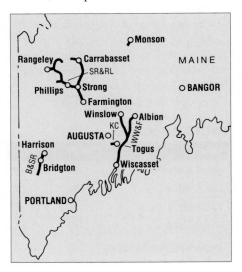

Savannah & Atlanta

Savannah & Atlanta train 2, the southbound mixed, pulls out of Sardis, Ga., about halfway between Camak and Savannah, behind Mikado 503.
C. M. Clegg

George M. Brinson began constructing a railroad northwest from Savannah, Ga., in 1906. The railroad—the Brinson Railway—reached Newington, Ga., 43 miles from Savannah in 1909. Brinson then acquired the Savannah Valley Railroad, which had a line from Egypt, Ga., through Newington and Sylvania to Mill Haven. At that point he ran out of money.

Control of the railroad company was acquired by a New York bank, though Brinson remained president. Construction resumed and the road reached Waynesboro and a connection with the Central of Georgia in 1911. It reached St. Clair and a connection with the Georgia & Florida in 1913. The road was renamed the Savannah & Northwestern in 1914.

The Savannah & Atlanta was incorporated in 1915 to build a connecting link between St. Clair and the Georgia Railroad's main line at Camak. Upon completion in 1916 the combination of the Georgia Railroad and the Savannah & Atlanta formed the shortest route between Atlanta and Savannah. In 1917 the Savannah & Atlanta absorbed the Savannah & Northwestern.

The company entered receivership in 1921 and emerged with its name unchanged in 1929. Its principal business was to serve as a Savannah extension of the Georgia Railroad. It was purchased by the Central of Georgia Railway in 1951 but continued to operate independently until 1971 with the formation of the Central of Georgia Railroad, a subsidiary of the Southern Railway.

In 1961 the S&A abandoned 36 miles of its line between Sylvania and Waynesboro and initiated joint operation with CofG, using S&A track between Savannah and Ardmore and CofG track between Ardmore and Waynesboro.

The S&A is remembered today chiefly for Pacific 750, purchased from the Florida East Coast in 1935 and given to the Atlanta Chapter of the National Railway Historical Society in 1962. For a number of years, the locomotive was a regular participant in the Southern's steam excursion program.

FACTS & FIGURES

Year	1929	1969
Miles operated	142	167
Locomotives	13	11
Passenger cars	7	—
Freight cars	58	781
Reporting marks: SA		

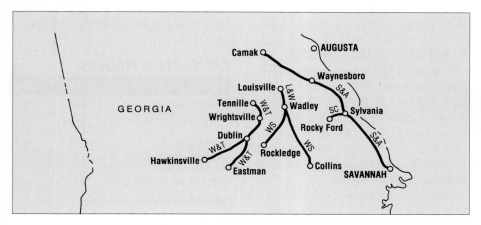

Seaboard Air Line

Three new EMD GP7s lead a Seaboard Air Line freight at Alberta, Va., at the joint SAL-Virginian station on Feb. 22, 1953. Built in September 1952, No. 1816 eventually became Seaboard Coast Line 996 and was retired in 1983. *Robert Milner*

The Portsmouth & Roanoke Rail Road was formed in 1832 to build a railroad from Portsmouth, Va., to Weldon, N. C., on the Roanoke River, shortcutting a long, three-sided water route. The line reached Weldon in 1837. The new railroad was not successful, and in 1846, it was purchased by the Virginia State Board of Public Works, leased to the town of Portsmouth, and reorganized as the Seaboard & Roanoke Railroad. In the early 1850s control of the road was acquired by a group of Philadelphians who also controlled the Richmond, Fredericksburg & Potomac and Richmond & Petersburg railroads.

The Raleigh & Gaston Railroad was completed in 1840 between Raleigh and Gaston, N. C., (not present-day Gaston, but a town a few miles up the Roanoke River from it). In 1853 the railroad was extended a few miles east to Weldon, connecting there with the Seaboard & Roanoke and several other railroads.

During the Civil War, portions of the railroad were torn up by both Union and Confederate troops, and parts were rebuilt and used by both sides, even though it was not a particularly strategic railroad.

In 1871 the Raleigh & Gaston acquired control of a railroad under construction south from Raleigh, the Raleigh & Augusta Air-Line Railroad. (An air-line is a straight beeline between two points, and a wonderful asset in advertising—even if the railroad is not perfectly straight, it can be drawn that way on timetable maps.) By 1877 that line had reached Hamlet, N. C., and a connection with the Carolina Central, a line from Wilmington through Charlotte to Shelby.

Seaboard Air-Line System

The Seaboard & Roanoke and the two Raleigh railroads were by then under the control of John M. Robinson, who was president of the RF&P and the Baltimore Steam Packet Co. In 1881 Robinson gained control of the Carolina Central. Robinson's railroads became known as the Seaboard Air-Line System.

The Seaboard system had had a friendly connection at Charlotte in the form of the Atlanta & Charlotte Air Line Railway. In 1881 that came under the control of the Richmond & Danville, a predecessor of the Southern Railway, and lost its friendly connection status. The Seaboard began construction in 1887 of a line from Monroe, N. C., between Hamlet and Charlotte, to Atlanta—the Georgia, Carolina & Northern Railway. It reached the Georgia capital in 1892. In the late 1890s the Richmond, Petersburg & Carolina Railroad was completed between Norlina, N. C., and Richmond, Va., and in 1900, it was renamed the Seaboard Air Line Railway.

SAL FACTS & FIGURES

Year	1929	1966
Miles operated	4,490	4,123
Locomotives	726	551
Passenger cars	474	414
Freight cars	22,483	28,778
Reporting marks: SAL		
Historical society: aclsal.org		

Train TT-23, running extra (note the white flags), is on the double-track main near Manson, N. C., in September 1965. The three GP30s are cruising at an easy 60 mph with their string of 56 piggyback cars. *Curt Tillotson Jr.*

Florida Central & Peninsular

The Florida Central & Peninsular traced its ancestry to the Tallahassee Railroad, organized in 1834 to build from Tallahassee to the Gulf of Mexico—its 22-mile line was opened in 1836. The Jacksonville–Tallahassee route, opened in 1860, was built by two companies that were eventually united as the Florida Central & Western Railroad.

The Florida Railroad opened in March 1861 from Fernandina through Baldwin and Gainesville to Cedar Key, Fla., to form a land bridge from the Atlantic to the Gulf. It became the Atlantic, Gulf & West India Transit company, then the Florida Transit Railroad ("transit" having its older, less-specific meaning, rather than referring to streetcars, nickel fares, and frequent service). In 1883 it was consolidated with two other companies to form the Florida Transit & Peninsular Railroad. In 1884 that company and the Florida Central & Western merged to form the Florida Railway & Navigation Co., which was succeeded in 1889 by the Florida Central & Peninsular Railway. In 1890 a line of the FC&P was extended south to Tampa, and in 1893 the company built a line north to Savannah, where it connected with the recently opened South Bound Railroad to Columbia, S. C.

John Skelton Williams

In 1896 John Skelton Williams of Richmond and a group of associates obtained control of the Georgia & Alabama Railway, a line completed in 1891 between Montgomery, Ala., and Lyons, Ga. Williams leased and built railroad lines to extend the G&A east to Savannah. In 1898 he acquired control of the Seaboard group of railroads, and in 1899 he took over the Florida Central & Peninsular Railroad, which had a line from Columbia, S. C., through Savannah and Jacksonville to Tampa, and another line west from Jacksonville through Tallahassee to a junction with the Louisville & Nashville at the Chattahoochee River.

In 1900, 91 miles of new railroad between Columbia and Cheraw, S. C., connected the Georgia & Alabama (Montgomery–Savannah) and the Florida Central & Peninsular with the "old" Seaboard. Williams proposed to build north from Richmond to connect with the Baltimore & Ohio, because the Richmond, Fredericksburg & Potomac was then controlled by the Atlantic Coast Line. The Pennsylvania Railroad and the state of Virginia, both owners of portions of the RF&P, applied pressure, and the Seaboard was allowed to sign a traffic agreement with the RF&P—and with the Pennsy too.

Twentieth-century expansion

Williams was out at the end of 1903—he went on to assemble the Georgia & Florida—but he had begun an extension west from Atlanta to Birmingham by a combination of new construction and the acquisition of the East & West Railroad.

In the early years of the twentieth century, the Seaboard acquired a number of branches and short lines. SAL entered a brief receivership in 1908, and the corporation underwent a reorganization in 1915 when the subsidiary Carolina, Atlantic & Western Railway was renamed the Seaboard Air Line Railway and took over the previous Seaboard Air Line.

In 1918 SAL opened a new line from Charleston, S. C., to Savannah. In conjunction with an existing line from Hamlet to Charleston, it formed a freight route with easier grades than the main line through Columbia. About that same time, SAL began to gather up short lines in the agricultural and phosphate-mining area of central Florida: the Tampa & Gulf Coast (Tampa to St. Petersburg and Tarpon Springs), the Charlotte Harbor & Northern (Mulberry to Boca Grande), and the Tampa Northern (Tampa to Brooksville).

SAL's principal project in Florida during the land boom of the early 1920s was a line from Coleman, just south of

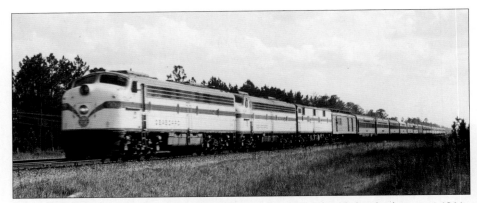

The *Silver Meteor*, train 58, cruises northward at 80 mph south of Baldwin, Fla., in August 1966. The railroad's only E9, No. 3060, is on the point with an E8A and E7B trailing. *David W. Salter*

Wildwood, southeast to West Palm Beach and Miami. SAL's first passenger train arrived in Miami on Jan. 8, 1927. A few months earlier, SAL had opened an extension down the west coast to Fort Myers and Naples. In 1928 Seaboard acquired the Georgia, Florida & Alabama Railway, a 194-mile line from Richland, Ga., south through Tallahassee to the Gulf.

The Florida land boom collapsed in 1926, just as SAL was completing its lines to Miami and Naples, and the stock market crashed in 1929. The Seaboard was not a strong railroad, and it was located between the Atlantic Coast Line and the Southern, both prosperous and well-established. Overextended by its expansion program in Florida, SAL collapsed into receivership in December 1930.

SAL undertook a modernization program, and revenues from World War II traffic lifted the road back to profitability and permitted it to install block signals and Centralized Traffic Control. The lack of signals on most of SAL's lines had caused several major accidents during the war years. The company was reorganized as the Seaboard Air Line Railroad in 1946.

Postwar prosperity

During the decade after World War II, the Seaboard prospered along with nearly every other railroad. Its position was bolstered by industrial development in the South and healthy traffic in phosphate rock—one-fifth of Seaboard's tonnage—used in the production of fertilizers. Seaboard's passenger business was also healthy, thanks to heavy traffic between the Northeast and Florida.

In 1958 SAL absorbed the Macon, Dublin & Savannah, which it had long owned, and in June 1959, SAL purchased the Gainesville Midland, a 42-mile line connecting the mill town of Gainesville, Ga., with the Seaboard at Athens.

Merger of the Seaboard with parallel—and rival—Atlantic Coast Line was proposed in 1958. The benefits of the Seaboard Coast Line merger, which took effect July 1, 1967, derived largely from eliminating duplicate lines and terminals.

Macon, Dublin & Savannah

The Macon, Dublin & Savannah began construction southeast from Macon, Georgia, in 1885. The line reached Dublin in 1891, and the decision was made not to build all the way to Savannah but only to Vidalia, where the MD&S could connect with the Georgia & Alabama Railway. The Georgia & Alabama became part of the SAL in 1900, forming its Savannah–Montgomery line, and the MD&S served as a Macon branch of that route.

In 1904 the Atlantic Coast Line purchased the outstanding stock and bonds of the MD&S but soon realized that the railroad was many miles from the nearest ACL track, an orphan. In 1906 ACL sold its holdings to the Seaboard. In 1930 SAL owned somewhat less than half of MD&S's stock but in the mid-1940s acquired the remainder. SAL absorbed the MD&S on March 1, 1958. The Georgia Central Railway purchased the line in 1990. The entire line is still in operation.

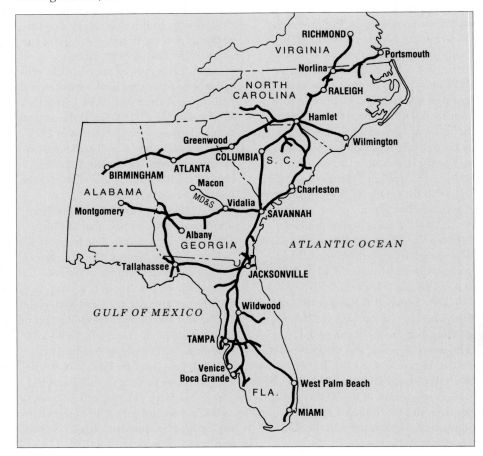

MD&S FACTS & FIGURES

Year	1929	1957
Miles operated	94	93
Locomotives	11	8
Passenger cars	7	—
Freight cars	21	107
Reporting marks: MD&S		

Seaboard Coast Line

Merger of the Seaboard Air Line and Atlantic Coast Line was proposed in 1958 and took effect July 1, 1967. Soon after the merger, some duplicate routes were rationalized. Among the abandonments were SAL's line between Charleston and Savannah, most of ACL's route into the Norfolk-Portsmouth area, and much of the dense network of branch lines in central Florida.

The most prevalent objection to the creation of SCL was over Atlantic Coast Line's control of Louisville & Nashville. Both Southern Railway and Illinois Central asked to purchase ACL's interest in L&N. The Southern and ACL plus SAL were about the same size, roughly 10,000 route miles, and adding 6,000-mile L&N to either would create a large railroad. Southern later dropped its objection when it gained control of Central of Georgia. Illinois Central was about the same size as Louisville & Nashville but had long been

Two GP40s lead a fast piggyback train through Neuse, N. C., a few miles north of Raleigh on the former Seaboard Air Line main, in June 1979. *Curt Tillotson Jr.*

eager to access the Southeast. Other protesters were Florida East Coast, which felt that ACL-SAL would surround it, and Gulf, Mobile & Ohio.

On July 1, 1969, SCL purchased the Piedmont & Northern, a former interurban line owned by the Duke interests, and on Sept. 1, 1976, SCL purchased the Durham & Southern, obtaining easier access to Durham, N. C.

Around 1974 SCL's advertising began to refer to SCL, Louisville & Nashville, Clinchfield, Georgia Railroad, and the West Point Route as "The Family Lines," but the title was simply a marketing device, not the name of a corporation. By then two other alliances had been formed south of the Ohio River and east of the Mississippi: Southern-Central of Georgia-Georgia & Florida-"old" Norfolk Southern and Illinois Central-Gulf, Mobile & Ohio. Unification of the members of the Family Lines could proceed. One Dec. 29, 1982, Seaboard Coast Line merged the Louisville & Nashville to form the Seaboard System Railroad.

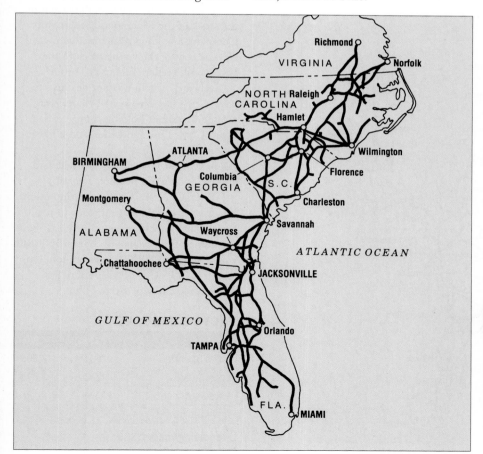

FACTS & FIGURES

Year	1967	1982
Miles operated	9,306	8,772
Locomotives	1,235	1,255
Passenger cars	729	—
Freight cars	63,405	59,335
Reporting marks: SCL		
Historical society: aclsal.org		

Seaboard System

A trio of B36-7s lead a manifest freight southbound near Collier, Va., in April 1986. Four months later, Seaboard System became part of CSX Transportation. *Michael S. Murray*

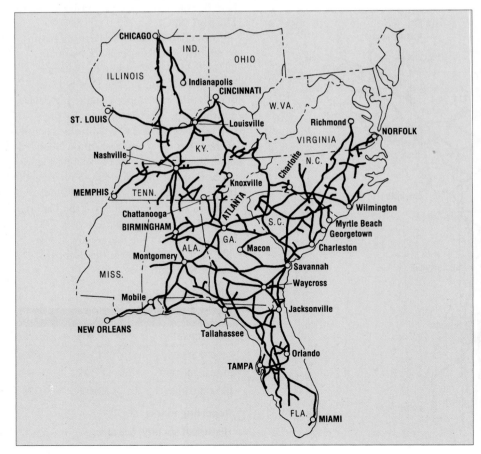

Seaboard System came into being on Dec. 29, 1982, when the Seaboard Coast Line Railroad merged the Louisville & Nashville Railroad. The Seaboard Coast Line had been formed in 1967 by the merger of the Atlantic Coast Line and the Seaboard Air Line; ACL had controlled the Louisville & Nashville since 1902.

On Jan. 1, 1983, the Clinchfield Railroad became the Clinchfield Division of the Seaboard System. That same year, Seaboard System purchased the Georgia Railroad, another member of the ACL-L&N family, and merged it. It also took over operations of the Atlanta & West Point Rail Road and the Western Railway of Alabama, both of which had long been affiliated with the Georgia Railroad.

Equipment received a new paint scheme, based on the old Family Lines scheme, but with new SBD initials and reporting marks.

Seaboard System owned 40 percent of the stock of the Richmond-Washington Company, a holding company that owned 63.6 percent of the voting stock of the Richmond, Fredericksburg & Potomac.

Seaboard System was not destined to have a long life. Two years before it was created, its parent holding company, Seaboard Coast Line Industries, and Chessie System, Inc., merged to form CSX Corporation ("C" for Chessie, "S" for Seaboard, and "X" for a multiplication symbol).

When CSX was formed, the intention was for the component railroads to retain their identities. However, on July 1, 1986, the name of the Seaboard System Railroad was changed to CSX Transportation. On Aug. 31, 1987, CSX Transportation merged the Chesapeake & Ohio.

FACTS & FIGURES

Year	1982	1986
Miles operated	15,294	13,506
Locomotives	2,426	2,093
Passenger cars	—	—
Freight cars	117,177	90,753
Reporting marks: SBD		

Soo Line (Minneapolis, St. Paul & Sault Ste. Marie)

In the 1870s the flour millers of Minneapolis sought a new outlet for their products to avoid the exorbitant freight rates charged by existing railroads through Chicago. James J. Hill, who later built the Great Northern, tried to persuade the Canadian Pacific to construct its line to the west through Sault Ste. Marie and Minneapolis, but nationalistic feeling in Canada dictated CP's all-Canada route north of Lake Superior.

In 1883 a group of Minneapolis men incorporated the Minneapolis, Sault Ste. Marie & Atlantic Railway to construct a line from the Twin Cities eastward to connect with the Canadian Pacific at Sault Ste. Marie. ("Sault" is pronounced "Soo." The area around the rapids of the St. Marys River is called "the Soo.")

A year later, the Minneapolis & Pacific Railway was incorporated by many of the same men to build northwestward into the wheat-growing areas of Minnesota and North Dakota. In 1888 these two roads and two others were consolidated to form the Minneapolis, St. Paul & Sault Ste. Marie Railway. Canadian Pacific acquired control of the railroad largely to block any attempt by CP's rival Grand Trunk Railway to build toward western Canada via the United States. In 1893 the Soo Line, as it was

Soo Line train 2, an all-day Minneapolis-Chicago local, rolls through Sussex, Wis., just west of Milwaukee. *David P. Morgan Library collection*

nicknamed, built northwest to connect with CP at Portal, N. D., and in 1904 completed a line north from Glenwood, Minn., to a connection with CP at Noyes, Minn.

In 1909 Soo Line leased the properties of the Wisconsin Central Railroad, a 1,000-mile road extending from Chicago to St. Paul, Duluth, and Ashland, Wis. In addition to gaining access to Chicago,

Soo Line also obtained routes to the industrial Fox River Valley of Wisconsin and the iron ore deposits in the northern part of the state.

The Duluth, South Shore & Atlantic Railway was formed by the merger of several lines along the south shore of Lake Superior. Its traffic consisted largely of iron ore and forest products. Its line ran east from Duluth along the south shore of Lake Superior to Sault Ste. Marie and to St. Ignace, where it connected via carferry to Mackinaw City at the northern tip of Michigan's lower peninsula. Canadian Pacific obtained control of the DSS&A in 1888 for the same reason it had bought into the Soo Line—to block possible construction by Grand Trunk. By 1930 the DSS&A shared officers with the Soo Line.

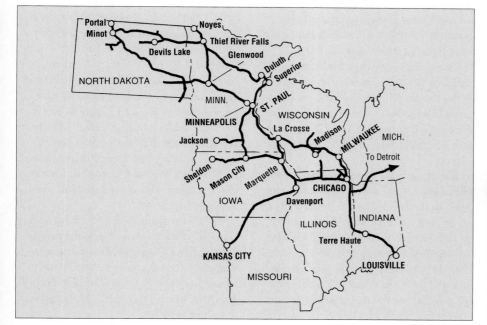

FACTS & FIGURES

Year	1929	1991
Miles operated	4,412	5,045
Locomotives	276	400
Passenger cars	270	—
Freight cars	15,161	12,695
Reporting marks: SOO		
Historical society: sooline.org		

Soo SD60 No. 6008, along with a GP38-2 and an SD40, leads eastbound train 208 at Lyndon Station, Wis., on the former Milwaukee Road main line, on July 7, 1989. The engines wear the red-and-white scheme that was standard from the 1960s through the '80s. *Howard Ande*

Soo Line

In 1961 the Minneapolis, St. Paul & Sault Ste. Marie; the Duluth, South Shore & Atlantic; and the Wisconsin Central merged to form the Soo Line Railroad (the corporate structure was that of the 1949 reorganization of the DSS&A). In 1982 Soo Line acquired the Minneapolis, Northfield & Southern Railway, a 74-mile line between Northfield, Minn., and the suburbs of Minneapolis.

Acquisition and divestment

Soo Line purchased the bankrupt Chicago, Milwaukee, St. Paul & Pacific Railroad in 1985 and merged it at the beginning of 1986. By then the Milwaukee, which had once reached west to Puget Sound, had shrunk to three principal routes: Chicago–Milwaukee–Minneapolis, Chicago–Kansas City, and Chicago–Louisville, Ky., (the last almost entirely by trackage rights). Soo Line also acquired trackage rights on Chessie System (now CSX) from Chicago

to Detroit, where it made a connection with parent CP Rail.

Soo briefly tried operating its light-density lines in Michigan and Wisconsin as Lake States Transportation Division (not to be confused with Michigan's Lake State Railway, the former Detroit & Mackinac Railway). Then Soo Line consolidated its Chicago–Twin Cities operations on the former Milwaukee Road main line and sold what had been its own lines to Wisconsin Central Ltd. in 1987, in many ways re-creating the pre-1909 Wisconsin Central.

For a long time, Canadian Pacific owned a little more than half of Soo's outstanding stock. In the late 1980s CP tried briefly to sell off Soo Line, but then decided to try for full ownership. By early 1990 CP Rail had acquired full ownership, and in early 1992 the separate listing for Soo Line disappeared from the *Pocket List of Railroad Officials*. CP briefly tried referring to Soo Line as its "Heavy Haul–U. S. Division" but

that didn't catch on. By the mid-1990s it was simply part of the CP Rail System—and "CP Rail" soon yielded to a restoration of the full Canadian Pacific name.

In 1990 Soo Line leased two routes in wheat-growing country totaling 293 miles to the Dakota, Missouri Valley & Western Railroad: Flaxton, N. D., to Whitetail, Mont., and Oakes, N. D., through Wishek and Bismarck to Washburn, N. D., plus a branch from Wishek to Ashley. In late 1996 CP sold a group of former Milwaukee Road lines to Montana Rail Link to operate as I&M Rail Link: Pingree Grove, Ill. (45 miles west of Chicago) to Kansas City branches serving northern Iowa and southern Minnesota.

All that remains of the Soo Line under Canadian Pacific ownership is the ex-Milwaukee Road Chicago–Milwaukee–Minneapolis line and a two-pronged route from Minneapolis to the Canadian border at Noyes, Minn., and Portal, N. D., plus a few short branches.

Southern

Three six-axle diesels, led by Southern Railway SD40 No. 3186, pull a southbound freight train out of Tunnel 26 on the Rat Hole line near Oakdale, Tenn., in May 1984. Most Southern diesels were set up to run long-hood forward. *John P. Baukus Jr.*

The earliest portion of the Southern Railway was the South Carolina Canal & Rail Road Company, which was chartered in 1828 to build from Charleston, S. C., to Hamburg, S. C., on the north bank of the Savannah River. Its purpose was to bring trade to the port of Charleston from inland points and divert trade that would otherwise move down the Savannah River to the port of Savannah, Ga. When the 136-mile line opened in 1833, it was the longest railroad in the world. By 1857 it was part of a line from Charleston to Memphis, Tenn.—at the time the longest connected system of railroads in the world. (Two of the railroads involved, the Georgia Railroad and the Western & Atlantic, are now part of CSX Transportation.)

The Southern Railway system, like many other railroads, grew by merger and acquisition, and the components retained their identities and corporate structure long after most other roads had absorbed their subsidiaries.

FACTS & FIGURES

Year	1929	1988
Miles operated	8,051	9,757
Locomotives	1,802	1,416
Passenger cars	1,037	22
Freight cars	60,423	58,929
Reporting marks: SOU		
Historical society: srha.net		

Brakeshoe smoke billows as a Southern freight descends Saluda grade, near Melrose, N. C., in the 1950s. The main line is to the right; the emergency runaway track is at left. *Linn Westcott*

Richmond & Danville–Richmond Terminal

The Richmond & Danville Railroad was the nucleus of the Southern Railway. It was chartered in 1847 and completed in 1856 from Richmond, Va., west 141 miles to Danville, Va. Its charter allowed it to acquire and control only railroads with which it connected directly. In 1880 interests connected with the R&D incorporated the Richmond & West Point Terminal Railway & Warehouse Co. ("Richmond Terminal") to acquire railroads that did not connect directly with the R&D. The majority owners of the R&D and the Richmond Terminal decided the existence of the Richmond Terminal was unnecessary (by then, the R&D's charter had been amended) and in 1886 leased the railroads controlled by the Richmond Terminal to the Richmond & Danville; then the Richmond Terminal acquired the Richmond & Danville.

In 1863 the R&D purchased a majority of the stock of the Piedmont Railroad, under construction from Danville to Greensboro, N. C. The line opened in 1864, and the R&D leased it in 1866. In 1871 the R&D leased the North Carolina Railroad, which was opened in 1856 from Goldsboro through Greensboro to Charlotte.

The R&D contracted to construct the Northwestern Railroad of North Carolina from Greensboro to Salem, and assisted the Atlanta & Richmond Air-Line Railroad with the construction of its line between Atlanta and Charlotte. Both those routes were opened in 1873. The Atlanta &

Charlotte Air-Line Railway was organized in 1877 as the successor to the Atlanta & Richmond. It was leased to the Richmond & Danville in 1881.

In 1881 the R&D purchased the Virginia Midland Railway from the Baltimore & Ohio to get a direct Danville–Washington route about 20 miles shorter than the route through Richmond. The Virginia Midland had begun as the Orange & Alexandria Railroad, opened from Alexandria, Va., across the Potomac River from Washington, D. C., southwest to Gordonsville, in 1854. Through trackage rights on a C&O predecessor and further construction, it reached Lynchburg in 1860. It came under control of the state of Virginia in 1867, and in 1872 the Virginia & North Carolina Railroad was organized to consolidate the Orange, Alexandria & Manassas Gap (successor to the O&A) and the Lynchburg & Danville Railroad, under construction between the cities of its name. The Baltimore & Ohio obtained control and named it the Washington City, Virginia Midland & Great Southern Railroad. The extension to Danville was completed in 1874, and in 1880, a cutoff from Orange to Charlottesville was opened. The company was reorganized as the Virginia Midland Railway in 1881.

In 1886 the R&D leased the Western North Carolina Railroad, which had been constructed from Salisbury west through Old Fort (1869) and Asheville (1879) to a connection at the Tennessee state line with the East Tennessee, Virginia & Georgia.

The Georgia Pacific Railway was chartered in 1881 to build a from Atlanta to a connection with the Texas & Pacific at Texarkana. It was opened as far as Columbus, Miss., in 1887. It was leased to the Richmond & Danville in January 1889, shortly before it completed its line as far as the Mississippi River at Greenville, Miss. The Mississippi portion of the GP, which had remained a separate entity, was cast off as the Columbus & Greenville in 1920.

In 1892 the Richmond Terminal and the railroads it controlled (Richmond & Danville; Virginia Midland; Charlotte, Columbia & Augusta; Western North Carolina; Georgia Pacific; and East Tennessee, Virginia & Georgia) entered receivership. The banking house of J. P. Morgan came to the rescue.

East Tennessee, Virginia & Georgia

In 1869 two railroads out of Knoxville, Tenn., the East Tennessee & Virginia and the East Tennessee & Georgia, were consolidated to form the East Tennessee, Virginia & Georgia Railroad. The East Tennessee & Virginia was built from Bristol, Va., to Knoxville, 131 miles, between 1850 and 1856. The East Tennessee & Georgia opened a line from Dalton, Ga., to Knoxville, 110 miles, and a branch from Cleveland, Tenn., to Chattanooga in 1859.

In 1881 the ETV&G acquired and constructed lines from Dalton to Brunswick, Ga., and Meridian, Miss. Three other major routes were more or less affiliated with the ETV&G: Chattanooga–Memphis, Mobile–Selma, Ala., and Louisville–Lexington, Ky.

Southern Railway

The Southern Railway was chartered in 1894 to acquire the properties of the Richmond Terminal. The system comprised lines from Alexandria, Va., to Columbus, Miss.; from Chattanooga through Atlanta to Brunswick, Ga.; from Memphis through Chattanooga to Bristol, Va.; from Selma, Ala., to Rome, Ga.; and from Danville, Va., to Richmond.

The Southern acquired other railroads; among the larger ones were the Georgia Southern & Florida Railway in 1895 and the Louisville, Evansville & St. Louis Consolidated Railroad in 1898.

The Southern acquired a number of subsidiaries over the years. Many retained independent status, and the continued existence of these subsidiaries was attested to by initials on locomotives and cars.

Queen & Crescent Route

The Alabama Great Southern Railway Company, Ltd., and the Alabama, New Orleans, Texas & Pacific Junction Railways, Ltd., were British-owned holding companies that owned five railroads forming the Queen & Crescent Route between Cincinnati (the Queen City) and New Orleans (the Crescent City). The five railroads were the Alabama Great Southern; the Cincinnati, New Orleans & Texas Pacific; the New Orleans & Northeastern; the Alabama & Vicksburg; and the Vicksburg, Shreveport & Pacific. In 1890 the Richmond & Danville and the East Tennessee, Virginia & Georgia acquired control of the AGS company.

The Alabama Great Southern was incorporated in 1877. It was the successor to the Alabama & Chattanooga Railroad, whose predecessors had been chartered in 1852 and 1853, consolidated in 1868, and opened in 1871. Its main line stretched from Chattanooga to Meridian, Miss., 292 miles. Southern acquired the minority interest in AGS in 1969.

The New Orleans & Northeastern Railroad was incorporated in 1868 but lay dormant until 1881, when control was acquired by the Alabama, New Orleans, Texas & Pacific Junction Railways Ltd. Construction began in 1882, and the line was opened between New Orleans and Meridian, Miss., 196 miles, in 1883. The Southern purchased the NO&NE in 1916. The Alabama Great Southern merged the NO&NE in 1969.

The Cincinnati Southern Railway was incorporated in 1869 to build from Cincinnati to Chattanooga, 336 miles. It opened in 1880. The railroad was owned (and still is) by the city of Cincinnati. The Cincinnati, New Orleans & Texas Pacific was chartered in 1881 and immediately leased the CS for operation. The CNO&TP was controlled by the two British-owned holding companies previously mentioned, which also controlled the Alabama Great Southern and the New Orleans & Northeastern. The Southern and the Cincinnati, Hamilton & Dayton (Baltimore & Ohio) acquired control of the CNO&TP in 1895, but through its control of the Alabama Great Southern, which held an interest in the CNO&TP, Southern effectively had

Green-and-gold Ps-4 Pacific No. 1395 pulls train 35, the Atlanta-New Orleans *Express*, out of Alexandria, Va., in June 1937. *Walter H. Thrall Jr.*

control. Southern acquired B&O's interest in 1954.

The two Vicksburg railroads, which were controlled by the Alabama, New Orleans, Texas & Pacific company, became part of the Illinois Central system in 1927. The Alabama Great Southern and the CNO&TP were considered Class 1 railroads in their own right until corporate simplifications took effect.

Georgia Southern & Florida

The Georgia Southern & Florida Railway was incorporated in 1895 under Southern Railway control as a reorganization of the Georgia Southern & Florida Railroad, which had opened in 1890 from Macon, Ga., through Valdosta, Ga., to Palatka, Fla. It was intended to be part of a route from Birmingham, Ala., to Florida that would bypass Atlanta. In 1902 it purchased the Atlantic, Valdosta & Western Railway line from Valdosta, Ga., to a point near Jacksonville, Fla. Southern acquired control in 1895.

Atlantic & Yadkin

The Cape Fear & Yadkin Valley Railway was an 1879 reorganization of the Western Railroad of North Carolina, which opened in 1860 from Fayetteville to Cumnock, 6 miles north of Sanford. By 1890 the CF&YV had a line from Wilmington through Fayetteville, Sanford, and Greensboro to Mount Airy and another from Fayetteville southwest to Bennettsville,

South Carolina. The company entered receivership in 1894.

In 1899 it was sold at foreclosure and split between the Atlantic Coast Line, which acquired the Wilmington–Sanford and Fayetteville–Bennettsville lines, and the Southern, which organized the Atlantic & Yadkin Railway to take over the rest, from Sanford to Mount Airy. The A&Y was operated by the Southern Railway, which controlled it, until 1916, when it assumed its own operation. The Southern merged the company and resumed operation of the road on Jan. 1, 1950.

Modern times and merger

In the 1970s the Southern was notable for staying out of Amtrak, continuing to run its remaining passenger trains and gradually trimming service to just the Washington-Atlanta-New Orleans *Southern Crescent*. Amtrak took over operation of that train on Feb. 1, 1979.

On March 25, 1982, the Interstate Commerce Commission approved the acquisition by Norfolk Southern Corporation, a newly organized holding company, of the Southern Railway and the Norfolk & Western. Merger took place on June 1, 1982. At the end of 1990 the Norfolk & Western Railway became a subsidiary of the Southern Railway (it had been a subsidiary of Norfolk Southern Corporation), and the Southern Railway changed its name to Norfolk Southern Railway.

Southern Pacific Lines

Train 99, the *Coast Daylight*, sails through Santa Barbara, Calif., in the early 1950s. Matching the colors of the train is GS-4-class 4-8-4 No. 4452, one of 28 built for Southern Pacific by Lima in 1941 and 1942. *Linn Westcott*

Until the supermergers of recent decades, Southern Pacific was one of the largest railroads in the U. S., ranking third behind Pennsylvania and New York Central in operating revenue and second behind Santa Fe in route mileage. SP's lines stretched over a greater distance than any other railroad—from New Orleans west to Los Angeles, then north to Portland, Ore., east from Sacramento to Ogden, Utah, and before 1951 down the west coast of Mexico to Guadalajara. It dominated transportation in California and was the only large railroad headquartered on the West Coast. Explaining Southern Pacific's history route by route, much as its passenger timetables were arranged years ago, makes it easier to understand.

Overland Route

California became a state in 1850. It would need a railroad to connect it to the rest of the country. The route that railroad should take posed a question: south toward the slave states or north toward the free states? The question was answered a decade later by the outbreak of the Civil War.

In 1852 the Sacramento Valley Rail Road engaged Theodore D. Judah to lay out its line from Sacramento east a few miles to Folsom and Placerville. The line was opened in 1856, but Judah had higher goals—a railroad over the Sierra Nevada to Virginia City, Nev. He scouted the mountains for a route and sought financial backing in San Francisco. That city considered itself a seaport, not the terminal of a railroad, but in Sacramento he obtained the backing of four merchants: Collis P. Huntington, Mark Hopkins, Charles Crocker, and Leland Stanford—collectively, the Big Four. They incorporated the Central Pacific Railroad in June 1861.

In 1862 Congress passed the Pacific Railroad Act. It provided for the incorporation of the Union Pacific Railroad to build westward (its eastern terminal, Omaha, was decided later), empowered the Central Pacific to build east, and provided loans and land for both efforts.

Construction of the CP began at Sacramento in January 1863. Its first train operated 18 miles east to what is now Roseville in November of that year. By 1867 CP had crossed the state line into Nevada, and on May 10, 1869, the Central Pacific and Union Pacific met at Promontory, Utah, creating the first transcontinental railroad.

California Lines

After meeting the UP at Promontory, the Central Pacific was extended west from Sacramento to San Francisco Bay, first by construction of the Western Pacific Railroad to Oakland over Altamont Pass (don't confuse this Western Pacific with the twentieth century railroad of the same name over the same pass, now part of Union Pacific), then by acquisition in 1876 of the California Pacific Railroad ("Cal-P") from Sacramento to Vallejo.

In 1879 Central Pacific completed a line from Port Costa, across the Carquinez Strait from Vallejo, along the shore of San Francisco Bay to Oakland. Train ferries made the connection between Port Costa and Benicia (just east of Vallejo) until the

SP FACTS & FIGURES

Year	1929	1994
Miles operated	13,848	8,991
Locomotives	2,388	1,682
Passenger cars	2,786	—
Freight cars	80,619	32,363
Reporting marks: SP		
Historical society: sphts.org		

construction of the bridge across Carquinez Strait in 1929.

The San Francisco & San Jose Railroad opened between the cities of its title in 1864, and in 1865, its owners incorporated the Southern Pacific Railroad to build south and east to New Orleans. History is unclear as to the next few years—who acquired whom, what was incorporated when—but by 1870 the Southern Pacific (possibly a new Southern Pacific) and the San Francisco & San Jose were in the hands of the Big Four. Construction started southeast from San Jose, and by 1871, the line had reached Tres Pinos, in the mountains east of Salinas and west—a long way west—of Fresno.

There was almost no population to support a railroad beyond Tres Pinos, so Southern Pacific changed its plans and started construction southeast through the San Joaquin Valley from Lathrop, 9 miles south of Stockton. The rails reached Fresno in 1872 and Sumner, across the Kern River from Bakersfield, at the end of 1874. The line was built by the Central Pacific as far south as Goshen Junction, 53 miles south of Fresno, where it intersected the original Southern Pacific survey. Beyond Goshen Junction, it was built by Southern Pacific.

The Tehachapi Mountains form the south end of the San Joaquin valley. To keep the grade over the mountains within limits, William Hood laid out a tortuous line that twists back and forth and at one point crosses over itself. The line reached a summit at Tehachapi, then descended directly to the northwest corner of the Mojave Desert. SP had intended to build southeast across the Mojave Desert to the Colorado River but it was induced to detour through Los Angeles (then barely more than a mission settlement).

The Coast Line, which was (and is) primarily a passenger route between San Francisco and Los Angeles, opened in 1901.

SP's line from Mojave to Los Angeles was a detour. SP returned to Mojave and built east across the Mojave Desert to the Colorado River at Needles, Calif., not with the intention of continuing eastward but to connect with the Atlantic & Pacific—meeting it at the state line and saying, "Welcome to Southern Pacific country." The eventual result of the line across the Mojave Desert was the Southern Pacific of Mexico.

Early SP freight-service diesels, such as F3 6133, wore the black, silver, red, and orange "black widow" paint scheme. *Linn Westcott*

Sunset, Golden State Routes

SP built east from Los Angeles, reaching the Colorado River at Yuma, Ariz., in 1877. Further construction, as the Galveston, Harrisburg & San Antonio Railway, put the line through Deming, N. M., and a Santa Fe connection in 1881. Later that same year, SP reached El Paso, Texas, and then, 90 miles farther east, Sierra Blanca, a connection with Texas & Pacific Railway. These connections created two more transcontinental U. S. railroad routes.

SP pushed on east, meeting the line from San Antonio at the banks of the Pecos River in 1883. The railroad there was later relocated, crossing the Pecos on the highest bridge on a U. S. common carrier (320 feet).

In the mid-1880s the Rock Island planned a line southwest from Kansas to El Paso, and in 1902, it met the El Paso & Rock Island Railway at Santa Rosa, N. M. The El Paso–Santa Rosa line was the Eastern Division of the El Paso & Southwestern System. EP&SW's Western Division consisted of a line from El Paso to Tucson, Ariz., parallel to SP but for much of the distance, 30 to 70 miles south of it. SP purchased the EP&SW in 1924.

Texas and Louisiana Lines

The SP lines east of El Paso grew from the Buffalo Bayou, Brazos & Colorado Railroad and the New Orleans, Opelousas & Great Western Railroad, both chartered in 1850. The BBB&C was reorganized as the Galveston, Harrisburg & San Antonio Railway in 1870. It reached San Antonio in 1877, engaged in some machinations with and against Jay Gould's Missouri Pacific system, and continued building west. The Opelousas, sold in 1869 to steamship magnate Charles Morgan and later resold and reorganized as Morgan's Louisiana & Texas Railroad, built across the bayou country west of New Orleans to form a New Orleans–Houston route in conjunction with the Louisiana Western and the Texas & New Orleans.

In 1934 all these railroads were consolidated as the Texas & New Orleans Railroad. Even after the repeal in 1967 of the article in the Texas constitution requiring railroads operating in Texas to be headquartered there, the T&NO lines were operated as a separate entity.

Shasta and Cascade Routes

In 1870 Central Pacific acquired the California & Oregon Railroad, which had built north from Marysville. It pushed north through Redding, Calif., up the Sacramento River canyon, and over the Siskiyou Range to connect with the Oregon & California Railroad at Ashland, Ore., in 1887. SP acquired the O&C at that time, extending its system north to Portland. In 1909 SP opened a line from Black Butte, Calif., at the foot of Mount Shasta, northeast across the state line to Klamath Falls, Ore.

Southern Pacific had more than 200 Cab-Forward steam locomotives (to keep smoke in tunnels away from crews). AC-10-class 4-8-8-2 4231 is at Oakland, Calif., in 1954. *Linn Westcott*

In 1926 SP opened the Natron Cutoff between Klamath Falls and Eugene, Ore. It had been conceived as a line southeast from Eugene to meet a proposed Union Pacific line west from the Idaho-Oregon border. That linkup never happened, but SP saw that extending this line south through the Klamath Basin might head off the Great Northern, which was constructing a line south from the Columbia River to connect with a Western Pacific line being pushed north from Keddie, Calif. As it turned out, GN wound up on SP rails between Chemult, Ore., and Klamath Falls. The new route had much easier grades and curves than the original route through Ashland, and it became SP's main route in Oregon.

About the same time, SP opened a line from Klamath Falls southeast to the Overland Route at Fernley, Nev. Some of the Modoc Line, as it is called, was new construction; for other portions of it, SP purchased and standard-gauged the 3-foot gauge Nevada-California-Oregon Railway.

Construction of Shasta Dam between 1938 and 1942 required relocation of much of SP's line in the lower Sacramento River canyon. The Pit River bridge, which carries both railroad and highway traffic, was at the time of its construction the highest in the U. S. (433 feet). Subsequent filling of Shasta Lake brought the water level up to just below the girders.

Southern Pacific, Central Pacific, and Mr. Harriman

The four men who controlled the Central Pacific also controlled the Southern Pacific, and the two roads were operated as a unified system. By 1884 it was clear that corporate simplification was necessary. The most logical proposal, consolidating the two companies, was rejected. A new Southern Pacific Company was formed to replace the Southern Pacific Railroad. The Central Pacific Railroad leased its properties to the SP and was reorganized as the Central Pacific Railway.

As the nineteenth century closed, control of SP rested with C. P. Huntington, last survivor of the Big Four. Huntington died in 1900, and his SP stock was purchased by the Union Pacific, which had recently come under the control of E. H. Harriman.

Harriman had acquired a UP that had fallen on hard times. It consisted essentially of lines from Omaha and Kansas City west through Cheyenne to Ogden. Harriman immediately undertook a complete rebuilding of the UP and reacquired the route northwest through Idaho to Portland, Ore., that UP had lost a few years before. Without ownership or control of the Central Pacific from Ogden to California, though, UP's line to Ogden was worthless.

The Southern Pacific was in good condition, but Harriman soon undertook three major improvements on SP's Overland Route: the Lucin Cutoff across the Great Salt Lake, shortening the Oakland–Ogden distance by 44 miles (and bypassing Promontory); a second track over the Sierra, in many places with an easier grade; and automatic block signaling. One of Harriman's improvements in California was the

Bayshore Cutoff south of San Francisco, which replaced a steep inland route with a water-level route along the shore of San Francisco Bay.

Meanwhile President Theodore Roosevelt had begun to consider the problems that big business posed for the free enterprise system. He focused his attention on Harriman, the Union Pacific, and the Southern Pacific.

The upshot was that UP had to sell its SP stock, and SP had to justify its retention of Central Pacific. Divestiture of Central Pacific would have ripped the heart out of Southern Pacific's network of lines in California and Oregon. Central Pacific's principal routes were from Oakland through Sacramento and Reno to Ogden; from Fernley, Nev., northwest to Susanville, Calif.; from Hazen, Nev., down to Mojave (mostly narrow gauge); from Roseville north to Hornbrook, Calif., on the Siskiyou Route and to Kirk, Ore., north of Klamath Falls; and from Stockton through Fresno to Goshen Junction. The Natron Cutoff and the Modoc line, both built in the late 1920s, were also Central Pacific routes. The process of justifying SP's ownership of Central Pacific to government agencies continued for years, consuming management time and creating an atmosphere of uncertainty. Central Pacific's corporate existence continued until 1959.

Merger with, um—who's available?

Southern Pacific and Santa Fe announced their merger proposal in May 1980, called it off later that year, and revived it in 1983. On Dec. 23, 1983, Santa Fe Industries and Southern Pacific Company, the parent companies of the two railroads, were absorbed by the new Santa Fe Southern Pacific Corporation. The two railroads remained separate but went so far as to paint and partly letter several locomotives for the Southern Pacific & Santa Fe Railway.

The Interstate Commerce Commission turned down the request for merger, rejected the subsequent appeal, and ordered SFSP Corp. to divest itself of one railroad. Offers to buy SP came from Kansas City Southern, Guilford Transportation Industries, SP management, and Rio Grande Industries, parent of the Denver & Rio Grande Western. On Aug. 9, 1988, the ICC approved sale of the SP to Rio

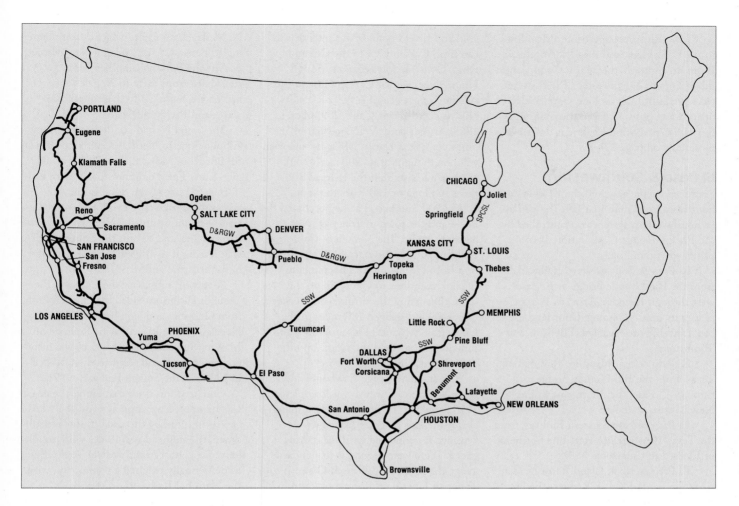

Grande Industries. The sale was completed on Oct. 13, 1988.

The name of the new system was Southern Pacific Lines. The identity and image of the Denver & Rio Grande Western were replaced by those of SP—much like Cotton Belt came to look like its parent, SP.

In 1991 SP sold its San Francisco–San Jose line and the commuter business it operated for the California Department of Transportation to San Francisco, San Mateo, and Santa Clara counties (retaining freight rights). The Peninsula Corridor Joint Powers Board assumed responsibility for funding and operating the service. Amtrak took over actual operation of the Peninsula commute trains on July 1, 1992.

Union Pacific purchased the Southern Pacific on Sept. 12, 1996. SP enthusiasts can take pleasure in knowing that technically SP merged UP, not the other way around. On Feb. 1, 1998, the Southern Pacific Transportation Company (a Delaware corporation) merged the Union Pacific Railroad and was then renamed the Union Pacific Railroad Company.

Cotton Belt

The St. Louis Southwestern Railway (the Cotton Belt) was SP's principal subsidiary. (The Cotton Belt is described fully in its own entry on page 261.)

After World War I, bridge traffic began to increase on the Cotton Belt. The Rock Island and the Kansas City Southern controlled it briefly before SP applied for control, which it got in 1932. The Cotton Belt essentially became a division of the SP, though its equipment was still lettered "Cotton Belt." In 1980 SSW acquired the former Rock Island line from St. Louis through Kansas City to Santa Rosa, N. M., (RI owned the line between Santa Rosa and Tucumcari, N. M., but it had long been leased to SP.) and trackage rights on Union Pacific's ex-Missouri Pacific route from Kansas City to St. Louis (the former RI line between Kansas City and St. Louis was part of a package).

SPCSL

Chicago, Missouri & Western Railway purchased Illinois Central Gulf's lines from Joliet to East St. Louis, Ill., and from Springfield, Ill., to Kansas City on April 28, 1987, essentially resurrecting the old Alton Railroad. Less than a year later, on April 1, 1988, the CM&W entered bankruptcy. Southern Pacific purchased the East St. Louis–Joliet line to operate as SPCSL Corporation (Southern Pacific Chicago St. Louis).

Other subsidiaries

In 1907 SP and Santa Fe formed the jointly owned Northwestern Pacific Railroad, which consolidated several lines north of San Francisco. NWP built north through the redwood country and down the canyon of the Eel River to Eureka, Calif. SP bought out Santa Fe's share in 1929, and sold the line in the 1980s and 1990s. (See Northwestern Pacific entry on page 231.)

SP had several subsidiary traction lines. The Portland, Eugene & Eastern served Oregon's Willamette Valley. The Interurban Electric Railway served the East Bay cities of Oakland, Berkeley, and Alameda and for a short period connected them with San Francisco via the Bay Bridge.

Pacific Electric, largest interurban line in the U. S., blanketed the Los Angeles Basin. In addition, the Marin County suburban lines of Northwestern Pacific were electrified until the Golden Gate Bridge opened and buses replaced the train-and-ferry service. (Pacific Electric is described more fully on page 234.)

El Paso & Southwestern

Southern Pacific acquired the El Paso & Southwestern system in 1924. The El Paso & Southwestern system was controlled by the Phelps-Dodge Corporation. It comprised several railroads:

• El Paso & Southwestern Railroad, from the Rio Grande bridge at El Paso west through Douglas, Ariz., to Tucson, plus branches to Deming, Courtland, Bisbee, Lowell, Fort Huachuca, Benson, and Tombstone

• El Paso & Southwestern Railroad of Texas, from the Rio Grande bridge through El Paso, then northeast to the New Mexico state line

• El Paso & Northeastern Railway, from the Texas–New Mexico state line northeast of El Paso to Carrizozo, N. M.

• El Paso & Rock Island Railway: Carrizozo to Santa Rosa, 128 miles (the line from Santa Rosa to Tucumcari was owned by the Rock Island but in later years leased to the Southern Pacific)

• Alamogordo & Sacramento Mountain Railway: Alamogordo and Russia, 32 miles (notable for its climb from 4,320 feet at Alamogordo to 8,600 feet at Cloudcroft, 20 miles out)

• Dawson Railway & Coal Co.: Tucumcari to Dawson, N. M., 132 miles

The EP&SW also controlled the Nacozari Railroad, from Douglas, Ariz., to Nacozari, Sonora, Mexico.

The eastern portion of the EP&SW formed an extension of the Rock Island's route southwest across Kansas, Oklahoma, Texas, and New Mexico—the Golden State Route in SP's advertising. West of El Paso the EP&SW was a second main line parallel to SP's own line but some distance south, close to the Mexican border. At Naco, the EP&SW turned north to Benson, then turned northwest, crossing and recrossing SP between Benson and Tucson.

SP narrow gauge lines

The Carson & Colorado Railroad was conceived in 1880 at the height of the Nevada gold and silver boom. It was intended to run from Carson City to the Colorado River. Construction began at Mound House, Nev., east of Carson City on the standard gauge Virginia & Truckee. Its rails reached Keeler, Calif., 299 miles, in 1883. At that point William Sharon, its promoter, asked Darius Mills, its financier, what he thought of it. Mills answered, "Either we have built the railroad 300 miles too long or 300 years too soon."

In 1900 Southern Pacific purchased the line—and the town of Tonopah, Nev., began to boom. The Nevada & California Railway, an SP subsidiary, built a connection from Hazen, on SP's Sacramento–Ogden main line, to Churchill on the C&C, bypassing the Virginia & Truckee, then standard-gauged 137 miles of the C&C from Mound House to Tonopah Junction. SP merged the C&C into the Nevada & California in 1905.

SP's standard gauge "Jawbone" line from Mojave to Owenyo was completed in 1910, largely to carry construction materials for the Los Angeles Aqueduct. At Owenyo it connected with the narrow gauge. There were proposals to standard-gauge the former C&C from Owenyo to Tonopah Junction to form a route from Los Angeles to Ogden, but uncertainty about the status of Southern Pacific control of Central Pacific kept the project from fruition.

In 1943 SP removed the narrow gauge rails between Mina, Nev., and Laws, Calif., having in 1938 ceased service between Tonopah Junction and Benton. The Laws–Keeler segment of the line was dieselized in 1954 and stayed in operation until April 29, 1960, carrying minerals and livestock.

Southern Pacific of Mexico

In 1881 and 1882 the Santa Fe built the Sonora Railway north from Guaymas, the principal Gulf of California port in the Mexican state of Sonora, to Nogales, on the U. S. border. The Santa Fe had already built southwest from Kansas to Deming, N. M. Trackage rights over SP from Deming to Benson, Ariz., and the New Mexico & Arizona Railroad, another Santa Fe subsidiary, from there to Nogales connected the Santa Fe to the Sonora Railway—and Pacific tidewater.

The Santa Fe had also built west from Albuquerque to Needles, Calif., meeting an SP line from Mojave. The SP line would give Santa Fe an entrance to southern California; SP saw in the Sonora Railway access to Mexico. The two roads worked a trade—Santa Fe got the Needles–Barstow–Mojave line, and SP got the Sonora Railway, leasing it in 1898 and purchasing it outright at the end of 1911.

A new SP subsidiary, the Cananea, Rio Yaqui & Pacific, extended the railroad south from Guaymas and built branches east of Nogales. The Southern Pacific Railroad of Mexico (Sud Pacifico de México) was incorporated in 1909 and acquired the CRY&P in 1909 and the Sonora Railway in 1912.

Construction southeast along the coast was hampered by uprisings and the Mexican revolution; by the time those settled down, the railhead was in the wild, rough barranca country southeast of Tepic. The SPdeM finally reached a connection with the National Railways of Mexico at Orendain Junction, 24 miles from Guadalajara, in 1927. Further revolutionary activity in 1929 destroyed bridges and interrupted service.

The SPdeM was a consistent money-loser for its parent, and at the beginning of 1940 Southern Pacific withdrew support, forcing the SPdeM to live on its own income. Losses continued, partly because of labor laws and partly because tariffs imposed by the U. S. on Mexican produce stifled traffic. Mexican authorities operated the line during a strike in 1947 and 1948. The status of foreign-owned holdings in Mexico became questionable, and there was a possibility of expropriation. In December 1951 SP sold the railroad to the Mexican government. It was renamed the Ferrocarril del Pacifico (Pacific Railroad).

SP NARROW GAUGE FACTS & FIGURES

Year	1929	1959
Miles operated	160	71
Locomotives	9	1
Passenger cars	9	—
Freight cars	284	222

SP OF MEXICO FACTS & FIGURES

Year	1929	1950
Miles operated	1,370	1,331
Locomotives	104	93
Passenger cars	129	88
Freight cars	1,513	618

Spokane International

Lumber provided much of Spokane International's local business. In this 1951 scene, the first three cars behind black-and-red RS-1 No. 205 are loaded with forest products. The SI also handled a great deal of bridge traffic. *Philip R. Hastings*

The Spokane International was built by D. C. Corbin from Spokane, Wash., north to the Canadian border at Eastport, Idaho, and Kingsgate, British Columbia. There it connected with Canadian Pacific's Kettle Valley route. The southern half of the line, from Spokane to Sandpoint, was parallel and within a few miles of Northern Pacific's main line; from Sandpoint to Bonners Ferry it virtually duplicated Great Northern's main line. (See the Spokane, Portland & Seattle map on the following page.)

The SI began operation on Nov. 1, 1906. It gave CPR a route to Spokane, or in conjunction with Soo Line, which it controlled, a route from St. Paul, Minn., to Spokane in competition with GN and NP. CPR purchased control of the SI in 1917.

Spokane International entered bankruptcy proceedings in 1933. Reorganization in 1941 as the Spokane International Railroad wiped out CPR's stock interest. During World War II, business increased and revenues climbed to give the railroad Class 1 status. After the war, it needed and got extensive rebuilding and dieselization. More than 80 percent of its business was bridge traffic between CPR and the connecting railroads at Spokane.

Union Pacific acquired control of SI on Oct. 6, 1958, by acquisition of nearly 90 percent of its stock, and gradually acquired the rest. The UP absorbed SI's operations, officially merging the SI in 1987.

FACTS & FIGURES

Year	1929	1958
Miles operated	166	150
Locomotives	11	12
Passenger cars	6	—
Freight cars	263	201
Reporting marks: SI		

Spokane, Portland & Seattle

James J. Hill announced in 1905 that he intended to build a railroad along the north bank of the Columbia River, partly to block the Milwaukee Road from doing the same and partly to invade Oregon, territory that belonged almost exclusively to E. H. Harriman's Union Pacific and Southern Pacific. The Portland & Seattle Railway was incorporated in 1905, and in 1908 Spokane was added to its name. The railroad was completed during 1908 from Pasco, Wash., to Portland, Ore., along the north bank of the Columbia River. In 1909 the line was opened from Spokane to Pasco. Jointly financing the construction of the SP&S were Great Northern and Northern Pacific.

Hill had already acquired a line along the south bank of the lower part of the Columbia River west of Portland; that plus NP's line from Portland to Goble, Ore., formed a route from Portland to Astoria where connection was made with Hill's steamships to San Francisco.

For most of its life, the SP&S functioned as an obscure extension of its two parents. Most of its steam locomotives were acquired second-hand from GN and NP. The road acquired a distinct identity during the diesel era with its heavy reliance on Alco power and a new slogan, "The Northwest's Own Railway." SP&S was

A westbound extra freight pulls out of Wishram, Wash., in June 1953 behind an FA/FB/FA trio (right) while an S-2 switcher works the yard. *David Plowden*

merged into Burlington Northern along with its parents, Northern Pacific and Great Northern, and Chicago, Burlington & Quincy on March 2, 1970.

Oregon Electric, Oregon Trunk

SP&S acquired the Oregon Electric Railway in 1910, two years after it had opened between Portland and Salem. The main line was extended south to Eugene in 1912. The OE was characterized by head-on competition with Harriman, with SP's electric lines in the Willamette Valley.

The Oregon Trunk was incorporated in 1909 and opened in 1911 between Wishram, Wash., on the Columbia River, and Bend, practically in the center of Oregon, 152 miles. Both OT and the Oregon-Washington Railroad & Navigation Co. (Union Pacific) built south up the canyon of the Deschutes River. The two railroads fought over occupancy of the canyon and eventually came to terms—trackage rights over portions of each other's line and abandonment of duplicate track.

United Railways

In 1906 the United Railways Company was incorporated and purchased the properties of Oregon Traction Company, which had a line from Linnton to Keasey, 54 miles. The line was operated primarily as a steam railroad and was notable for a 4,100-foot tunnel west of Portland. SP&S absorbed the company in 1943.

FACTS & FIGURES

Year	1929	1969
Miles operated	555	922
Locomotives	99	112
Passenger cars	100	54
Freight cars	698	3,216
Reporting marks: SPS		
Historical society: spshs.org		

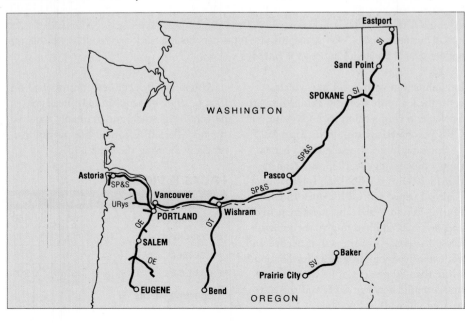

Sumpter Valley

The Sumpter Valley was incorporated in 1890 to tap the forests of the Blue Mountains of eastern Oregon. Much of the rolling stock for the line came from Union Pacific 3-foot gauge lines in Utah and Idaho that had just been standard-gauged. The first portion of the line from Baker to McEwen opened for service in 1892, and the line reached the town of Sumpter (which was in the midst of a gold-mining boom) in 1897.

The line reached Austin in 1905 and Prairie City, a cattle-raising center, in 1910. There were proposals to extend the line to Burns and also southwest to a connection with the Nevada-California-Oregon, which was building north from Reno, Nev. The latter would have created a narrow gauge route all the way from California's Owens Valley to Baker, except for a short stretch of the standard gauge Virginia & Truckee, and it would have traversed some of the emptiest country in the U. S. The Sumpter Valley got no farther than Prairie City, but it connected with an extensive network of logging railroads centered on Austin.

In 1932 the western 20 miles of the line from Bates to Prairie City were abandoned. In 1940 the SV bought two 2-6-6-2 articulated locomotives from the Uintah Railway (in western Colorado). SV converted them from tank engines to tender engines and used them for seven years.

By 1946 a reduction by the U. S. Forestry Service in the amount of timber that could be cut and the necessity to transfer lumber from narrow gauge to standard gauge cars at Baker caused the Sumpter

Sumpter Valley 2-6-6-2 No. 250 rolls a long train of lumber along the Powder River in the Blue Mountains of eastern Oregon in 1946. *Henry R. Griffiths*

Valley to petition for abandonment, even though it was still profitable and free of debt. The last scheduled run was on April 11, 1947, and official abandonment came on Aug. 31, 1948. The articulateds were sold to International Railways of Central America.

A two-mile portion of the railroad at Baker remained in switching service until the end of 1961. The sole remaining locomotive, a 30-ton Davenport diesel switcher built in 1937, was sold to the Denver & Rio Grande Western in 1963 for service at Durango as D&RGW No. 50.

FACTS & FIGURES

Year	1929	1945
Miles operated	80	58
Locomotives	11	3
Passenger cars	4	—
Freight cars	236	227
Reporting marks: SVR		

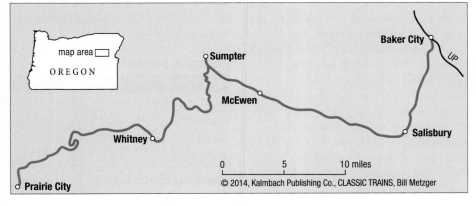

map area
OREGON

Baker City
UP
Sumpter
McEwen
Salisbury
Whitney
0   5   10 miles
Prairie City

© 2014, Kalmbach Publishing Co., CLASSIC TRAINS, Bill Metzger

Tennessee, Alabama & Georgia

Tennessee, Alabama & Georgia's entire diesel roster appears in this 1970 scene at the road's Chattanooga yard: GP38 No. 80, GP7 No. 709, GP18 No. 50, and GP7s 708 and 707, all painted a dark green. *William J. Husa Jr.*

Construction of the Chattanooga Southern Railway began in 1890 and was completed in 1891, creating a new line between Chattanooga, Tenn., and Gadsden, Ala. Backing the project was Russell Sage, a New York financier. The company entered receivership in 1892 and was reorganized as the Chattanooga Southern Railroad in 1896.

Receivers again took it over between 1907 and 1910; it was reorganized in 1911 as the Tennessee, Alabama & Georgia Railway—it, too, was reorganized in 1920. During the 1920s the Interstate Commerce Commission approved a proposal to extend the line southwest to a connection with Seaboard's Atlanta–Birmingham line, but the idea never bore fruit.

The TA&G was sold, reorganized, and sold again, this time to a syndicate headed by W. H. Coverdale of Coverdale & Colpitts, the railroad engineering firm. The new management immediately undertook a long-needed rehabilitation. Much of the line was still laid with the original 56-pound rail; it was upgraded with 100-pound rail. As business increased, TA&G had to replace its small, low-drivered Consolidations with secondhand Mikados and a pair of ex-Boston & Albany Berkshires. The company was reorganized again in 1937.

The original purpose of the road was to tap the iron, coal, and timber resources of northeastern Alabama, but gradually the TA&G's principal purpose came to be serving the steel mills at Gadsden.

On Jan. 1, 1971, the Southern Railway purchased the TA&G. The middle portion of the line was abandoned about 1980, and the south end in the early '90s. NS sold the northernmost 19 miles of line to the Chattooga & Chickamauga Railway in 1989. The C&C quit in 2008; part of the line was abandoned and part reverted to NS.

FACTS & FIGURES

Year	1929	1970
Miles operated	95	87
Locomotives	8	5
Passenger cars	2	—
Freight cars	8	94
Reporting marks: TA&G		

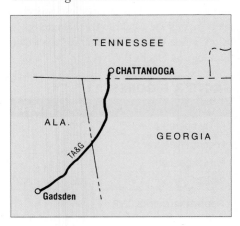

Tennessee Central

The Tennessee & Pacific Railroad was organized in 1871 and built eastward from Nashville to Lebanon, Tenn. By 1894 the line had extended east to Monterey with the intention of tapping coal mines; by 1900 the line had been pushed east to a connection with the Southern (Cincinnati, New Orleans & Texas Pacific) at Emory Gap by the Tennessee Central Railway (the road's history includes several Tennessee Central companies, railroads, and railways). In 1904 the TC was complete, with a 2-mile extension from Emory Gap to Harriman and an 83-mile line constructed from Nashville northwest to Hopkinsville, Ky.

The TC was the only direct route from Nashville to eastern Tennessee, albeit through topography requiring 3-percent grades, 10-degree curves, and several spectacular trestles. The road was intended to be a coal carrier—and by 1950 the principal commodity carried by the TC was indeed coal, but more coal was received from connecting railroads than was originated on line. TC provided access to Nashville for Illinois Central from Hopkinsville and for Southern from Harriman. Its tracks formed a belt line around Nashville, a city that was otherwise the exclusive province of Louisville & Nashville and its subsidiary Nashville, Chattanooga & St. Louis. During World War II, TC's traffic was boosted considerably by the Army installation at Fort Campbell near Hopkinsville.

Between a brief receivership in 1904 and a longer one from 1913 to 1917, the road was divided at Nashville and operated by IC and Southern, but neither IC nor

An Alco FA1/FB1 set leads a westbound extra freight out of a tunnel near Rockwood, Tenn., east of Crossville toward the eastern end of the Tennessee Central. *R. D. Sharpless*

Southern wished to continue the arrangement. The road was reorganized in 1922, and in 1946 control was assumed by a group of investors from Philadelphia. Net operating income became a deficit in 1963; from 1957 to 1966 the TC posted a net profit for only two years, 1958 and 1959. In May 1968 the ICC authorized abandonment of the Tennessee Central.

Portions of Tennessee Central's main line were acquired by other roads: Hopkinsville–Nashville by Illinois Central; Nashville–Crossville by Louisville & Nashville; and Crossville–Harriman by Southern. The Hopkinsville–Nashville segment has had a succession of operators and has been trimmed back to a 19-mile stub out of Nashville. About two-thirds of the line east of Nashville is still in service.

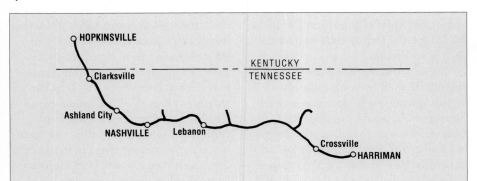

FACTS & FIGURES

Year	1929	1966
Miles operated	296	280
Locomotives	41	21
Passenger cars	33	—
Freight cars	663	557
Reporting marks: TC		
Historical society: tcry.org		

Texas & Pacific

Texas & Pacific's F units, including these F7s awaiting assignment at Fort Worth, Texas, in the mid-1950s, followed parent Missouri Pacific's Eagle blue scheme but with a T&P nose logo and "Texas & Pacific" side lettering. *Linn Westcott*

The southernmost of the routes surveyed between 1853 and 1855 for a transcontinental railroad led across central Texas. Although it was the shortest and lowest route between the Atlantic and the Pacific and the one least subject to the rigors of winter, the Civil War eliminated it from consideration.

After the war, though, a transcontinental route between the 32nd and 35th parallels was again feasible and desirable. In 1871 Congress chartered the Texas Pacific Railroad to build from Marshall, Texas, to San Diego, Calif., via El Paso, Texas. The name of the company was soon changed to Texas & Pacific Railway. Its first president was Thomas Scott, who had been vice-president and general manager of the Pennsylvania Railroad, and its first chief engineer was Grenville M. Dodge, the former chief engineer of the Union Pacific.

The new road purchased the properties and franchises of two early railroads, including a rail line in operation between Shreveport, La., and Longview, Texas. Construction west from Longview, begun in October 1872, was plagued by low water in the Red River (hindering the transportation of supplies), disease that killed off the mules used in construction, and yellow fever. Even so, the line reached Dallas in less than a year.

By the beginning of 1874, the T&P was operating from Shreveport west to Dallas, from Marshall north to Texarkana, and from Sherman east to Brookston (near Paris). In July 1876 the line from Shreveport reached Fort Worth. (To keep its charter in effect, the T&P had to reach Fort Worth before the state legislature ended its session; Fort Worth's representative kept the session going for several extra days.) Less than a month later, the Texarkana–Sherman line was completed.

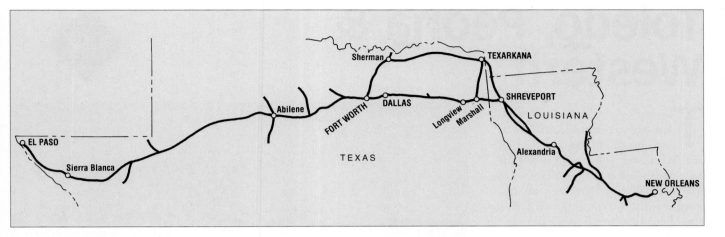

Fort Worth remained T&P's western terminus for several years. Construction had resumed in 1880, and the line proceeded rapidly across west Texas. On Dec. 15, 1881, at Sierra Blanca, about 90 miles east of El Paso, the T&P met the Southern Pacific, which had been building east from Los Angeles, completing the second transcontinental rail route.

By September 1882 T&P had purchased and built a line east from Shreveport to New Orleans, essentially completing the road. In the decades before and after the turn of the century, T&P upgraded some of the more-hastily constructed portions of its main line and acquired a number of short branches, but did nothing to alter the basic shape of its map.

In January 1880 Jay Gould and Russell Sage joined T&P's board of directors; in April of the next year Scott, sold his interests in the T&P to Gould, who became president of the road. The T&P was in receivership from 1885 to 1888 and entered receivership again in 1916. Fortunately for T&P, oil was discovered at Ranger, Texas, in 1918. T&P's revenues from the oil boom underwrote a rehabilitation program and put the road back in the black in 1924. Oil continued to be a major item of traffic until the completion of pipelines in the late 1940s.

In 1962 the Muskogee Co. authorized the sale of all its railroad stocks to the Texas & Pacific. In September 1964 T&P acquired control of the three Muskogee roads but immediately sold the Oklahoma City-Ada-Atoka to the Santa Fe. Midland Valley was merged into T&P on April 1, 1967, and the same happened to Kansas, Oklahoma & Gulf exactly three years later.

During reorganization in 1923, Texas & Pacific issued preferred stock to Missouri Pacific in exchange for mortgage bonds held by MP. By the beginning of 1930, Missouri Pacific owned all T&P's preferred stock and more than half its common stock. After many years of controlling T&P, MoPac finally merged the Texas & Pacific on Oct. 15, 1976.

A 2-10-4—known as a "Texas" because T&P had the first ones—powers a freight up Baird Hill in west Texas. The T&P owned 70 locomotives with this wheel arrangement. *Texas & Pacific*

FACTS & FIGURES

Year	1929	1975
Miles operated	1,956	2,139
Locomotives	372	153
Passenger cars	234	—
Freight cars	9,517	13,366

Reporting marks: T&P, TP

Historical society: mopac.org

Toledo, Peoria & Western

The first Toledo, Peoria & Warsaw Railway was chartered in 1863. It was opened in 1868 from the Indiana-Illinois state line at what is now Effner through Peoria to Warsaw, Ill., on the Mississippi River. In 1880 the road was reorganized as the Toledo, Peoria & Western Railroad and leased to the Wabash, St. Louis & Pacific for a term of 49 years—the lease lasted only until 1884.

The Toledo, Peoria & Western Railway was chartered in 1887 to take over the railroad. In 1893 the Pennsylvania Railroad and a predecessor of the Chicago, Burlington & Quincy each acquired a large stock interest in the TP&W, which by then had been extended across the Mississippi to Keokuk, Iowa. In 1927 the TP&W made a connection with the Santa Fe at Lomax, Ill., over a 10-mile line from La Harpe, Ill.

In 1927 George P. McNear Jr. purchased the TP&W at foreclosure. He saw the road's potential as a bridge route bypassing Chicago and St. Louis, and he began to improve its physical plant. In 1941 McNear refused to go along with an industry-wide pay increase, proposing hourly wages and the elimination of inefficient practices. A bitter strike ensued, followed by government operation during World War II and the 1947 murder of McNear. That year new management took over and the TP&W resumed operation after a 19-month work stoppage.

Another Toledo, Peoria & Western was incorporated in 1952. In 1960 the Santa Fe purchased the railroad and sold a half interest to the Pennsy. The TP&W formed a Chicago bypass for traffic moving between the Pennsy and the Santa Fe.

An eastbound TP&W local behind olive-green-and-gold Alco RS-2 No. 204 rolls across a steel bridge near Forrest, Ill., on Feb. 27, 1960. *J. Parker Lamb Jr.*

The formation of Conrail changed traffic patterns, and TP&W didn't fit into Conrail's plans. In 1976 TP&W bought the former Pennsylvania line from Effner east to Logansport, Ind., where it could interchange traffic with the Norfolk & Western. In 1979 the Pennsylvania Company, a subsidiary of Penn Central, sold its half interest in the TP&W back to the Santa Fe. Merger with Santa Fe took place on Dec. 31, 1983.

In 1986 the Keokuk Junction Railway, a terminal railroad at Keokuk, Iowa, bought the westernmost 33 miles of the line, from La Harpe to Warsaw and Keokuk. On Feb. 1, 1989, a group of investors purchased the Logansport-Lomax line from the Santa Fe, and yet another Toledo, Peoria & Western Railway began operating. Ownership went to Delaware Otsego Corporation in 1996, to RailAmerica in 1999, and Genesee & Wyoming in 2012.

FACTS & FIGURES

Year	1929	1980
Miles operated	239	301
Locomotives	24	29
Passenger cars	13	—
Freight cars	348	608
Reporting marks: TPW		

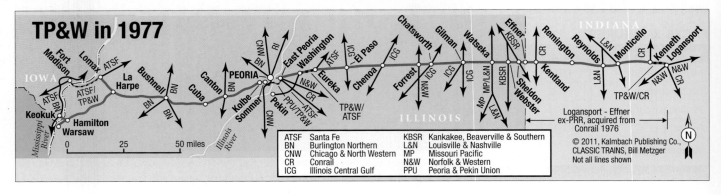

TP&W in 1977

ATSF	Santa Fe	KBSR	Kankakee, Beaverville & Southern
BN	Burlington Northern	L&N	Louisville & Nashville
CNW	Chicago & North Western	MP	Missouri Pacific
CR	Conrail	N&W	Norfolk & Western
ICG	Illinois Central Gulf	PPU	Peoria & Pekin Union

Logansport - Effner ex-PRR, acquired from Conrail 1976

© 2011, Kalmbach Publishing Co., CLASSIC TRAINS, Bill Metzger
Not all lines shown

Tonopah & Goldfield

In 1900 the discovery of silver in south-central Nevada created a boom town: Tonopah. Several rail proposals followed, including a branch of Southern Pacific's narrow gauge Carson & Colorado and southward extensions of the Nevada Central, the Eureka & Palisade and the Nevada Northern.

On July 25, 1903, the Tonopah Railroad was organized by the Tonopah Mining Co. Work began promptly from Tonopah Junction, 9 miles south of Mina on the C&C, and the 3-foot gauge track reached Tonopah, 60 miles from the junction, on July 23, 1904. A week later, a cloudburst washed out part of the line. More rain followed, and it was Sept. 7 before service was restored.

In October 1904 SP began standard-gauging its line from Mound House, the junction with the Virginia & Truckee, to Mina. The Tonopah Railroad proceeded to standard-gauge its own line, completing the job on Aug. 15, 1905.

Meanwhile, gold had been discovered in 1902 south of Tonopah, creating another boom town, Goldfield. The board of directors of the mining company declared the company had no interest in Goldfield affairs. As individuals, however, they did—and organized the standard gauge Goldfield Railroad.

On Sept. 12, 1905, the first train rolled into Goldfield. At that point the directors decided that it would be better to have

World War II brought a last surge of operation to the T&G. Here, two Consolidations haul several cars of aviation fuel bound for the air base at Tonopah. *C. M. Clegg*

one railroad than two. The Tonopah and Goldfield railroads were consolidated as the Tonopah & Goldfield Railroad on Nov. 1, 1905.

Also in 1905 T&G interests organized the improbably named Bullfrog Goldfield Railroad to build south to Beatty to head off the Las Vegas & Tonopah and the Tonopah & Tidewater. It reached Beatty in April 1907, six months after the Las Vegas & Tonopah had arrived. The LV&T pushed north parallel to the BG and reached Goldfield in October 1907, just in time for the collapse of the mining boom and a nationwide business slump. In 1908 the Tonopah & Tidewater took over operation of the Bullfrog Goldfield.

There followed a long period of declining business and belt-tightening through which the T&G continued to operate at a profit, if not a large one. The Las Vegas & Tonopah ceased operation in 1918, and the last Bullfrog Goldfield train departed Goldfield Jan. 7, 1928, leaving the T&G alone in Goldfield. The T&G endured a receivership from 1932 to 1937, and in 1942, the Tonopah Mining Co. sold its interest in the railroad to Dulien Steel Products of Seattle. Dismantling and scrapping appeared likely.

In 1942 the Army Air Force established an air base at Tonopah. Movements of troops and aviation gasoline suddenly brought boom times to the Tonopah & Goldfield.

When the air base was deactivated at the end of the war and the Army asked for the return of its three Alco RSD-1s, the T&G found itself with no serviceable steam locomotives. The railroad embargoed freight traffic on Oct. 1, 1946, and began handling mail and express by truck. Operators of mines protested the abandonment and promised carloads of ore if the road continued in operation, but the railroad said that it could not exist on an occasional carload of ore with most other commodities moving by truck. The Tonopah & Goldfield was formally abandoned on Oct. 15, 1947.

FACTS & FIGURES

Year	1929	1946
Miles operated	100	104
Locomotives	7	7
Passenger cars	1	2
Freight cars	104	—
Reporting marks: T&G		

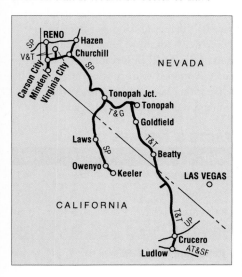

Tonopah & Tidewater

In the late 1920s the owners of the Tonopah & Tidewater tried to develop Death Valley as a winter tourist resort. Part of their program was the purchase of a gas-electric, which would cost less to operate than a steam-powered passenger train. Twice a week, a Pullman sleeper ran from Los Angeles to Death Valley Junction, with Union Pacific handling it between LA and Crucero. *Arthur C. Davis collection*

Francis Marion Smith's Pacific Coast Borax Co. had a borate mine in the Funeral Mountains east of Death Valley, California. The nearest railroad was the California Eastern at Ivanpah, Calif. (That line became a branch of Santa Fe, with which it connected at Goffs; it was abandoned in 1921.) Smith built a wagon road 100 miles north to the Lila C. Mine and tried out a steam traction engine as a replacement for his 20-mule teams. The traction engine lasted all of 14 miles. Smith decided a railroad was necessary.

The Tonopah & Tidewater Railway was incorporated on July 19, 1904, to build a railroad to Rhyolite, Calif. Construction began on May 29, 1905, at Las Vegas, a location suggested by Senator William Clark, the Montana copper magnate and builder of the San Pedro, Los Angeles & Salt Lake (which became Union Pacific's route from Salt Lake City through Las Vegas to southern California). After hearing of the gold and silver discoveries at Tonopah, Clark refused to let the T&T connect with the SPLA&SL and he started his own railroad to Tonopah, the Las Vegas & Tonopah.

Smith moved his base of operations to Ludlow, Calif., on the Santa Fe east of Barstow, and started construction in the fall of 1905. The relocated T&T crossed the SPLA&SL at Crucero, opened a branch from Death Valley Junction to the Lila C. Mine on Aug. 16, 1907, and reached Gold Center on Oct. 30. The remaining 2 miles to Beatty were on the rails of the Bullfrog Goldfield. (See the map on the previous page.) By then the Panic of 1907 was in progress and Rhyolite was already losing population. (Except for the former LV&T station and a few scattered buildings in Rhyolite, Beatty is all that remains today of that cluster of mining boom towns.)

In June 1908 ownership of the T&T and the Bullfrog Goldfield was transferred to a common holding company, with the blithe hope that the profits and losses of the two railroads would offset each other. In 1914 the Lila C. mine closed, and the owners moved the borax operations to a new location at Ryan. The branch to the Lila C. mine was abandoned and a new 3-foot gauge railroad, the Death Valley Railroad, was built from Ryan to the T&T at Death Valley Junction.

Also in 1914 the BG shifted its allegiance to the Las Vegas & Tonopah, and the two roads consolidated their parallel lines between Beatty and Goldfield. When the LV&T ceased operation in 1918, the Tonopah & Tidewater once again took over the Bullfrog Goldfield and in 1920 acquired the majority of its stock.

The borax mines, which provided nearly all the T&T's traffic, were nearly exhausted by the late 1920s. The Bullfrog Goldfield was abandoned in 1928, and the Death Valley Railroad, which had been operated as a branch of the T&T, closed in 1931. Traffic on the T&T continued to decline. In 1933 T&T abandoned the Ludlow-Crucero portion of its line and moved its shop facilities from Ludlow to Death Valley Junction.

Floods had occasionally disrupted service on the line, and a major flood in March 1938 destroyed much of the south end of the T&T. In December 1938 the road petitioned to discontinue service. Operation ceased on June 14, 1940, and the railroad was scrapped in 1942 and 1943.

FACTS & FIGURES

Year	1929	1939
Miles operated	169	143
Locomotives	5	5
Passenger cars	5	5
Freight cars	29	29
Reporting marks: T&T		

Toronto, Hamilton & Buffalo

In the 1880s the Canadian Pacific Railway wanted access to the growing industrial city of Hamilton, Ontario, and a connection with U. S. railroads at Buffalo, N. Y. Moreover, the city of Hamilton wanted the competitive benefits of a second railroad, and existing routes from Hamilton to Buffalo were circuitous.

The Toronto, Hamilton & Buffalo was incorporated in 1884 to build a railroad from Toronto through Hamilton to a point on the Niagara River. In 1890, before construction began, the road modified its goal and aimed the line at Welland, Ontario, on the main line of the Michigan Central.

Meanwhile the citizens of Brantford, Ontario, which was west of Hamilton and which had been bypassed by the Great Western Railway, incorporated the Brantford, Waterloo & Lake Erie Railway to build a line from Brantford south to a connection with the Michigan Central. The line was in operation by 1889. In 1892 the road undertook an extension from Brantford to Hamilton. Its finances ran out a few miles west of Hamilton, and the TH&B purchased it and began operating trains, even if it still hadn't begun work on its line to Welland.

In 1895 four railroads agreed to buy the TH&B: Canadian Pacific, 27 percent; New York Central, 37 percent; Michigan Central, 18 percent; and Canada Southern, 18 percent. The last two were part of the New York Central System, so ownership was effectively three-fourths NYC and one-fourth CPR. In April 1896, the CPR was granted trackage rights on Grand Trunk from Toronto almost to Hamilton. The TH&B dropped its plans to build to

Maroon-and-cream GP7 No. 76 and GP9 No. 402 lead a Toronto–Cobourg freight on the rails of parent CP Rail on April 28, 1976. *A. J. Sutherland*

Toronto and laid a mile and a half of track to connect its Hamilton terminal with the GTR near Bayview Junction, then turned that track over to CPR. In mid-1896 Michigan Central took over operation of the road, but in 1897 TH&B resumed its own operation.

The Hamilton-Welland portion of the TH&B (38 miles) opened in December 1895. It formed the middle third of a Buffalo–Toronto route for its owners. In 1905 TH&B agreed with Michigan Central to pool locomotives and crews between Hamilton and Buffalo, and in 1912 the locomotive pool was expanded to include Canadian Pacific.

A TH&B subsidiary, the Erie & Ontario Railway, completed a line from Smithville to Dunnville, 15 miles, in 1914. The TH&B merged the company in 1915 and extended it another 4 miles to Port Maitland in 1917.

A subsidiary, the Toronto, Hamilton & Buffalo Navigation Co., was incorporated in 1916 to operate a car ferry across Lake Erie between Port Maitland, Ontario, and Ashtabula, Ohio. Ferry service ended in 1932.

The TH&B continued as part of a Buffalo-Toronto route through the 1960s. Passenger service diminished little by little until in 1964 just one train was left, the main purpose of which was to convey a New

York–Toronto sleeping car. In 1970 the schedule was changed to create a daytime service between New York and Toronto. Freight business grew as passenger business declined.

When Conrail was formed in 1976, majority ownership of the TH&B remained with Penn Central (the ex-New York Central, Michigan Central, and Canada Southern interests in the road). In 1977 CP Rail purchased the Penn Central interest and assumed sole ownership. The last passenger service, a Toronto–Buffalo RDC (Rail Diesel Car) that operated in conjunction with CPR and Conrail, was discontinued April 25, 1981. (Amtrak's *Maple Leaf* began running between New York and Toronto the next day, using Canadian National rails between Niagara Falls and Toronto.)

On January 1, 1987, Canadian Pacific absorbed the TH&B.

FACTS & FIGURES

Year	1929	1979
Miles operated	111	110
Locomotives	31	18
Passenger cars	17	—
Freight cars	1,357	1,167
Reporting marks: THB		
Historical society: thbrailway.ca		

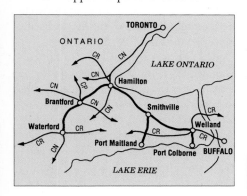

Union Pacific

Union Pacific Big Boy 4013 leaves Cheyenne, Wyo., headed for Sherman Hill, with a solid train of Pacific Fruit Express refrigerator cars in the mid-1950s. The 4-8-8-4 was one of 20 built for the UP by Alco in 1941; five more came in 1944. *Robert A. Caflisch; Helen Caflisch collection*

Union Pacific is still doing business at the same stand in Omaha, although it's much larger than it used to be—and in fact currently stands as the longest railroad in the nation. Over the years UP has merged and absorbed many other major railroads, including Western Pacific, Missouri Pacific, Missouri-Kansas-Texas, Chicago & North Western, and Southern Pacific to name a few. To understand how it came to pass, let's go back to the railroad's beginnings.

The Union Pacific was chartered by an act of Congress in 1862. The act provided subsidies and land grants to UP, which was to build west from Omaha, and to the Central Pacific, which was to build east from Sacramento, Calif. Construction began in 1865, and the two roads met at Promontory, Utah, on May 10, 1869. Ceremonies and a golden spike celebrated the completion of the first railroad across North America.

The ensuing three decades were difficult for Union Pacific. Bad management, over-extension, the effect of the Crédit Mobilier scandal, and the debt owed the federal government took their toll.

During that period UP affiliated or subsidiary lines were extended north from Ogden, Utah, to Butte, Mont. (Utah & Northern), and northwest from Granger, Wyo., to Portland, Ore. (Oregon Short Line). In 1880 the Union Pacific merged the Kansas Pacific Railway, which had opened from Kansas City to Denver in 1870, and the affiliated Denver Pacific, which connected Denver with the UP main line at Cheyenne. About that same time Union Pacific gained control of several railroads in Colorado that later became the Colorado & Southern Railway—meaning for a few years (until 1893) the Union Pacific system reached down into Texas.

The Harriman era

In 1897 E. H. Harriman purchased the Union Pacific at a public auction and assembled a system that included Southern Pacific, Illinois Central, and Chicago & Alton. Harriman embarked on an improvement program that included double track from Omaha west to Granger, Wyo., and a new line over Sherman Hill between Cheyenne and Laramie, Wyo.

In 1905 the Los Angeles & Salt Lake Railroad was completed between its namesake cities, but severe floods in several successive years in Nevada and western Utah destroyed much of the line in the Meadow Valley Canyon. The line was rebuilt and placed in service in 1912.

After Harriman

In 1912 the federal government required UP to divest itself of its Southern Pacific stock, but close cooperation continued between the two railroads aided by a 1924 agreement that permitted SP to control Central Pacific and required SP to solicit traffic to move via Ogden and the UP.

For the first three-quarters of the twentieth century the map of the Union Pacific remained the same: Omaha to Ogden, Ogden to Los Angeles, Ogden to Butte, Granger, Wyo., to Portland (and on to Seattle, by trackage rights), with a branch to Spokane, and Kansas City through Denver to Cheyenne, plus branches. Chicago, the railroad center of the United States, was 500 miles east of the east end of the main line, but Chicago & North Western's double-track route between

Chicago and Omaha had been practically an eastern extension of the UP since before 1900.

The Union Pacific of those years was even then a fast, long-haul, heavy-duty railroad. It had networks of traffic-gathering branches in Kansas, Nebraska, Utah, Idaho (it was the only railroad in the southern part of Idaho), Oregon, and eastern Washington, but its principal business was moving freight across a generally unpopulated area of the West. An hour spent at trackside in Wyoming would demonstrate this: frequent trains running fast on double track. It was equally competent in the passenger department. Its yellow streamliners moved in fleets, and its dining car service was as good as the Santa Fe's—better if you factor in UP's dome dining cars.

In 1955 UP suddenly shifted its streamliners to the Milwaukee Road east of Omaha. Eight years later UP petitioned to merge the Rock Island, primarily for its Omaha–Chicago line. The Rock Island merger case dragged on for 12 years before the involved parties gave up.

Expansion by merger

While UP was considering the Rock Island as a merger partner, four major western railroads got together to form an even bigger railroad—Burlington Northern. That merger was no surprise—it had been sixty-some years in the making. In 1977 Burlington Northern began merger discussions with the Frisco. In early January 1980 Union Pacific surprised the railroad industry by announcing that it intended to acquire the Missouri Pacific and later that month announced an offer to acquire the Western Pacific.

What triggered UP's move? BN's merger of Frisco? Southern Pacific's desire to push toward Kansas City by acquiring part of the Rock Island? A hunch that railroads were soon going to choose up sides and UP wanted to be a chooser, not the chosen?

The announcements constituted a major realignment of the western railroads. Union Pacific and Southern Pacific had long been considered logical merger partners, and Missouri Pacific and Western Pacific were part of the old Gould empire—as was the Denver & Rio Grande Western, which linked the MP and WP. More recently, WP and

Extra 2317 West, behind an MK-8-class Mikado, heads west across the Nebraska prairie in the early 1950s. The former Oregon Short Line 2-8-2 was built by Baldwin in 1918. *Linn Westcott*

SD70M 4059 and two mates lead a long westbound double-stack container train into a curve on the two-track former SP main line east of Vail, Ariz., in February 2001. *Jeff Wilson*

D&RGW had been good friends with the Burlington.

Acquisition of WP would take UP into San Francisco Bay area; the MP would give UP access to lucrative oil and chemical traffic in Texas and the long-coveted route to Chicago—Kansas City to St. Louis on MP, then up to Chicago on the former Chicago & Eastern Illinois.

On Dec. 22, 1982, Union Pacific merged the Missouri Pacific and the Western Pacific, more than doubling the original UP in size. The name Pacific Rail Systems was used briefly to describe the combined railroads, but it did not catch on. Western Pacific was absorbed immediately. Missouri Pacific was to remain separate, but within a year, yellow paint

began to replace blue on MP locomotives, and not long after that "Union" replaced "Missouri" in the lettering diagrams. The MP diesel shop at North Little Rock, Ark., became a valued asset.

In 1987 Union Pacific Railroad simplified its corporate structure by merging a number of its subsidiaries: Los Angeles & Salt Lake Railroad, Oregon Short Line Railroad, Oregon-Washington Railroad & Navigation Co., St. Joseph & Grand Island, Spokane International, Yakima Valley Transportation Co. (a traction line at Yakima, Wash.), Western Pacific, Sacramento Northern, and Tidewater Southern.

The Interstate Commerce Commission approved the purchase of the Missouri-

Kansas-Texas ("Katy") by the Missouri Pacific Railroad on May 16, 1988. UP absorbed the Katy's operations on Aug. 12, 1988. Meanwhile, UP had been buying into Chicago & North Western for its access into Chicago as well as Wyoming's Powder River Basin coal reserves (which UP had partnered with C&NW to build).

UP merged C&NW on April 24, 1995. The transition did not go well: Union Pacific offered buyouts to C&NW employees, and more people than anticipated took up UP on its offer, leaving the railroad short of train crews.

Meanwhile, Southern Pacific and Santa Fe began actions to merge on the assumption the Interstate Commerce Commission would continue to be as liberal about such matters as it had been before, but the ICC rejected their proposed combination. On the rebound, Santa Fe paired up with Burlington Northern, and Southern Pacific was acquired by Rio Grande Industries on Sept. 12, 1988. On Oct. 13, 1988, the two railroads began operating as one under the name Southern Pacific.

Southern Pacific fell on hard times and obviously had to merge but not with Burlington Northern & Santa Fe. Been there, done that. On Sept. 11, 1996, Union Pacific announced it would acquire Southern Pacific, completing what E. H. Harriman had started. Early in the process Union Pacific reassured regulatory authorities and shippers that there would not be operating problems of the magnitude experienced when UP absorbed the Chicago & North Western. The railroad still had difficulties swallowing Southern Pacific, however, and it took months to sort out all of the operational issues. Merger with the 13,000-mile SP created the largest railroad in the nation by track miles, 31,000, and reunited the partners of the original transcontinueal railroad 125 years later. In 2012, Union Pacific celebrated its 150th birthday.

FACTS & FIGURES

Year	1929	1981
Miles operated	9,878	9,096
Locomotives	1,674	1,665
Passenger cars	1,374	345
Freight cars	58,214	64,263
Reporting marks: UP		
Historical society: uphs.org		

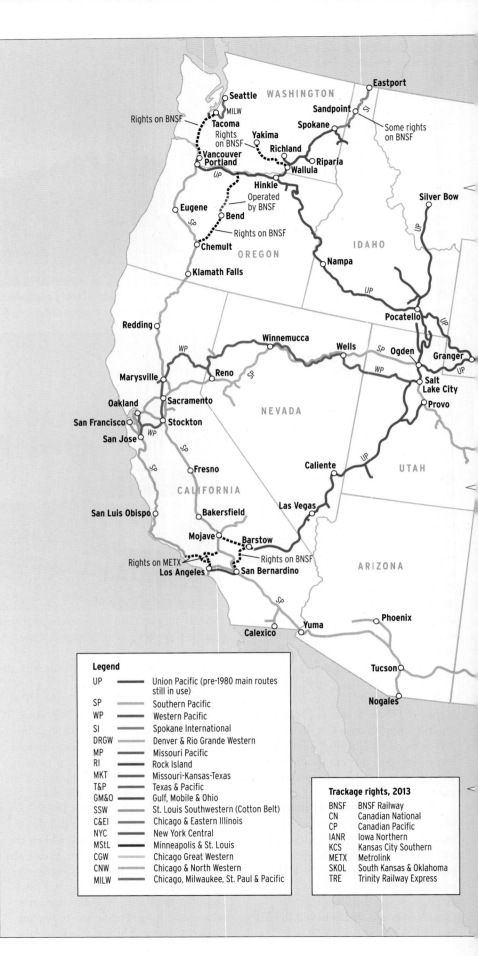

Legend

UP		Union Pacific (pre-1980 main routes still in use)
SP		Southern Pacific
WP		Western Pacific
SI		Spokane International
DRGW		Denver & Rio Grande Western
MP		Missouri Pacific
RI		Rock Island
MKT		Missouri-Kansas-Texas
T&P		Texas & Pacific
GM&O		Gulf, Mobile & Ohio
SSW		St. Louis Southwestern (Cotton Belt)
C&EI		Chicago & Eastern Illinois
NYC		New York Central
MStL		Minneapolis & St. Louis
CGW		Chicago Great Western
CNW		Chicago & North Western
MILW		Chicago, Milwaukee, St. Paul & Pacific

Trackage rights, 2013

BNSF	BNSF Railway
CN	Canadian National
CP	Canadian Pacific
IANR	Iowa Northern
KCS	Kansas City Southern
METX	Metrolink
SKOL	South Kansas & Oklahoma
TRE	Trinity Railway Express

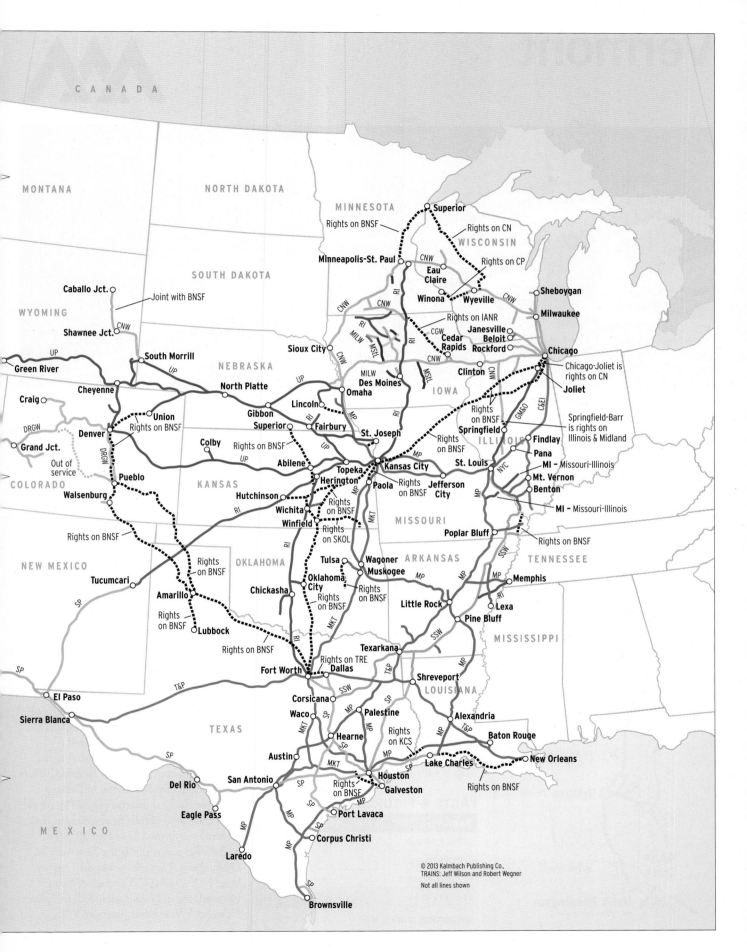

CANADA

MONTANA

NORTH DAKOTA

MINNESOTA
Superior
Rights on BNSF
Rights on CN
WISCONSIN
Minneapolis-St. Paul
CNW
Eau Claire
Rights on CP
Sheboygan
SOUTH DAKOTA
CNW
Winona
Wyeville
CNW
Milwaukee
Caballo Jct.
Joint with BNSF
CNW
Rights on IANR
Janesville
Beloit
WYOMING
Shawnee Jct.
CNW
RI
CNW
MILW
MSTL
CGW
Cedar Rapids
Rockford
Chicago
UP
Sioux City
CNW
Chicago-Joliet is rights on CN
Green River
MILW
Des Moines
Joliet
South Morrill
UP
MSTL
IOWA
Clinton
CNW
GM&O
C&EI
North Platte
Omaha
Rights on BNSF
Springfield-Barr is rights on Illinois & Midland
Craig
UP
Lincoln
Rights on BNSF
Springfield
Cheyenne
Gibbon
RI
Fairbury
St. Joseph
Rights on BNSF
ILLINOIS
Findlay
DRGW
Union
Rights on BNSF
Superior
Kansas City
St. Louis
Pana
Denver
Colby
Abilene
Topeka
NYC
MI – Missouri-Illinois
Grand Jct.
DRGW
Rights on BNSF
UP
Herington
Paola
Rights on BNSF
Jefferson City
Mt. Vernon
Benton
Out of service
Hutchinson
MP
COLORADO
Pueblo
KANSAS
Wichita
MKT
MI – Missouri-Illinois
Walsenburg
RI
Winfield
Rights on BNSF
MISSOURI
Poplar Bluff
Rights on BNSF
Rights on SKOL
SSW
TENNESSEE
Rights on BNSF
NEW MEXICO
Tulsa
Wagoner
Muskogee
MP
MP
Memphis
Tucumcari
Rights on BNSF
Oklahoma City
ARKANSAS
MP
Lexa
Amarillo
Chickasha
Rights on BNSF
Little Rock
RI
Rights on BNSF
SP
Lubbock
Pine Bluff
MISSISSIPPI
Rights on BNSF
MKT
Texarkana
MP
RI
Rights on TRE
Dallas
SP
T&P
Shreveport
El Paso
Fort Worth
SSW
LOUISIANA
Corsicana
MP
Palestine
Alexandria
Sierra Blanca
Waco
SP
Rights on KCS
T&P
Baton Rouge
TEXAS
Hearne
MP
MP
SP
Austin
MKT
SP
Lake Charles
New Orleans
Del Rio
San Antonio
SP
Houston
Rights on BNSF
Rights on BNSF
Galveston
Eagle Pass
MP
SP
Port Lavaca
MEXICO
MP
Corpus Christi
Laredo
SP
© 2013 Kalmbach Publishing Co.,
TRAINS: Jeff Wilson and Robert Wegner
Not all lines shown
Brownsville

— 295 —

Vermont

Vermont Railway 310, a former Canadian National GP40-2LW, leads a train south near Ludlow, Vt., on sister Vermont Rail System road Green Mountain Railroad in September 2011. It was the first post-Hurricane Irene train on the line following a nearby washout. *Kevin Burkholder*

Today's Vermont Railway had its beginning with the 1843 charter of the Rutland Railroad, which had all the characteristics that railroad enthusiasts appreciate and find interesting: a picturesque setting, a past that included control by other railroads (Central Vermont and New York Central), bankruptcy and receivership, and a series of adversities, each worse than the previous one, including floods, labor troubles, loss of a connecting Great Lakes boat line, and various stockholder and bondholder proposals for salvation. The Rutland's lines extended from Bellows Falls, Vt., and Chatham, N. Y., to Ogdensburg, N. Y., via Rutland and Burlington, Vt., and Rouses Point, N. Y. (For more on the Rutland, see pages 254-255.)

A 1961 strike shut down the Rutland, and it was abandoned two years later, leaving much of Vermont without rail service. There was still a need for such, so the state of Vermont bought the railroad in 1963 and engaged Jay Wulfson to operate the portion between White Creek, N. Y., and Burlington. Vermont Railway was incorporated in 1963 and began operation in January 1964.

Freed of the Rutland's worst problems, such as labor difficulties and the long tentacle of line across the Lake Champlain islands and the top of New York state to Ogdensburg, the Vermont (VTR) regained lost business and attracted new. It bought many of Rutland's boxcars and acquired a large fleet of piggyback trailers. Soon more businesses were shipping and receiving tonnage on VTR than had used the entire Rutland before the 1961 strike.

C&P and Green Mountain

In 1972, VTR purchased from Vermont Marble Co. the Clarendon & Pittsford, a short line running from Rutland and West Rutland a few miles north to Proctor and Florence and a nearby quarry. All but a bit of C&P trackage near Florence has been abandoned, but in 1983 VTR, through the C&P, bought 24 miles of Delaware & Hudson's line from Rutland to Whitehall, N. Y., which connects with D&H successor Canadian Pacific at Whitehall.

In 1997, the Vermont expanded again, buying the Green Mountain Railroad, which runs from Rutland southeast to Bellows Falls (see Rutland map on page 255). At the same time, an umbrella firm, Vermont Rail System, was formed to oversee all three roads. VRS also controls the New York & Ogdensburg (Norfolk-Norwood-Ogdensburg, N. Y.) and the Washington County Railroad (the old Montpelier & Barre plus Newport-White River Junction, Vt.).

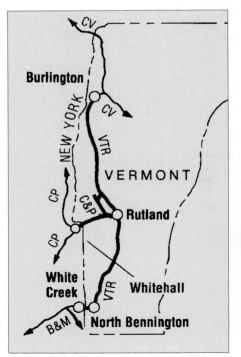

FACTS & FIGURES

Year	1965	2013
Miles operated	124	129
Locomotives	8	14
Passenger cars	—	—
Freight cars	358	27
Reporting marks: VTR		

Virginia & Truckee

During the California gold rush of 1849, Nevada was simply a place to pass through on the way west. In 1849 the Mormons established a settlement at Genoa, east of Lake Tahoe. Gold placers were discovered nearby, followed by the discovery of the Comstock Lode and the establishment of Virginia City. The boom was on. The miners were hampered by large amounts of a blue rock surrounding the gold, and for some time no one realized that the blue rock was silver ore.

By 1865 the Comstock mines were ready to produce on a larger scale. Machinery and timbers for deeper workings were expensive. William Sharon, local representative of the Bank of California, recognized the need for a railroad to bring in mining machinery and timbers and to take ore to reducing mills located along the Carson River. He asked an engineer if a railroad could be built from Virginia City to the Carson River. The engineer said "Yes."

The Virginia & Truckee Railroad was incorporated on March 5, 1868. Construction began almost a year later, and the first train from Carson City rolled into Gold Hill, just south of Virginia City, on Dec. 21, 1869. A month later the line reached Virginia City. The line from Carson City to Reno and a connection with the Central Pacific was completed on Aug. 24, 1872. (See the Tonopah & Goldfield map on page 289.)

The railroad's fortunes followed those of Virginia City and its mines. The destruction of most of Virginia City by fire in 1875 simply brought more business in the form of building materials, but ore production began to decline toward the end of the decade.

Carson & Colorado

In 1880 the Carson & Colorado was chartered by some of V&T's directors. Its narrow gauge track took off from the V&T at Mound House, northeast of Carson City, to head south 300 miles into California's Owens Valley.

Southern Pacific acquired the C&C in 1900. Two months later, silver was

Virginia & Truckee 2-8-0 No. 5 brings the daily-except-Sunday mixed train across the highway at Washoe on Aug. 7, 1948. *Fred H. Matthews Jr.*

discovered at Tonopah, and the C&C became a key link in the route to Tonopah. SP standard-gauged the C&C as far south as Tonopah Junction, and the new Tonopah Railroad did the same. SP considered purchasing the V&T as a connection between the C&C and the SP main line at Reno, but V&T's price was too high and SP instead built a connection south from Hazen, bypassing the V&T.

Gentle decline

The V&T was reorganized in 1905 as the Virginia & Truckee Railway. In 1906 it opened a 15-mile extension south from Carson City to Minden, and there was talk of electrifying the Reno–Minden line. Mining continued, but the V&T came to depend more on agriculture.

In 1924 the V&T paid its last dividend. Motor cars and mixed trains replaced the passenger trains, and the Minden line became the main route. Traffic continued to dwindle. Following the death of Ogden L. Mills, sole owner of the road since 1933, the V&T entered receivership. The Virginia City line was abandoned in 1939, and the V&T sold some of its old-time

rolling stock to Hollywood film companies (surplus cars and locomotives had simply been stored and the dry climate of Nevada kept them from deteriorating).

Railroad enthusiasts discovered the railroad, and their excursion trains reminded Nevadans that the V&T still existed. More equipment was sold to Hollywood, providing needed dollars in V&T's treasury. The railroad showed a modest profit in 1939, and the scrap value of the Virginia City line kept the road alive through World War II.

It is open to question whether V&T's postwar management was intent on keeping the road alive or abandoning it. That was 50 years ago, and question or not, the V&T ended service on May 31, 1950.

FACTS & FIGURES

Year	1929	1949
Miles operated	67	46
Locomotives	8	3
Passenger cars	19	4
Freight cars	32	9
Reporting marks: V&T		

Virginian

The Virginian was the creation of one man, Henry Huttleston Rogers, and was a one-commodity railroad—practically a conveyor belt to move coal from the mountains of West Virginia to ships at Norfolk, Va.

The Deepwater Railway was incorporated in West Virginia to build a line south into the mountains from Deepwater, W. Va., a station on the Chesapeake & Ohio 30 miles southeast of Charleston. By 1902, Rogers, vice-president of Standard Oil, had acquired an interest in the 4-mile line, which served lumber mills and coal mines. Neither C&O nor Norfolk & Western would agree on freight rates, so Rogers decided to build his own railroad from the coalfields to tidewater at Norfolk. He got the Deepwater's charter amended to allow construction to the Virginia state line, and he incorporated the Tidewater Railway in Virginia in February 1904 to build a railroad between Norfolk and the West Virginia state line.

In March 1907 the name of the Tidewater Railway was changed to Virginian Railway; in April of that year, the Virginian acquired the property of the Deepwater Railway. The line was completed between Norfolk and Deepwater at the beginning of 1909. From Roanoke to Norfolk, the railroad was as close as possible to a straight line, and it had an almost constant gentle descent. West of Roanoke, though, lay the Blue Ridge Mountains, with grades in both directions. The steepest eastbound grade was 2 percent for 14 miles from Elmore to Clarks Gap, W. Va.

The Virginian was built as a heavy-duty railroad. Before World War I, when the standard coal car was a 50-ton hopper, Virginian was using 120-ton, 12-wheel

Three-unit electric locomotive 103 rolls downgrade with tonnage at Oakvale, W. Va., on Sept. 4, 1953. *Richard J. Cook*

gondolas. In 1909 the road bought 2-6-6-0s, its first Mallets, and within a decade rostered 2-8-8-2s and 2-10-10-2s. It even experimented with a 2-8-8-8-4 that was unable to generate steam fast enough for its six cylinders. In the 1920s the Virginian electrified its line between Mullens, W. Va., and Roanoke. The new electric locomotives could haul heavier trains than the best steam locomotives and move them twice as fast.

In 1925 the N&W agreed to lease the Virginian if the Interstate Commerce Commission approved, which it did not. Other suitors included the Pennsylvania, the New York Central, and the Chesapeake & Ohio. In 1929 the Virginian applied to the ICC for permission to build a one-mile line across the Kanawha River at Deepwater to connect with New York Central's Kanawha & Michigan Railway. The ICC approved over the protest of the C&O.

Jan. 29, 1956 was the final run of the last passenger schedule, a Norfolk–Roanoke daytime local.

In 1948 Virginian received four two-unit electric locomotives to begin replacing the aging side-rod motors. In 1956 and 1957, 12 more electrics joined the roster. The new units were basically six-axle diesel hood units with Ignitron rectifiers instead of diesel engines. Shortly after they arrived, Virginian dumped the fire on its last steam engine. The diesels that replaced steam were all Fairbanks-Morse products, except for a General Electric 44-tonner purchased second-hand in 1954.

The Virginian and the Norfolk & Western had not forgotten the idea of merger. By 1959 the regulatory climate was different. The stockholders of the two railroads and the ICC approved, and on Dec. 1, 1959, they merged, with the Virginian disappearing into the N&W. An almost immediate casualty of the merger was Virginian's electrification. N&W developed a one-way traffic pattern to take advantage of the best grades, and the electrics had only eastbound work to do. The electrification was shut down at the end of June 1962.

FACTS & FIGURES

Year	1929	1958
Miles operated	545	608
Locomotives	175	120
Passenger cars	62	—
Freight cars	10,273	17,143
Reporting marks: VGN		
Historical society: nwhs.org		

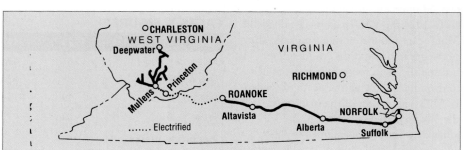

Wabash

"Follow the Flag"
WABASH

A northbound passenger train (either the *Banner Blue* or *Wabash Cannon Ball*, likely the former) rolls out of Decatur, Ill., behind blue, white, and gray E8 No. 1007 on June 1, 1952. *George Krambles; Krambles-Peterson Archive*

The Wabash seems to have gone through more reorganizations and name changes than most railroads its size. The term "Wabash" refers to the company in this history, unless clarity requires the full title.

In 1851 the North Missouri Railroad was chartered to build northwest from St. Louis to the Iowa state line at Coatesville, Mo. The railroad, completed in 1858, required a ferry crossing of the Missouri River at St. Charles, 19 miles from St. Louis, until a bridge was completed in 1871. In the 1860s the road acquired a branch to Brunswick; the town of Moberly was established at the junction and became the location of the road's shops. The Brunswick line was extended to Kansas City in 1868. The main route was extended north to Ottumwa, Iowa, in 1870, and construction of a line from Brunswick to Omaha was begun that same year (it reached Council Bluffs, Iowa, in 1879). The North Missouri ran into financial difficulty in 1871. It was succeeded in 1872 by the St. Louis, Kansas City & Northern Railroad.

In 1853 two railroad companies were organized: the Toledo & Illinois to build from Toledo, Ohio, to the Ohio-Indiana state line, and the Lake Erie, Wabash & St. Louis to continue the line across Indiana to Attica, following the route of the Wabash & Erie Canal. The two companies merged in 1856 as the Toledo, Wabash & Western Railroad, and they were succeeded in 1858 by the Toledo & Wabash Railway. By then the company had absorbed the Great Western of Illinois (a successor to the Northern Cross Railroad, chartered about 1837 to run from Quincy, Ill., east to the Indiana state line) and reached from Toledo to the Mississippi River at Quincy and at Keokuk, Iowa.

Jay Gould

In 1879 Jay Gould obtained control of the Toledo & Wabash and the St. Louis, Kansas City & Northern and merged them to form the Wabash, St. Louis & Pacific Railroad. To the new railroad, he soon added the Chicago & Paducah, whose line from Streator to Effingham crossed the Wabash at Bement. Within a year Gould

FACTS & FIGURES

Year	1929	1963
Miles operated	2,524	2,422
Locomotives	660	307
Passenger cars	412	101
Freight cars	26,633	15,028
Reporting marks: WAB		
Historical society: wabashrhs.org		

had constructed a line north to Chicago from a point on the Chicago & Paducah, and a line from Butler, Ind., northeast to Detroit.

Gould continued to add to the Wabash. By 1884 it had 3,549 miles of road extending from Detroit to Omaha and from Fonda in northwestern Iowa to Cairo, Ill. Financially the Wabash was overextended, and Gould's frequent rate wars with other railroads reduced the road's income. In May 1884 the Wabash defaulted in interest payments and entered receivership, with Gould as the receiver. The leased lines—like the Des Moines North Western and the Cairo & Vincennes—were returned to their owners. The Wabash itself was reorganized as several separate railroads, which were reunited in 1889 as the Wabash Railroad.

In 1889 the Wabash acquired trackage rights from Detroit through southern Ontario to Buffalo over the rails of the Grand Trunk. The Canadian portion of the system was connected with the rest by ferries across the Detroit River between Detroit and Windsor. A line from Butler to New Haven, Ind., east of Fort Wayne, opened in 1902, allowing Detroit–St. Louis trains to be routed through Fort Wayne, Huntington, and Wabash, Ind. The older, more direct route along the Eel River was sold to the Pennsylvania Railroad.

Twentieth century

In 1904 the Wabash reached Pittsburgh from Toledo over the rails of the Wheeling & Lake Erie and the Wabash Pittsburgh Terminal (predecessor of the Pittsburgh & West Virginia). The WPT was part of George Gould's plan to assemble the transcontinental system that his father had almost put together. The Wabash wasn't in Pittsburgh very long—receivership overtook it again in 1911, followed by reorganization in 1915 as the Wabash Railway.

The automobile industry was growing, and the Wabash found itself in the middle of it. One of the road's biggest assets was its direct line from Detroit to Kansas City, bypassing Chicago and St. Louis. The key portion of the route was the Decatur, Ill.– Moberly, Mo. line. Decatur was the hub of the Wabash and the site of its principal shops. The Hannibal–Moberly portion of the line was built by the Missouri-Kansas-Texas, but in 1894 the Wabash made arrangements to operate the line jointly,

A Wabash Detroit-Decatur, Ill., freight departs Oakwood Yard outside the Motor City behind 4-8-2 No. 2812 in 1940. *Robert A. Hadley*

with costs proportionate to use. The Wabash found itself paying 90 percent of the costs and leased the line in 1923.

In 1925 the Wabash acquired control of the Ann Arbor, and by the end of 1962 owned all but a few shares of Ann Arbor's stock. In 1928 the Pennsylvania Company gained control of the Wabash, largely to protect itself after the Wabash and the Delaware & Hudson bought control of the Lehigh Valley.

Wabash passenger service had several distinct personalities. Between St. Louis and Kansas City, Wabash operated the easternmost segment of Union Pacific's *City of St. Louis* and its own *City of Kansas City*. That was also mixed-train territory: Well into the 1960s several mixed trains a day connected the university town of Columbia, Mo., with the main line at Centralia, and in later years the St. Louis– Council Bluffs train was a mixed. On the Chicago–St. Louis run the Wabash competed with Gulf, Mobile & Ohio and Illinois Central and had the best rolling stock—the Vista-Dome *Blue Bird*. The second Chicago–St. Louis train, the *Banner Blue*, was one of the last trains to carry an open-platform parlor-observation car. Between Detroit and St. Louis the night and day trains were not glossy streamliners or extensions of someone else's train or plug locals—they were just plain, comfortable trains. In its last two decades the daytime run carried a legendary name from folk music, *Wabash Cannon Ball*.

The Wabash was unique in extending across the imaginary line dividing the country—a line from Chicago through Peoria to St. Louis, then down the Mississippi River to New Orleans. The Wabash was more a bridge railroad than an originator of traffic, a paradoxical situation in that most railroads had to shorthaul themselves to turn over traffic to the Wabash. The only major railroads that could give Wabash the long haul without sacrifice were the Union Pacific and the Kansas City Southern at Kansas City, UP at Council Bluffs, Iowa, and the Lackawanna and Lehigh Valley at Buffalo.

Norfolk & Western era

At the end of 1963, the Pennsylvania Company owned nearly 87 percent of Wabash's stock. When the Pennsylvania and the New York Central planned their merger, it was clear that the Wabash would not be included. Penn Central was large enough, and the Interstate Commerce Commission probably wouldn't allow it anyway. Wabash found a niche in the Norfolk & Western-Nickel Plate merger, but Wabash subsidiary Ann Arbor was kept in the Pennsy family (N&W didn't want it) by selling it to the Detroit, Toledo & Ironton on Aug. 31, 1963.

The expanded N&W leased Wabash on Oct. 16, 1964, and on March 31, 1970, N&W acquired control of Wabash from the Pennsylvania Company; by the end of 1980, N&W had almost complete ownership of Wabash, and its three main trunk lines in the U. S. remain busy under NS.

Waterloo, Cedar Falls & Northern

Freight motor 182 leads a train across the Cedar River bridge south of Waterloo. The first car is a meat refrigerator car from the Rath plant in Waterloo. *William D. Middleton*

The Waterloo & Cedar Falls Rapid Transit Co. was incorporated in December 1895. In 1896 it purchased the Waterloo Street Railway. Faced with difficulty obtaining a franchise to operate in Cedar Falls, it arranged to electrify and operate a branch of the Chicago Great Western. The CGW and the electric line were closely associated for several years.

In 1904 the company changed its name to Waterloo, Cedar Falls & Northern Railway. It expanded to the southeast in 1913 with a line to Cedar Rapids and built a

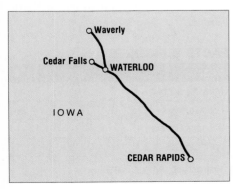

freight belt line around Waterloo to serve such industries as John Deere and Rath Packing Co. The WCF&N early recognized the benefits of interchanging carload freight with the steam railroads—indeed, it handled much of its freight with steam locomotives until 1915, and it actively promoted industrial development in Waterloo.

By 1927 WCF&N's freight revenue exceeded its passenger revenue. The road's passenger service was notable for its steam-road-size parlor-observation cars, which were later rebuilt as coaches, though they retained the observation platform.

A fire in the Waterloo roundhouse in October 1954 destroyed most of the passenger equipment, several locomotives, and the shop machinery that was necessary to maintain the electric cars and locomotives.

WCF&N discontinued passenger service in 1956. (The Waterloo city cars were replaced by buses in 1936; WCF&N operated the buses until 1953, when the city took over the service.) In March 1955 the stockholders approved sale of the line to

the Waterloo Railroad, which had recently been organized by the Illinois Central and the Rock Island.

The Waterloo Railroad took over the property of the WCF&N on July 1, 1956. Diesel operation was phased in gradually, and electric operation ended in August 1958. Illinois Central purchased Rock Island's half interest in July 1968, and in 1970 the Waterloo Railroad became simply a part of IC's Iowa Division. Most of WCF&N's line was later abandoned, and in 1985 IC used the corporate structure of the Waterloo Railroad for a subsidiary line in Mississippi.

FACTS & FIGURES

Year	1929	1955
Miles operated	138	98
Locomotives	7	10
Passenger cars	41	2
Freight cars	120	28
Reporting marks: WCF&N		

Wellsville, Addison & Galeton

The Wellsville, Addison & Galeton Railroad was incorporated in October 1954 by Murray M. Salzberg to puchase a segment of the Baltimore & Ohio from Galeton, Pa., to Wellsville and Addison, N. Y., and Ansonia, Pa. Salzberg took possession on Jan. 1, 1956.

For motive power, Salzberg acquired seven uniquely styled center-cab General Electric diesels built between 1937 and 1940 for Ford Motor Company's River Rouge works. WA&G also gathered a fleet of several hundred interchange freight cars from Boston & Maine. These cars were rebuilt and repainted and lettered with WA&G's slogan, "The Sole Leather Line," a reference to the tanneries sited along the railroad.

In 1959 the line to Addison was abandoned north of Elkland, Pa., because of a weakened bridge; the interchange at Addison was with the same railroad—Erie—as the interchange at Wellsville. In 1964 Salzberg purchased the 26-mile

Wellsville, Additon & Galeton GE center-cab diesel 1700 has a string of the road's wood boxcars in tow at Ansonia, Pa., in March 1970. *David H. Hamley*

Coudersport & Port Allegany, which connected with the Wellsville line.

The GE diesels began to wear out, and in 1968 and 1969, WA&G acquired a fleet of former Southern Pacific F7s. About the same time, freight car per diem rules changed and revenue from WA&G's fleet of boxcars dropped. WA&G petitioned to abandon the Wellsville line and rely solely on interchange with Penn Central at Ansonia. (The C&PA ceased operation in December 1970.) Floods in 1972 ended service on the Wellsville line, and it was officially abandoned in 1973.

The road petitioned the Interstate Commerce Commission to discontinue service on the remainder of the line, and the last run was on March 16, 1979. General Electric center-cab No. 1700, the last of its type, has been preserved by the Lake Shore Railway Historical Society in North East, Pa.

FACTS & FIGURES

Year	1956	1978
Miles operated	91	40
Locomotives	4	6
Passenger cars	—	—
Freight cars	3	17
Reporting marks: WAG		

Western Maryland

Three red-and-white EMD hood units—two GP35s and a GP40—lead an eastbound freight across the steel viaduct over the Baltimore & Ohio at Meyersdale, Pa., in July 1973. *Victor Hand*

On May 27, 1852, the Maryland General Assembly granted a charter to the Baltimore, Carroll & Frederick Rail Road to build a line from Baltimore northwest through Westminster, then west toward Hagerstown, Md. The name of the enterprise was soon changed to Western Maryland Rail Road.

The line opened to Union Bridge in November 1862, and it was seized briefly by the Union Army during the Battle of Gettysburg in July 1863. Construction resumed in 1868. The line reached Hagerstown in 1872 and was extended a few miles to a connection with the Chesapeake & Ohio Canal at Williamsport in 1873.

In 1881 WM leased a line north to Shippensburg, Pa., and in 1886 established a connection there with a predecessor of the Reading. Also in 1886 WM gained a

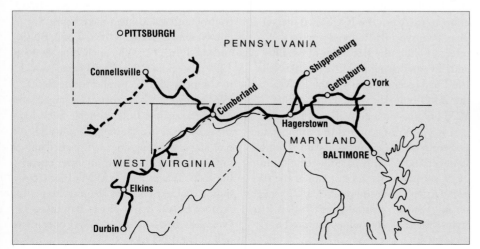

FACTS & FIGURES

Year	1929	1982
Miles operated	878	1,152
Locomotives	259	109
Passenger cars	78	—
Freight cars	11,481	6,836
Reporting marks: WM		
Historical society: moosevalley.org		

branch north from Emory Grove to Hanover and Gettysburg, Pa. That line was soon extended southwest from Gettysburg to meet WM's main line at Highfield, Md.

The main line was extended from Williamsport to Big Pool, Md., and across the Potomac River to Cherry Run, West Virginia, where it connected with the Baltimore & Ohio. B&O, WM, and Reading joined forces to operate a through freight route between Cumberland, Md., and Allentown, Pa., via Harrisburg.

The Gould era

WM's stock was largely owned by the city of Baltimore, which also held its mortgage bonds. By the turn of the century WM's debt to Baltimore was substantial and the city sought a buyer for the railroad. Bids were submitted in 1902. The syndicate representing George Gould was the lowest bidder but guaranteed full payment of WM's debt, extension west of Cumberland, and creation of a major tidewater terminal at Baltimore. On May 7, 1902, the city accepted the Gould syndicate's offer.

WM immediately built the marine terminal, Port Covington, and began construction westward along the Potomac (where all the good locations had been taken by the Baltimore & Ohio Railroad, the Chesapeake & Ohio Canal, and the National Turnpike). The line reached Cumberland in 1906. There it met the Cumberland & Piedmont Railway, which with the West Virginia Central & Pittsburg, another Gould road, formed a route southwest from Cumberland through Elkins to Durbin and Belington, W. Va. In 1907 Gould acquired control of the Georges Creek & Cumberland Railway, which had a line from Cumberland north through the Cumberland Narrows.

B&O and Reading broke their traffic agreement with WM in 1902, with the result that coal from Gould's West Virginia Central bypassed the WM and went instead over the Pennsy, which at the time controlled the B&O. The rest of Gould's empire was in trouble too, and in 1908, the Western Maryland entered receivership, as did the Wabash Pittsburg Terminal and the Wheeling & Lake Erie.

The Western Maryland Railway took over the Western Maryland Rail Road at the beginning of 1910 and immediately began constructing an 86-mile extension

Challengers pull and push Western Maryland tonnage around Helmstetter's Curve a few miles west of Cumberland. *George C. Corey*

northwest from Cumberland to a connection with the Pittsburgh & Lake Erie at Connellsville, Pa.

B&O ownership

When the Gould empire collapsed John D. Rockefeller acquired control of the Western Maryland. Because the ICC merger plan of 1921 grouped WM with Baltimore & Ohio, in 1927 B&O bought Rockefeller's WM interest and soon increased its WM holdings to 43 percent. Frank Taplin, who controlled the Pittsburgh & West Virginia, protested B&O's action. The Interstate Commerce Commission charged B&O with violating antitrust laws—in its effort to carry out the ICC's own merger plan. Pennsylvania Railroad interests offered to help the B&O out of its difficulty by purchasing its WM interests (the PRR had recently acquired the P&WV), but B&O refused to sell and placed its WM holdings in a nonvoting trust.

In 1944 WM acquired the Cumberland & Pennsylvania, a short coal carrier out of Cumberland. WM began dieselization in 1949, starting with the east end of the system, farthest from the coalfields. Passenger service, which consisted of coach-only local trains, lasted barely long enough to be dieselized.

As the large railroads of the East formulated their merger plans WM could envision its traffic disappearing. Merger of the Pennsylvania and New York Central could shift traffic from the Pittsburgh & Lake Erie (part of the NYC) to the Pennsy. Norfolk & Western could easily move traffic off the P&WV onto its own lines, circuitous though they were, right into Hagerstown. WM decided to forsake independence and join the Baltimore & Ohio-Chesapeake & Ohio alliance—after all, B&O was almost a half owner of WM. B&O and C&O applied to control WM, and the ICC approved their bid in 1967.

There was little evidence of C&O-B&O control until 1973, when the Chessie System was incorporated to own C&O, B&O, and WM. In 1973 WM applied to abandon 125 miles of main line from Hancock, Md., to Connellsville, Pa., parallel to the B&O. WM's single track had better clearances and easier grades than B&O's double track, but the expense of maintaining the line and building connecting lines outweighed any saving that might result from lower operating costs. That same year WM's Port Covington coal terminal was abandoned in favor of B&O's newer pier in Baltimore. Gradually B&O absorbed WM's operations and in late 1983 merged WM.

Western Pacific

An F7 A-B-B set leads a Western Pacific freight down Third Street in Oakland in the 1960s on track that has since been abandoned. Orange-and-silver F7 916-D was built in 1950. *Jim McClellan*

In 1900 the Gould railroads (Western Maryland, Wabash, Missouri Pacific, and Denver & Rio Grande chief among them) stretched from Baltimore, Md., to Ogden, Utah, with only a short gap in Pennsylvania. The Southern Pacific connection at Ogden furnished considerable traffic to the system until E. H. Harriman obtained control of the Union Pacific and the Southern Pacific, effectively shutting Denver & Rio Grande out of the Ogden Gateway. At the same time California shippers and merchants considered themselves at the mercy of Southern Pacific, which had a near-monopoly in the state.

From time to time railroads had been proposed and surveyed across the Sierra Nevada, the mountain range along much of the eastern border of California. Some of those routes followed the canyon of the Feather River to Beckwourth Pass, which was 2,000 feet lower than the Central Pacific (later Southern Pacific) route over Donner Pass.

One such survey had been made by W. H. Kennedy, assistant to the chief engineer of the Union Pacific when Jay Gould controlled UP. Arthur Keddie used the Kennedy survey to obtain a franchise for a railroad along that route. Keddie's partner,

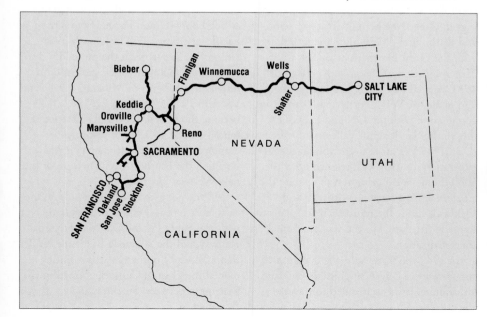

FACTS & FIGURES

Year	1929	1981
Miles operated	1,055	1,436
Locomotives	169	144
Passenger cars	86	—
Freight cars	9,470	6,077

Reporting marks: WP

Historical society: wplives.com

The steam era was ending as Mikado 308 waited with an eastbound freight train at Altamont, Calif., the summit of WP's climb over the hills between San Francisco Bay and the Central Valley. *Arthur Lloyd*

Walter J. Bartnett, signed an agreement with George Gould, Jay Gould's eldest son and successor, to take over the surveys, franchises, and incorporations.

The Western Pacific Railway was incorporated in 1903 to build a railroad from Salt Lake City to San Francisco (the name chosen was also that of the railroad that originally extended the Central Pacific from Sacramento to Oakland). Gould's Denver & Rio Grande underwrote $50 million in bonds for construction. The last spike was driven in 1909 on the Spanish Creek trestle at Keddie, Calif.

The new railroad had no branches to feed traffic to it, and revenue didn't cover operating expenses and construction costs. WP entered bankruptcy in 1915 and pulled the Rio Grande in with it. At the same time, the eastern end of Gould's empire collapsed as the cost of building the Wabash Pittsburgh Terminal (later the Pittsburgh & West Virginia) bankrupted the Wabash.

Reorganization and expansion

The Western Pacific Railway was sold in 1916 and reorganized as the Western Pacific Railroad. In 1917 the WP purchased control of the Tidewater Southern, an interurban that ran south from Stockton, Calif., and took over the south end of the narrow gauge Nevada-California-Oregon to gain entry to Reno, Nev. With the payment it received from the government for damages during the period of

operation by the United States Railroad Administration—chiefly the result of lack of maintenance—WP purchased control of the Sacramento Northern, an electric railroad from Sacramento to Chico, Calif. In 1927 WP bought the San Francisco-Sacramento Railroad, an interurban between the two cities of its name, and merged it with Sacramento Northern.

The USRA introduced paired-track operation with Southern Pacific between Winnemucca and Wells, Nev., 182 miles. The arrangement was discontinued after the USRA relinquished control, but resumed in 1924.

In 1926 Arthur Curtiss James acquired control of WP; he already had large holdings in Great Northern, Northern Pacific, and Burlington. WP built a line to link up with the Great Northern at Bieber, Calif. The completion of the project on Nov. 10, 1931, created the Inside Gateway route and made the WP a north-south carrier in conjunction with the GN and Santa Fe's line in the San Joaquin Valley.

In 1935 WP underwent voluntary reorganization. In 1939 WP teamed up with Rio Grande and Burlington to operate the *Exposition Flyer* between Chicago and Oakland, Calif. The railroads made plans to upgrade the train, but the war postponed their realization.

In 1949 the three railroads inaugurated the *California Zephyr*, a Chicago–Oakland streamliner. It was scheduled to traverse the most scenic parts of the trip by day and

was equipped with Vista-Domes—five per train—so passengers could enjoy the scenery. The train was an immediate success. Soon afterward WP equipped the secondary train on its line with Budd Rail Diesel Cars called *Zephyrettes* (not to be confused with the *CZ*'s train hostesses, who had the same title).

Independence and merger

In 1962 Southern Pacific and Santa Fe sparred for control of Western Pacific. Neither won, and WP remained independent. The road dropped its segment of the *California Zephyr* on March 21, 1970. WP continued to roll along as it had, very much a regional-size railroad with giants as neighbors (Union Pacific, Southern Pacific, and Santa Fe). In January 1980 Union Pacific surprised the railroad industry by announcing in quick succession its impending mergers of Missouri Pacific and Western Pacific. On Dec. 22, 1982, WP became the Fourth Operating District of Union Pacific. In 1985 in response to employee requests the former WP was renamed the Feather River Division of the new Western District.

WP owned two switching roads on the east shore of San Francisco Bay jointly with the Santa Fe: the Oakland Terminal Railway and the Alameda Belt Line. WP, Santa Fe, and Southern Pacific jointly owned the Central California Traction Co., which ran between Stockton and Sacramento.

Wheeling & Lake Erie

The Wheeling & Lake Erie Rail Road was incorporated in 1871 to build a line from Martins Ferry, Ohio, near Wheeling, W. Va., through the coalfields of southeastern Ohio to the Lake Erie ports of Sandusky and Toledo. Construction began—in narrow gauge—in 1873, but soon ceased. Construction resumed in 1881, this time in standard gauge and with the backing of Jay Gould. In 1882 the W&LE acquired the Cleveland & Marietta Railroad and began service between Toledo and Marietta. A year later, the C&M was in receivership and back on its own.

The W&LE reorganized in 1886 and continued construction eastward, reaching Wheeling in 1891. The road prospered until a depression and a long strike by coal miners in 1896 threw it into receivership.

Myron T. Herrick was appointed receiver of the W&LE in 1897. He added to it the Cleveland, Canton & Southern, a run-down, former narrow gauge line from Cleveland to Zanesville, Ohio. Turn-of-the-century prosperity embraced the new W&LE, largely because of coal traffic. In 1906 the W&LE chartered the Lorain & West Virginia Railway to build a branch from Wellington, on the W&LE, to Lorain, on Lake Erie. In 1907 the Gould empire collapsed. The W&LE fell once again into receivership.

The growth of the automobile industry helped bring the W&LE up from the depths. In 1927 the Nickel Plate, Baltimore & Ohio, and New York Central teamed up to buy the W&LE stock held

Wheeling & Lake Erie Berkshire 6430 has the 75 cars of train 95 rolling toward Toledo along the Sandusky River north of Fremont, Ohio, on June 20, 1950. *Bob Lorenz*

by John D. Rockefeller. The Van Sweringen brothers, who controlled the NKP, bought more stock on their own to ensure that the W&LE would remain out of the reach of Leonor F. Loree of the Delaware & Hudson, who was trying to build a rail system, and to keep the Pittsburgh & West Virginia from buying the W&LE.

The Interstate Commerce Commission ordered NKP, B&O, and NYC to sell their W&LE stock. The Van Sweringens' Alleghany Corporation bought NYC's shares and traded its interest in the Buffalo, Rochester & Pittsburgh for Baltimore & Ohio shares. By 1929 the Van Sweringens owned the W&LE but were not

allowed to exercise control.

The W&LE was one of the first railroads to drop passenger service, becoming freight-only in July 1938.

In 1946 and 1947 the Nickel Plate purchased approximately 80 percent of the stock of the W&LE, and on Dec. 1, 1949, the Nickel Plate leased the W&LE. NKP's control and lease passed to the Norfolk & Western in 1964.

On April 9, 1988, the Ohio Central Railroad began operating between Harmon and Zanesville. On Sept. 16 of that year, the N&W merged the W&LE. On May 17, 1990, a new Wheeling & Lake Railway leased and began operation on most of the rest of the old W&LE (plus the Akron, Canton & Youngstown and the Pittsburgh & West Virginia).

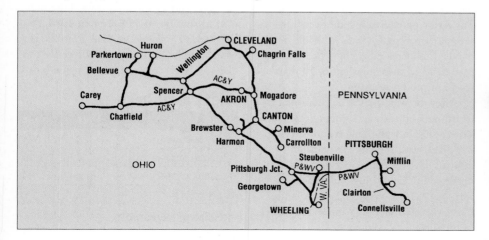

FACTS & FIGURES

Year	1929	1948
Miles operated	512	506
Locomotives	185	161
Passenger cars	66	—
Freight cars	11,626	13,646

Reporting marks: WLE

Historical society: or4c.com/wlehs

White Pass & Yukon

The White Pass & Yukon was born in the Yukon gold rush of 1898. A railroad was necessary to carry machinery and supplies from tidewater at Skagway, Alaska, over the Coast Mountains to the Yukon River in Canada's Yukon Territory.

Construction of the 3-foot gauge railroad began in 1898, and crews working from Skagway and from Whitehorse, Y. T., met at Carcross, Y. T., on July 29, 1900. The road's destination at one time was Fort Selkirk, Y. T., at the confluence of the Pelly and Lewes (or Upper Yukon) rivers.

WP&Ys corporate structure encompassed three railroads: the Pacific & Arctic Railway & Navigation Co. (Alaska, 20.4 miles), the British Columbia-Yukon Railway (British Columbia, 32.2 miles), and the British Yukon Railway (Yukon Territory, 58.1 miles), all three operated by the White Pass & Yukon.

The WP&Y prospered for a few years, then gold mining slackened and the company entered reorganization. The belligerence of Japan and the approach of World War II roused the economy of the Yukon.

One of White Pass & Yukon's original yellow-and-green General Electric diesels leads a passenger train across one of the many trestles above Skagway. *David P. Morgan Library collection*

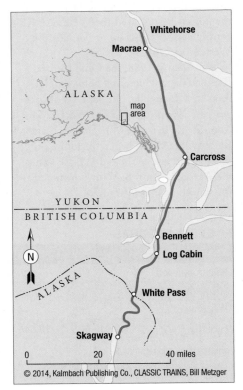

© 2014, Kalmbach Publishing Co., CLASSIC TRAINS, Bill Metzger

The railroad's business increased and in 1937 it even inaugurated air services (WP&Y had operated steamboats for many years between Whitehorse and Dawson and between Carcross and Atlin).

The bombing of Pearl Harbor in 1941 triggered the construction of the Alaska Highway. One of the jumping-off places for construction crews was Whitehorse, the northern terminus of the railroad. The WP&Y found itself with too big a job to do, so the U. S. Army's Military Railway Service moved in to operate the railroad. The Army purchased locomotives from several narrow gauge lines in the U. S. to handle the increased traffic—in 1943 the road handled the equivalent of 10 years' worth of prewar tonnage.

After the war, the WP&Y returned to its primary business of bringing the necessities of life into the Yukon and carrying out silver, lead, and zinc. In addition the railroad developed a tourist business, connecting with cruise ships calling at Skagway. In 1951 the White Pass & Yukon Corp. was chartered to acquire ownership of the subsidiary companies.

To reduce the cost of transferring cargo between ships, trucks, and trains, the White Pass developed a container that would fit on the narrow gauge cars and flatbed trucks. In 1954 WP&Y designed and bought a ship, the *Clifford J. Rogers*, to carry the containers between Vancouver, B. C., and Skagway. The company also acquired a trucking operation and a pipeline parallel to the railroad.

In 1982 a slump in the mining industry and the construction of a highway between Skagway and Whitehorse caused the railroad to shut down. However, in 1988 the southern 67 miles of the line, from Skagway through the summit of White Pass to Carcross, was reopened for excursion trains.

FACTS & FIGURES

Year	1929	1984
Miles operated	123	111
Locomotives	14	20
Passenger cars	n/a	34
Freight cars	n/a	399
Reporting marks: WPY		

Winston-Salem Southbound

Winston-Salem Southbound time freights 209 and 212 meet at night at Eller, N. C., in 1956. Mikado 827, at right, is a former Atlantic Coast Line engine with a Norfolk & Western tender. *Philip R. Hastings*

The Winston-Salem Southbound was incorporated in 1905—late as North American railroad history goes—to build a railroad from Winston-Salem, N. C., to the South Carolina state line. Construction began in 1909 after the railroad's principal connections, Norfolk & Western and Atlantic Coast Line,

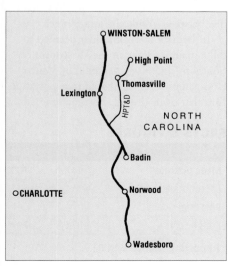

guaranteed its bonds and became its joint owners.

The reason for the road's existence was probably to form a shortcut for coal moving south to fuel ACL locomotives and U. S. Navy ships at Charleston, S. C. WSS's rails reached Whitney in December 1910 and few months later Wadesboro, where it connected with ACL.

WSS depended on parent Norfolk & Western for maintenance of its line and for supervision of its operations. It relied on Atlantic Coast Line for accounting and marketing. In the early 1950s, WSS's motive power fleet consisted of two half-century-old ex-N&W 2-8-0s, two ex-ACL Mikados, and two similar 2-8-2s purchased new. In 1957 the Southbound replaced steam with four GP9s, two in WSS gray and maroon and two in ACL black.

In 1960 WSS acquired control of the High Point, Thomasville & Denton Railroad, a 34-mile line from High Point to a connection with the WSS at High Rock. The WSS merged it in 2010.

About 1967 the GP9s disappeared, two each, into the rosters of N&W and Seaboard Coast Line. Thereafter WSS leased power from its parents. About the same time, WSS no longer had any interchange freight cars of its own, although three cabooses remained in service into the mid-1980s. The year 1967 signifies the end date appearance-wise for the railroad, but it really marks the transition to paper-railroad status. WSS maintains a degree of independence even though its allegiance is split between the two giants of southeastern railroading, Norfolk Southern and CSX Transportation.

FACTS & FIGURES

Year	1929	1967
Miles operated	98	95
Locomotives	11	—
Passenger cars	3	—
Freight cars	203	—
Reporting marks: WSS		

Wisconsin & Southern

In 1978 Milwaukee Road was considering abandoning several branches that served the area northwest of its namesake city. FSC Corp. of Pittsburgh, Pa., (which operated the Upper Merion & Plymouth, a switching road at Conshohocken, Pa.) won the bidding to operate the lines, purchased them with state and federal aid, and organized the Wisconsin & Southern Railroad (WSOR), which began on July 1, 1980.

In 1988 the Wisconsin & Southern was purchased by Railroad Acquisition Corporation, owned by Milwaukee-area industrialist William Gardner. On Aug. 21, 1992, Railroad Acquisition Corp. bought the Wisconsin & Calumet Railroad (WICT), which operated former Milwaukee and Illinois Central Gulf lines in south central Wisconsin (see the CMStP&P entry). The lines included Madison–Prairie du Chien, Madison–Janesville, and Janesville–Fox Lake, Ill. WICT continued to operate as a separate railroad until 1997, when it was merged and became part of WSOR, which thus gained access to Chicago, on trackage

Two Wisconsin & Southern SD40-2s head east with a train of windmill turbine blades near Palmyra, Wis., in May 2011, bound for Waukesha and eventually Cambria. *Andy Cummings*

rights to Clearing Yard.

In the late 1990s, WSOR leased from Union Pacific several former Chicago & North Western lines in the Madison area.

WSOR also bought from Soo Line the ex-MILW line from Madison to Watertown.

In 2005, when Wisconsin Central Ltd. successor CN planned to abandon its Saukville–Kiel line (also ex-MILW) north of Milwaukee, the state of Wisconsin bought it and WSOR leased it, plus a connecting ex-C&NW branch from Plymouth to Sheboygan Falls. WSOR also obtained overhead-traffic (only) rights on CP from Milwaukee to Rondout, Ill.

WSOR operates its two portions as separate divisions (Northern and Southern), connecting them by trackage rights on Canadian National's former WC main line between Waukesha and Slinger.

In January 2012, Gardner decided to sell a majority stake in the Wisconsin & Southern, and it was acquired by Watco Companies, a Kansas-based transportation firm that owns several shortline railroads.

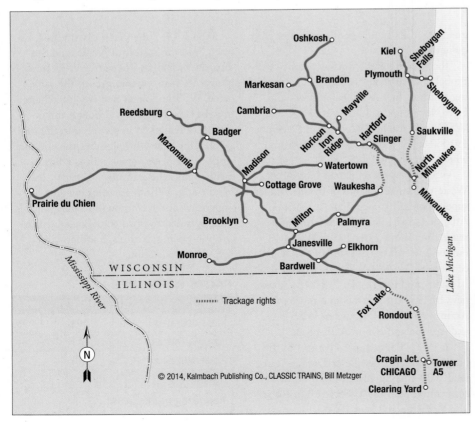

© 2014, Kalmbach Publishing Co., CLASSIC TRAINS, Bill Metzger

FACTS & FIGURES

Year	1981	2012
Miles operated	147	700
Locomotives	4	41
Passenger cars	—	—
Freight cars	1,375	797
Reporting marks: WSOR		

Wisconsin Central Ltd.

W hen Soo Line purchased the Milwaukee Road in 1985, it acquired a double-track Chicago-Twin Cities line that was 50 miles shorter than its own single-track route. Soo Line consolidated operations on the former Milwaukee, and briefly tried operating its light-density lines in Michigan and Wisconsin as Lake States Transportation Division (not to be confused with Michigan's Lake State Railway, the former Detroit & Mackinac Railway), but was unable to change work-rules to cut costs on LSTD lines. Milwaukee Road's dowry included debt accumulations and deferred maintenance. Soo found itself short of cash and offered the Lake States lines for sale.

A new firm headed by Edward Burkhardt and Thomas Power bought the lines in 1987, naming the new entity Wisconsin Central Ltd. Its map (and emblem) looked much like those of the original Wisconsin Central Railway (see the Soo Line entry): the Chicago-Twin Cities main; branches from Neenah to Manitowoc and Argonne, and from Spencer north to Ashland (in two pieces); and from Owen to Superior. Along with the old WC came ex-MILW lines from Milwaukee to Green Bay and from New Lisbon to Tomahawk; nearly all the original (1883) Soo from St. Paul to Sault Ste. Marie, Ontario; and two pieces

Two Wisconsin Central SD45s, in WC's Soo Line-like livery, plus WC's lone ex-Southern SD35, roll a southbound freight across a trestle near Vernon, Wis., in May 1995. *Tom Danneman*

of the old Duluth, South Shore & Atlantic main line. WCL began on Oct. 11, 1987 (the map shows the system circa 1990).

In August 1989 WCL bought Lake Superior & Ishpeming's long-isolated 5-mile Munising Junction-Munising spur. In July 1992 WCL purchased Chicago & North Western's 98-mile Cameron–Superior line, giving WC a second Superior route. Part of its original purchase agreement was that if WC acquired its own rails

to Superior, Soo would have to sell and WC would have to buy the Ladysmith–Superior line, on which WC had trackage rights. WC did so, then combined the best of the two: the ex-Soo from Ladysmith to Gordon, Wis., and the ex-C&NW from Gordon to Superior. In 1993 WC acquired the Green Bay & Western and the Fox River Valley, combining them as Fox Valley & Western; two years later WC bought the Algoma Central (all have their own entries in this book). In 1996, WCL bought from UP 18 miles of an ex-C&NW branch into Hayward, Wis., and, through its Sault Ste. Marie Bridge Co. entity (SSAM), 220 ex-C&NW miles from Green Bay north to Ishpeming, Mich., including branches to Palmer and Iron Mountain, Mich., and to Niagara, Wis. In 2001, Wisconsin Central Ltd. was purchased by Canadian National, which absorbed WCL into its system.

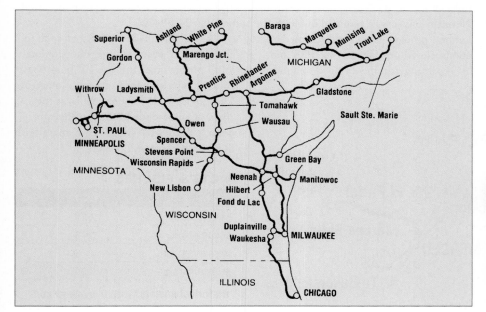

FACTS & FIGURES

Year	1988	2001
Miles operated	2,134	2,850
Locomotives	96	228
Passenger cars	—	—
Freight cars	5,183	7,852
Reporting marks: WC, SSAM		

Yosemite Valley

Yosemite National Park was established in 1890, and soon afterward, railroad routes were surveyed into the valley. A group of men from San Francisco and Oakland incorporated the Yosemite Valley Railroad in 1902, choosing a route that simply followed the Merced River Canyon to the park. Grading got underway in 1905 from the city of Merced, Calif., and early in 1906, service began as far as Merced Falls.

In May 1907 the railroad reached a point about 12 miles from the east end of the valley and established a station named El Portal at the park entrance. From there the railroad built a wagon road into the park itself, and passengers could ride a stage coach (motor coach after 1913) into the park. Service over the full length of the line began on May 15, 1907. Railway Post Officie service began in March 1908.

By 1910, Pullmans were being operated over the Southern Pacific from Los Angeles and Oakland to Merced. In 1912 the Yosemite Lumber Co. opened a sawmill at Merced Falls as well as a logging operation across the river from El Portal. The tourist business grew, and visiting royalty and Hollywood stars rode the YV.

Construction of the Exchequer Dam on the Merced River beginning in 1924 required a major line relocation, with almost 17 miles of track moved, a 1,600-foot long bridge, and four tunnels. The YV also benefited from the project, hauling materials for the dam, and the YV's business peaked in 1925. Paved roads reached El Portal in

In 1940 Yosemite Valley train 3, a 4-4-0 with a steel baggage-mail car and wood observation car, pauses at El Portal before its run down the Merced River Canyon. *Harre W. Demoro*

1926, and YV's passenger traffic dropped 78 percent from 1925 to 1928. The Yosemite Lumber Co. suspended operations in 1927.

The Depression drove YV into bankruptcy in 1935, and on Jan. 1, 1936 the company was reorganized as the Yosemite Valley Railway. Freight traffic increased, and the railroad showed a small profit, but a flood in December 1937 wiped out 30 miles of line in the Merced River canyon. Nevertheless, service resumed in 1938. The lumber company, which had resumed operations, closed permanently in 1938, and YV's passenger traffic dropped to almost

nothing during World War II. The closing of the Yosemite Portland Cement Co. (at Merced) in July 1944 resulted in more lost traffic. The trustees petitioned for abandonment in August 1944.

Another flood in 1945 further weakened the Yosemite Valley's finances, and a bridge fire in August of that year stranded some of the rolling stock on the east end of the line. The railroad's last run occurred on Aug. 24, 1945.

The railroad made a profit before fixed charges in 32 of its 38 years of operation. With proper financing, the YV might have endured long enough to take advantage of California's postwar boom. Now, as the crush of automobile traffic threatens to destroy Yosemite National Park, many wish the railroad were still operating.

FACTS & FIGURES

Year	1929	1945
Miles operated	78	78
Locomotives	8	8
Passenger cars	8	7
Freight cars	255	73
Historical society: yosemitevalleyrr.com		

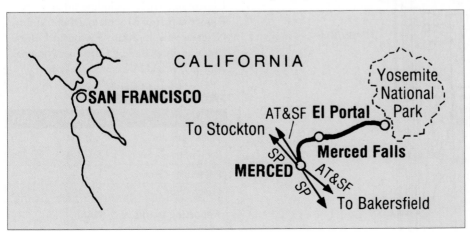

Index

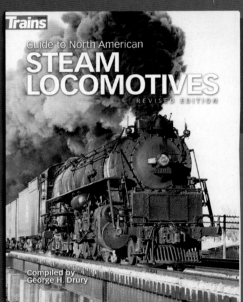
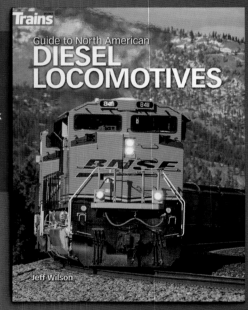
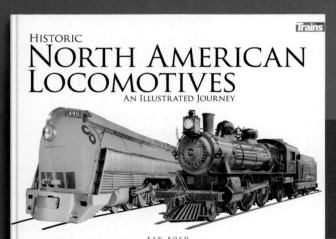